FIFTH EDITION

Traditions & Encounters

A Brief Global History

VOL. 2: FROM 1500 TO THE PRESENT

Jerry H. Bentley
UNIVERSITY OF HAWAI'I

Herbert F. Ziegler
UNIVERSITY OF HAWAI'I

Heather E. Streets-Salter
NORTHEASTERN UNIVERSITY

Craig Benjamin
GRAND VALLEY STATE UNIVERSITY

McGraw Hill

TRADITIONS & ENCOUNTERS: A BRIEF GLOBAL HISTORY: VOLUME 2 FROM 1500 TO THE PRESENT, FIFTH EDITION

1 2 3 4 5 6 7 8 9 LWI 27 26 25 24 23 22

ISBN 978-1-264-33955-6 (bound edition)
MHID 1-264-33955-0 (bound edition)
ISBN 978-1-264-33956-3 (loose-leaf edition)
MHID 1-264-33956-9 (loose-leaf edition)

Senior Portfolio Manager: *Jason Seitz*
Product Developer Manager: *Dawn Groundwater*
Senior Product Developer: *Lauren A. Finn*
Senior Marketing Manager: *Michael Gedatus*
Content Project Managers: *Sandy Wille; Vanessa McClune*
Senior Buyer: *Sandy Ludovissy*
Associate Content Licensing Manager: *Brianna Kirschbaum*

Cover Images: Arp 273: Egyptian Studio/Shutterstock; finger: chaoss/Shutterstock; fern fiddlehead: Zoonar GmbH/Alamy Stock Photo; Cave of Hands painting: Eduardo Rivero/Shutterstock; shell pattern: andreahast/123RF; Egyptian Rosetta Stone: Photos.com/Getty Images; marble inlay: Glow Images; textile fragment: The Metropolitan Museum of Art, New York, Gift of Henry G. Marquand, 1882; fish mosaics: Lissa Harrison; tunic: The Walters Art Museum, Baltimore, Gift of Georgia and Michael de Havenon, 2016; Greek vase: Digital image courtesy of the Getty's Open Content Program; mosaic of triangles: Alfredo Venturi/Alamy; Roman mosaic: neil harrison/ iStock/Getty Images; Ardabil carpet: LACMA -Los Angeles County Museum of Art; Pont du Gard: Bertl123/Shutterstock; Jameh Mosque: Andrea Ricordi, Italy/Moment/Getty Images; Moroccan tile: AlxeyPnferov/iStock/Getty Images; Celtic knot tombstone: Robin Bath/Alamy; Buddhist mani stone: Egmont Strigl/Imagebroker RF/age footstock; bowl: The Metropolitan Museum of Art; New York, The Michael C. Rockefeller Memorial Collection, Purchase, Nelson A. Rockefeller Gift; Vitruvian Man: Janaka Dharmasena/Shutterstock; Romanian carpet; Europeana Collections / INP - National Heritage Institute, Bucharest; dot painting: Paul Pegler/E+/Getty Images; distemper on cloth: The Metropolitan Museum of Art, New York, Purchase, Lita Annenberg Hazen Charitable Trust Gift, 1987; barkcloth: LACMA - Los Angeles County Museum; Moroccan tiles: AlxeyPnferov/iStock/Getty Images; mosaic floor: Digital image courtesy of the Getty's Open Content Program; Pair of Parfleches: The Metropolitan Museum of Art, New York, Ralph T. Coe Collection, Gift of Ralph T. Coe Foundation for the Arts, 2011; Moroccan tile: AlxeyPnferov/iStock/Getty Images; fabric pattern: ADELART/Shutterstock; El Castillo: Kitti Boonnitrod/Getty Images; Buddhist temple: Melba Photo Agency/Alamy; tile: LACMA - Los Angeles County Museum; fan patterns: Jenny Dettrick/Moment/Getty Images; molecules: McGraw Hill; spiral staircase: Rob Tilley/Spaces Images/Blend Images LLC; ceremonial skirt: The Metropolitan Museum of Art, Rogers Fund, 2004; Fleur-de-lis: Exactostock/ SuperStock; Saint Basil's Cathedral: Dave and Les Jacobs/Blend Images LLC; Japanese maple leaf pattern: Photosindia.Com, Llc/Glow Images; DNA: Jezper/Shutterstock; farming village: KingWu/ iStockphoto; silk sari: jayk7/Getty Images; bark cloth: Yale University Art Gallery, Photo Credit: Christopher Gardner; silk brocade: Kevin McNeill/ iStock/360/Getty Images; Lozenge composition: The Art Institute of Chicago, Gift of Edgar Kaufmann, Jr.; blue technology background: SkillUp/Shutterstock

Compositor: Aptara, Inc.

Library of Congress Cataloging-in-Publication Data

Names: Bentley, Jerry H., 1949–2012, author. | Ziegler, Herbert F., 1949- author. | Streets-Salter, Heather, author.

Title: Traditions & encounters : a brief global history Jerry H. Bentley, University of Hawai'i ; Herbert F. Ziegler, University of Hawai'i ; Heather E. Streets-Salter, Northeastern University.

Other titles: Traditions and encounters

Description: Fifth edition. | New York, NY : McGraw Hill Education, [2023] | Includes bibliographical references and index | Contents: v. 1. – v. 2.

Identifiers: LCCN 2022009113 (print) | LCCN 2022009114 (ebook) | ISBN 9781264339532 (v. 1 ; hardcover) | ISBN 9781264339549 (v. 1 ; spiral bound) | ISBN 9781264339556 (v. 2 ; hardcover) | ISBN 9781264339563 (v. 2 ; spiral bound) | ISBN 9781260070286 (hardcover) | ISBN 9781264339617 (spiral bound) | ISBN 9781264339587 (ebook) | ISBN 9781264339525 (ebook other) | ISBN 9781264339587 (v. 1 ; ebook) | ISBN 9781264339525 (v. 1 ; ebook other) | ISBN 9781259283772 (v. 2 ; ebook) | ISBN 9781260112467 (v. 2 ; ebook other)

Subjects: LCSH: World history–Textbooks. | Intercultural communication–History–Textbooks.

Classification: LCC D21 .B46 2023 (print) | LCC D21 (ebook) | DDC 909–dc23/eng/20220328

LC record available at https://lccn.loc.gov/2022009113

LC ebook record available at https://lccn.loc.gov/2022009114

Brief Contents

Contents

Maps

Sources from the Past

Connecting the Sources

Preface

How do the themes of traditions and encounters continue to help make sense of the entire human past in the twenty-first century?

As Jerry Bentley and Herb Zeigler noted in their original Preface to this book, world history is about both diversity and connections. They began this text with a simple goal: to help our students understand the unique histories of the world's rich variety of peoples, while at the same allowing them to see the long histories of connections and interactions that have shaped all human communities for millennia. To do this, the authors wrote a story around the dual themes of traditions and encounters to highlight the many different religions and customs embraced by the world's peoples while exploring the encounters with other cultures that brought about inevitable change.

It is the interaction of these traditions and encounters that continues to provide the key to making sense of our past. Human communities furthered themselves not by remaining isolated but by interacting with others and exploring the benefits and risks of reaching out. The vitality of history—and its interpretation—lies in understanding the nature of individual cultural traditions and the scope of encounters that punctuated every significant event in human history.

This fifth edition of *Traditions & Encounters: A Brief Global History* provides a genuinely global vision of history that is increasingly meaningful in the shrinking world of the twenty-first century. The theme of *traditions* draws attention to the formation, maintenance, and sometimes collapse of so many distinctive, individual societies. Because the world's peoples have also interacted regularly with one another since the earliest days of human history, the theme of *encounters* directs attention to communications, interactions, networks, and exchanges that have linked individual societies to their neighbors and others in the larger world. Despite many changes in the way world historians have tried to conceptualize the past and present since the appearance of the first edition of *Traditions & Encounters* decades ago, the twin themes of traditions and encounters remain at the heart of every chapter in the text, no matter how extensive revisions might have been. They provide a lens through which to interpret the affairs of humankind and the pressures that continue to shape history. All aspects of the text support these themes—from the organization of chapters and engaging stories of the world's peoples to the robust map program, updated primary sources, and critical-thinking features that permeate the text.

Some of the changes authors Heather Streets-Salter and Craig Benjamin have introduced to the brief fifth edition of *Traditions & Encounters* are the following.

We have worked hard to eliminate any gendered or out-of-date language throughout the book, in line with most historical writing being done today.

We decided to eliminate the Part openers and Part closers to help provide a more seamless narrative and to downplay the somewhat compartmentalized and episodic structure that was more common when earlier editions were prepared.

We have changed the old Eyewitness feature to *Zooming in on Traditions* or *Zooming in on Encounters* to further emphasize the key organizational lens of the book. And we have streamlined the opening stories featured in these *Zooming* features to give greater voice to the many individuals from the past they include. We have also separated these stories from a new *Chapter Overview* that helps better prepare readers for the contents of the chapter that follows.

We have changed the titles of a number of chapters to reflect recent thinking within the field and, in some cases, to be more geographically and politically inclusive. For example, chapter 21 has been renamed to The Integration of the Americas and Oceania with the Wider World to emphasize the relations of these regions with the rest of the world. We have also made numerous changes to headers and sub-headers throughout, both to reflect new interpretations of how we should "label" various peoples and historical processes and to make the structure of each chapter clearer.

We have replaced and updated a number of sources in the *Sources from the Past* and *Connecting the Sources* features and have selected many new images to better illustrate the text. In chapter 28, we added a new *Sources from the Past* by Queen Lili'uokulani. We have added in-line comprehension questions to the sources and updated reflection questions on most sources, maps, and images to help students practice both their comprehension and their analytical thinking skills.

We have changed the old *Reverberations* feature to *Why It Matters*, both to further enhance the flow of historical processes and also to more clearly emphasize the continuing relevance of each of the themes explored to the global world of today. For example, in chapter 22, we discuss the profound and long-term effects of pandemic disease during the Columbian Exchange and how it permanently altered human populations in the Americas. In chapter 30, we discuss the ways the destruction of World War I shifted popular and intellectual culture in Europe from an optimistic belief in social progress to pessimism about the human condition—a feature of popular culture that has persisted right up to the present.

We have changed the old *Summary* feature to a *Conclusion* and modified the language in each to more succinctly sum up the developments described in the chapter. We have also added new and more relevant secondary sources to the *For Further Reading* section at the end of each chapter.

New to this edition, we have added a feature called *What's Left Out?* to call attention to issues most texts do not usually have space to discuss. Its purpose is to remind students that history is far more complicated and nuanced than any brief narrative can provide. For example, in chapter 24, we give greater context on non-elite women in southwest Asia because most textbooks focus on elite women associated with the imperial harem, while in chapter 32 we help students understand that the rivalries of the Cold War, in fact, originated much earlier in the interwar period.

CHAPTER-BY-CHAPTER CHANGES

The following is a chapter-by-chapter list of topics that are new to this edition or elements that have been substantially revised or updated.

Chapter 19: Transoceanic Encounters and Global Connections

- Reversed subsections in the first section, so that Technology of Exploration precedes Motives of Exploration.
- Reversed the sections Trade and Conflict in Early Modern Asia and Ecological Exchanges, so that Ecological Exchanges comes first.
- Added a "What's Left Out?" on the reasons spices were so coveted in European societies.
- Deepened the context for the "Sources from the Past" about Christopher Columbus.
- Updated section Ecological Exchanges to reflect current scholarship.

Chapter 20: The Transformation of Europe

- Changed title of section Western Christendom to Western European Christendom to be more specific.
- Added a "What's Left Out?" on the desperate conditions for ordinary Europeans caused by the Thirty Years' War.

Chapter 21: The Integration of the Americas and Oceania with the Wider World

- Changed title to emphasize the relations of these regions with the rest of the world.
- Changed the subsection Conquest of Mexico and Peru to simply Mexico and Peru to de-emphasize the idea that conquest was inevitable.
- Changed introductory vignette on Doña Marina to complicate her story.

- Emphasized the critical role of epidemic disease in the devastation of the populations of the Americas.
- Emphasized the brutal treatment of Native American peoples by European conquerors and settlers, as well as resistance to such treatment.
- Added a "What's Left Out?" on the widespread practice of British settlers enslaving Native American peoples in the eastern colonies.
- Streamlined and clarified section Colonial Society in the Americas to reflect current scholarship.
- Added clarity regarding competition among Native American groups in North America.

Chapter 22: Africa and the Atlantic World

- Removed several instances of Eurocentric text.
- Brought the sections on the trans-Saharan slave trade and Atlantic slave trade up to date.
- Updated section on consequences of the Atlantic slave trade in Africa to reflect current scholarship.
- Updated section on the African diaspora to reflect current scholarship.
- Added a "What's Left Out?" on the ways women experienced slavery differently than men.
- Updated the section on African diaspora cultures to reflect current scholarship.
- Rewrote the Conclusion.

Chapter 23: Tradition and Change in East Asia

- Clarified and updated section on foot binding.
- Added a "What's Left Out?" on the parallels between Chinese foot binding and the use of corsets in western Europe.
- Rewrote the section Government and Technology to minimize Eurocentrism.
- Eliminated comparisons of Chinese and European merchants to eliminate Eurocentrism.

Chapter 24: Empires in South and Southwest Asia

- Changed title to de-emphasize Islam for a focus on the region.
- Reversed the two subheads in the section Empires in Transition to tell the story more clearly.
- Updated the section Dynastic State to reflect current thinking on succession.
- Reversed subheads Steppe Traditions and Women in Politics in the section Dynastic State.
- Added a new "Sources from the Past" by Emperor Akbar of the Moghul dynasty.
- Added a "What's Left Out?" on the lives of ordinary Muslim women in the Ottoman empire.
- Added detail to section Food Crops.
- Significantly updated section Economic Difficulties and Military Decline to reflect current scholarship.
- Deleted section Cultural Conservatism because of Eurocentrism and bias.

Chapter 25: Revolutions and National States in the Atlantic World

- Rewrote Chapter Overview to reflect extensive changes in the chapter.
- Changed title of first section to Revolutionary Ideas.
- Added new section Revolutions to cover the American, French, Haitian, and Latin American revolutions.
- Added a new heading called Consequences and Implications of the Revolutions.
- Changed first subhead under the Consequences section to The Emergence of New Ideologies.
- Changed final section to New Nations and Nationalism in Europe.
- De-emphasized the revolutionary potential of ideas and emphasized the importance of war as a factor in instigating the revolutions of this period.
- Rewrote the subhead Tightened British Control of the Colonies to reflect the importance of the experience of war.
- Clarified the reasons behind the start of the American revolution.
- Rewrote the section on why the British lost the American revolution, with an emphasis on the role of the French.
- Clarified that the French philosophes were deeply inspired by the American revolution.
- Updated section Haitian revolution.
- Wrote introduction to new section on the consequences of the revolutions.
- Added a "What's Left Out?" on women's participation in the revolutions.
- Rewrote Conclusion.

Chapter 26: The Making of Industrial Society

- Added more on the environmental impact of the Industrial Revolution.
- Updated section on the origins of the industrial revolution to reflect current scholarship.
- Added a new "Sources from the Past" on Ned Ludd.
- Added a "What's Left Out?" on the introduction of clock time.
- Revised subheads Big Business and Corporations for greater clarity.
- Deleted claim about the strong link between industrialization and the abolition of slavery.
- Updated and clarified subheads New Social Classes and Work and Play.
- Updated subheads on women and gender to reflect current scholarship.
- Updated and rewrote subhead Global Division of Labor and Economic Interdependence to reflect current scholarship.

Chapter 27: The Americas in the Age of Independence

- Added more in-depth indigenous perspectives to chapter content.
- Clarified and streamlined lead-up to the U.S. Civil War.
- Clarified the process of Canada gaining dominion status.
- Updated and streamlined subhead Mexico.
- Rewrote the introduction to American Economic Development.
- Significantly rewrote the section Latin American Investments.
- Added a "What's Left Out?" on child removal in Australia, Canada, and the United States.
- Updated the section Societies in the United States to reflect recent scholarship.

Chapter 28: The Apex of Global Empire Building

- Changed title to reflect content changes in chapter.
- Wrote a new introductory story on Menelik II of Ethiopia.
- Rewrote the Chapter Overview to reflect content changes in the chapter.
- Changed subhead Political Motives for Imperialism to Geopolitical Motives for Imperialism.
- Substantially rewrote subheads Geopolitical Motives for Imperialism, Economic Motives for Imperialism, and Cultural Justifications for Imperialism.
- Moved subheads within the section Foundations of Empire for better flow.
- Rewrote most of the section on the Indian mutiny.
- Added new "Sources from the Past" by Queen Lili'uokulani.
- Deleted some material on European explorers in Africa and added material on King Leopold's Congo.
- Changed subhead Ottoman Military Decline to Ottoman Military Difficulties.
- Updated section The Emergence of New Imperial Powers to reflect current scholarship.
- Updated subhead Scientific Racism to reflect current scholarship.
- Added a "What's Left Out?" on the unintended consequences of colonialism on gender relations.

Chapter 29: The Great War: The World in Upheaval

- Under the section Global War, added sections Battles in Southwest Asia and Africa and Africans in the War.
- Clarified introduction to the section Understandings and Alliances.
- Clarified the establishment of the western front.
- Added a "What's Left Out?" on the German Committee for Indian Independence.
- Added material on battles in southwest Asia.
- Added material on Africa in the war.

Chapter 30: Anxieties and Experiments in Postwar Europe and the United States

- Changed title to reflect content within chapter.
- Shortened introductory story on Hitler.
- Changed section Probing Cultural Frontiers to New Intellectual Frontiers.
- Significantly rewrote the section on communism in Russia.
- Added a "What's Left Out?" on the popularity of eugenics in the United States.

Chapter 31: Revolutionaries and Nationalists in the Colonial and Neocolonial World

- Changed title to reflect new content in the chapter.
- Changed section Asian Paths to Autonomy to Paths to Autonomy in East and Southeast Asia.
- Changed subhead China's Search for Order to China's Campaigns to End Foreign Domination.
- Changed section Africa under Colonial Domination to Sub-Saharan Africa under Colonial Domination.
- Deleted section Africa and Africans in the Great War.
- Significantly rewrote the material on China and India to reflect current scholarly understandings.
- Updated section on sub-Saharan Africa to reflect current scholarship.
- Added a "What's Left Out?" on the League Against Imperialism.
- Updated and clarified subhead Neighborly Cultural Exchanges.
- Added a new ending to chapter.

Chapter 32: New Conflagrations: World War II and the Cold War

- Updated subhead on Chinese resistance to Japanese invasion to reflect current scholarship.
- Updated subhead Italian and German Aggression by adding material on Ethiopian invasion.
- Nuanced the philosophy of appeasement.
- Clarified and rewrote the chain of events in the German conquest of western Europe.
- Added to subhead Women's Roles by adding information about Soviet women.
- Added a "What's Left Out?" on the long history of anti-communism.
- Added material in the section on the cold war that clarifies the Soviet perspective.
- Updated section Cracks in the Soviet-Chinese Alliance to reflect current scholarship.

Chapter 33: The End of Empire in an Era of Cold War

- Changed title to reflect importance of cold war in decolonization.

- Streamlined introductory story on Gandhi and significantly rewrote the Chapter Overview to reflect new content in the chapter.
- Rewrote introduction to Independence in Asia.
- Rewrote material on partition in India.
- Rewrote section on nationalism in Vietnam.
- Updated section on Palestine to reflect recent scholarship.
- Rewrote section on the Suez Crisis.
- Substantially rewrote the section on French decolonization in North Africa.
- Added material on apartheid in South Africa.
- Streamlined and updated the material on Mao's China.
- Updated material on postcolonial India to reflect current scholarship.
- Updated material on Islamism and the Iranian revolution.
- Deleted text on African disunity.
- Added "Sources from the Past" on China's marriage law.
- Added a "What's Left Out?" on the combination of decolonization and the cold war in Angola.

Chapter 34: Into the Twenty-First Century

- Changed title to make it sound more current.
- Updated all dates and material to bring them in line with the second decade of the twenty-first century.
- Rewrote Chapter Overview to reflect content changes in the chapter.
- Changed title of section The End of the Cold War to The End of the Cold War and the Emergence of a Unipolar World.
- Added subhead The Unipolar Moment.
- Moved the subhead International Organizations to the section on Cross-Cultural Exchanges.
- Renamed the section Global Problems to Urgent Global Issues in the Twenty-First Century.
- Added subheads The Continuing Inequality of Women, Migration, and Global Diseases.
- Deleted final section Crossing Boundaries.
- Added a new introduction to the section End of the Cold War.
- Added new text on the end of the cold war through 2020.
- Clarified information on GATT and WTO.
- Updated section Rise of China.
- Added new material on the EU to Brexit.
- Updated material on OPEC.
- Deleted subhead on Pan-American culture and added material on cultural globalization.
- Deleted subhead on the age of access and added material on the networked world.
- Deleted subheads Prominence of the English Language and Adaptations of Technology.
- Deleted information on population pressure.
- Added material on climate change.

- Added new material on global diseases, specifically the COVID-19 pandemic, to bring content up to the present.
- Updated material on global terrorism.
- Added new material on women's inequality globally.
- Added a new "Sources from the Past" by Malebogo Molefhe.
- Added a "What's Left Out?" on the difficulties of writing the history of the very recent past.
- Added new material on migrants in a global context as well as the recent conflict between Russia and Ukraine.

PRIMARY SOURCES HELP STUDENTS THINK CRITICALLY ABOUT HISTORY

Primary sources help students think critically about history and expose them to contrasting perspectives of key events. The fifth edition of *Traditions & Encounters* provides four different ways to use primary source documents.

Power of Process for Primary Sources

Power of Process is a critical thinking tool for reading and writing about primary sources. As part of Connect History, McGraw Hill's learning platform, Power of Process contains a database of more than 400 searchable primary sources in addition to the capability for instructors to upload their own sources. Instructors can then select a series of strategies for students to use to analyze and comment on a source. The Power of Process framework helps students develop essential academic skills such as understanding, analyzing, and synthesizing readings and visuals such as maps, leading students toward higher-order thinking and writing.

The Power of Process landing page makes it easy for instructors to find pre-populated documents or to add their own.

Sources from the Past

These features showcase a significant primary source document of the period, such as a poem, journal account, religious writing, or letter. Thought-provoking questions prompt readers to analyze key issues raised in the document.

Connecting the Sources

This feature helps students recognize that historiography is based on scholars' interpretation of historical information. It focuses on two documents or images, asking students to think critically about the different ways information can be interpreted.

McGraw Hill Create

Because no two history courses are the same, you can select primary sources that meet the unique needs of your course.

Using McGraw Hill's Create® allows you to quickly and easily create custom course materials with cross-disciplinary content. Here's what you can do:

- Choose your own content: Create a book that contains only the chapters you want, in the order you want. Create will even renumber the pages for you!
- Add readings: Add readings from our collection or add your own original content such as syllabus or history major requirements.
- Choose your format: Print or ebook? Softcover, spiral, or loose-leaf? Black-and-white or color?
- Customize your cover: Pick your own cover image and include your name and course information right on the cover. Students will know they're purchasing the right book—and using everything they purchase!
- Review your creation: When you are all done, you'll receive a free PDF to review in just minutes. To get started, go to create.mheducation.com and register today.

SMARTBOOK TAILORS CONTENT TO THE INDIVIDUAL STUDENT

SMARTBOOK® Available within Connect History, SmartBook has been updated with improved learning objectives to ensure that students gain foundational knowledge while learning to make connections to help them formulate a broader understanding of historical events. SmartBook personalizes learning to individual student needs, continually adapting to pinpoint knowledge gaps and focus learning on topics that need the most attention. Study time is more productive, and as a result, students are better prepared for class and coursework. For instructors, SmartBook tracks student progress and provides insights that can help guide teaching strategies.

WRITING ASSIGNMENT

McGraw Hill's new Writing Assignment Plus tool delivers a learning experience that improves students' written communication skills and conceptual understanding with every assignment. Assign, monitor, and provide feedback on writing more efficiently and grade assignments within McGraw Hill Connect®. Writing Assignment Plus gives you time-saving tools with a just-in-time basic writing and originality checker.

Features include

- Grammar/writing checking with McGraw Hill learning resources.
- Originality checker with McGraw Hill learning resources.
- Writing stats.
- Rubric building and scoring.
- Ability to assign draft and final deadline milestones.
- Tablet ready and tools for all learners.

CONTEXTUALIZE HISTORY

Help students experience history in a whole new way with our new Podcast Assignments. We've gathered some of the most interesting and popular history podcasts currently available and built assignable questions around them. These assignments allow instructors to bring greater context and nuance to their courses while engaging students through the storytelling power of podcasts.

INSTRUCTOR RESOURCES

Traditions & Encounters offers an array of instructor resources for the world history course.

Instructor's Manual

The Instructor's Manual provides a wide variety of tools and resources for presenting the course, including learning objectives and ideas for lectures and discussions.

Test Bank

Each question has been tagged for level of difficulty, Bloom's taxonomy, and topic coverage. Organized by chapter, the questions are designed to test factual, conceptual, and higher-order thinking.

Test Builder

New to this edition and available within Connect, Test Builder is a cloud-based tool that enables instructors to format tests that can be printed and administered within a Learning Management System. Test Builder offers a modern, streamlined interface for easy content configuration that matches course needs, without requiring a download.

Test Builder enables instructors to
- Access all Test Bank content from a particular title.
- Easily pinpoint the most relevant content through robust filtering options.
- Manipulate the order of questions or scramble questions and/or answers.
- Pin questions to a specific location within a test.
- Determine your preferred treatment of algorithmic questions.
- Choose the layout and spacing.
- Add instructions and configure default settings.

PowerPoint

The PowerPoint presentations highlight the key points of the chapter and include supporting visuals. New to this edition, all slides are WCAG compliant.

PROCTORIO

Remote Proctoring & Browser-Locking Capabilities

Remote proctoring and browser-locking capabilities, hosted by Proctorio within Connect, provide control of the assessment environment by enabling security options and verifying the identity of the student.

Seamlessly integrated within Connect, these services allow instructors to control the assessment experience by verifying identification, restricting browser activity, and monitoring student actions.

Instant and detailed reporting gives instructors an at-a-glance view of potential academic integrity concerns, thereby avoiding personal bias and supporting evidence-based claims.

About the Authors

Jerry H. Bentley was professor of history at the University of Hawai'i and editor of the *Journal of World History*. His research on the religious, moral, and political writings of the Renaissance led to the publication of *Humanists and Holy Writ: New Testament Scholarship in the Renaissance* (Princeton, 1983) and *Politics and Culture in Renaissance Naples* (Princeton, 1987). More recently, his research concentrated on global history and particularly on processes of cross-cultural interaction. His book *Old World Encounters: Cross-Cultural Contacts and Exchanges in Pre-Modern Times* (New York, 1993) examines processes of cultural exchange and religious conversion before the modern era, and his pamphlet *Shapes of World History in Twentieth-Century Scholarship* (1996) discusses the historiography of world history. His most recent publication is *The Oxford Handbook of World History* (Oxford, 2011), and he served as a member of the editorial team preparing the forthcoming *Cambridge History of the World*. Jerry Bentley passed away in July 2012, although his legacy lives on through his significant contributions to the study of world history. The World History Association recently named an annual prize in his honor for outstanding publications in the field.

Herbert F. Ziegler is an associate professor of history at the University of Hawai'i. He has taught world history since 1980; he previously served as director of the world history program at the University of Hawai'i as well as book review editor of the *Journal of World History*. His interest in twentieth-century European social and political history led to the publication of *Nazi Germany's New Aristocracy: The SS Leadership, 1925-1939* (Princeton, 1990) and to his participation in new educational endeavors in the history of the Holocaust, including the development of an upper-division course for undergraduates. He is at present working on a study that explores from a global point of view the demographic trends of the past ten thousand years, along with their concomitant technological, economic, and social developments. His other current research project focuses on the application of complexity theory to a comparative study of societies and their internal dynamics.

Heather Streets-Salter is Professor and Director of World History Programs at Northeastern University in Boston, Massachusetts. She is the author of *World War One in Southeast Asia: Colonialism and Anticolonialism in an Era of Global Conflict* (Cambridge University Press, 2017); *Martial Races: The Military, Martial Races, and Masculinity in British Imperial Culture, 1857-1914* (Manchester University Press, 2004); and *Empires and Colonies in the Modern World* (Oxford University Press, 2015) with Trevor Getz. Her next book is called *The Chill before the Cold War: Communism and Anti-Communism in Colonial Southeast Asia in the Interwar Period*.

Craig Benjamin is Professor of History Emeritus at Grand Valley State University in Michigan. He is the author of *The Yuezhi: Origin, Migration and the Conquest of Northern Bactria* (Brepols, 2007) and *Empires of Ancient Eurasia: The First Silk Roads Era 100 BCE-250 CE* (Cambridge University Press, 2018) and co-author of *Big History: Between Nothing and Everything* (McGraw Hill, 2014). He is the editor of Volume 4 of the *Cambridge History of the World* (Cambridge University Press, 2015) and co-editor of *The Routledge Companion to Big History* (Routledge, 2019). Craig served as president of the World History Association and chair of both the Advanced Placement and SAT World History Test Committees.

Acknowledgments

Many individuals have contributed to this book, and the authors take pleasure in recording deep thanks for all the comments, criticism, advice, and suggestions that helped improve the work. The editorial, marketing, and production teams at McGraw Hill did an outstanding job of seeing the project through to publication. Special thanks go to Jason Seitz, Stephanie Ventura, and Sandy Wille, who provided crucial support by helping the authors work through difficult issues and solve the innumerable problems of content, style, and organization that arise in any project to produce a history of the world. Many colleagues at the University of Hawai'i at Mānoa, most notably the late Professor Margot A. Henriksen, and elsewhere aided and advised the authors on matters of organization and composition. Finally, we would like to express our appreciation for the advice of the following individuals, who read and commented on the previous edition of *Traditions & Encounters* and helped inform this revision.

Stephanie N. Allen, *Alabama A&M University*
Milan Andrejevich, *Ivy Tech Community College of Indiana*
Kevin Brady, *Tidewater Community College*
Matthew Brent, *Rappahannock Community College*
Lucas Bruff, *Davidson-Davie Community College*
Brian Carriere, *Mississippi Gulf Coast Community College*
William Cavert, *University of Hawai'i-West O'ahu*
Camille Dantzler, *Middlesex College*
John Diffley, *Springfield Technical Community College*
Allen Fromherz, *Georgia State University*
Jim Frutchey, *Marywood University*
Wayne Girard, *Middlesex College*
Ashley Giugliano, *Middlesex College*
Lanette Gonzalez, *Ivy Tech Community College of Indiana*
Scott Gurman, *University of Wisconsin-Platteville*
Aimee Harris-Johnson, *El Paso Community College*
Caroline Hasenyager, *Virginia State University*
Elizabeth Horodowich, *New Mexico State University*
Andrey Ivanov, *University of Wisconsin-Platteville*
Jason Kennedy, *West Georgia Technical College*
Marc Lane, *Middlesex College*

Thomas Lansburg, *Middlesex College*
Rebecca Leber-Gottberg, *Pierce College*
Mark Lee, *University of Nebraska-Lincoln*
Darin D. Lenz, *Biola University*
Mary Lyons-Carmona, *Metropolitan Community College*
Meredith May, *Kilgore College*
Kelli Y. Nakamura, *Kapi'olani Community College*
Kevin Nehil, *Mid Michigan College*
Sarah Pacelli, *Siena College*
Chris Powers, *Fort Hays State University*
Julie Rancilio, *Kapi'olani Community College*
Martina Saltamacchia, *University of Nebraska at Omaha*
Charles Sanft, *University of Tennessee, Knoxville*
Stacey Schneider, *Thomas Nelson Community College*
Jason Shows, *Mississippi Gulf Coast Community College*
David Simonelli, *Youngstown State University*
Benjamin Sorensen, *Cape Fear Community College*
Martin Spence, *Cornerstone University*
Shih-chieh (Jay) Su, *Delaware Valley University*
Lawrence Wallis, *Mercer County Community College*

Special thanks and gratitude to the McGraw Hill Academic Integrity Board of Advisors who were instrumental in providing guidance on chapter content, illustration program, and language and conventions. Our advisors include:

Susan Bragg, *Georgia Southwestern State University*
Jennifer Epley Sanders, *Texas A & M*
Eileen Ford, *California State University, Los Angeles*
Nicholas Fox, *Houston College*
Rudy Jean-Bart, *Broward Community College*
Darnell Morehand-Olufade, *University of Bridgeport*
Sharon Navarro, *University of Texas at San Antonio*
Jeffrey Ogbar, *University of Connecticut*
Andrea Oliver, *Tallahassee Community College*
Birte Pfleger, *California State University, Los Angeles*
Linda Reed, *University of Houston*

Traditions & Encounters

A Brief Global History

19 Transoceanic Encounters and Global Connections

ZOOMING IN ON ENCOUNTERS

Vasco da Gama's Search for Spices

On 8 July 1497 the Portuguese mariner **Vasco da Gama** led a small fleet of four armed merchant vessels with 170 crewmen out of the harbor at Lisbon. His destination was India, which he planned to reach by sailing around the continent of Africa and through the Indian Ocean, and his goal was to enter the highly lucrative trade in spices dominated in Europe by the merchants of Venice. He carried letters of introduction from the king of Portugal as well as cargoes of gold, pearls, wool textiles, bronzeware, iron tools, and other goods that he hoped to exchange for spices in India.

Before there would be an opportunity to trade, however, da

Vasco da Gama (VAS-koh duh GAM-uh)

Vasco da Gama's flagship, the *San Rafael,* on the journey to India in 1497.
Photo Researchers/Science History Images/Alamy Stock Photo

Gama and his crew sailed south from Portugal to the Cape Verde Islands off the west coast of Africa, where they took on water and fresh provisions. On 3 August they headed south into the Atlantic Ocean to take advantage of the prevailing winds. For the next ninety-five days, the fleet saw no land. In October, da Gama came across westerly winds in the southern Atlantic, which helped propel him around the Cape of Good Hope and into the Indian Ocean. The fleet slowly worked its way up the east coast of Africa, engaging in hostilities with local authorities at Mozambique and Mombasa, as far as Malindi, where da Gama secured the services of an Indian Muslim pilot to guide his ships across the Arabian Sea. On 20 May 1498—more than ten months after its departure from Lisbon—the fleet anchored at Calicut in southern India.

In India the Portuguese fleet encountered a wealthy, cosmopolitan society. Upon its arrival local authorities in Calicut dispatched a pair of Tunisian merchants who spoke Spanish and Italian to serve as translators for the newly arrived party. The markets of Calicut offered not only pepper, ginger, cinnamon, and other spices sought so eagerly by da Gama but also gems, gold, and fine textiles. But apart from gold and some striped cloth, the merchants at Calicut were not interested in the goods that da Gama had brought to trade.

Nevertheless, da Gama managed to exchange gold for a cargo of pepper and cinnamon, which turned a handsome profit when the fleet returned to Portugal in August 1499. Da Gama's expedition opened the door to direct maritime trade between European and Asian peoples and helped establish permanent links between the world's various regions.

CHAPTER OVERVIEW

Cross-cultural interactions and encounters have been a persistent feature of historical development. Even in ancient times, mass migration, campaigns of imperial expansion, and long-distance trade deeply influenced societies throughout the world. But after 1500 C.E. cross-cultural interactions took place on a much larger geographic scale, and encounters thus affected greater numbers of people than in earlier centuries. Equipped with a variety of technologies and a powerful military arsenal, western

CHRONOLOGY	
1394–1460	Life of Prince Henry the Navigator of Portugal
1488	Bartolomeu Dias's voyage around the Cape of Good Hope into the Indian Ocean
1492	Christopher Columbus's first voyage to the western hemisphere
1497–1499	Vasco da Gama's first voyage to India
1519–1522	Ferdinand Magellan's circumnavigation of the world
1565–1575	Spanish conquest of the Philippines
1768–1780	Captain James Cook's voyages in the Pacific Ocean

European peoples began to cross the world's oceans in large numbers during the early modern era (ca. 1500–ca. 1800). At the same time, Russian adventurers built an enormous Eurasian empire and ventured into the Pacific Ocean.

Europeans were not the only peoples who actively explored the larger world during the early modern era. In the early fifteenth century the Ming emperors of China sponsored a series of seven massive maritime expeditions that visited all parts of the Indian Ocean basin. In the sixteenth century Ottoman mariners also ventured into the Indian Ocean. Although other peoples also made their way into the larger world, it was Europeans who, initially by chance, linked the lands and peoples of the eastern hemisphere, the western hemisphere, and Oceania. Because they began to travel regularly between the world's major geographic regions, in this period European peoples benefited from unparalleled opportunities to increase their power, wealth, and influence. By 1800 the projection of European influence had brought about a decisive shift in the global balance of power.

The expansion of European influence also resulted in the establishment of truly global networks of transportation, communication, and exchange. A worldwide diffusion of plants, animals, diseases, and human communities followed European ventures across the oceans, and intricate trade networks eventually gave birth to a global economy. The consequences to the peoples of the Americas and Oceania were disastrous, as epidemic diseases killed millions of people. Over much of the rest of the world, however, the spread of food crops and domesticated animals contributed to a dramatic surge in global population. The establishment of global trade networks established in this period ensured that interactions between the world's peoples would continue and intensify.

EXPLORATION OF THE WORLD'S OCEANS

Between 1400 and 1800 European mariners launched a remarkable series of exploratory voyages that took them to nearly all the earth's waters. Those voyages were very expensive affairs. Yet private investors and government authorities had strong motives to underwrite the expeditions and outfit them with the latest nautical technology. The voyages of exploration paid large dividends: they enabled European mariners to chart the world's ocean basins and develop an accurate understanding of world geography. On the basis of that knowledge, European merchants and mariners established global networks of communication, transportation, and exchange that had dramatic consequences for the whole world.

The Technology of Exploration

Without advanced nautical technology and navigational skills, European mariners would not have been able to explore the world's oceans. They also needed sturdy ships, good navigational equipment, and knowledge of sailing techniques. These they devised by creatively combining Chinese and Arabic technologies with technologies from the Mediterranean and northern Europe.

Ships and Sails From their experiences in the rough coastal waters of the Atlantic, European sailors learned to construct ships strong enough to survive most adverse conditions. Beginning about the twelfth century, they increased the maneuverability of their craft by building a rudder onto the stern. (The sternpost rudder was a Chinese invention that had diffused across the Indian Ocean.) They outfitted their vessels with two types of sails: square sails (which enabled them to take full advantage of a wind blowing from behind) and triangular lateen sails (which could catch winds from the side as well as from behind). With a combination of square and lateen sails, European ships were able to use whatever winds arose. Their ability

astrolabe (AS-truh-leyb)

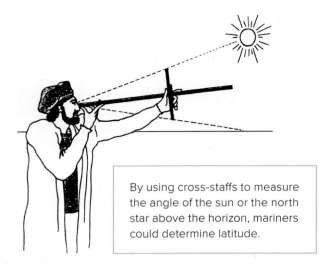

By using cross-staffs to measure the angle of the sun or the north star above the horizon, mariners could determine latitude.

to tack—to advance against the wind by sailing across it—was crucial for the exploration of regions with uncooperative winds.

Navigational Instruments The most important navigational equipment on board these vessels were the **magnetic compass** (which determined heading) and the **astrolabe** (which determined latitude). The compass was a

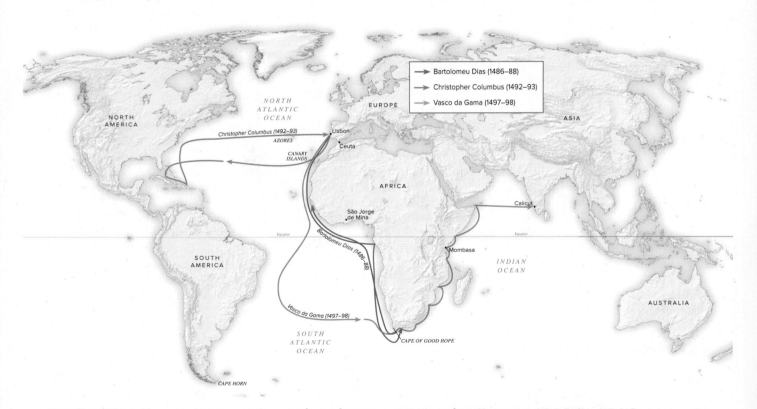

MAP 19.1   European exploration in the Atlantic Ocean, 1486–1498

Observe the difference between Bartolomeu Dias's journey and Vasco da Gama's journey around the Cape of Good Hope.

Why did da Gama go so far out into the Atlantic before rounding the cape?

Chinese invention that had diffused throughout the Indian Ocean basin in the eleventh century and had reached European mariners by the mid-twelfth century. The astrolabe was a simplified version of an instrument used by Greek and Persian astronomers to measure the angle of the sun or the north star above the horizon. In the late fifteenth century, however, Portuguese mariners encountered Arab sailors in the Indian Ocean using simpler and more serviceable instruments for determining latitude, which the Portuguese then used as models for the construction of cross-staffs and back-staffs.

Knowledge of Winds and Currents European mariners' ability to determine direction and latitude enabled them to assemble a vast body of data about the earth's geography and to find their way around the world's oceans with tolerable accuracy and efficiency. Equipped with the latest technological hardware, European mariners ventured into the oceans and gradually compiled a body of practical knowledge about winds and currents. Critical to this body of knowledge was the strategy devised by Portuguese mariners called the *volta do mar* ("return through the sea"), which involved using prevailing winds and currents to reach destinations across the oceans. Although the *volta do mar* forced mariners to take indirect routes to their destinations—which at times required going hundreds of miles out of their way—experience soon taught that sailing around contrary winds was more reliable than butting up against them. When Vasco da Gama sailed for India in 1497, for example, he sailed south to the Cape Verde Islands and then allowed the trade winds to carry him southwest into the Atlantic Ocean until he approached the coast of Brazil. Only then did da Gama catch the prevailing westerlies, which allowed him to sail east around the Cape of Good Hope. As they became familiar with the wind systems of the world's oceans, European mariners developed variations on the *volta do mar* that enabled them to travel reliably to coastlines around the world.

Motives for Exploration

A complex combination of motives prompted Europeans to explore the world's oceans. Most important of those motives were the search for basic resources and lands suitable for the cultivation of cash crops, the desire to establish new trade routes to Asian markets, and the aspiration to expand the influence of Christianity.

Portuguese Exploration Mariners from the relatively poor kingdom of Portugal were most prominent in the search for fresh resources and lands. Beginning in the thirteenth century Portuguese seamen ventured away from the coasts and into the open Atlantic Ocean to supplement their own meager resources. By the early fourteenth century they had discovered the uninhabited Azores and Madeiras Islands and called frequently at the Canary Islands, inhabited by the indigenous Guanche people. These Atlantic islands proved ideal for the cultivation of sugar, a product that enjoyed a strong European demand. In the fifteenth century Italian investors—who had organized sugar plantations in the Mediterranean since the twelfth century—helped Portuguese mariners establish plantations in the Atlantic islands using slave labor. Continuing Portuguese voyages also led to the establishment of plantations on the Cape Verde Islands, São Tomé, Principe, and Fernando Po.

Trade Even more important than the exploitation of fresh lands and resources was the goal of establishing maritime trade routes to the markets of Asia. During the era of the Mongol empires, European merchants often traveled over land as far as China to trade for Asian goods. When the Mongol empires collapsed and bubonic plague spread across Eurasia in the fourteenth century, however, travel on what are now called the Silk Roads became much more dangerous. As a result, Europeans relied on Arab mariners to take Asian goods through the Indian Ocean and the Red Sea to Cairo, where Italian merchants purchased them for distribution in western Europe. But prices at Cairo were high, and Europeans sought ever-larger quantities of Asian goods, particularly spices.

By the fourteenth century the wealthy classes of Europe regarded Indian pepper and Chinese ginger as expensive necessities, and they especially prized cloves and nutmeg from the spice islands of Maluku. Merchants and monarchs alike realized that by gaining direct access to Asian markets and eliminating Muslim intermediaries, they could increase the quantities of spices and other Asian goods available in Europe while making enormous profits.

Europeans were also interested in African trade. Since the twelfth century camel caravans had delivered west African gold, ivory, and enslaved people to north African ports, where Europeans—along with many others—took part in their trade. Gold was an especially important commodity, because the precious metal from west Africa was Europeans' principal form of payment for Asian luxury goods. As in the case of Asian trade, European merchants were interested in maritime routes that eliminated Muslim intermediaries and offered more direct access to African markets.

Missionary Efforts Alongside material incentives, the goal of expanding the boundaries of Christianity drove Europeans into the larger world. Like Buddhism and Islam, Christianity is a missionary religion that directs believers to spread the faith. Sometimes such efforts

CALECHVT CELEBERRI:
MVM INDIÆ EMPORIVM.

A depiction of the Indian port of Calicut in 1572, when Portugal dominated the pepper trade.
FLHC A20/Alamy Stock Photo

were attempted through peaceful persuasion. At other times the expansion of Christianity could be quite violent. Beginning in the eleventh century, for example, western Europeans launched a series of crusades against Muslims in Palestine, the Mediterranean islands, and Iberia. In Iberia, in fact, the Muslim kingdom of Granada fell to Spanish Christian forces just weeks before Christopher Columbus set sail on his famous first voyage to the western hemisphere in 1492. Whether through persuasion or violence, overseas voyages offered fresh opportunities for western Europeans to spread their faith.

In practice, the various motives for exploration combined and reinforced one another. When Vasco da Gama reached the Indian port of Calicut in 1498, local authorities asked him what he wanted there. His reply was "Christians and spices." The goal of spreading Christianity thus became a powerful justification and reinforcement for the more material motives for the voyages of exploration.

What's Left Out?

In Europe during the late Middle Ages, spices such as pepper, cloves, and nutmeg were extremely expensive, costing approximately 1 to 3 English shillings per pound. Compare this to a whole cow, which cost between 6 and 10 shillings. An ordinary soldier's wages, by comparison, were about a shilling a day, whereas a kitchen servant's wages were between 2 and 4 shillings for a whole year. What was it about the spices that made people want to pay such high prices for them, and for others to risk their lives and all their material possessions to trade them? Spices were used to enhance the taste and smell of many foods and drinks, to mask bad odors, and as medicines. Pepper and cinnamon, for example, were used to treat a myriad of ailments, including headache, insomnia, and digestive problems. But scholars now believe it was the very rarity of spices that was the real source of their value. Precisely because they came from so far away and were thus so expensive, spices were viewed as the ultimate status symbols. In addition, many Europeans believed fantastic stories about the way spices were procured. Pepper, for example, was thought to come from trees guarded by serpents that poisoned anyone attempting to harvest the peppercorns that grew on them. Stories such as these added to the allure of spices, which in turn helped explain the very high prices Europeans were willing to pay for them.

Source: John Keay. *The Spice Route: A History.* Berkeley: University of California Press, 2006.

European Voyages of Exploration: From the Mediterranean to the Atlantic

Prince Henry of Portugal Although European exploratory voyaging began as early as the thirteenth century, the pace quickened decisively after 1415. In that year, Prince Henry of Portugal (1394–1460), often called **Prince Henry the Navigator**, conquered the Moroccan port of **Ceuta** and sponsored a series of voyages down the west African coast. Portuguese merchants soon established fortified trading posts at São Jorge da Mina (in modern Ghana) and other strategic locations. There they exchanged European horses and goods for gold and, increasingly, enslaved people. Portuguese explorations continued after Henry's death, and in 1488 Bartolomeu Dias rounded the Cape of Good Hope and entered the Indian Ocean. He did not proceed farther because of storms and a restless crew, but the route to India, China, and the spice-bearing islands of southeast Asia lay open. The sea route to the Indian Ocean offered European merchants the opportunity to buy silk, spices, and pepper at the source, rather than through Muslim intermediaries, and to take part in the flourishing trade of Asia.

Vasco da Gama As we have already seen, in 1497 Vasco da Gama departed Lisbon with a fleet of four armed merchant ships bound for India. His experience was not altogether pleasant. His fleet went more than three months without seeing land, and his cargoes excited little interest in Indian markets. Moreover, more than half of his crew died slow and painful deaths from scurvy (vitamin C deficiency) before making it back to Portugal. Yet his cargo of pepper and cinnamon was hugely profitable, and Portuguese merchants began immediately to organize further expeditions. By 1500 they had built a trading post at Calicut, and Portuguese mariners soon called at ports throughout the Indian Ocean basin. By the late sixteenth century English and Dutch mariners had followed suit.

Christopher Columbus While Portuguese navigators plied the sea route to India, the Genoese mariner Cristoforo Colombo, known in English as Christopher Columbus (1451–1506), proposed sailing to the markets of Asia by a western route. On the basis of wide reading in the existing geographic literature, Columbus believed that the earth was a relatively small sphere with a circumference of about 17,000 nautical miles. (In fact, the earth's circumference is almost 25,000 nautical miles.) By Columbus's calculations, Japan should have been less than 2,500 nautical miles west of the Canary Islands. (The actual distance is more than 10,000 nautical miles.) This geography suggested that sailing west from Europe to Asian markets would be profitable, and Columbus sought royal sponsorship for a voyage to prove his ideas.

Eventually, Fernando and Isabel of Spain agreed to underwrite Columbus's expedition, and in August 1492 his fleet of three ships departed southern Spain. He sailed south to the Canaries, picked up supplies, and then turned west with the trade winds. On the morning of 12 October 1492, he made landfall at an island in the Bahamas that the native **Taino** inhabitants called **Guanahaní** and that Columbus renamed San Salvador (also known as Watling Island). Thinking that he had arrived in the spice islands known familiarly as the Indies, Columbus called the Tainos "Indians." He sailed around the Caribbean for almost three months in search of gold, and at the large island of Cuba he sent a delegation to seek the court of the emperor of China. When Columbus returned to Spain, he reported to his royal sponsors that he had reached islands just off the coast of Asia.

Hemispheric Links In spite of what he believed, Columbus never reached the riches of Asia. Moreover, he obtained very little gold in the Caribbean. Yet news of his voyage spread rapidly throughout Europe, and hundreds of Spanish, English, French, and Dutch mariners soon followed in his wake. Initially, many of them continued to seek the passage to Asian waters that Columbus himself had pursued. Over the longer term, however, it became clear that the American continents and the Caribbean islands themselves held abundant opportunities for entrepreneurs. Thus Columbus's voyages to the western hemisphere had unintended but profound consequences, because they established links between the eastern and western hemispheres and paved the way for the conquest, settlement, and exploitation of the Americas by European peoples.

European Voyages of Exploration: From the Atlantic to the Pacific

While some Europeans sought opportunities in the Americas, others continued to seek a western route to Asian markets. However, in the early sixteenth century no one suspected the vast size of the Pacific Ocean, which covers one-third of the earth's surface.

Ferdinand Magellan The initial exploration of the Pacific Ocean basin began with the Portuguese navigator Fernão de Magalhães (1480–1521), better known as **Ferdinand Magellan**. While sailing in the service of Portugal, Magellan had visited ports throughout the Indian Ocean basin and had traveled east as far as the spice islands of

---

Ceuta (SYOO-tuh)
São Jorge da Mina (sou hor-hay da meena)
Bartolomeu Dias (bahr-tol-uh-MEY-oh dee-as)
Taino (tah-EE-no)
Guanahaní (Gwah-nah-nee)
Ferdinand Magellan (FUR-dih-nand muh-JEHL-uhn)

Christopher Columbus's First Impressions of American Peoples

Christopher Columbus kept journals of his experiences during his voyages to the western hemisphere. These journals were not meant to be private but, instead, were to be shared with his benefactors, Ferdinand and Isabel of Spain, as well as to record his accomplishments for posterity. The journal of his first voyage survives mostly in summary, but it clearly communicates Columbus's first impressions of the peoples he met in the Caribbean islands. The following excerpts show that Columbus, like other European mariners, had both Christianity and commerce in mind when exploring distant lands. Keep in mind that Columbus treated the indigenous Taino with brutality, even from the first day of his arrival, when he had six people seized as servants. Look for places in the text in which Columbus uses dehumanizing language or suggests how the Taino could be useful to Europeans.

Thursday, 11 October [1492]. . . .

I . . . in order that they would be friendly to us—because I recognized that they were people who would be better freed [from error] and converted to our Holy Faith by love than by force—to some of them I gave red caps, and glass beads which they put on their chests, and many other things of small value, in which they took so much pleasure and became so much our friends that it was a marvel. Later they came swimming to the ships' launches where we were and brought us parrots and cotton thread in balls and javelins and many other things, and they traded them to us for other things which we gave them, such as small glass beads and bells. In sum, they took everything and gave of what they had willingly.

But it seemed to me that they were a people very poor in everything. All of them go as naked as their mothers bore them; and the women also, although I did not see more than one quite young girl. And all those that I saw were young people, for none did I see of more than 30 years of age. They are very well formed, with handsome bodies and good faces. Their hair [is] coarse—almost like the tail of a horse—and short. They wear their hair down over their eyebrows except for a little in the back which they wear long and never cut. . . .

They do not carry arms nor are they acquainted with them, because I showed them swords and they took them by the edge and through ignorance cut themselves. They have no iron. Their javelins are shafts without iron and some of them have at the end a fish tooth and others of other things. All of them alike are of good-sized stature and carry themselves well. I saw some who had marks of wounds on their bodies and I made signs to them asking what they were; and they showed me how people from other islands nearby came there and tried to take them, and how they defended themselves and I believed and believe that they come here from *tierra firme* [the continent] to take them captive. They should be good and intelligent servants, for I see that they say very quickly everything that is said to them; and I believe that they would become Christians very easily, for it seemed to me that they had no religion. . . .

> On what basis might Christopher Columbus have been making such an observation about religious faith? What might he have been missing?

Monday, 12 November. . . .

They are very gentle and do not know what evil is; nor do they kill others, nor steal; and they are without weapons and so timid that a hundred of them flee from one of our men even if our men are teasing them. And they are credulous and aware that there is a God in heaven and convinced that we come from the heavens; and they say very quickly any prayer that we tell them to say, and they make the sign of the cross. So that Your Highnesses ought to resolve to make them Christians: for I believe that if you begin, in a short time you will end up having converted to our Holy Faith a multitude of peoples and acquiring large dominions and great riches and all of their peoples for Spain. Because without doubt there is in these lands a very great quantity of gold; for not without cause do these Indians that I bring with me say that there are in these islands places where they dig gold and wear it on their chests, on their ears, and on their arms, and on their legs; and they are very thick bracelets. And also there are stones, and there are precious pearls and infinite spicery. . . . And also here there is probably a great quantity of cotton; and I think that it would sell very well here without taking it to Spain but to the big cities belonging to the Grand [Mongol] Khan.

> Does this statement contradict Columbus's earlier assertion that the people he encountered "had no religion"?

For Further Reflection

■ On the basis of Columbus's account, what inferences can you draw about his plans for American lands and peoples? Based on this small excerpt, is it possible to surmise how contemporary Taino people might have described Columbus and his men?

Source: Christopher Columbus. *The* Diario *of Christopher Columbus's First Voyage to America.* Trans. by Oliver Dunn and James E. Kelley Jr. Norman: University of Oklahoma Press, 1989, pp. 65–69, 143–45. Used with permission.

Maluku. He believed that the spice islands and Asian markets lay fairly close to the western coast of the Americas, and he decided to pursue Christopher Columbus's goal of establishing a western route to Asian waters. Because Portuguese mariners had already reached Asian markets through the Indian Ocean, they had little interest in Magellan's proposed western route. Thus, on his Pacific expedition and circumnavigation of the world (1519–1522), Magellan sailed in the service of Spain.

The Circumnavigation Magellan's voyage was an exercise in endurance. He began by probing the eastern coast of South America in search of a strait leading to the Pacific. Eventually he found and sailed through the treacherous Strait of Magellan near the southern tip of South America. His fleet then sailed almost four months before taking on fresh provisions at Guam. During that period crewmen survived on worm-ridden biscuits and water gone foul. Lacking fresh fruits and vegetables in their diet, many of the crew fell victim to the dreaded disease scurvy, which caused painful rotting of the gums, loss of teeth,

abscesses, hemorrhaging, and in most cases death. Scurvy killed twenty-nine members of Magellan's crew during the Pacific crossing.

Conditions improved after the fleet called at Guam, but its ordeal had not come to an end. From Guam, Magellan proceeded to the Philippine Islands, where he and 40 of his crew were killed in a local political dispute. The survivors continued on to the spice islands of Maluku, where they took on a cargo of cloves. They then sailed home through the familiar waters of the Indian Ocean—and thus completed the first circumnavigation of the world—returning to Spain after a voyage of almost exactly three years. Of Magellan's five ships and 280 men, only one ship with 18 of the original crew returned. (An additional 17 crewmen returned later by other routes.)

Exploration of the Pacific The Pacific Ocean is so vast that it took European explorers almost three centuries to chart its features. Spanish merchants built on information gleaned from Magellan's expedition and established a trade route between the Philippines and

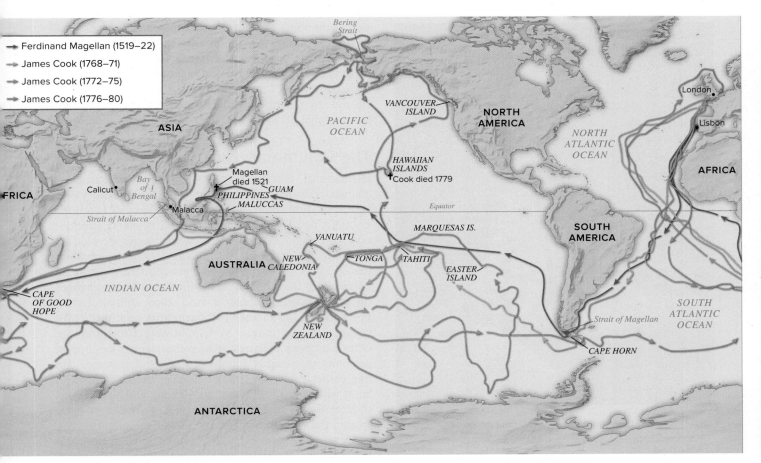

MAP 19.2   Pacific voyages of Magellan and Cook, 1519–1780

What made exploration of the Pacific Ocean so daunting? What fate befell Magellan and Cook?

Mexico, but they did not continue to explore the ocean basin itself. English navigators, however, ventured into the Pacific in search of a northwest passage from Europe to Asia. While searching for a passage, English mariners mapped many of the details of Pacific geography. In the sixteenth century, for example, Sir Francis Drake scouted the west coast of North America as far north as Vancouver Island.

Russian expansion was mostly a land-based affair in early modern times, but by the eighteenth century Russians also were exploring the Pacific Ocean. Russian officials commissioned the Danish navigator Vitus Bering to undertake two maritime expeditions (1725–1730 and 1733–1742) in search of a northeast passage to Asian ports. Bering sailed through the icy Arctic Ocean and the Bering Strait, which separates Siberia from Alaska.

Other Russian explorers made their way from Alaska down the western Canadian coast to northern California. By 1800 Russian mariners were scouting the Pacific Ocean as far south as the Hawaiian Islands. Indeed, they built a small fort on the island of Kaua'i and engaged in trade there for a few years in the early nineteenth century.

A portrait of Captain James Cook, painted by William Hodges about 1775, depicts a serious and determined man.
Ian Dagnall/Alamy Stock Photo

Captain James Cook Alongside Magellan, however, the most important of the Pacific explorers was **Captain James Cook** (1728–1779), who led three expeditions to the Pacific and died in a scuffle with the indigenous people of Hawai'i. Cook charted eastern Australia and New Zealand, and he added New Caledonia, Vanuatu, and Hawai'i to European maps of the Pacific. He probed the frigid waters of the Arctic Ocean and spent months at a time in the tropical islands of Tahiti, Tonga, and Hawai'i. By the time Cook's voyages came to an end, European geographers had compiled a reasonably accurate understanding of the world's ocean basins, their lands, and their peoples.

ECOLOGICAL EXCHANGES

European explorers and those who followed them established links between all the lands and peoples of the world. Interaction between peoples in turn resulted in an unprecedented volume of exchange across the boundaries of societies and cultural regions. Some of that exchange involved biological species: plants, food crops, animals, human populations, and disease pathogens all spread to regions they had not previously visited. These biological exchanges had differing and dramatic effects on human populations, destroying some of them through epidemic diseases while enlarging others through increased food supplies and richer diets. Commercial exchange also flourished in the wake of the voyages of exploration as European merchants traveled to ports throughout the world in search of trade. Indeed, by the mid-eighteenth century they had established global networks of trade and communication.

The Columbian Exchange

Biological Exchanges Processes of biological exchange were prominent features of world history well before modern times. The early expansion of Islam, for example, had facilitated the diffusion of plants and food crops throughout much of the eastern hemisphere during the period from about 700 to 1100 C.E., some of which helped spark demographic and economic growth in the lands where they took root. Yet the **Columbian exchange**— the global diffusion of plants, food crops, animals, human populations, and disease pathogens that took place after voyages of exploration by Christopher Columbus and other European mariners—had consequences much more profound than earlier rounds of biological exchange. Unlike earlier processes, the Columbian exchange involved lands with radically different flora, fauna, and diseases. For thousands of years the various species of the eastern hemisphere, the western hemisphere, and Oceania had evolved along separate lines. By creating links between these biological zones, the European voyages of exploration set off a round of biological exchange that permanently altered the world's human geography and natural environment.

Why It Matters ▷▷▷▷▷▷▷

Short-Term and Long-Term Effects of the Columbian Exchange

Have you ever wondered why the world is the way it is today? If so, you would need to go back all the way to the years around 1500 C.E. for the answer. Can you imagine Italian food without tomatoes? Ireland without potatoes? Can you imagine Italian food without tomatoes? Ireland without potatoes? American prairies without cows or horses? North American lawns without dandelions? Before the Columbian exchange, all of these plants and animals were missing from these cultures, because they only existed in either the Americas or Afro-Eurasia. Once all of the world's peoples were brought into contact around 1500 C.E., exchanges of plants and animals transformed landscapes and societies around the world.

Some, such as dandelions introduced in the Americas or pigs introduced on the island of Barbados, became invasive in their new environments and threatened existing plants and animals. Others brought about fundamental cultural changes when introduced to other parts of the world. Foods from the Americas such as potatoes, corn, chocolate, and tomatoes altered the cuisine of people from Europe to Africa to Asia so profoundly that it is hard to imagine many cultures without them.

Nonfood crops that were part of the Columbian exchange also transformed the world in ways that we can still see today. One of the most significant of these crops was tobacco, which was introduced to the rest of the world from the Americas in the sixteenth century and quickly spread to Europe, Asia, west Africa, and the Near East. In the present, approximately 1.1 billion of the world's people are smokers, and about 25 percent of smokers die from smoke-related causes—a health crisis that can only be explained by events that happened more than five hundred years ago.

In the Americas, the very societies that we see all around us in the present are a direct result of the most devastating aspect of the Columbian exchange: disease. In this chapter we have already seen that the introduction of diseases by Europeans to populations indigenous to the Americas resulted in 50 to 90 percent mortality across the entire region. Such high mortality was a key factor in allowing European invaders to conquer, settle, and expand throughout the Americas—a process discussed in chapter 21. In other words, if disease had not ravaged indigenous populations, it seems likely that Europeans would not have been able to use American lands for their own purposes on such a large scale and that the population of the present-day Americas would be composed of many more peoples whose ancestors were native to the area. A longer-term consequence of disease during the Columbian exchange was that there were simply not enough laborers in large parts of the Americas to carry out the work required by large-scale agricultural enterprises developed by Europeans after conquest. As a result, first the Portuguese and then many other Europeans began to import enslaved African laborers to the Americas, a process discussed in chapter 22. The Atlantic slave trade, in turn, had profound effects on the eventual composition of populations in the Americas.

No matter where you are in the world today, all you need to do is look around to see how the momentous changes that occurred during the Columbian exchange are still with us. Its effects are in landscapes, food, cultures, and people. It helped, in large and small ways and at great cost in human life, to make the world we live in now.

Beginning in the early sixteenth century, infectious and contagious diseases brought devastating demographic losses to indigenous peoples of the Americas and the Pacific islands. The most virulent disease was smallpox, but measles, diphtheria, whooping cough, and influenza also took heavy tolls. Before the voyages of exploration, none of the peoples of the western hemisphere or Oceania possessed inherited or acquired immunities to those pathogens. In the eastern hemisphere, these diseases were endemic: they claimed a certain number of victims from the ranks of infants and small children, but survivors gained immunity to the diseases through exposure at an early age. In some areas of Europe, for example, smallpox was responsible for 10 to 15 percent of deaths, but most victims were younger than age ten. Although its individual effects were tragic, smallpox did not pose a threat to European society as a whole because it did not carry away economically and socially productive adults.

Epidemic Diseases and Population Decline

When infectious and contagious diseases traveled to previously unexposed populations, however, they touched off ferocious epidemics that sometimes destroyed entire societies. Beginning in 1519, epidemic smallpox ravaged the Aztec empire in combination with other diseases. Although scholars do not agree about the scale of mortality because preconquest population data are incomplete, many believe that within a century the indigenous

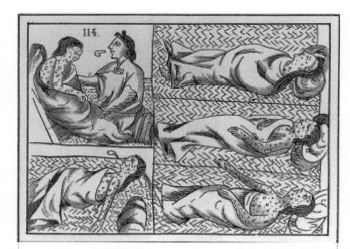

Smallpox victims in the Aztec empire. The disease killed most of those it infected and left disfiguring scars on survivors.

Peabody Museum, Harvard University (2004.24.29636)

population of Mexico declined by as much as 90 percent, from about 17 million to 1.3 million. By that time Spanish conquerors had imposed their rule on Mexico, and many of the political, social, and cultural traditions of the indigenous peoples had either disappeared or fallen under Spanish domination.

Imported diseases took their worst tolls in densely populated areas such as the Aztec and Inca empires, but they did not spare other regions. Smallpox and other diseases were so easily transmissible that they raced to remote areas of North and South America and sparked epidemics well before the first European explorers arrived in those regions. By the 1530s smallpox may have spread as far from Mexico as the Great Lakes in the north and the pampas of Argentina in the south.

When introduced to the Pacific islands, infectious and contagious diseases struck vulnerable populations with the same horrifying effects as in the Americas. All told, disease epidemics sparked by the Columbian exchange probably caused the worst demographic calamity in all of world history. Between 1500 and 1800, upward of one hundred million people may have died of diseases imported by Europeans into the Americas and Pacific islands.

Food Crops and Animals   Over a longer term, however, the Columbian exchange increased rather than diminished human population because of the global spread of food crops and animals that it sponsored. In the long term, a better-nourished world was an important contributing factor in the growth of the world's population, which began in the eighteenth century and continues in the present. Out of Eurasia to the western hemisphere traveled wheat, rice, sugar, bananas, apples, cherries, peaches,

peas, and citrus fruits. Africa contributed yams, okra, collard greens, and coffee. Animals such as horses, cattle, pigs, sheep, goats, and chickens also went from Europe to the Americas, where they sharply increased the availability of food and animal resources.

Food crops native to the Americas also played prominent roles in the Columbian exchange. American crops that took root in Africa, Asia, and Europe include maize, potatoes, beans, tomatoes, peppers, peanuts, manioc, papayas, guavas, avocados, tobacco, pineapples, and cacao, to name only a few. Residents of the eastern hemisphere only gradually developed a taste for American crops, but by the eighteenth century maize and potatoes had contributed to a sharply increased number of calories in Eurasian diets. In tropical regions, peanuts and manioc flourished in soils that otherwise would not produce large yields or support large populations.

Population Growth   The Columbian exchange of plants and animals fueled a surge in world population. In 1500, as Eurasian peoples were recovering from epidemic bubonic plague, world population stood at about 425 million. By 1600 it had increased more than 25 percent, to 545 million. By 1750 human population stood at 720 million, and by 1800 it had surged to 900 million, having grown by almost 50 percent during the previous century. Much of the rise was due to the increased nutritional value of diets enriched by the global exchange of food crops and animals.

Migration   Alongside disease pathogens and plant and animal species, the Columbian exchange involved the spread of human populations through transoceanic migration, both voluntary and forced. During the period from 1500 to 1800, the largest contingent of migrants consisted of enslaved Africans transported against their will to the Americas. A smaller migration involved Europeans who traveled to the Americas as settlers. In some cases, they settled on lands that had previously been depopulated by infectious and contagious diseases while in others they forced out existing populations through violence and forced relocation. During the nineteenth century, European peoples traveled in huge numbers to the western hemisphere and to south Africa, Australia, and the Pacific islands, and equal numbers of Asian peoples migrated to tropical and subtropical destinations throughout much of the world. In combination, those migrations have profoundly influenced modern world history.

The Origins of Global Trade

Besides stimulating commerce in the eastern hemisphere, the voyages of European merchant mariners encouraged the emergence of a genuinely global trading system. European manufactured goods traveled west across the Atlantic in exchange for silver from Mexican and Peruvian

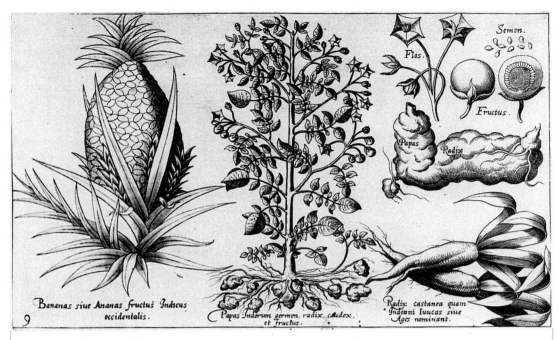

Illustrations in an early-seventeenth-century book depict pineapple, potatoes, and cassava—all plants native to the Americas and unknown to Europeans before the sixteenth century.
From the James Ford Bell Library, University of Minnesota, Minneapolis, Minnesota

mines and agricultural products such as sugar and tobacco, both of which were in high demand among European consumers. Trade in human beings also figured in Atlantic commerce. European manufactured goods went south to west Africa, where merchants exchanged them for enslaved Africans, who then were forcibly transported to the tropical and subtropical regions of the western hemisphere to work on plantations.

The Manila Galleons The experience of the **Manila galleons** illustrates the early workings of the global economy in the Pacific Ocean basin. For 250 years, from 1565 to 1815, Spanish galleons—sleek, fast, heavily armed ships capable of carrying large cargoes—regularly plied the waters of the Pacific Ocean between Manila in the Philippines and Acapulco on the west coast of Mexico. From Manila they took Asian luxury goods to Mexico and exchanged them for silver. Most of the precious metal made its way to China, where a thriving domestic economy demanded increasing quantities of silver. Meanwhile, some of the Asian luxury goods from Manila remained in Mexico or went to Peru, where they contributed to a comfortable way of life for Spanish ruling elites. Most, however, went overland across Mexico and then traveled by ship across the Atlantic to Spain and European markets.

Environmental Effects of Global Trade As the demand for silver fueled growing volumes of global trade,

pressures increased on several animal species that had the misfortune to become commodities on the world market. Fur-bearing animals came under particularly intense pressure, as hunters sought their pelts for sale to consumers in China, Europe, and North America. During the seventeenth century an estimated two hundred to three hundred thousand sable pelts flowed annually from Siberia to the global market, and during the eighteenth century, more than sixteen million North American beaver pelts fed consumers' demands for fur hats and cloaks. Wanton hunting of fur-bearing animals soon drove many species into extinction or near extinction, permanently altering the environments they had formerly inhabited. Early modern hunters also harvested enormous numbers of deer, codfish, whales, walruses, and seals as merchants sought to supply animal products for global consumers.

In the seventeenth and eighteenth centuries, the volume of global trade expanded rapidly. During the seventeenth century, for example, Dutch merchants imported, among other commodities, wheat from south Africa, cowry shells from India, and sugar from Brazil. The wheat fed domestic consumers, who increasingly worked as merchants, bankers, or manufacturers rather than as cultivators. English, Dutch, and other merchants eagerly purchased the cowry shells—which served as currency in much of sub-Saharan Africa—and exchanged them for enslaved people destined for plantations in the western hemisphere. The sugar went on the market at Amsterdam and found its way to

An artist's rendering of a Spanish galleon. Galleons were large, multidecked, highly stable, and maneuverable sailing ships used by Europeans for war or commerce. The Spanish and the Portuguese built the largest types for their profitable overseas trade.
Bettmann/Getty Images

consumers throughout Europe. And that was just the beginning. By 1750 all parts of the world except Australia participated in global networks of commercial relations in which European merchant mariners played prominent roles.

TRADE AND CONFLICT IN EARLY MODERN ASIA

The voyages of exploration taught European mariners how to sail to almost any coastline in the world and return safely. Once they arrived at their destinations, they sought commercial opportunities. In the eastern hemisphere they built a series of fortified trading posts that offered footholds in regions where established commercial networks had held sway for centuries. They even attempted to control the spice trade in the Indian Ocean, but with limited success. For the most part, they did not have the human numbers or the military power to impose their rule in the eastern hemisphere. In a parallel effort involving expansion across land rather than the sea, Russian explorers and adventurers established a presence in central Asia and Siberia, thus laying the foundations for a vast Eurasian empire. Commercial and political rivalries in both the eastern and the western hemispheres also led to conflict between European

peoples, which resulted in numerous wars between competing powers for both territory and resources.

Trading-Post Empires

Portuguese Trading Posts Portuguese mariners built the earliest trading-post empire. Their goal was not to conquer territories but to control trade routes by forcing merchant vessels to call at fortified trading sites and pay duties there. Vasco da Gama obtained permission from local authorities to establish a trading post at Calicut when he arrived there in 1498. By the mid-sixteenth century, Portuguese merchants had built more than fifty trading posts between west Africa and east Asia.

Afonso d'Albuquerque Equipped with heavy artillery, Portuguese vessels were able to overpower most other craft they encountered, and they sometimes bombarded coastal communities with their cannons. The architect of their aggressive policy was **Afonso d'Albuquerque**, commander of Portuguese forces in the Indian Ocean during the early sixteenth century. Albuquerque's fleets seized Hormuz in 1508, Goa in 1510, and Melaka in 1511. From these strategic sites, Albuquerque sought to control Indian Ocean trade by forcing all merchant ships to purchase safe-conduct passes and present them at Portuguese trading posts. Ships without passes were subject to confiscation, along with their cargoes. Albuquerque's forces punished violators of

Afonso d'Albuquerque (al-FAWN-soo d'AL-buh-kur-kee)

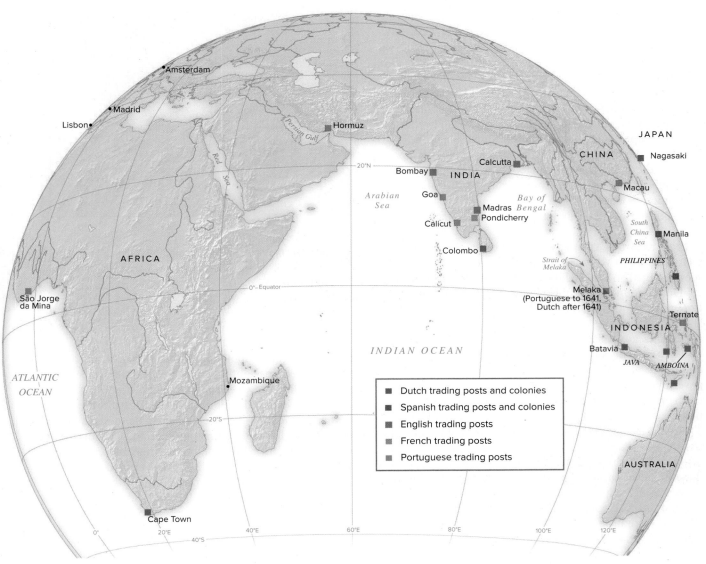

MAP 19.3   European trading posts in Africa and Asia, ca. 1700

Note how many more trading posts there were in Asia than in Africa. What accounts for the difference?

his policy by executing them or cutting off their hands. Albuquerque was confident of Portuguese naval superiority and its ability to control trade in the Indian Ocean.

In reality, however, Portuguese forces did not have enough vessels to enforce their commander's orders. Arab, Indian, and Malay merchants continued to play prominent roles in Indian Ocean commerce, usually without taking the precaution of securing a safe-conduct pass. Indeed, Arab vessels continued to deliver shipments of pepper and spices through the Red Sea, which Portuguese forces never managed to control, to Cairo and Mediterranean trade routes.

By the late sixteenth century, Portuguese hegemony in the Indian Ocean was growing weak. Portugal was a small country with a small population—about one million in 1500—and was unable to sustain its large seaborne trading empire. In addition, by the late sixteenth century, investors in other lands had begun to organize expeditions to Asian markets. Most prominent of those who followed the Portuguese into the Indian Ocean were English and Dutch mariners.

English and Dutch Trading Posts Like their predecessors, English and Dutch merchants built trading posts on Asian coasts and sought to channel trade through them, but they did not attempt to control shipping on the high seas. They also occasionally seized Portuguese sites, although Portuguese authorities held many of their trading posts into the twentieth century. Meanwhile, English and Dutch entrepreneurs established parallel networks. English merchants concentrated on India and built trading posts at Bombay, Madras, and Calcutta, whereas the Dutch operated more broadly from Cape Town, Colombo, and Batavia (modern Jakarta on the island of Java).

English and Dutch merchants enjoyed two main advantages over their Portuguese predecessors. They sailed faster, cheaper, and more powerful ships, which offered both an economic and a military edge over their competitors. Furthermore, they conducted trade through an exceptionally efficient form of commercial organization—the **joint-stock company**—which enabled investors to realize handsome profits while limiting the risk to their investments.

The Trading Companies English and Dutch merchants formed two especially powerful joint-stock companies: the English **East India Company**, founded in 1600, and its Dutch counterpart, the United East India Company, known from its initials as the **VOC** (Vereenigde Oost-Indische Compagnie), established in 1602. Private merchants advanced funds to launch these companies, outfit them with ships and crews, and provide them with commodities and money to trade. Although they enjoyed government support, the companies were privately owned enterprises. Unhampered by political oversight, company agents concentrated strictly on profitable trade. Their charters granted them the right to buy, sell, and build trading posts, and even make war.

The English and Dutch companies experienced immediate financial success. In 1601, for example, five English ships set sail from London with cargoes mostly of gold and silver coins valued at thirty thousand pounds sterling. When they returned in 1603, the spices they carried were worth more than one million pounds sterling. Because of their advanced nautical technology, powerful military arsenal, efficient organization, and relentless pursuit of profit, the English East India Company and the VOC contributed to the early formation of a global network of trade.

European Conquests in Southeast Asia

Following voyages of exploration to the western hemisphere, the massive demographic catastrophe caused by the introduction of contagious diseases to indigenous peoples enabled Europeans to build territorial empires and establish colonies settled by European migrants. In the eastern hemisphere, however, they were mostly unable to force their will on large Asian populations and powerful centralized states. With the decline of the Portuguese

Miguel López de Legazpi (mee-GEHL
LOH-pess de le-GAHS-pee)

Mindanao (min-duh-NAH-oh)

Modern image of Fort Tolukko, a trading fortification originally built by the Portuguese on the spice island of Ternate. The Dutch occupied it in the early seventeenth century.

Ali Trisno Pranoto/Getty Images

effort to control shipping in the Indian Ocean, Europeans mostly traded peacefully in Asian waters alongside Arab, Indian, Malay, and Chinese merchants.

Yet in two island regions of southeast Asia—the Philippines and Indonesia—Europeans were able to make limited conquests during the early modern period. Though densely populated, neither the Philippines nor Indonesia were ruled by a single state when Europeans arrived there in the sixteenth century. Nor did imperial authorities in China or India lay claim to the island regions. Heavily armed ships enabled Europeans to use violence and to establish imperial regimes that favored the interests of European merchants.

Conquest of the Philippines Spanish forces approached the Philippines in 1565 under the command of Miguel López de Legazpi, who named the islands after King Philip II of Spain. Because the Philippines had no central government, there was no organized resistance to the intrusion. By 1575 Spanish forces controlled the coastal regions of the central and northern islands, and during the seventeenth century they extended their authority to most parts of the archipelago except the southern island of Mindanao, where a large Muslim community stoutly resisted Spanish expansion.

Manila Spanish policy in the Philippines revolved around trade and Christianity. Manila soon emerged as a bustling, multicultural port city—an entrepôt for trade, particularly in silk—and it quickly became the hub of Spanish commercial activity in Asia. Chinese merchants were especially prominent in Manila. They occupied a specially designated commercial district of the city and supplied silk goods that Spanish traders shipped to Mexico in the Manila galleons. Their commercial success brought suspicion on the Chinese community, however, and resentful Spanish and Filipino residents massacred Chinese merchants in several eruptions of violence over the next few hundred years. Meanwhile, the Spanish also sought to Christianize the Philippines. Spanish rulers and missionaries pressured prominent Filipinos to convert to Christianity in hopes of persuading others to follow their example. They opened schools to teach the fundamentals of Christian doctrine, along with basic literacy, in densely populated regions throughout the islands. Although Spanish missionaries initially faced resistance, over the long term Filipinos turned increasingly to Christianity, and by the nineteenth century the Philippines had become one of the most fervent Roman Catholic lands in the world.

Conquest of Java Dutch mariners who imposed their rule on the islands of Indonesia did not worry about seeking converts to Christianity but concentrated instead on the trade in spices, particularly cloves, nutmeg, and mace. The architect of Dutch policy was Jan Pieterszoon Coen, who in 1619 founded Batavia on the island of Java to serve as an entrepôt for the VOC. Coen's plan was to establish a VOC monopoly over spice production and trade, thus enabling Dutch merchants to reap enormous profits in European markets. Coen brought his naval power to bear on the small Indonesian islands and forced them to deliver spices only to VOC merchants. By the late seventeenth century the VOC controlled all the ports of Java as well as most of the important spice-bearing islands throughout the Indonesian archipelago.

Dutch numbers were too few for them to rule directly over their whole southeast Asian empire. They made alliances with local authorities to maintain order in most regions, reserving only Batavia and the most important spice-bearing islands for direct Dutch rule. The Dutch did not embark on campaigns of conquest for purposes of adding to their holdings, but they uprooted spice-bearing plants on islands they did not control and mercilessly attacked peoples who sold their spices to merchants not associated with the VOC. Eventually, monopoly profits from the spice trade not only enriched the VOC but also made the Netherlands the most prosperous land in Europe throughout most of the seventeenth century.

Foundations of the Russian Empire in Asia

While western European peoples were building maritime empires, Russians were laying the foundations for a vast land empire that embraced most of northern Eurasia. This round of expansion began in the mid-sixteenth century as Russian forces took over several Mongol khanates in central Asia. Those acquisitions resulted in Russian control over the Volga River and offered opportunities for trade with the Ottoman empire, Iran, and even India through the Caspian Sea. In the eighteenth century, Russian forces extended their presence in the Caspian Sea region by absorbing much of the Caucasus, a vibrant, multiethnic region embracing the modern-day states of Georgia, Armenia, and Azerbaijan.

Siberia Far more extensive were Russian acquisitions in northeastern Eurasia. The frozen tundras and dense forests of Siberia posed formidable challenges, but explorers and merchants made their way into the region in a quest for fur. In the late sixteenth century, Russian explorers pushed into the interior regions of Siberia by way of the region's great rivers. By 1639 they had made their way across the Eurasian landmass and reached the Pacific Ocean.

Peoples of Siberia Siberia was home to about twenty-six major ethnic groups that lived by hunting, trapping, fishing, or herding reindeer. These indigenous peoples varied widely in language and religion, and they responded in different ways to the arrival of Russian adventurers who sought to exact tribute from them by coercing them to supply animal pelts on a regular basis. Some groups readily accepted iron tools, woven cloth, flour, tea, and liquor for the skins of fur-bearing animals such as otter, lynx, and especially sable. Others resented the ever-increasing demands for tribute and resisted Russian encroachment on their lands. For example, the Yakut people of the Lena and Aldan river valleys in central Siberia mounted a revolt against Russian oppression in 1642. The Russian response was brutal: over a period of forty years, Russian forces drove many Yakut out of their settlements and reduced their population by an estimated 70 percent. Quite apart from military violence, like people in the Americas, the peoples of Siberia reeled from epidemic diseases that reduced many populations by more than half.

The Russian Occupation of Siberia Despite the region's harsh climate, Russian migrants—some of whom were adventurers or convicted criminals—gradually filtered into Siberia and thoroughly altered its demographic complexion. Small agricultural settlements grew up near many trading posts, particularly in the fertile Amur River valley. Over time, Siberian trading posts developed into Russian towns with Russian-speaking populations attending Russian Orthodox churches. By 1763 some 420,000 Russians lived in Siberia, nearly double the number of indigenous inhabitants. In the nineteenth century, large numbers of additional migrants moved east to mine Siberian gold, silver, copper, and iron. By this time, the Russian state was well on the way toward consolidating its control over the region.

Jan Pieterszoon Coen (yahn PEE-tuhr-sohn KOH-uhn)

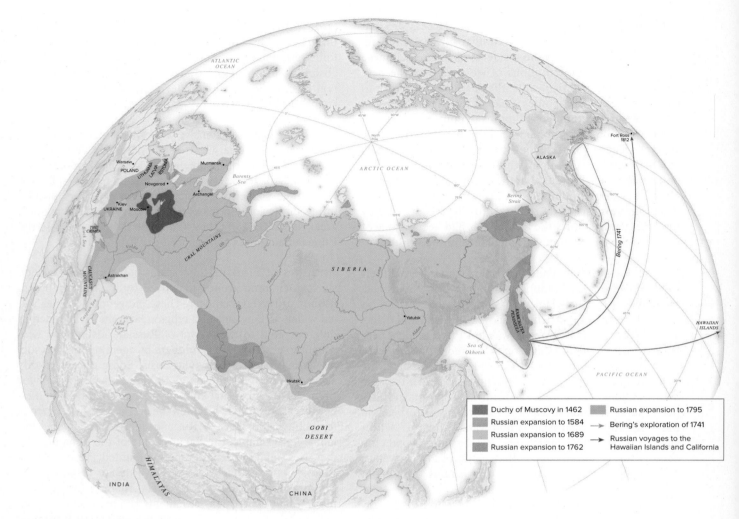

MAP 19.4   Russian expansion, 1462–1795

Observe how vast the empire became after it added the territory of Siberia.

How did Russians exert their control over such a huge and unforgiving territory?

European Commercial Rivalries

Exploration and imperial expansion led to conflicts not only between Europeans and Asians but also among the Europeans. Mariners competed vigorously for trade in Asia and the Americas, and their efforts to establish markets—and sometimes monopolies—led frequently to clashes with their counterparts from different lands.

Competition and Conflict Indeed, throughout the seventeenth and early eighteenth centuries, commercial and political rivalries led to running wars between ships flying different flags. Dutch vessels were most numerous in the Indian Ocean, and they enabled the VOC to dominate the spice trade. Dutch forces expelled most Portuguese merchants from southeast Asia and prevented English mariners from establishing secure footholds there. By the early

eighteenth century, trade in Indian cotton and tea from Ceylon had begun to overshadow the spice trade, and English and French merchants working from trading posts in India became the dominant carriers in the Indian Ocean. Fierce competition again generated violence: in 1746, French forces seized the English trading post at Madras, one of the three principal centers of British operations in India.

Commercial competition led to conflict also in the Caribbean and the Americas. English pirates and privateers preyed on Spanish shipping from Mexico, often seizing vessels carrying cargoes of silver. English and French forces constantly skirmished and fought over sugar islands in the Caribbean while contesting territorial claims in North America. In addition, almost all conflicts between European states in the eighteenth century spilled over into the Caribbean and the Americas.

CONCLUSION

Global commercial and biological exchanges and encounters arose from the efforts of European mariners to explore the world's waters and establish sea lanes that would support long-distance trade. Their search for sea routes to Asia accidentally led them to the western hemisphere and the vast expanse of the Pacific Ocean. The geographic knowledge that they accumulated enabled them to link the world's regions into an ever more finely articulated network of trade. But commercial exchange was not the only result of this global network. Food crops, animal stocks, disease pathogens, and human migrants also traveled the sea lanes and dramatically influenced societies throughout the world.

Europeans did not achieve global dominance in early modern times. However, their voyages of exploration and consequent development of transoceanic trading networks meant that European peoples now played a more prominent role in world affairs than any of their ancestors had. In addition, their efforts helped foster the development of an increasingly interdependent world.

STUDY TERMS

Afonso d'Albuquerque (340)
astrolabe (330)
Captain James Cook (336)
Ceuta (333)
Columbian exchange (336)
East India Company (342)
Ferdinand Magellan (333)
Guanahaní (333)
joint-stock company (342)

magnetic compass (330)
Manila galleons (339)
Prince Henry the Navigator (333)
Taino (333)
Vasco da Gama (328)
Vitus Bering (336)
VOC (342)
volta do mar (331)

FOR FURTHER READING

Rene J. Barendse. *The Arabian Seas.* Eastgate, N.Y., 2002. A pathbreaking and complex work that emphasizes the long predominance of Asia in the world economy.

Jerry Brotton. *A History of the World in 12 Maps.* New York, 2013. A cross-cultural sampling of maps, both ancient and current, and the ideas and beliefs that shaped them.

Christopher Columbus. *The* Diario *of Christopher Columbus's First Voyage to America.* Trans. by O. Dunn and J. E. Kelley Jr. Norman, Okla., 1989. A careful translation.

Dorothy Crawford. *Deadly Companions: How Microbes Shaped Our History.* Oxford, 2007. Explores how microbes and humans evolved together from earliest humanity to the present.

Alfred W. Crosby. *The Columbian Exchange: Biological and Cultural Consequences of 1492.* Westport, Conn., 1972. Focuses on early exchanges of plants, animals, and diseases between Europe and America.

Charles C. Mann. *1493: Uncovering the New World Christopher Columbus Created.* New York, 2011. A thorough account of the ways ecological and economic exchanges fundamentally transformed societies in the Americas, Europe, east Asia, and Africa.

Lincoln Paine. *The Sea and Civilization: A Maritime History of the World.* New York, 2013. An accessible, enjoyable, and refreshing maritime history of the world.

John F. Richards. *The Unending Frontier: An Environmental History of the Early Modern World.* Berkeley, 2003. Thoroughly explores the environmental effects of the global historical processes that shaped the early modern world.

Yuri Slezkine. *Arctic Mirrors: Russia and the Small Peoples of the North.* Ithaca, N.Y., 1994. Thoughtful analysis of Russian relations with the hunting, fishing, and herding peoples of Siberia.

Heather Streets-Salter and Trevor Getz. *Empires and Colonies in the Modern World.* New York, 2015. A globally focused exploration of imperialism and colonialism from the fourteenth century to the present.

ZOOMING IN ON TRADITIONS
Martin Luther Challenges the Church

I n 1517 an obscure German monk posed a challenge to the Roman Catholic church. **Martin Luther** of Wittenberg denounced the church's sale of indulgences, a type of pardon that excused individuals from doing penance for their sins. Indulgences had been available since the eleventh century, but to raise funds for the reconstruction of St. Peter's basilica in Rome, church authorities began to sell indulgences aggressively in the early sixteenth century. From their point of view, indulgences were splendid devices: they encouraged individuals to reflect piously on their behavior while bringing large sums of money into the church's treasury.

To Martin Luther, however, indulgences were signs of greed, hypocrisy, and moral rot in the Roman Catholic church. Luther believed that no human being had the power to absolve individuals of their sins and grant them admission to heaven, so for him the sale of indulgences constituted a moral and religious fraud. In October 1517, following academic custom, he offered to debate publicly with anyone who wished to dispute his views, and he denounced the sale of indulgences in a document called the *Ninety-five Theses*.

This detail from a sixteenth-century painting by François Dubois depicts the brutal murder of French Protestants in Paris during the St. Bartholomew's Day Massacre on 23 August 1572.
Alfredo Dagli Orti/Shutterstock

Contrary to popular legend, Luther did not nail his work to the church door in Wittenberg. Nevertheless, news of the *Ninety-five Theses* spread rapidly: within a few weeks, printed copies were available throughout Europe. Luther's challenge galvanized both strong support and severe criticism. Religious and political authorities seeking to maintain the established order were especially critical. Church officials judged Luther's views erroneous, and in 1520 Pope Leo X excommunicated him. In 1521 the Holy Roman emperor Charles V, a devout Roman Catholic, summoned Luther and demanded that he publicly renounce his views. Luther's response: "I cannot and will not recant anything, for it is neither safe nor right to act against one's conscience. Here I stand. I can do no other. God help me. Amen."

Martin Luther's challenge held enormous religious and political implications. Though expelled from the church, Luther still considered himself Christian, and he held religious services for a community of devoted followers. By the 1520s religious dissent had spread through much of Germany and Switzerland. During the 1530s these dissenters—who became known as Protestants because of their protest against the established church—organized movements in France, England, the Low Countries, Italy, and Spain. By mid-century Luther's act of individual rebellion had mushroomed into the **Protestant Reformation**, which shattered the religious unity of western European Christendom.

CHAPTER OVERVIEW

For all its unsettling effects, the Protestant Reformation was only one of several powerful movements that transformed European society during the early modern era. Another was the consolidation of strong, centralized states, which took shape partly because of the Reformation. Between the sixteenth and eighteenth centuries monarchs in western Europe took advantage of religious quarrels to tighten control over their societies. By the mid-eighteenth century some rulers had concentrated so much power in their own hands that historians refer to them as absolute monarchs.

Alongside religious conflict and the building of powerful states, capitalism and early modern science profoundly influenced western European society in early modern times. Early capitalism—an economic system based on free market conditions and private ownership of goods and services—encouraged European merchants and manufacturers to reorganize their businesses in search of maximum efficiency. Early modern science challenged traditional ways of understanding the world and the universe and prompted European intellectuals to seek an entirely rational understanding of the natural world.

CHRONOLOGY	
1473–1543	Life of Nicolaus Copernicus
1478	Foundation of the Spanish Inquisition
1483–1546	Life of Martin Luther
1517	Publication of the *Ninety-five Theses*
1540	Foundation of the Society of Jesus
1545–1563	Council of Trent
1564–1642	Life of Galileo Galilei
1571–1630	Life of Johannes Kepler
1618–1648	Thirty Years' War
1642–1727	Life of Isaac Newton
1643–1715	Reign of King Louis XIV
1648	Peace of Westphalia
1694–1778	Life of Voltaire
1723–1790	Life of Adam Smith

As a result of these phenomena, between 1500 and 1800, western Europe underwent a thorough transformation. Although the changes were unsettling and often disruptive, they also strengthened European society. Indeed, by 1800 several European states had become especially powerful, wealthy, and dynamic. They stood poised to play major roles in world affairs during the nineteenth and twentieth centuries.

THE FRAGMENTATION OF WESTERN EUROPEAN CHRISTENDOM

Although the peoples of western Europe spoke different languages and observed different customs, the church of Rome provided them with a common religious and cultural heritage. During the sixteenth and seventeenth centuries, however, revolts against the Roman Catholic church shattered the religious unity of western Europe. Followers of Martin Luther and other Protestant reformers established a series of churches independent of Rome, and Roman Catholic leaders strengthened their own church against the challengers. Throughout early modern times, religious controversies fueled social tensions.

The Protestant Reformation

Martin Luther Martin Luther (1483-1546) quickly attracted enthusiastic support from others who resented the policies of the Roman church. Luther was a talented writer, and he published numerous works condemning the Roman church. His cause benefited enormously from the printing press, which had first appeared in Europe in the mid-fifteenth century. A sizable literate public inhabited European cities and towns, and readers eagerly consumed printed works on religious as well as secular themes. Printed editions of Luther's writings appeared throughout Europe and sparked spirited debates on theological issues. His supporters and his critics took their own works to the printers, and religious controversies kept the presses busy churning out pamphlets and treatises for a century and more. Luther attacked the Roman church for a wide range of abuses and called for thorough reform of Christendom. He advocated the closure of monasteries, translation of the Bible from Latin into vernacular languages, and an end to priestly authority, including the authority of the pope himself. Most important, Luther believed that salvation could never be earned through good works or the prayers of others. Instead, he argued, humans could be saved only through faith in the promises of God as revealed in the Bible. This idea of "justification by faith alone" became the core of Protestant belief. When opponents pointed out that Luther's reform program ran counter to church policy, he rejected the authority of the church hierarchy and proclaimed that the Bible was the only source of Christian religious authority.

Reform outside Germany Luther's works drew an enthusiastic popular response, and in Germany they fueled a movement to reform the church along the lines of Luther's teachings. Lay Christians flocked to hear Luther preach in Wittenberg, and several princes of the Holy Roman Empire warmed to Luther's views—partly because of personal conviction but partly also because religious controversy offered opportunities for them to build their own power bases. Although German enthusiasm for Lutheranism was not monolithic, many of the most important German cities—Strasbourg, Nuremberg, and Augsburg, among others—passed laws requiring all religious services to follow Protestant doctrine and procedures during the 1520s and 1530s. By the mid-sixteenth century about half the German population had adopted Lutheran Christianity, and reformers had launched Protestant movements and established alternative churches in other lands as well. By the late 1520s the prosperous cities of Switzerland—Zurich, Basel, and Geneva—had fledgling Protestant churches. The heavily urbanized Low Countries also responded enthusiastically to Protestant appeals. Protestants appeared even in Italy and Spain, although authorities in those lands handily suppressed their challenge to the Roman church.

John Calvin Meanwhile, an even more influential reformation was taking shape in France and French-speaking Switzerland. The initiator was a French lawyer, John Calvin (1509-1564), who in the 1530s converted to Protestant Christianity. Because the French monarchy sought to suppress Protestants, Calvin moved to French-speaking Geneva in Switzerland, where he organized a tight-knit Protestant community. Calvin also composed an influential treatise, *Institutes of the Christian Religion* (first published in 1536), that presented Protestant teachings as a coherent and organized package. Although Calvin believed in the basic elements of Luther's Protestant teachings, his ideas differed from those of Luther in important ways. Most fundamentally, Calvin emphasized the awesome power of God more than Luther did. Indeed, he believed not only that humans could never earn salvation through prayers and good works but also that God had, in fact, already determined which individuals would be saved from damnation before they were even born. These individuals, known as "the elect," were predestined to salvation regardless of their deeds on earth. This doctrine of "predestination," as it became known, grew increasingly important to the Calvinist church in the generations after Calvin's death.

Calvin's Geneva was based on a strict code of morality and discipline. **Calvinists** were supposed to dress simply, to study the Bible regularly, and to refrain from activities such as playing cards and dancing. It was, in effect, a model Protestant community. Geneva also became an important missionary center from which Calvinist doctrine spread to other parts of Europe. Calvinist missionaries were most active in France, where they attracted strong interest in the cities, but they also ventured to Germany, the Low Countries, England, Hungary, and—most successfully—the Netherlands and Scotland.

---

vernacular (ver-NA-kyoo-lar)

The English Reformation In England a reformation took place for political as well as religious reasons. Lutherans and other Protestants worked to build a following in England from the 1520s on, but they faced significant government resistance until King Henry VIII (reigned 1509–1547) came into conflict with the pope. Henry wanted to divorce his wife, who had not given birth to a male heir, but the pope refused to allow him to do so. Henry's response was to cut off relations with the Roman church and make himself supreme head of the Anglican church—an English pope, as it were. While Henry reigned, the theology of the English church changed little, but his successors replaced Roman Catholic with Protestant doctrines and rituals. By 1560 England had permanently left the Roman Catholic community. Indeed, by the late sixteenth century, Lutherans, Calvinists, and **Anglicans** in Europe had built communities large enough that a return to religious unity in western Europe was inconceivable.

The Catholic Reformation

In response to the Protestant Reformation, Roman Catholic authorities undertook a wide-ranging reform effort of their own in the sixteenth century. Their purpose was to clarify differences between Roman and Protestant churches, to correct abuses within the church (such as the ability of wealthy men to purchase clerical offices), to persuade Protestants to return to the Roman church, and to deepen the sense of spirituality and religious commitment in their own community. Taken together, their efforts constituted the **Catholic Reformation**.

The Council of Trent Two institutions were especially important for defining the Catholic Reformation and advancing its goals—the **Council of Trent** and the **Society of Jesus**. The Council of Trent was an assembly of high church officials who met intermittently between 1545 and 1563 to address matters of doctrine and reform. During the meetings, the council defined the elements of Roman Catholic theology in detail. The council also took steps to reform the church by demanding that church authorities observe strict standards of morality and requiring them to establish schools and seminaries to prepare priests properly for their roles.

St. Ignatius of Loyola While the Council of Trent dealt with doctrine and reform, the Society of Jesus sought to extend the boundaries of the reformed Roman church. The society's founder was St. Ignatius Loyola (1491–1556), a Basque nobleman and soldier who in 1521 suffered a leg wound that ended his military career. While recuperating he read spiritual works and popular accounts of saints' lives, and he resolved to put his energy into religious work. In 1540, together with a small band of disciples, he founded the Society of Jesus.

The Society of Jesus Ignatius required that members of the society, known as Jesuits, complete a rigorous and advanced education in theology, philosophy, languages, history, literature, and science. As a result of that preparation, the Jesuits made extraordinarily effective missionaries. They also acquired a reputation for discipline and determination, and they often served as counselors to kings and other rulers. They also were the most prominent of the early Christian missionaries outside Europe: in the wake of the European reconnaissance of the world's oceans, Jesuits attracted converts in India, China, Japan, the Philippines, and the Americas, thus making Christianity a genuinely global religion.

Witch Hunts and Religious Wars

Europeans took religion seriously in the sixteenth century, and religious divisions helped fuel social and political conflict. Apart from wars, the most destructive violence that afflicted early modern Europe was the hunt for witches, which was especially prominent in regions such as the Rhineland, where tensions between Protestants and Roman Catholics ran high.

Like many other peoples, Europeans had long believed that certain individuals possessed unusual or supernatural powers. During the late fifteenth century, theologians developed a theory that some of these people were witches who derived their powers—such as the ability to fly through the night on brooms or pitchforks—from the devil. Theorists believed that witches regularly flew off to distant places to attend the witches' Sabbath, a gathering that featured devil worship and the concoction of secret potions and culminated in sexual relations with the devil himself. Indeed, witchcraft became a convenient explanation for any unpleasant turn of events—failure of a crop, an unexpected death, or the inability to conceive a child.

Witch-Hunting In the sixteenth and seventeenth centuries, fears that individuals were making alliances with the devil sparked a widespread hunt for witches beginning in the sixteenth century. About 110,000 individuals underwent trial as suspected witches, and about 60,000 of them were executed either by hanging or by burning at the stake. Most of the victims—perhaps 95 percent—were poor, old, single, or widowed women who lived on the margins of their societies and thus were easy targets for accusers. Although the fear of witches had largely diminished by 1700, the intermittent pursuit of witches for the better part of two centuries clearly revealed the stresses and strains—both secular and religious—that afflicted European society during early modern times.

Religious Wars Religious tensions also led to outright war between Protestant and Roman Catholic communities. Religious wars wracked France for thirty-six years

The Burning of Three Witches (1585), by Johann Jakob Wick. This illustration depicts the execution by burning of three accused "witches" in Baden, Switzerland, on 4 November 1585.

The History Collection/Alamy Stock Photo

(1562–1598), for example, and they complicated relations between Protestant and Roman Catholic states. In 1588 King Philip II of Spain (reigned 1556–1598) attempted to force England to return to the Roman Catholic church by sending the Spanish Armada—a huge flotilla consisting of 130 ships and 30,000 men—to dethrone Protestant Queen Elizabeth. The effort collapsed, however, when English forces disrupted the Spanish fleet by sending blazing, unmanned ships into its midst. Then a ferocious gale scattered Spanish vessels throughout the North Sea.

Religious convictions also aggravated relations between the Netherlands and Spain by fueling the revolt of the Dutch provinces from their overlord, the king of Spain. In 1567 resistance escalated into a full-scale rebellion. By 1610 the seven northern provinces (the modern Netherlands) had won their independence and formed a republic known as the United Provinces, leaving ten southern provinces (modern Belgium) under Spanish and later Austrian rule until the late eighteenth century.

The Thirty Years' War The religious wars culminated in a great continental conflict known as the **Thirty Years' War** (1618–1648). The war opened after the Holy Roman emperor attempted to force his Bohemian (in modern Czechoslovakia) subjects to return to the Roman Catholic church, although the main battleground was the emperor's territory in Germany. By the time the war ended, however, Spanish, French, Dutch, German, Swedish, Danish, Polish, Bohemian, and Russian forces had taken part in the conflict. The war itself was the most destructive European conflict before the twentieth century. Quite apart from violence and brutalities committed by undisciplined soldiers, the war damaged economies and societies throughout Europe and led to the deaths of about one-third of the German population. And though religious differences were not the only issues of the war, they complicated other issues and made them more difficult to resolve.

What's Left Out? ■■■ ■■■ ■■ ■■ ■■

The Thirty Years' War was the most destructive European conflict until the even more brutal World Wars of the twentieth century. But the need to cover many topics often means that textbooks cannot delve into the details of what such a claim might have meant for the ordinary people who lived through the war. In German territories alone, nearly a quarter of the population died as a result of the war, and in some places the toll was closer to 50 percent. The incredible destruction of the war was due to a number of reasons that had little to do with religion or loyalties. Among the most important was the lack of separation between battle fronts and home fronts, which meant that civilians often found themselves directly in the path of invading or defending armies. In addition, both invading and defending armies required food, clothing, and shelter, and these frequently were taken from civilians by both friendly and enemy troops. Moreover, when civilians had to endure the destruction of their crops, homes, and food stores, famines and food shortages became a grim reality. Weakened individuals then died from sickness and disease on a vast scale. People such as Hans Heberle—a cobbler from what is now southern Germany—endured staggering losses during the war. He and his wife and children were driven from their home and lost all of their possessions. They were then forced to take refuge in forests, in neighboring towns, and in a fortress to protect themselves from invading armies. Heberle watched as those around him were reduced to famine conditions, eating grass and weeds as well as dogs, cats, mice, and horses. In 1635, just one year in the war, fifteen thousand people died from famine and disease in his hometown of Ulm. Over the course of the war, approximately eight million soldiers and civilians died, each of whom could have told an equally horrific story of fear, loss, and brutality.

Source: Hans Medick and Benjamin Marschke. *Experiencing the Thirty Years War: A Brief History with Documents.* New York: Bedford St. Martin's, 2013.

THE CONSOLIDATION OF SOVEREIGN STATES

Although fundamentally a religious movement, the Reformation had strong political implications, and centralizing monarchs readily made use of religious issues in their efforts to strengthen their states and enhance their authority. Indeed, after the devastation of the Thirty Years' War, rulers of these states devised a diplomatic system that sought to maintain order among the many independent and competitive European states.

The Attempted Revival of Empire

After the dissolution of the Carolingian empire in the ninth century C.E., there was no effective imperial government in western Europe. The Holy Roman Empire emerged in the tenth century, but its authority extended only to Germany and northern Italy, and even there its power was contested. During the early sixteenth century it seemed that **Emperor Charles V** (reigned 1519–1556) might establish the Holy Roman Empire as the preeminent political authority in Europe, but by mid-century it was clear that there would be no revival of empire. Thus, unlike China, India, and the Ottoman empire, early modern Europe developed as a region of independent states.

Charles V After 1438 the Habsburg family, with extensive dynastic holdings in Austria, dominated the Holy Roman Empire. Through marriage alliances, the **Habsburgs** accumulated rights and titles to lands throughout Europe and beyond. Indeed, when Charles V became emperor in 1519, his empire stretched from Vienna in Austria to Cuzco in Peru. In spite of his far-flung holdings, Charles did not extend his authority throughout Europe. Part of the reason was that throughout his reign Charles had to devote much of his attention and energy to the Lutheran movement and to putting down imperial princes who took advantage of religious controversy to assert their independence. Foreign difficulties also played a role, because Charles's neighbors to the west and east—in France and the Ottoman empire, respectively—actively opposed the creation of a powerful Holy Roman Empire.

To ensure that Charles's territories remained in disarray, for example, the Roman Catholic French kings aided German Lutherans in their rebellion against the Holy Roman Empire. The French kings even allied with the Muslim Ottoman Turks against the emperor, who did not want a powerful Christian empire to threaten their holdings in eastern Europe and the Mediterranean basin.

Thus domestic and foreign problems prevented Charles V from establishing his vast empire as the supreme political authority in Europe. In 1556, disappointed especially in his inability to suppress the Lutherans in his territories, the emperor abdicated his throne and retired to a monastery in Spain. His empire did not survive. Charles bestowed his holdings in Spain, Italy, the Low Countries,

Carolingian (kar-uh-LIHN-jee-uhn)

MAP 20.1 Sixteenth-century Europe

Note the extent of Habsburg territories and the wide boundaries of the Holy Roman Empire.

With such powerful territories, what prevented the Habsburgs from imposing imperial rule on most of Europe?

and the Americas on his son, King Philip II of Spain, and his brother Ferdinand inherited the Habsburg family lands in Austria and the imperial throne.

The New Monarchs

In the absence of effective imperial power, public affairs fell to the various regional states that had emerged during the middle ages. In this period, however, the most

powerful European states were the kingdoms of England, France, and Spain. During the late fifteenth and sixteenth centuries, rulers of these lands, known as the "new monarchs," marshaled their resources, curbed the nobility, and built strong, centralized regimes.

Finance The new monarchs included Henry VIII of England, Louis XI and Francis I of France, and Fernando and Isabel of Spain. All the new monarchs sought to enhance their treasuries by developing new sources of finance. The French kings levied direct taxes on sales,

Louis (LOO-ee)

arose. That, in turn, resulted in increased control over the nobility, who could no longer compete with the power and wealth of the state.

The Spanish Inquisition The debates and disputes launched by the Protestant Reformation also helped monarchs increase their power. Whereas monarchs in Protestant lands—including England, much of Germany, Denmark, and Sweden—expropriated church wealth to expand their powers, others relied on religious justifications to advance state ends. The **Spanish Inquisition** was the most distinctive institution of that kind. Fernando and Isabel founded the Spanish Inquisition in 1478, and they obtained papal license to operate the institution as a royal agency. Its original task was to ferret out those who secretly practiced Judaism or Islam, but Charles V charged it with responsibility also for detecting Protestant heresy in Spain.

Inquisitors had broad powers to investigate suspected cases of heresy. Popular legends have created an erroneous impression of the Spanish Inquisition as an institution running amok, framing innocent victims and routinely subjecting them to torture. In fact, inquisitors usually observed rules of evidence, and they released many suspects after investigation. Yet when they detected heresy, inquisitors could be ruthless. They sentenced hundreds of victims to hang from the gallows or burn at the stake and imprisoned many others for extended periods of time. Fear of the Inquisition deterred nobles from adopting Protestant views out of political ambition, and inquisitors also used their influence to silence those who threatened the Spanish monarchy. From 1559 to 1576, for example, inquisitors imprisoned the archbishop of Toledo—the highest Roman Catholic church official in all of Spain—because of his political independence.

Constitutional States

During the seventeenth and eighteenth centuries, as European states sought to restore order after the Thirty Years' War, they developed along two lines. Rulers in England and the Netherlands shared authority with representative institutions and created **constitutional states**, whereas monarchs in France, Spain, Austria, Prussia, and Russia concentrated power in their own hands and created a form of state known as absolute monarchy.

During the seventeenth century the island kingdom of England and the maritime Dutch republic evolved governments that recognized rights pertaining to individuals and representative institutions. Their constitutional states took different forms: in England a constitutional monarchy emerged, whereas in the Netherlands a republic based on representative government emerged. In neither land did constitutional government come easily into being: in England it followed a civil war (1642–1649), and in the Netherlands it followed a long strug-

This engraving, *Judgment Scene at Spanish Inquisition,* depicts an auto-da-fé, or "act of faith," involving the execution of Jews by burning at the stake. An auto-da-fé more specifically was a ritual of public penance and punishment of condemned heretics. In 1492 the Catholic monarchy of Spain ordered the expulsion of Jews from Spain.
Bettmann/Getty Images

households, and the salt trade. A new sales tax dramatically boosted Spanish royal income in the sixteenth century, and English kings increased revenues by raising fines and fees for royal services. Moreover, after Henry VIII severed ties between the English and Roman churches, he confiscated all church properties in England, which dramatically increased the size and wealth of the state.

State Power With their increased income the new monarchs enlarged their administrative staffs, which enabled them to collect taxes and implement royal policies more reliably than before. Increased wealth also allowed the new monarchs to raise powerful armies when the need

gle for independence in the late sixteenth century. In both lands, however, constitutional government strengthened the state and provided a political framework that enabled merchants to flourish as never before in European experience.

The English Civil War Constitutional government came to England after political and religious disputes led to the **English Civil War**. Politically, disputes arose between the king and the parliament over the king's ability to institute new taxes without parliamentary approval, and religious tensions between the Anglican king and a vocal group of zealous, reform-minded Calvinists in Parliament created a deep rift between the two branches of

In this contemporary painting, the executioner holds up the just-severed head of King Charles I of England. The sight of a royal execution overcomes one woman, who faints (at bottom).
Art Collection 2/Alamy Stock Photo

government. By 1641 both King Charles I and Parliament had raised armies to fight against one another. In the conflicts that followed, Parliamentary forces captured Charles and in 1649 executed him for tyranny. Yet English problems of government continued through a dictatorial Puritan regime as well as restoration of the monarchy in 1660, until in 1688 Parliament deposed King James II and invited his daughter Mary and her Dutch husband, William of Orange, to assume the throne. The resulting arrangement provided that kings would rule in cooperation with Parliament, thus guaranteeing that nobles, merchants, and other constituencies would enjoy representation in government affairs. It also provided a momentous precedent in European affairs about the power of a people to replace its government if it is not perceived to be acting in the best interests of its people.

The Dutch Republic As in England, a combination of political and religious tensions led to conflict from which constitutional government emerged in the Netherlands. In the mid-sixteenth century, authority over the Low Countries, including modern-day Belgium as well as the Netherlands, rested with King Philip II of Spain. In 1566 Philip, a devout Roman Catholic, moved to suppress an increasingly popular Calvinist movement in the Netherlands—a measure that provoked large-scale rebellion against Spanish rule. In 1581 a group of Dutch provinces proclaimed themselves the independent United Provinces. Representative assemblies organized local affairs in each of the provinces, and on that foundation political leaders built a Dutch republic. Although Spain did

not officially recognize the independence of the United Provinces until 1648, the Dutch republic was effectively organizing affairs in the northern Low Countries by the early seventeenth century.

In both England and the Dutch republic, merchants were especially prominent in political affairs, and state policy in both lands favored maritime trade and the building of commercial empires overseas. The constitutional states allowed entrepreneurs to pursue their economic interests with minimal interference from public authorities, and during the late seventeenth and eighteenth centuries both states experienced extraordinary prosperity as a result of those policies. Indeed, in many ways the English and Dutch states represented an alliance between merchants and rulers that worked to the benefit of both. Merchants supported the state with the wealth they generated through trade—especially overseas trade—and rulers followed policies that looked after the interests of their merchants.

Absolute Monarchies

Whereas constitutional states devised ways to share power and authority, absolute monarchies stood on a theoretical foundation known as the divine right of kings. This theory held that kings derived their authority from God and served as "God's lieutenants upon earth." There was no role in divine-right theory for common subjects or even nobles in public affairs: the monarch made law and determined policy. In practice, absolute monarchs always relied on support from nobles and other social groups, but

King Louis XIV and his entourage approach the main gate of Versailles (bottom right). Though only partially constructed at the time of this painting (1668), Versailles was already a spacious and luxurious retreat for Louis and his court.
Everett Collection/Shutterstock

the claims of divine-right theory clearly reflected efforts at royal centralization.

The most conspicuous absolutist state was the French monarchy. The architect of French **absolutism** was a prominent church official, **Cardinal Richelieu**, who served as chief minister to King Louis XIII from 1624 to 1642. Richelieu worked systematically to undermine the power of the nobility and enhance the authority of the king. He destroyed nobles' castles and ruthlessly crushed aristocratic conspiracies. As a counterweight to the nobility, Richelieu built a large bureaucracy staffed by commoners loyal to the king. He also appointed officials to supervise the implementation of royal policy in the provinces.

The Sun King The ruler who best epitomized royal absolutism was **King Louis XIV** (reigned 1643–1715). In fact, Louis XIV once reportedly declared that he was himself the state: *"l'état c'est moi."* Known as *le roi soleil*—"the sun king"—Louis surrounded himself with splendor befitting

one who ruled by divine right. During the 1670s he built a magnificent residence at **Versailles**, and in the 1680s he moved his court there. Louis's palace at Versailles was the largest building in Europe, with 230 acres of formal gardens and fourteen hundred fountains. All prominent nobles established residences at Versailles for their families and entourages. Louis strongly encouraged them to live at court, where he and his staff could keep an eye on them, and ambitious nobles gravitated there anyway in hopes of winning influence with the king. While nobles living at Versailles mastered the intricacies of court ritual and attended banquets, concerts, operas, balls, and theatrical performances, Louis and his ministers ran the state, maintained a huge army, waged war, and promoted economic development. In effect, Louis provided the nobility with luxurious accommodations and endless entertainment in exchange for absolute rule.

Richelieu (RISH-uh-loo)
Versailles (vehr-SEYE)

Absolutism in Russia under Peter I Louis XIV was not the only absolute monarch of early modern Europe: Spanish, Austrian, and Prussian rulers embraced similar policies. Yet the potential of absolutism to increase state power was particularly conspicuous in the case of Russia, where czars of the **Romanov** dynasty (1613-1917) tightly centralized government functions. Most important of the Romanov czars was Peter I (reigned 1682-1725), widely known as **Peter the Great**, who inaugurated a thorough-going process of state transformation. Peter had a burning desire to transform Russia, a huge but underpopulated land, into a great military power like those that had recently emerged in western Europe. In 1697-1698 he led a large party of Russian observers on a tour of Germany, the Netherlands, and England to learn about western European administrative methods and military technology. His traveling companions often behaved crudely by western European standards: they consumed beer, wine, and brandy in quantities that astonished their hosts, and King William III sent Peter a bill for damages done by his entourage at the country house where they lodged in England.

On his return to Moscow, Peter set Russia spinning. He reformed the army by providing his forces with extensive training and equipping them with modern weapons. He ordered aristocrats to study mathematics and geometry, so that they could calculate how to aim cannons accurately, and he began the construction of a navy. He also overhauled the government bureaucracy to facilitate tax collection and improve administrative efficiency. He even commanded his aristocratic subjects to wear western European fashions and ordered men to shave their traditional beards. These measures provoked spirited protest among those who resented the influence of western European ways. Yet Peter was so insistent on the observance of his policies that he reportedly went into the streets and personally hacked the beards off recalcitrants' faces. Perhaps the best symbol of his policies was St. Petersburg, a newly built seaport that Peter opened in 1703 to serve as a magnificent capital city and a haven for Russia's fledgling navy.

Catherine II and the Limits of Reform The most able of Peter's successors was Catherine II (reigned 1762-1796), also known as **Catherine the Great**. Like Peter, Catherine sought to make Russia a great power. She worked to improve governmental efficiency, and she promoted economic development in Russia's towns. For a while, she even worked to improve the conditions of Russia's oppressed peasantry by restricting the punishments—such as torture, beating, and mutilation—that noble landowners could inflict on the serfs who worked their lands.

However, Catherine's interest in social reform cooled rapidly when it seemed to inspire challenges to her rule. She faced a particularly unsettling rebellion in 1773 and 1774, when a disgruntled former soldier named **Yemelian Pugachev** mounted an uprising in the steppe lands north of the Caspian Sea. Pugachev raised a motley army of adventurers, exiles, peasants, and serfs who killed thousands of noble landowners and government officials before imperial forces crushed the uprising. Government authorities took the captured Pugachev to Moscow in chains, beheaded him, quartered his body, and displayed its parts throughout the city as a warning against rebellion. Thereafter, Catherine's first concern was the preservation of autocratic rule rather than the transformation of Russia according to western European models.

Thus in Russia as in other European lands, absolutist policies resulted in tight centralization and considerable strengthening of the state. The enhanced power that flowed from absolutism became dramatically clear in the period 1772 to 1797, when Austria, Prussia, and Catherine II's Russia picked the weak kingdom of Poland apart. In a series of three "partitions," the predatory absolutist states seized Polish territory and absorbed it into their own realms, ultimately wiping Poland entirely off the map. The lesson of the partitions was clear: any European state that hoped to survive needed to construct an effective government that could respond promptly to challenges and opportunities.

The European States System

Whether they relied on absolutist or constitutional principles, European governments of early modern times built states much more powerful than those of their medieval predecessors. This round of state development led to difficulties within Europe, since conflicting interests fueled interstate competition and war. In the absence of an imperial authority capable of imposing and maintaining order in Europe, sovereign states had to find other ways to resolve conflicts.

The Peace of Westphalia The Thirty Years' War demonstrated the chaos and devastation that conflict could bring. In an effort to avoid tearing their society apart, European states ended the Thirty Years' War with the **Peace of Westphalia** (1648), which laid the foundations for a system of independent, competing states. By the treaty's terms, the European states regarded one another as sovereign and equal. They also mutually recognized their rights to organize their own domestic and religious affairs and agreed that political and diplomatic affairs were to be conducted by states acting in their own

Romanov (ruh-MAH-nuhf)
Yemelian Pugachev (yehm-eel-ian puh-gah-chehf)
Westphalia (west-FEY-lee-uh)

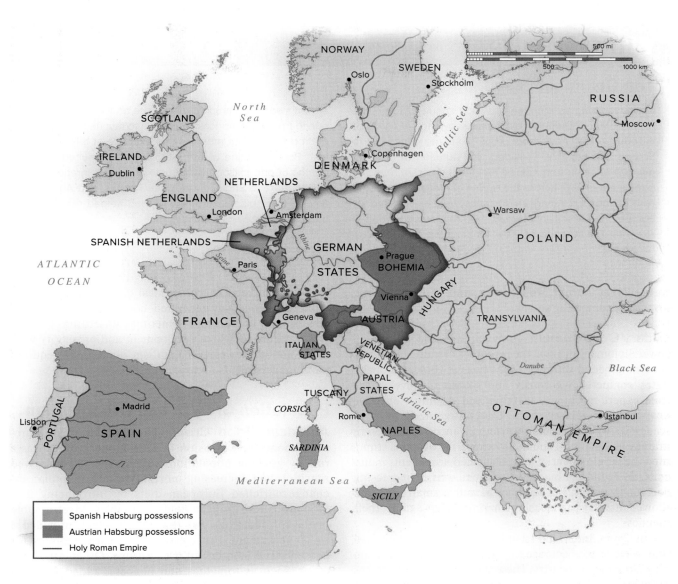

MAP 20.2   Europe after the Peace of Westphalia, 1648

Both England and the Netherlands became constitutional states with strong commercial interests. Compare this map with map 20.1.

How have the boundaries of the Holy Roman Empire changed, and why?

interests. European religious unity had disappeared, and the era of the sovereign state had arrived.

The Peace of Westphalia did not bring an end to war. Indeed, war was almost constant in early modern Europe. Most conflicts were minor affairs, but some grew to sizable proportions. Most notable among them were the wars of Louis XIV and the Seven Years' War. Between 1668 and 1713 the sun king sought to expand his borders east into Germany and to absorb Spain and the Spanish Netherlands into his kingdom. That prospect prompted England, the United Provinces, and Austria to mount a coalition against Louis. Later the Seven Years' War (1756–1763)

pitted France, Austria, and Russia against Britain and Prussia, and it merged with conflicts between France and Britain in India and North America to become a global war for imperial supremacy.

The Balance of Power These shifting alliances illustrate the principal foundation of European diplomacy in early modern times—the balance of power. No ruler wanted to see another state dominate all the others. Thus when any particular state began to grow too strong, others formed coalitions against it. By playing balance-of-power politics, statesmen prevented the building of empires and

Why It Matters ▷▷▷▷▷▷▷

The Columbian Exchange

Can something as mundane as food shape history? The history of the Columbian exchange shows that it can. The introduction of new food crops from the Americas to Europe, for example, provided vital nutrition to ordinary people, which in turn helped fuel an impressive round of population growth across the region at precisely the same time indigenous American societies were devastated by European diseases. In this way, food reinforced European strength. But reliance on new foods could be a double-edged sword: too much dependence on food crops introduced from the Americas could lead to famine in the event of crop failure. The most famous example of this was the Irish Potato Famine of 1845–1852, which resulted in the deaths of one million Irish people and the migration of a million more to England, the United States, and Australia, among other places. In this way, food helped restructure the makeup of whole societies.

---

ensured that Europe would be a land of independent, sovereign, competing states.

Military Development Frequent wars and balance-of-power diplomacy drained the resources of individual states but strengthened European society as a whole. European states competed vigorously and sought to develop the most expert military leadership and the most effective weapons for their arsenals. States organized military academies where officers received advanced education in strategy and tactics. Demand for powerful weapons stimulated the development of a sophisticated armaments industry. Gun foundries manufactured cannons of increasing size, range, power, and accuracy as well as small arms that allowed infantry to unleash withering volleys against their enemies.

In China, India, and Islamic lands, imperial states had little incentive to encourage similar technological innovation in the armaments industry. These states possessed the forces and weapons they needed to maintain order within their boundaries, and they rarely encountered foreign threats backed up with superior armaments. In Europe, however, failure to keep up with the latest improvements in arms technology could lead to defeat on the battlefield and decline in state power. Thus Europeans continuously sought to improve their military arsenals, and as a result, by the eighteenth century European armaments were outperforming all others.

EARLY CAPITALIST SOCIETY

While the Protestant Reformation and the emergence of sovereign states brought religious and political change, a rapidly expanding population and economy encouraged the development of capitalism, which in turn led to a restructuring of the European economy and society. Technologies of communication and transportation enabled businessmen to profit from distant markets, and merchants and manufacturers increasingly organized their affairs with the market rather than local communities in mind. Although capitalism generated considerable wealth, its effects were uneven and sometimes unsettling. Even in western Europe, where development and prosperity were most noticeable, early capitalism sometimes required painful adjustments to new conditions.

Population Growth and Urbanization

American Food Crops The foundation of European economic expansion in early modern times was a rapidly growing population, which reflected improved nutrition and decreasing mortality. The Columbian exchange enriched European diets by introducing new food crops to European fields and tables. Most notable of the introductions was the potato, which provided a welcome and inexpensive source of carbohydrates for peasants and laborers all over Europe. Other American crops, such as tomatoes and peppers, added vitamins and tangy flavor to European diets.

Since better-nourished populations are less susceptible to illness, new food crops also improved the overall resistance of Europeans to old diseases such as smallpox, dysentery, influenza, and typhus. Bubonic plague, a devastating epidemic killer during the fourteenth and fifteenth centuries, also receded from European society. Although plague made periodic appearances throughout the early modern era, epidemics were rare and isolated events after the mid-seventeenth century.

Although European birthrates did not rise dramatically in early modern times, decreasing mortality resulted in rapid population growth. In 1500 the population of Europe, including Russia, was about 81 million. By 1700 the population had risen to 120 million, and in the next century it reached 180 million. Such rapid population growth drove a process of equally rapid urbanization. In the mid-sixteenth century, for example, the population of Paris was about 130,000, and that of London was about 60,000. A century later the populations of both cities had risen to 500,000. Other European cities also experienced rapid growth, including Madrid, Amsterdam, Berlin, Copenhagen, Dublin, Stockholm, and Vienna, to name only a few.

Early Capitalism and Protoindustrialization

The Nature of Capitalism Population growth and rapid urbanization helped spur a round of remarkable economic development. That economic growth coincided with the emergence of **capitalism**—an economic system in which private parties make their goods and services available on a free market and seek to take advantage of market conditions to profit from their activities. Private parties own the land, machinery, tools, equipment, buildings, workshops, and raw materials needed for production. Private parties also hire workers and decide for themselves what to produce: economic decisions are the prerogative of capitalist businesspeople, not governments or social superiors. The center of a capitalist system is the market in which businesspeople compete with one another, and the forces of supply and demand determine the prices received for goods and services. The goal is to realize handsome profits from these activities.

Supply and Demand The desire to accumulate wealth and realize profits was by no means new. Indeed, for several thousand years before the early modern era, merchants in China, southeast Asia, India, southwest Asia, the Mediterranean basin, and sub-Saharan Africa had pursued commercial ventures in hopes of realizing profits. During early modern times, however, European merchants and entrepreneurs transformed their society in a way that none of their predecessors had done. The capitalist economic order developed as individuals learned to take advantage of market conditions in distant places via efficient networks of transportation and communication. For example, Dutch merchants might purchase cheap grain from Poland, store it in Amsterdam until they learned about a famine in the Mediterranean, and then transport it and sell it in southern France or Spain at an enormous profit.

Private parties organized an array of institutions and services to support early capitalism. Banks, for example, appeared in all the major commercial cities of Europe: they held funds on account for safekeeping and granted loans to merchants or entrepreneurs launching new business ventures. Insurance companies mitigated financial losses from risky undertakings such as transoceanic voyages, and stock exchanges provided markets where investors could buy and sell shares in joint-stock companies and trade in other commodities as well.

Joint-Stock Companies Joint-stock companies were especially important institutions in early capitalist society. Large trading companies such as the English East India Company and its Dutch counterpart, the Vereenigde Oost-Indische Compagnie (VOC), spread the risks attached to expensive business enterprises and took advantage of extensive communications and transportation networks. The trading companies organized commercial ventures on a larger scale than ever before in world history. They were the principal foundations of the global economy that emerged in early modern times, and they were the direct ancestors of contemporary multinational corporations.

Politics and Empire Capitalism did not develop in a political vacuum. On the contrary, it emerged with the active support of government authorities who saw a capitalist order as the one best suited to their individual and

The Old Stock Exchange of Amsterdam, depicted here in a painting of the mid-seventeenth century, attracted merchants, investors, entrepreneurs, and businesspeople from all over Europe. There they bought and sold shares in joint-stock companies such as the VOC and dealt in all manner of commodities traded in Amsterdam.
Historic Images/Alamy Stock Photo

SOURCES FROM THE PAST

Adam Smith on the Capitalist Market

Adam Smith (1723–1790) was a Scottish economist, philosopher, and author who devoted special thought to the nature of early capitalist society and the principles that made it work. In 1776 he published a lengthy book titled An Inquiry into the Nature and Causes of the Wealth of Nations, *a vastly influential work that championed free, unregulated markets and capitalist enterprise as the principal ingredients of prosperity. Smith's optimism about capitalism sprang from his conviction that society as a whole benefits when individuals pursue their own economic interests and trade on a free market.*

Every individual is continually exerting himself to find out the most advantageous employment for whatever capital he can command. It is his own advantage, indeed, and not that of the society, which he has in view. . . .

As every individual, therefore, endeavours as much as he can both to employ his capital in the support of domestic industry, and so to direct that industry that its produce may be of the greatest value, every individual necessarily labours to render the annual revenue of the society as great as he can. He generally, indeed, neither intends to promote the public interest, nor knows how much he is promoting it. By preferring the support of domestic to that of foreign industry, he intends only his own security; and by directing that industry in such a manner as its produce may be of the greatest value, he intends only his own gain, and he is in this, as in many other cases, led by an invisible hand to promote an end which was no part of his intention. Nor is it always the worse for the society that it was no part of it. By pursuing his own interest he frequently promotes that of the society more effectually than when he really intends to promote it. I have never known much good done by those who affected to trade for the public good. It is an affectation, indeed, not very common among merchants, and very few words need be employed in dissuading them from it.

> Smith's notion of an "invisible hand"' operating on the economy is famous. What do you think Smith meant by this?

What is the species of domestic industry which his capital can employ, and of which the produce is likely to be of the greatest value, every individual, it is evident, can, in his local situation, judge much better than any statesman or lawgiver can do for him. The statesman, who should attempt to direct private people in what manner they ought to employ their capitals, would not only load himself with a most unnecessary attention, but assume an authority which could safely be trusted, not only to no single person, but to no council or senate whatever, and which would nowhere be so dangerous as in the hands of a man who had folly and presumption enough to fancy himself fit to exercise it.

> Why, according to Smith, are individuals better able to judge how to spend their money than representatives of the state?

To give the monopoly of the home market to the produce of domestic industry, in any particular art or manufacture, is in some measure to direct private people in what manner they ought to employ their capitals, and must, in almost all cases, be either a useless or a hurtful regulation. If the produce of domestic industry can be brought there as cheap as that of foreign industry, the regulation is evidently useless. If it cannot, it must generally be hurtful. It is the maxim of every prudent master of a family, never to attempt to make at home what it will cost him more to make than to buy. The tailor does not attempt to make his own shoes, but buys them of the shoemaker. The shoemaker does not attempt to make his own clothes, but employs a tailor. The farmer attempts to make neither the one nor the other, but employs those different artificers. All of them find it for their interest to employ their whole industry in a way in which they have some advantage over their neighbours, and to purchase with a part of its produce, or, what is the same thing, with the price of a part of it, whatever else they have occasion for.

For Further Reflection

■ To what extent do you think Adam Smith's analysis reflected the experiences of his own times, and to what extent did it represent universally valid observations?

Source: Adam Smith. *An Inquiry into the Nature and Causes of the Wealth of Nations.* Edinburgh: 1863, pp. 198–200.

collective interests. Merchants were especially influential in the affairs of the English and Dutch states, so it is not surprising that these lands adopted policies that were most favorable to capitalist enterprises throughout the early modern era. The English and Dutch states recognized individuals' rights to possess private property and protected their financial interests. They also authorized joint-stock companies to explore and colonize distant lands in search of commercial opportunities. Indeed, imperial expansion and colonial rule were crucial for the development of capitalism, since they enabled European merchants to gain access to the natural resources and commodities that they distributed so effectively through their transportation networks.

The Putting-Out System Quite apart from its influence on trade and the distribution of goods, capitalism also encouraged European entrepreneurs to organize new ways to manufacture goods. For centuries, craft guilds had monopolized the production of goods such as textiles and metalwares in European towns and cities. Guilds fixed prices and wages, and they sought not to realize profits so much as to protect markets and preserve their members' places in society. As a result, they actively discouraged competition. Because of this, capitalist entrepreneurs side-stepped the guilds and moved production into the country-side. There they organized a "putting-out system" by which they delivered unfinished materials such as raw wool to rural households. Men and women in the countryside spun and wove the wool into cloth and then cut and assembled the cloth into garments. The entrepreneur picked up the finished goods, paid the workers, and sold the items on the market for a handsome profit. The putting-out system represented an early effort to organize efficient industrial production, and some historians even refer to the seventeenth and eighteenth centuries as an age of **protoindustrialization**.

Social Change in Early Modern Europe

Capitalist economic development brought significant change to European lands. In western Europe, the putting-out system introduced considerable sums of money into the countryside, which tended to undermine long-established patterns of rural life even as it brought material benefits such as improved food, clothing, and furnishings to rural households. Increased wealth meant that individuals suddenly acquired incomes that enabled them to become financially independent of their families and neighbors, and many feared that these individuals—especially young adults and women—might abandon their kin and way of life altogether as a result.

In eastern Europe, the putting-out system did not become a prominent feature of production, but early capitalism prompted deep social change there as well. Eastern

Europe had very few cities in early modern times, so in agrarian states such as Poland, Bohemia, and Russia most people had no alternative to working in the countryside. Landlords took advantage of this situation by forcing peasants to work under extremely harsh conditions.

Serfdom in Russia Russia, in particular, was a vast but sparsely populated empire with little trade or manufacturing. Out of a concern to retain the allegiance of the powerful nobles who owned most of Russia's land, the Romanov czars restricted the freedoms of most Russian peasants and tied them to the land as serfs. The institution of serfdom had emerged in the early middle ages as a labor system that required peasants to provide labor services for landowners and prevented them from marrying or moving away without their landlords' permission. Although serfdom came to an end in western Europe after the fifteenth century, in eastern Europe landowners and rulers tightened restrictions on peasants during the sixteenth century. In Russia, for example, landlords commonly sold serfs to one another as if they were private property. In effect, the Romanovs won the support of the Russian nobles by ensuring them that laborers would be available to work their estates, which otherwise would have been worthless. Under these conditions, landlords operated estates with inexpensive labor and derived enormous incomes from the sale of agricultural products on the market.

These arrangements played crucial roles in the emergence of capitalism. In the larger economy of early modern Europe, eastern European lands produced agricultural products and raw materials based on semifree labor, which were then exported to western Europe to sustain its large and growing free wage labor force. Already by the early sixteenth century, consumers in the Netherlands depended for their survival on grains imported from Poland and Russia through the Baltic Sea. Thus it was possible for capitalism to flourish in western Europe only because the peasants and semifree serfs of eastern Europe provided inexpensive foods and raw materials that fueled economic development. From its earliest days, capitalist economic organization had implications for peoples and lands far removed from the centers of capitalism itself.

Profits and Ethics Capitalism also posed moral challenges. Medieval theologians had regarded profit making as morally dangerous, since profiteers looked to their own advantage rather than to the welfare of the larger community. But capitalism found advocates who sought to explain its principles and portray it as a socially beneficial form of economic organization. Most important of the early apostles of capitalism was the Scottish philosopher Adam Smith, who argued that society would prosper when individuals pursued their own economic interests.

Nevertheless, prosperity was unattainable for all or even most early modern Europeans, which meant that the transition to capitalist economic practices was a long and painful process that generated deep social strains throughout Europe. Those strains often manifested themselves in violence: bandits plagued the countryside of early modern Europe, and muggers turned whole sections of large cities into danger zones. Some historians believe that witch-hunting activities reflected social tensions generated by early capitalism and that accusations of witchcraft represented hostility toward women who were becoming economically independent of their husbands and families.

The Nuclear Family   In some ways capitalism favored the nuclear family as the principal unit of society. Although for centuries European couples had set up independent households, early capitalism offered further opportunities for independent families to increase their wealth by producing goods for sale on the market. As nuclear families became more important economically, they also became more socially and emotionally independent. Love between a man and a woman became a more important consideration in the making of marriages than the interests of the larger extended families, and affection between parents and their children became a more important ingredient of family life. Capitalism did not necessarily cause these changes in family life, but it may have encouraged developments that helped define the nature and role of the family in modern European society.

TRANSFORMATIONS IN SCIENTIFIC THINKING

While experiencing religious, political, economic, and social change, western Europe also underwent intellectual and cultural transformation. Astronomers and physicists rejected Greek and Roman authorities, whose theories had dominated scientific thought during the middle ages, and based their understanding of the natural world on direct observation and mathematical reasoning. During the seventeenth and eighteenth centuries they elaborated a new vision of the earth and the larger universe in a process known as the **scientific revolution**. In the process, they weakened the influence of churches in western Europe and encouraged the development of secular values.

The Reconception of the Universe

The Ptolemaic Universe   Until the seventeenth century European astronomers based their understanding of the universe on the work of the Greek scholar Claudius Ptolemy of Alexandria. In the middle of the second century C.E. Ptolemy produced a work known as the *Almagest*,

A woodcut illustration depicts the Ptolemaic universe with the earth at the center surrounded by spheres holding the planets and the stars.
Pictorial Press Ltd/Alamy Stock Photo

which envisioned a motionless earth surrounded by a series of nine hollow, concentric spheres that revolved around it. Each of the first seven spheres had one of the observable heavenly bodies embedded in its shell. The eighth sphere held the stars, and an empty ninth sphere surrounded the whole cosmos and provided the spin that kept all the others moving. Beyond the spheres, Christian astronomers located heaven, the realm of God.

Following Ptolemy, astronomers believed that the heavens consisted of a pure substance that did not experience change or corruption and was not subject to the physical laws that governed the world below the moon. They also held that heavenly bodies followed perfectly circular paths in making their revolutions around the earth.

Planetary Movement   This cosmology, however, did not mesh readily with the erratic movements of the planets, which sometimes slowed down, stopped, or even turned back on their courses. Astronomers went to great lengths to explain planetary behavior as the result of perfectly circular movements. The result was an awkward series of

Ptolemaic (TAWL-oh-may-ihk)

adjustments known as epicycles—small, circular revolutions that planets made around a point in their spheres, even while the spheres themselves revolved around the earth.

The Copernican Universe In 1543, however, the Polish astronomer **Nicolaus Copernicus** published *On the Revolutions of the Heavenly Spheres,* which broke with Ptolemaic theory. Copernicus argued that the sun, rather than the earth, stood at the center of the universe and that the planets, including the earth, revolved around the sun. Although this new theory harmonized much better with observational data, it did not receive a warm welcome. Copernicus's ideas not only challenged prevailing scientific theories but also threatened cherished religious beliefs, which held that the earth and humanity were unique creations of God.

The Scientific Revolution

In time, though, Copernicus's theory inspired some astronomers to examine the heavens in fresh ways, using precise observational data and mathematical reasoning. Gradually, they abandoned the Ptolemaic in favor of the Copernican model of the universe. Some also began to apply their analytical methods to mechanics—the branch of science that deals with moving bodies—and by the mid-seventeenth century accurate observation and mathematical reasoning dominated both mechanics and astronomy. Indeed, reliance on observation and mathematics transformed the study of the natural world and brought about the process we now call the scientific revolution.

Galileo Galilei The works of two mathematicians—**Johannes Kepler** of Germany and **Galileo Galilei** of Italy—rang the death knell for the Ptolemaic universe. Kepler (1571–1630) demonstrated that planetary orbits are elliptical, not circular as in Ptolemaic theory. Galileo (1564–1642) showed that the heavens are not the perfect, unblemished realm that Ptolemaic astronomers assumed. Using the recently invented telescope, Galileo was able to observe spots on the sun and mountains on the moon. He also caught sight of distant stars previously undetectable to the naked eye, which implied that the universe was much larger than anyone had previously suspected.

Isaac Newton The new approach to science culminated in the work of the English mathematician **Isaac Newton** (1642–1727), who depended on accurate observation and mathematical reasoning to construct a powerful synthesis of astronomy and mechanics. Newton outlined his views on the natural world in an epoch-making volume in 1687 titled *Mathematical Principles of Natural Philosophy.* Newton's work united the heavens and the earth in a vast, cosmic system. He argued that a law of universal gravitation regulates the motions of bodies throughout the universe, and he offered precise mathematical explanations of the laws that govern movements of bodies on the earth. His laws also allowed him to explain a vast range of seemingly unrelated phenomena, such as the ebb and flow of the tides and the eccentric orbits of planets and comets. Until the twentieth century, Newton's universe served as the unquestioned framework for the physical sciences.

Inspired by the dramatic discoveries of astronomers and physicists, other scientists began to construct fresh approaches to understanding the natural world. During the seventeenth and eighteenth centuries, anatomy, physiology, microbiology, chemistry, and botany underwent a thorough overhaul as scientists tested their theories against direct observation of natural phenomena and explained them in rigorous mathematical terms.

Women and Science

In the sixteenth and seventeenth centuries, Europe's learned men challenged some of the most hallowed

Émilie du Châtelet was perhaps the most exceptional female scientist of the eighteenth century. Although she had to contend with the conventional demands on women, she remained committed to her study of Newton and science.
DEA/G. Dagli Orti/De Agostini/Getty Images

traditions concerning the nature of the physical universe and supplanted them with new scientific principles. Yet when male scientists studied female anatomy, female physiology, and women's reproductive organs, they were commonly guided not by scientific observation but by tradition, prejudice, and fanciful imagination. William Harvey (1578–1657), the English physician who discovered the principles of the circulation of human blood, also applied his considerable talents to the study of human reproduction. After careful dissection and observation of female deer, chickens, and roosters, he hypothesized that women, like hens, served as mere receptacles for the "vivifying" male fluid. According to him, it was the male semen—endowed with generative powers so potent that it did not even have to reach the uterus to work its magic—from which the unfertilized egg received life and form. Anatomy, physiology, and limited reproductive function seemed to confirm the innate inferiority of women, adding a "scientific" veneer to the traditionally limited images, roles, and functions of women. With the arrival of printing, men were able to disseminate more widely those negative conclusions about women.

Émilie du Châtelet Despite prevailing critical attitudes, some women found themselves drawn to the new intellectual currents of the time. One of the most notable female scientists of her age was **Émilie du Châtelet** (1706–1749), a French mathematician and physicist. Long famous for being the mistress of the celebrated French intellectual Voltaire (chapter 25), she was a talented intellectual and scientist in her own right. A precocious child, du Châtelet was apparently fluent in six languages at the age of twelve, and she benefited from having an unusually enlightened father who provided his rebellious daughter with an education more typical for boys.

Du Châtelet's crowning achievement was her translation of Isaac Newton's monumental work *Principia Mathematica,* which has remained the standard French translation of the work. She did not simply render Newton's words into another language, however; she explained his complex mathematics in graceful prose, transformed his geometry into calculus, and assessed the current state of Newtonian physics. She finished her work in the year of her death, at age forty-three, six days after giving birth to a child. Underscoring the difficulty of reconciling a woman's reproductive duties with her intellectual aspirations was her lover Voltaire's commentary. He declared in a letter to his friend Frederick II, king of Prussia (reigned 1740–1786), that du Châtelet was "a great man whose only fault was being a woman."

Science and Society

Newton's vision of the universe was so powerful and persuasive that its influence extended well beyond science. His work suggested that rational analysis of human behavior and institutions could lead to fresh insights into the human as well as the natural world. Thus from Scotland to Sicily and from Philadelphia to Moscow, European and Euro-American thinkers launched an ambitious project to use scientific principles and reason to transform the world. Like the early modern scientists, they abandoned Aristotelian philosophy, Christian theology, and other traditionally recognized authorities, and they sought to subject the human world to purely rational analysis. For example, the English philosopher John Locke (1632–1704) worked to discover natural laws of politics. He attacked divine-right theories that served as a foundation for absolute monarchy and advocated constitutional government on the grounds that sovereignty resides in the people rather than the state or its rulers. Adam Smith turned his attention to economic affairs and held that laws of supply and demand determine what happens in the marketplace. Using the techniques of scientific inquiry, thinkers like Locke and Smith helped constitute a movement called the Enlightenment (chapter 25), which itself provided the justification for momentous social and political change around the world.

CONCLUSION

During the early modern era, European society experienced a series of profound and sometimes painful changes. The Protestant Reformation ended the religious unity of western Europe, and intermittent religious conflict disrupted European society for a century and more. Centralizing monarchs strengthened their realms and built a society of sovereign, autonomous, and intensely competitive states with distinctive traditions. Capitalist entrepreneurs reorganized the production and distribution of manufactured goods, and although their methods led to increased wealth, their quest for efficiency and profits clashed with traditional values. Modern science based on direct observation and mathematical explanations emerged as a powerful tool for the investigation of, and encounters with, the natural world. At just the time that European merchants, colonists, and adventurers were seeking new opportunities and encounters in the larger world, European society was becoming more powerful, more experimental, and more competitive than ever before. Given that Europeans now possessed the latest armaments and were willing to use them to achieve political and economic goals, this combination would have profound effects for many regions of the world in the future.

STUDY TERMS

absolutism (354)
Anglicans (349)
Calvinists (348)
capitalism (359)
Cardinal Richelieu (355)
Catherine the Great (356)
Catholic Reformation (349)
constitutional states (353)
Council of Trent (349)
Émilie du Châtelet (364)
Emperor Charles V (351)
English Civil War (354)
Galileo Galilei (363)
Habsburgs (351)
Isaac Newton (363)
Johannes Kepler (363)

King Louis XIV (355)
Martin Luther (346)
Nicolaus Copernicus (363)
Ninety-five Theses (346)
Peace of Westphalia (356)
Peter the Great (356)
Protestant Reformation (347)
protoindustrialization (361)
Romanov (356)
scientific revolution (362)
Society of Jesus (349)
Spanish Inquisition (353)
Thirty Years' War (350)
Versailles (355)
Yemelian Pugachev (356)

FOR FURTHER READING

Paul Dukes. *The Making of Russian Absolutism, 1613-1801.* 2nd ed. London, 2015. A succinct study of two disparate centuries, the seventeenth and eighteenth, and two influential czars, Peter and Catherine.

Patricia Fara. *Pandora's Breeches: Women, Science, and Power in the Enlightenment.* London, 2004. An engaging account of the contributions women made to science in the seventeenth and eighteenth centuries.

Philip S. Gorski. *The Disciplinary Revolution: Calvinism and the Rise of the Early Modern State.* Chicago, 2003. Argues that the formation of strong European states was a result of religious and social control policies initiated by the Protestant Reformation.

Thomas S. Kuhn. *The Structure of Scientific Revolutions.* 3rd ed. Chicago, 1997. An influential theoretical work that views scientific thought in larger social and cultural contexts.

Brian P. Levack. *The Witch-Hunt in Early Modern Europe.* New York, 2006. A compact but comprehensive survey of European witchcraft beliefs and the pursuit of witches in the sixteenth and seventeenth centuries.

Jerry Z. Muller. *The Mind and the Market: Capitalism in Modern European Thought.* New York, 2002. A broad history of the development of capitalism through the eyes of major European thinkers, including Adam Smith, Joseph Schumpeter, and Karl Marx.

Andrew Pettegree. *Reformation and the Culture of Persuasion.* Cambridge, 2005. Investigates why people chose to support the Reformation in an era before mass literacy.

Paolo Rossi. *The Birth of Modern Science.* Malden, Mass., 2001. Explores specific seventeenth-century value systems and traditions that were central to the rise of modern science.

Merry Wiesner-Hanks. *Women and Gender in Early Modern Europe.* 4th ed. Cambridge, 2019. A comprehensive overview of women's lives and of ideas about gender in the early modern period, with attention to race, migration, and global issues.

Peter Wilson. *The Thirty Years' War: Europe's Tragedy.* Cambridge, Mass., 2011. A comprehensive study of the destructiveness of the war and its social, political, and economic causes as well as its religious causes.

The Integration of the Americas and Oceania with the Wider World

ZOOMING IN ON ENCOUNTERS

The Complicated Choices of Doña Marina

A remarkable young woman played a pivotal role in the Spanish conquest of Mexico. Sometimes called **Malintzin**, she is better known by her Spanish name, **Doña Marina**. Born about 1500 to a noble family in central Mexico, Doña Marina's mother tongue was **Nahuatl**, the principal language of the Aztec empire. When she was a girl, Doña Marina's family sent her to the Mexican coast as an enslaved person. Her slaveholders later passed her on to their neighbors on the Yucatan peninsula, where she also became fluent in the Mayan language.

When **Hernán Cortés** arrived on the Mexican coast in 1519, only one of his soldiers could speak the Mayan language spoken by coastal peoples. But he had no way to communicate with the Nahuatl-speaking peoples of central Mexico until a Maya chieftain presented him with twelve young women, including Doña Marina, when he entered

A contemporary mural by Tlaxala artist Desiderio Hernández Xochitiotzin—which is based on a sixteenth-century indigenous painting—suggests the central place of Doña Marina in facilitating encounters between Hernán Cortés (on the right) and the indigenous peoples of Mexico.
Benson Latin American Collection, General Libraries, University of Texas at Austin

Malintzin (mal-een-tzeen)
Nahuatl (na-watl)
Hernán Cortés (er-NAHN kawr-TEZ)

into an alliance with Cortés against the Aztec. Doña Marina's linguistic abilities enabled Cortés to communicate through an improbable chain of languages—from Spanish to Mayan to Nahuatl and then back again—while making his way to the Aztec capital of Tenochtitlan. (Doña Marina learned Spanish and thus eliminated the Maya link in the linguistic chain.)

Doña Marina provided Cortés with information and diplomatic as well as linguistic services. On several occasions she learned of plans by indigenous peoples to destroy the tiny Spanish army, and she alerted Cortés to the danger in time for him to prevent an attack. She also helped Cortés negotiate with emissaries from the major cities of central Mexico. In fact, without Doña Marina's help, it is difficult to see how Cortés's small band could have survived to see the Aztec capital.

Precisely because of her pivotal role in aiding Cortés in his invasion of the Aztec empire, Doña Marina earned another name commonly bestowed on her in Mexican history: La Malinche, or the traitor. The belief that she betrayed her people by collaborating with the Spanish underscores the complicated choices Doña Marina was faced with in her encounters with Europeans. In particular, it is important to remember her lack of power as an enslaved woman. After being given to Cortés, she may have felt the need to protect her new membership in his group by making herself valuable. Using her linguistic and diplomatic talents to aid Cortés may have been a means of survival. Whatever her motives, it is clear that Doña Marina's aid was crucial to the success of Cortés's small group.

In addition to facilitating the Spanish conquest of the Aztec empire, Doña Marina played a role in the formation of a new society in Mexico. In 1522, one year after the fall of Tenochtitlan, she gave birth to a son fathered by Cortés, and in 1526 she bore a daughter to a Spanish captain whom she had married. Given her status as an enslaved person, historians have no way of knowing whether Doña Marina conceived her children willingly or not. Nevertheless, although her offspring were not the first children born in the western hemisphere of indigenous and Spanish parentage, they symbolize the early emergence of a mestizo population in Mexico. Doña Marina died soon after the birth of her daughter, probably in 1527, but during her short life she contributed to the thorough transformation of Mexican society.

CHAPTER OVERVIEW

Until 1492 the peoples of the eastern and western hemispheres had few dealings with one another. After 1492, however, the voyages of European mariners led to permanent and continuous contact between the peoples of all these areas. The resulting encounters brought profound and often violent change to both American and Pacific lands. European peoples possessed powerful weapons, horses, and ships that provided them with technological advantages over the peoples they encountered in the Americas and the Pacific islands. Moreover, most Europeans also enjoyed complete or partial immunity to diseases that caused devastating epidemics when introduced to the western hemisphere and Oceania. Because of their technological advantages and the depopulation that followed from epidemic diseases, European peoples were able to establish a strong presence throughout the Americas and much of the Pacific Ocean basin.

COLLIDING WORLDS

When European peoples first sought to establish their presence in the Americas, they brought technologies unavailable to the peoples they encountered in the western hemisphere. Even more important than technology, however, was the combination of devastating epidemic disease Europeans brought with them and European willingness to exploit existing divisions between indigenous peoples. With the help of technology, disease, and ruthless political maneuvering, Spanish conquerors toppled the Aztec and Inca empires and imposed their own rule in Mexico and Peru. In later decades Portuguese planters built sugar plantations on the Brazilian coastline. French, English, and Dutch migrants displaced indigenous peoples in North America and established settler colonies under the rule of European peoples.

The Spanish Caribbean

Tainos When Spanish mariners arrived in the Caribbean, the Taino (also known as the Arawak) were the

---

Tenochtitlan (teh-noch-tee-TLAHN)
Taino (tah-EE-noh)

CHRONOLOGY

1492	First voyage of Christopher Columbus to the western hemisphere
1494	Treaty of Tordesillas
1500	Brazil claimed for Portugal by Pedro Alvarez de Cabral
1500–1527	Life of Doña Marina
1518	Smallpox epidemic in the Caribbean
1519–1521	Spanish conquest of Mexico
1532–1540	Spanish conquest of Peru
1545	Spanish discovery of silver near Potosí
1604	Foundation of Port Royal (Nova Scotia)
1607	Foundation of Jamestown
1608	Foundation of Quebec
1619	First enslaved Africans brought to Virginia
1623	Foundation of New Amsterdam
1630	Foundation of the Massachusetts Bay Colony
1688	Smallpox epidemic on Guam
1768–1779	Captain James Cook's exploration of the Pacific Ocean
1788	Establishment of the first European colony in Australia

most prominent people in the region. The Taino cultivated manioc and other crops, and they lived in small villages under the authority of chiefs who allocated land to families and supervised community affairs. Although at first the Taino received the Spanish warmly, within a few months relations between the Taino and the Spanish turned sour when it became clear that the Spanish were not satisfied with the amount of gold they were getting through trade alone.

Spanish Arrival Christopher Columbus and his immediate followers made the island of Hispaniola (modern Haiti and the Dominican Republic) the base of Spanish operations in the Caribbean. Columbus's original plan was to build forts and trading posts where merchants could trade with local peoples for products desired by European consumers. However, it soon became clear that the Caribbean region offered no silks or spices for the European market. If Spanish settlers wanted to maintain their presence in the Caribbean, they would need to find some way to make a living.

encomienda (ehn-koh-MYEN-dah)

The settlers first attempted to support their society by mining gold. Spanish settlers were few in number and were not inclined to perform heavy labor, so they recruited the labor they needed from the ranks of the Taino. This was done through an institution known as the *encomienda,* which involved *encomenderos* (Spanish settlers) forcing the Taino to work in their mines or fields. In return for labor, *encomenderos* were supposed to look after their workers' welfare and encourage their conversion to Christianity.

Conscription of Taino labor was a brutal business that, in practice, functioned like a system of slavery. *Encomenderos* worked their charges hard and punished them severely. The Taino occasionally organized rebellions, but their bows, arrows, and slings had little effect against horse-mounted Spanish forces wielding steel swords and firearms. By about 1515 enslavement and physical abuse had caused Taino populations to decline dramatically on the large Caribbean islands of Hispaniola, Jamaica, Puerto Rico, and Cuba.

Smallpox Another serious demographic decline set in after 1518, when **smallpox** reached the Caribbean and touched off devastating epidemics. To replace laborers lost to disease, *encomenderos* resorted to kidnapping and enslaving the Taino and other peoples. That tactic, however, only exposed additional victims to disease. As a result of epidemic disease, the indigenous population of the Caribbean plummeted from about four million in 1492 to a few thousand in the 1540s. Entire societies passed out of existence. Only a few Taíno cultural elements survived: canoe, hammock, hurricane, barbecue, maize, and tobacco all derive from Taíno words, but the society that generated them had largely disappeared by the middle of the sixteenth century.

From Mining to Plantation Agriculture After the mid-sixteenth century, when it was clear that gold supplies in the region were not plentiful, the Caribbean became a much less important part of the Spanish empire. In the 1640s, French, English, and Dutch settlers began to take the place of the Spanish and flocked to the Caribbean with the intention of establishing plantations. Indeed, they found that the Caribbean offered ideal conditions for the cultivation of cash crops, particularly sugar and tobacco. Meanwhile, because indigenous populations had been decimated,Europeans solved the labor shortage by forcibly importing several million enslaved people from Africa. By 1700 Caribbean society consisted of a small class of European landowners and large numbers of enslaved Africans.

One of the earliest European depictions of Native Americans was this engraving of 1505. The caption informed readers that American peoples lived in communal society, where men took several wives but none had private possessions and that they routinely smoked and consumed the bodies of slain enemies. How might such representations have shaped European ideas about Native Americans?

North Wind Picture Archives/Alamy Stock Photo

Mexico and Peru at the Time of Contact

Spanish interest shifted quickly from the Caribbean to the American mainland in the quest for resources. During the early sixteenth century, Spanish *conquistadores* ("conquerors") pressed west into Mexico and south into Panama and Peru. Aided especially by the spread of epidemic disease, between 1519 and 1521 Hernán Cortés and a small band of men brought down the Aztec empire in Mexico, and between 1532 and 1533 Francisco Pizarro and his followers toppled the Inca empire in Peru. Those conquests laid the foundations for colonial regimes that would transform the Americas.

In Mexico and Peru, Spanish explorers found societies quite different from those of the Caribbean islands. Both Mexico and Peru had been sites of agricultural societies, cities, and large states for more than a millennium. In the early fifteenth century both lands fell under the sway of powerful imperial states: the Mexica people and their allies founded the Aztec empire, which expanded to embrace most of Mesoamerica, and the Inca imposed their rule on a vast realm extending from modern Ecuador in the north to modern Chile in the south.

Hernán Cortés The conquest of Mexico began in 1519 when Cortés led about 450 soldiers from Veracruz on the Gulf coast to the island city of Tenochtitlan, the large and vibrant Aztec capital situated in Lake Texcoco. They seized the emperor, **Motecuzoma II**, who died in 1520 during a skirmish between Spanish forces and residents of Tenochtitlan. Fierce Aztec resistance soon drove the *conquistadores* from the capital, but Cortés built a small fleet of ships, placed Tenochtitlan under siege, and in 1521 starved the city into surrender.

---

conquistadores (kon-kees-tah-DOH-rayz)

Motecuzoma (mo-tec-oo-ZO-ma)

Why It Matters

The Columbian Exchange

Do people shape history, or do events such as natural disasters or pandemics? The European conquest of the Americas raises questions about the importance of individual action versus forces like disease. Recall that the spread of epidemic diseases such as smallpox and influenza from Eurasia to the Americas was one of the key features of the Columbian exchange. When indigenous Americans were exposed to Eurasian diseases, they had almost no acquired immunity. As a result, diseases took a staggering toll: in some places the mortality rate may have been as high as 90 percent. If epidemic disease had not caused such high mortality among indigenous Americans, in what ways might the history of the Americas in the sixteenth and seventeenth centuries have been different? In other words, did individuals such as Hernan Cortés or Motecuzoma shape history, or did viruses?

Spanish weapons and horses offered Cortés and his soldiers some advantage over the forces they met and help account for the Spanish conquest of the Aztec empire. Yet weaponry alone clearly was not enough to overcome such a large, densely populated society. Indeed, Cortés's expedition also made important alliances with peoples who resented Aztec domination. Indigenous allies reinforced the small Spanish army with thousands of veteran warriors and provided Spanish forces with logistical support and secure bases in friendly territory.

Epidemic Disease Epidemic disease also aided Spanish efforts. During the siege of Tenochtitlan, smallpox raged through the city, killing inhabitants by the tens of thousands. It then spread beyond the capital and raced through Mexico, killing so many people that Aztec society was unable to function. Only in the context of this enormous depopulation is it possible to understand the Spanish conquest of Mexico.

Francisco Pizarro **Francisco Pizarro** experienced similar results when he led a Spanish expedition from Central America to Peru. Pizarro set out in 1530 with 180 soldiers, later joined by reinforcements to make a force of about 600. The *conquistadores* arrived in Peru just after a bitter dispute within the Inca ruling house, and it was easy for them to exploit differences between the factions. By 1533 they had taken the Inca capital at Cuzco. Under pretext of holding a conference, they called the Inca ruling elites together, seized them, and killed most of them. They spared the Inca ruler **Atahualpa** until he had delivered a large quantity of gold to Pizarro. Then they strangled him and decapitated his body. Pizarro and his *conquistadores* proceeded to loot gold and silver from Cuzco's temples and public buildings, and even to loot jewelry and ornaments from the embalmed bodies of deceased Inca rulers.

As Cortés's expedition had done to the Aztec in Mexico, Pizarro's tiny force toppled the Inca empire by exploiting divisions among indigenous peoples. Many Inca subjects despised their overlords and thus either allied with or did not resist Pizarro's forces. In addition, smallpox had spread to the Inca empire in the 1520s, long before Pizarro's arrival, and had already significantly weakened Andean populations. By 1540 Spanish forces had established themselves securely in Peru.

Spanish and Portuguese Empires in the Americas

Spanish Colonial Administration The conquests of Mexico and Peru were the results not of Spanish royal policy but, rather, of individual efforts by freelance

Tlaxcalan allies of the Spanish on their way to the Aztec capital of Tenochtitlan. A Spanish warrior is at the front right of the drawing on his horse. Taken from the sixteenth-century *Lienzo de Tlaxcala* manuscript.
The Picture Art Collection/Alamy Stock Photo

Cuzco (KOOS-koh)
Atahualpa (ah-tah-WAHL-pah)

SOURCES FROM THE PAST

First Impressions of Spanish Forces

As the Spanish army made its way to Tenochtitlan, Motecuzoma dispatched a series of emissaries to communicate with Cortés and learn his intentions. The following document, based on indigenous accounts but filtered through the Spanish sensibilities of Bernardino de Sahagun, suggests that Motecuzoma reacted with fright when presented with reports that were less than reassuring because they focused on the fearsome weapons and animals of the Spanish. Given the vigorous resistance by the Aztec to the Spanish invaders, it seems highly likely that the source exaggerated Motecuzoma's terror. At the same time, at the very least it suggests that Motecuzoma took the threat posed by the Spanish very seriously.

And when [Motecuzoma] had heard what the messengers reported, he was terrified, he was astounded. . . .

Especially did it cause him to faint away when he heard how the gun, at [the Spaniards'] command, discharged [the shot]; how it resounded as if it thundered when it went off. It indeed bereft one of strength; it shut off one's ears. And when it discharged, something like a round pebble came forth from within. Fire went showering forth; sparks went blazing forth. And its smoke smelled very foul; it had a fetid odor which verily wounded the head. And when [the shot] struck a mountain, it was as if it were destroyed, dissolved. And a tree was pulverized; it was as if it vanished; it was as if someone blew it away. ——

> For someone who had never seen a firearm in action before, does this description seem to do an adequate job of relaying its effects?

All iron was their war array. In iron they clothed themselves. With iron they covered their heads. Iron were their swords. Iron were their crossbows. Iron were their shields. Iron were their lances.

And those which bore them upon their backs, their deer [that is, horses], were as tall as roof terraces.

And their bodies were everywhere covered; only their faces appeared. They were very white; they had chalky faces; they had yellow hair, though the hair of some was black. Long were their beards; they also were yellow. They were yellow-headed. [The Black men's hair] was kinky, it was curly. ——

> Why might the Aztec have paid particular attention to the Europeans with blond hair?

And their food was like fasting food—very large, white, not heavy like [tortillas]; like maize stalks, good-tasting as if of maize stalk flour; a little sweet, a little honeyed. It was honeyed to eat; it was sweet to eat.

And their dogs were very large. They had ears folded over; great dragging jowls. They had fiery eyes—blazing eyes; they had yellow eyes—fiery yellow eyes. They had thin flanks—flanks with ribs showing. They had gaunt stomachs. They were very tall. They were nervous; they went about panting, with tongues hanging out. They were spotted like ocelots; they were varicolored.

And when Motecuzoma heard all this, he was much terrified. It was as if he fainted away. His heart saddened; his heart failed him.

For Further Reflection

■ What did the Spanish and their indigenous allies hope to gain by presenting this image of Motecuzoma?

Source: Bernardino de Sahagún. *Florentine Codex: General History of the Things of New Spain,* 13 vols. Trans. by A. J. O. Anderson and C. E. Dibble. Salt Lake City: University of Utah Press, 1950–1982, 13:19–20. (Translation slightly modified.)

adventurers. Gradually, however, the Spanish monarchy extended its control over the growing American empire, and by about 1570 it had established formal rule under the Spanish monarchy. Spanish administrators established two main centers of authority in the Americas—Mexico (which they called New Spain) and Peru (known as New Castile)—each governed by a viceroy who was responsible to the king of Spain. In Mexico they built a new capital,

Mexico City, on top of Tenochtitlan. In Peru they moved the seat of government from the high-altitude Inca capital of Cuzco to the Peruvian coast and in 1535 founded the new capital of Lima.

The viceroys were the king's representatives in the Americas, and they wielded considerable power. The kings of Spain attempted to hold them in check by subjecting them to the review of courts, known as *audiencias,* staffed by university-educated lawyers. The *audiencias* heard appeals against the viceroys' decisions and policies and had the right to address their concerns directly to the Spanish king. Furthermore, the *audiencias* conducted reviews of viceroys' performance at the end of their terms, and negative reviews could lead to severe punishment.

In spite of this structure, in many way Spanish administration in the Americas was often ineffective. Transportation and communication difficulties limited the ability of viceroys to supervise their own extensive territories. The jurisdiction of the viceroyalty of New Spain, for example, reached from Mexico City north to St. Augustine in Florida (founded in 1565). Distance also prevented Spanish monarchs from exercising much influence on American affairs. It often took two years for the central government in Spain to respond to a query from Mexico or Peru, and when viceroys received clear orders that they did not like, it was easy to procrastinate.

The Portuguese in Brazil While the Spanish built a territorial empire in Mexico and Peru, Portuguese forces established an imperial presence in Brazil. The Portuguese presence came about by an odd twist of diplomatic convention. In 1494 Spain and Portugal signed the Treaty of Tordesillas, which divided the world along an imaginary north-south line 370 leagues west of the Azores and Cape Verde Islands. According to this agreement, Spain could claim any non-Christian lands west of that line and Portugal gained the same rights for lands east of the line. Of course, this treaty completely disregarded preexisting indigenous claims to any of these lands—an indication of the conceit of both the Spanish and the Portuguese. By its terms, however, Portugal gained territory along the northeastern part of the South American continent, a region known as Brazil from the many brazilwood trees that grew along the coast, and the remainder of the western hemisphere fell under Spanish control. Yet Brazil did not attract significant Portuguese interest until entrepreneurs began establishing sugar plantations on the coast after the mid-sixteenth century. Once it was clear the plantations would be profitable, Portuguese interest—and settlement—surged.

audiencias (AW-dee-uhns-cee-ahs)
Guaraní (gwahr-uh-NEE)
Quiché (keesh-AY)
Quechua (keh-CHUA)

Colonial American Society Both the Spanish and the Portuguese rapidly established cities throughout their territories. Like their compatriots in Europe, colonists preferred to live in cities even when they derived their income from the agricultural production of their landed estates, and they made every attempt to model their new cities along European lines. Away from urban areas, however, indigenous ways of life largely persisted. In places such as the Amazon basin and Paraguay, for example, where there were no mineral deposits to attract European migrants, European visitors learned to adapt to indigenous societies and customs: they ate bread made of manioc flour, made use of native hammocks and canoes, and communicated in the Guaraní and Tupí languages. Indeed, indigenous languages flourish even today throughout much of Latin America: among the more prominent are Nahuatl in Mexico, Quiché in Mexico and Guatemala, Guaraní in Paraguay, and Quechua in the Andean highlands of Peru, Ecuador, and Bolivia.

Spanish and Portuguese peoples always saw the western hemisphere more as a land to exploit and administer than as a place to settle and colonize. Nevertheless, upward of five hundred thousand Spaniards and one hundred thousand Portuguese settled permanently in the Americas between 1500 and 1800. Their presence contributed to the making of a much more globalized world—a world characterized by intense interaction among the peoples of Europe, Africa, and the Americas—in the western hemisphere.

Settler Colonies in North America

Throughout the sixteenth century, Spanish explorers sought opportunities north of Mexico and the Caribbean. They established towns, forts, and missions from modern Florida as far north as Virginia, and they scouted shorelines off Maine and Newfoundland. On the west coast they established a fort on Vancouver Island in modern Canada. By mid-century, however, French, English, and Dutch mariners were dislodging Spanish colonists north of Florida. Originally, they came in a fruitless search for a northwest passage to Asia. Instead, they found immense quantities of codfish, which they exploited from the banks off Labrador, Newfoundland, Nova Scotia, and New England.

Foundation of Colonies In the early seventeenth century explorers began to establish permanent colonies on the North American mainland. French settlers established colonies at Port Royal (Nova Scotia) in 1604 and Quebec in 1608. During the seventeenth and eighteenth centuries French migrants settled in eastern Canada, and French explorers and traders scouted the St. Lawrence, Ohio, and Mississippi rivers, building forts all the way to the Gulf of Mexico. Meanwhile, English migrants founded Jamestown in 1607 and the Massachusetts Bay

MAP 21.1 European empires and colonies in the Americas about 1700

Locate the major cities and settlements of each imperial power.

What factors decided where settlements would be placed? Why are so few settlements in the interior of either North or South America?

Colony in 1630, and proceeded to establish colonies along the east coast of the present-day United States of America. Dutch entrepreneurs built a settlement at New Amsterdam in 1623, but in 1664 an English fleet seized and rechristened it New York and absorbed it into English colonial holdings.

Life in those early settlements was extremely difficult. Most of the settlers hoped to sustain their communities not through farming but by producing valuable commodities such as fur, pitch, tar, or lumber, if not silver and gold. They relied heavily on provisions sent from Europe, and when supply ships did not arrive as expected, they sometimes avoided starvation only because indigenous peoples provided them with food. In Jamestown, food shortages and disease became so severe that only sixty of the colony's five hundred inhabitants survived the winter of 1609–1610.

Colonial Government The French and English colonies in North America differed in several ways from Iberian territories to the south. Whereas Iberian explorations had royal backing, private investors played larger roles in French and English colonial efforts. Because of that, individuals retained much more control over their colonies' affairs than did their Iberian counterparts. Thus settlers in the English colonies—though ultimately subject to royal authority—maintained their own assemblies and influenced the choice of royal governors: there were no viceroys or *audiencias* in the North American colonies.

Relations with Indigenous Peoples French and English colonies differed from Iberian territories also in their relationships with indigenous peoples. French and English migrants did not find large, densely settled, centralized states like the Aztec and Inca empires. Although many of the indigenous societies in eastern North America practiced agriculture, most also relied on hunting and consequently moved their villages frequently in pursuit of game. They did not claim ownership of precisely bounded territories, but they regularly migrated between well-defined regions and utilized the resources of the land as they did so.

When European settlers saw forested lands not bearing crops or supporting villages, they viewed them as "empty" and unclaimed. Even when lands had been in use by multiple Native American groups over many hundreds of years, Europeans believed they had the right to claim such lands. Thus they staked out farms for themselves and excluded indigenous peoples from those lands. The availability of fertile farmland soon attracted large numbers of European migrants. Upward of one hundred fifty thousand English migrants moved to North America during the seventeenth century alone, and sizable French, German, Dutch, and Irish contingents soon joined them.

European migrants took pains to justify their claims to American lands. English settlers, in particular, brought with them English legal structures such as property deeds that suggested land could be permanently transferred to individuals or groups. They fundamentally did not understand that the Native American way of life in the region depended on a very different way of using land. For Native American groups, using the land productively entailed keeping hunting grounds healthy, whereas for Europeans land could only be considered productive if under cultivation. Such justifications did not convince indigenous peoples, who frequently clashed with colonists over the right to use their hunting grounds, whether treaties existed or not. In 1622, for example, indigenous peoples angry over European intrusions killed almost one-third of the English settlers in the Chesapeake region.

Such conflict did not stem the tide of European migrants, however. Between 1600 and 1800, about one million European migrants arrived in North America, many of whom actively sought to displace indigenous peoples from their lands. Violent conflict, indeed, took a heavy toll on indigenous populations. Yet as in the Iberian territories, epidemic disease also dramatically reduced the

A painting of the English settlement at Jamestown in the early seventeenth century illustrates the precarious relations between European settlers and indigenous peoples. Note the heavy palisades surrounding the settlement.
MPI/Archive Photos/Getty Images

indigenous population of North America in early modern times. In 1492 the indigenous population of the territory now embraced by the United States was greater than five million, perhaps as high as ten million. By the mid-sixteenth century, however, smallpox and other diseases had spread north from Mexico and ravaged indigenous societies in the plains and eastern woodlands of North America. By 1800 only six hundred thousand indigenous peoples remained, as against almost five million settlers of European ancestry and about one million enslaved people of African ancestry. As with the Iberian incursions in the south, the European settlement of North America fundamentally transformed the western hemisphere.

COLONIAL SOCIETY IN THE AMERICAS

The European migrants who flooded into the western hemisphere interacted both with the indigenous inhabitants and with African peoples whom they forcibly imported as enslaved laborers. Throughout the Americas, relations between individuals of American, European, and African ancestry soon led to the emergence of what were known at the time as *mestizo* ("mixed") populations. Notwithstanding such intercultural mixing, European peoples and their Euro-American offspring increasingly dominated political and economic affairs in the Americas. Using enslaved labor and Native American knowledge, they mined precious metals, cultivated cash crops such as sugar and tobacco, and trapped fur-bearing animals to supply capitalist markets that met the voracious demands of European and Asian consumers. Over time they also established their Christian religion as the dominant faith of the western hemisphere.

The Formation of Multicultural Societies

Many parts of the Americas remained outside European control until the nineteenth century. Only rarely did Europeans venture into the interior regions of the American continents in the sixteenth century, and those who did often found themselves at the mercy of the indigenous inhabitants. But even though their influence reached the American interior only gradually, European migrants radically transformed the social order in the regions where they established colonies.

Mestizo Societies All European territories became multicultural societies where peoples of varied ancestry lived together under European or Euro-American dominance. Spanish and Portuguese territories soon became not only multicultural but ethnically mixed as well, largely because of migration patterns. Migrants to the Iberian

colonies were overwhelmingly men: about 85 percent of the Spanish migrants were men, and the Portuguese migration was even more male-dominated than the Spanish. Because of the small numbers of European women, many Spanish and Portuguese migrants entered into relationships with indigenous women, which soon gave rise to an increasingly *mestizo* society.

Most Spanish migrants went to Mexico, where there was soon a growing population of *mestizos*—those of Spanish and native parentage, like the children of Doña Marina. Women were more prominent among the migrants to Peru than to Mexico, and most Spanish colonists there lived in cities, where they maintained a more distinct community than did their counterparts in Mexico. In the colonial cities, Spanish migrants married among themselves and re-created a European-style society. In less settled regions, however, Spanish men associated with indigenous women and gave rise to *mestizo* society.

With few European women available in Brazil, Portuguese men readily entered into relations—some consensual and some forced—both with indigenous women and with enslaved African women. Brazil soon had large populations not only of *mestizos* but also of people known as mulattoes, who were born of Portuguese and African parents; those known as *Zambos*, who were born of indigenous and African parents; and other combinations arising from these groups. Indeed, marriages between members of different racial and ethnic communities became common in colonial Brazil and generated a society even more thoroughly mixed than that of Mexico.

The Social Hierarchy In both the Spanish and the Portuguese colonies, migrants born in the Iberian peninsula in Europe (known as *peninsulares*) stood at the top of the social hierarchy. They were followed by *criollos,* or creoles, individuals born in the Americas of Iberian parents. As the numbers of *mestizos* grew, they also became essential contributors to their societies, especially in Mexico and Brazil. Meanwhile, mulattoes, *Zambos,* and other individuals of mixed parentage became prominent groups in Brazilian society, although they were usually subordinate to *peninsulares,* creoles, and *mestizos.* In all the Iberian colonies, enslaved and indigenous peoples stood at the bottom of the social hierarchy.

Sexual Hierarchies Race and ethnicity were crucial in shaping a person's position and role in colonial society. But the defining factor in both Spanish and Portuguese America was the existence of a clear sexual hierarchy that

---

mestizo (mehs-TEE-soh)
Zambos (SAHM-bohs)
peninsulares (pehn-IHN-soo-LAH-rayz)
criollos (KRYO-yohs)

Indigenous Zapotec painter Miguel Mateo Maldonado y Cabrera (1695–1768) created this domestic portrait of a multicultural family in the viceroyalty of New Spain, today's Mexico. A Spanish man gazes at his indigenous Mexican wife and their *mestizo* daughter.

Album/Alamy Stock Photo

their elite position to their advantage. By necessity, women of color and of the lower classes became part of the colonial labor force, performing tasks such as food preparation, laundering, and weaving. Although poor, these women were freer to move about in public and to interact with others than were their elite counterparts. The most disadvantaged women were Black, mulatta, and *Zamba* enslaved women, who were required to perform hard physical tasks such as planting and cutting cane or working as laundresses. Such women were also frequently the targets of forced sexual relationships with European men.

North American Societies The social structure of the French and English colonies in North America differed markedly from that of the Iberian colonies. Women were more numerous, especially among the English migrants, and settlers tended to marry within their own groups. Although French fur traders often associated with indigenous women and generated *métis* (the French equivalent of *mestizos*) in regions around trading posts, such arrangements were less common in French colonial cities such as Port Royal and Quebec.

Mingling between peoples of different ancestry was least common in the English colonies of North America. Colonists regarded the indigenous peoples they encountered as heathens who did not exert themselves to cultivate the land. Later they also scorned enslaved Africans as inferior beings. Those attitudes fueled a virulent racism, and English settlers worked to maintain sharp boundaries between themselves and peoples of Native American and African ancestry.

Yet English settlers readily borrowed useful cultural elements from other communities. From indigenous communities, for example, they learned about American plants and animals, and they adapted moccasins and deerskin clothes. From their enslaved Africans they borrowed African food crops and techniques for the cultivation of rice. Yet, unlike their Iberian neighbors, English settlers discouraged relationships between individuals of different ancestry and mostly refused to accept offspring of mixed parentage.

Mining and Agriculture in the Spanish Empire

From the Spanish perspective, the greatest attractions of the Americas were precious metals. Once the *conquistadores* had thoroughly looted the treasures of the Aztec and Inca empires, their followers opened mines to extract the mineral wealth of the Americas in a more systematic fashion.

Silver Mining Silver was the most abundant American treasure, and much of Spain's American enterprise focused on its extraction. Silver production concentrated on

privileged men. Women lived in a patriarchal world, where men occupied positions of power and delineated the boundaries of acceptable female behavior. Although there were exceptions to the rule, women's power tended to be expressed informally through their influence on relationships and in domestic duties.

Gender alone, however, did not explain the diverse experiences of women in colonial society. Commonly, the ratio of men to women in a given community either enhanced or limited women's choices. Race and class also usually figured as powerful forces shaping women's lives. Women of European descent, though under strict patriarchal control and under pressure to conform to the stereotype of female dependence and passivity, sometimes used

métis (may-TEE)

Mining operations at Potosí in South America gave rise to a large settlement that housed miners and others who supplied food, made charcoal, fashioned tools, and supported the enterprise. In this illustration from the mid-1580s, llamas laden with silver ore descend the mountain (background) while laborers work in the foreground to crush the ore and extract pure silver from it.
Courtesy of the Hispanic Society of America, New York

two areas: the thinly populated Mexican north, particularly the region around Zacatecas, and the high central Andes, particularly the stunningly rich mines of Potosí. Both sites employed large numbers of indigenous laborers. Many laborers went to Zacatecas voluntarily to escape the pressures of conquest and disease. Over time they became professional miners, spoke Spanish, and lost touch with the communities of their birth.

Meanwhile, Spanish prospectors discovered a large vein of silver near Potosí in 1545 and began large-scale mining there in the 1580s. By 1600 Potosí had a booming population of one hundred fifty thousand. Such rapid growth created an explosive demand for labor. As in the Mexican mines, Spanish administrators relied mostly on voluntary labor, but they also adapted the Inca practice of requisitioning draft labor, known as the *mita* **system**, to recruit workers for particularly difficult and dangerous chores. Under the *mita* system, each village was required to send one-seventh of its male population to work for four months in the mines at Potosí. Draft laborers received

very little payment for their work, and conditions were extremely harsh. Death rates of draft laborers were high, and many men sought to evade *mita* obligations by fleeing to cities or hiding in distant villages.

The Global Significance of Silver The mining industries of Mexico and Peru powered the Spanish economy in the Americas and even stimulated the world economy of early modern times. Indeed, the Spanish government's share—one-fifth of all silver production, called the *quinto*—represented the principal revenue the monarchy derived from its American possessions. Most American silver made its way across the Atlantic to Spain, where it financed Spain's army and bureaucracy and lubricated markets throughout Europe. From Europe, merchants

Zacatecas (sah-kah-TEH-kahs)
Potosí (paw-taw-SEE)
quinto (KEEN-toh)

used it to trade for silk, spices, and porcelain in the markets of Asia. Silver also traveled from Acapulco on the west coast of Mexico across the Pacific in the Manila galleons, and from Manila it made its way to Asian markets—especially China. No matter which direction it went, American silver powerfully stimulated global trade.

The Hacienda   Apart from mining, the principal occupations in Spanish America were farming, stock raising, and craft production. By the seventeenth century the most prominent site of agricultural and craft production in Spanish America was the **hacienda**, or estate, which produced goods for sale to local markets in nearby mining districts, towns, and cities. Bordering the large estates were smaller properties owned by Spanish migrants or creoles as well as sizable tracts of land held by indigenous peoples who practiced subsistence agriculture.

Labor Systems   The major source of labor for the haciendas was the indigenous population. As in the Caribbean, Spanish conquerors first organized indigenous workforces under the *encomienda* system. Yet from the 1520s to the 1540s, this system led to rampant abuse, as Spanish landowners overworked their laborers and skimped on their maintenance. After mid-century, *encomenderos* in agriculturally productive regions increasingly required their subject populations to provide tribute but not labor. That did not solve the problem of labor, however, so Spanish landowners resorted to a system of debt peonage to recruit workers for their haciendas. Under this system, landowners advanced loans to indigenous peoples, so that they could buy seeds, tools, and supplies for their farms. The debtors then repaid the loans with labor, but wages were so low that they were never able to pay off their debts. Thus landowners helped create a cycle of debt that ensured them a dependent labor force to work their estates.

Resistance to Spanish Rule   The Spanish regimes in the Americas met considerable resistance from indigenous peoples. Resistance took various forms: armed rebellion, work slowdowns, and retreat into the mountains and forests. On some occasions, indigenous peoples turned to Spanish law in search of aid against oppressive colonists. In 1615, for example, Felipe Guaman Poma de Ayala, a native of Peru, fired off a twelve-hundred-page-page letter to King Philip III of Spain asking for protection for indigenous peoples against greedy colonists. He wrote passionately of men ruined by overtaxation and women driven to prostitution, of Spanish colonists who grabbed the lands of indigenous peoples and Spanish priests who preyed sexually on the wives of indigenous men. Guaman Poma warned the king that if Philip wanted anything to remain of his Andean empire, he should intervene and protect the indigenous peoples of the land. Unfortunately for Guaman Poma, the king never saw the letter. Instead, it ended up in Denmark, where it remained unknown in a library until 1908.

Sugar and Slavery in Brazil

Whereas the Spanish American empire concentrated on the extraction of silver, the Portuguese empire in Brazil depended on the production and export of sugar. The different economic and social foundations of the Spanish and Portuguese empires led to different patterns of labor recruitment. The Spanish forced indigenous peoples to provide labor; the Portuguese relied instead on enslaved Africans. Because of that, Africans and their descendants became the majority of the population in Brazil.

The *Engenho*   Colonial Brazilian life revolved around the *engenho,* or sugar mill, which came to represent a complex of land, labor, buildings, animals, capital, and technical skills related to the production of sugar. Unlike other crops, sugarcane required extensive processing to yield molasses or refined sugar. Thus *engenhos* needed both heavy labor for the planting and harvesting of cane and specialized skills for the intricacies of processing.

The Search for Labor   Like their Spanish counterparts, Portuguese colonists first tried to enlist local populations as laborers. Unlike the inhabitants of Mexico and Peru, however, the peoples of Brazil were not sedentary cultivators. They resisted efforts to commandeer their labor and evaded the Portuguese simply by retreating to interior lands. In addition, in Brazil as elsewhere in the Americas, epidemic diseases devastated indigenous populations. After smallpox and measles ravaged the Brazilian coast in the 1560s, Portuguese settlers had a hard time even finding potential laborers, let alone forcing them to work.

Slavery   Faced with those difficulties, the colonists turned to another labor source: enslaved Africans. Portuguese plantation managers imported enslaved people as early as the 1530s, but they began to rely on African labor on a large scale only in the 1580s. The toll on enslaved communities was extremely heavy: arduous working conditions, mistreatment, poor nutrition, and inadequate housing combined to produce high rates of disease and mortality. Indeed, *engenhos* typically lost 5 to 10 percent of their enslaved laborers annually, so there was a constant demand for more people from Africa.

Owners had little economic incentive to improve conditions for enslaved people or to encourage them to reproduce naturally. If an enslaved person lived five to six years, the investment of the average owner doubled and permitted him to purchase a new and healthy laborer without

---

hacienda (ah-SYEN-dah)
engenho (en-GEHN-ho)

taking a monetary loss. To them the balance sheet of sugar production was about profit, not about enslaved people's lives. All told, the business of producing Brazilian sugar was so brutal that every ton of the sweet substance cost one human life.

Fur Traders and Settlers in North America

The Fur Trade European mariners first frequented North American shores in search of fish. Over time, though, trade in furs became far more lucrative. After explorers found a convenient entrance to rich fur-producing regions through the Hudson Strait and Hudson Bay, they began to connect large parts of the North American interior by a chain of forts and trading posts. Indigenous peoples trapped animals for Europeans and exchanged the pelts for manufactured goods. Most of the hides went to Europe, where there was strong demand for beaver skin hats and fur clothing.

Effects of the Fur Trade The **fur trade** generated tremendous conflict in North America. American beaver populations, which were the chief targets of the trade, declined so rapidly that trappers constantly had to push farther inland. When hunting grounds became depleted, indigenous peoples poached or invaded others' territories, which sometimes led to war. The fur trade also took place in the context of competition between European states. This competitive atmosphere contributed to further conflict as indigenous peoples became embroiled in their patrons' rivalries.

Settler Society European settler-cultivators posed an even more serious challenge to indigenous ways of life than the fur traders, since they displaced indigenous peoples from the land and turned hunting grounds into plantations. And, as colonists' numbers increased, they sought to integrate their American holdings into the larger economy of the Atlantic Ocean basin by producing cash crops—such as tobacco, rice, and indigo—that they could market in Europe.

Tobacco In the English colonies of Virginia and Carolina, settlers concentrated on the cultivation of tobacco, a plant they learned about from Native American societies. Although originally hailed for its medicinal uses, this plant quickly became wildly popular with Europeans as a recreational drug. Indeed, just a few decades after English settlers cultivated the first commercial crop of tobacco in Virginia in 1612, Europeans were smoking tobacco socially in huge numbers. This widespread popularity was due to the addictive nature of nicotine: an oily, toxic substance present in tobacco leaves. As a result, it was easy for tobacco users to become dependent on nicotine, which in turn kept demand for tobacco high. Moreover, merchants

This painting features the "first smoke" of Sir Walter Raleigh (1552–1618). He was an English aristocrat, writer, poet, soldier, courtier, spy, and explorer. He is also well known for popularizing tobacco in England.
The Picture Art Collection/Alamy Stock Photo

and mariners soon spread the use of tobacco throughout Europe and to all parts of the world that European ships visited—a process that helped, at least in the short term, to expand the markets for American tobacco.

Indentured Labor Cash-crop plantations created high demand for inexpensive labor. Colonists in North America enslaved indigenous peoples in large numbers, but still the demand for labor grew. By the seventeenth century colonists had begun to recruit **indentured servants** from Europe to increase the supply of labor. Under this system, people who had little future in Europe—the chronically unemployed, orphans, and criminals—received free passage across the Atlantic in exchange for providing four to seven years of labor. Although thousands of indentured servants came to the American colonies with high hopes for making a new start, the system was far from ideal—many died of disease or overwork before completing their terms of labor, and others found only marginal employment.

Slavery in North America English settlers in North America also found uses for enslaved Africans. In 1619 a group of about twenty Africans reached Virginia, where they worked alongside European laborers as indentured servants. After about 1680, however, planters increasingly replaced indentured servants with enslaved Africans. By 1750 some one hundred twenty thousand enslaved Africans tilled Chesapeake tobacco, and one hundred eighty thousand more cultivated Carolina rice.

Plantation labor was not prominent in the northern colonies, mostly because the land and the climate were not suitable for the cultivation of labor-intensive cash crops. Nevertheless, the economies of these colonies also profited handsomely from slavery. Many New England merchants traded in enslaved people destined for the West Indies: by the mid-eighteenth century, half the merchant fleet of Newport carried human cargo. The economies of New York and Philadelphia also benefited from the building and outfitting of slave vessels, and the seaports of New England became profitable centers for the distillation of rum. The chief ingredient of that rum was slave-produced sugar from the West Indies, and merchants traded much of the distilled spirits for enslaved people on the African coast. Thus, although the southern plantation societies became most directly identified with slavery, all the North American colonies participated in and profited from the slave trade.

Christianity and Indigenous Religions in the Americas

Like Buddhists and Muslims in earlier centuries, Christian explorers, conquerors, merchants, and settlers took their religious traditions with them when they traveled overseas. Centuries of warfare against Muslims had convinced Spanish monarchs that non-Christians should be converted to Christianity. Thus when Spanish *conquistadores,* colonists, and priests came to the Americas, they came both as conquerors and as evangelists. In the long term their conversion efforts succeeded, but in the process Catholicism evolved into a religion that integrated Christian concepts with aspects of indigenous beliefs and traditions.

Spanish Missionaries From the beginning of Spanish colonization in Mexico and Peru, Franciscan, Dominican, and Jesuit missionaries campaigned to Christianize indigenous peoples. Over time, and despite considerable initial resistance, Christianity did win adherents in Spanish America. In the wake of conquest and epidemic disease, many indigenous leaders in Mexico concluded that their

Famed Mexican painter Miguel Cabrera crafted this eighteenth-century depiction of the Virgin of Guadalupe. Recognized as the greatest painter in New Spain, he featured in this work one of Mexico's most powerful religious icons.
Album/Alamy Stock Photo

gods had abandoned them, and they looked to the missionaries for spiritual guidance. When indigenous peoples adopted Christianity, however, they blended their own interests and traditions with the faith taught by Spanish missionaries. When they learned about Roman Catholic saints, for example, they revered saints with qualities like those of their inherited gods or those whose feast days coincided with traditional celebrations.

The Virgin of Guadalupe In Mexico, Christianity became especially popular after the mid-seventeenth century as an increasingly *mestizo* society took the **Virgin of Guadalupe** almost as a national symbol. According to legends, the Virgin Mary appeared before a peasant near Mexico City in 1531. The site of the apparition soon became a popular local shrine visited mostly by Spanish settlers. By the 1640s the shrine was attracting pilgrims from all parts of Mexico, and the Virgin of Guadalupe had gained a reputation for working miracles on behalf of individuals who visited her shrine. The popularity of the Virgin of Guadalupe helped ensure not only that Roman Catholic Christianity would dominate cultural and religious matters in Mexico but also that Mexican religious faith would retain strong indigenous influences.

French and English Missions French and English missionaries did not attract nearly as many converts to Christianity in North America as their Spanish counterparts did in Mexico and Peru. In part this was because French and English colonists did not rule over sedentary cultivators: it was much more difficult to conduct missions among peoples who frequently moved about the countryside than among those who lived permanently in villages, towns, or cities. Even so, French missionaries did work actively among indigenous communities in the St. Lawrence, Mississippi, and Ohio river valleys and experienced

Virgin of Guadalupe (gwah-dah-LOO-pay)

What's Left Out? ■ ■ ■ ■ ■ ■

The history of slavery in North America has, until recently, focused mainly on enslaved Africans in what became the American south. Although many textbooks acknowledge that the northern colonies also permitted slavery for a time, these colonies have nevertheless usually been depicted as less dependent on slave labor. Moreover, a large body of historical work once argued that Native Americans were unwilling or unable to tolerate slavery, and thus were not commonly enslaved by Europeans. Recent scholarship, however, is revising these long-standing perceptions. Indeed, during the seventeenth and eighteenth centuries, New England colonists enslaved many thousands of Native Americans and depended on their labor to build new lives for themselves. During both the Pequot War (1630s) and King Philip's War (1670s), thousands of Native Americans were captured and sold into slavery. King Philip's War, in fact, had erupted in part because a Wampanoag-led coalition protested the use of forced Native American labor. But the war ended in defeat for the Wampanoag and did not end the practice of enslaving indigenous peoples. Instead, one study shows that after the war nearly 40 percent of the Native Americans remaining in the southern portion of New England were enslaved or were indentured servants in English households. In addition, European colonists in Virginia, North Carolina, and South Carolina similarly enslaved and traded indigenous peoples. These practices continued until the late eighteenth century, when large numbers of enslaved Africans began to displace enslaved indigenous people. In what ways can new information such as this add nuance or even alter our perceptions about the early history of the United States?

Source: Margaret Ellen Newell. *Brethren by Nature: New England Indians, Colonists, and the Origins of American Slavery.* Ithaca: Cornell University Press, 2015.

modest success for their efforts. English colonists, in contrast, displayed little interest in converting indigenous peoples to Christianity, nor did they welcome indigenous converts into their agricultural and commercial society. However, even without indigenous conversion to Christianity, the growing settlements of French and especially English colonists guaranteed that European religious traditions would figure prominently in North American society.

EUROPEANS IN THE PACIFIC

Though geographically distant from the Americas, the peoples of Australia and the Pacific islands underwent experiences similar to those that transformed the western hemisphere in early modern times. Like their American counterparts, the peoples of Oceania had no inherited or acquired immunities to diseases that were common to peoples throughout the eastern hemisphere, and their numbers plunged when epidemic disease struck their populations. For the most part, however, the peoples of Australia and the Pacific islands experienced epidemic disease and the arrival of European migrants later than did those in the Americas. European mariners thoroughly explored the Pacific basin between the sixteenth and eighteenth centuries, but only in Guam and the Mariana Islands did they establish permanent settlements before the late eighteenth century. Nevertheless, their scouting of the region laid a foundation for much more intense interactions among European, Euro-American, Asian, and Oceanic peoples during the nineteenth and twentieth centuries.

Australia and the Larger World

Dutch Exploration At least from the second century C.E. European geographers had speculated about *terra australis incognita*—"unknown southern land"—that they thought must exist in the world's southern hemisphere to balance the huge landmasses north of the equator. Although Portuguese mariners most likely charted much of the western and northern coasts of Australia as early as the 1520s, Dutch sailors based in the Indonesian islands made the first recorded European sighting of the southern continent in 1606. The Dutch VOC authorized exploratory voyages, but mariners found little to encourage further efforts. In 1623, after surveying the landscape of western Australia, the Dutch mariner Jan Carstenzs described the land as "the most arid and barren region that could be found anywhere on earth."

Nevertheless, Dutch mariners continued to visit Australia. By the mid-seventeenth century they had scouted the continent's northern, western, and southern coasts and had fleeting encounters with indigenous populations. However, because those peoples were nomadic foragers rather than sedentary cultivators, Europeans did not hold them in high regard. In the absence of tempting opportunities to trade, European mariners made no effort to establish permanent settlements in Australia.

British Colonists Only after **James Cook** charted the eastern coast in 1770 did European peoples become seriously interested in Australia. Cook dropped anchor for a week at Botany Bay (near modern Sydney) and reported that the region was suitable for settlement. In 1788

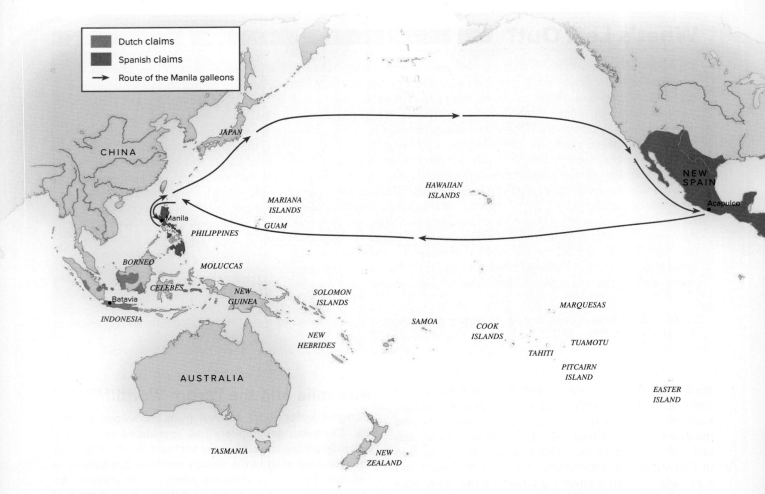

MAP 21.2   Manila galleon route and the lands of Oceania, 1500–1800

Note the route taken by the Manila galleons in relation to the majority of the Pacific islands.

Why did Spanish mariners not explore the Hawaiian Islands and the more southerly Pacific islands as they made their way to the Philippines?

a British fleet arrived at Sydney carrying about one thousand passengers, eight hundred of them convicts, who established the first European settlement in Australia as a penal colony. For half a century Europeans in Australia numbered only a few thousand, most of them convicts. In fact, free settlers did not outnumber convicted criminal migrants until the 1830s. Thus, despite early fleeting encounters between European and aboriginal Australian peoples, it was only in the nineteenth and twentieth centuries that a continuing stream of European settlers linked Australia more directly to the larger world.

The Pacific Islands and the Larger World

The entry of European mariners into the Pacific Ocean basin did not bring immediate change to most of the Pacific islands. In these islands, as in Australia, European merchants and settlers did not arrive in large numbers until the late eighteenth century. However, in Guam and the Mariana Islands, dramatic change was already under way by the sixteenth century.

Spanish Voyages in the Pacific Ferdinand Magellan and his crew became the first Europeans to cross the Pacific Ocean in 1521. Before reaching the Philippines, they encountered only one inhabited island group—the Marianas, dominated by Guam. In 1565 Spanish mariners inaugurated the Manila galleon trade between Manila and Acapulco. Because their primary goal was to link New Spain to Asian markets, they rarely went out of their way to explore the Pacific Ocean or to search for other islands. Although a few Spanish vessels visited some of the other Pacific islands in the sixteenth century, Spanish mariners found little to interest them and did not establish regular communications with island peoples.

Guam The only Pacific islands that attracted substantial Spanish interest in the sixteenth century were Guam and the Marianas. Manila galleons called regularly at Guam, which lay directly on the route from Acapulco to Manila. For more than a century they took on fresh provisions and engaged in mostly peaceful trade with the indigenous Chamorro people. Then, in the 1670s and 1680s, Spanish authorities decided to bring the Mariana Islands under the control of the viceroy of New Spain in Mexico. They dispatched military forces to the islands to impose Spanish rule and subject the Chamorro to the spiritual authority of the Roman Catholic church. The Chamorro strongly opposed those efforts, but a smallpox epidemic in 1688 severely reduced their numbers and crippled their resistance. By 1695 the Chamorro population had declined from about fifty thousand at mid-century to five thousand, mostly because of smallpox. By the end of the seventeenth century, Spanish forces had established garrisons throughout the Mariana Islands and relocated surviving Chamorro into communities supervised by Spanish authorities.

Visitors and Trade By the late eighteenth century, growing European and Euro-American interest in the Pacific Ocean basin had led to sharply increased interactions between islanders and mariners. English and French mariners explored the Pacific basin in search of commercial opportunities and the elusive northwest passage from Europe to Asia. They frequently visited Tahiti after 1767, and they soon began to trade with the islanders, whose societies were complex and highly stratified by social class and by occupation. European mariners received provisions and engaged in sexual relations with Tahitian women in exchange for nails, knives, iron tools, and textiles.

Captain Cook and Hawai'i After 1778 the published writings of Captain James Cook, who happened across the Hawaiian Islands in that year, galvanized even greater interest in the Pacific. European whalers, missionaries, and planters came in large numbers in search of opportunities. As a result, by the early nineteenth century, European and Euro-American peoples had become prominent figures in all the major Pacific island groups. In the next two centuries, interactions among islanders, visitors, and migrants brought rapid and often unsettling change to Pacific island societies.

Chamorro (chuh-MAWR-oh)

CONCLUSION

The Americas underwent thorough transformation in early modern times. Smallpox and other diseases sparked ferocious epidemics that devastated indigenous populations and undermined their societies. In the wake of severe depopulation, European peoples toppled imperial states, established mining and agricultural enterprises, imported enslaved African laborers, and founded colonies throughout much of the western hemisphere. Some indigenous peoples disappeared entirely as distinct groups. Others maintained their communities, identities, and cultural traditions but fell increasingly under the influence of European migrants and their Euro-American offspring. In Oceania only Guam and the Mariana Islands felt the full effects of epidemic disease and migration in the early modern era. By the late eighteenth century, however, European and Euro-American peoples with advanced technologies had thoroughly explored the Pacific Ocean basin, and epidemic diseases featured largely in their encounters with the peoples of Australia and the Pacific islands. As a result, during the nineteenth and twentieth centuries, Oceania underwent a social transformation similar to the one experienced earlier by the Americas. These encounters in both regions profoundly shaped the course of their history into the modern era.

STUDY TERMS

Atahualpa (370)	Malintzin (366)
audiencias (372)	*mestizo* (375)
conquistadores (369)	*métis* (376)
criollos (375)	*mita* system (377)
Doña Marina (366)	Motecuzoma II (369)
encomienda (368)	Nahuatl (366)
engenho (378)	*peninsulares* (375)
Francisco Pizarro (370)	*quinto* (377)
fur trade (379)	smallpox (368)
hacienda (378)	Virgin of Guadalupe
Hernán Cortés (366)	(380)
indentured servants (379)	*Zambos* (375)
James Cook (381)	

FOR FURTHER READING

Rolena Adorno. *Guaman Poma: Writing and Resistance in Colonial Peru.* Austin, 2000. A native Andean, who came of age after the fall of the Inca empire, tells Philip III of Spain of the evils of colonialism and the need for reform.

William Cronon. *Changes in the Land: Indians, Colonists, and the Ecology of New England.* Rev. ed. New York, 2003. A brilliant study concentrating on the different ways English colonists and indigenous peoples in colonial New England used the environment.

John H. Elliot. *Empires of the Atlantic World: Britain and Spain in America 1492–1830*. New Haven, 2006. An excellent comparative study of Spanish and English colonies in the Americas.

K. R. Howe. *Where the Waves Fall: A New South Sea Island History from First Settlement to Colonial Rule*. Honolulu, 1984. A thoughtful survey of Pacific island history emphasizing interactions between islanders and visitors.

John E. Kicza. *Resilient Cultures: America's Native Peoples Confront European Colonization, 1500–1800*. Upper Saddle River, N.J., 2002. A comprehensive comparative study assessing the impact of colonization on Native American peoples and indigenous influences on American colonial history.

Karen Ordahl Kupperman. *Indians and English: Facing Off in Early America*. Ithaca, N.Y., 2000. A fascinating reconstruction of the early encounters between English and indigenous American peoples, drawing on sources from all parties to the encounters.

Kathleen Ann Meyers. *Neither Saints nor Sinners: Writing the Lives of Women in Spanish America*. New York, 2003. Examines female self-representation through the life writings of six seventeenth-century women in Latin America.

Matthew Restall, Lisa Sousa, and Kevin Terraciano, eds. *Mesoamerican Voices: Native Language Writings from Colonial Mexico, Yucatan, and Guatemala*. Cambridge, 2005. Composed between the sixteenth and eighteenth centuries, this collection of texts offers access to an important historical source.

Daniel Richter. *Facing East from Indian Country: A Native History of North America*. Cambridge, 2003. Explores the active ways Native American communities engaged with European colonization efforts into the interior of North America.

Richard White. *The Middle Ground: Indians, Empires, and Republics in the Great Lakes Region, 1650–1815*. Cambridge, 1991. An insightful study of relations among French, English, and indigenous peoples in the Great Lakes region.

ZOOMING IN ON TRADITIONS AND ENCOUNTERS

An Enslaved Man's Trip Back to Africa

Between 1760 and 1792, a west African man known as Thomas Peters crossed the Atlantic Ocean four times. In 1760 slave raiders captured Peters, whose original African name is unknown, marched him to the coast, and sold him to French slave merchants. He traveled in a slave ship to the French colony of Louisiana, where he probably worked on a sugar plantation. But Peters was not a docile servant. He attempted to escape at least three times, and his slaveholder punished him by beating him and branding him with a hot iron. During the 1760s his French slaveholder sold Peters to an English planter, and about 1770 a Scottish landowner in North Carolina purchased him.

During the 1770s, as English colonists in North America prepared to rebel against the British government, enslaved people of African ancestry considered their own prospects and looked for ways to obtain personal freedom. Peters was among them. When war broke out, he made his way with his wife and daughter to British lines and joined the Black Pioneers, a company of formerly enslaved people who fought to maintain British rule in the

SLAVES PACKED BELOW AND ON DECK.

Young people held on board an illegal slave ship captured by the British in 1857.
Historia/Shutterstock

colonies. When the colonists won the war, Peters escaped to Nova Scotia with his family and many other formerly enslaved people.

Slavery was illegal in Nova Scotia, but the white ruling elites forced people of African ancestry to till marginal lands and live in segregated villages. In hopes of improving their lot, some two hundred Black families sent Peters to London in 1790, where he promoted the establishment of a colony for formerly enslaved people in Sierra Leone. His efforts succeeded, and the next year he returned to Nova Scotia to seek recruits for the colony. In 1792 he led 1,196 formerly enslaved people aboard a convoy of fifteen ships and began his fourth crossing of the Atlantic Ocean. The colonists arrived safely at Freetown, where Peters served as a leader of the new community. Although he lived less than four months after arriving in Sierra Leone, his life and experiences personified the links connecting the lands and peoples of the Atlantic Ocean basin.

CHAPTER OVERVIEW

The establishment of global trade networks in the early modern period brought deep change to sub-Saharan Africa. Commercial opportunities drew Europeans to the coasts of west Africa, and maritime trade soon turned the attention of west African leaders to the Atlantic. Maritime commerce also helped promote the emergence of prosperous port cities and the establishment of powerful coastal kingdoms that traded through the ocean rather than the desert. In central Africa and south Africa, European merchants brought the first substantial opportunities for long-distance trade, since Muslim merchants had not previously ventured to those regions in large numbers.

Trade through the Atlantic profoundly affected African society because it involved human beings. Slavery had been a part of African societies for centuries, and Africans had long supplied enslaved people to Muslim merchants involved in trans-Saharan trade networks. The Atlantic slave trade, however, operated on a vastly larger scale than the trans-Saharan slave trade, and it had more serious consequences for African society. Between the fifteenth and nineteenth centuries, it not only siphoned millions of people from their own societies but also provoked turmoil in large portions of sub-Saharan Africa.

The vast majority of Africans sold into the Atlantic slave trade went to the Caribbean or the Americas. Most worked on plantations cultivating cash crops for export, although some worked as domestic servants, miners, or laborers. Together they made up the largest migration in history before the nineteenth century and gave rise to an African diaspora in the western hemisphere. Under the restrictive conditions of slavery, they could not reconstitute African societies, but they preserved some African traditions and blended them with European and American traditions to create hybrid societies.

CHRONOLOGY	
1441	Beginning of the Portuguese slave trade
1464–1493	Reign of Sunni Ali
1464–1591	Songhay empire
1506–1542	Reign of King Afonso I of Kongo
1623–1663	Reign of Queen Nzinga of Ndongo
1706	Execution of Doña Beatriz
1745–1797	Life of Olaudah Equiano
1793–1804	Haitian revolution
1807	End of the British slave trade
1865	Abolition of slavery in the United States

AFRICAN POLITICS AND SOCIETY IN EARLY MODERN TIMES

At the start of the early modern era, African peoples lived under a variety of political organizations, including small groups based on kinship, regional kingdoms, city-states, and large imperial states that drew their power from the trans-Saharan trade. In the early modern era, however, the influence of maritime trade across the Atlantic and Indian oceans changed patterns of state development. In west Africa, regional kingdoms replaced imperial states as peoples organized their societies to take advantage of Atlantic as well as trans-Saharan commerce. In east Africa, Swahili city-states fell under the domination of Portuguese merchant-mariners seeking commercial opportunities in the Indian Ocean basin. The extension of trade networks also led to the formation of regional kingdoms in central Africa and south Africa. As the volume of long-distance trade grew, both Islam and Christianity became more prominent in sub-Saharan African societies.

The States of West Africa and East Africa

Between the eighth and sixteenth centuries, powerful kingdoms and imperial states ruled the savannas of west

Africa. The earliest was the kingdom of **Ghana**, which originated as early as the fourth or fifth century and established its dominance in the region in the eighth century. By controlling and taxing the trans-Saharan trade in gold, the kings of Ghana gained the resources they needed to field a large army and influence affairs in much of west Africa. In the thirteenth century the **Mali empire** replaced Ghana as the preeminent power in west Africa and continued the Ghana policy of controlling trans-Saharan trade.

The Songhay Empire

In the fifteenth century the expansive state of Songhay emerged to take Mali's place as the dominant power of the western grasslands. Based in the trading city of Gao, Songhay rulers built a flourishing city-state as early as the eighth century. In the early fifteenth century, they rejected Mali authority, and in 1464 the Songhay ruler **Sunni Ali** (reigned 1464–1493) conquered his neighbors and consolidated the **Songhay empire** (1464–1591). He brought the important trading cities of **Timbuktu** and **Jenne** under his control and used their wealth to dominate the central Niger valley.

Songhay Administration

Sunni Ali built an elaborate administrative and military apparatus to oversee affairs in his realm. He instituted a hierarchy of command that turned his army into an effective military force. He also created an imperial navy to patrol the Niger River, which was an extremely important commercial highway. Songhay military might enabled Sunni Ali's successors to extend their authority north into the Sahara, east toward Lake Chad, and west toward the upper reaches of the Niger River.

The Songhay emperors presided over a prosperous land. The capital city of Gao had about seventy-five thousand residents, many of whom participated in the lucrative trans-Saharan trade that brought salt, textiles, and metal goods south in exchange for gold and enslaved people. The emperors were all Muslims: they supported mosques, built schools to teach the Quran, and maintained an Islamic university at Timbuktu. Like the rulers of Ghana and Mali, the Songhay emperors valued Islam as a cultural foundation for cooperation with Muslim merchants and Islamic states in north Africa.

Ghana (GAH-nuh)
Songhay (song-AHY)
Sunni Ali (soon-ee ah-lee)
Timbuktu (tim-buhk-TOO)
Jenne (jehn-neh)
Diula (dih-uh-lah)
Mande (MAHN-dey)
Swahili (swah-HEE-lee)

Fall of Songhay

The Songhay empire dominated west Africa for most of the sixteenth century, but it was the last of the great imperial states of the grasslands. In 1591 a musket-bearing Moroccan army trekked across the Sahara and attacked the previously invincible Songhay military machine. Songhay forces withered under the assault, and subject peoples took the opportunity to revolt against Songhay domination.

As the Songhay empire crumbled, a series of small, regional kingdoms and city-states emerged in west Africa. On the coasts, Diula, Mande, and other trading peoples established a series of states that entered into commercial relations with European merchant-mariners who called at west African ports after the fifteenth century. The increasing prominence of Atlantic trade in west African society worked against the interests of imperial states such as Mali and Songhay, which had relied on control of trans-Saharan trade to finance their empires.

Swahili Decline

While regional states displaced the Songhay empire in west Africa, the Swahili city-states of east Africa fell on hard times. In 1505 a huge Portuguese naval expedition subdued all the Swahili cities from Sofala to Mombasa. Portuguese forces built administrative centers at Mozambique and Malindi and constructed forts throughout the region in hopes of controlling trade in east

Timbuktu, the commercial and cultural center of the Mali and Songhay empires, as sketched by a French traveler in 1828. Though Timbuktu was in decline by that time, its mosques, mud-brick dwellings, and crowds of people suggest the prosperous city of an earlier era.
Everett Historical/Shutterstock

Africa. They did not succeed in that effort, but they disrupted trade patterns enough to send the Swahili cities into a decline from which they never fully recovered.

The Kingdoms of Central Africa and South Africa

The Kingdom of Kongo
As trade networks multiplied and linked all regions of sub-Saharan Africa, an increasing volume of commerce encouraged state building in central and south Africa. In central Africa the principal states were the kingdoms of Kongo, **Ndongo**, Luba, and Lunda in the Congo River basin. Best known of them was the kingdom of **Kongo**, which emerged in the fourteenth century. Its rulers built a centralized state with officials overseeing military, judicial, and financial affairs, and by the late fifteenth century Kongo embraced much of the modern-day Republic of the Congo and Angola.

In 1483 a small Portuguese fleet initiated commercial relations with Kongo. Within a few years, Portuguese merchants had established a close political and diplomatic relationship with the kings of Kongo. They supplied the kings with advisors, provided a military garrison to support the kings and protect Portuguese interests, and brought artisans and priests to Kongo.

The kings of Kongo converted to Christianity and thus established closer commercial and diplomatic relations with the Portuguese. The kings appreciated the fact that Christianity offered a strong endorsement of their monarchical rule and found similarities between Roman Catholic saints and the spirits recognized in Kongolese religion. **King Nzinga Mbemba** of Kongo, also known as King Afonso I (reigned 1506–1542), became a devout Roman Catholic and sought to convert all his subjects to Christianity. Portuguese priests in Kongo reported that he attended religious services daily and studied the Bible so zealously that he sometimes neglected to eat.

Slave Raiding in Kongo
Relations with Portugal brought wealth and foreign recognition to Kongo but led eventually to the destruction of the kingdom. In exchange for their goods and services, Portuguese merchants sought high-value merchandise such as copper, ivory, and, most of all, enslaved people. They sometimes embarked on slaving expeditions themselves, but more often they made alliances with local authorities in interior regions and provided them with weapons in exchange for captured people. Such tactics undermined the authority of the kings, who appealed repeatedly for the Portuguese to cease or at least to limit their trade in enslaved people.

Over time, relations between Kongo and Portugal deteriorated, particularly after Portuguese agents began to pursue opportunities south of Kongo. In 1665 Portuguese colonists to the south even went to war with Kongo. Portuguese forces quickly defeated the Kongolese army and

decapitated King Antonio I (also called Nvita a Nkanga) the same year. Soon thereafter, Portuguese merchants began to withdraw from Kongo in search of more profitable business in the kingdom of Ndongo to the south. By the eighteenth century the kingdom of Kongo had largely disintegrated.

The Kingdom of Ndongo
Meanwhile, Portuguese explorers were developing a brisk trade in enslaved people to the south in the kingdom of Ndongo, which the Portuguese referred to as Angola from the title of the king, *ngola*. During the sixteenth century, Ndongo had grown from a small chiefdom subject to the kings of Kongo to a powerful regional kingdom in its own right, largely on the basis of the wealth it was able to attract by trading directly with Portuguese merchants rather than through Kongolese intermediaries. After 1611 the Portuguese steadily increased their influence inland by allying with neighboring peoples who delivered increasing numbers of war captives to feed the growing slave trade. Over the next several decades, Portuguese forces campaigned in Ndongo in an effort to establish a colony that would support large-scale trading in human beings.

Queen Nzinga
The conquest of Ndongo did not come easily. For forty years **Queen Nzinga** (reigned 1623–1663)

An engraving from 1626 showing Queen Nzinga of Matamba, who is sitting on a prostrate man while having an audience with a group of Portuguese men. Fotosearch/Stringer/Getty Images

Mozambique (moh-zam-BEEK)
Malindi (mah-LIN-dee)
Ndongo (n'DAWN-goh)
Nzinga Mbemba (IN-zinga MEHM-bah)

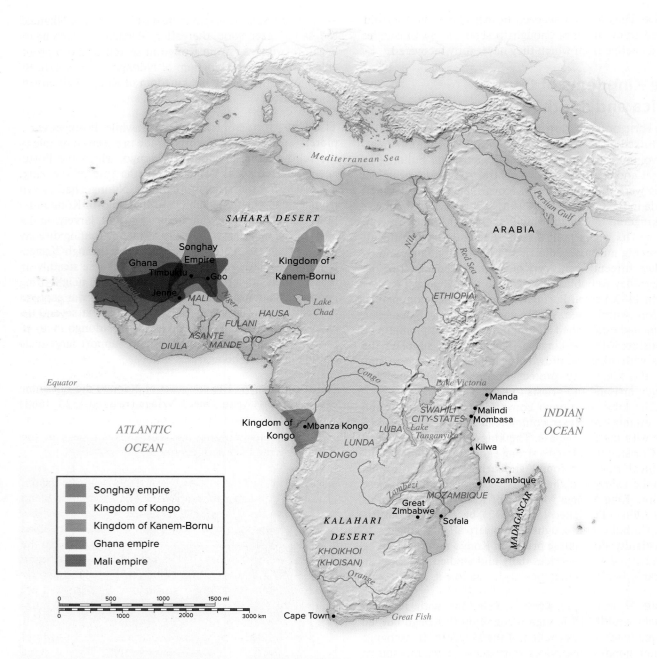

MAP 22.1 African states, 1500–1650

Locate the three largest states of Songhay, Kongo, and Kanem-Bornu.

What was it about their respective locations that favored the development of such large polities?

led spirited resistance against Portuguese forces. Nzinga came from a long line of warrior-kings. She dressed as a male warrior when leading troops in battle and insisted that her subjects refer to her as king rather than queen. She mobilized central African peoples against her Portuguese adversaries, and she allied with Dutch mariners who also traded on the African coast. Her aim was to drive the

Portuguese from her land, expel the Dutch, and then to create a central African empire embracing the entire lower Congo basin.

The Portuguese Colony of Angola Although she was an effective military leader, Nzinga was unable to oust Portuguese forces from Ndongo. When Nzinga died in

1663, Portuguese forces faced less capable resistance, and they both extended and tightened their control over the region now called Angola, the first European colony in sub-Saharan Africa.

Regional Kingdoms in South Africa In south Africa, as in central Africa, regional kingdoms dominated political affairs. Kingdoms had begun to emerge as early as the eleventh century, largely as a result of increasing trade. Merchants from the Swahili city-states of coastal east Africa sought gold, ivory, and people to enslave from the interior regions of south Africa. By controlling commerce, chieftains increased their wealth, enhanced their power, and extended their authority. By 1300 rulers of one such kingdom had built a massive, stone-fortified city, known as Great Zimbabwe, near the city of Nyanda in modern Zimbabwe, and they dominated the gold-bearing plain between the Zambesi and Limpopo rivers until the late fifteenth century.

European Arrival in South Africa After the fifteenth century a series of smaller kingdoms displaced the rulers of Great Zimbabwe, and Portuguese and Dutch mariners began to play a role in South African affairs. They became especially active after Dutch mariners built a trading post at Cape Town in 1652. With the aid of firearms, they claimed lands for themselves and forcibly commandeered the labor of indigenous **Khoikhoi** peoples. By 1700 large numbers of Dutch colonists had begun to arrive in South Africa, and by mid-century they had established settlements in the region. Their conquests laid the foundation for a series of prosperous Dutch and British colonies in sub-Saharan Africa.

Islam and Christianity in Early Modern Africa

Indigenous religions remained influential throughout sub-Saharan Africa in early modern times. Although many Africans recognized a supreme, remote creator god, they also devoted attention to powerful spirits who were thought to intervene directly in human affairs. Many of these spirits were associated with geographic features such as mountains, waters, or forests, and others were believed to be the spirits of ancestors who roamed the world.

Islam in Sub-Saharan Africa Although most Africans continued to observe indigenous religions, both Islam and Christianity attracted increasing interest in sub-Saharan Africa. Islam was most widely adopted in the commercial centers of west Africa and the Swahili city-states of east Africa. In the sixteenth century the trading city of Timbuktu had a prominent Islamic university and 180 schools that taught the Quran. Students flocked to Timbuktu by the thousands from all parts of west Africa.

African Muslims often blended Islam with indigenous beliefs and customs. The result was a syncretic style of Islam that not only made a place for African beliefs but also permitted men and women to associate with one another on much more familiar terms than was common in north Africa and Arabia. This syncretic Islam frequently struck many devout Muslims as impure. Muslim merchants and travelers from north Africa and Arabia often commented on their shock at seeing women in tropical Africa who went out in public with bare breasts and socialized freely with men outside their own families.

The Fulani and Islam Some Muslims in sub-Saharan Africa also shared these concerns about the purity of Islam. Most important of them were the **Fulani** of the west African savannas, who observed a strict form of Islam like that practiced in north Africa and Arabia. Beginning about 1680 and continuing through the nineteenth century, the Fulani led a series of military campaigns to establish Islamic states and impose their own style of Islam in west Africa. They founded powerful states in what is now Guinea, Senegal, Mali, and northern Nigeria, and they promoted the spread of Islam beyond the cities to the countryside by establishing Islamic schools in remote towns and villages. Their campaigns did not stamp out African religions, but they strengthened Islam in sub-Saharan Africa and laid a foundation for new rounds of Islamic state building and conversion efforts in the nineteenth and twentieth centuries.

Christianity in Sub-Saharan Africa Like Islam, Christianity in sub-Saharan Africa was a syncretic blend of Christian doctrine and indigenous traditions and beliefs. A particularly influential form of Christianity was the **Antonian movement** in Kongo, which flourished in the early eighteenth century. The Antonian movement began in 1704 when an aristocratic woman named **Doña Beatriz** proclaimed that St. Anthony of Padua had possessed her and chosen her to communicate his messages. St. Anthony was a thirteenth-century Franciscan missionary and popular preacher, and he became the patron saint of Portugal. Doña Beatriz gained a reputation for working miracles and curing diseases, and she used her prominence to promote an African form of Christianity. She taught that Jesus Christ had been a Black African man, that Kongo was the true holy land of Christianity, and that heaven was for Africans. She urged Kongolese to ignore European missionaries and heed her disciples instead, and she sought to harness the widespread popular interest in her teachings and use it to end the wars plaguing Kongo.

Zimbabwe (zihm-BAHB-way)
Khoikhoi (KOY-koy)
Fulani (foo-LAH-nee)

Doña Beatriz's movement was a serious challenge to Christian missionaries in Kongo. In 1706 they persuaded King Pedro IV of Kongo to arrest the charismatic prophet on suspicion of heresy. After examining her, the missionaries determined that Doña Beatriz knowingly taught false doctrine. On their recommendation the royal government sentenced her to death and burned her at the stake. Yet the Antonian movement did not disappear: in 1708 an army of almost twenty thousand Antonians challenged King Pedro, whom they considered an unworthy ruler. Their efforts illustrate clearly the tendency of Kongolese Christians to fashion a faith that reflected their own needs and concerns.

Social Change in Early Modern Africa

Despite increased state-building activity and political turmoil, African societies followed long-established patterns during the early modern era. Kinship groups, for example, continued to serve as the basis of social organization and sometimes political organization as well. Within agricultural villages throughout sub-Saharan Africa, clans under the leadership of prominent individuals organized the affairs of their kinship groups and disciplined those who violated community standards. Even in lands ruled by formal states, clan leaders usually implemented state policy at the village level.

American Food Crops in Sub-Saharan Africa In the mid-sixteenth century, American crops such as manioc, maize, and peanuts arrived in Africa aboard Portuguese ships. These crops supplemented bananas, yams, rice, and millet, the principal staple foods of sub-Saharan Africa. The most important American crop was manioc because of its high yield and because it thrived in tropical soils not well suited to cultivation of the other crops.

Population Growth By the eighteenth century, bread made from manioc flour had become a staple food in much of west Africa and central Africa, where it helped provide a foundation for steady population growth. In 1500 C.E. the population of sub-Saharan Africa was about thirty-four million. By 1600 it had increased to forty-four million, and it continued climbing, to sixty million in 1800. This strong demographic expansion is all the more remarkable because it took place precisely when millions of Africans underwent involuntary, forced migration to destinations in the Caribbean and the Americas as part of the Atlantic slave trade.

THE ATLANTIC SLAVE TRADE

Of all the processes that linked Africa to the larger Atlantic world in early modern times, the most momentous was the **Atlantic slave trade**. From the fifteenth to the nineteenth centuries, millions of Africans were brutally enslaved and sent to the Americas to work on European-owned agricultural plantations. In exchange for providing enslaved people, African slave traders sought European manufactured products—most notably firearms. Only in the nineteenth century did the Atlantic slave trade and, in most places, slavery itself come to an end.

Foundations of the Slave Trade

Slavery in Africa Until the nineteenth century many settled peoples of the world utilized slave labor in some form. Slavery was common throughout Africa after Bantu-speaking people spread agriculture to all parts of the continent. As in other societies, most enslaved people in Africa were war captives, although criminals and individuals expelled from their clans also fell into slavery. Once enslaved, an individual had no personal or civil rights. Owners could punish enslaved people at will and sell them as chattel. Enslaved Africans usually worked as cultivators in societies far from their homes, although some worked as administrators, soldiers, or even highly placed advisors. The Songhay emperors, for example, often employed enslaved people as administrators and soldiers, since the rulers distrusted free nobles, whom they considered excessively ambitious and undependable.

Yet despite similarities with slavery in other places like Europe and Asia, African slavery was also distinct in some ways. African law did not recognize private property but, rather, vested ownership of land in communities. Thus wealth and power in Africa came not from the possession of land but from control over the human labor that made land productive. Enslaved people were thus an important means of measuring wealth. Those who controlled large numbers of enslaved people were able to harvest more crops and accumulate more wealth than others. Africans routinely purchased enslaved people to enlarge their families, and they often assimilated them into their kinship groups so that within a generation an enslaved person might obtain both freedom and an honorable position in a new family or clan.

The Trans-Saharan Slave Trade After the eighth century, Muslim merchants from north Africa, Arabia, and Persia sought enslaved Africans for sale and distribution to destinations in the Mediterranean basin, southwest Asia, India, and even southeast Asia and China. When demand for enslaved people outstripped supply, merchants resorted to raiding villages and capturing innocent individuals. Merchants then transported the victims of these raids across the Sahara desert or boarded them on ships at the Swahili port cities of east Africa. Between the eighth and the twentieth centuries, as many as ten million Africans may have been enslaved as part of the Islamic slave trade.

By the time Europeans ventured to sub-Saharan Africa in the fifteenth and sixteenth centuries, traffic in enslaved people was a well-established feature of African

Why It Matters

The Columbian Exchange

What are the long-term effects of pandemic disease? The answer is always highly complex, but the massive depopulation caused by pandemic diseases during the Columbian exchange also helped create the conditions that later led Europeans to seek an alternate labor force to work their plantations in the Americas. As we know, this labor force was brought forcibly from Africa. Over the course of three centuries, more than twelve million people were forced into slavery thousands of miles from their homes. If pandemic disease could help set the conditions for the Atlantic slave trade, can you imagine ways that pandemic disease in the present could shape the long-term future?

society, and a system for capturing, selling, and distributing them had functioned effectively for more than five hundred years. After 1450 European peoples initially tapped existing networks and then dramatically expanded commerce in enslaved Africans even as they shifted its focus to the Atlantic Ocean basin. This Atlantic slave trade profoundly influenced the development of societies throughout the Atlantic Ocean basin.

Human Cargoes

The Atlantic slave trade began small, but it grew steadily and eventually reached enormous proportions. The earliest European slave traders were Portuguese explorers who, in 1441, seized and enslaved twelve African men and took them to Portugal. Portuguese mariners encountered stiff resistance when they attempted to capture Africans to enslave, as African warriors fired thousands of poison-tipped arrows at gangs of would-be slave raiders. Soon, however, the mariners learned that they could purchase enslaved people rather than capture them. By 1460 they were delivering five hundred enslaved people per year to Portugal and Spain, where they usually worked as miners, porters, or domestic servants.

The Early Slave Trade Slave traders also delivered their human cargoes to Portuguese island colonies in the Atlantic. There was no supply of labor to work plantations in the Azores, the Madeiras, the Cape Verde Islands, and São Tomé, all of which were uninhabited when explorers discovered them in the fifteenth century. Sugar planters on the island of São Tomé, in particular, called for slave labor to solve this labor shortage. By the 1520s some two thousand enslaved people per year went to São Tomé, which allowed sugar production on the island to soar. By the 1530s Portuguese entrepreneurs had extended the use of slave labor to Brazil, which eventually became the wealthiest of the sugar-producing lands of the western hemisphere.

Spanish explorers and conquerors also sought laborers to work lands in the Caribbean and the Americas. As imported diseases ravaged indigenous populations, the conquerors found themselves with few laborers to work

the land. Gradually, Spanish settlers began to rely on enslaved people from Africa as well. In 1518 the first shipment of enslaved Africans went directly from west Africa to the Caribbean, where they worked on recently established sugar plantations. By the early seventeenth century, English colonists had introduced enslaved Africans also to the North American mainland.

Triangular Trade The demand for labor in the western hemisphere stimulated a profitable commerce known as the **triangular trade**, since European ships often undertook voyages of three legs. On the first leg they carried horses and European manufactured goods—especially firearms—which they exchanged in Africa for enslaved people. The second leg took enslaved Africans to Caribbean and American destinations.

On arrival merchants sold their human cargoes to plantation owners for two to three times what they had cost in Africa. In sugar-producing regions they often bartered enslaved Africans for sugar or molasses. Then they filled their vessels' hulls with American products before embarking on their voyage back to Europe.

At every stage of the process, the slave trade was a brutal and inhumane business. The original capture of Africans into slavery was almost always a violent affair. As European demand for enslaved people grew, some African chieftains organized raiding parties to seize individuals from neighboring societies. Others launched wars for the purpose of capturing victims for the slave trade. They often snatched individuals right out of their homes, fields, or villages: millions of lives changed instantly, as slave raiders grabbed their victims and then immediately spirited them away in captivity.

The Middle Passage Following capture, enslaved individuals underwent a forced march to the coast, where they lived in holding pens until a ship arrived to transport them

Azores (uh-ZAWRZ)
Madeiras (muh-DEER-uhs)
São Tomé (SOU tuh-MEY)

SOURCES FROM THE PAST

Olaudah Equiano on the Middle Passage

Olaudah Equiano (1745–1797) was a native of Benin in west Africa. When he was ten years old, slave raiders seized him and his sister at their home while their parents were tending the fields. He spent the next twenty-one years in slavery. Eventually, Equiano purchased his freedom and worked against the slave trade for the rest of his life. In his autobiography, published in of 1789, Equiano described the horrors of the middle passage.

The first object which saluted my eyes when I arrived on the coast was the sea, and a slave ship which was then riding at anchor and waiting for its cargo. These filled me with astonishment, which was soon converted into terror when I was carried on board. I was immediately handled and tossed up to see if I were sound by some of the crew, and I was now persuaded that I had gotten into a world of bad spirits and that they were going to kill me. . . .

I was not long suffered to indulge my grief; I was soon put down under the decks, and there I received such a salutation in my nostrils as I had never experienced in my life: so that with the loathsomeness of the stench and crying together, I became so sick and low that I was not able to eat, nor had I the least desire to taste anything. I now wished for the last friend, death, to relieve me; but soon, to my grief, two of the white men offered me eatables, and on my refusing to eat, one of them held me fast by the hands and laid me across I think the windlass and tied my feet while the other flogged me severely. I had never experienced anything of this kind before, and although not being used to the water I naturally feared that element the first time I saw it, yet nevertheless if I could have gotten over the nettings I would have jumped over the side, but I could not; and besides, the crew used to watch very closely over those of us who were not chained down to the decks, lest we should leap into the water: and I have seen some of these poor African prisoners most severely cut for attempting to do so, and hourly whipped for not eating. This indeed was often the case with myself. . . .

One day when we had a smooth sea and moderate wind, two of my wearied countrymen who were chained together (I was near them at the time), preferring death to such a life of misery, somehow made through the nettings and jumped into the sea: immediately another quite dejected fellow, who on account of his illness was suffered to be out of irons, also followed their example; and I believe many more would very soon have done the same if they had not been prevented by the ship's crew, who were instantly alarmed. Those of us that were the most active were in a moment put down under the deck, and there was such a noise and confusion amongst the people of the ship as I never heard before, to stop her and get the boat to go after the slaves. However, two of the wretches were drowned, but they got the other and afterwards flogged him unmercifully for thus attempting to prefer death to slavery. In this manner we continued to undergo more hardships than I can now relate, hardships which are inseparable from this accursed trade.

> Why was it so important to the ship's crew that the Africans on board eat?

> Consider how terrible the conditions on board the ship must have been to encourage some of the Africans on board to choose death over survival.

For Further Reflection

■ On the basis of Equiano's account, what measures did the crews of slave ships take to ensure maximum profits from their business of transporting human cargoes?

Source: Olaudah Equiano. *The Interesting Narrative of the Life of Olaudah Equiano, or Gustavus Vassa, the African, Written by Himself.* 2 vols. London, 1789. (Translation slightly modified.)

Belowdecks on an illegal slave ship seized by a British antislavery patrol in 1846. Note the extremely cramped quarters in which captives were forced to spend most of their time. They were deeply uncomfortable, and the close quarters contributed to dangerously unsanitary conditions. The Art Archive/Shutterstock

seventeenth century, the trade in humans from Africa rose dramatically to twenty thousand per year. The high point of the slave trade came in the eighteenth century, when the number of enslaved people exported to the Americas averaged fifty-five thousand per year. During the 1780s arrivals of enslaved Africans averaged eighty-eight thousand per year, and in some individual years they exceeded one hundred thousand. From beginning to end the Atlantic slave trade brought about twelve million Africans to the western hemisphere. An additional four million or more died before arriving.

The impact of the slave trade varied over time and from one African society to another. Some societies largely escaped the slave trade because their lands were distant from the major slave ports on the west African coast. Those societies that raided, took captives, and sold enslaved Africans to Europeans profited handsomely from the trade, as did the port cities and the states that coordinated trade with European merchants. Asante, Dahomey, and Oyo peoples, for example, took advantage of the slave trade to obtain firearms from European merchants and build powerful states in west Africa.

Social Effects of the Slave Trade

On the whole, however, sub-Saharan Africa suffered serious losses from the slave trade. The Atlantic slave trade alone deprived African societies of about sixteen million individuals, in addition to several million others forced into the continuing trans-Saharan slave trade during the early modern era. Although total African population rose during the early modern era, partly because American food crops enriched diets, several individual societies experienced severe losses because of the slave trade. West African societies between Senegal and Angola were especially vulnerable to slave raiding because of their proximity to the most active slave ports.

While diverting labor from Africa to other lands, the slave trade also distorted African sex ratios, since approximately two-thirds of all exported enslaved people were males. Slavers preferred young men between ages fourteen and thirty-five, since they had the best potential to provide heavy labor over an extended period of time. This preference for

to the western hemisphere. Then they embarked on the dreadful **middle passage**, the trans-Atlantic journey aboard filthy and crowded slave ships. Enslaved passengers traveled belowdecks in hideously cramped quarters. Conditions were so bad that many individuals attempted to starve themselves to death or mounted revolts. Ship crews often treated the unwilling passengers with cruelty and contempt. Crew members used tools to pry open the mouths of those who refused to eat and pitched sick individuals into the ocean rather than have them waste limited supplies of food.

In good sailing conditions, the journey to Caribbean and American destinations took four to six weeks, during which heat, cold, and disease levied a heavy toll on the enslaved people aboard the ships. During the early days of the slave trade, mortality could exceed 50 percent. As the volume of the trade grew, slavers provided better nourishment and facilities for the enslaved people aboard their ships, and mortality eventually declined to about 5 percent per voyage. Over the course of the Atlantic slave trade, however, approximately 25 percent of individuals enslaved in Africa died during the middle passage.

The Impact of the Slave Trade in Africa

Volume of the Slave Trade

Before 1600 the Atlantic slave trade operated on a modest scale: on average about two thousand enslaved people left Africa annually during the late fifteenth and sixteenth centuries. During the

---

Asante (uh-SAN-tee)

Dahomey (dah-HO-meh)

Oyo (OH-yoh)

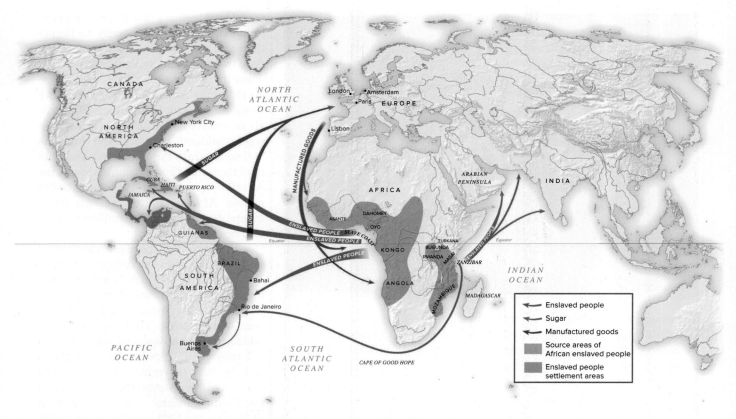

MAP 22.2   The Atlantic slave trade, 1500–1800

Note the triangular pattern of the Atlantic trade routes between Europe, Africa, and the Americas.

Why were most enslaved people in the Atlantic system taken from west/central Africa, and where were they taken?

Volume of the Slave Trade. This table depicts the number of enslaved people forcibly sent to locations around the Atlantic world by century.

	Europe	Mainland N. America	British Caribbean	French Caribbean	Dutch Americas	Danish West Indies	Spanish Americas	Brazil	Africa	Totals
1501–1600	903	0	0	0	0	0	241,917	34,686	0	277,506
1601–1700	3,639	19,956	405,117	50,356	145,980	22,610	313,301	910,361	4,312	1,875,631
1701–1800	6,256	358,845	2,139,819	1,178,518	339,559	81,801	175,438	2,210,931	3,451	6,494,619
1801–1866	0	93,581	218,475	99,549	28,654	25,455	860,589	2,376,141	171,137	3,873,580
Totals	**10,798**	**472,381**	**2,763,411**	**1,328,422**	**514,192**	**129,867**	**1,591,245**	**5,532,118**	**178,901**	**12,521,336**

Source: *Emory University. "The Trans-Atlantic Slave Trade Database." Accessed Jan 10, 2020. https://slavevoyages.org/assessment/estimates*

enslaved males had social implications for their places of origin in Africa. By the late eighteenth century, for example, women made up more than two-thirds of the adult population of Angola. This sexual imbalance encouraged Angolans to practice polygamy and forced women to take on duties that in earlier times had been the responsibility of men.

Political Effects of the Slave Trade Apart from its demographic and social effects, the slave trade brought turmoil to African societies. Violence escalated especially after the late seventeenth century, when African states and kingdoms increasingly exchanged enslaved people for European firearms. When the kingdom of Dahomey obtained effective firearms, for example, its armies were able to capture people from unarmed neighboring societies and exchange them for more weapons. During the eighteenth century, Dahomey expanded rapidly and absorbed neighboring societies by increasing its arsenal of firearms and maintaining a constant flow of enslaved people to the coast. By no means did all African states take such advantage of the slave trade, but Dahomey's experience illustrates the potential of the slave trade to alter the patterns of African politics and society.

Connecting the Sources

Using indirect sources to reconstruct the lives of enslaved people

The problem   Sometimes historians want to find out about the experiences of groups that may not have had much power in the past, such as women, peasants, or enslaved people. This can be difficult, however, because such groups frequently did not leave many textual records behind. In the case of enslaved people who became part of the Atlantic slave trade, it is difficult to find primary sources created by individual enslaved people themselves, particularly in the seventeenth and eighteenth centuries. Many enslaved people were not literate in European languages, and even when enslaved people were literate, the documents they created may not have been saved for later inclusion in historical archives. Some voices—such as Olaudah Equiano's—have survived from that period, as we see in this chapter. However, to understand the varieties of experiences enslaved people might have had, historians must use many primary sources written by others, including those written by slave traders, slaveholders, courts, and governments. Let us consider two such sources as a way of thinking about what indirect sources can and cannot tell us about the experience of slavery in the eighteenth century.

FL Historical 28/Alamy Stock Photo

The documents   Read the following documents, and consider carefully the questions that follow.

Document 1:

This advertisement comes from the New London Summary *(Connecticut) on March 30, 1764.*

> *The text reads:*
> *Ran away from me the subscriber, the 14th instant, a Molatto named Bilhah, a tall, thick-built well-proportioned Wench; had on a brown short stuff Gown, batt'd with Yellow, a blue camblet Quilt, and check'd linnen Apron, black silk Bonnet, a large pair flower'd silver Shoe-Buckles; may possibly pretend to be a Free Woman, or may Change her Apparel for Men's Cloathing. All Masters of Vessels are cautioned from carrying off said Molatto—Any Person who shall secure said Molatto Wench in any of His Majesty's Goals, shall have FOUR DOLLARS Reward, and necessary Charges paid by Jared Eliot. Killingworth, Mar. 21, 1764.*

Why might Bilhah have tried to dress like a man? Does the fact that this is included in the ad suggest it was a common practice?

Document 2:

This broadside advertisement was posted in Charlestown, South Carolina, in 1769.

The text reads:

CHARLESTOWN, April 27, 1769
TO BE SOLD,
On Wednesday the Tenth Day of
May next,
A CHOICE CARGO OF
Two Hundred & Fifty
NEGROES:

ARRIVED in the Ship
Countess of Sussex, Thomas Davies,
Master, directly from Gambia, by
JOHN CHAPMAN, & Co.

THIS is the Vessel that had the Small-Pox on Board at the Time of her Arrival the 31st of
March last: Every necessary Precaution hath since been taken to cleanse both Ship and
Cargo thoroughly, so that those who may be inclined to purchase need not be under the least
Apprehension of Danger from Infliction.

> How might the ship's crew have cleansed a cargo of people, and what can this phrase tell us about the nature of the slave trade?

The NEGROES are allowed to be the likeliest Parcel that have been imported this Season.

Questions

1. What can these advertisements definitively tell you about their respective situations? What facts can be gleaned from these brief sources?
2. In Document 1, what might this advertisement imply about the experience of slavery from Bilhah's point of view? For example, does it imply that Bilhah was unhappy with her status as an enslaved woman, or is it simply impossible to know?
3. Also in Document 1, what might this advertisement imply about Bilhah's treatment prior to her departure? Are there any clues that indicate how she lived under Jared Eliot's care?
4. In Document 2, what kinds of information can you glean about the possible experience of the enslaved captives held aboard the *Countess of Sussex*? For example, what might it have been like to cross the Atlantic with smallpox aboard?
5. Taking both documents together, what kinds of contextual information would you need in order to understand these advertisements more fully? For example, would your conclusions about the meaning of Document 1 change if you knew that hundreds of enslaved people ran away every year or, alternatively, if Bilhah was a rare exception? Would your conclusions regarding Document 2 be different if you knew that the *Countess of Sussex* was one of many slave ships to arrive in port at Charlestown in 1769, or if you knew such a landing was a rare occurrence? What further information would you need in order to use these documents to interpret the experience of enslaved people in North America in the eighteenth century?
6. Sources such as these make up the building blocks on which historians base their interpretations of the past. In most cases, however, historians discover that they must use a variety of primary and secondary sources in order to make accurate interpretations.

Source Websites: **Document 1:** http://www.yale.edu/glc/citizens/stories/module1/documents/runaway_slave.html. **Document 2:** http://www.pbs.org/wgbh/aia/part1/1h304.html.

THE AFRICAN DIASPORA

Some enslaved people worked as urban laborers or domestic servants, and in Mexico and Peru many worked as miners. The vast majority, however, worked as agricultural laborers on plantations in the Caribbean or the Americas. There they cultivated cash crops that made their way into commercial arteries linking lands throughout the Atlantic Ocean basin. Although deprived of their freedom and frequently treated with brutality, enslaved people often resisted their bondage, and they built hybrid cultural traditions compounded of African, European, and American elements. Most European and American states ended the slave trade and abolished slavery during the nineteenth century. By that time the **African diaspora**—the dispersal of African peoples and their descendants—had left a permanent mark throughout the western hemisphere.

Plantation Societies

Most enslaved Africans went to plantations in the tropical and subtropical regions of the western hemisphere. Spanish colonists established the first of these plantations in 1516 on the island of Hispaniola (modern Haiti and the Dominican Republic) and soon extended them to Mexico as well. Beginning in the 1530s Portuguese entrepreneurs organized plantations in Brazil, and by the early seventeenth century English, Dutch, and French settlers had also established plantations in the Caribbean and the Americas.

Cash Crops Many of these plantations produced sugar, which was one of the most lucrative cash crops of early modern times. But plantations produced other crops as well, including tobacco, rice, and indigo (a dye). By the eighteenth century many plantations concentrated on the cultivation of cotton, and coffee had begun to emerge as a plantation cash crop.

Regardless of the crops they produced, Caribbean and American plantations had certain elements in common. All of them specialized in the production and export of commercial crops. They all also relied almost exclusively on slave labor. Plantations also featured a sharp, racial division of labor: small numbers of European or Euro-American supervisors governed plantation affairs, and large numbers of enslaved Africans or people of African descent performed most of the community's physical labor.

Regional Differences In spite of their structural similarities, plantation societies differed considerably from one region to another. In the Caribbean and South America, populations of enslaved people usually were unable to sustain their numbers by natural means. This was due partly to the impact of tropical diseases such as malaria and yellow fever and partly to the brutal working conditions enslaved people faced on the plantations. Moreover, since most enslaved people were male, their communities did not reproduce quickly.

Thus, in the Caribbean and South America, plantation owners demanded a continuous supply of enslaved Africans to maintain their workforces. Of all the enslaved people delivered from Africa to the western hemisphere, about half went to Caribbean destinations, and a third more went to Brazil.

Only about 5 percent of enslaved Africans went to North American destinations. Diseases there were less threatening than in the Caribbean and Brazil. Moreover, North American planters imported larger numbers of enslaved women and encouraged them to form families and bear children. Their support for natural reproduction was especially strong in the eighteenth century, when the prices of individuals direct from Africa rose dramatically.

Resistance to Slavery No matter where they lived, enslaved people did not meekly accept their status but, like Thomas Peters, whom we met in the introduction, resisted it in numerous ways. Some forms of resistance were mild but costly to slaveholders: individuals might purposefully work slowly for their slaveholders but diligently in their own gardens, for example. Some enslaved people might also sabotage plantation equipment or work routines. More seriously, enslaved people resisted by running away. Runaways known as maroons gathered in remote regions and built their own self-governing communities. Many maroons had gained military experience in Africa, and they organized fellow runaways into effective military forces. Maroon communities flourished throughout slaveholding regions of the western hemisphere, and some of them survived for centuries. In present-day Suriname, for example, the Saramaka people maintain an elaborate oral tradition that traces their descent from eighteenth-century maroons.

Slave Revolts The most dramatic form of resistance to slavery was the organized revolt. Enslaved people far outnumbered others in most plantation societies, and thus slave revolts brought stark fear to plantation owners and supervisors. Yet these revolts almost never brought slavery itself to an end, because the European and Euro-American ruling elites had access to military forces that extinguished most rebellions. Only in the French sugar colony of Saint-Domingue did a revolt abolish slavery as an institution (1793). Indeed, the enslaved people of Saint-Domingue declared independence from France, renamed the land **Haiti**, and established a self-governing republic (1804). The Haitian revolution terrified slaveholders and inspired enslaved people throughout the western hemisphere, but no other rebellion matched its accomplishments.

Slavery and Economic Development The physical labor of enslaved people made crucial contributions to the

diaspora (dahy-AS-per-uh)
Suriname (SOOR-uh-nahm)
Saramaka (sar-ah-MAH-kah)
Saint-Domingue (san doe-MANG)

Enslaved people were vulnerable to cruel treatment that often provoked them to run away from their plantations or even mount revolts. A French visitor to Brazil in the early nineteenth century depicted a Portuguese overseer administering a brutal whipping to a bound man on a plantation near Rio de Janeiro. What function might the branch behind this enslaved man's knees have had?
Pictorial Press Ltd/Alamy Stock Photo

building of new societies in the Americas and to the making of the early modern world as a whole. Enslaved people cultivated many of the crops and extracted many of the minerals that made their way around the world in the global trade networks of the early modern era. Although they themselves did not enjoy the fruits of their labors, without them it would have been impossible for prosperous new societies to emerge in the Americas during the early modern era.

The Making of Hybrid Cultural Traditions

When Africans were forced into slavery, they could not bring material items such as clothing, artwork, furniture, or tools. Once in the Americas and Caribbean, individuals found themselves enslaved with other Africans from many regions who spoke a wide variety of languages. As a result, it was difficult for enslaved Africans to maintain their cultural traditions in the western hemisphere. Instead, enslaved people adapted by constructing hybrid languages and religions based on many African traditions combined with new European and American elements.

Gullah (GUHL-uh)
Geechee (GEE-chee)
Voudou (voo-doo)
Santeria (sahn-tuh-REE-uh)
Candomblé (kan-duhm-BLEH)

African and Creole Languages European languages were dominant tongues in the plantation societies of the western hemisphere, but enslaved people frequently spoke a creole tongue that drew on several African and European languages. In the low country of South Carolina and Georgia, for example, enslaved people made up about three-quarters of the population in the eighteenth century and regularly communicated in the **creole languages** Gullah and Geechee, respectively.

African-Influenced Religions Like their languages, religions of enslaved Africans combined elements from different societies. Some enslaved people from Africa were Muslims, some were Christians, and many others converted to Christianity after their arrival in the western hemisphere. Most Africans and African descendants, however, practiced a syncretic faith that made considerable room for African interests and traditions. Because they developed mostly in plantation societies under conditions of slavery, these syncretic religions usually did not create an institutional structure or establish a hierarchy of priests and officials. Yet in several cases—most notably Voudou in Haiti, Santeria in Cuba, and Candomblé in Brazil—they became exceedingly popular.

All the syncretic religions with African influences drew inspiration from Christianity: they met in parish churches, sought personal salvation, and made use of Christian paraphernalia such as holy water, candles, and statues. Yet they also preserved African traditions. They associated

What's Left Out? ■■ ■■ ■■ ■■ ■

There were important differences in the ways enslaved women and enslaved men experienced slavery. In the case of enslaved women, European slave traders and settlers often wrongly believed that African women were hypersexual and that they were uninhibited about sexual encounters. These beliefs, combined with the power of ownership over enslaved women's bodies, contributed to a strong sense of entitlement over their reproductive capacities. Indeed, slaveholders viewed enslaved women not only as laborers but also as profitable vessels for producing additional enslaved people. Sexual violence by Europeans was a routine part of enslaved women's lives and resulted in many unwanted pregnancies. Even when enslaved women gave birth to children by partners of their own choosing, their children were subject to sale, and thus they could not control basic aspects of their futures. Enslaved women often resisted these practices, but the structure of slave societies meant that they could not turn to the law or to the larger society for assistance. It is important to remember that the practice of slavery in the Americas and the Caribbean involved control over the most intimate aspects of daily life. For women, this involved significant loss of control over their bodies and their reproductive capacities.

Source: Jennifer Morgan. *Laboring Women: Reproduction and Gender in New World Slavery.* Philadelphia: University of Pennsylvania Press, 2004.

African deities with Christian saints and relied heavily on African rituals such as drumming, dancing, and sacrificing animals. They also preserved beliefs in spirits and supernatural powers: magic, sorcery, witchcraft, and spirit possession all played prominent roles in the new hybrid religions.

African-American Music As in language and religion, enslaved people relied on African traditions in creating musical forms. Once in the Americas, enslaved people adapted African musical traditions, including both rhythmic and lyrical elements. Under the brutal circumstances of slavery, music may have been one of the means by which enslaved people resisted their new lives and survived its brutal conditions. In the process, they created new musical forms that influenced not only enslaved communities but also the multicultural societies of the Caribbean and the Americas.

Enslaved people fashioned new identities in part by adapting west African instruments and musical traditions to suit European languages, Christian religion, and the work routines of American plantations. Enslaved musicians played drums and stringed instruments like banjos that closely resembled traditional African instruments. They also adapted west African call-and-response patterns of singing to the rhythms of field work on plantations. Indeed, from work songs and spirituals to the blues, jazz, and soul, African-inspired music evolved to mirror the difficult and often brutal circumstances of Black life in the Americas.

African-Inspired Cultural Traditions African traditions also made their effects felt throughout much of the western hemisphere. Enslaved people introduced African foods to Caribbean and American societies and helped give rise to distinctive hybrid cuisines. They combined African okra, for example, with European-style sautéed vegetables and American shellfish to produce magnificent gumbos, which found their way to Euro-American tables and the tables of Africans and their descendants. Enslaved people introduced rice cultivation to tropical and subtropical regions. They also built houses, fashioned clay pots, and wove grass baskets in west African styles. In many ways the African diaspora influenced the ways all people lived in plantation societies.

The End of the Slave Trade and the Abolition of Slavery

Olaudah Equiano Almost as old as the Atlantic slave trade itself were voices calling for its abolition. The American and French revolutions, with their calls for liberty and universal human rights, stimulated the abolitionist cause. Africans also took up the struggle to abolish commerce in human beings. Frequent revolts in the eighteenth and nineteenth centuries made the institution of slavery an expensive and dangerous business. Some formerly enslaved people contributed to the abolitionist cause by writing books that exposed the brutality of institutional slavery. Most notable among them was the west African **Olaudah Equiano** (1745–1797), who in 1789 published an autobiography detailing his experiences as an enslaved and as a free man. Captured at age ten in his native Benin (in modern Nigeria), Equiano was enslaved in the West Indies, Virginia, and Pennsylvania. He accompanied one of his slaveholders on several campaigns of the Seven Years' War before purchasing his freedom in 1766. The book became a best-seller, and Equiano traveled throughout the British Isles giving speeches and

Olaudah Equiano (oh-LAU-duh ay-kwee-AHN-oh)

Enslaved people in chains on the island of Zanzibar (off the east coast of modern Tanzania), where slavery was abolished on 5 March 1873. Zanzibar had served as east Africa's principal port for the slave trade between Africa and Asia.
Bojan Brecelj/Corbis Historical/Getty Images

denouncing slavery as an evil institution. He lobbied government officials and members of Parliament, and his efforts strengthened the antislavery movement in England, which after 1789 was spearheaded by the social reformer and Parliamentarian William Wilberforce.

The Economic Costs of Slavery Quite apart from moral and political arguments, economic forces contributed to the end of slavery and the slave trade. Indeed, it gradually became clear that slave labor did not come cheap. The possibility of rebellion forced plantation societies to maintain expensive military forces. Even in peaceful times enslaved people were often unwilling and unproductive workers. Furthermore, in the late eighteenth century a rapid expansion of Caribbean sugar production led to declining prices. About the same time, African slave traders and European merchants sharply increased the prices they charged for individual enslaved people.

As the profitability of slavery declined, Europeans began to shift their investments from sugarcane and other agricultural products to newly emerging manufacturing industries. Investors soon found that wage labor in factories was less expensive than slave labor on plantations. As

an additional benefit, free workers spent much of their income on manufactured goods. Meanwhile, European investors realized that leaving Africans in Africa, where they could secure raw materials and buy manufactured goods in exchange, was good business.

End of the Slave Trade Denmark abolished trade in slaves in 1803, and other lands followed suit: Great Britain in 1807, the United States in 1808, France in 1814, the Netherlands in 1817, and Spain in 1820. The end of the slave trade did not abolish the institution of slavery itself, however, and as long as plantation slavery continued, a clandestine trade shipped enslaved people across the Atlantic. British naval squadrons sought to prevent this trade by conducting search-and-seizure operations, and gradually the illegal slave trade ground to a halt. The last documented ship that carried enslaved people across the Atlantic arrived in Cuba in 1867.

The abolition of the institution of slavery itself was a long, drawn-out process: emancipation of all enslaved people came in 1833 in British colonies, 1848 in French colonies, 1865 in the United States, 1886 in Cuba, and 1888 in Brazil. Saudi Arabia and Angola abolished slavery in the 1960s. Officially, slavery no longer exists, but millions of people live in various forms of slavery even today. According to the Anti-slavery Society for the Protection of Human Rights, debt bondage, contract labor, sham adoptions, servile marriages, and other forms of forced servitude still oppress more than two hundred million people, mostly in Africa, south Asia, and Latin America. Meanwhile, the legacy of the Atlantic slave trade remains visible throughout much of the western hemisphere, where the African diaspora has given rise to distinctive communities as well as cultural traditions that have shaped societies as a whole throughout the Americas and the Caribbean.

CONCLUSION

During the early modern era, many sub-Saharan Africans continued the tradition of living in small kinship groups while others built states and traded with Muslim societies. Yet Africans also experienced dramatic changes as they participated in the formation of an integrated Atlantic Ocean basin. Among the agents of change were European merchant-mariners who sought to trade in sub-Saharan Africa. They brought European manufactured goods and introduced American food crops that fueled population growth throughout Africa. But they also encouraged a vast expansion of existing slave-trading networks as they sought unfree laborers for plantations in the western hemisphere. The Atlantic slave trade violently removed sixteen million or more individuals from their home societies, which led to political turmoil and social disruption throughout much of sub-Saharan Africa. Once in the Americas, enslaved Africans formed an African diaspora from multiple encounters between peoples from all over sub-Saharan Africa and, as a result, were able to maintain some African traditions and to build new ones inspired by African knowledge. The individuals who made up the African diaspora profoundly influenced the development of societies in all slaveholding regions of the Caribbean and the Americas. Ultimately, Africans and African-descended people collaborated with others to bring about an end to the slave trade and the abolition of slavery itself.

STUDY TERMS

African diaspora (399)
Antonian movement (391)
Atlantic slave trade (392)
creole language (400)
Doña Beatriz (391)
Fulani (391)
Ghana (388)
Haiti (399)
Jenne (388)
Khoikhoi (391)
King Nzinga Mbemba (389)
Kongo (389)
Mali empire (388)
middle passage (395)
Ndongo (389)
Olaudah Equiano (401)
Queen Nzinga (389)
Songhay empire (388)
Sunni Ali (388)
Timbuktu (388)
triangular trade (393)

FOR FURTHER READING

Vince Brown. *The Reaper's Garden: Death and Power in the World of Atlantic Slavery.* Cambridge, Mass., 2008. A fascinating exploration of the ways death shaped multiple aspects of life in Jamaica in the time of slavery.

Michael L. Conniff and Thomas J. Davis. *Africans in the Americas: A History of the Black Diaspora.* New York, 2002. A comprehensive survey of African-European relations, the slave trade, and the African diaspora.

Christopher Ehret. *The Civilizations of Africa: A History to 1800.* Charlottesville, Va., 2002. An important contribution that views Africa in the context of world history.

Olaudah Equiano and Vincent Carretta. *The Interesting Life of Olaudah Equiano.* Rev. ed. New York, 2003. The autobiography of an enslaved man who turned into an abolitionist, with an informative introduction and editorial comments.

Philip Gould. *Barbaric Traffic: Commerce and Antislavery in the Eighteenth-Century Atlantic World.* Cambridge, 2003. A compelling study of Anglo-American antislavery literature that suggests the discourse was less a debate over the morality of slavery than a concern with the commercial aspects of the slave trade.

Patrick Manning. *The African Diaspora: A History through Culture.* New York, 2010. A truly global exploration of the connections wrought between Africans as they interacted across the continents after 1400.

Stephanie Smallwood. *Saltwater Slavery: A Middle Passage from Africa to American Diaspora.* Cambridge, Mass., 2008. A harrowing look at the process of becoming enslaved from the perspective of enslaved people themselves.

James H. Sweet. *Recreating Africa: Culture, Kinship, and Religion in the African-Portuguese World, 1441-1770.* Chapel Hill, N.C., 2006. An engaging study of African slave culture in Portuguese Brazil and the process of creolization.

Dale W. Tomich. *Through the Prism of Slavery: Labor, Capital, and World Economy.* Lanham, Md., 2004. A brief overview of slavery's role in the development of global capitalism.

Jan Vansina. *Paths in the Rainforest: Toward a History of Political Tradition in Equatorial Africa.* Madison, 1990. A thoughtful analysis that considers both indigenous traditions and external influences on African history.

ZOOMING IN ON ENCOUNTERS
Matteo Ricci and Chiming Clocks in China

In January 1601 a mechanical clock chimed the hours for the first time in the city of Beijing. In the early 1580s, devices that Chinese people called "self-ringing bells" had arrived at the port of Macau with Portuguese merchants. Reports of them soon spread to the emperor in Beijing. The Roman Catholic missionary **Matteo Ricci** conceived the idea of impressing the emperor with mechanical clocks and then persuading him and his subjects to convert to Christianity. From his post at Macau, Ricci let imperial authorities know that he could supply the emperor with a chiming clock. When the emperor **Wanli** (reigned 1572–1620) granted him permission to travel to Beijing and establish a mission, Ricci took with him a large mechanical clock intended for public display and a smaller clock for the emperor's personal use.

Emperor Wanli was enchanted by the chiming clocks, and they soon became the rage in elite society throughout China. Wealthy Chinese merchants paid handsome sums

Matteo Ricci (maht-TAY-oh REET-chee)
Wanli (wahn-LEE)

European-style buildings on the waterfront in eighteenth-century Guangzhou, where foreign merchants conducted their business.
The Picture Art Collection/Alamy Stock Photo

for them, and Europeans often found that business went better if they presented clocks to the government officials they dealt with. In the eighteenth century the imperial court maintained a workshop to manufacture and repair mechanical clocks and watches. Although most Chinese people could not afford to purchase mechanical clocks, commoners could admire the large, chiming clock Matteo Ricci installed outside his residence in Beijing.

Chiming clocks did not have the effect that Ricci desired. The emperor showed no interest in Christianity, and the missionaries attracted only small numbers of Chinese converts. However, by opening the doors of the imperial court to the missionaries, the self-ringing bells symbolized the increasing engagement between east Asian and European peoples.

CHAPTER OVERVIEW

By linking all the world's regions and peoples, the European voyages of exploration inaugurated a new era in world history. Yet transoceanic connections influenced different societies in very different ways. In contrast to sub-Saharan Africa, where the Atlantic slave trade provoked turmoil, for the most part east Asian lands benefited greatly from long-distance trade, since it brought silver, which stimulated their economies. East Asian societies benefited also from American plant crops that made their way across the seas as part of the Columbian exchange.

Unlike societies in the Americas, where Europeans profoundly influenced historical development from the time of their arrival, east Asian societies controlled their own affairs until the nineteenth century. Because of its political and cultural preeminence, China remained the dominant power in east Asia. China was also a remarkably prosperous land. Indeed, with its huge population, enormous productive capacity, and strong demand for silver, China was a leading economic powerhouse driving world trade in early modern times. By the late eighteenth century, however, China was experiencing social and economic change that eventually caused instability.

During the seventeenth and eighteenth centuries, Japan also underwent major transformations. The **Tokugawa** *shoguns* unified the Japanese islands for the first time and laid a foundation for long-term economic growth. While tightly restricting contacts and relations with the larger world, Tokugawa Japan generated a distinctive set of social and cultural traditions. Those developments helped fashion a Japan that would play a decisive role in global affairs by the twentieth century.

CHRONOLOGY	
1368–1644	Ming dynasty (China)
1368–1398	Reign of Hongwu
1403–1424	Reign of Yongle
1552–1610	Life of Matteo Ricci
1572–1620	Reign of Emperor Wanli
1600–1867	Tokugawa shogunate (Japan)
1616–1626	Reign of Nurhaci
1642–1693	Life of Ihara Saikaku
1644–1911	Qing dynasty (China)
1661–1722	Reign of Kangxi
1736–1795	Reign of Qianlong

THE QUEST FOR POLITICAL STABILITY

During the thirteenth and fourteenth centuries, China was ruled by the Yuan dynasty (1279–1368) of nomadic Mongol warriors. Mongol overlords ignored Chinese political and cultural traditions, and they displaced Chinese bureaucrats in favor of foreign administrators. When the Yuan dynasty came to an end, the Ming emperors who succeeded it sought to erase all signs of Mongol influence and restore traditional ways to China. Looking to the Tang and Song dynasties for inspiration, they built a powerful imperial state, revived the civil service staffed by Confucian scholars, and promoted Confucian thought. Rulers of the succeeding Qing dynasty were themselves **Manchus** of nomadic origin, but they, too, worked zealously to promote Chinese ways. Ming and Qing emperors alike were deeply conservative: their principal concern was to maintain stability in a large, agrarian society, so they adopted policies that favored Chinese political and cultural traditions. The state they fashioned governed China for more than half a millennium.

The Ming Dynasty

Ming Government When the Yuan dynasty collapsed, the Ming dynasty (1368–1644) restored Han Chinese rule to

Tokugawa (TOH-koo-GAH-wah)
shogun (SHOH-gun)
Qing (chihng)

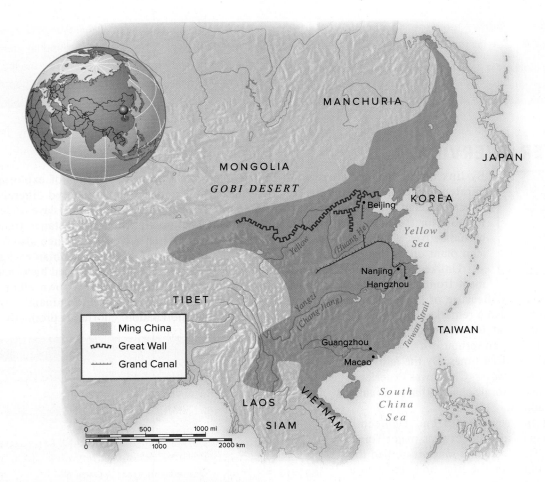

MAP 23.1 Ming China, 1368-1644

Locate the old Ming capital at Nanjing and the new Ming capital at Beijing.

Why would the Ming emperors have wanted to move so far north?

China. Hongwu (reigned 1368-1398), founder of the Ming ("brilliant") dynasty, built a tightly centralized state. As emperor, Hongwu made extensive use of mandarins, imperial officials who oversaw the implementation of government policies throughout China. He also placed great trust in eunuchs, on the assumption that they could not generate families who might one day challenge imperial authority. The emperor Yongle (reigned 1403-1424) launched a series of naval expeditions that went as far as Malindi in east Africa. Yongle's successors discontinued the expeditions but maintained the centralized state that Hongwu had established.

The Great Wall The Ming emperors were determined to prevent new invasions. In 1421 Yongle moved the capital

from Nanjing in the south to Beijing to keep closer watch on the Mongols and other nomadic peoples in the north. The later Ming emperors sought to protect their realm by building new fortifications, including the **Great Wall** of China, along the northern border. The Great Wall had precedents dating back to the fourth century B.C.E., but its construction was a Ming dynasty project. Workers by the hundreds of thousands labored throughout the late fifteenth and sixteenth centuries to build a stone and brick barrier that ran some 2,500 kilometers (1,550 miles). The Great Wall was 10 to 15 meters (33 to 49 feet) high, and it featured watch towers, signal towers, and accommodations for troops stationed at the border.

The Ming emperors also set out to eradicate Mongol and other foreign influences and to create a stable society in the image of the Chinese past. Respect for Chinese traditions facilitated the restoration of institutions that the Mongols had ignored or suppressed. The government sponsored study of Chinese cultural traditions, especially

Hongwu (hawng-woo)
eunuch (YOO-nuhk)
Yongle (yong-lay)

A portion of the Great Wall in Jinshanlang, Hebei province.

Benjamin B/Shutterstock

Confucianism and the reestablishment of imperial academies and regional colleges. Most important, the Ming state restored the system of **civil service examinations** that Mongol rulers had neglected.

Ming Decline The vigor of early Ming rule did not survive beyond the mid-sixteenth century, when a series of problems weakened the dynasty. From the 1520s to the 1560s, pirates and smugglers operated almost at will along the east coast of China. Suppression of the pirates took more than forty years, partly because of an increasingly inept imperial government. The later Ming emperors lived extravagantly in the **Forbidden City**, a vast complex in Beijing that was isolated from the outside world and only received news about what was happening in the rest of China from eunuch servants and administrators. The emperors sometimes ignored government affairs for decades, and powerful eunuchs won favor by providing for their amusement. Over time, corruption and inefficiency spread throughout the government and weakened the Ming state.

Ming Collapse When a series of famines struck China during the early seventeenth century, the government was unable to organize effective relief efforts. During the 1630s peasants organized revolts throughout China. To complicate matters further, Manchu forces invaded from the north. In 1644 Chinese rebel forces captured the Ming capital at Beijing. Manchu invaders allied with an army loyal to the Ming, crushed the rebels, and recovered Beijing. The Manchus portrayed themselves as avengers who saved the capital from dangerous rebels, but instead of restoring Ming rule they moved their own capital to Beijing and displaced the Ming dynasty.

The Qing Dynasty

The Manchus When the Ming dynasty fell, Manchus poured south into China from their homeland of Manchuria. The victors proclaimed a new dynasty, the Qing ("pure"), which ruled China until the early twentieth century (1644-1911). The Manchus were primarily pastoral nomads whose remote ancestors had traded with China since the Qin dynasty. During the late sixteenth and early seventeenth centuries, an ambitious chieftain named **Nurhaci** (reigned 1616-1626) unified Manchu tribes into a centralized state and organized a powerful military force. During the 1620s and 1630s, the Manchu army captured Korea and Mongolia and launched small-scale invasions into China. After their seizure of Beijing in 1644, the Manchus moved to extend their authority throughout China. By the early 1680s they had consolidated the Qing dynasty's hold throughout the land.

Establishment of the Qing dynasty was due partly to Manchu military might and partly to Chinese support for the Manchus. During the 1630s and 1640s, many Chinese generals and Confucian scholar-bureaucrats deserted the Ming dynasty because of its corruption and inefficiency. The Manchu ruling elites were schooled in the Chinese language and Confucian thought, and they were often more respected by the Chinese than the high administrators of the Ming dynasty itself.

Yet the Manchus were also careful to preserve their own ethnic and cultural identity. They outlawed intermarriage between the Manchus and Chinese and forbade the Chinese to travel to Manchuria or to learn the Manchurian language. Qing authorities also forced Chinese men to shave the front of their heads and grow a Manchu-style queue (somewhat like a ponytail) as a sign of submission to the dynasty.

Kangxi and His Reign The long reigns of two particularly effective emperors, **Kangxi** (1661-1722) and **Qianlong** (1736-1795), helped mute the tensions between the Manchus and Chinese and allowed the Manchus to consolidate their hold on China. Kangxi was a Confucian scholar as well as an enlightened ruler. He studied the Confucian classics and sought to apply their teachings through his policies. For example, he organized flood-control and irrigation projects on the Confucian precept that rulers should look after the welfare of their subjects and promote agriculture. He also generously patronized Confucian schools and academies.

Kangxi was also a conqueror, and he oversaw the construction of a vast empire. He conquered the island of Taiwan, where Ming loyalists had retreated after being expelled

Nurhaci (NOOR-hacheh)
Kangxi (kahng-shee)
Qianlong (chyahn-lawng)

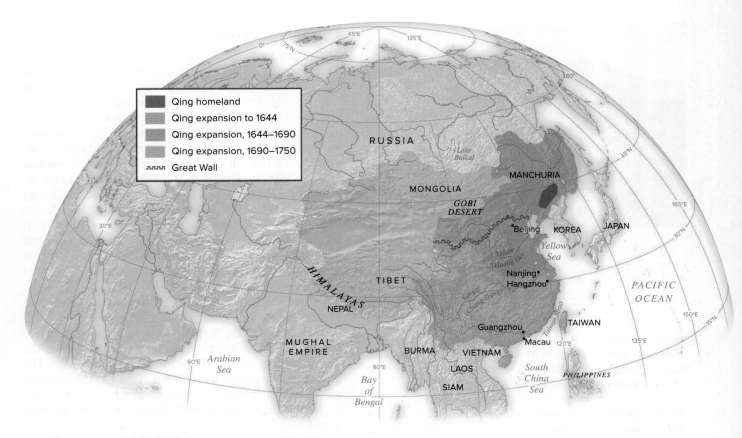

MAP 23.2 The Qing empire, 1644–1911

Compare this map with Map 23.1.

Why would the Qing emperors have wanted to incorporate such extensive territories in Mongolia and Tibet into their empire?

from southern China, and absorbed it into his empire. Like his predecessors of the Han and Tang dynasties, Kangxi sought to forestall problems with nomadic peoples by projecting Chinese influence into central Asia. His conquests in Mongolia and central Asia extended almost to the Caspian Sea, and he imposed a Chinese protectorate over Tibet. Kangxi's grandson Qianlong continued this expansion of Chinese influence by consolidating Kangxi's conquests in central Asia and by making Vietnam, Burma, and Nepal tributary states of the Qing dynasty.

Qianlong and His Reign Qianlong's reign marked the height of the Qing dynasty. Like Kangxi, Qianlong was a sophisticated and learned man. During his long, stable, and prosperous reign, the imperial treasury collected so much wealth that on four occasions Qianlong canceled tax collections. Toward the end of his reign, however, Qianlong delegated many responsibilities to his favorite eunuchs. His successors continued that practice, and by the nineteenth century the Qing dynasty faced serious difficulties. Throughout the reign of Qianlong, however, China remained a wealthy and well-organized land.

The Son of Heaven and the Scholar-Bureaucrats

Although Qing rulers usually appointed Manchus to the highest political posts, they relied on the same governmental apparatus that the Ming emperors had established. Indeed, for more than five hundred years, the autocratic state created by the Ming emperor Hongwu governed China's fortunes.

The Son of Heaven If the emperor of China during the Ming and Qing dynasties was not quite a god, he was more than a mere mortal. Chinese tradition held that he was the **Son of Heaven**, the human being designated by heavenly powers to maintain order on the earth. He led a privileged life within the walls of the Forbidden City. Hundreds of concubines resided in his harem, and thousands of eunuchs looked after his every need. Everything about his person and the institution he represented conveyed a sense of awesome authority. The imperial wardrobe and personal effects bore designs no one else was allowed to wear, for instance, and it was forbidden throughout the realm to write the characters of the emperor's name. Individuals who had the rare privilege of a personal audience with the emperor had to perform the **kowtow**—three kneelings and nine head knockings. Those who gave even minor offense faced having their bare buttocks flogged with bamboo canes.

The Scholar-Bureaucrats

Day-to-day governance of the empire fell to scholar-bureaucrats appointed by the emperor. With few exceptions these officials came from the class of well-educated and highly literate men known as the scholar-gentry. These men had earned academic degrees by passing rigorous civil service examinations, and they dominated China's political and social life.

Preparations for the examinations began at an early age, either in local schools or with private tutors. By the time students were eleven or twelve years old, they had memorized several thousand characters that were necessary to deal with the Confucian curriculum, including the *Analects* of Confucius and other standard works. They followed those studies with instruction in calligraphy, poetry, and essay composition.

Though painted in the nineteenth century, this portrait depicts Kangxi in his imperial regalia as he looked at about age fifty. Kangxi reigned for sixty-one years, making him the longest-ruling emperor in Chinese history.

Universal History Archive/Getty Images

Civil Service Examinations The examinations consisted of a battery of tests administered at the district, provincial, and metropolitan levels. Stiff official quotas restricted the number of successful candidates in each examination—only three hundred students could pass metropolitan examinations—and students frequently took the examinations several times before earning a degree.

The Examination System and Chinese Society The possibility of bureaucratic service—with prospects for rich social and financial rewards—ensured that competition for degrees was ferocious at all levels. Yet a degree did not ensure government service. During the Qing dynasty the empire's one million degree holders competed for twenty thousand official civil service positions, and only those who passed the metropolitan examinations could look forward to powerful positions in the imperial bureaucracy.

Yet the examination system was a pivotal institution. By opening the door to honor, power, and rewards, the

examinations encouraged serious pursuit of a formal education. Furthermore, since the system did not erect social barriers before its recruits, it provided an avenue for upward social mobility. Finally, in addition to selecting officials for government service, the education and examination system molded the personal values of those who managed day-to-day affairs in imperial China. By concentrating on Confucian classics and neo-Confucian commentaries, the examinations guaranteed that Confucianism would be at the heart of Chinese education and that Confucians would govern the state.

ECONOMIC AND SOCIAL CHANGES

By modeling their governmental structure on the centralized imperial states of earlier Chinese dynasties, the Ming and Qing emperors succeeded in their goal of restoring and maintaining traditional ways in China. They also sought to preserve the traditional hierarchical and patriarchal social order. However, while the emperors promoted conservative political and social policies, China experienced economic and social changes, partly as a result of influences and encounters from abroad. Agricultural production increased dramatically and fueled rapid population growth, and global trade brought China enormous wealth. These developments deeply influenced Chinese society and partly undermined the stability that the Ming and Qing emperors sought to preserve.

The Patriarchal Family

Filial Piety Moralists portrayed the Chinese people as one large family, and they extended family values to the larger society. **Filial piety**, for example, implied not only duties of children toward their parents but also loyalty of subjects toward the emperor. Like the imperial government, the ideal Chinese family was hierarchical, patriarchal, and authoritarian. The father was head of the household, and he passed leadership of the family to his eldest son. The veneration of ancestors, which the state

kowtow (kou-tou)

promoted, strengthened the authority of the patriarchs by honoring the male line of descent. Filial piety was the cornerstone of family values. Children had the duty to look after their parents' happiness and well-being, especially in their old age. Young children heard stories of sons who went so far as to cut off parts of their bodies to ensure that their parents had enough to eat.

The ideal Chinese family extended into patrilineal (tracing descent through the male line) descent groups such as the clan. Clans—whose members sometimes numbered in the thousands—assumed responsibilities such as the maintenance of local order, organization of local economies, and provision for welfare. Clan-supported education gave poor but promising relatives the opportunity to succeed in the civil service examinations. Finally, clans served as a means for the transmission of Confucian values from the gentry leaders to all social classes within the clan.

Gender Relations Within the family, Confucian principles subjected women to the authority of men. The subordination of females began at an early age. Chinese parents preferred boys over girls. Whereas a boy might have the opportunity to take the official examinations and become a government official, parents regarded a girl as a social and financial liability. Under those circumstances some people even resorted to female infanticide when a girl was born to them.

During the Ming and Qing dynasties, patriarchal authority over females probably became tighter than ever before in China. Since ancient times, relatives had discouraged widows from remarriage, but social pressures increased during the Ming dynasty. Friends and relatives not only encouraged widows to honor the memory of their departed husbands but also heaped honors on those who committed suicide and followed their spouses to the grave.

Foot binding, a custom that probably originated in the Song dynasty, became popular during the late Ming and Qing dynasties. Because small and dainty feet were considered attractive and even erotic, some families bound the feet of girls with strips of linen to make their feet even smaller. Bound feet could not grow naturally and so would not support the weight of an adult woman. For this reason, the practice of foot binding became most widespread among the wealthy classes, since it demonstrated an ability to support women who could not perform physical labor. Sometimes, however, commoners bound the feet of girls who they hoped could attract marriage prospects that would enhance the family's social standing.

Marriage itself was a contractual affair whose principal purpose was to continue the male line of descent. A bride became a member of the husband's family, and her position there was one of unambiguous subservience. Women could not divorce their husbands, but men could divorce their wives in cases where there were no offspring or where the wife was guilty of adultery, theft, or disobedience.

Thus custom and law combined to strengthen patriarchal authority in Chinese families during the Ming and Qing dynasties. However, while family life continued to develop along traditional lines, the larger Chinese society underwent considerable change between the sixteenth and eighteenth centuries.

Population Growth and Economic Development

China was a predominantly agricultural society, a fact that meshed agreeably with the Confucian view that land was

What's Left Out? ▪ ▪▪ ▪▪ ▪▪ ▪▪ ▪▪▪

The practice of foot binding in China was painful for the (mostly elite) women who underwent the process. There is also no doubt that it permanently limited women's mobility, increasing their dependency on others around them. Western observers certainly saw the practice as oppressive. But it is important to remember that foot binding was only one example of many around the world in which women altered or deformed their bodies in the name of beauty. In fact, in the eighteenth and nineteenth centuries—the very same period westerners were pointing out the cruelties and pain associated with foot binding—middle-class and elite western European women were wearing whale-bone corsets around their torsos to alter their shapes. Like foot binding, corseting was painful and could permanently deform women's bodies. Corseting also had significant adverse health effects for women, including breathing and lung disorders, prolapsed uteruses, digestive problems, and back pain. The point is that although ideals of female beauty differed from place to place, Chinese society during the Qing period was not distinctive for encouraging some women to alter their bodies to achieve a physical ideal. Moreover, many of the methods for attaining these ideals of female beauty, including foot binding and corseting, also had secondary effects of limiting the mobility of women.

Sources: John Robert Shepherd. *Foot-Binding as Fashion: Ethnicity, Labor, and Status in Traditional China.* Seattle: University of Washington Press, 2019; Leigh Summers. *Bound to Please: A History of the Victorian Corset.* Oxford: Berg, 2001.

the source of everything praiseworthy. Yet only a small fraction of China's land is suitable for planting: even today only about 11 percent is in cultivation. To feed the country's large population, China's farmers relied on intensive, garden-style agriculture that was highly productive. On its strong agrarian foundation, China supported a large population and built the most highly commercialized economy of the preindustrial world.

American Food Crops By intensively cultivating every available parcel of land, Chinese peasants increased their yields of traditional food crops—especially rice, wheat, and millet—until the seventeenth century. As peasants approached the upper limits of agricultural productivity, Spanish merchants coming by way of the Philippines introduced American food crops to China. American maize (corn), sweet potatoes, and peanuts permitted Chinese farmers to take advantage of soils that previously had gone uncultivated. The introduction of new crops increased the food supply and supported further population growth.

Population Growth In spite of recurring epidemic diseases such as plague, China's population rose rapidly from 100 million in 1500 to 160 million in 1600. By 1750 it had surged to 225 million. However, this rapid demographic growth set the stage for future economic and social problems, since agricultural production could not keep pace with population over a long term.

Although an increasing population placed pressure on Chinese resources, it offered opportunities for entrepreneurs. Indeed, entrepreneurs had access to a large, mobile labor force, which meant they were able to recruit workers readily at low cost. After the mid-sixteenth century the Chinese economy benefited also from the influx of Japanese and American silver, which stimulated trade and financed further commercial expansion.

Foreign Trade Global trade brought tremendous prosperity to China, especially during the early Qing dynasty. Chinese workers produced vast quantities of silk, porcelain, lacquerware, and tea for consumers in the Indian Ocean basin, central Asia, and Europe. Chinese imports were relatively few, and thus the most important form of payment for exports was silver bullion, which supported the silver-based Chinese economy and fueled manufacturing.

Economic growth and commercial expansion took place mostly in an atmosphere of tight government regulation. Although the Ming emperor Yongle had sponsored a series of maritime expeditions (1405–1433) in the Indian Ocean basin, his successors withdrew their support for such activities and even tried to prevent Chinese subjects from dealing with foreign peoples. In its effort to pacify southern China during the later seventeenth century, the Qing government tried to end maritime activity altogether. An imperial edict of 1656 forbade "even a plank from drifting to the sea," and in 1661 the emperor Kangxi ordered the evacuation of the southern coastal regions. Those policies had only a limited effect, and when Qing forces pacified southern China in the 1680s, government authorities rescinded the strictest measures. Thereafter, however, Qing authorities closely supervised the activities of foreign merchants in China. Portuguese merchants were allowed to operate only at the port of Macau, and British agents had to deal exclusively with the official merchant guild in Guangzhou.

Government policies also discouraged the organization of large-scale commercial ventures by Chinese merchants. As a result, it was impossible to maintain shipyards that could construct large sailing ships capable of traveling long distances. Similarly, it was impossible to organize large trading firms like the English East India Company or the Dutch VOC.

Trade and Migration to Southeast Asia Nevertheless, thousands of Chinese merchants worked

Why It Matters

The Columbian Exchange

Did you know that the Columbian exchange was one of the factors that led to dramatic population growth in China during the sixteenth century? Even though Chinese people were not involved in the initial period of contact between Europeans and the people of the Americas, the Columbian exchange nevertheless had an impact on China. Beginning in the sixteenth century, food crops native to the Americas—such as corn, sweet potatoes, and peanuts—made their way to China via trade networks. These crops both changed Chinese cuisine and allowed more land to be cultivated. The result was dramatic population growth, which had both positive and negative effects for Chinese people over the long term. In this case, consider the ways that events and processes that occurred in the Americas played an important but unforeseen role in shaping historical developments in east Asia.

SOURCES FROM THE PAST

Qianlong on Chinese Trade with England

Qing administrators tightly restricted foreign trade. Foreign merchants had to deal with government-approved agents outside the city walls of Guangzhou and had to depart as soon as they had completed their business. In 1793 a British diplomat representing King George III of England bestowed gifts on the emperor Qianlong (reigned 1735–1796) and petitioned for the right to trade at ports other than Guangzhou. In a letter to King George, Qianlong outlined his views on Chinese trade with England. His letter also clearly demonstrates the active role of the imperial government in the formation of commercial and economic policies.

You, O king, from afar have yearned after the blessings of our civilization, and in your eagerness to come into touch with our influence have sent an embassy across the sea bearing a memorandum. I have already taken note of your respectful spirit of submission, have treated your mission with extreme favor and loaded it with gifts, besides issuing a mandate to you, O king, and honoring you with the bestowal of valuable presents. . . .

Yesterday your ambassador petitioned my ministers to memorialize me regarding your trade with China, but his proposal is not consistent with our dynastic usage and cannot be entertained. Hitherto, all European nations, including your own country's barbarian merchants, have carried on their trade with our Celestial Empire at Guangzhou. Such has been the procedure for many years, although our Celestial Empire possesses all things in prolific abundance and lacks no product within its own borders. There was therefore no need to import the manufactures of outside barbarians in exchange for our own produce. But as the tea, silk, and porcelain which the Celestial Empire produces are absolute necessities to European nations and to yourselves, we have permitted, as a signal mark of favor, that trading agents should be established at Guangzhou, so that your wants might be supplied and your country thus participate in our beneficence. But your ambassador has now put forward new requests which completely fail to recognize our throne's principle to "treat strangers from afar with indulgence," and to exercise a pacifying control over barbarian tribes the world over. . . . Your England is not the only nation trading at Guangzhou. If other nations, following your bad example, wrongfully importune my ear with further impossible requests, how will it be possible for me to treat them with easy indulgence? Nevertheless, I do not forget the lonely remoteness of your island, cut off from the world by intervening wastes of sea, nor do I overlook your excusable ignorance of the usages of our Celestial Empire. I have consequently commanded my ministers to enlighten your ambassador on the subject, and have ordered the departure of the mission. . . .

If, after the receipt of this explicit decree, you lightly give ear to the representations of your subordinates and allow your barbarian merchants to proceed to Zhejiang and Tianjin, with the object of landing and trading there, the ordinances of my Celestial Empire are strict in the extreme, and the local officials, both civil and military, are bound reverently to obey the law of the land. Should your vessels touch the shore, your merchants will assuredly never be permitted to land or to reside there, but will be subject to instant expulsion. In that event your barbarian merchants will have had a long journey for nothing. Do not say that you were not warned in due time! Tremblingly obey and show no negligence! A special mandate!

> Does the language of Emperor Qianlong here signal an attitude of deference or an attitude of superiority to the English?

> What will the consequences be for English traders who try to trade outside Guangzhou in spite of the emperor's ban?

For Further Reflection

■ What considerations might have prompted the Chinese government to take such a restrictive approach to foreign trade?

Source: J. O. P. Bland. *Annals and Memoirs of the Court of Peking.* Boston: Houghton Mifflin, 1914, pp. 325–31. (Translation slightly modified.)

A Ming-era vase painting depicts a woman weaving silk as an attendant pours tea. Silk and tea were among the exports China produced for global trade.
DeAgostini/Getty Images

formation of economic and social policies. During the Tang and Song dynasties, the imperial government had encouraged technological innovation as a foundation of military and economic strength. In contrast, the Ming and Qing regimes favored political and social stability over technological innovation.

Alongside government policy, the abundance of skilled workers discouraged technological innovation. When employers wanted to increase production, they found that hiring additional workers was cost-effective, and thus there was little need for new technologies. In the short run this tactic kept most of China's population gainfully employed. Over the longer term, however, the fact that Europeans were investing in a variety of technological innovations by the late eighteenth century meant that there would be an imbalance in technological knowledge that would favor Europeans by the nineteenth century.

Gentry, Commoners, Soldiers, and "Mean" People

Privileged Classes Aside from the emperor and his family, scholar-bureaucrats and gentry (people from the highest social classes) occupied the most exalted positions in Chinese society. Scholar-bureaucrats had much in common with the gentry: they came largely from gentry ranks, and after leaving government service they usually rejoined gentry society. The scholar-bureaucrats and the gentry functioned as intermediaries between the imperial government and local society. By organizing water-control projects and public security measures, they played a crucial role in the management of local society.

Scholar-bureaucrats and gentry wore distinctive clothing—black gowns with blue borders adorned with various rank insignia—and commoners addressed them with honorific terms. They also received favorable legal treatment and enjoyed immunity from corporal punishment as well as exemption from labor service and taxes.

Most of the gentry owned land, which was their major source of income. Some were also silent business partners of merchants and entrepreneurs. Their principal source of income, however, was the government service to which their academic degrees gave them access. In contrast to landed elites elsewhere, who often lived on rural estates, China's gentry resided largely in cities and towns, where they tended to political, social, and financial affairs.

either individually or in partnerships, plying the waters of the China seas to link China with global trade networks. Chinese merchants were especially prominent in Manila (in the Philippines), where they exchanged silk and porcelain for American silver that came across the Pacific Ocean from Mexico. They were also frequent visitors at the Dutch colonial capital of Batavia, where they supplied the VOC with silk and porcelain in exchange for silver and Indonesian spices. Entrepreneurial Chinese merchants ventured also to lands throughout southeast Asia in search of tropical products for Chinese consumers. Indeed, the early modern era was an age when merchants established a prominent Chinese presence throughout southeast Asia.

Government and Technology During the Tang and Song dynasties, Chinese engineers had produced a veritable flood of inventions, and China was the world's leader in technology. However, by early Ming times technological innovation had slowed. Part of the explanation for the slowdown had to do with the role of the government in the

Working Classes Confucian tradition ranked three broad classes of commoners below the gentry: peasants, artisans or workers, and merchants. By far the biggest class consisted of peasants: a designation that covered everyone from day laborers to small landlords. Confucian principles regarded peasants as the most honorable of the three classes, because they supplied the entire population with food.

Chinese peasants plowing, ca. 1770.
Chronicle/Alamy Stock Photo

bureaucrats in the highest command positions, even at the expense of military effectiveness.

THE CONFUCIAN TRADITION AND NEW CULTURAL INFLUENCES

The Ming and Qing emperors looked to Chinese traditions for guidance in framing their cultural as well as their political and social policies. They provided generous support for Confucianism, and they ensured that formal education in China revolved around Confucian thought and values. Yet demographic and urban growth also encouraged the emergence of a vibrant popular culture in Chinese cities, and European missionaries introduced the Chinese to Roman Catholic Christianity and European science and technology as well.

Neo-Confucianism and Pulp Fiction

Imperial sponsorship of Chinese cultural traditions meant primarily support for the Confucian tradition, especially as systematized by the Song dynasty scholar **Zhu Xi**, the most prominent architect of neo-Confucianism. Zhu Xi combined the moral, ethical, and political values of Confucius with the logical rigor and speculative power of Buddhist philosophy. He emphasized the values of self-discipline, filial piety, and obedience to established rulers, all of which appealed to Ming and Qing emperors seeking to maintain stability in their vast realm. To promote Confucian values, the Ming and Qing emperors supported educational programs at many levels throughout the land.

Popular Culture While the imperial courts promoted Confucianism, a lively popular culture took shape in the cities of China. Most urban residents did not have an advanced education and knew little about Confucius. Many were literate, however, and they found that popular novels were more intellectually engaging and met their needs for entertainment and diversion. Although Confucian scholars thought popular novels were crude, printing made it possible to produce them cheaply and in large numbers, and urban residents eagerly consumed them. Many of the novels had little literary merit, but their tales of conflict, horror, wonder, excitement, and sometimes unconcealed pornography appealed to readers.

Popular Novels Some popular novels, however, did offer thoughtful reflections on the world and human affairs. The historical novel *The Romance of the Three Kingdoms*, for example, explored the political intrigue that followed the collapse of the Han dynasty. *The Dream of the Red Chamber* told the story of cousins deeply in love who could not marry because of their families' wishes. Through the prism of a sentimental love story, the novel explored the complicated dynamics of wealthy scholar-gentry families.

The category of artisans and workers encompassed a wide spectrum of occupations. Despite their lower status, crafts workers, tailors, barbers, and physicians generally enjoyed higher income than peasants. Artisans and workers were usually employees of the state or of gentry and merchant families, but they also pursued their occupations as self-employed persons.

Merchants Merchants, from street peddlers to individuals of enormous wealth and influence, ranked at the bottom of the Confucian social hierarchy. Because moralists looked on them as unscrupulous social parasites, merchants enjoyed little legal protection. Yet Chinese merchants often garnered official support for their enterprises through bribery of government bureaucrats or through profit-sharing arrangements with gentry families. Indeed, the participation of gentry families in commercial ventures such as warehousing, moneylending, and pawnbroking blurred the distinction between gentry and merchants. In addition, merchants blurred the distinction further by preparing their sons for government examinations, which could result in appointment to civil service positions and promotion to gentry status. Although Qing China was still a basically agricultural land, the increasing wealth of the merchant classes signaled that manufacturing and commerce had become much more economically important than in ancient times.

Lower Classes Beyond the Confucian social hierarchy were members of the military forces and "mean" people, such as enslaved people, indentured servants, entertainers, and prostitutes. Confucian moralists regarded armed forces as a wretched but necessary evil and attempted to avoid military dominance of society by placing civilian

Zhu Xi (ZHOO SHEE)
neo-Confucianism (NEE-oh kuhn-FYEW-shuhn-iz′m)

The Return of Christianity to China

Nestorian Christians had established churches and monasteries in China as early as the seventh century C.E., and Roman Catholic communities were prominent in Chinese commercial centers during the Yuan dynasty. After the outbreak of epidemic plague and the collapse of the Yuan dynasty in the fourteenth century, however, Christianity disappeared from China. When Roman Catholic missionaries returned in the sixteenth century, they had to start from scratch in their efforts to win converts.

Matteo Ricci Founder of the mission to China was the Italian Jesuit Matteo Ricci (1552–1610), who had the ambitious goal of converting China to Christianity, beginning with the Ming emperor Wanli. Ricci was a brilliant and learned man as well as a polished diplomat, and he became a popular figure at the Ming court. On arrival at Macau in 1582, Ricci immersed himself in the study of the Chinese language and the Confucian classics. By the time he first traveled to Beijing and visited the imperial court in 1601, Ricci was able to write learned Chinese and converse fluently with Confucian scholars.

Ricci's mastery of the Chinese language and literature opened doors for the **Jesuits**, who then impressed their hosts with European science and mechanical gadgetry such as glass prisms, harpsichords, and especially—as we saw in the introduction to this chapter—"self-ringing bells."

Confucianism and Christianity The Jesuits sought to capture Chinese interest with European science and technology, but their ultimate goal was to win converts. Ricci, for example, tried to make Christianity seem familiar by arguing that the doctrines of Confucius and Jesus were very similar, if not identical. The Jesuits also held religious services in the Chinese language and allowed converts to continue the time-honored practice of venerating their ancestors.

In spite of their tolerance, flexibility, and genuine respect for their hosts, the Jesuits attracted few converts in China. By the mid-eighteenth century, Chinese Christians numbered about two hundred thousand—a tiny proportion of the Chinese population of 225 million. Many Chinese people hesitated to adopt Christianity partly because of its exclusivity: like Islam, Christianity claimed to be the only true religion, so conversion implied that the time-honored traditions of Confucianism, Daoism, and Buddhism were fallacious creeds—a proposition most Chinese people were unwilling to accept.

End of the Jesuit Mission Ultimately, the Roman Catholic mission in China came to an end because of squabbles between the Jesuits and members of the Franciscan and Dominican orders, who also sought converts in China. Jealous of the Jesuits' presence at the imperial court, they complained to the pope about their rivals' tolerance of Chinese traditions. The pope sided with the critics and in the early eighteenth century issued several proclamations ordering missionaries in China to conduct services according to European standards. In response, the emperor Kangxi ordered an end to the preaching of Christianity in China. By the mid-eighteenth century, the mission had weakened so much that it had effectively come to an end.

The Roman Catholic mission to China did not attract large numbers of converts; nonetheless, it had important cultural effects. In letters, reports, and other writings distributed widely throughout Europe, the Jesuits described China as an orderly and rational society. The rational morality of Confucianism appealed to the Enlightenment intellectuals, who sought alternatives to Christianity as the foundation for ethics and morality. Thus for the first time since Marco Polo, strong European interest in east Asian societies was stimulated.

THE UNIFICATION OF JAPAN

During the late sixteenth and early seventeenth centuries, the political unification of Japan ended an extended period of civil disorder. Like the Ming and Qing emperors in China, the Tokugawa leaders sought to lay a foundation for long-term political and social stability by promoting conservative values and tightly restricting foreign influence in Japan. As in China, however, demographic expansion and economic growth fostered social and cultural change in Japan, and merchants introduced Chinese and European influences into Japan.

The Tokugawa Shogunate

From the twelfth through the sixteenth century, a shogun (military governor) ruled Japan through retainers who received political rights and large estates in exchange for military services. Theoretically, the shogun ruled as a temporary stand-in for the Japanese emperor. In fact, however, the emperor was nothing more than a figurehead. After the fourteenth century the conflicting ambitions of *shoguns* and retainers led to constant turmoil, and by the sixteenth century, Japan was in a state of civil war. Japanese historians often refer to the sixteenth century as the era of *sengoku*—"the country at war."

Tokugawa Ieyasu Toward the end of the sixteenth century, a series of military leaders brought about the unification of the land. In 1600 the last of those leaders, **Tokugawa Ieyasu** (reigned 1600–1616), established

---

Buddhism (BOO-diz'm)
Tokugawa (TAW-koo-GAH-wah)
sengoku (sehn-goh-koo)

a military government known as the Tokugawa **bakufu** (tent government, because it theoretically was only a temporary replacement for the emperor's rule). Ieyasu and his descendants ruled the bakufu as *shoguns* from 1600 until the end of the Tokugawa dynasty in 1867.

The principal aim of the Tokugawa *shoguns* was to prevent the return of civil war. Consequently, the *shoguns* needed to control the **daimyo** (great names), powerful territorial lords who ruled most of Japan from their vast, hereditary landholdings. Each maintained a government, an independent judiciary, and schools, and each circulated paper money. Moreover, after the mid-sixteenth century, many daimyo established relationships with European mariners, from whom they learned how to manufacture and use gunpowder weapons, which they turned against one another.

bakufu (bah-kuh-fuh)
daimyo (DEYEM-yoh)

Control of the Daimyo From the castle town of Edo (modern Tokyo), the *shogun* sought to extend his control over the daimyo through the policy of "alternate attendance," which required daimyo to maintain their families at Edo and spend every other year at the Tokugawa court. This policy enabled the *shoguns* to keep an eye on the daimyo, and it encouraged daimyo to spend their money on comfortable lives in Edo rather than on military forces that could challenge the bakufu. The *shoguns* also discouraged the daimyo from visiting one another and even required daimyo to obtain permission to meet with the emperor.

Control of Foreign Relations In an effort to prevent European influences from destabilizing the land, the Tokugawa *shoguns* closely controlled relations between Japan and the outside world. A primary concern was that Europeans might threaten the bakufu by making alliances

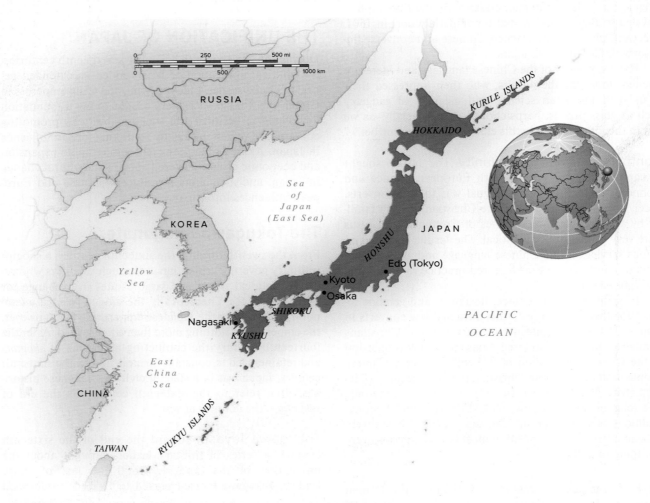

MAP 23.3 Tokugawa Japan, 1600–1867

Consider Japan's position in relation to China, Korea, and Russia.

Would it have been easy or difficult to enforce the ban on foreign trade during most of the period?

with daimyo and supplying them with weapons. Thus during the 1630s the *shoguns* issued a series of edicts sharply restricting Japanese relations with other lands.

These policies forbade Japanese people from going abroad on pain of death and prohibited the construction of large ships. It expelled Europeans from Japan and prohibited foreign merchants from trading in Japanese ports. But the policies did allow carefully controlled trade with Asian lands, and it permitted small numbers of Chinese and Dutch merchants to trade under tight restrictions at the southern port city of Nagasaki. As a result, Japan was never completely isolated from the outside world.

Economic and Social Change

By ending civil conflict and maintaining political stability, the Tokugawa *shoguns* set the stage for economic growth in Japan. Ironically, peace and a booming economy encouraged social change that undermined the order that the bakufu sought to preserve. Economic growth had its roots in increased agricultural production, especially of rice, cotton, silk, and indigo. In many parts of Japan, villages moved away from subsistence farming in favor of production for the market.

Population Growth Increased agricultural production brought about rapid demographic growth: during the seventeenth century the Japanese population rose by almost one-third, from twenty-two million to twenty-nine million. Thereafter, however, many families practiced population control to maintain or raise their standard of living. Between 1700 and 1850 the Japanese population grew only moderately, from twenty-nine million to thirty-two million. Contraception, late marriage, and abortion all played roles in limiting population growth, but the principal method of control was infanticide, euphemistically referred to as "thinning out the rice shoots." Japanese families resorted to these measures primarily because Japan was land poor, which made it easy for populations to strain available resources.

Social Change The Tokugawa era was an age of social as well as demographic change in Japan. Because of Chinese cultural influence, the Japanese social hierarchy followed Confucian precepts in ranking the ruling elites—including the daimyo and samurai warriors—as the most privileged class of society, followed by peasants and artisans. As in China, merchants ranked at the bottom. Yet the extended period of peace ushered in by Tokugawa rule undermined the social position of the ruling elites, who found their traditional role as local administrators redundant. Many of the ruling elite also fell into financial difficulty in this period because of rising prices and lavish lifestyles. As a result, many became indebted to rice brokers and gradually declined into genteel poverty.

Dutch sailing ships and smaller Japanese vessels mingle in Nagasaki Harbor, the only place the Japanese government allowed the Dutch to trade. Dutch merchants conducted their business on the artificial island of Deshima, at left.
CPA Media Pte Ltd/Alamy Stock Photo

Meanwhile, as in China, merchants in Japan became increasingly wealthy and prominent. Japanese cities flourished throughout the Tokugawa era—the population of Edo approached one million by 1700—and merchants prospered in the vibrant urban environment. Rice dealers, pawnbrokers, and sake merchants soon controlled more wealth than the ruling elites.

Neo-Confucianism, "Native Learning," and Floating Worlds

Neo-Confucianism in Japan Japanese culture had long been indebted to Chinese culture, and the influence of China continued throughout the Tokugawa era. Formal education began with the study of Chinese language and literature. As late as the nineteenth century, many Japanese scholars wrote their philosophical, legal, and religious works in Chinese. The common people embraced Buddhism, which had come to Japan from China, and Confucianism was the most influential philosophical system. Indeed, by the early eighteenth century, neo-Confucianism had become the official ideology of the Tokugawa bakufu.

"Native Learning"
However, even with Tokugawa sponsorship, neo-Confucianism did not dominate intellectual life in Japan. Some scholars sought to establish a sense of Japanese identity that did not depend on cultural kinship with China. Particularly during the eighteenth century, scholars of "native learning" scorned neo-Confucianism and even Buddhism as alien cultural imports and emphasized instead the importance of folk traditions and the indigenous Shinto religion for Japanese identity. Many scholars of native learning viewed Japanese people as superior to all others and glorified the supposed purity of Japanese society before its corruption by Chinese and other foreign influences.

Meanwhile, the emergence of a prosperous merchant class encouraged the development of a vibrant popular culture. During the seventeenth and eighteenth centuries, an exuberant middle-class culture flourished in cities such as Kyoto, Edo, and Osaka. In those and other cities, Japan's finest creative talents catered to middle-class appetites.

Floating Worlds
The centers of Tokugawa urban culture were the *ukiyo* (**"floating worlds"**), entertainment and pleasure quarters where teahouses, theaters, brothels, and public baths offered escape from the rigid rules of conduct that governed public behavior in Tokugawa society. In contrast to the solemn, serious proceedings of the imperial court and the bakufu, the popular culture of urban residents was secular and satirical. The main expressions

A colored woodcut by Okumura Masanobu depicts the audience at a seventeenth-century kabuki theater. Enthusiastic actors often ran down wooden ramps and played their roles among the audience.
Universal History Archive/Getty Images

of this lively culture were prose fiction and new forms of theater.

Ihara Saikaku (1642–1693), one of Japan's most prolific poets, helped create a new genre of prose literature, the "books of the floating world." Much of his fiction revolved around the themes of sex and love. In *The Life of a Man Who Lived for Love,* for example, Ihara chronicled the experiences of a townsman who devoted his life to a quest for sexual pleasure. Ihara's treatment of love stressed the erotic, and the brief, episodic stories that made up his work appealed to literate urban residents who were not inclined to pore over dense neo-Confucian treatises.

Beginning in the early seventeenth century, two new forms of drama became popular in Japanese cities. One was **kabuki** theater, which usually featured several acts consisting of lively and sometimes bawdy skits in which stylized acting combined with lyric singing, dancing, and spectacular staging. The other new dramatic form was **bunraku**, the puppet theater. In bunraku, chanters accompanied by music told a story acted out by puppets. Manipulated by a team of three, each puppet could execute the subtlest and most intricate movements, such as brushing a tear from the eye with the sleeve of a kimono. Both kabuki and bunraku attracted enthusiastic audiences in search of entertainment and diversion.

Christianity and Dutch Learning

Christian Missions Christian missionaries and European merchants also contributed their own distinctive threads to the cultural fabric of Tokugawa Japan. The Jesuit **Francis Xavier** opened the first Roman Catholic mission in 1549 and for a few decades experienced remarkable success. Several powerful daimyo adopted Christianity and ordered their subjects to do likewise. Many Japanese converts became enthusiastic Christians and worked to convert their compatriots to the new faith. By the 1580s about one hundred fifty thousand Japanese had converted to Christianity, and by 1615 Japanese Christians numbered about three hundred thousand.

Although Christians were only a tiny minority of the Japanese population, the popularity of Christianity generated a backlash among those seeking to preserve Japanese religious and cultural traditions. The Tokugawa *shoguns* restricted European access to Japan largely because of concerns that Christianity might serve as a cul-

tural bridge for alliances between daimyo and European adventurers, which in turn could threaten the bakufu. Meanwhile, Buddhist and Confucian scholars resented the Christian conviction that their faith was the only true doctrine.

Anti-Christian Campaign Between 1587 and 1639, *shoguns* promulgated several decrees ordering a halt to Christian missions and commanding Japanese Christians to renounce their faith. In 1612 the *shoguns* began rigorous enforcement of these decrees. They tortured and executed European missionaries who refused to leave the islands as well as Japanese Christians who refused to abandon their faith. The campaign was so effective that even some European missionaries abandoned Christianity. Most notable was the Portuguese Jesuit **Christovão Ferreira**, head of the Jesuit mission in Japan, who gave up Christianity under torture, adopted Buddhism, and interrogated many Europeans who fell into Japanese hands in the mid-seventeenth century. By the late seventeenth century, the anti-Christian campaign had claimed tens of thousands of lives, and Christianity survived only as a secret, underground religion.

Dutch Learning Tokugawa policies ensured that Christianity would not soon reappear in Japan, but they did not entirely prevent contacts between Europeans and the Japanese. After 1639 Dutch merchants trading at Nagasaki became Japan's principal source of information about the world beyond east Asia. A small number of Japanese scholars learned Dutch to communicate with the foreigners. Their studies, which they called **Dutch learning**, brought considerable knowledge of the outside world to Japan. After 1720 Tokugawa authorities lifted the ban on foreign books, and Dutch learning—especially European art and science—began to play a significant role in Japanese intellectual life. Indeed, by the mid-eighteenth century the Tokugawa *shoguns* themselves had become enthusiastic proponents of Dutch learning, and schools of European medicine and Dutch studies flourished in several Japanese cities.

---

kabuki (kah-BOO-kee)
bunraku (boon-RAH-koo)
Francis Xavier (fran-sis ZEY-vee-er)
Christovão Ferreira (chris-STOH-voh feh-RAY-rah)

CONCLUSION

Both China and Japan controlled their own affairs throughout the early modern era and avoided the turmoil that afflicted societies in the Americas and much of sub-Saharan Africa. Rulers of the Ming dynasty built a powerful, centralized state in China. They worked diligently to restore traditional ways by reviving Chinese political institutions and providing state sponsorship for neo-Confucianism. In the interest of stability, authorities also restricted encounters with foreigners by limiting foreign merchants' access to China and the activities of Christian missionaries. The succeeding Qing dynasty pursued similar policies. The Ming and Qing dynasties both brought political stability, but China experienced considerable social and economic change in early modern times. American food crops helped increase agricultural production, which fueled rapid population growth, and global trade stimulated the Chinese economy, which improved the position of merchants and artisans in society. The experience of the Tokugawa era in Japan was much like that of the Ming and Qing eras in China. The Tokugawa bakufu brought political order to the Japanese islands and closely controlled encounters with foreigners, but a vibrant economy promoted social change, which enhanced the status of merchants and artisans.

STUDY TERMS

bakufu (416)
bunraku (419)
Christovāo Ferreira (419)
civil service examinations (407)
daimyo (416)
Dutch learning (419)
filial piety (409)
floating worlds (418)
Forbidden City (407)
Francis Xavier (419)
Great Wall (406)
Jesuits (415)
kabuki (419)
Kangxi (407)
kowtow (409)
Manchus (405)
Matteo Ricci (404)
Nurhaci (407)
Qianlong (407)
sengoku (415)
Son of Heaven (408)
Tokugawa Ieyasu (415)
Tokugawa shoguns (405)
Wanli (404)
Zhu Xi (414)

FOR FURTHER READING

Timothy Brook. *The Troubled Empire: China in the Yuan and Ming Dynasties.* Cambridge, Mass., 2010. A readable and intriguing account of the Yuan and Ming dynasties.
——. *The Confusions of Pleasure: Commerce and Culture in Ming China.* Berkeley, 1998. A fascinating social and cultural analysis of Ming China focusing on the role of commerce as an agent of social change.
Adam Clulow. *The Company and the Shogun: The Dutch Encounter with Tokugawa Japan.* New York, 2013. Explores the Dutch East India Company's clashes with Tokugawa Japan over trade and diplomacy.
Mark C. Elliott. *The Manchu Way: The Eight Banners and Ethnic Identity in Late Imperial China.* Stanford, 2001. An important scholarly study focusing on relations between the Manchus and Chinese during the Qing dynasty.
Benjamin A. Elman. *A Cultural History of Civil Examinations in Late Imperial China.* Berkeley, 2000. A meticulous study of one of the most important institutions in Chinese history.
Susan Mann and Yu-Ying Cheng, eds. *Under Confucian Eyes: Writings on Gender in Chinese History.* Berkeley, 2001. A rich anthology of primary texts documenting the lives of women in imperial China.
Kenneth Pomeranz. *The Great Divergence: China, Europe, and the Making of the Modern World Economy.* Princeton, 2000. A pathbreaking scholarly study that illuminates the economic history of the early modern world through comparison of economic development in Asian and European lands.
William T. Rowe. *China's Last Empire: The Great Qing.* Cambridge, Mass., 2009. Revisionist history that challenges ideas of the Qing empire as inward-looking.
Ronald P. Toby. *State and Diplomacy in Early Modern Japan: Asia in the Development of the Tokugawa Bakufu.* Princeton, 1984. An important study dealing with Japanese trade and relations with other lands under Tokugawa rule.
H. Paul Varley. *Japanese Culture.* 4th ed. Honolulu, 2000. Places the cultural history of the Tokugawa era in its larger historical context.

ZOOMING IN ON TRADITIONS

Shah Jahan's Monument to Love and Allah

In 1635 Shah Jahan, the emperor of Mughal India, took his seat on the Peacock Throne. Seven years in the making, the Peacock Throne is probably the most spectacular seat on which any mortal human being has rested. Shah Jahan ordered the throne encrusted with ten million rupees' worth of diamonds, rubies, emeralds, and pearls. Atop the throne itself stood a magnificent, golden-bodied peacock with a huge ruby and a fifty-carat, pear-shaped pearl on its breast and a brilliant tail fashioned of sapphires and gems.

However, for all its splendor, the Peacock Throne ranks a distant second among the artistic projects Shah Jahan sponsored: pride of place goes to the Taj Mahal. Built over a period of eighteen years as a tomb for Shah Jahan's beloved wife, Mumtaz Mahal, who died during childbirth in 1631, the Taj Mahal is a graceful and elegant monument both to the departed empress and to Shah Jahan's Islamic faith.

Shah Jahan (shah jah-han)
Mumtaz Mahal (moom-tahz muh-HAHL)

The Taj Mahal, a sumptuous mosque and tomb built between 1632 and 1649 by Shah Jahan in memory of his wife, Mumtaz Mahal.
Andrea Pistolesi/The Image Bank/Getty Images

The emperor and his architects conceived the Taj Mahal as a vast allegory in stone symbolizing the day when Allah would cause the dead to rise and undergo judgment. Its gardens represented the gardens of paradise, and the four water channels running through them symbolized the four rivers of the heavenly kingdom. The domed marble tomb of Mumtaz Mahal represented the throne of Allah. The main gateway to the structure features the entire text of the chapter promising that on the day of judgment, Allah will punish the wicked and gather the faithful into his celestial paradise.

CHAPTER OVERVIEW

The Peacock Throne and the Taj Mahal testify to the wealth of the Mughal empire, and the tomb of Mumtaz Mahal highlights the Islamic character of the ruling dynasty. But the Mughal realm was not the only well-organized empire in south and southwest Asia in early modern times. The Ottoman dynasty ruled a powerful empire that expanded from its base in Anatolia to embrace much of eastern Europe, Egypt, and north Africa. The Safavid dynasty challenged the Ottomans for dominance in southwest Asia and prospered from its role in trade networks linking China, India, Russia, southwest Asia, and the Mediterranean basin. Between them, the Mughal, Ottoman, and Safavid empires ruled over most of south and southwest Asia in the early modern period.

All three empires in this broad region had dynasties that originated with nomadic, Turkic-speaking peoples from the steppes of central Asia. All three dynasties retained political and cultural traditions that their ancestors had adopted on the steppes, but they also adapted readily to the city-based agricultural societies that they conquered. The Ottoman dynasty made especially effective use of gunpowder weapons, and the Safavids and the Mughals also incorporated gunpowder weapons into their arsenals. All three dynasties officially embraced Islam and drew cultural guidance from long-held Islamic values.

During the sixteenth and early seventeenth centuries, the three empires presided over expansive and prosperous societies. Each controlled important trade routes that linked peoples across thousands of miles, and each produced sought-after commodities that were traded in distant markets. About the mid-seventeenth century, however, they all began to weaken. Each empire waged long, costly wars that drained resources without bringing compensating benefits. The empires also faced domestic difficulties. Each of them was an ethnically and religiously diverse realm, and each experienced tensions when conservative Muslim leaders lobbied for strict observance of Islam while members of other communities sought greater freedom for themselves. All three empires—especially the Mughal and Ottoman—relied increasingly on trade with Europeans, who came to their lands with textiles, food items, and armaments. Although it could not have been predicted initially, such reliance eventually put the empires at both an economic and a technological disadvantage to Europeans, who increasingly sought to dominate the world around them. By the mid-eighteenth century the Safavid empire had collapsed, and the Ottoman and Mughal realms were rapidly falling under European influence.

CHRONOLOGY	
1289–1923	Ottoman dynasty
1451–1481	Reign of Mehmed the Conqueror
1453	Ottoman conquest of Constantinople
1501–1524	Reign of Shah Ismail
1501–1722	Safavid dynasty
1502–1558	Life of Hürrem Sultana
1514	Battle of Chaldiran
1520–1566	Reign of Süleyman the Magnificent
1526–1858	Mughal dynasty
1556	Construction of Suleymaniye Mosque
1556–1605	Reign of Akbar
1588–1629	Reign of Shah Abbas the Great
ca. 1600	Introduction of tobacco to the Ottoman empire
1659–1707	Reign of Aurangzeb
1632–1649	Construction of the Taj Mahal

FORMATION OF THE EMPIRES OF SOUTH AND SOUTHWEST ASIA

By the sixteenth century Turkic warriors had transformed much of south and southwest Asia into vast, regional empires. These empires divided up the greater part of the Islamic world at the time: the **Ottoman empire**, which was distinguished by its multiethnic character; the **Safavid empire** of Persia, which served as the center of Shiite Islam; and the **Mughal empire**, which had been imposed over a predominantly Hindu Indian subcontinent. The creation of these durable and powerful political entities attempted centralization throughout south and southwest Asia.

All three empires developed from small, Turkic warrior principalities in frontier areas of central Asia. As they grew, they devised elaborate administrative and military institutions. Under the guidance of talented and energetic rulers, each empire organized an effective governmental apparatus

Osman Bey (oz-MAHN beh)
ghazi (GAH-zee)
Byzantine (BIHZ-uhn-teen)

and presided over a diverse and prosperous society that maintained connections with distant lands ranging from east and southeast Asia to western Europe.

The Ottoman Empire

Osman The Ottoman empire was an unusually successful frontier state. The term *Ottoman* derived from **Osman Bey**, founder of the dynasty that continued in unbroken succession from 1289 until the dissolution of the empire in 1923. Osman was *bey* (chief) of a band of seminomadic Turks who migrated to northwestern Anatolia in the thirteenth century. Osman and his followers sought above all to become *ghazi*, Muslim religious warriors who fought in the name of Islam against non-Muslims.

Ottoman Expansion The Ottomans' location on the borders of the Byzantine empire afforded them ample opportunity to wage war against non-Muslims. Their first great success came in 1326 with the capture of the Anatolian city of Bursa, which became the capital of the Ottoman principality. About 1352 they established a foothold in Europe when they seized the fortress of Gallipoli. The city of Edirne (Adrianople) became a second Ottoman capital and served as a base for further expansion into the Balkans. As

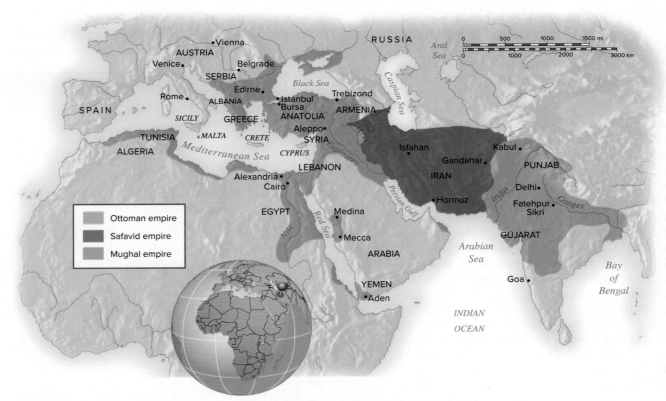

MAP 24.1 The empires of South and Southwest Asia

Locate the Ottoman capital of Istanbul, the Safavid capital of Isfahan, and the Mughal capital of Delhi.

What strategic or commercial purposes did each of these capitals fulfill, and how would their locations have aided or hindered imperial administration?

warriors settled in frontier districts and pushed their boundaries forward, they took spoils and gathered revenues that enriched both the *ghazi* and the central government.

Driving Ottoman expansion was a formidable military machine, which included light cavalry, volunteer infantry, and—as the state grew larger—heavy cavalry. After expanding into the Balkans, the Ottomans created an important force composed of troops of enslaved people. Through an institution known as the *devshirme,* the Ottomans required the Christian population of the Balkans to contribute young boys to become enslaved to the sultan. The boys received special training, learned Turkic, and converted to Islam. According to individual ability, they entered either the Ottoman civilian administration or the military. Those who became soldiers were known as **Janissaries**, from the Turkic *yeni cheri* ("new troops"). The Janissaries quickly gained a reputation for esprit de corps, loyalty to the sultan, and readiness to employ new military technology. The Ottomans also outfitted their forces with gunpowder weapons and used them effectively in battles and sieges.

Mehmed the Conqueror The capture of Constantinople in 1453 by Mehmed II (reigned 1451–1481)—known as **Mehmed the Conqueror**—opened a new chapter in Ottoman expansion. With its superb location and illustrious heritage, Constantinople became the new Ottoman capital, subsequently known as **Istanbul**. With the capture of the great city behind him, Mehmed presented himself not just as a warrior-sultan but as a true emperor. He laid the foundations for a tightly centralized, absolute monarchy, and his army faced no serious rival. He completed the conquest of Serbia, moved into southern Greece and Albania, eliminated the last Byzantine outpost at Trebizond (on the Black Sea), captured Genoese ports in the Crimea, initiated a naval war with Venice in the Mediterranean, and reportedly hoped to march on Rome and capture the pope. Toward the end of his life, he launched an invasion of Italy and briefly occupied Otranto, but his successors abandoned plans for expansion in western Europe.

Süleyman the Magnificent The Ottomans continued their expansion in the early sixteenth century by occupying Syria and Egypt. The occupation of both areas represented a shift in Ottoman expansionist goals from a focus on non-Muslim areas to areas that were governed by other Muslims. In Syria and Egypt, for example, Ottomans waged war against the Muslim Mamluks who had ruled the area for over two centuries. The reason the Ottomans gave for this campaign was that the Mamluks were no longer able to protect Muslim holy sites, particularly Mecca and Medina, from foreigners. Of special concern to the Ottomans were the Christian Portuguese, who had begun their aggressive style of trade in the Indian Ocean and Red Sea after Vasco da Gama circumnavigated Africa in 1498. By 1516 the Ottoman conquest of Mamluk territories meant that it not

Sultan Süleyman (center, on horse) leads Ottoman forces as they march on Europe.
Leemage/Universal Images Group/Newscom

only controlled Islam's holiest sites but also controlled some of the wealthiest trade routes in Eurasia, particularly those that went through Cairo (in modern Egypt) and Damascus (in modern Syria).

Ottoman expansion climaxed in the reign of **Süleyman the Magnificent** (reigned 1520–1566). In 1534 Süleyman conquered Baghdad and added the Tigris and Euphrates valleys to the Ottoman domain. In Europe he kept the rival Habsburg empire on the defensive throughout his reign. He captured Belgrade in 1521, defeated and killed the king of Hungary at the battle of Mohács in 1526, and in 1529 subjected the Habsburgs' prized city of Vienna to a brief siege.

Istanbul (iss-TAHN-bull)
Süleyman (SOO-lehy-mahn)

Under Süleyman, the Ottomans also became a major naval power. In addition to their own Aegean and Black sea fleets, the Ottomans inherited the navy of the Mamluk rulers of Egypt. A Turkic corsair, Khayr al-Din Barbarossa Pasha, placed his pirate fleet under the Ottoman flag and became Süleyman's leading admiral. With such resources and leadership, Süleyman was able to challenge Christian vessels throughout the Mediterranean as well as Portuguese fleets in the Red Sea and the Indian Ocean.

The Safavid Empire

In 1499 a twelve-year-old boy named Ismail left the swamps of Gilan near the Caspian Sea, where he had hidden from the enemies of his family for five years, to seek his revenge. Two years later he entered Tabriz (in modern Iran) at the head of an army and laid claim to the ancient Persian imperial title of shah. The young **Shah Ismail** (reigned 1501–1524) also proclaimed that the official religion of his realm would be Twelver Shiism, and he proceeded to impose it, by force when necessary, on the formerly Sunni population. Over the next decade he seized control of the Iranian plateau and launched expeditions into the Caucasus, Anatolia, Mesopotamia, and central Asia.

The Safavids Shah Ismail and his successors traced their ancestry back to Safi al-Din (1252–1334), leader of a Sufi religious order in northwestern Persia. The famous tomb and shrine of Safi al-Din at Ardabil became the home of Shah Ismail's family (named "Safavids" after the holy man himself), the headquarters of his religious movement, and the center of a determined, deliberate campaign to win political power for his descendants. The Safavids changed their religious preferences several times in the hope of gaining popular support before settling on a form of Shiism that appealed to the nomadic Turkic tribes who were moving into the area.

Twelver Shiism **Twelver Shiism** held that there had been twelve infallible imams (religious leaders) after Muhammad, beginning with the prophet's cousin and son-in-law, Ali. The twelfth, or "hidden," imam had gone into hiding about 874 to escape persecution, but the Twelver Shiites believed he was still alive and would one day return to take power and spread the true religion. Ismail's father had instructed his Turkic followers to wear a distinctive red hat with twelve pleats in memory of the twelve Shiite imams, and they subsequently became known as the *qizilbash* ("red heads"). Safavid propaganda also suggested that Ismail was himself the hidden imam, or even an incarnation of Allah.

Although most Muslims would have regarded those claims as utterly blasphemous, the *qizilbash* enthusiastically accepted them, because they resembled traditional Turkic conceptions of leadership that associated military leaders with divinity. The *qizilbash* believed that Ismail would make them invincible in battle, and they became extremely loyal to the Safavid cause.

Shah Ismail's curious blend of Shiism and Turkic traditions created some powerful enemies. Foremost among them were the staunchly **Sunni** Ottomans, who believed that the first legitimate successor to Mohammed was Mohammed's father-in-law, Abu Bakr, not Ali as the Safavids believed. The Ottoman Sunni feared not only Safavid territorial expansion but also the spread of Safavid propaganda among the nomadic Turks in their own territory. As a result, Ottomans launched a full-scale invasion of Safavid territory in the early sixteenth century.

Shah Ismail and the *qizilbash*. This miniature painting from a Safavid manuscript depicts the shah and his *qizilbash* warriors wearing the distinctive red pleated caps that were their emblem of identity.
Album/Alamy Stock Photo

Shah Ismail (shah IZ-may-el)

Shiism (SHEE-izm)

Sunni (SOON-nee)

Safavid (SAH-fah-vihd)

qizilbash (gih-ZIHL-bahsh)

Battle of Chaldiran At a battle on the plain of Chaldiran (1514), the Ottomans deployed heavy artillery and thousands of Janissaries equipped with firearms behind a barrier of carts. Although the Safavids knew about gunpowder technology, the Ottomans maintained a clear technological advantage. Trusting in the protective charisma of Shah Ismail, the *qizilbash* cavalry attacked the Ottoman line and suffered devastating casualties. Ismail had to slip away, and the Ottomans temporarily occupied his capital at Tabriz. The Ottomans badly damaged the Safavid state but lacked the resources to destroy it, and the two empires remained locked in intermittent conflict for the next two centuries.

Shah Abbas the Great Later Safavid rulers prudently abandoned the extreme Safavid ideology that associated the emperor with Allah in favor of more conventional Twelver Shiism, from which they still derived legitimacy as descendants and representatives of the imams. In the late sixteenth century, **Shah Abbas the Great** (reigned 1588–1629) fully revitalized the Safavid empire. He moved the capital to the more central location of Isfahan, encouraged trade with other lands, and reformed the administrative and military institutions of the empire. With newly strengthened military forces, Shah Abbas led the Safavids to numerous victories. He attacked and defeated the nomadic Uzbeks in central Asia, expelled the Portuguese from Hormuz, and engaged the Ottomans in a series of wars from 1603 to the end of his reign. His campaigns brought most of northwestern Iran, the Caucasus, and Mesopotamia under Safavid rule.

The Mughal Empire

Babur In 1523 Zahir al-Din Muhammad, known as **Babur** ("the Tiger"), a Chagatai Turk who claimed descent from both Chinggis Khan and Tamerlane, appeared in northern India. Unlike the Ottomans or Safavids, who fought on behalf of Islam, Babur made little pretense to be anything more than a soldier of fortune in the manner of his illustrious ancestors. His father had been the prince of Farghana (in modern Uzbekistan), and Babur's great ambition was to transform his inheritance into a glorious central Asian empire. Yet envious relatives and Uzbek enemies frustrated his ambitions.

Unable to accomplish his goals in central Asia, Babur turned his attention to India. With the aid of gunpowder weapons, including artillery and firearms, Babur conquered Delhi in 1526. Ironically, Babur cared little for the land he had conquered. Many in his entourage wanted to take their spoils of war and leave the hot and humid Indian climate, which ruined their finely crafted compound bows, but Babur elected to stay. By the time of his death in 1530, Babur had built a loosely knit empire that stretched from Kabul through the Punjab to the borders of Bengal. He founded a dynasty called the *Mughal* (a Persian term for "Mongol"), which eventually embraced all the Indian subcontinent.

Akbar The real architect of the Mughal empire was Babur's grandson **Akbar** (reigned 1556–1605), a brilliant and charismatic ruler. During his reign, Akbar created a centralized administrative structure with ministries regulating the various provinces of the empire. His military campaigns

Chaldiran (chahld-ih-rahn)
Mughal (MOO-guhl)
Zahir al-Din Muhammad (zah-here ahl-dihn muh-HAHM-mud)
Babur (BAH-ber)
Chagatai (chah-guh-TAHY)

This manuscript illustration from about 1590 depicts Akbar (at top, shaded by attendants) inspecting the construction of a new imperial capital at Fatehpur Sikri.
Picturenow/Universal Images Group/Getty Images

consolidated Mughal power in Gujarat to the west and Bengal to the east. He destroyed the Hindu kingdom of Vijayanagar, thus laying the foundation for later Mughal expansion in southern India.

Akbar was a thoughtful, reflective man deeply interested in religion and philosophy. He pursued a policy of religious toleration that he hoped would reduce tensions between Hindu and Muslim communities in India. Although illiterate (probably due to dyslexia), he was extremely intelligent and had books read to him daily. Instead of imposing Islam on his subjects, he encouraged the elaboration of a syncretic religion called the "divine faith," which focused attention on the emperor as a ruler common to all the religious, ethnic, and social groups of India.

SOURCES FROM THE PAST

The *Ain I Akbari* on Akbar's Imperial Harem

From 1590 until his death in 1602, Abu'l-Fazl—Akbar's court historian—wrote a history of Akbar's reign, which became known as the Akbar Nama (Chronicle of Akbar). *Book three of this expansive, three-volume work is called the* Ain I Akbari (Institutes of Akbar) *and presents a detailed look at both Mughal institutions and Mughal India more generally. Abu'l-Fazl used vast quantities of imperial records in his work and set the standard for royal chronicles in the region for centuries. Throughout the* Akbar Nama, *Abu'l-Fazl presented Akbar as a semidivine ruler who presided over a multiethnic and multireligious empire. Here he describes Akbar's harem.*

His majesty forms matrimonial alliances with princes of Hindustan, and of other countries; and secures by these ties of harmony the peace of the world.

As the sovereign, by the light of his wisdom, has raised fit persons from the dust of obscurity, and appointed them to various offices, so does he also elevate faithful persons to the several ranks in the service of the seraglio [women's apartments], . . . "The saying of the wise is true that the eye of the exalted is the elixir for producing goodness." Such also are the results flowing from the love of order of his majesty [Akbar], from his wisdom, insight, regard to rank, his respect for others, his activity, his patience. . . .

His majesty has made a large enclosure with fine buildings inside, where he reposes. Though there are more than five thousand women, he has given to each a separate apartment. He has also divided them into sections, and keeps them attentive to their duties. Several chaste women have been appointed as *daroghas* [officials], and superintendents over each section, and one has been appointed as a writer [record-keeper] . . . .

The inside of the Harem is guarded by sober and active women; the most trustworthy of them are placed about the apartments of his Majesty. Outside of the enclosure the eunuchs are placed; and at a proper distance, there is a guard of faithful *Rajputs* [soldiers from a Hindu military caste], beyond whom are the porters of the gates. . . . Notwithstanding the great number of faithful guards, his Majesty does not dispense with his own vigilance, but keeps the whole in proper order.

> Why would marriage with women from princely Hindu families have secured "peace" in Akbar's realm?

> What is the author trying to say about Akbar's ideas about merit versus birth?

For Further Reflection

■ Why was it so important to keep Akbar's harem under such heavy guard? Was he more concerned with keeping people out of the harem or keeping people in? Was there reason to be concerned about maintaining armed order inside the harem, given the many conflicts over succession in the Mughal empire?

Source: This translation taken from Abul Fazl'Allami. *Ain I Akbari*, volume I. Trans. by H. Blockman. Calcutta, 1873, pp. 44–45. Available on the Hathi Trust website: https://babel.hathitrust.org/cgi/pt?id=mdp.39015005602431&view=image&seq=7.

Aurangzeb The Mughal empire reached its greatest extent under **Aurangzeb** (reigned 1659–1707). During his long reign, Aurangzeb waged a relentless campaign of expansion. By the early eighteenth century, Mughals ruled the entire subcontinent except for a small region at the southern tip. Although he greatly expanded Mughal boundaries, Aurangzeb presided over a troubled empire. Aurangzeb was a devout Muslim, and he broke with Akbar's policy of religious toleration. He demolished several famous Hindu temples and replaced them with mosques. He also imposed a tax on Hindus in an effort to encourage conversion to Islam. His promotion of Islam appealed strongly to Indian Muslims, but it provoked deep hostility among Hindus and enabled local leaders to organize movements to resist or even rebel against Mughal authority.

IMPERIAL SOCIETY

Despite many differences, there were striking similarities in the development of Ottoman, Safavid, and Mughal societies. All relied on bureaucracies that drew inspiration from the steppe traditions of Turkic and Mongol peoples as well as from the heritage of Islam. They adopted similar economic policies and sought ways to maintain harmony in societies that embraced many different religious and ethnic groups. Rulers of all the empires also sought to enhance the legitimacy of their regimes by providing for public welfare and associating themselves with literary and artistic talent. Finally, all of the empires became centers of long-distance trade and, thus, were areas of cross-cultural interaction.

The Dynastic State

The Ottoman, Safavid, and Mughal empires were all military creations, regarded by their rulers as personal possessions by right of conquest. The rulers exercised personal command of the armies, appointed and dismissed officials at will, and adopted whatever policies they wished. In theory, the emperors owned all land and granted use of it in return for the payment of fixed taxes. The emperors and their families derived revenues from crown lands, and revenues from other lands supported military and administrative officials.

The Emperors and Islam In the Ottoman, Safavid, and Mughal empires, the prestige and authority of the dynasty derived from the personal piety and the military prowess of the ruler and his ancestors. Devotion to Islam encouraged rulers to extend their faith to new lands. Moreover, the *ghazi* ideal of spreading Islam by fighting nonbelievers or heretics resonated with the traditions of Turkic and Mongolian peoples, which emphasized the glory of battle.

Women and Politics Even though Muslim theorists agreed that women should have no role in public affairs, in practice women played important roles in managing all three empires. Many Ottoman, Safavid, and Mughal emperors followed the example of Chinggis Khan, who bestowed special privileges and authority on his mother and his first, and favorite, wife. Ottoman courtiers often complained loudly about the "rule of women," thus offering eloquent testimony to the power that women could wield. Süleyman the Magnificent, for example, fell in love with **Hürrem Sultana** (also known as Roxelana), a concubine of Ukrainian origin who

What's Left Out? ▮ ▮ ▮ ▮ ▮

In textbook overviews such as this, women in the empires of south and southwest Asia tend to appear only briefly, usually in the context of imperial harems. But it would be a mistake to imagine that the lives of most women in the Ottoman, Mughal, and Safavid empires were similar to the lives of women in imperial harems. If we take the Ottoman empire during the seventeenth century as an example, we see that only a tiny proportion of Ottoman women lived in the secluded and isolated conditions of harems. Instead, Ottoman women were visible in multiple contexts. As was the case in many parts of the world, elite women were more constrained in their mobility than were those from laboring classes; nevertheless, they could be seen moving through towns and cities with their bodies covered. Women of the farming and agricultural classes, in contrast, were visible in the fields, driving horses and threshing grain. In cities and large towns, laboring women could be seen selling crafts on the streets. And in both rural and urban areas, enslaved women were constantly visible in public doing a wide variety of tasks. In the realm of law, Ottoman women were highly visible in the courts, where they frequently brought suits against others. Additionally, Ottoman law allowed women to own property in their own names and to dispose of it as they pleased. Thus, although it is important to remember that Ottoman women were not considered equal to men (such a status did not exist anywhere in the world at this time), they also were not the invisible, secluded, highly controlled creatures that images of the harem tend to suggest.

Source: Ebru Boyar and Kate Fleet, eds. *Ottoman Women in Public Space.* Leiden: Brill, 2016.

had been brought to the sultan's harem as a slave. Eventually, Süleyman elevated her to the status of a legal wife, consulted her on state policies, and deferred to her judgment on a variety of matters.

Women also played prominent political roles in the Safavid and Mughal empires. In Safavid Persia, Khayr al-Nesa, better known as Mahd-e Olya and mother of the future Shah Abbas I, gained enormous influence over her husband. Her efforts to limit the power of the *qizilbash* so enraged them that in 1579 they murdered her. The aunt of another shah scolded the ruler for neglecting his duties and used her own money to raise an army to put down a revolt. The Mughal emperor Jahangir was content to let his wife Nur Jahan run the government, and Muslim Aurangzeb listened to his daughter's political advice.

Steppe Traditions The autocratic authority wielded by the rulers of all three empires also reflected steppe traditions. The early emperors largely did as they pleased, regardless of religious and social norms in the areas they conquered. The Ottoman sultans, for example, unilaterally issued numerous legal edicts, and Safavid and Mughal rulers unabashedly asserted their spiritual authority over their subjects. Yet steppe practices also brought problems to the Islamic empires, especially regarding succession issues. In the steppe empires the ruler's relatives often managed components of the states, and succession to the throne became a hot contest between competing members of the family. Problems of succession were compounded by the fact that rulers of all three empires maintained large harems that could include many wives and concubines as well as their children, and thus rivalry for succession was deeply intertwined with the desire of different wives to maintain their position at court. This was reflected in the Mughal empire, where conflicts among princes and rebellions of sons against fathers were recurrent features throughout its history. The Safavids also engaged in murderous struggles for the throne. Shah Abbas himself lived in fear that another member of the family would challenge him. He kept his sons confined to the palace and killed or blinded relatives he suspected, almost wiping out his family in the process.

Succession issues also became a problem for the Ottomans. After the fifteenth century, the sultans increasingly moved to protect their position by eliminating family rivals. Mehmed the Conqueror decreed that a ruler could legally kill off his brothers—many of whom would have been half-siblings by different mothers—after taking the throne. His successors observed that tradition until 1595, when the new sultan executed nineteen brothers, many of them infants, as well as fifteen expectant mothers. After that episode, sultans confined their sons in special quarters of the imperial harem and forbade them to go outside except to take the throne.

Agriculture and Trade

Food Crops Productive agricultural economies were the foundations of all three empires. Each extracted sur-

A sixteenth-century portrait of Hürrem Sultan (1510–1588), born Aleksandra Lisowska and also known as Roxelana.
ART Collection/Alamy Stock Photo

plus agricultural production and used it to finance armies and bureaucracies. For the most part, all three empires relied on crops of wheat and rice that had flourished for centuries in the lands they ruled. In addition, European merchants introduced maize, potatoes, tomatoes, and other crops from the Americas to each of the empires, and the new arrivals soon enlivened regional cuisines with new tastes and textures.

Two products introduced by global trade networks that caught on extremely well in both the Ottoman and Safavid empires were coffee and tobacco. Although native to Ethiopia and cultivated in southern Arabia, coffee did not become popular in Islamic lands until the sixteenth century. Like sugar, coffee became a cash crop in the Americas, which then was sold for profit in markets around the world. By the eighteenth century, American producers and European merchants supplied Muslim markets with coffee as well as sugar.

Tobacco According to the Ottoman historian Ibrahim Pechevi, English merchants introduced tobacco about 1600, claiming it was useful for medicinal purposes. Within a few decades it had spread throughout the Ottoman empire. The increasing popularity of coffee drinking and pipe smoking

Why It Matters

The Columbian Exchange

When we think of tobacco use today, we tend to think of it as an individual activity strongly associated with cigarette smoking. But one of the reasons tobacco became so popular outside the Americas after the eighteenth century was that it was experienced as an intensely social occurrence. In the empires of south and southwest Asia, people gathered in coffeehouses to smoke tobacco from hookahs, drink coffee, and talk. Over time it became a matter of good etiquette to offer tobacco to household visitors as soon as they arrived. Because of these practices, tobacco became an integral part of social rituals in this region, allowing its addictive effects to reach substantial numbers of people at many levels of society. Consider the long-term health effects of tobacco use in this region for the millions of consumers over the centuries who became familiar with smoking as a social activity.

encouraged entrepreneurs to establish coffeehouses, where customers could indulge their appetites for caffeine and nicotine at the same time. The popularity of coffeehouses provoked protest from moralists who worried that these popular attractions were dens of iniquity. Pechevi himself complained about the odor of tobacco and the messy ashes, and religious leaders claimed that it was worse to frequent a coffeehouse than a tavern that served alcohol. Sultan Murad IV (reigned 1623–1640) went so far as to outlaw coffee and tobacco and to execute those who continued to partake. That effort, however, was a losing battle. Both pastimes eventually won widespread acceptance, and the coffeehouse became a prominent social institution in all three empires.

Population Growth The population of India surged during early modern times, growing from 105 million in 1500 to 190 million in 1800. This population growth resulted more from intensive agriculture along traditional lines than from any other factor. The Safavid population grew less rapidly, from five million in 1500 to eight million in 1800. Ottoman numbers grew from nine million in 1500 to about twenty-four million about 1800, but those numbers reflect territorial additions more than fertility increases. Even in the Ottoman heartland of Anatolia, population did not expand nearly as dramatically as it did in other lands in early modern times. From six million in 1500, the population of Anatolia rose to just nine million in 1800.

Trade All three empires ruled lands that had figured prominently in long-distance trade for centuries and participated actively in global trade networks in early modern times. In the Ottoman empire, for example, the early capital at Bursa was also the terminus of a caravan route that brought raw silk from Persia to supply the Italian market. The Ottomans also granted special trading concessions to merchants from England and France to cement alliances against common enemies in Spain and central Europe, and the city of Aleppo became an emporium for foreign merchants engaged primarily in the spice trade.

Shah Abbas promoted Isfahan as a commercial center and extended trading privileges to foreign merchants to help create a favorable environment for trade. European merchants sought Safavid raw silk, carpets, and ceramics. The English East India Company, the French East India Company, and the Dutch VOC all traded actively with the

This nineteenth-century depiction of a coffeehouse in Istanbul demonstrates the centrality of tobacco smoking to the experience. In the Ottoman empire, men socialized in coffeehouses while smoking from elaborate water pipes called hookahs.
Historical Picture Archive//Corbis/Getty Images

Safavids. To curry favor, the English company even sent military advisors to help introduce gunpowder weapons to Safavid armed forces and provided a navy to help them retake Hormuz in the Persian Gulf from the Portuguese.

The Mughals did not pay as much attention to foreign trade as the Ottomans and the Safavids, partly because of the enormous size and productivity of the domestic Indian economy and partly because the Mughal rulers had little interest in maritime affairs. Nevertheless, the Mughal treasury derived significant income from foreign trade. The Mughals allowed the creation of trading stations and merchant colonies by Portuguese, English, French, and Dutch merchants. Meanwhile, Indian merchants formed trading companies of their own, venturing both overland as far as Russia and by sea to ports all over the Indian Ocean. In fact, Indian merchants from Gujarat had been among the first to bring Islam to the island of Sumatra, in southeast Asia, in the late thirteenth century. By the middle of the fifteenth century, Indian merchants and southeast Asian Muslim converts had already spread the faith to Malacca and other surrounding areas even before the creation of the Mughal empire in the sixteenth century.

Religious Affairs

Religious Diversity Each of the empires had a population that was religiously and ethnically diverse, and imperial rulers had the daunting challenge of maintaining harmony among different religious communities. The Ottoman empire included large numbers of Christians and Jews in the Balkans, Armenia, Lebanon, and Egypt. The Safavid empire embraced sizable Zoroastrian and Jewish communities as well as many Christian subjects in the Caucasus. The Mughal empire was especially diverse. Most Mughal subjects were Hindus, but large numbers of Muslims lived alongside smaller communities of Jains, Zoroastrians, Christians, and Sikhs.

Akbar's Divine Faith In India, Akbar was especially tolerant of diverse religions and worked to find a religious synthesis that would serve as a cultural foundation for unity in his diverse empire. As part of that effort, he supported the early **Sikhs**, who combined elements of Hinduism and Islam in a new syncretic faith. He also attempted to elaborate his own "divine faith," which emphasized loyalty to the emperor while borrowing eclectically from different religious traditions. Akbar never explained his ideas systematically, but it is clear that they drew most heavily on Islam. The divine faith was strictly monotheistic, and it reflected the influence of Shiite and Sufi teachings. But it also glorified the emperor: Akbar even referred to himself as the "lord of wisdom," who would guide his subjects to an understanding of god. The divine faith was tolerant of Hinduism, and it even drew inspiration from Zoroastrianism in its effort to bridge the gaps between Mughal India's many cultural and religious communities.

Status of Religious Minorities Each of the empires relied on a long-established model to deal with subjects who were not Muslims. They did not require conquered peoples to convert to Islam but extended to them the status of *dhimmi* (a protected people). In return for their loyalty and payment of a special tax known as *jizya*, *dhimmi* communities retained their personal freedom, kept their property, practiced their religion, and handled their own legal affairs. In the Ottoman empire, for example, autonomous religious communities known as **millet** retained their own civil laws, traditions, and languages. *Millet* communities usually also assumed social and administrative functions in matters concerning birth, marriage, death, health, and education.

The situation in the Mughal empire was different, because its large number of religious communities made a *millet* system impractical. Mughal rulers reserved the most powerful military and administrative positions for Muslims, but in the day-to-day management of affairs, Muslims and Hindus cooperated closely. Some Mughal emperors, such as Akbar, worked particularly hard to forge links between religious communities and to integrate Muslim and Hindu elites. Indeed, in an effort to build bridges between the different religious communities of his realm, he abolished the *jizya* and sponsored discussions and debates among Muslims, Hindus, Jains, Zoroastrians, and Christians.

Promotion of Islam Some Indian Muslims worried that policies of religious toleration would lead to the loss of their religious identity or that they might be absorbed into Hindu society. Some therefore insisted that Mughal rulers create and maintain an Islamic state based on Islamic law. When Aurangzeb reached the Mughal throne in 1659, these ideas gained strength. Aurangzeb reinstated the *jizya* and promoted Islam as the official faith of Mughal India. His policy satisfied zealous Muslims but at the cost of deep bitterness among his Hindu subjects. Tension between Hindu and Muslim communities in India persisted throughout the Mughal dynasty and beyond.

Cultural Patronage

As the empires matured, the rulers of all three empires sought to enhance their prestige through public works projects and patronage of scholars. They competed to attract outstanding religious scholars, artists, and architects to their courts and lavished resources on public buildings.

Istanbul Capital cities and royal palaces were the most visible expressions of imperial majesty. The Ottomans took particular pride in Istanbul, which quickly revived after

---

Sikhs (SIHKS)
dhimmi (DIHM-mee)
jizya (JIHZ-yuh)

The massive Süleymaniye mosque built for Sultan Süleyman the Magnificent by the Ottoman architect Sinan Pasha in 1556.
Anadolu Agency/Getty Images

The Royal Mosque of Isfahan, centerpiece of the city as rebuilt by Shah Abbas at the end of the sixteenth century. With its combination of an open space flanked by markets, the palace, and religious structures, Isfahan stands as a unique example of urban planning in Islamic lands.
DrRave/E+/Getty Images

conquest and became a bustling, prosperous city of more than a million people. At its heart was the great **Topkapi Palace**, which housed government offices and meeting places for imperial councils. At its core was the sultan's residence with its harem, gardens, and pleasure pavilions, as well as a repository for the most sacred possessions of the empire, including the mantle of the prophet Muhammad. Sultan Süleyman the Magnificent was fortunate to be able to draw on the talents of the architectural genius **Sinan Pasha** (1489–1588) to create the vast religious complex called the **Süleymaniye**, which blended Islamic and Byzantine architectural elements. It combined tall, slender minarets with large, domed buildings supported by half domes in the style of the Byzantine church Hagia Sofia (which the Ottomans converted into the mosque of Aya Sofya).

Isfahan Shah Abbas made his capital, Isfahan, into one of the leading Persian cities and the prime center of urban architectural development anywhere in the world. Abbas concentrated markets, the palace, and the royal mosque around a vast polo field and public square. Broad, shaded avenues and magnificent bridges linked the central city to its suburbs. Safavid architects made use of monumental entryways, vast arcades, spacious courtyards, and intricate, colorful decoration. Unlike the sprawling Ottoman and Mughal palaces, the Safavid palaces in Isfahan were relatively small and emphasized natural settings with gardens, pools, and large, open verandas. The point was not only to enable the shah to observe outside activities but also to emphasize his visibility and accessibility, qualities long esteemed in the Persian tradition of kingship.

Fatehpur Sikri In India, Mughal architects skillfully blended central Asian traditions with elements of Hindu architecture, and they built on a scale that left no doubt about their wealth and resources. They constructed scores

of mosques, fortresses, and palaces and sometimes created entire cities. The best example was Fatehpur Sikri, a city planned and constructed by Akbar that served as his capital from 1569 to 1585. With its mint, records office, treasury, and audience hall, the new city demonstrated Akbar's strength and imperial ambitions. Fatehpur Sikri was also a private residence and retreat for the ruler, reproducing in stone a royal encampment with exquisite pleasure palaces where Akbar indulged his passions for music and conversation with scholars and poets. At yet another level, it was a dramatic display of Mughal piety and devotion, centered on the cathedral mosque and the mausoleum of Akbar's Sufi spiritual teacher, **Shaykh Salim Chishthi**. Despite their intensely Islamic character, many of the buildings consciously incorporated Indian elements, such as verandas supported by columns and decorations of stone elephants. Unfortunately, Akbar had selected a poor site for the city and soon abandoned it because of its bad water supply.

Topkapi (TOHP-kah-pih)
Sinan Pasha (sih-NAHN pah-cha)
Fatehpur Sikri (fah-teh-poor SIH-kree)
Shaykh Salim Chishthi
(sheyk sah-LEEM CHEESH-tee)

This city was built by Akbar in the 1570s to commemorate the emperor's military conquests and house the tomb of his religious guide. It included a palace, an audience hall where Akbar attended religious and philosophical debates, and a great mosque.
Gavin Hellier/robertharding/Alamy Stock Photo

The Taj Mahal The most famous of the Mughal monuments was the **Taj Mahal**, which we read about in the introduction to this chapter. Shah Jahan had twenty thousand workers toil for eighteen years to erect the exquisite white marble mosque and tomb. He originally planned to build a similar mausoleum out of black marble for himself, but his son Aurangzeb deposed him before he could carry out the project. Shah Jahan spent his last years confined to a small cell with a tiny window, and only with the aid of a mirror was he able to catch sight of his beloved wife's final resting place.

THE EMPIRES IN TRANSITION

The empires of south and southwest Asia underwent dramatic change between the sixteenth and eighteenth centuries. The Safavid empire disappeared entirely. In 1722 a band of Afghan tribesmen marched all the way to Isfahan, blockaded the city until its starving inhabitants resorted to cannibalism, forced the shah to abdicate, and executed thousands of Safavid officials as well as many members of the royal family. After the death of Aurangzeb in 1707, Mughal India experienced provincial rebellions and foreign invasions. By mid-century the subcontinent was falling under British imperial rule. By 1700 the Ottomans, too, were on the defensive: the sultans lost control over

provinces such as Lebanon and Egypt, and throughout the eighteenth and nineteenth centuries European and Russian states placed political, military, and economic pressure on the shrinking Ottoman realm.

Economic and Military Decline

In the sixteenth century, each of the empires had a strong domestic economy and played a prominent role in global trade networks. By the eighteenth century, however, domestic economies were under great stress, and foreign trade had declined dramatically or had fallen under the control of European powers. The empires were well on their way to becoming dependent on goods produced elsewhere.

Economic Difficulties The high cost of maintaining an expensive military and administrative apparatus helped bring about economic decline in each of the empires. As long as the empires were expanding, they were able to finance their armies and bureaucracies with fresh resources extracted from newly conquered lands. When expansion slowed, ceased, or reversed, however, they faced the problem of supporting their institutions with limited resources. The long, costly, and unproductive wars fought by the Ottomans with the Habsburgs in central Europe, by the Safavids and Ottomans in Mesopotamia, and by Aurangzeb in southern

Each of the empires in south and southwest Asia fought numerous wars, many of which exhausted resources without adding to the productive capacities of the empire. This illustration depicts Ottoman forces (right) clashing with heavily armored Austrian cavalry near Budapest in 1540.
Images & Stories/Alamy Stock Photo

expansion of their business in India. Imperial authorities were content to have foreign traders come to them. Only later did it become clear that welcoming European traders to their lands gave Europeans the leverage to become economically dominant and, in the case of India, conquerors.

Military Decline As they lost initiative to western European peoples in economic and commercial affairs, the empires of south and southwest Asia also experienced military decline. During the sixteenth and early seventeenth centuries, the Islamic empires were able to purchase European weapons in large numbers and attract European expertise that kept their armies supplied with powerful gunpowder weapons. Although each of the empires of south and west Asia continued to be able to purchase European weapons and expertise, this ready availability was one of the reasons none of them developed large armament industries of their own. When combined with financial difficulties within each of the empires, the result was an inability to buy the latest technologies. Over time, their equipment and arsenals became increasingly dated. By the late eighteenth century, even the once-influential Ottoman navy had closed its shipbuilding operations. From then on, the Ottomans ordered all new military ships from European shipyards.

The Deterioration of Imperial Leadership

Strong and effective central authority had long been essential to the empires of south and southwest Asia, and Muslim political theorists never tired of emphasizing the importance of rulers who were diligent, virtuous, and just. Weak, negligent, and corrupt rulers would allow the social order to break down. The Ottomans were fortunate in having a series of talented sultans for three centuries, and the Safavids and the Mughals produced their share of effective rulers as well.

Dynastic Decline Eventually, however, all three dynasties had rulers who were incompetent or irresponsible about tending to affairs of state. Moreover, all three dynasties faced difficulties because of suspicion and fighting among competing members of their ruling houses. In the Ottoman empire alone, notorious examples of problem rulers included Süleyman's successor, Selim the Sot (reigned 1566–1574) and Ibrahim the Crazy (reigned 1640–1648), who taxed and spent to such excess that government officials deposed and murdered him. Indeed, after the late seventeenth century, weak rule increasingly provoked mutinies in the army, provincial revolts, political corruption, and insecurity throughout the Ottoman realm.

India exhausted the treasuries of the empires without making fresh resources available to them.

As expansion slowed and the empires lost control over remote provinces, officials reacted to the loss of revenue by raising taxes, selling public offices, accepting bribes, or resorting to simple extortion. All those measures did long-term economic damage. Foreign trade initially seemed to provide a partial solution, as the goods they brought provided extra revenue for the state and helped satisfy consumer demands for things such as textiles and tobacco. The Ottomans therefore expanded the privileges enjoyed by foreign merchants, whereas the Mughals encouraged the establishment of Dutch and English trading outposts and welcomed the

Religious Tensions Political troubles often arose from religious tensions. Conservative Muslim clerics had considerable influence in each of the empires because of their monopoly on education and their deep involvement in the everyday lives and legal affairs of ordinary subjects. The clerics mistrusted the emperors' interests in unconventional forms of Islam such as Sufism, objected when women or subjects who were not Muslims played influential political roles, and protested any exercise of royal authority that contradicted Islamic law.

In the Ottoman empire, disaffected religious students often joined the Janissaries in revolt. A particularly serious threat came from the **Wahhabi** movement in Arabia, which denounced the Ottomans as dangerous religious innovators who were unfit to rule. Conservative Muslims fiercely protested the construction of an astronomical observatory in Istanbul and forced the sultan to demolish it in 1580. In 1742 they also forced the closure of the Ottoman printing press, which they regarded as an impious technology.

In the Safavid empire, rulers fell under the domination of conservative Shiite clerics. Shiite leaders pressured the shahs to persecute Sunnis, non-Muslims, and even the Sufis who had helped establish the dynasty. Religious tensions also afflicted Mughal India. In the mid-eighteenth century, as Aurangzeb struggled to claim the Mughal throne, he drew on conservative Islamic ideas when he required non-Muslims to pay the poll tax and ordered the destruction of Hindu temples. Those measures inflamed tensions among the various Sunni, Shiite, and Sufi branches of Islam and fueled animosity among Hindus and other Mughal subjects who were not Muslims.

Wahhabi (wuh-HAH-bee)
Sufis (SOO-fees)

CONCLUSION

Like China and Japan, the empires of south and southwest Asia remained strong and powerful throughout the early modern era. Ruling elites of the Ottoman, Safavid, and Mughal empires came from nomadic Turkic stock, and they all drew on steppe traditions in organizing their governments. But the rulers also adapted steppe traditions to the needs of the settled agricultural societies they encountered and devised institutions that maintained order over the long term. During the sixteenth and seventeenth centuries, each of the empires enjoyed a productive economy and participated actively in the global trade networks of early modern times. Their leaders sponsored magnificent architectural and artistic projects as well as campaigns for expansion, and their populations boomed. Each of the empires was religiously and ethnically diverse, and their leaders devised policies to accommodate non-Muslims. By the early eighteenth century, however, the same empires were experiencing difficulties that led to political and military decline. Extensive military campaigns eventually drained the imperial treasuries, and slowed territorial expansion decreased imperial revenues. The diversity that characterized each of the realms also led to religious tensions, and a series of weak rulers encouraged resistance and rebellion. By the late eighteenth century, the Safavid empire had collapsed, and economic difficulties and cultural insularity had severely weakened the Ottoman and Mughal empires and made them vulnerable to outside influences.

STUDY TERMS

Akbar (428)	Safavid empire (424)
Aurangzeb (429)	Shah Abbas the Great (427)
Babur (427)	Shah Ismail (426)
dhimmi (432)	Shaykh Salim Chishthi (433)
ghazi (424)	Sikhs (432)
Hürrem Sultana (429)	Sinan Pasha (433)
Istanbul (425)	Süleyman the Magnificent (425)
Janissaries (425)	Süleymaniye (433)
jizya (432)	Sunni (426)
Mehmed the Conqueror (425)	Taj Mahal (434)
millet (432)	Topkapi Palace (433)
Mughal empire (424)	Twelver Shiism (426)
Osman Bey (424)	Wahhabi (436)
Ottoman empire (424)	
qizilbash (426)	

FOR FURTHER READING

Giancarlo Casale. *The Ottoman Age of Exploration.* New York, 2010. Argues convincingly that the Ottoman Turks were important players in the maritime explorations of the sixteenth century.

Stephen F. Dale. *The Muslim Empires of the Ottomans, Safavids, and Mughals.* Cambridge, 2010. A learned but approachable comparative study of three Islamic empires from 1300 to 1923.

Andrew de la Garza. *The Mughal Empire at War: Babur, Akbar and the Indian Military Revolution, 1500–1605*. London, 2016. Argues that the military innovations introduced in the early Mughal empire constituted a fundamental military revolution.

Carter Vaughn Findley. *The Turks in World History*. New York, 2005. A highly readable account that connects the two-thousand-year history of the Turkic peoples with larger global processes.

Douglas Howard. *A History of the Ottoman Empire*. Cambridge, 2017. Covers the entire social and political history of the Ottoman empire from its origins to the twentieth century.

Kemal H. Karpat. *The Politicization of Islam: Reconstructing Identity, State, Faith, and Community in the Late Ottoman State*. New York, 2001. A scholarly study of the Ottoman state's role in constructing Muslim identity.

Moazzen Maryam. *Formation of a Religious Landscape: Shii Higher Learning in Safavid Iran*. Leiden, 2017. Explores the ways religious information was produced and transmitted during the second half of Safavid rule via institutions of higher learning.

Andrew J. Newman. *Safavid Iran: Rebirth of a Persian Empire*. London and New York, 2008. Based on meticulous scholarship, the definitive single-volume work on the subject.

Leslie Pierce. *The Imperial Harem: Women and Sovereignty in the Ottoman Empire*. Oxford, 1993. Challenges many stereotypes about the role of women in the imperial Ottoman elite.

John F. Richards. *The Mughal Empire*. Cambridge, 1993. A concise and reliable overview of Mughal history, concentrating on political affairs.

Chapter 25 Revolutions and National States in the Atlantic World

ZOOMING IN ON TRADITIONS

Olympe de Gouges Declares the Rights of Women

Marie Gouze was a French butcher's daughter who educated herself by reading books before moving to Paris and marrying a junior army officer. Under the name **Olympe de Gouges** she won fame as a journalist, actress, and playwright. Gouges was as flamboyant as she was talented, and her well-publicized love affairs scandalized Parisian society.

Gouges was also a revolutionary and a strong advocate of women's rights. She responded enthusiastically when the French revolution broke out in July 1789, and she applauded in August when revolutionary leaders proclaimed freedom and equality for all citizens in the **Declaration of the Rights of Man and the Citizen**. It soon became clear, however, that freedom and equality pertained only to male citizens. Revolutionary leaders welcomed women's contributions to the revolution but refused to grant them political and social rights.

Gouges demanded that women share equal rights in family property and campaigned for equal education. She

Olympe de Gouges (oh-LIM-peh de gouj)

Liberty, personified as a woman, leads the French people in a famous painting by Eugène Delacroix.
The Picture Art Collection/Alamy Stock Photo

even appealed to Queen Marie Antoinette to use her influence to advance women's rights. In 1791 Gouges published a **Declaration of the Rights of Woman and the Female Citizen**, which claimed the same rights for women that revolutionary leaders had granted to men in August 1789. She insisted on the rights of women to vote, speak their minds freely, participate in the making of law, and hold public office.

Gouges's declaration attracted a great deal of attention but little support. Revolutionary leaders dismissed her appeal, and in 1793 they executed her because of her affection for Marie Antoinette and her persistent crusade for women's rights. Yet Gouges's campaign illustrated the power of the ideals of the eighteenth-century Enlightenment movement, which emphasized freedom and equality. Indeed, once revolutionaries in France and elsewhere had proclaimed freedom and equality as universal human rights, they were unable to suppress demands to extend them to other groups— such as women, enslaved people, and people of color—whom the revolutionaries often originally intended to exclude.

CHAPTER OVERVIEW

A series of violent revolutions based on Enlightenment principles brought dramatic political and social change to lands throughout much of the Atlantic Ocean basin in the late eighteenth and early nineteenth centuries. And although each revolution was different, they all shared several features. First, all were at least partially inspired by Enlightenment ideals. Second, wars fought between the major imperial powers created the conditions for each of the revolutions to erupt. Finally, the revolutions were deeply interlinked: in fact, beginning with the **American revolution**, each successive revolution helped create the conditions for the next. Revolution broke out first in the British colonies of North America, where colonists founded a new republic. Partly as a result of the lavish spending of the French on helping the American revolutionaries, revolution broke out in France just a few years later. There, revolutionaries abolished the French monarchy and thoroughly reorganized French society. During the French revolution, enslaved people in the French sugar island of St. Domingue seized the opportunity to revolt against French rule and establish their independence.The Napoleonic wars (1799–1815) then created the conditions for the peoples of Latin America to seek independence from Spain and Portugal. By the 1830s, societies had reorganized political and social structures throughout western Europe and the Americas.

The revolutions of the late eighteenth and early nineteenth centuries had two results of deep global significance. First, they helped spread a cluster of Enlightenment ideas concerning freedom, equality, and popular sovereignty. Revolutionary leaders argued that political authority arose from the people rather than the rulers and often sought to establish republican forms of government in which the people selected delegates to represent their interests. In fact, early revolutionaries extended political rights only to a privileged group of white men, but they justified their actions in general terms that prompted disenfranchised groups to seek freedom, equality, and a political voice as well. Indeed, such ideas spread globally in the nineteenth and twentieth centuries as social reformers and revolutionaries struggled to make freedom and equality a reality for oppressed groups throughout the world.

Second, while promoting Enlightenment values, the revolutions of this period encouraged the consolidation of national states as the principal form of political organization. As people defended their states from enemies and sometimes mounted attacks on foreign lands, they developed a powerful sense of identity with their compatriots. During the nineteenth century, strong national identities led to movements to build national states, which in turn profoundly influenced the political experiences of European states. During the late nineteenth and twentieth centuries, efforts to harness nationalist sentiments and form states based on national identity became one of the most powerful and dynamic movements in world history.

CHRONOLOGY	
1694–1778	Life of Voltaire
1744–1803	Life of Toussaint Louverture
1748–1793	Life of Olympe de Gouges
1753–1811	Life of Miguel de Hidalgo
1756–1763	Seven Years' War
1769–1821	Life of Napoleon Bonaparte
1774–1793	Reign of King Louis XVI
1775–1781	American revolution
1783–1830	Life of Simón Bolívar
1789–1799	French revolution
1791–1803	Haitian revolution
1799–1814	Reign of Napoleon
1810–1825	Wars of independence in Latin America
1814–1815	Congress of Vienna

REVOLUTIONARY IDEAS

Revolutionaries of the eighteenth and nineteenth centuries sought to fashion equitable societies by instituting governments that were responsive to the peoples they governed. In justifying their policies, revolutionaries argued for popular sovereignty—the idea that legitimate political authority resides not in kings but, rather, in the people who make up a society. In North America, colonists declared independence from British rule and instituted a new government founded on the principle of popular sovereignty. Soon thereafter, French revolutionaries abolished the monarchy and restructured the social order. Their goals resonated with many others in the Atlantic basin, including people in the Caribbean and Latin America, who fought their own revolutions in the name of liberty and freedom. Meanwhile, Napoleon Bonaparte's invasions of states in western Europe helped spread revolutionary ideas to much of the region.

The Enlightenment

Isaac Newton's conception of the universe during the scientific revolution (discussed in chapter 20) had been so powerful and persuasive that its influence extended well beyond science and into the realm of politics and human relationships. Newton's work on the rationality of the laws of physics suggested that human behavior and institutions might also be guided by rational laws. Inspired by this idea, during the seventeenth and eighteenth centuries European and Euro-American thinkers launched an ambitious project to discover the laws that governed humanity. Some, such as the English philosopher **John Locke** (1632–1704), sought the natural laws of politics. Others, such as Adam Smith (1723–1790), sought to comprehend the laws of economics. Like the early modern scientists, however, they all abandoned Aristotelian philosophy and Christian religion as sources of authority in their quest to subject the human world to purely rational analysis. The result of their work was a movement known as the **Enlightenment**.

The center of Enlightenment thought was France, where prominent intellectuals known collectively as **philosophes** ("philosophers") advanced the cause of reason. The philosophes addressed their works more to the educated public than to scholars: instead of formal philosophical treatises, they mostly composed histories, novels, dramas, satires, and pamphlets on religious, moral, and political issues.

philosophes (fil-uh-sofs)
Voltaire (vohl-TAIR)

Voltaire More than any other philosophe, François-Marie Arouet (1694–1778) epitomized the spirit of the Enlightenment. Writing under the pen name **Voltaire**, he championed individual freedom and attacked any institution sponsoring intolerant or oppressive policies. Targets of his often caustic wit included the French monarchy and the Roman Catholic church. When the king of France sought to save money by reducing the number of horses kept in royal stables, for example, Voltaire suggested that it would be more effective to get rid of the asses who rode the horses. Voltaire also waged a long literary campaign against the Roman Catholic church, which he held responsible for fanaticism, intolerance, and incalculable human suffering.

The Theory of Progress Most philosophes were optimistic about the future of the world and humanity. In fact, they believed that rational understanding of human and natural affairs would bring about a new era of progress and individual freedom and would lead to the construction of a prosperous, just, and equitable society. Although those fond wishes did not come to pass, the Enlightenment did indeed help bring about a thorough cultural transformation of European society. For one thing, it weakened the influence of organized religion by encouraging the replacement of Christian values with a new set of secular values. Furthermore, the Enlightenment encouraged political and cultural leaders to subject society to rational analysis and intervene actively in its affairs in the interests of promoting progress and prosperity. Perhaps most importantly, the Enlightenment encouraged thinkers and activists to question the social, political, and economic order around them and offered concrete ideas about how societies could be reordered more effectively.

Popular Sovereignty

One of the ideas that Enlightenment thinkers questioned most consistently was the long-held idea that European monarchs possessed a divine right to rule. Instead, philosophes and other advocates of Enlightenment ideas argued that kings should be responsible to the people they governed. John Locke, for example, regarded government as a contract between rulers and ruled. In his *Second Treatise of Civil Government,* published in 1690, Locke held that individuals granted political rights to their rulers but retained personal rights to life, liberty, and property. Furthermore, according to Locke, rulers derived their authority from the consent of those they governed. If rulers broke the contract, the people had the right to replace their rulers. In effect, Locke's political thought relocated sovereignty, removing it from rulers as divine agents and vesting it in the people of a society.

Individual Freedom Enlightenment thinkers addressed issues of freedom and equality as well as sovereignty. Philosophes resented the persecution of religious minorities as well as royal censorship. Philosophes called for religious toleration and freedom to express their views openly. Thus, when censors prohibited the publication of their writings in France, they often published their books in Switzerland or the Netherlands and smuggled them across the border into France.

Political and Legal Equality Many Enlightenment thinkers also called for equality. They argued that privileged aristocrats made no more contribution to the larger society than peasants, artisans, or workers and recommended the creation of a society in which all individuals would be equal before the law. The most prominent advocate of political equality was the French-Swiss thinker **Jean-Jacques Rousseau** (1712–1778). In his influential book *The Social Contract* (1762), Rousseau argued that members of a society were collectively the sovereign. In an ideal society all individuals would participate directly in the formulation of policy and the creation of laws.

Global Influence of Enlightenment Values Most Enlightenment thinkers were of common birth but comfortable means. Though seeking to limit the prerogatives of ruling and aristocratic classes, they did not envision a society in which they would share political rights with women, children, peasants, laborers, or enslaved people. Nevertheless, Enlightenment thought constituted a serious challenge to long-established notions of political and social order. Although arguments for freedom, equality, and popular sovereignty originally served the interests of relatively privileged European and Euro-American men, many other groups made effective use of them in seeking the extension of political rights. Indeed, Enlightenment ideas became the foundation of and justification for a series of revolutions that rocked the Atlantic world in the late eighteenth and early nineteenth centuries.

REVOLUTIONS
The American Revolution

In the mid-eighteenth century there were few signs that North America would become a center of revolution. Residents of the thirteen British colonies there regarded themselves as British subjects: they recognized British law, read English-language books, and they benefited handsomely from British rule. Trade brought prosperity to the colonies, and British military forces protected the colonists' interests. From 1754 to 1763, for example, British forces waged an expensive conflict in North America known as the French and Indian War. That conflict merged with a larger contest for imperial supremacy, the **Seven Years' War** (1756–1763), in which British and French forces battled each other in Europe and India as well as North America. Victory in the Seven Years' War ensured that Britain would dominate global trade and that British North America would prosper.

Tightened British Control of the Colonies But the Seven Years' War also provided the circumstances in which American colonists became increasingly discontented with British rule. The war had been enormously expensive for the British government and had increased the tax burden of ordinary people living in Britain, so when it was over the British government wanted the American colonists to help pay their fair share—via increased taxes—for the continuing maintenance and protection of the colonies. But new taxes proved extremely unpopular in North America. Colonists especially resented the imposition of taxes on molasses by the Sugar Act (1764), on publications and legal documents by the Stamp Act (1765), on a variety of imported items by the Townshend Act (1767), and on tea by the Tea Act (1773). Colonists also took offense at the Quartering Act (1765), which required them to provide housing and accommodations for British troops.

Colonists argued that they should pay such taxes only if the North American colonies were represented in the British parliament, arguing that there should be "no taxation without representation." They boycotted British products, physically attacked British officials, and mounted protests. They also organized the **Continental Congress** (1774), which coordinated resistance to British policies across the thirteen colonies. By 1775 tensions were so high that British troops and a colonial militia skirmished at the village of Lexington, near Boston. The American revolution had begun.

The Declaration of Independence On 4 July 1776 the Continental Congress adopted a document titled "The unanimous Declaration of the thirteen united States of America." This **Declaration of Independence** drew deep inspiration from Enlightenment political thought in its insistence "that all men are created equal, that they are endowed by their Creator with certain unalienable Rights, that among these are Life, Liberty, and the pursuit of Happiness." It echoed John Locke's contractual theory of government in arguing that governments derive their power and authority from "the consent of the governed." When any government infringes on individuals' rights, the document continued, "it is the Right of the People to alter or abolish it, and to institute new Government." The Declaration of Independence presented a long list of specific abuses charged to the British crown and concluded by proclaiming the colonies "Free and Independent States."

MAP 25.1 The American revolution, 1781

Note the location of both the major towns and cities in the colonies and the location of the major battles that occurred during the revolution.

Why were both situated so close to the eastern coast?

It was one thing to declare independence but a different matter to make independence a reality. Britain enjoyed many advantages over the rebels: a strong government, the most powerful navy in the world, a competent army, and a sizable population of loyalists in the colonies. But in spite of Britain's many advantages, it nevertheless lost the war. This can be explained in part by the distance between Britain and the colonies. **George Washington** (1732–1799)

also provided strong and imaginative military leadership for the colonial army, and local militias used guerrilla tactics effectively against British forces. Most important, however, was the eventual support rival European powers—especially France—gave to the American colonists. The French had reason to help the colonists; they wanted revenge against the British for their recent losses in the Seven Years' War. By 1780, the French were providing the

Washington Crossing the Delaware is an 1851 oil on canvas by German-American artist Emanuel Leutze. It commemorates Washington's crossing of the Delaware on 25 December 1776, during the American revolutionary war. A copy of this painting hangs in the West Wing reception area of the White House. The painting emphasizes the mythological qualities of Washington as hero.

The Metropolitan Museum of Art, New York, Gift of John Stewart Kennedy, 1897.

Americans with not only substantial sums of money but also naval support and a large force of trained soldiers and officers. In fact, the French were critical in forcing the British to surrender at Yorktown in October 1781. Although the war continued into 1782, Cornwallis's surrender ensured an eventual American victory. In September 1783 diplomats concluded the Peace of Paris, by which the British government formally recognized American independence, thanks in very large measure to French aid.

Building an Independent State The leaders of the fledgling republic organized a state that reflected Enlightenment principles. In 1787 a constitutional convention drafted the Constitution of the United States, which emphasized the rights of individuals. American leaders based the federal government on popular sovereignty, and they agreed to guarantee individual liberties such as freedom of speech, of the press, and of religion. Full political and social rights, however, were accorded only to men of property: landless men, women, and enslaved and indigenous peoples were not included. Yet in spite of its imperfections, the early American republic served as an inspiration to others around the Atlantic basin, who similarly sought to create governments based on popular sovereignty.

The French Revolution

Among those most inspired by the success of the American revolution were the French philosophes and their followers, who had long argued in favor of popular sovereignty and greater social and political equality. But although French Enlightenment thinkers drew inspiration from the American example, the **French revolution** that began in 1789 was a more radical affair than its American counterpart. Unlike the Americans, French revolutionary leaders repudiated existing society, which

they called the **ancien régime** ("the old order") and sought to replace it with new political, social, and cultural structures.

The Estates General Serious financial, political, and social problems within the French government provided the opportunity for French revolutionaries to put their ideas into practice. In the 1780s approximately half of the French royal government's revenue went to pay off war debts—nearly a quarter of which were amassed as a result of French support for colonists in the war of American independence. Combined with the need to maintain the French armed forces and the lavish spending of the French court, by 1789 the French government faced complete bankruptcy. King **Louis XVI** (reigned 1774–1793) was unable to raise more revenue from the overburdened peasantry, so he sought to increase taxes on the French nobility. The nobility, which had traditionally been exempt from taxation, protested. This then forced Louis to summon the **Estates General**, an assembly that represented the entire French population through groups known as estates, to get the money he needed. In the ancien régime there were three estates, or political classes. The first estate consisted of about one hundred thousand Roman Catholic clergy, and the second included some four hundred thousand nobles. The third estate embraced the rest of the population—about twenty-four million serfs, free peasants, and urban residents ranging from laborers, artisans, and shopkeepers to physicians, bankers, and attorneys. Though founded in 1303, the Estates General had not met since 1614. The third estate had as many delegates as the

ancien régime (ahn-syan rey-ZHEEM)
Louis (LOO-ee)

A contemporary print depicts the storming of the Bastille in 1789. The deeds of common people working in crowds became a favorite theme of artists after the outbreak of the French revolution.
PRISMA ARCHIVO/Alamy Stock Photo

other two estates combined, but that numerical superiority offered no advantage when the assembly voted on issues, because voting took place by estate—one vote for each—rather than by individuals.

In May 1789 King Louis called the Estates General into session at the royal palace of Versailles in hopes that it would authorize new taxes. Louis never controlled the assembly. Representatives of the third estate arrived at Versailles demanding political and social reform. Although some members of the lower clergy and a few prominent nobles supported reform, in general the first and second estates actively thwarted efforts at pushing reform measures through the Estates General.

The National Assembly On 17 June 1789, after several weeks of fruitless debate, representatives of the third estate took the dramatic step of seceding from the Estates General and proclaiming themselves to be the **National Assembly**. Three days later, meeting in an indoor tennis court, members of the new Assembly swore not to disband

until they had provided France with a new constitution. On 14 July 1789 a Parisian crowd, fearing that the king sought to undo events of the previous weeks, stormed the Bastille, a royal jail and arsenal, in search of weapons. The military garrison protecting the Bastille surrendered to the crowd, but only after killing many of the attackers. To vent their rage, members of the crowd hacked the defenders to death. One assailant used his pocketknife to sever the garrison commander's head, which the victorious crowd mounted on a pike and paraded around the streets of Paris. News of the event soon spread, sparking insurrections in cities throughout France.

Emboldened by popular support, the National Assembly undertook a broad program of political and social reform. The *Declaration of the Rights of Man and the Citizen,* which the National Assembly promulgated in August 1789, articulated its guiding principles. Reflecting the influence of American revolutionary ideas, the *Declaration of the Rights of Man and the Citizen* proclaimed the equality of all men, declared that sovereignty resided in the

SOURCES FROM THE PAST

Declaration of the Rights of Man and the Citizen

This declaration, which became part of the official revolutionary platform in France in August 1789, was written in close collaboration with Thomas Jefferson, the principal author of the American Declaration of Independence and the U.S. ambassador to France that year. Thus it is not surprising that the Declaration of the Rights of Man and the Citizen *reflects the influence of American revolutionary ideas.*

First Article. Men are born and remain free and equal in rights. Social distinctions may be based only on common utility.

Article 2. The goal of every political association is the preservation of the natural and inalienable rights of man. These rights are liberty, property, security, and resistance to oppression.

Article 3. The principle of all sovereignty resides essentially in the nation. No body and no individual can exercise authority that does not flow directly from the nation. ——————

> According to this statement, was it possible for kings to be sovereign?

Article 4. Liberty consists in the freedom to do anything that does not harm another. The exercise of natural rights of each man thus has no limits except those that assure other members of society their enjoyment of the same rights. These limits may be determined only by law.

Article 6. Law is the expression of the general will. All citizens have the right to participate either personally or through their representatives in the making of law. The law must be the same for all, whether it protects or punishes. Being equal in the eyes of the law, all citizens are equally eligible for all public honors, offices, and occupations, according to their abilities, without any distinction other than that of their virtues and talents.

Article 7. No person shall be accused, arrested, or imprisoned except in the cases and according to the forms prescribed by law. Any one soliciting, transmitting, executing, or causing to be executed, any arbitrary order, shall be punished. But any citizen summoned or arrested in virtue of the law shall submit without delay, as resistance constitutes an offense.

Article 9. As all persons are held innocent until they shall have been declared guilty, if arrest shall be deemed indispensable, all harshness not essential to the securing of the prisoner's person shall be severely repressed by law.

> Is it possible to learn something of French society under the ancien régime by reading these articles?

Article 11. The free communication of thoughts and opinions is one of the most precious rights of man: every citizen may thus speak, write, and publish freely, but will be responsible for abuse of this freedom in cases decided by the law. ——————

Article 13. For the maintenance of public military force and for the expenses of administration, common taxation is necessary: it must be equally divided among all citizens according to their means.

Article 15. Society has the right to require from every public official an accounting of his administration.

Article 16. Any society in which guarantees of rights are not assured and separation of powers is not defined has no constitution at all.

Article 17. Property is an inviolable and sacred right. No one may be deprived of property except when public necessity, legally determined, clearly requires it, and on condition of just and prearranged compensation.

For Further Reflection

■ In what ways do the principles established in the declaration reflect the political transformations taking place throughout the age of Atlantic revolutions?

Source: Déclaration des droits de l'homme et du citoyen. Translated by Jerry H. Bentley.

people, and asserted individual rights to liberty, property, and security.

Liberty, Equality, and Fraternity

Between 1789 and 1791 the National Assembly reconfigured French society. Taking the Enlightenment ideals of "liberty, equality, and fraternity" as its goals, the Assembly abolished the old social order. It seized church lands, abolished the first estate, defined clergy as civilians, and required clergy to take an oath of loyalty to the state. It also produced a constitution that left the king in place but deprived him of legislative authority. France became a constitutional monarchy in which men of property—about half the adult male population—had the right to vote in elections to choose legislators. In these ways, the French revolution represented an effort to put Enlightenment political thought into practice.

The Convention

The revolution soon took a radical turn. The French nobility, who were not happy with their diminished status, sought to mobilize foreign powers in support of the king and the ancien régime. This gave the Assembly the pretext to declare war against Austria and Prussia in April 1792. Adding to the military burden of France, revolutionary leaders declared war on Spain, Britain, and the Netherlands. Fearing military defeat and counterrevolution, revolutionary leaders created the Convention, a new legislative body elected by universal manhood suffrage, which abolished the monarchy and proclaimed France a republic. The Convention rallied the French population by instituting the *levée en masse,* a "mass levy" that drafted people and resources for use in the war against invading forces. The Convention also rooted out enemies at home by making frequent use of the guillotine. In 1793 King Louis XVI and his wife, Queen Marie Antoinette, themselves were killed by the guillotine when the Convention found them guilty of treason.

Revolutionary chaos reached its peak in 1793 and 1794 when **Maximilien Robespierre** (1758-1794) and the radical Jacobin party dominated the Convention. A lawyer by training, Robespierre had emerged during the revolution as a ruthless but popular radical known as "the Incorruptible," and he dominated the Committee of Public Safety, the executive authority of the republic. The Jacobins believed passionately that France needed complete restructuring, and they unleashed a campaign of terror to promote their revolutionary agenda. They sought to eliminate the influence of Christianity in French society by closing churches, forcing priests to take wives, and promoting a new, secular "cult of reason." They reorganized the calendar, replacing seven-day weeks with ten-day units that recognized no day of religious observance. The

Jacobins also encouraged citizens to display their revolutionary zeal by wearing working-class clothes and granted increased rights to women by permitting them to inherit property and divorce their husbands. The Jacobins made especially frequent use of the guillotine: in a yearlong **reign of terror** between the summer of 1793 and the summer of 1794, they executed about forty thousand people and imprisoned three hundred thousand others as suspected enemies of the revolution.

The Directory

Eventually, such political purges undermined confidence in the regime itself. In July 1794 the Convention arrested Robespierre and his allies, convicted them of tyranny, and sent them to the guillotine. A group of conservative men of property then seized power and ruled France under a new institution known as the Directory (1795-1799). However, the Directory was unable to resolve the economic and military problems that plagued revolutionary France. In seeking a middle way between the ancien régime and radical revolution, it lurched from one policy to another and faced constant challenges to its authority. The Directory came to an end in November 1799 when a young general named Napoleon Bonaparte staged a coup d'état and seized power.

The Reign of Napoleon

Born to a minor noble family on the Mediterranean island of Corsica, **Napoleon Bonaparte** (1769-1821) studied at French military schools and became an officer in the army of King Louis XVI. A brilliant military leader, he became a general at age twenty-four. He was a fervent supporter of the revolution and defended the Directory against a popular uprising in 1795. In a campaign of 1796-1797, he drove the Austrian army from northern Italy and established French rule there. In 1798 he mounted an invasion of Egypt, but the campaign ended in a French defeat. Politically ambitious, Napoleon returned to France in 1799 and joined the Directory. When Austria, Russia, and Britain formed a coalition to attack France and end the revolution, he overthrew the Directory, imposed a new constitution, and named himself first consul. In 1802 he became consul for life, and two years later he crowned himself emperor.

Napoleonic France

Napoleon brought political stability to a land torn by revolution and war. He made peace with the Roman Catholic church and reversed the most radical religious policies of the Convention. In 1804 Napoleon issued the **Civil Code**, a revised body of civil law, which also helped stabilize French society. The Civil Code affirmed the political and legal equality of all adult men and established a merit-based society in which individuals advanced in education and employment because of talent

---

Napoleon Bonaparte (nuh-POH-lee-uhn BOH-nuh-pahrt)

rather than birth or social standing. The Civil Code confirmed many of the moderate revolutionary policies of the National Assembly but retracted measures passed by the more radical Convention. The code restored patriarchal authority in the family, for example, by making women and children subservient to male heads of households.

Although he approved of the Enlightenment ideal of equality, Napoleon was no champion of intellectual freedom or representative government. He limited free speech and routinely censored newspapers and other publications. He established a secret police force that relied heavily on spies and detained suspected political opponents by the

MAP 25.2 Napoleon's empire in 1812

Observe the number of states dependent on or allied with Napoleon as opposed to those that were at war with him.

Were there geographic conditions that allowed some states to resist Napoleon's efforts at conquest better than others?

thousands. He made systematic use of propaganda to manipulate public opinion. He ignored elective bodies and founded a dynasty that set his family above the people in whose name they ruled.

Napoleon's Empire While working to stabilize France, Napoleon also sought to extend his authority throughout Europe. Napoleon's armies conquered Spain, Portugal, and Italy; occupied the Netherlands; and inflicted humiliating defeats on Austrian and Prussian forces. Napoleon sent his brothers and other relatives to rule the conquered and occupied lands, and he forced Austria, Prussia, and Russia to ally with him and respect French hegemony in Europe.

However, Napoleon's empire began to unravel in 1812, when he decided to invade Russia. Convinced that the czar was conspiring with his British enemies, Napoleon led an army of six hundred thousand soldiers to Moscow. He captured the city, but the czar withdrew and set Moscow ablaze, leaving Napoleon's vast army without adequate shelter or supplies. Napoleon ordered a retreat, but the bitter Russian winter destroyed his army, and only a battered remnant of thirty thousand soldiers managed to limp back to France. By the end of the campaign, more than four hundred thousand French soldiers had died.

The Fall of Napoleon Napoleon's disastrous Russian campaign emboldened his enemies. A coalition of British, Austrian, Prussian, and Russian armies converged on France and forced Napoleon to abdicate his throne in April 1814. The victors restored the French monarchy and exiled Napoleon to the tiny Mediterranean island of Elba. But in March 1815 Napoleon escaped from Elba, returned to France, and ruled France for a hundred days before a British army defeated him at Waterloo in Belgium. This time, European powers banished Napoleon to the remote and isolated island of St. Helena in the South Atlantic Ocean, where he died of natural causes in 1821.

The Haitian Revolution

The success of the American revolution appealed not only to French social reformers but also to enslaved people and free people of color in the Caribbean. But on the French portion of the island of Hispaniola it was the French revolution that provided the immediate inspiration and the opportunity for the revolution that broke out there in 1791. Indeed, the only successful slave revolt in history took place on the island in the midst of the French Revolution. The Spanish colony of Santo Domingo occupied the eastern part of the island (modern Dominican Republic), and the French colony of Saint-Domingue occupied the western part (modern Haiti). Saint-Domingue was one of the richest of all European colonies in the Caribbean: sugar, coffee, and cotton produced there accounted for almost one-third of France's foreign trade.

Saint-Domingue Society In 1790 the population of Saint-Domingue included about forty thousand white

A French depiction of the Battle of Crête à Pierrot (4–12 March 1802) during the Haitian revolution.
Niday Picture Library/Alamy Stock Photo

French settlers, thirty thousand *gens de couleur* (free people of color), and some five hundred thousand enslaved people, most of whom were born in Africa. Led by wealthy planters, white Europeans stood at the top of society. *Gens de couleur* farmed small plots of land, sometimes with the aid of a few enslaved people, or worked as artisans in the island's towns. Most of the colony's enslaved population toiled in the fields under brutal conditions. Many enslaved people ran away into the mountains to escape such treatment. By the late eighteenth century, Saint-Domingue had many large communities of maroons (former enslaved people who had escaped).

The American and French revolutions both inspired and helped ignite violent political and social revolution in Saint-Domingue (in what became known as the **Haitian revolution**). Because the French government supported North American colonists against British rule, colonial governors in Saint-Domingue sent about five hundred *gens de couleur* to fight in the American war of independence. Having seen revolutionary ideals in practice, they returned to Saint-Domingue with the intention of reforming society. Then, when the French revolution broke out a few years later in 1789, white settlers in Saint-Domingue sought the right to govern themselves, but they opposed proposals to grant political and legal equality to the *gens de couleur.* By May 1791 civil war had broken out between white settlers and *gens de couleur.*

Slave Revolt

The conflict expanded dramatically when a charismatic Voudou priest named Boukman organized a revolt. In August 1791 some twelve thousand enslaved people began a campaign of killing white settlers, burning their homes, and destroying their plantations. Within a few weeks the numbers of enslaved people in revolt had grown to almost one hundred thousand. Saint-Domingue quickly descended into chaos as white, *gens de couleur,* and slave factions battled one another. Foreign armies soon complicated the situation: French troops arrived in 1792 to restore order, and British and Spanish forces intervened in 1793 in hopes of benefiting from France's difficulties.

Toussaint L'Ouverture

Eventually, slave forces overcame white settlers, *gens de couleur,* and foreign armies. Their successes were due largely to the leadership of François-Dominique Toussaint (1744–1803), who after 1791 called himself **Louverture**—from the French *l'ouverture,* meaning "the opening." The son of enslaved parents, he himself had been a free man since 1776. Toussaint was a skilled organizer, and by 1793 he had built a strong, disciplined army. He shrewdly played French, British, and Spanish forces against one another while jockeying for power with other Black and mixed-race generals. By 1797 he was leading an army of twenty thousand that controlled most of Saint-Domingue. In 1801 he issued a constitution that granted equality and citizenship to all residents of Saint-Domingue. He stopped short of declaring independence from France, however, because he did not want to provoke Napoleon—who had by that time seized power in France—into attacking the island.

The Republic of Haiti

Toussaint's worries about Napoleon were well founded. In 1802 Napoleon dispatched forty thousand troops to restore French authority in Saint-Domingue. Toussaint attempted to negotiate a peaceful settlement, but the French commander arrested him and sent him to France, where he died in jail of maltreatment in 1803. By the time he died, however, the generals who succeeded Toussaint had defeated the remaining French troops and driven them out of the colony. Late in 1803 they declared independence, and on 1 January 1804 they proclaimed the establishment of Haiti, meaning "land of mountains," which became the second independent republic in the western hemisphere after the United States.

Wars of Independence in Latin America

Latin American Society

Revolutionary ideals also traveled to the Spanish and Portuguese colonies in the Americas. Though governed by *peninsulares* (colonial officials from Spain or Portugal), the Iberian colonies all had a large, wealthy, and powerful class of Euro-American *criollos* (creoles), or people of European descent who had been born in the Americas. In 1800 the *peninsulares* numbered about 30,000, with a creole population of 3.5 million. The Iberian colonies also had a large population—about 10 million in all—of less privileged classes such as enslaved people of African descent, indigenous peoples, and mixed-race peoples.

Creoles prospered during the eighteenth century as they established plantations in the colonies and participated in trade with Spain and Portugal. Yet the creoles also had grievances. Like British colonists in North America, the creoles resented administrative control and economic regulations imposed by the Iberian powers. Although they drew inspiration from Enlightenment political thought, the creoles desired neither radical social reform nor the establishment of an egalitarian society. Instead, they sought to displace the *peninsulares* but retain their privileged position in society. Their opportunity came as a result of the Napoleonic Wars in Europe, because Napoleon invaded and conquered Portugal in 1807 and Spain in

peninsulares (peh-neen-soo-LAH-rehs)

criollos (kree-OH-lohs)

Miguel de Hidalgo was a priest and a leader of the Mexican War of Independence in 1810. Although he was executed by royalist forces in 1811, in Mexico he is seen as the father of the nation.

The Art Archive/Superstock

1808. In the Spanish case, this effectively left Spanish settlers in the Americas to rule themselves until Napoleon was defeated and the Spanish king was restored in 1814. As a result of their experiences with self-rule, between 1810 and 1825, creoles led movements that brought independence to all Spanish colonies in the Americas—except Cuba and Puerto Rico—and established creole-dominated republics.

Mexican Independence By 1810 weakened royal authority in the Americas spurred revolts against Spanish rule in Argentina, Venezuela, and Mexico. The most serious was a peasant rebellion in Mexico led by a parish priest, **Miguel de Hidalgo** (1753–1811), who rallied indigenous peoples and *mestizos*—people of mixed European and indigenous descent—against colonial rule. Conservative creoles who feared revolution by the masses soon

Miguel de Hidalgo (mee-GEL de hee-DHAHL-goh)

captured Hidalgo and executed him, but his rebellion continued to flare for three years after his death. Hidalgo became the symbol of Mexican independence, and the day on which he proclaimed his revolt—16 September 1810—is Mexico's principal national holiday.

Colonial rule actually came to an end in 1821, when the creole general Augustín de Iturbide (1783–1824) declared independence from Spain. In the following year, he declared himself emperor of Mexico. Iturbide was an incompetent administrator, however, and in 1823 creole elites deposed him and established a republic. Two years later the southern regions of the Mexican empire declared their own independence. They formed a Central American Federation until 1838, then split into the independent states of Guatemala, El Salvador, Honduras, Nicaragua, and Costa Rica.

Simón Bolívar In South America, creole elites such as **Simón Bolívar** (1783–1830) led the movement for independence. Born in Caracas (in modern Venezuela), Bolívar was a fervent republican steeped in Enlightenment ideas about popular sovereignty. Inspired by the example of George Washington, he took up arms against Spanish rule in 1811, during the period of weakened royal authority when the Spanish king had been deposed. In 1819, after many reversals, he assembled an army that surprised and crushed the Spanish army in Colombia. Later he campaigned in Venezuela, Ecuador, and Peru, coordinating his efforts with other creole leaders such as José de San Martín (1778–1850) in Argentina and Bernardo O'Higgins (1778–1842) in Chile. By 1825 creole forces had overcome Spanish armies and deposed Spanish rulers throughout South America.

Bolívar's goal was to weld the former Spanish colonies of South America into a confederation like the United States. During the 1820s, independent Venezuela, Colombia, and Ecuador formed a republic called Gran Colombia, and Bolívar attempted to bring Peru and Bolivia into the confederation as well. By 1830, however, strong political and regional differences led to the breakup of Gran Colombia. As the confederation disintegrated, a bitterly disappointed Bolívar—who died shortly afterward—pronounced South America "ungovernable."

Brazilian Independence Independence came to Portuguese Brazil at the same time as to Spanish colonies, but by a different process. When Napoleon invaded Portugal in 1807, the royal court fled Lisbon and established a government-in-exile in Rio de Janeiro. In 1821 the king returned to Portugal, leaving his son Pedro in Brazil as regent. The next year Brazilian creoles called for independence from Portugal, and Pedro agreed to their demands. In 1822 Pedro declared Brazil's independence and accepted appointment as Emperor Pedro I (reigned 1822–1834).

Creole Dominance In Brazil as in the former Spanish colonies, creole elites dominated both politics and society. Indeed, independence brought little social change in Latin America: although the *peninsulares* returned to Europe, Latin American society remained stratified and unequal. The newly independent states granted military authority to local strongmen, known as **caudillos**, who allied with creole elites. The new states also allowed the continuation of slavery, confirmed the wealth and authority of the Roman Catholic church, and repressed the poor. The principal beneficiaries of independence in Latin America were the creole elites.

CONSEQUENCES AND IMPLICATIONS OF THE REVOLUTIONS

The ideals of the Atlantic revolutions resulted in the birth of new ideologies, including especially the ideologies of conservatism and liberalism. Whereas **conservatism** sought to justify the current state of affairs, **liberalism** sharply criticized the status quo and argued for the need to improve society. The revolutions also encouraged social reformers to organize broader programs of liberation, including the extension of rights to women and enslaved people of African ancestry. During the nineteenth century all European and American states abolished slavery, but formerly enslaved people and their descendants remained an underprivileged and oppressed class in most of the Atlantic world. The quest for women's rights also proceeded slowly during the nineteenth century.

The Emergence of New Ideologies

Conservatism The modern ideology of conservatism arose as political and social theorists responded to the challenges of the American and especially the French revolutions. Conservatives believed that social change, if necessary at all, must be undertaken gradually and with respect for tradition. The English political philosopher Edmund Burke (1729–1797), for example, condemned radical or revolutionary change, which in his view could only lead to anarchy. Thus Burke approved of the American revolution, which he viewed as a natural and logical change, but he denounced the French revolution as a chaotic and irresponsible assault on society.

Liberalism In contrast to conservatives, liberals viewed change as the agent of progress. Conservatism, they argued, was just a means to justify the status quo and maintain the privileges enjoyed by favored classes. For liberals the trick was not to stifle change but, rather, to manage it in the best interests of society. Liberals such as the English political philosopher John Stuart Mill (1806–1873) championed the Enlightenment values of freedom and equality, which liberals believed would lead to higher standards of morality and increased prosperity for the whole society. They usually favored republican forms of government in which citizens elected representatives to legislative bodies, and they called for written constitutions that guaranteed freedom and equality for all citizens. Although some liberals, such as Mill, advocated universal suffrage (and in Mill's case even woman suffrage), many liberals during the nineteenth century did not go so far: for most, universal suffrage still seemed dangerous, because it allowed the uneducated masses to participate in politics.

Testing the Limits of Revolutionary Ideals: Slavery and Women's Rights

The Enlightenment ideals of freedom and equality were watchwords of revolution in the Atlantic Ocean basin. Yet different revolutionaries understood the implications of freedom and equality in very different ways, and the Atlantic revolutions had produced widely varying results. Nevertheless, in the wake of the revolutions, social activists in Europe and the Americas considered the possibility that the ideals of freedom and equality would have further implications as yet unexplored. They turned their attention especially to the issues of slavery and women's rights.

Movements to End the Slave Trade The campaign to end the slave trade and abolish slavery began in the eighteenth century. Only after the American, French, and Haitian revolutions, however, did the antislavery movement gain momentum. The leading spokesman of the movement was **William Wilberforce** (1759–1833), a prominent English philanthropist elected in 1780 to a seat in Parliament. There he tirelessly attacked slavery on moral and religious grounds. After the Haitian revolution he attracted supporters who feared that continued reliance on enslaved labor would result in more and larger revolts, and in 1807 Parliament passed Wilberforce's bill to end the slave trade. Under British pressure, other states also banned international commerce in enslaved people: the United States in 1808, France in 1814, the Netherlands in 1817, and Spain in 1845. The slave trade died slowly, but the British navy, which dominated the North Atlantic Ocean, patrolled the west coast of Africa to ensure compliance with the law.

Movements to Abolish Slavery The abolition of slavery itself was a much bigger challenge than ending the slave trade, because owners had property rights in the people they enslaved and strongly resisted efforts to alter the system. In some places, revolution hastened slavery's end: Haiti abolished the institution in 1801 and Mexico in 1829, and in South America Simón Bolívar freed enslaved people who joined his forces and provided constitutional

---

caudillos (KAHW-dee-yohs)

MAP 25.3   Latin America in 1830

Note the date each state won its independence.

Since most states became independent in very close succession, what conditions prevented Latin American states from joining together in a federation like that in the United States?

guarantees of free status for all residents of Gran Colombia. In other areas slavery was abolished as a result of extensive campaigns by antislavery activists such as Wilberforce. In 1833, one month after Wilberforce's death, Parliament provided twenty million pounds sterling as compensation to slaveholders and abolished slavery throughout the British empire. Other states followed the British example: France abolished slavery in 1848, the United States in 1865, Cuba in 1886, and Brazil in 1888.

Freedom without Equality Abolition brought legal freedom for African and African-descended enslaved people, but it did not bring political equality. In most places, African-descended peoples were prevented from voting through property requirements, literacy tests, and campaigns of intimidation. Nor did emancipation bring social and economic improvements for former enslaved people and their descendants. White creole elites owned most of the property in the Americas, and they kept formerly enslaved people in subordination by forcing them to accept low-paying work.

Enlightenment Ideals and Women Meanwhile, women who participated alongside men in the movement to abolish slavery came to believe that women suffered many of the same legal disabilities as enslaved people: they had little access to education, they could not enter professional occupations that required advanced education, and they were legally deprived of the right to vote. In making the case for their own rights, women drew on Enlightenment ideas about liberty and equality. For example, the English writer Mary Astell (1666–1731) used the political thought of John Locke to argue that absolute sovereignty was no more appropriate in a family than in a state. Astell also reflected Enlightenment influence in asking why, if all men were born free, all women were born enslaved. **Mary Wollstonecraft** (1759–1797), another British writer, similarly drew on Locke's ideas, especially in her 1792 essay titled *A Vindication of the Rights of Woman*. Like Astell, Wollstonecraft argued that women possessed all the rights that Locke had granted to men. She especially insisted on the right of women to education: it would make them better mothers and wives, she said, and would enable them to contribute to society by preparing them for professional occupations and participation in political life.

Women and Revolution Women played crucial roles in the revolutions of the late eighteenth and early nineteenth centuries, from making bandages to managing farms to actively taking up arms. Even so, they did not win political or social rights. In France, where women did gain rights to property, education, and divorce in the early years of the French revolution, they were consistently denied the right to vote or to hold public office. In the later years of the revolution, under the Directory and Napoleon's rule, women lost even the limited rights they had won earlier. In other places, women never gained as much as they did in revolutionary France. In the United States and the independent states of Latin America, revolution brought

What's Left Out? ■■■ ■■■ ■■■ ■■■ ■■■

In the eighteenth century women were barred from serving in the military almost everywhere in the world. Whereas some women defied this restriction by disguising themselves as men and fighting alongside them, many more played active roles in military conflicts as spies. Female secret agents were particularly active during the American revolution and provided critical intelligence for both the American and the British sides. Spying was dangerous work, because the punishment for being caught was death. But women took advantage of the fact that they were seldom suspected of espionage. As a result, women were often able to carry out their work in plain sight, by hiding messages in their clothing, by posing as peddlers in army camps, and by serving food and drink to officers planning their next moves. One example was Anna Smith Strong, whose main job was to let other agents know where to pick up secret messages and anti-British intelligence. Her system was simple: when information was ready to be picked up, she hung a black petticoat outside on her laundry line. The location of the pickup was signaled by the number of handkerchiefs she hung out to dry, which corresponded to various locations. Sometimes the information provided by female spies changed the course of the war. For example, a woman still known only as "Agent 355" provided information to the Continental Army that the British planned to attack French forces in Newport, Rhode Island; American forces then used this information to prevent the surprise attack from occurring. Anna Strong and Agent 355 are only two examples of many, which should help us remember that even before women were permitted to join national military forces in the twentieth century, they were still able to play active roles in military conflicts.

Source: Jeanne Munn Bracken, ed. *Women in the American Revolution*. Auburndale, Mass.: History Compass, 2009.

legal equality and political rights only for adult white men, who retained patriarchal authority over their wives and families.

Women's Rights Movements Nevertheless, throughout the nineteenth century social reformers pressed for women's rights as well as the abolition of slavery. The American **Elizabeth Cady Stanton** (1815–1902) was an especially prominent figure in this movement. In 1840 Stanton went to London to attend an antislavery conference but found that the organizers barred women from participation. Infuriated, Stanton returned to the United States and organized a conference of women at Seneca Falls, New York, in 1848. The conference passed twelve resolutions demanding that lawmakers grant women the right to vote, to attend public schools, to enter professional occupations, and to participate in public affairs. The women's rights movement experienced only limited success in the nineteenth century: some women gained access to education, but nowhere did they win the right to vote. However, by seeking to extend the promises of Enlightenment political thought to people of color and women as well as white men, social reformers of the nineteenth century laid a foundation that would lead to large-scale social change in the twentieth century.

THE NEW NATIONS AND NATIONALISM IN EUROPE

The Enlightenment ideals of freedom, equality, and popular sovereignty inspired political revolutions in much of the Atlantic Ocean basin, and the revolutions in turn helped spread Enlightenment values. The wars of the French revolution and the Napoleonic era also inspired the development of a particular type of community identity that had little to do with Enlightenment values—**nationalism**. Revolutionary wars involved millions of French citizens in the defense of their country against foreign armies and the extension of French influence to neighboring states. Wartime experiences encouraged peoples throughout Europe to think of themselves as members of distinctive national communities. Throughout the nineteenth century, European nationalist leaders worked to fashion states based on national identities and mobilized citizens to work in the interests of their own national communities, sometimes by fostering jealousy and suspicion of other national groups. By the late nineteenth century, national identities were so strong that peoples throughout Europe responded enthusiastically to ideologies of nationalism, which promised glory and prosperity to those who worked in the interests of their national communities.

Nations and Nationalism

One of the most influential concepts of modern political thought is the idea of the nation. At various times and places in history, individuals have associated themselves primarily with families, clans, cities, regions, and religious faiths. However, during the nineteenth century, European peoples came to identify strongly with communities they called nations. Members of a nation considered themselves a distinctive people that spoke a common language, observed common customs, inherited common cultural traditions, held common values, and shared common historical experiences.

Intense feelings of national identity fueled ideologies of nationalism. Advocates of nationalism insisted that the nation must be the focus of political loyalty. Zealous nationalist leaders maintained that members of their national communities had a common destiny that they could best advance by organizing independent national states. Ideally, in their view, the boundaries of the national state embraced the territory occupied by the national community, and its government promoted the interests of the national group, sometimes through conflict with other peoples.

Cultural Nationalism Early nationalist thought often sought to deepen appreciation for the historical experiences of the national community and foster pride in its cultural accomplishments. During the late eighteenth century, for example, **Johann Gottfried von Herder** (1744–1803) sang the praises of the German *Volk* ("people") and their powerful and expressive language. In reaction to Enlightenment thinkers and their quest for a scientific, universally valid understanding of the world, early cultural nationalists such as Herder emphasized the uniqueness of their societies through the study of history, literature, and song.

Political Nationalism During the nineteenth century, nationalist thought became much more strident. In lands where they were minorities or where they lived under foreign rule, nationalists demanded loyalty and solidarity from the national group and sought to establish independent states. In Italy, for example, the nationalist **Giuseppe Mazzini** (1805–1872) formed a group called **Young Italy**, which promoted independence from Austrian and Spanish rule and the establishment of an Italian national state. Austrian and Spanish authorities forced Mazzini to lead much of his life in exile, but he used the opportunity to encourage the organization of nationalist movements in new places. By the mid-nineteenth century, Young Italy had inspired the development of nationalist movements in Ireland, Switzerland, and Hungary.

Johann Gottfried von Herder (YOH-hahn GAWT-freet fuhn HER-duhr)

Giuseppe Mazzini (joo-ZEP-pe maht-TSEE-nee)

During the late nineteenth and twentieth centuries, millions of Jews migrated to other European states or to North America to escape persecution and violence. Anti-Semitism was not as violent in France as in central and eastern Europe, but it reached a fever pitch there after a military court convicted Alfred Dreyfus, a Jewish army officer, of spying for Germany in 1894. Although he was innocent of the charges and eventually had the verdict reversed on appeal, Dreyfus was the focus of bitter debates about the trustworthiness of Jews in French society.

Zionism   Among the reporters at the Dreyfus trial was a Jewish journalist from Vienna, **Theodor Herzl** (1860–1904). As Herzl witnessed mobs shouting "Death to the Jews" in what was supposed to be the land of enlightenment and liberty, he concluded that anti-Semitism could not be solved by assimilation into the larger society. In 1896 Herzl published the pamphlet *Judenstaat,* which argued that the only defense against anti-Semitism lay in the mass migration of Jews from all over the world to a land that they could call their own. In the following year, Herzl organized the first Zionist Congress in Basel, Switzerland, which founded the World Zionist Organization. The delegates at Basel formulated the basic platform of the Zionist movement, declaring that "Zionism seeks to establish a home for the Jewish people in Palestine," the location of the ancient kingdom of Israel.

The Emergence of National Communities

The French revolution and the wars that followed it heightened feelings of national identity throughout Europe. In France the establishment of a republic based on liberty, equality, and fraternity inspired patriotism and encouraged citizens to rally to its defense when foreign armies threatened it. Revolutionary leaders took the tricolored flag as a symbol of the French nation, and they adopted a rousing marching tune, the "Marseillaise," as an anthem that inspired pride and identity with the national community. In Spain, the Netherlands, Austria, Prussia, and Russia, national consciousness surged in reaction to the invasions and occupations of revolutionary and Napoleonic armies. Opposition to Napoleon, and especially fears over French invasion, also inspired national feeling in Britain.

The Congress of Vienna   After the fall of Napoleon, conservative political leaders feared that heightened national consciousness and ideas of popular sovereignty

A determined Theodor Herzl (1860–1904) founded the Zionist movement, which sought to confront anti-Semitism in Europe by establishing a home for the Jews in Palestine.

The History Collection/Alamy Stock Photo

Nationalism and Anti-Semitism   Although it encouraged political leaders to work toward the establishment of national states for their communities, nationalism also had strong potential to stir up conflict between different groups of people. The more nationalists identified with their own national communities, the more they distinguished themselves both from peoples in other lands and from minority groups within their own societies. This divisive potential of nationalism helps explain the emergence of **Zionism**, a political movement that holds that the Jewish people constitute a nation and have the right to their own national homeland. Unlike Mazzini's Italian compatriots, Jews did not inhabit a well-defined territory but, rather, lived in states throughout Europe. As national communities tightened their bonds, nationalist leaders often became distrustful of minority populations. Suspicion of Jews fueled violent **anti-Semitism** in many parts of Europe, including Austria-Hungary, Germany, and eastern Europe. In Russia and the Russian-controlled areas of Poland, the persecution of Jews climaxed in a series of anti-Jewish riots called pogroms (organized massacres), which claimed the lives and property of thousands of Jews.

Theodor Herzl (TEY-aw-dohr HER-tsuhll)
Judenstaat (juh-dehn-STAHT)

Why It Matters

▷▷▷▷▷▷▷

The Birth of Nationalism

Why do people fight and die for their nation? Why do people get emotional when they hear their national anthem? These things may seem natural to us now, but, in fact, they are the legacies of events and processes that began only in the late eighteenth century. Prior to that time, individuals might have local, regional, or religious loyalties, or they might serve particular monarchs or leaders. But the idea that there was an abstract community and culture—a nation—to whom individuals owed their loyalty regardless of who was in charge was new, and it began in this period.

The consequences of this new way of thinking about human communities were enormous, not only in the period when it began but also right down to the present. What were the sources of its power? From its beginnings, nationalism was intimately linked with folk traditions, songs, modes of dress, language, and literature that symbolized a common heritage and common values. These cultural expressions had the power to awaken deep feelings of love and unity among people who felt connected to them. Such feelings often spurred individuals to work on behalf of the nation even at the expense of their own interests, such as fighting in a war to defend the nation even when an individual was not immediately threatened. These feelings also encouraged individuals to exclude—sometimes brutally—those they defined as "outside the nation" and to see the interests of their own nation in competition with the interests of other nations. As a result, people around the world have done extraordinary things—both altruistic and cruel—in the name of nationalism.

In this chapter, we have already seen some of the first instances (in Italy and Germany) of individuals using the power of nationalism to create unified state governments where there were none before—a process that has been attempted multiple times since then. We have also seen that nationalism was used from its beginnings as a tool to exclude unwelcome groups—in this case, European Jews. In fact, nationalism has often served as the double-edged sword of unity. On one side, its symbols and myths have been used by diverse populations as the glue uniting them into one people. On the other side, by emphasizing particular languages and heritages, nationalism often inspires some groups to seek the exclusion of others.

States have frequently exploited the emotive power of nationalism for their own self-interested reasons. In Europe, for example, states played upon nationalist sentiments among their citizens—especially the specter of being bested by other nations—to garner support for imperial expansion in Asia and Africa. By framing expansionist programs in terms of national aggrandizement, states were able to win support for imperial conquests. Somewhat ironically, European imperial expansion ensured that people all over the world would be introduced to the concept of nationalism during the nineteenth and twentieth centuries, with consequences that would ultimately bring down all of the European empires.

The birth of nationalism profoundly shaped identities, loyalties, and both individual and state actions around the world from the late eighteenth century onward, with effects that continue to be felt in the present. As you look around, think about the many and varied ways that the force of nationalism, born in the context of the Atlantic revolutions, still matters in the world we live in today.

---

would undermine European stability. In response, representatives of Britain, Austria, Prussia, and Russia attempted to restore the prerevolutionary order at a meeting known as the **Congress of Vienna** (1814–1815). Under the guidance of the influential foreign minister of Austria, Prince **Klemens von Metternich** (1773–1859), the Congress dismantled Napoleon's empire, returned sovereignty to Europe's royal families, restored them to the thrones they had lost during the Napoleonic era, and created a diplomatic order based on a balance of power that prevented any one state from dominating the others. One of Metternich's central goals was to suppress national consciousness, which he viewed as a serious threat to the multicultural Austrian empire. Yet the efforts of the Congress of Vienna to restore the ancien régime had limited success. Although the European balance of power established at Vienna survived for almost a century, it had become impossible to suppress national consciousness and ideas of popular sovereignty.

Nationalist Rebellions From the 1820s through the 1840s, a wave of rebellions inspired by nationalist sentiments swept through Europe. The first uprising occurred in 1821 in the Balkan peninsula, where the Greek people sought independence from the Ottoman

Klemens von Metternich (kleh-men fuhn MET-er-nik)

The German realist painter Franz von Lenbach (1836–1904) painted many contemporary leaders, including the German chancellor Otto von Bismarck, depicted here. Bismarck is commonly credited with the unification of Germany and creation of the German empire in 1871. Bismarck is wearing a Pickelhaube, a spiked helmet worn by German military, firefighters, and police in the nineteenth and twentieth centuries.
ART Collection/Alamy Stock Photo

sovereignty remained active, and the potential of their ideals to mobilize popular support was crucial in the unification of two new European states: Italy by 1870 and Germany by 1871.

The Unifications of Italy and Germany

The most striking demonstration of the power that national sentiments could unleash involved the unifications of Italy and Germany. A variety of regional kingdoms, city-states, and ecclesiastical states ruled the Italian peninsula for more than a thousand years, and princes divided Germany into more than three hundred semiautonomous jurisdictions.

Cavour and Garibaldi The unification of Italy came about when practical political leaders such as Count **Camillo di Cavour** (1810–1861), prime minister to King **Vittore Emmanuele** II of Piedmont and Sardinia, combined forces with nationalist advocates of independence. Cavour was a cunning diplomat, and the kingdom of Piedmont and Sardinia was the most powerful of the Italian states. In alliance with France, Cavour expelled Austrian authorities—who had gained control of the region through the Congress of Vienna—from most of northern Italy in 1859. Then he turned his attention to southern Italy, where **Giuseppe Garibaldi** (1807–1882), a charismatic soldier for hire and a passionate nationalist, led the unification movement. With an army of about one thousand men outfitted in distinctive red shirts, Garibaldi swept through Sicily and southern Italy, outmaneuvering government forces and attracting enthusiastic recruits. In 1860 Garibaldi met King Vittore Emmanuele near Naples. Not ambitious to rule, Garibaldi delivered southern Italy into Vittore Emmanuele's hands, and the kingdom of Piedmont and Sardinia became the kingdom of Italy. During the next decade the new monarchy absorbed several additional territories, including Venice, Rome, and their surrounding regions.

Otto von Bismarck In Germany as in Italy, unification came about when political leaders harnessed nationalist aspirations. The Congress of Vienna created a German confederation composed of thirty-nine states dominated by Austria. In 1862 King Wilhelm I of Prussia—one of the thirty-nine states—appointed a wealthy landowner, **Otto von Bismarck** (1815–1898), as his prime minister. Bismarck was a master of realpolitik ("the politics of reality") who

Turks. With the aid of Britain, France, and Russia, the rebels won formal recognition of Greek independence in 1830. In the same year, liberal revolutionaries in France, Spain, Portugal, and some of the German principalities called for constitutional government based on popular sovereignty. In Belgium, Italy, and Poland, they demanded independence and the formation of national states as well as popular sovereignty. Revolution in Paris drove Charles X from the throne, and uprisings in Belgium resulted in independence from the Netherlands. In 1848 a new round of rebellions shook European states, where they brought down the French monarchy and seriously threatened the Austrian empire. Uprisings also rocked cities in Italy, Prussia, and German states in the Rhineland.

By the summer of 1849, the veteran armies of conservative rulers had put down the last of the rebellions. However, advocates of national independence and popular

Vittore Emmanuele (vih-tor-reh i-MAHN-yoo-uhl)

Giuseppe Garibaldi (juh-SEP-eh gar-uh-BAWL-dee)

Otto von Bismarck (oht-toh fuhn BIZ-mahrk)

MAP 25.4 The unification of Italy

The unifications of Italy and Germany (see Map 25.5) as national states in the nineteenth century fundamentally altered the balance of power in Europe.

Why did unification result from diplomacy and war conducted by conservative statesmen rather than popular nationalist action?

argued that "the great questions of the day will not be settled by speeches or majority votes . . . but by blood and iron." It was indeed blood and iron that brought about the unification of Germany. As prime minister, Bismarck reformed and expanded the Prussian army. Between 1864 and 1870 he intentionally provoked three wars—with Denmark, Austria, and France—and whipped up German sentiment against the enemies. In all three conflicts Prussian forces quickly shattered their opponents, swelling German pride. In 1871 the Prussian king proclaimed himself emperor of the Second Reich—meaning the second German empire, following the Holy Roman Empire—which embraced almost all German-speaking

peoples outside Austria and Switzerland in a powerful and dynamic national state.

The unifications of Italy and Germany made it clear that when coupled with strong political, diplomatic, and military leadership, nationalism had enormous potential to mobilize people who felt a sense of national kinship. Italy, Germany, and other national states went to great lengths to foster a sense of national community. They adopted national flags to serve as symbols of unity, national anthems to inspire patriotism, and national holidays to focus public attention on individuals and events of special importance for the national community. They established bureaucracies that took censuses of national populations

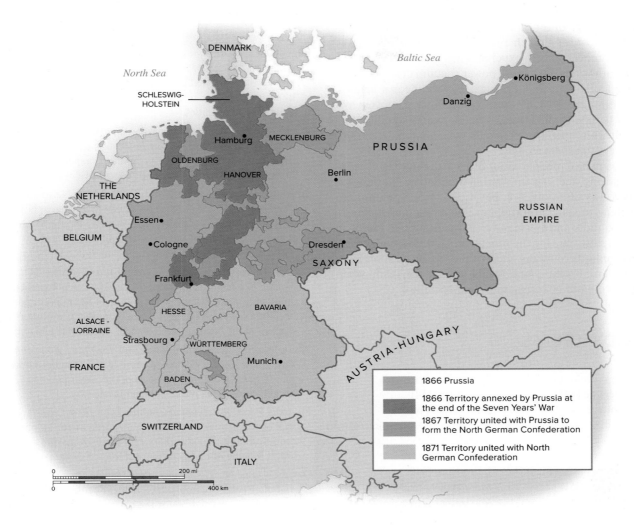

MAP 25.5   The unification of Germany

Note the vast size of the territory in central Europe that united to become Germany in just five years.

Does the map give a sense of why the state of Prussia dominated the newly unified nation?

and tracked vital national statistics involving birth, marriage, and death. They built schools that instilled patriotic values in students, and they recruited young men into armies that defended national interests and sometimes went on the offensive to enhance national prestige. By the end of the nineteenth century, the national state had proven to be a powerful model of political organization in Europe.

CONCLUSION

The Enlightenment ideals of freedom, equality, and popular sovereignty inspired revolutionary movements throughout much of the Atlantic Ocean basin in the late eighteenth and early nineteenth centuries. Although Enlightenment ideals may have served as inspiration, war provided the opportunity and dictated the timing of the revolutions. Just as important, each successive revolution drew inspiration from those that went before. In North America, tensions caused by the Seven Years' War provided the context in which colonists threw off British rule and founded an independent federal republic. In France, where aid to the American revolutionaries helped cause a massive financial crisis, revolutionaries abolished the monarchy, established a republic, and abandoned traditions to refashion the social order. In Saint-Domingue, rebellious enslaved people who were inspired by revolutionary ideas took advantage of the chaos caused by the French revolution to throw off French rule. In Latin America, creole elites led movements to expel Spanish and Portuguese colonial authorities during the power vacuum created by the invasion of Spain and Portugal by Napoleon's armies. And although most of these revolutionary movements sought to extend the ideals of freedom and equality only to adult white men, reformers launched campaigns to extend them to others as well.

Meanwhile, people around the Atlantic basin developed strong feelings of national identity. Nationalist thought was often divisive, but it had strong potential to contribute to state-building movements such as the unifications of Italy and Germany or the aspiration to establish a Jewish state. During the nineteenth and twentieth centuries, peoples throughout the world drew inspiration from egalitarian revolutionary ideals and nationalism when seeking to build or restructure their societies.

STUDY TERMS

American revolution (439)
ancien régime (443)
anti-Semitism (455)
Camillo di Cavour (457)
caudillos (451)
Civil Code (446)
Congress of Vienna (456)
conservatism (451)
Continental Congress (441)
Declaration of Independence (441)
Declaration of the Rights of Man and the Citizen (438)
Declaration of the Rights of Woman and the Female Citizen (438)
Elizabeth Cady Stanton (454)
Enlightenment (440)
Estates General (443)
French revolution (443)
gens de couleur (449)
George Washington (442)
Giuseppe Garibaldi (457)
Giuseppe Mazzini (454)
Haitian revolution (449)
Jean-Jacques Rousseau (441)

Johann Gottfried von Herder (454)
John Locke (440)
Klemens von Metternich (456)
liberalism (451)
Louis XVI (443)
Louverture (449)
Mary Wollstonecraft (453)
Maximilien Robespierre (446)
Miguel de Hidalgo (450)
Napoleon Bonaparte (446)
National Assembly (444)
nationalism (454)
Olympe de Gouges (438)
Otto von Bismarck (457)
philosophes (440)
reign of terror (446)
Seven Years' War (441)
Simón Bolívar (450)
Theodor Herzl (455)
Vittore Emmanuele (457)
Voltaire (440)
William Wilberforce (451)
Young Italy (454)
Zionism (455)

FOR FURTHER READING

Benedict Anderson. *Imagined Communities: Reflections on the Origin and Spread of Nationalism.* Rev. ed. London, 1991. A pioneering work that analyzes the means and the processes by which peoples came to view themselves as members of national communities.

David A. Bell. *The First Total War: Napoleon's Europe and the Birth of Warfare as We Know It.* Boston, 2007. A fine work that argues that nearly every "modern" aspect of war was born in the Revolutionary and Napoleonic wars.

Suzanne Desan, Lynn Hunt, and William Max Nelson, eds. *The French Revolution in Global Perspective.* Ithaca, N.Y., 2013. A collection of essays that offers a new approach to the understanding of the international origins and worldwide effects of this seminal revolution.

Laurent Dubois. *Avengers of the New World: The Story of the Haitian Revolution.* Cambridge, Mass., 2005. A comprehensive study of how the French slave colony of Saint-Domingue became a unique example of a successful Black revolution that challenged the boundaries of freedom, citizenship, and empire.

Susan Dunn. *Sister Revolutions: French Lightning, American Light.* New York, 1999. An accessible and stimulating work that traces the different legacies of the American and French revolutions of the eighteenth century.

François Furet. *Revolutionary France 1770-1880.* Oxford, 1995. In a brilliant work of synthesis, a leading historian places the revolutions of 1789, 1830, 1848, and 1871 within the grand scheme of democratic traditions.

David Geggus, ed. *The Impact of the Haitian Revolution in the Atlantic World.* Columbia, S.C., 2001. Focuses on the wider impact of the revolution for the region in terms of ideology, economics, and precedent.

Jay Kinsbruner. *Independence in Spanish America: Civil Wars, Revolutions, and Underdevelopment.* 2nd ed. Albuquerque, 2000. A compelling reinterpretation of the independence movements of sixteen nations, their similarities, and their regional differences.

Robert Middlekauff. *The Glorious Cause: The American Revolution, 1763-1789.* 2nd ed. Oxford, 2005. A masterful exploration of the causes, events, and consequences of the revolution.

Anthony Pagden. *The Enlightenment: And Why It Still Matters.* New York, 2013. This sweeping and fascinating work is an enlightening look at the Enlightenment that argues for the continuing relevance of this intellectual movement.

ZOOMING IN ON TRADITIONS AND ENCOUNTERS

Betty Harris: A Woman Chained in the Coal Pits

In 1827, shortly after marrying at age twenty-three, Betty Harris took a job as a drawer in a coal pit near Manchester, England. A drawer's job involved crawling down narrow mine shafts and hauling loads of coal from the bottom of the pit to the surface. Drawers performed unskilled labor for low wages, but their work was essential for obtaining the coal that fueled the factories and mills of early industrial society.

An 1831 painting by D. O. Hill depicting the St. Rollox Chemical Works in Glasgow, Scotland, on the occasion of the opening of the Garnkirk and Glasgow railway. Note the juxtaposition between the picnicking spectators and the black smoke emanating from the St. Rollox factory chimney stacks.
FLHC 15/Alamy Stock Photo

While working, Harris wore a heavy belt around her waist. Hitched to the belt was a chain that passed between her legs and attached to the coal cart that she pulled through the steep and slippery mine shafts, often on hands and knees. Every workday, even when she was pregnant, Harris strapped on her belt and chain at 6:00 A.M., removing her bindings only at the end of the shift twelve hours later.

Harris reported that drawing coal was "very hard work for a woman," and she did not exaggerate. The belts and chains worn by drawers often chafed their skin raw, and miners contributed to their physical discomfort by beating them for slow or clumsy work. The miners, many of whom worked naked in the hot, oppressive coal pits, also sometimes sexually abused the women and girl drawers: Harris personally knew several women who became pregnant after being raped in the coal pits.

Harris's work schedule made comfortable family life impossible. A cousin cared for her two children during the day, and Harris tended to them and her husband at night after a twelve-hour workday with only a single one-hour break to eat bread and butter. At age thirty-seven, after fourteen years in the mines, Harris put it mildly when she said, "I am not so strong as I was."

CHAPTER OVERVIEW

Not all industrial workers worked in such difficult conditions, but Betty Harris's experience nonetheless illustrates some of the deep changes that industrialization wrought in patterns of work and family life. First in Britain, then in parts of western Europe, North America, Russia, and Japan, machines and factories transformed agricultural societies into industrial societies. At the heart of this transformation were technological changes that led to the extensive use of machinery in manufacturing. Industrial machinery transformed economic production by turning out high-quality products quickly, cheaply, and efficiently. The process of industrialization encouraged rapid technological innovation and over the long term raised material standards of living in much of the world.

But the impact of industrialization went beyond economics. Perhaps most importantly, the use of fossil fuels and the transition to industrial production had enormous environmental consequences. By the turn of the twentieth century, many of the world's soils and waters were deeply polluted, and the air near industrial areas posed a serious health risk. Social change was also far-reaching. Early industrialists created a new work environment, the factory, which concentrated large numbers of workers under one roof to operate complicated machinery. By moving work outside the home, however, factories drew fathers, mothers, and children in different directions, altered traditional patterns of domestic life, and strained family relations.

Industrialization also encouraged rapid urbanization and migration. New cities mushroomed to house workers who left the countryside for jobs in factories. Millions of migrants even crossed the seas in search of opportunities in new lands. Often, however, early industrial workers found themselves living in squalor and toxic pollution while laboring under dangerous conditions.

Social critics and reformers worked to alleviate the social problems caused by early industrial society. Despite their appeals, however, capitalism and industrialization flourished and spread rapidly from Britain to continental Europe, North America, and Asia. In some areas, notably western Europe and North America, industrialization was encouraged, so that states could gain the economic advantages of industrialization. In other places, including Russia and Japan, industrialization was undertaken as part of a larger program of social, political, and economic reform to avoid domination by western European and American powers. Elsewhere, industrialization created a new international division of labor that made most of Africa, Asia, and Latin America economically dependent on the export of raw materials that supplied the factories and cities of the industrialized world. Thus, although industrialization spread unevenly and for different reasons, it profoundly influenced social and economic conditions all over the globe.

CHRONOLOGY	
1733	John Kay develops the flying shuttle
1765	James Watt patents an improved steam engine
1779	Samuel Crompton develops the spinning mule
1785	Edmund Cartwright develops the power loom
1797	Eli Whitney introduces interchangeable parts to the manufacturing process
1829	George Stephenson's locomotive, the Rocket, attains a speed of 45 kilometers (28 miles) per hour
1848	Karl Marx and Friedrich Engels publish *Manifesto of the Communist Party*
1849–1915	Life of Sergei Witte
1851	Crystal Palace exhibition in London
1853	Arrival of Commodore Perry in Japan
1853–1856	Crimean War
1855–1881	Reign of Czar Alexander II
1856	Bessemer converter developed
1861	Emancipation of the Russian serfs
1868	Meiji restoration
1913	Henry Ford introduces the assembly line to the manufacture of automobiles

PATTERNS OF INDUSTRIALIZATION

Industrialization refers to a process that transformed economies previously centered around agriculture and handicrafts to those distinguished by industry and machine manufacture. Critical to industrialization were productivity-increasing technological developments that made it possible to produce goods by machines rather than by hand and that harnessed inanimate sources of energy such as coal and petroleum. Also critical was the development of factory production, in which workers assembled under one roof to produce goods in mass quantities. The need to invest in expensive factory equipment in turn encouraged the formation of large businesses: by the mid-nineteenth century many giant corporations had joined together to control trade through trusts and cartels.

Foundations of Industrialization

By the mid-eighteenth century several areas of the world—Great Britain in western Europe, the Yangzi delta in China, and Japan—exhibited dynamic economies that shared many features. High agricultural productivity resulted in significant population growth, and high population densities encouraged occupational specialization outside of agriculture. Navigable rivers and networks of canals facilitated trade and transport, and cities and towns supported sophisticated banking and financial institutions. At the same time, these dynamic economies ran up against difficult ecological obstacles—especially soil depletion and deforestation—that threatened continued population growth and consumption levels. Despite their common features, Great Britain was the first to transcend these ecological constraints by exploiting coal deposits found near large centers of population and by utilizing natural resources found abroad.

Coal and Colonies Until the eighteenth century, wood served as Great Britain's primary source of fuel for iron production, home heating, and cooking. Such extensive use of wood resulted in serious wood shortages. However, geographic luck had placed some of western Europe's largest coal deposits in Great Britain, within easy reach of water transport, centers of commerce, and pools of skilled labor. Humans in many parts of the world had known for at least a millennium that coal can burn. In Britain, however, it did not seem necessary to seek it out in large quantities until wood became scarce. Once it became clear that wood was in increasingly short supply, the fortunate combination encouraged the substitution of coal for wood, thus creating a promising framework for industrialization. If coal had not been easily accessible in Britain, it is unlikely that the economy could have supported expanding iron production and the application of steam engines to mining and industry—both crucial to the industrial process in Great Britain. In that respect Britain's experience differed from that of China. In China, the largest coal deposits were hundreds of miles from the area in the Yangzi delta where large populations of skilled laborers lived. As a result, it did not make sense to shift to a reliance on coal in China in this period.

The unique economic relationship between Europe and the Americas gave Great Britain in particular an additional resource to overcome ecological obstacles. After decimating the indigenous populations of the Americas and then settling the land, European colonizers overcame land constraints by supplying European societies with a growing volume of primary products. During the eighteenth century slavery-based plantations supplied Europe with huge amounts of sugar and cotton; the former increased available food calories, and the latter kept emerging textile industries going. Neither of those products could have been grown in Europe. The significance of valuable American resources grew after 1830, when large amounts of grain, timber, and beef grown on colonial acreage were sent across the Atlantic to European destinations. In addition, American lands served as outlets for European manufactured goods as well as Europe's surplus population.

Mechanization of the Cotton Industry Among the first industries to mechanize was British textile manufacturing. During the seventeenth century English consumers had become fond of calicoes—inexpensive, brightly printed cotton textiles from India. Cotton cloth came into demand because it was lighter and easier to wash than wool, which was the principal fabric of European clothes before the nineteenth century. Although British wool producers tried to protect their industry through a series of laws designed to prohibit imports of cotton cloth from India in 1720 and 1721, they could not stifle public demand.

In fact, demand for cotton was so strong that producers had to speed up spinning and weaving to supply growing markets. To increase production they turned to inventions that rapidly mechanized the cotton textile industry. The first important technological breakthrough came in 1733 when Manchester mechanic John Kay invented the **flying shuttle**, which sped up the weaving process. Within a few years, inventors created several mechanical spinning devices, the most important of which was Samuel Crompton's spinning **mule**, built in 1779. In 1790 the mule was adapted for steam power, and it became the device of choice for spinning cotton. A worker using a steam-driven mule could produce a hundred times more thread than a worker using a manual spinning wheel.

The new spinning machines necessitated new weaving machines, so that weavers could keep up with the

This 1835 engraving depicts female workers at a textile factory. The shift to machine-based manufacturing commonly started with the mechanization of the textile industries, not only in Great Britain but also in other industrializing lands such as the United States and Japan. What cannot be communicated by images like this was the deafening clatter made by the machines while they were being operated throughout the day.
Bettmann/Getty Images

production of thread. In 1785 Edmund Cartwright, a clergyman without experience in either mechanics or textiles, patented a water-driven **power loom**. Within two decades steam moved the power loom, and by the 1820s hand weavers were nearly obsolete. A young boy working on two power looms could produce fifteen times more cloth than the fastest hand weaver. Collectively, these technological developments permitted the mass production of inexpensive textile goods. By 1830 half a million people worked in the cotton business, Britain's leading industry, which accounted for 40 percent of exports.

Steam Power Among the most crucial technological breakthroughs of the early industrial era was the development of a general-purpose steam engine in 1765 by **James Watt**, an instrument maker at the University of Glasgow in Scotland. Even before Watt's time, primitive steam engines had powered pumps that drew water out of coal mines, but those devices consumed too much fuel to be useful for other purposes. Watt's version relied on steam to force a piston to turn a wheel, whose rotary motion converted a simple pump into an engine. By

1800 more than a thousand of Watt's steam engines were in use in the British Isles. They were especially prominent in the textile industry, where they allowed greater productivity for manufacturers and cheaper prices for consumers.

Iron and Steel The iron and steel industries also benefited from technological refinement in this period, and the availability of inexpensive, high-quality iron and steel reinforced the move toward mechanization. After 1709 British smelters began to use coke (a purified form of coal) rather than more expensive charcoal as a fuel to produce iron. As a result, British iron production skyrocketed during the eighteenth century, and prices to consumers fell. Inexpensive iron fittings and parts made industrial machinery stronger, and iron soon became common in bridges, buildings, and ships.

Steel is much harder, stronger, and more resilient than iron, but until the nineteenth century it was very expensive to produce. In 1856, however, Henry Bessemer—an English inventor—built a refined blast furnace, known as the Bessemer converter, that made it possible to produce large quantities of steel cheaply. Steel production rose sharply, and steel quickly began to replace iron in tools, machines, and structures that required high strength.

Transportation Steam engineering and metallurgical innovations both contributed to improvements in transportation technology. In 1815 **George Stephenson**, a self-educated Englishman, built the first steam-powered locomotive. In 1829 his Rocket won a contest by reaching a speed of 45 kilometers (28 miles) per hour. By the mid-nineteenth century, refined steam engines of high efficiency also began to drive steamships.

Because they had the capacity to carry huge cargoes, steam trains and steamships dramatically lowered transportation costs. They also contributed to the creation of transportation networks that linked remote interior regions and distant shores more closely than ever before in history. Between 1830 and 1870, British entrepreneurs laid about 20,000 kilometers (13,000 miles) of railroads, which carried some 322 million passengers as well as cargoes of raw materials and manufactured goods. Meanwhile, steamships proved their versatility by advancing up rivers to points that sailboats could not reach because of inconvenient twists or turns.

The Factory System

The Factory The **factory system** became the characteristic method of production in industrial economies. It emerged in the late eighteenth century, when technological advances transformed the British textile industry, and by the mid-nineteenth century most cotton production took place in factories. Many of the newly developed machines were too large and expensive for home use, so it became necessary to move work to centralized locations.

That centralization of production brought together more workers doing specialized tasks than ever before.

Working Conditions The factory system with its new machines demanded a rational organization of job functions. Thus the factory became associated with a new division of labor that called for a production process in which each worker performed a single task, rather than one in which a single worker completed the entire job, as was typical of handicraft traditions. This new division of labor allowed managers to improve worker productivity and realize spectacular increases in the output of manufactured goods. But the new environment also had unsettling effects on the nature of work. For instance, the factory system led to the emergence of an owner class whose capital financed equipment and machinery that were too expensive for workers to acquire. As a result, industrial workers became mere wage earners who depended on their employers for their livelihood. The repetitive and boring nature of many industrial jobs, moreover, left many workers alienated from their work and the products of their labor. In addition, any broad-range skills that workers might have previously acquired as artisans often became obsolete in the factory work environment. Between 1811 and 1816 that situation prompted organized bands of English handicraft workers known as **Luddites** to destroy textile machines, which they blamed for their low wages and unemployment. Nevertheless, by hanging fourteen Luddites in 1813, the government served notice that it was unwilling to tolerate violence even against machines, and the movement gradually died out.

Equally disturbing was the new work discipline and the pace of work. Those accustomed to rural labor found that the seasons and fluctuations in the weather no longer dictated work routines. Instead, clocks, machines, and

What's Left Out? ■■■ ■■■ ■■■ ■■■ ■■■

How might you experience time if you had no clocks—no way to know the exact time to wake up, eat lunch, or go home from work? It is difficult to imagine now, but prior to the industrial revolution, time was dictated by the rhythm of the seasons, tasks that needed to be completed, and the progression of the day. However, with the advent of railroads, it became important to know exactly when a train would arrive and depart. To solve the problem of widely varying local times, in 1847 the railroads in Britain uniformly adopted Greenwich Mean Time. Over the next few decades, most towns adopted this single, standardized time. The factory system also revolutionized the way people experienced time. Unlike earlier forms of work, the scale of the workforce in factories and the expense of running complicated machines prompted factory owners to insist that workers arrive to work, take breaks, and leave from work at exact times. Suddenly, people needed to know precisely when to get up, go to work, eat, and sleep. Towns erected large clocks, which loudly chimed the hour, so that all could hear, and those who could afford it purchased pocket watches or clocks for their homes. As a result, people began to experience time not in terms of natural rhythms but almost exclusively as something dictated by the discipline of clocks—a discipline that has become a permanent part of modern life right into the present.

Source: Trish Ferguson. *Victorian Time: Technologies, Standardizations, Catastrophes.* 3rd ed. London: Palgrave Macmillan, 2013.

SOURCES FROM THE PAST

Ned Ludd's Angry Letter to a Shearing Frame Holder

Many ordinary people in Britain were not happy with the mechanization that accompanied industrialization in the early nineteenth century. Skilled artisans such as weavers rightly worried that the new machines would put them out of a job. In fact, it was true that a single person could do the work of several people by operating one of the shearing frames being introduced into the weaving industry. Between 1811 and 1816, groups of men claiming to be led by "Ned Ludd" or "General Ludd" banded together to destroy the new machines and to protest cuts in their wages. They sent threatening letters to business owners who utilized the new machines, broke into factories to break the machines, attacked employers, and fought with government soldiers. Although some of these protesters were caught and executed, most Luddites escaped capture, because local communities seem to have protected them. The following letter was written around 9 March 1812 to a Mr. Smith, an owner of a factory with shearing frames in Yorkshire.

Information has just been given in that you are a holder of those detestable Shearing Frames, and I was desired by my Men to write to you and give you fair Warning to pull them down, and for that purpose I desire you will now understand I am now writing to you. you will take Notice that if they are not taken down by the end of next Week, I will detach one of my Lieutenants with at least 300 Men to destroy them and furthermore take Notice that if you give us the Trouble of coming so far we will increase your misfortune by burning your Buildings down to Ashes and if you have Impudence to fire upon any of my Men, they have orders to murder you, & burn all your Housing, you will have the Goodness to your Neighbours to inform them that the same fate awaits them if their Frames are not speedily taken down as I understand their are several in your Neighbourhood, Frame holders.

> What will happen to Mr. Smith and his fellow industrialists if they do not voluntarily take down their shearing frames, according to the letter?

And as the Views and Intentions of me and my Men have been much misrepresented I will take this opportunity of stating them, which I desire you will let all your Brethren in Sin know of. I would have the Merchants, Master Dressers, the Government & the public to know that the Grievances of such a Number of Men are not to be made sport of for by the last Returns there were 2782 Sworn Heroes bound in a Bond of Necessity either to redress their Grievances or gloriously perish in the Attempt in the Army of Huddersfield alone, nearly double sworn Men in Leeds . . . We hope for assistance from the French Emperor in shaking off the Yoke of the Rottenest, Wickedest and most Tyranious Government that ever existed; then down come the Hanover Tyrants [the current line of British kings], and all our Tyrants from the greatest to the smallest. And we will be governed by a just Republic, and may the Almighty hasten those happy Times is the Wish and Prayer of Millions in this Land, but we won't only pray but we will fight, the Redcoats shall know that when the proper time comes We will never lay down our Arms.

> What indication is there that the author of this letter has only a basic education? Can that tell us anything about who he might have been?

Signed by the General of the Army of Redressers
Ned Ludd Clerk

Redressers for ever Amen,
You may make this Public
[9 or 10 March]

For Further Reflection

■ What is the ultimate goal of Ned Ludd and his army of redressers, according to this letter, and how will they achieve it?
■ What can this document tell us about how ordinary people might have viewed the changes associated with the industrial revolution?

Source: Ned Ludd Clerk. *Letter from "Ned Ludd Clerk" Addressed "To Mr Smith Shearing Frame Holder at Hill End Yorkshire."* 1812. http://ludditebicentenary.blogspot.com/2012/03/9th-march-1812-letter-from-ned-ludd.html

shop rules established new rhythms of work. Industrial workers commonly labored six days a week, twelve to fourteen hours a day. The factory whistle sounded the beginning and the end of each working day, and throughout the day workers had to keep pace with the movements of machines. At the same time, they faced strict and immediate supervision. Floor managers pressured men, women, and children to speed up production and punished them when they did not meet expectations. In addition, dangerous work conditions often meant that early industrial workers faced exposure to toxic chemicals, harmful levels of noise, and the possibility of accidents—some of which could be fatal.

The Early Spread of Industrialization

For fifty years industrialization occurred only in Britain. Aware of their head start, British entrepreneurs and government officials forbade the export of machinery, manufacturing techniques, and skilled workers to other lands. Yet Britain's monopoly on industrialization did not last, because enterprising entrepreneurs ignored government regulations and sold machinery and technical know-

how abroad. Moreover, European and North American businesspeople did not hesitate to bribe or even kidnap British engineers to learn the secrets of industrialization, and they smuggled advanced machinery out of the British Isles.

Industrialization in Western Europe As a result, by the mid-nineteenth century industrialization had spread to parts of France, Germany, Belgium, and the United States. The earliest continental center of industrial production was Belgium, where coal, iron, textile, glass, and armaments production flourished in the early nineteenth century. About the same time, France also moved toward industrialization. By the mid-nineteenth century, French engineers and inventors were devising refinements and innovations that led to greater efficiencies, especially in metallurgical industries. Although German industrialization started off more slowly than in France or Belgium, German coal and iron production soared after the 1840s, and by the 1850s an extensive railroad network was under construction. After unification in 1871, Bismarck's government sponsored rapid industrialization in Germany, especially of heavy industry.

Workers tend to a massive steam hammer, which was used for forging metal. Note the proximity of the workers to the molten metal.
Ann Ronan Pictures/Print Collector/Getty Images

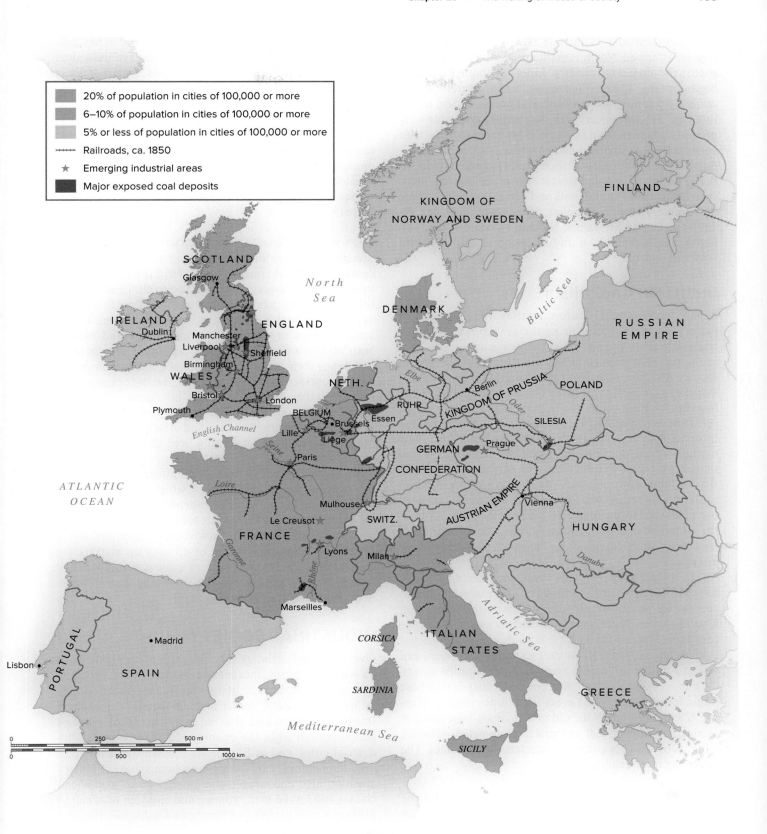

20% of population in cities of 100,000 or more

6–10% of population in cities of 100,000 or more

5% or less of population in cities of 100,000 or more

┈┈┈┈ Railroads, ca. 1850

★ Emerging industrial areas

Major exposed coal deposits

MAP 26.1 Industrial Europe, ca. 1850

Locate the places marked as emerging industrial areas.

Are there any features those areas have in common? If so, what are they?

Industrialization in North America Industrialization transformed North America as well as western Europe in the nineteenth century. American industrialization began in the 1820s when entrepreneurs lured British crafts workers to New England and built a cotton textile industry. By mid-century well over a thousand mills were producing fabrics from raw cotton grown in the southern states, and New England had emerged as a site for the industrial production also of shoes, tools, and handguns. In the 1870s heavy iron and steel industries emerged in areas such as western Pennsylvania and central Alabama where there were abundant supplies of iron ore and coal. By 1900 the United States had become an economic powerhouse, and industrialization had begun to spill over into southern Canada.

Industrial Capitalism

Mass Production Cotton textiles were the major factory-made products during the early phase of industrialization, but the factory system soon spread to other industries. An important contribution to the evolving factory system came from the American inventor **Eli Whitney** (1765–1825). Though best remembered as the inventor of the cotton gin (1793), Whitney also developed the technique of using machine tools to produce interchangeable parts in the making of firearms. This method meant that unskilled workers made only a particular part that fit every musket of the same model. Before long, entrepreneurs applied Whitney's method to the manufacture of everything from clocks and sewing machines to uniforms and shoes. By the middle of the nineteenth century, mass production of standardized items was becoming the hallmark of industrial societies.

In 1913 **Henry Ford** improved manufacturing techniques further when he introduced the assembly line to automobile production. Instead of organizing production around a series of stations where workers assembled whole cars using standardized parts, Ford designed a conveyor system that allowed each worker to perform a specialized task at a fixed point on the assembly line. With the assembly line, workers churned out a complete chassis (the base frame for an automobile) every 93 minutes instead of every 728 minutes under the old system. Such huge gains in productivity meant that car prices plummeted, allowing millions of ordinary people to purchase automobiles. The age of the motor car had arrived.

The Corporation As the factory evolved, so did the organization of business. Industrial machinery and factories were expensive investments, and they encouraged businesses to organize on a large scale. During the 1850s and 1860s government authorities in Britain and France laid the legal foundations for the modern corporation, which quickly became the most common form of business organization in industrial societies. Instead of individual or small partnerships owning businesses, **corporations** were formed as legal entities that were separate and distinct from their owners. This meant that individual people could not be held liable for claims or losses incurred, thus spreading financial risk. It also allowed groups of people to raise money by selling shares, which allowed large sums of capital to be raised for expensive ventures. By the late nineteenth century, corporations controlled most businesses requiring large investments in land, labor, or machinery.

Monopolies, Trusts, and Cartels To protect their investments, some big businesses of the late nineteenth century sought not only to outperform their competitors in the capitalist marketplace but also to eliminate competition. Business firms formed associations to restrict markets or establish monopolies in their industries. Large-scale business organizations formed **trusts** and **cartels**, both of which aimed to control the supply of a product and hence its price in the marketplace. Trusts commonly sought control of industries through vertical organization, by which they would dominate all facets of a single industry. John D. Rockefeller's Standard Oil Company and Trust, for example, controlled almost all oil drilling, processing, refining, marketing, and distribution in the United States.

Cartels, in contrast, tried to eliminate competition by means of horizontal organization, which involved the consolidation or cooperation of independent companies in the same business. Thus cartels sought to ensure the prosperity of their members by absorbing competitors, fixing prices, regulating production, or dividing up markets. By the end of the nineteenth century some governments had outlawed trusts and cartels. However, monopolistic practices continued even into the present.

INDUSTRIAL SOCIETY

Over time, industrialization brought material benefits in its wake, including inexpensive manufactured products and rising standards of living. Yet industrialization also unleashed dramatic social and environmental change. Immense internal and external migrations took place as people moved from the countryside to work in new industrial cities, and as Europeans crossed the Atlantic to seek opportunities in the western hemisphere. Industrialization also encouraged the emergence of new social classes and forced men, women, and children to adjust to distinctly new patterns of family and work life. Reformers sought to alleviate the social, economic, and environmental problems that accompanied industrialization and worked toward the building of a more equitable and just society.

Exhibitors from around the world displayed fine handicrafts and manufactured goods at the Crystal Palace exhibition of 1851 in London. Industrial products from Britain and the United States particularly attracted the attention of visitors to the enchanting and futuristic exhibition hall.

World History Archive/Alamy Stock Photo

The Fruits of Industry

Industrialization brought efficiencies in production that flooded markets with affordable manufactured goods. Indeed, industrialization raised material standards of living in many ways. Industrial production led to dramatic reductions in the cost of clothing, for example, so by the early nineteenth century all but the desperately poor could afford several changes of clothes. Industrial factories turned out tools that facilitated agricultural work, and steam-powered locomotives delivered produce quickly and cheaply to distant markets. Consumers in early industrial Europe also filled their homes with more furniture, porcelain, and decorative objects than had any but the most wealthy of their ancestors.

Population Growth The populations of European and Euro-American peoples rose sharply during the eighteenth and nineteenth centuries, reflecting the rising prosperity and standards of living that came with industrialization. Between 1700 and 1900 the population of Europe increased from 105 to 390 million. Demographic growth in the Americas—fueled by migration from Europe—was even more remarkable. Between 1700 and 1900 the population of North America and South America rose from 13 million to 145 million.

The rapid population growth in Europe and the Americas reflected changing patterns of fertility and mortality. In most preindustrial societies fertility was high, but so was child mortality, which held population growth in check. High birthrates were common also in early industrializing societies, but death rates fell markedly because better diets and improved disease control reduced child mortality. By the late nineteenth century better diets and improved sanitation led to declining levels of adult as well as child mortality. In combination, these two factors allowed populations to expand rapidly.

The Demographic Transition Beginning in the nineteenth century, however, industrializing lands experienced a social change known as the **demographic transition**. As industrialization transformed societies, fertility—the number of children born—declined. In the short run, mortality fell even faster than fertility, so the populations of industrial societies continued to increase. Over time, however, declining birthrates led to lower population growth and relative demographic stability. The principal reason for declining fertility in industrial lands was voluntary birth control through contraception, perhaps because raising children cost more in industrial societies or because more children were likely to survive to adulthood than in the past.

Urbanization and Migration

Industrialization and population growth strongly encouraged migration and urbanization. Within industrial societies, migrants flocked from the countryside to urban centers in search of work. For example, in 1800 about one-fifth of the British population lived in towns and cities of ten thousand or more inhabitants. By 1900 three-fourths of the population worked and lived in cities. That pattern repeated itself elsewhere: by 1900 at least half of the population in industrialized lands lived in towns with populations of two thousand or more. The increasing size of cities reflected this internal migration. In 1800 there were barely twenty cities in Europe with populations as high as one hundred thousand, and there were none in the western hemisphere. By 1900 there were more than one hundred and fifty large cities in Europe and North America combined.

The Urban Environment

With urbanization came intensified environmental pollution. Although cities have always been unsanitary places, the rapid increase in urban populations during the industrial age dramatically increased the magnitude and severity of water and air pollution. The widespread burning of fossil fuels fouled the air with vast quantities of chemicals and particulate matter. This pollution led to occupational diseases in some trades. Chimney sweeps, for instance, contracted cancer of the scrotum from hydrocarbon deposits found in soot. Effluents from factories and mills as well as untreated sewage dirtied virtually every major river. No part of a city was immune to the constant stench coming from air and water pollution. Worse, tainted water supplies and unsanitary living conditions led to periodic epidemics of cholera and typhus. Until the latter part of the nineteenth century, urban environments remained dangerous places in which death rates commonly exceeded birthrates, and only the constant stream of new arrivals from the country kept cities growing.

Income determined the degree of comfort and security offered by city life. The wealthy typically tried to insulate themselves from urban discomforts by retreating to their elegant homes in newly growing suburbs. The working poor, in contrast, occupied overcrowded tenements lacking in comfort and amenities. The cramped spaces in apartments obliged many to share the same bed, increasing the ease of disease transmission. The few open spaces outside the buildings were usually home to herds of pigs living in their own dung or were depositories for pools of stagnant water and human waste.

By the later nineteenth century, though, government authorities were tending to the problems of the early industrial cities. They improved the safety of municipal water supplies, expanded sewage systems, and introduced building codes that outlawed the construction of rickety tenements to accommodate poorly paid workers. Those measures made city life safer and brought improved sanitation. City authorities also built parks and recreational facilities to make cities more livable. Nevertheless, the emissions from fossil-fuel combustion that accompanied industrialization and rapid economic development were responsible for the increased amount of greenhouse gases, hence the rise in the average temperature of earth's atmosphere and oceans that continues to this day.

Transcontinental Migration

Rapid population growth in Europe also encouraged massive migration to the Americas, especially to the United States. During the nineteenth and early twentieth centuries, about fifty million Europeans migrated to the western hemisphere, which accounts for much of the stunning demographic growth of the Americas. Many of the migrants intended to stay for only a few years and fully expected to return to their homelands with a modest fortune made in the Americas. The vast majority, however, remained in the western hemisphere.

Industry and Society

New Social Classes

Industrialization radically altered traditional social structures and helped bring new social classes into being. Enterprising businesspeople became fabulously wealthy and powerful enough to overshadow the traditionally privileged classes. Less powerful than this new elite was the **middle class**, consisting of small business owners, factory managers, engineers, and professionals such as teachers, physicians, and attorneys. A large portion of industrial wealth flowed to the middle class, which benefited greatly from industrialization. Meanwhile, laborers who worked in factories and mines constituted a new **working class**. Less skilled than the artisans and crafts workers of earlier times, the new workers tended to machines or provided heavy labor for low wages.

Industrial Families

The most basic unit of social organization—the family—also underwent fundamental change during the industrial age. In preindustrial societies the family was the basic productive unit. Whether engaged in agriculture, domestic manufacturing, or commerce, family members worked together and contributed to the welfare of the larger group. Industrialization challenged the family economy and reshaped family life by moving economic production outside the home and introducing a sharp distinction between work and family life. Workers left their homes each day to labor an average of fourteen hours in factories, and family members led increasingly separate lives.

Men and the Industrial Revolution

Men gained increased stature and responsibility in the industrial age as work dominated public life. Upper-class and middle-class men enjoyed especially increased prestige at home, since

In 1872 Gustave Doré, a French book illustrator, sketched an image of Wentworth Street, Whitechapel, in London. By the middle of the nineteenth century, population shifts from rural areas to London made Whitechapel synonymous with poverty and overcrowding. Small, dark avenues such as Wentworth Street epitomized the suffering of the poorest classes during the industrial revolution.
Historical Picture Archive/Corbis Historical/Getty Images

At the same time, middle-class men increasingly insisted that women should not leave the household to work but, rather, that they should devote themselves to raising children and managing the home.

For middle-class women, then, industrialization brought stringent confinement to the domestic sphere and pressure to conform to new models of behavior revolving around their roles as mothers and wives. Popular books such as *Woman in Her Social and Domestic Character* (1833) insisted that the ideal woman "knows that she is the weaker vessel" and takes pride in her ability to make the home a happy place. Meanwhile, in addition to working in factories, millions of working-class women were employed as domestic servants for the growing middle class. In fact, one of every three European women became a domestic servant at some point in her life.

Child Labor Industrialization profoundly influenced children's lives as well. Children in preindustrial societies had always worked in and around the family home. However, industrial work, which took children away from home and parents for long hours with few breaks, made abuse and exploitation of child labor more likely. Early reports from British textile mills described overseers who forced children to work from dawn until dark and beat them to keep them awake. In the 1840s the British Parliament began to pass laws regulating child labor and ultimately restricted or removed children from the industrial workforce. In the long term, urban industrial societies redefined the role of children. Motivated in part by the recognition that modern society demanded a skilled and educated labor force, governments established the legal requirement that education, and not work for monetary gain, was the principal task of childhood. In England, for instance, education for children ages five to ten had become mandatory by 1881.

they usually were the sole providers who made their families' comfortable existence possible. Working-class men also enjoyed increased prestige because they tended to make wages far in excess of those of working-class women. As a result, their earnings usually constituted the bulk of their families' income.

Women and the Industrial Revolution Industrialization dramatically changed the terms of work for women. When industry moved production from the home to the factory, married women with children had no choice but to leave their children in someone else's care.

The Socialist Challenge

Among the most vocal and influential critics of early industrial society were the socialists, who worked to alleviate the social and economic problems generated by

This 1909 photograph shows a young girl being instructed by a male supervisor on how to use a spinning machine. Women, not men, made up the bulk of the early labor force in the textile industry, principally because it was presumed that women were easier to discipline than men and because women's smaller hands allegedly made them better suited for working with machines.
Bettmann/Getty Images

capitalism and industrialization. Socialists deplored economic inequalities, as represented by the vast difference in wealth between a captain of industry and a factory laborer, and they condemned the system that permitted the exploitation of laborers, including women and children. Early socialists sought to expand the Enlightenment understanding of equality: they understood equality to have an economic as well as a political, legal, and social dimension, and they looked to the future establishment of a just and equitable society. Although most socialists shared this general vision, they held very different views on the best way to establish and maintain an ideal socialist society.

Utopian Socialists The term **socialism** first appeared around 1830, when it referred to the ideas of social critics such as Robert Owen (1771–1858). Often called **utopian socialists**, these reformers and their followers worked to establish ideal communities that would point the way to an equitable society. Owen, for example, was a successful businessman who transformed a squalid Scottish cotton mill

town called New Lanark into a model industrial community. At New Lanark, Owen raised wages, reduced the workday from seventeen to ten hours, built spacious housing, and opened a store that sold goods at fair prices. Despite the costs of those reforms, the mills of New Lanark generated profits. Owen also kept young children out of the factories and sent them to a school he opened in 1816. Owen's indictment of competitive capitalism, his stress on cooperative control of industry, and his advocacy of improved educational standards for children left a lasting imprint on the socialist tradition.

The ideas of the utopian socialists resonated widely in the nineteenth century, and their disciples established experimental communities from the United States to Romania. But in spite of the enthusiasm of the founders, most of the communities soon encountered economic difficulties and political problems that forced them to fold. By the mid-nineteenth century, most socialists looked not to utopian communities but to large-scale organization of working people as the best means to bring about a just and equitable society.

Marx and Engels Most prominent of the nineteenth-century socialists were the German theorists **Karl Marx** (1818–1883) and **Friedrich Engels** (1820–1895). Marx and Engels believed that the social problems of the nineteenth century were inevitable results of a capitalist economy. They held that capitalism divided people into two main classes, each with its own economic interests and social status: the capitalists, who owned industrial machinery and factories (which Marx and Engels called the means of production), and the proletariat, consisting of wageworkers who had only their labor to sell. Intense competition between capitalists trying to realize a profit resulted in ruthless exploitation of the working class. Moreover, according to Marx and Engels, the state and its coercive institutions, such as police forces and courts of law, functioned to enable capitalists to continue their exploitation of the proletariat. Even music, art, literature, and religion served the purposes of capitalists, according to Marx and Engels, since they amused the working classes and diverted attention from their misery.

The Communist Manifesto Marx developed those views fully in a long, theoretical work called *Capital.* Together with Engels, Marx also wrote a short, spirited tract titled *Manifesto of the Communist Party* (1848). In the *Manifesto,* Marx and Engels aligned themselves with the communists, who worked toward the abolition of private property and the institution of a radically egalitarian society. *The Communist Manifesto* asserted that all human history was the history of struggle between social classes. It also argued that the future lay with the working class. Crises of overproduction, underconsumption, and diminishing profits would shake the foundations of the capitalist order. Meanwhile, members of the proletariat would come to view the forcible overthrow of the existing system as the only alternative available to them. Marx and Engels believed that a socialist revolution would result in a "dictatorship of the proletariat," which would abolish private property and destroy the capitalist order. After the revolution was secure, the state would wither away. Coercive institutions would also disappear, since there would no longer be an exploiting class. Thus socialism would lead to a fair, just, and egalitarian society infinitely more humane than the capitalist order.

The doctrines of Marx and Engels came to dominate European and international socialism, and socialist parties grew rapidly throughout the nineteenth century. Political parties, trade unions, newspapers, and educational associations all worked to advance the socialist cause. Yet socialists disagreed strongly on the best means to reform society. Revolutionary socialists such as Marx and Engels urged workers to forcibly seize control of the state. In contrast, evolutionary socialists placed their hopes in representative governments and called for the election of legislators who supported socialist reforms.

Contemporary photograph of Karl Marx (1818–1883), German political philosopher and founder of modern socialism. His most important theoretical work, *Das Kapital* (*Capital,* in the English translation), is an extensive treatise on political economy that offers a highly critical analysis of capitalism.
Bettmann/Getty Images

Social Reform Although socialists did not win control of any government until the Russian revolution of 1917, their critiques helped persuade government authorities to attack the abuses of early industrialization and provide more security for the working classes. In Britain, for example, Parliament prohibited underground employment for women and stipulated that children under age nine not work more than nine hours a day. Beginning in 1832, a series of parliamentary acts also expanded the franchise for men by reducing property qualifications, preparing the way for universal male suffrage. In Germany in the 1880s, Otto von Bismarck introduced medical insurance, unemployment compensation, and retirement pensions to provide social security for working people in industrial society. Yet Bismarck's reforms were hardly universal: they did not apply to women or agricultural workers, and they were paid for by expensive contributions from employers as well as from workers' salaries.

Trade Unions **Trade unions** also sought to advance the quest for a just and equitable society. As governments regulated businesses and enhanced social security, workers struggled to improve their lives by organizing to seek higher wages and better working conditions for their members. Through most of the nineteenth century, both employers and governments considered trade unions illegal associations whose purpose was to restrain trade. Yet trade unions persisted, and over the long run they improved the lives of working people and reduced the likelihood that a disgruntled proletariat would mount a revolution to overthrow industrial capitalist society.

GLOBAL EFFECTS OF INDUSTRIALIZATION

Although early industrialization was a British, western European, and North American affair, it had deep global implications. In part this was because industrial powers used their tools, technologies, business organization, financial influence, and transportation networks to obtain raw materials from societies around the world. Many places that possessed natural resources were unable to maintain control over them, because representatives of industrial countries dominated the commercial and financial institutions associated with their trade. Other societies—in particular, Russia and Japan—saw the writing on the wall and embarked on huge industrialization programs of their own to stave off Euro-American domination.

The International Division of Labor

Industrialization influenced the economic and social development of many societies, because it promoted a new international division of labor. Industrial societies needed minerals, agricultural products, and other raw materials to supply their factories, and they frequently obtained them from distant regions of the world.

Although large-scale global trade in agricultural products such as sugar, tea, and cotton was nothing new, industrial society fueled the demand for additional products as industrialists sought the natural resources and agricultural products of Africa, the Americas, Asia, Australia, and eastern Europe. The mechanization of the textile industry, for example, produced a demand for large quantities of raw cotton, which came mostly from India, Egypt, and the southern rim of the United States. Similarly, new industrial technologies increased demand for products such as rubber, the principal ingredient of the belts and tires that were essential to industrial machinery, which came from Brazil, Malaya, and the Congo River basin.

Economic Development In some places specialization in the production and export of primary goods paved the way for economic development and eventual industrialization. This pattern was especially noticeable in European settler colonies, including Canada, South Africa, Australia, and New Zealand, each of which enjoyed a special relationship with Great Britain. Britons directly controlled the government in each of these colonies, and British investors were directly and heavily invested in their infrastructure and economies. European migrants flocked to the settler colonies, where they set up businesses that exported primary products to feed the economies of the industrial states. European settlers commanded high wages, and the spending power of these incomes created flourishing markets for industrial goods within the settler colonies. Over time, European entrepreneurs in the settler colonies developed mechanized industries themselves based on technologies brought from Europe.

Economic Dependence Other places did not benefit from the same advantages as European settler colonies. In most of Latin America, sub-Saharan Africa, south Asia, and southeast Asia, representatives of industrialized states sought to impose their will either by outright colonial conquest or by using economic and political pressure. In most areas, they sought raw materials—especially sugar, cotton, and rubber—and encouraged whole economies to move toward an export-oriented agricultural economy based on cash crops. They actively discouraged industrialization, seeking instead to create reliable supplies of raw materials to feed their own industrial economies. They often set controls on the prices of agricultural goods, thus keeping prices—and thus the profits for producers—artificially low. Over time, these conditions created a new geographic division of labor, in which some of the world's peoples provided raw materials while others processed and consumed them.

The Continuing Spread of Industrialization: Russia and Japan

Industrialization brought great economic and military strength to societies that reconfigured themselves and relied on mechanized production. Their power encouraged other societies to seek their own paths to industrialization. Indeed, by the late nineteenth century it had become clear to leaders in many preindustrial societies that unless they undertook programs of social, political, and economic reform, they would grow progressively weaker in relation to industrial powers. Faced with such a reality, after 1870 both Russia and Japan embarked on campaigns of rapid industrialization to strengthen their societies and enable them to resist military and economic pressures from western Europe and the United States.

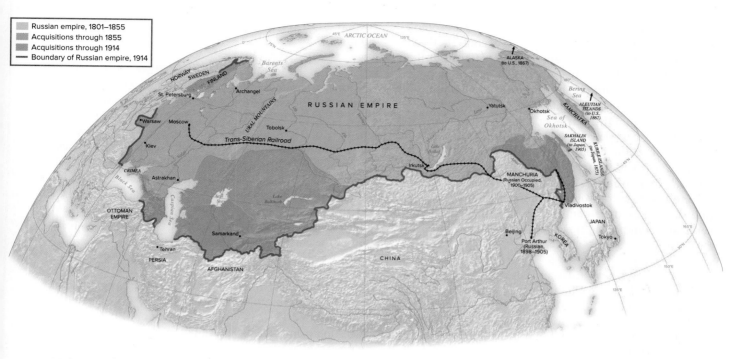

Russian empire, 1801–1855
Acquisitions through 1855
Acquisitions through 1914
Boundary of Russian empire, 1914

MAP 26.2 The Russian empire, 1801–1914

Note the sheer size of Russian territory in this period and that the state included parts of Europe, central Asia, and east Asia.

How would straddling so much space and so many cultures have affected the process of industrialization and nationalism in Russia?

Russia in 1870 was a multiethnic, multilingual, multi-cultural empire that stretched from Poland to the Pacific Ocean. The Romanov czars ruled their diverse and sprawling realm through an autocratic regime in which all initiative came from the central administration. The czars enjoyed the support of a powerful class of nobles who owned most of the land and were exempt from taxes and military duty. Peasants made up the vast majority of the population, and most of them were serfs bound to the lands they cultivated.

Although the Russian army in the nineteenth century was huge, conflict with France and Britain in the Crimean War (1853–1856) clearly revealed the inability of Russian forces—based as they were on an agrarian economy—to compete with the industrial powers of western Europe. Military defeat compelled the czarist autocracy to reevaluate the Russian social order and undertake an extensive program of reform along western European lines.

After signing the Treaty of Paris in 1856, ending the Crimean War, Alexander abolished serfdom in the Russian empire.
Universal History Archive/UIG/Shutterstock

Emancipation of the Serfs The most significant social reform in Russia was emancipation of the serfs (1861), an institution many believed had become an obstacle to economic development. Indeed, **Czar Alexander II** (reigned 1855–1881) emancipated the serfs partly with the intention of creating a mobile labor force for emerging industries, and the czarist government encouraged industrialization as a way of strengthening the Russian empire. Thus, although Russian industrialization took place within a framework of capitalism, it differed from western European industrialization in that the motivation for development was political and military, and the driving force was government policy rather than entrepreneurial initiative. Industrialization proceeded slowly at first, but it surged during the last two decades of the nineteenth century.

Romanov (ROH-muh-nawf)

czar (zahr)

Railroads In Russia the czarist government promoted industrialization by encouraging the construction of railroads to link the distant regions of the far-flung empire. In 1860 Russia had fewer than 1,100 kilometers (700 miles) of railroads, but by 1900 there were more than 58,000 kilometers (36,000 miles). Most impressive of the Russian railroads was the trans-Siberian line, constructed between 1891 and 1904, which stretched more than 9,000 kilometers (5,600 miles) and linked Moscow with the port of Vladivostok on the Pacific Ocean. Apart from drawing the regions of the Russian empire together, railroads stimulated the development of coal, iron, and steel industries and enabled Russia to serve as a commercial link between western Europe and east Asia.

The Witte System Russian industry experienced explosive growth when Count **Sergei Witte** served as finance minister (1892–1903). Witte oversaw construction of the trans-Siberian railroad, and he worked to push Russian industrialization by reforming commercial law, protecting infant industries, supporting steamship companies, and promoting nautical and engineering schools. He invited foreign investors to bring their capital and expertise to Russia, and he encouraged the establishment of savings banks to raise additional investment funds at home. By 1900 Russia produced half the world's oil, and Russian steel production ranked fourth in the world, behind that of the United States, Germany, and Britain. As a result of Witte's efforts, Russia also developed enormous coal and iron industries, and government

---

Sergei Witte (SAYR-gay VIHT-tee)
Tokugawa (TOH-koo-GAH-wah)

demand for weapons also supported a huge armaments industry.

Industrial Discontent Although Russia successfully began a program of industrialization, such efforts came at a high cost. As in other places, industrial growth generated an urban working class, which endured miserable working and living conditions. Employers kept the wages of overworked and poorly housed workers at the barest minimum. Moreover, economic exploitation and the lack of political freedom made workers increasingly receptive to socialist and revolutionary propaganda, which—when combined with further military defeat and political oppression—eventually undermined the Russian state itself in the early twentieth century.

Foreign Pressure In Japan, too, imperial authorities promoted industrialization, although under very different circumstances from those in Russia. Until 1853 Japan had largely closed itself off from interaction with European and American traders. The situation changed abruptly in that year, however, with the arrival of a U.S. naval squadron in Tokyo Bay. The American commander, **Commodore Matthew C. Perry**, trained his guns on the bakufu capital of Edo (modern Tokyo) and demanded that the shogun open Japan to diplomatic and commercial relations and sign a treaty of friendship. The shogun had no good alternative and so acquiesced to Perry's demands. Representatives of Britain, the Netherlands, and Russia soon won similar rights, all of which opened Japanese ports to foreign commerce, deprived the government of control over tariffs, and granted foreigners extraterritorial rights.

The sudden intrusion of foreign powers precipitated a domestic crisis in Japan that eventually resulted in the collapse of the Tokugawa bakufu and the restoration of imperial rule. After years of conflict and a brief civil war, the

---

Why It Matters ▷▷▷▷▷▷▷

The Birth of Nationalism

Does it matter if nationalism is promoted from the top down rather than from a groundswell of popular sentiment? Consider the case of Japan. Nationalism came to Japan as a result of contact with the aggressive trade policies of the United States and European nations. An elite group of reformers believed that in order to avoid domination by western powers, they had to modernize and industrialize on the western model—which included embracing the idea of a Japanese nation whose citizens

would work together to promote the interests of the new state. Part of the way this was accomplished was through mandatory, state-funded education programs to teach both literacy and an appreciation of state-sanctioned national values. But what is lost when the state decides national values? Is there a danger that state-sanctioned national values might restrict the ability of ordinary people to express ideas of nationhood in opposition to those of the state?

Japanese women boiling cocoons and reeling silk at a silk factory during the 1880s.

MeijiShowa/Alamy Stock Photo

boy emperor **Mutsuhito**—known by his regnal name, Meiji ("Enlightened Rule")—took the reins of power on 3 January 1868.

The Meiji Restoration The **Meiji restoration** returned authority to the Japanese emperor and marked the birth of a new Japan. Determined to gain equality with foreign powers, a conservative coalition of daimyo (feudal lords), imperial princes, court nobles, and samurai formed a new government dedicated to the twin goals of prosperity and strength: "rich country, strong army." The Meiji government looked to the industrial nations of Europe and the United States to obtain the knowledge and expertise to strengthen Japan. The Meiji government sent many students and officials abroad to study everything from technology to constitutions, and it hired foreign experts to facilitate economic development and the creation of internal Japanese expertise.

Economic Development Economic initiatives were critical to the process of Meiji reconstruction. Convinced that a powerful economy was the foundation of national strength, the Meiji government created a modern transportation, communications, and educational infrastructure. The establishment of telegraph, railroad, and steamship lines tied local and regional markets into a national economic network. Aiming to improve literacy rates, the government introduced a system of universal primary and secondary education. Universities provided advanced instruction for the best students, especially in scientific and technical fields. This infrastructure supported rapid industrialization and economic growth. Although most economic enterprises were privately owned, the government

Mutsuhito (MOO-tsoo-HE-taw)
Meiji (MAY-jee)
daimyo (DEYEM-yoh)

controlled military industries and established pilot programs to stimulate industrial development. During the 1880s the government sold most of its enterprises to private investors who had close ties to government officials. The result was a concentration of enormous economic power in the hands of a small group of people, collectively known as *zaibatsu*, or financial cliques. By the early twentieth century, Japan had joined the ranks of the major industrial powers.

Costs of Economic Development As in Russia, economic development came at a price, as the Japanese people bore the social and political costs of rapid industrialization. During this period, hundreds of thousands

zaibatsu (zeye-BAHT-soo)

of rural families lived in destitution, many malnourished to the point of starvation. In addition, those who took up work in the burgeoning industries learned that working conditions were difficult and that the state did not tolerate labor organizations that promoted the welfare of workers.

Nevertheless, the desire to achieve political and economic equality with Euro-American industrial powers—and to avoid the domination and dependence experienced by preindustrial societies elsewhere—transformed Japan into a powerful industrial society in a single generation. Serving as symbols of Japan's remarkable development were the conclusion of an alliance with Britain as an equal power in 1902 and convincing displays of military power in victories over the Chinese empire (1894–1895) and the Russian empire (1904–1905).

CONCLUSION

The process of industrialization involved the harnessing of inanimate sources of energy, the replacement of handicraft production with machine-based manufacturing, and the generation of new forms of business and labor organization. Along with industrialization came demographic growth, large-scale migration, and rapid urbanization, which increased the demand for manufactured goods by working people, who formed the majority of the population. Societies that underwent industrialization enjoyed sharp increases in economic productivity: they produced large quantities of high-quality goods at low prices, and their increased productivity eventually translated into higher material standards of living. Yet industrialization brought costs as well as benefits. Family life changed dramatically in the industrial age as men, women, and children increasingly left their homes to work in factories and mines, often under appalling conditions. In response, socialist critics sought to bring about a more just and equitable society, and government authorities eventually responded by curtailing the worst abuses of the early industrial era. Meanwhile, industrialization increasingly touched the lives of peoples around the world. To avoid being dominated, Russia and Japan followed the lead of Britain, western Europe, and North America into industrialization, whereas many African, Asian, and Latin American states were coerced into dependence on the export of raw materials to industrial societies.

STUDY TERMS

cartels (470)
Commodore Matthew C. Perry (478)
corporations (470)
Czar Alexander II (477)
demographic transition (471)
Eli Whitney (470)
factory system (467)
flying shuttle (464)
Friedrich Engels (475)
George Stephenson (467)
Henry Ford (470)
James Watt (465)
Karl Marx (475)
Luddites (467)
Meiji restoration (479)
middle class (472)
mule (464)
Mutsuhito (479)
power loom (465)
Sergei Witte (478)
socialism (474)
The Communist Manifesto (475)
trade unions (476)
trusts (470)
utopian socialists (474)
working class (472)
zaibatsu (480)

FOR FURTHER READING

Barbara Hahn. *Technology in the Industrial Revolution.* Cambridge, 2020. Takes a global approach to the industrial revolution in Britain and offers new perspectives on the relationship between society and technology.

Daniel R. Headrick. *Power over Peoples: Technology, Environments, and Western Imperialism, 1400 to the Present.* Princeton, 2009. Explores the important relationship between technology and imperialism.

Penelope Lane, Neil Raven, and K. D. M. Snell, eds. *Women, Work and Wages in England, 1600–1850.* Rochester, N.Y., 2004. A study of women's contributions to British industrialization and how they were rewarded.

Karl Marx and Friedrich Engels. *The Communist Manifesto.* Trans. by S. Moore. Harmondsworth, 1967. An English translation of the most important tract of nineteenth-century socialism, with an excellent introduction by historian A. J. P. Taylor.

Kenneth Pomeranz. *The Great Divergence: China, Europe, and the Making of the Modern World Economy.* Princeton, 2000. Argues that the fortuitous location of coal deposits and access to the resources of the Americas created a uniquely advantageous framework for English industrialization.

Hans Rogger. *Russia in the Age of Modernisation and Revolution, 1881–1917*. New York, 1983. An important study of Russian social and economic development.

William Rosen. *The Most Powerful Idea in the World: A Story of Steam, Industry, and Invention*. New York, 2010. Dismissing traditional explanations for the origins of British industrialization, the author argues that England's patent system proved the decisive factor.

Peter N. Stearns. *The Industrial Revolution in World History*. 4th ed. Boulder, Colo., 2012. A concise account placing industrialization and its effects in a global perspective.

Masayuki Tanimoto, ed. *The Role of Tradition in Japan's Industrialization: Another Path to Industrialization*. New York, 2006. Traditional or indigenous industries take center stage in this examination of Japan's early industrial development.

Louise A. Tilly. *Industrialization and Gender Inequality*. Washington, D.C., 1993. A brief historiographical survey of debates on gender and industrialization in England, France, Germany, the United States, Japan, and China.

27 The Americas in the Age of Independence

ZOOMING IN ON ENCOUNTERS

Fatt Hing Chin Searches for Gold from China to California

Fatt Hing Chin was a village fish peddler who lived in a coastal town in southern China. One day at the wharves, he heard people talking about a place across the ocean where the mountains were laden with gold. Chin was nineteen years old and full of energy, and he longed for the chance to see if he could find some of this gold for himself. He learned that he could purchase passage on a foreign ship, and in 1849 he boarded a Spanish ship to sail to California and join the gold rush.

Once at sea, Chin was surprised at the large number of young Chinese men crammed in with him in the ship's hold, where the smell of vomit was overpowering. Ninety-five difficult days and nights passed before the hills of San Francisco came into view. On arrival the travelers met Chinese veterans of life in the United States who explained the strategy of sticking together in order to survive and prosper.

Chin hired himself out as a gold miner, and after two years he accumulated his own little pile of gold. He wrote to his brothers and cousins, urging them to join him, and thus helped fuel a large-scale overseas migration that brought twenty-four thousand Chinese workers to California in the four years between 1849 and 1853. Having made his

Seven miners stand near a sluice box in California around 1852. Note the four Chinese miners standing to the right.
Fotosearch/Stringer/Archive Photos/Getty Images

fortune, though, Chin decided to return to China. Indeed, California gold provided him with the means to take a wife, build a house, and buy some land in his home country.

Although settled and prosperous, Chin longed to return to California. Leaving his pregnant wife, he sailed for California again after only a year. He returned to mining with his brother (who had also made the trip to California), but the gold had become more difficult to find. Inspired by the luck of another migrant, Tong Ling, who managed to get one dollar for each meal he sold, Chin's cousins in San Francisco decided to open a restaurant. Chin found the city much more comfortable than the mountains. "Let the others go after the gold in the hills," he said. "I'll wait for the gold to come to the city."

Fatt Hing Chin was one of the earliest Chinese migrants to settle in the Americas. His career path—from a miner in search of quick riches to an urban resident committed to a new homeland—was typical of Chinese migrants to the United States. Along with millions of others from Europe and Asia, Chinese migrants increased the ethnic diversity of American populations and stimulated political, social, and economic development in the western hemisphere.

CHAPTER OVERVIEW

During the late eighteenth and early nineteenth centuries, almost all the territories of the western hemisphere won their independence from European colonial powers. The American peoples then struggled throughout the nineteenth century to build their own states and societies. The United States embarked on a westward push that brought most of the temperate regions of North America under U.S. control. Canada built a federal state under British Canadian leadership. The varied lands of Latin America built smaller states, many of which fell under the sway of local military leaders. One issue that most American peoples wrestled with, regardless of their region, was the legacy of the Enlightenment. The effort to build societies based on freedom, equality, and constitutional government was a monumental challenge that remained only partially realized. Indeed, Asian and European migrants joined native-born workers and formerly enslaved people in labor systems—from plantations and factories to debt peonage—that often demonstrated the hollowness of American promises of welcome and freedom.

The age of independence for the United States, Canada, and Latin America was a contentious era characterized by continuous mass migration and explosive economic growth, occasionally followed by deep economic stagnation, and punctuated with civil war, ethnic violence, class conflict, and battles for racial and sexual equality. Goals to build effective states, enjoy economic prosperity, and attain cultural cohesion were elusive throughout the nineteenth century (and in many ways remain so even in the present day). Nevertheless, the histories of these first territories to win independence from colonial powers inspired other peoples who later sought freedom from imperial rule.

CHRONOLOGY	
1803	Louisiana Purchase
1804–1806	Lewis and Clark expedition
1812–1814	War of 1812
1838–1839	Trail of Tears
1845–1848	Mexican-American War
1848	Seneca Falls Convention
1849	California gold rush
1850s	*La Reforma* in Mexico
1861–1865	U.S. Civil War
1867	Establishment of the Dominion of Canada
1867	French troops withdraw from Mexico
1867–1877	Reconstruction in the United States
1869	Completion of the transcontinental railroad line in the United States
1876	Battle of Little Bighorn
1876–1911	Rule of Porfirio Díaz in Mexico
1885	Completion of the Canadian Pacific Railroad
1885	Northwest Rebellion
1890	Massacre at Wounded Knee
1911–1920	Mexican revolution

THE BUILDING OF AMERICAN STATES

After winning independence from Britain in 1783, the United States fashioned a government and began to expand rapidly to the west. Yet the United States was an unstable society composed of varied regions with diverse economic and social structures. Differences over slavery and the rights of individual states as opposed to the federal government sparked a bloody civil war in the 1860s. That conflict resulted in the abolition of slavery and the strengthening of the federal state. The experience of Canada was very different from that of the United States. Canada gained independence from Britain without fighting a war, and despite also being a land of great diversity, avoided fighting a civil war. Canada established a relatively weak federal government, which presided over provinces that had considerable power over local affairs. Latin American lands were even more diverse than their counterparts to the north, and in spite of the efforts of some individuals they were unable to join together in a confederation. Throughout the nineteenth century Latin America was politically fragmented, and many individual states faced serious problems and divisions within their own societies.

The United States: Westward Expansion and Civil War

After gaining independence the United States faced the need to construct a government. During the 1780s leaders

from the rebellious colonies drafted a constitution that entrusted responsibility for general issues to a federal government, reserved authority for local issues for individual states, and provided for the admission of new states and territories to the confederation. Originally most states limited the vote to men of property, but the Enlightenment ideal of equality encouraged political leaders to extend the franchise: by the mid-nineteenth century almost all adult white men were eligible to vote.

Westward Expansion and Manifest Destiny

While working to settle constitutional issues, Americans also began to expand to the west. After the American Revolution, Britain ceded to the new republic all lands between the Appalachian Mountains and the Mississippi River, and the United States doubled in size. In 1803 Napoleon Bonaparte allowed the United States to purchase France's Louisiana Territory, which extended from the Mississippi River to the Rocky Mountains. Overnight the United States doubled in size again. Between 1804 and 1806 a

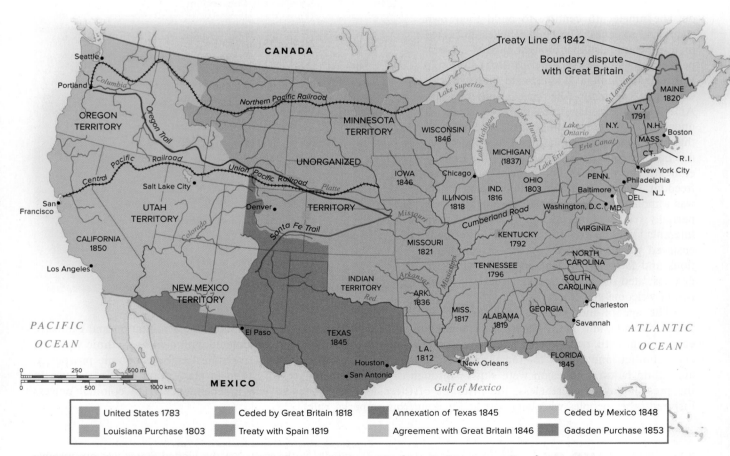

MAP 27.1 Westward expansion of the United States during the nineteenth century

Note the large land claims ceded by Britain, France, and Mexico.

Why were there no portions of North America purchased from or ceded by Native Americans?

geographic expedition led by Meriwether Lewis and William Clark mapped the territory and surveyed its resources. Settlers soon began to flock west in search of cheap land to cultivate. By the 1840s many Americans spoke of a **manifest destiny** to occupy all of North America from the Atlantic to the Pacific Ocean.

Conflict with Indigenous Peoples Although gaining territory from Britain and France gave westward expansion legal legitimacy from the American point of view, from the perspective of indigenous peoples it was nothing less than forcible conquest of lands on which they had lived for thousands of years. Indeed, westward expansion brought settlers and government forces into conflict with the indigenous peoples of North America, who resisted efforts to push them from their ancestral lands and hunting grounds. However, U.S. officials and military forces supported Euro-American settlers and violently forced the continent open to white expansion. Then, with the **Indian Removal Act of 1830**, the U.S. government determined to move all Native Americans west of the Mississippi River onto marginal lands they called "Indian Territory" (Oklahoma). Among the native groups affected by this forced removal from the east were the Cherokee, who suffered a harrowing 800-mile migration from the eastern woodlands to Oklahoma on the **Trail of Tears** (1838–1839), so known because thousands died from disease, starvation, and the difficulties of relocation.

After 1840 the site of conflict between Euro-American and indigenous peoples shifted to the plains region west of the Mississippi River. Settlers and ranchers in the trans-Mississippi west encountered peoples such as the Sioux, the Comanche, the Pawnee, and the Apache, who possessed firearms and outstanding equestrian skills. The indigenous peoples of the plains offered effective resistance to encroachment by white settlers and at times won powerful victories over U.S. forces. In 1876, for example, thousands of Lakota Sioux and their allies defeated an army under the command of Colonel George Armstrong Custer in the **battle of Little Bighorn** (in southern Montana). Ultimately, however, Native Americans on the plains lost the war against the forces of U.S. expansionism. U.S. forces employed cannons and deadly, rapid-fire Gatling guns against native American peoples, which opened the western plains to U.S. conquest.

One last symbolic conflict took place in 1890 at Wounded Knee Creek in South Dakota. U.S. cavalry forces, hoping to suppress Sioux religious ceremonies that envisioned the disappearance of white people, chased the Sioux who were fleeing to safety in the South Dakota Badlands. At Wounded Knee Creek, a Sioux man accidentally shot off a gun, and the cavalry overreacted badly, slaughtering more than two hundred men, women, and children with machine guns. Emblematic of harsh U.S. treatment of native peoples, **Wounded Knee** represented

Sitting Bull (ca. 1831–1890) was a Hunkpapa Lakota Sioux holy man who also led his people as a war chief during years of resistance to U.S. government policies. The battle of the Little Bighorn, also known by the indigenous Americans as the battle of Greasy Grass Creek, was the most famous action of the Great Sioux War against the U.S. cavalry in 1876–1877. It was an overwhelming victory for the Lakota and Northern Cheyenne, overseen by Sitting Bull.
CSU Archive/Everett Collection Inc./age fotostock

the place where "a people's dream died," as one Native American leader put it.

The Mexican-American War Westward expansion also generated tension between the United States and Mexico, whose territories included most of what is now the American southwest. Texas declared independence from Mexico in 1836, largely because the many American migrants who had settled there wanted to run their own affairs. In 1845 the United States accepted Texas as a new state—against vigorous Mexican protest—and moved to

Sioux (soo)

consolidate its hold on the territory. Those moves led to conflicts that rapidly escalated into the **Mexican-American War** (1845–1848). U.S. forces instigated the war by sending troops into a disputed zone along the Rio Grande. When Mexican cavalry attacked U.S. soldiers in this zone, the United States sent in reinforcements and inflicted a punishing defeat on the Mexican army. By the Treaty of **Guadalupe Hidalgo** (1848), the United States took possession of approximately one-half of Mexico's territory, paying a mere fifteen million dollars in exchange for Texas north of the Rio Grande, California, and New Mexico. Thousands of U.S. and Mexican soldiers died in this conflict, and thousands of Mexican families found themselves stranded in territories annexed by the United States. Some moved to be within the new borders of Mexico, but most stayed where they were and attained U.S. citizenship. This conflict, nonetheless, fueled Mexican nationalism, as well as Mexican disdain for the United States.

Westward expansion also created problems within the republic by aggravating tensions between regions. The most divisive issue had to do with slavery, which had been a serious problem in American politics since independence. The Enlightenment ideal of equality clearly suggested that the appropriate policy was to abolish slavery, but the framers of the Constitution recognized the sanctity of private property, which legally included enslaved people. American independence initially promoted a surge of antislavery sentiment, and states north of Delaware abolished slavery within their jurisdictions. That move hardened divisions between slave and free states. Westward expansion aggravated tensions further by raising the question of whether settlers could extend slavery to newly acquired territories.

Sectional Conflict

The election of **Abraham Lincoln** to the presidency in 1860 was the spark that ignited war between the states (1861–1865). Lincoln was an explicitly sectional candidate who was convinced that slavery was immoral and who was committed to the idea of free soil—territories without slavery. Fundamentally, slavery was at the center of the conflict that erupted into the **Civil War**. At the same time, the issue of slavery was also deeply intertwined with other important issues such as the nature of the Union, states' rights as opposed to the federal government's authority, and the needs of a budding

The grotesquely twisted bodies of dead Confederate soldiers lay near a fence outside Antietam, Maryland, in 1862. The Civil War was the most costly in U.S. history in number of lives lost.
Library of Congress, Prints & Photographs Division [LC-DIG-cwpb-01097]

industrial-capitalist system against those of an export-oriented plantation economy.

The U.S. Civil War Eleven southern states withdrew from the Union in 1860 and 1861, affirming their right to dissolve the Union and their support for states' rights. Northerners saw the situation differently. They viewed secession as illegal insurrection and an act of betrayal. They fought not only against slavery but also against the concept of a state subject to blackmail by its constituent parts. They also fought for a way of life—their emerging industrial society—and an expansive western agricultural system based on free labor.

Ultimately the northern states prevailed. They brought considerable resources to the war effort—some 90 percent of the country's industrial capacity and approximately two-thirds of its railroad lines—but still they fought four bitter years against a formidable enemy. The consequences of that victory were enormous, for it ended slavery in the United States. Indeed, once Abraham Lincoln signed the **Emancipation Proclamation** on 1 January 1863, which made the abolition of slavery an explicit goal of the war, it was clear that a northern victory would entail radical changes in southern life. Moreover, the victory of the northern states ensured that the United States would remain politically united, and it enhanced the authority of the federal government in the American republic. Thus, as European lands were building powerful states on the foundations of revolutionary ideals, liberalism, and nationalism, the United States also forged a strong central government to oversee settler colonialism to the west and to deal with the political and social issues that divided the American republic.

Guadalupe Hidalgo (gwahd-l-OOP hee-DAHL-goh)

The Canadian Dominion: Independence without War

Autonomy and Division Canada did not fight a war for independence, and in spite of deep regional divisions, it did not experience bloody internal conflict. Instead, Canadian independence came gradually as Canadians and the British government agreed on general principles of autonomy. The distinctiveness of the two dominant European ethnic groups, the British Canadians and the French Canadians, ensured that the process of building an independent society would not be smooth, but intermittent fears about the possibility of a U.S. invasion from the south helped submerge ethnic differences. By the late nineteenth century, Canada was a state in control of its own destiny.

Originally colonized by trappers and settlers from both Britain and France, the colony of New France was incorporated into the British empire after the British victory in the Seven Years' War (1756–1763). Until the late eighteenth century, however, French Canadians outnumbered British Canadians, so imperial officials made a number of concessions to their subjects of French descent to forestall unnecessary strife. After 1781, however, large numbers of British loyalists fled the newly formed United States and sought refuge in Canada, thus greatly enlarging the size of the English-speaking community there.

The War of 1812 Ethnic divisions and political differences could easily have splintered Canada, but the **War of 1812** stimulated a sense of unity against an external threat. The United States declared war on Britain in retaliation for encroachments on U.S. rights during the Napoleonic wars, and the British colony of Canada formed one of the front lines of the conflict. U.S. military leaders assumed that they could easily invade and conquer Canada to pressure Britain. Despite the greater resources of the United States, however, Canadian forces repelled U.S. incursions. Their victories promoted a sense of Canadian pride, and anti-U.S. sentiments became a means for covering over differences among French and British Canadians.

After the War of 1812, Canada experienced an era of rapid growth. Expanded business opportunities drew English-speaking migrants, who swelled the population. This influx threatened the identity of French Canadians in Quebec, and discontent in Canada reached a critical point in the 1830s. The British imperial governors of Canada did not want a repeat of the American Revolution, so between 1840 and 1867 they defused tensions by expanding home rule in Canada and permitting the provinces to govern their internal affairs.

Dominion Over the next few decades, Canadians developed a federal structure for their developing state. The **British North America Act of 1867** joined Quebec, Ontario, Nova Scotia, and New Brunswick and recognized them as the **Dominion of Canada** (other provinces joined the Dominion later). Under this arrangement, each province had its own seat of government, provincial legislature, and lieutenant governor representing the British crown. The act created a federal government headed by a governor-general, who acted as the British representative. An elected House of Commons and an appointed Senate rounded out the framework of governance. Without waging war, the Dominion of Canada had won control over all Canadian internal affairs, and Britain retained jurisdiction over foreign affairs until 1931.

John A. Macdonald (1815–1891) became the first prime minister of Canada, and he moved to incorporate all of British North America into the Dominion. He negotiated the purchase of the huge Northwest Territories from the Hudson's Bay Company in 1869, and he persuaded Manitoba, British Columbia, and Prince Edward Island to join the Dominion. Then, to strengthen the union, he oversaw construction of a transcontinental railroad, completed in 1885. The railroad facilitated transportation and communications throughout Canada and eventually helped bring new provinces into the Dominion: Alberta and Saskatchewan in 1905 and Newfoundland in 1949. Although maintaining ties to Britain and struggling to forge an identity distinct from its powerful neighbor to the south, Canada developed as a culturally diverse yet politically unified society.

Latin America: Fragmentation and Political Experimentation

Political unity was short-lived in Latin America. Simón Bolívar (1783–1830), hailed as the region's liberator, worked for the establishment of a large confederation that would provide Latin America with the political, military, and economic strength to resist encroachment by foreign powers. The wars of independence that he led encouraged a sense of solidarity in Latin America. But Bolívar once admitted, "I fear peace more than war," and after the defeat of the common colonial enemy, most of Latin America fragmented into numerous independent states. An important exception was the state of Brazil, which, under the leadership of Dom Pedro I (1798–1834) and his son, Dom Pedro II (1825–1891), managed to maintain stability and economic prosperity through most of the nineteenth century.

Creole Elites and Political Instability Following the example of the United States, creole (people of European descent born in the Americas) elites in most newly independent states of Latin America established republics with written constitutions. Yet Latin American leaders had less experience with self-government, because Spanish and Portuguese colonies were ruled far more directly by representatives of the crown than the British colonies in North America. As a result, several Latin American states lurched from one constitution to another as leaders

MAP 27.2 The Dominion of Canada in the nineteenth century

Note the provinces that make up the modern state of Canada and the dates in which they were incorporated into the Dominion.

On what date were eastern and western Canada geographically united?

struggled to create a machinery of government that would lead to political and social stability.

Creole elites themselves were part of the problem, because they dominated the newly independent states and effectively prevented mass participation in public affairs. Less than 5 percent of the male population was active in Latin American politics in the nineteenth century, and millions of indigenous peoples lived entirely outside the political system. Those disillusioned with

the system, then, had little choice beyond rebellion. To make matters worse, elites were divided by vocation—urban merchants versus rural landowners—as well as by ideology, whether liberalism, conservatism, secularism, or Roman Catholicism.

Conflicts with Indigenous Peoples Like their neighbors in the United States, one thing elites agreed on was the policy of claiming land for agriculture and ranching

Edouard Manet's painting (one of a series painted between 1867 and 1869) depicts the execution by firing squad of Emperor Maximilian, whose death in 1867 ended attempted French rule in Mexico. World History Archive/Alamy Stock Photo

by pushing aside indigenous peoples. Conflict was most intense on the plains of Argentina and Chile. During the mid-nineteenth century, as the United States was crushing indigenous resistance to western expansion in North America, Argentine and Chilean forces brought modern weapons to bear in their campaign to conquer the indigenous peoples of the South American plains. By the 1870s colonists had forced indigenous peoples on the most productive lands to retreat to marginal lands or to assimilate to Euro-American society.

Caudillos Although creole elites agreed on the policy of conquering indigenous peoples, division in the newly independent states helped *caudillos,* or regional military leaders, come to power in much of Latin America. The wars of independence had lasted well over a decade, and they provided Latin America with military rather than civilian heroes. After independence, military leaders took to the political stage by exploiting the discontent of the masses. One of the most notable caudillos was **Juan Manuel de Rosas**, who from 1835 to 1852 ruled an Argentina divided between the cattle-herding society of the pampas (the interior grasslands) and the urban elite of Buenos Aires. Rosas called for regional autonomy in an attempt to reconcile competing interests, but at the same time he worked to centralize the government he now controlled. He quelled rebellions, but he did so in bloody fashion: one writer counted 22,404 victims murdered under Rosas's rule.

Rosas did what caudillos did best: he restored order. In doing so, however, he made terror a tool of the govern-

ment, and he ruled as a despot through his own personal army. Yet although caudillo rule limited freedom and undermined republican ideals, it also sometimes gave rise to liberal opposition movements in favor of democratic forms of government.

Mexico: War and Reform Independent Mexico was a case in point. The Mexican-American War (1846–1848) caused political turmoil in Mexico and helped the caudillo General **Antonio López Santa Anna** (1794–1876) come to power. After the defeat and disillusion of the war, however, a liberal reform movement attempted to reshape Mexican society. Led by President **Benito Juárez** (1806–1872), a Mexican of indigenous ancestry, *La Reforma* of the 1850s aimed to limit the power of the military and the Roman Catholic church in Mexican society. The Constitution of 1857 set forth the ideals of *La Reforma*. It curtailed the prerogatives of priests and military elites, and it guaranteed universal male suffrage and other civil liberties, such as freedom of speech.

Mexico: Revolution *La Reforma* challenged the conservatism of Mexican elites, who led a determined opposition against it. In fact, divisions were so deep that conservatives forced the Juárez government out of Mexico

caudillos (KAHW-dee-yohs)
Juan Manuel de Rosas (HWAHN mahn-WEL de roh-sahs)
Buenos Aires (BWE-naws AHY-res)
Benito Juárez (beh-nee-toh WAHR-ez)

MAP 27.3   Latin America in the nineteenth century

Date is year of independence. Note the many states that emerged from the independence movements early in the century.

Why was it difficult for large, federated republics, such as the Republic of Colombia, founded by Simón Bolívar, to survive?

City until 1861. During those difficult times, Juárez chose to suspend loan payments to foreign powers to lessen Mexico's financial woes, and that led to French, British, and Spanish intervention as Europeans sought to protect their investments in Mexico. In 1862, France's Napoleon III even sent tens of thousands of troops to Mexico and proclaimed a Mexican empire. However, he was forced to withdraw French forces in 1867, and in the same year a Mexican firing squad killed the man he had appointed emperor, the Austrian archduke Maximilian (1832–1867). Juárez managed to restore a semblance of liberal government after the French invasion, but Mexico remained beset by political divisions.

By the early twentieth century, Mexico was a divided land moving toward civil war. The Mexican revolution (1911–1920), a bitter and bloody conflict, broke out when middle-class Mexicans joined with peasants and workers to overthrow the powerful dictator **Porfirio Díaz** (1830–1915). The revolt, which attempted to topple the grossly unequal system of landed estates—in which fully 95 percent of all peasants remained landless—turned increasingly radical as rebels engaged in guerrilla warfare against government forces. The lower classes took up weapons and followed the revolutionary leaders **Emiliano Zapata** (1879–1919) and **Francisco (Pancho) Villa** (1878–1923), charismatic men of agrarian backgrounds who organized huge armies fighting for *tierra y libertad* (land and liberty). Zapata, the son of a mestizo peasant, and Villa, the son of a field worker, embodied the ideals and aspirations of the indigenous Mexican masses and enjoyed tremendous popular support. They discredited what they saw as timid governmental efforts at reform and challenged governmental political control. For example, Zapata himself confiscated hacienda lands and began distributing the lands to the peasants, and Villa attacked and killed U.S. citizens in retaliation for U.S. support of Mexican government officials.

Despite the power and popularity enjoyed by Zapata and Villa, they did not command the resources and wealth of the government. The Mexican revolution came to an end soon after government forces ambushed and killed Zapata in 1919. Villa likewise was assassinated, on his ranch in 1923. Government forces regained control over a battered and devastated Mexico: as many as two million Mexicans may have died in the revolution. Although radicals such as Zapata and Villa were ultimately defeated, the Mexican government that came to power in 1917 issued a constitution that did, in fact, address some of the concerns of the revolutionaries by providing for land redistribution, universal suffrage, state-supported education, minimum wages and maximum hours for workers, and restrictions on foreign ownership of Mexican land and resources.

Instability and conflict plagued Latin America throughout the nineteenth century in the form of division, rebellion, caudillo rule, and civil war. Many Latin American peoples lacked education, profitable employment, and

political representation. Simón Bolívar himself once said that "independence is the only blessing we have gained at the expense of all the rest."

AMERICAN ECONOMIC DEVELOPMENT

During the nineteenth and early twentieth centuries, two principal influences—mass migration and British investment—shaped economic development throughout the Americas. But American states reacted in different ways to migration and foreign investment. The United States and Canada absorbed waves of migrants, exploited British capital, built industrial societies, and established economic independence. But the results of mass migration and financial investment were much more mixed in Latin America. In both South America and the Caribbean, migrants tended to arrive as contract or indentured laborers to take the place of enslaved people after abolition, and thus remained quite poor. Additionally, in much of Latin America financial investments tended to benefit only the investors themselves and the small elite classes that controlled most countries.

Migration to the Americas

Underpinning the economic development of the Americas was the mass migration of European and Asian peoples to the United States, Canada, and Latin America. Gold discoveries in California and Canada drew prospectors hoping to make a quick fortune, but outnumbering gold prospectors were millions of European and Asian migrants who made their way to the factories, railroad construction sites, and plantations of the Americas. Following them were others who offered the support services that made life for migrant workers more comfortable and at the same time transformed the ethnic and cultural landscape of the Americas.

Industrial Migrants After the mid-nineteenth century, European migrants flocked to North America, where they filled the factories of the growing industrial economy of the United States. Their lack of skills made them attractive to industrialists seeking workers to operate machinery or perform heavy labor at low wages. By keeping labor costs down, migrants helped increase the profitability and fuel the expansion of U.S. industry. In the 1850s 2.3 million Europeans migrated to the United States—almost as many as had crossed the Atlantic during the half century from 1800 to 1850—and the volume of migration continued to surge until the early twentieth century. In the first half of the century, migrants came mostly from Ireland,

Porfirio Díaz (pawr-FEER-eeo DEE-ahs)
Emiliano Zapata (eh-mee-LYAH-no zuh-PAH-tuh)
Francisco Villa (frahn-SEES-kow VEE-uh)

Italian migrants construct a railway in New York. Italians were just one of many migrant groups coming to the Americas in the nineteenth century, including the Irish and Chinese.

Michael Maslan/Corbis Historical/Getty Images

both China and Japan migrated to Peru, where they worked on cotton plantations, mined guano deposits, and helped build railroad lines. After the middle of the nineteenth century, expanding U.S. influence in the Pacific islands also led to Chinese, Japanese, Filipino, and Korean migrations to Hawai'i, where planters sought indentured laborers to tend sugarcane. About twenty-five thousand Chinese went to Hawai'i during the 1850s and 1860s, and later one hundred eighty thousand Japanese also made their way to island plantations.

Economic Expansion in the United States

British Capital British investment capital in the United States proved crucial to the early stages of industrial development by helping businesspeople establish a textile industry. In the late nineteenth century, it also helped spur a vast expansion of U.S. industry by funding entrepreneurs who opened coal and iron ore mines, built iron and steel factories, and constructed railroad lines. The flow of investment monies was a consequence of Britain's own industrialization, which generated enormous wealth and created a need for investors to find profitable outlets for their funds.

Railroads Perhaps the most important economic development of the later nineteenth century was the construction of railroad lines that linked all U.S. regions and helped create an integrated national economy. Because of its enormous size and environmental diversity, the United States offered an abundance of natural resources for industrial exploitation. But vast distances made it difficult to maintain close economic ties between regions until a boom in railroad construction created a dense transportation, communication, and distribution network. Before the Civil War the United States had about 50,000 kilometers (31,000 miles) of railroad lines, most of them short routes east of the Mississippi River. By 1900 there were more than 320,000 kilometers (200,000 miles) of track, and the American rail network stretched from coast to coast.

Railroads decisively influenced American economic development. They provided cheap transportation for agricultural commodities, manufactured goods, and individual travelers. Railroads hauled grain, beef, and hogs from the plains states, cotton and tobacco from the south, lumber from the northwest, iron and steel from Pittsburgh, and finished products from the eastern industrial cities. In addition to the transportation services they provided, railroads

Scotland, Germany, and Scandinavia to escape high rents and indebtedness. By the late nineteenth century, most European migrants were coming from southern and eastern Europe and included Poles, Russian Jews, Slavs, Italians, Greeks, and Portuguese. Without their labor, the remarkable industrial expansion that the United States experienced in the late nineteenth century would not have been possible.

Chinese migration grew rapidly after the 1840s, when British gunboats opened China to foreign influences. Between 1852 and 1875 some two hundred thousand Chinese people migrated to California. Some, like Fatt Hing Chin, negotiated their own passage, but most traveled on indentured labor contracts that required them to cultivate crops or work on the Central Pacific Railroad. An additional five thousand Chinese people entered Canada to search for gold in British Columbia or work on the Canadian Pacific Railroad.

Plantation Migrants Whereas migrants to the United States contributed to the development of an industrial society, most of those who went to Latin American lands worked on agricultural plantations. Some Europeans figured among these migrants. About four million Italians sought opportunities in Argentina in the 1880s and 1890s, for example, and the Brazilian government paid Italian migrants to cross the Atlantic and work for coffee growers after the abolition of slavery there in 1888.

Asian laborers also worked on plantations in the western hemisphere. More than fifteen thousand indentured laborers from China worked in the sugarcane fields of Cuba during the nineteenth century, and Indian migrants traveled to Jamaica, Trinidad, Tobago, and Guyana. Laborers from

In this lithograph of Frances F. Palmer's well-known painting *American Express Train* (ca. 1864), the railroad is depicted as a cheerful and industrious master of the landscape.

Yale University Art Gallery

spurred the development of other industries, because they required huge amounts of coal, wood, glass, and rubber. Indeed, by the 1880s some 75 percent of U.S. steel went to the railroad industry. Railroads also required the development of new managerial skills to operate large, complicated businesses with multiple employees.

Space and Time Railroads led to drastic changes in the landscape. Indeed, the westward expansion driven by the railroad led to large-scale land clearing and the extension of farming and mining lands and brought about both human suffering for indigenous peoples and environmental damage through soil erosion and pollution. Railroads even shaped the American sense of time. Until rapid and regular rail transportation became available, communities set their clocks by the sun. As a result, New York time was eleven minutes and forty-five seconds behind Boston time. Those differences in local sun times created scheduling nightmares as well as the potential for train accidents. To simplify matters, in 1883 railroad companies divided the North American continent into four zones in which all railroad clocks read precisely the same time. The general public quickly adopted **railroad time**, and in 1918 the U.S. government legally established the four time zones as the national standard.

Economic Growth Led by railroads, the U.S. economy expanded rapidly between 1870 and 1900. Inventors designed new products and brought them to market: electric lights, telephones, typewriters, phonographs, film photography, motion picture cameras, and electric motors all made their appearance during this era. By the early twentieth century the United States had emerged as one of the world's major industrial powers.

Canadian Prosperity

British investment deeply influenced the development of the Canadian as well as the U.S. economy in the nineteenth and early twentieth centuries. Canadian leaders, like U.S. leaders, took advantage of British capital to industrialize without allowing their economy to fall under British control.

The National Policy After the establishment of the Dominion of Canada in 1867, politicians started a program of economic development known as the **National Policy**. The idea was to attract migrants, protect nascent industries through tariffs, and build national transportation systems. The centerpiece of the transportation network was the transcontinental **Canadian Pacific Railroad**, built largely with British investment capital and completed in 1885. The Canadian Pacific Railroad opened the western prairie lands to commerce, stimulated the development of other industries, and promoted the emergence of a Canadian national economy. The National Policy created some violent conflicts with indigenous peoples who resisted encroachment on their lands and with trappers who resented disruption of their way of life, but it also promoted economic growth and independence.

As a result of the National Policy, Canada experienced booming agricultural, mineral, and industrial production in the late nineteenth and early twentieth centuries. Canadian population surged as a result of both migration and natural increase. Migrants flocked to Canada's shores from Asia and especially from Europe: between 1903 and 1914 some 2.7 million eastern European migrants settled in Canada. Fueled in part by this population growth, Canadian economic expansion took place on the foundation of rapidly increasing wheat production and the extraction of rich mineral resources, including gold, silver, copper, nickel, and asbestos. Industrialists also tapped Canadian rivers to produce the hydroelectric power necessary for manufacturing.

U.S. Investment Canada remained wary of its powerful neighbor to the south but did not keep U.S. economic influence entirely at bay. By 1918, Americans owned 30 percent of all Canadian industry, and thereafter the U.S. and Canadian economies became increasingly interdependent. Canada began to undergo rapid industrialization after the early twentieth century, as the province of Ontario benefited from the spillover of U.S. industry in the northeast.

Latin American Dependence

Latin American states did not undergo industrialization or enjoy economic development as the United States and Canada did. When the colonies of Spain and Portugal became independent in the early nineteenth century, European investors from Britain, France, and Germany jumped at the chance to establish trading relationships in a region where they had long been prevented from investing. Both Central and South America offered attractive prospects for extracting raw materials such as wheat, beef, and fish, and European investors were happy to supply the investment for railroads and other types of infrastructure necessary to bring raw materials to ports. Since Latin American elites retained control over local economies, European investors only needed to make sure their economic plans were attractive to them. And, indeed, elites profited handsomely from European trade and investment and thus had little incentive to work toward industrialization.

British Investment British investors were particularly active in Latin America in the nineteenth century. In Argentina, for example, British investors encouraged the development of cattle and sheep ranching. After the 1860s and the invention of refrigerated cargo ships, meat became Argentina's largest export and Britain its principal market. Because British investors controlled the industry at almost every stage, they also reaped the profits.

Attempted Industrialization Latin American elites did make attempts to encourage industrialization in a few places, but these had limited success. The most notable of those efforts was when the dictatorial general Porfirio Díaz ruled Mexico (1876–1911). Díaz represented the interests of large landowners, wealthy merchants, and foreign investors. Under his rule, railroad tracks and telegraph lines connected all parts of Mexico and the production of mineral resources surged. A small steel industry produced railroad track and construction materials, and entrepreneurs established glass, chemical, and textile industries. The capital, Mexico City, underwent a transformation during the Díaz years: it acquired paved streets, streetcar lines, and electric streetlights. But the profits from Mexican enterprises did not support continuing industrial development. Instead, they went into the pockets of the Mexican elite and foreign investors who supported Díaz while a growing and discontented urban working class seethed with resentment at low wages, long hours, and foreign managers. Even as agriculture, railroad construction, and mining were booming, the standard of living for average Mexicans was declining in the late nineteenth century. Frustration with that state of affairs helps explain the sudden outbreak of violent revolution in 1911.

Latin American economies expanded rapidly in the late nineteenth century. Exports drove this growth: copper and silver from Mexico, bananas from Central America, rubber and coffee from Brazil, beef and wheat from Argentina, copper from Chile, and tobacco and sugar from Cuba. Because foreign investors controlled the markets and their infrastructure, however, they were also able to keep prices for commodities low. Latin American economies were thus subject to decisions made in the interests of foreign investors, and unstable governments could do little in the face of strong foreign intervention. Controlled by the very elites who profited from foreign intervention at the expense of their citizens, Latin American governments helped promote the region's economic dependence, despite growth in industrial and export economies.

AMERICAN CULTURAL AND SOCIAL DIVERSITY

Much of the allure of the Americas derived from their vast spaces and diverse populations. Although diversity distinguished the Americas, it also provided abundant fuel for conflicts between ethnic groups, social classes, and those segregated by race or gender. The social and cultural diversity of American societies challenged their ability to achieve cultural cohesion as well as democratically inclusive states. The lingering legacies of European conquest, slavery, migration, and patriarchy highlighted contradictions between the Enlightenment ideals of freedom and equality and the realities of life for indigenous and African-American peoples as well as recent migrants and women. In efforts to maintain their own position and preserve social stability, the dominant political forces in the Americas often repressed demands for recognition by dispossessed groups.

Multicultural Society in the United States

By the late nineteenth century, the United States had become a boisterous multicultural society whose population included indigenous peoples, Euro-Americans, African-Americans, and growing numbers of migrants from Europe and Asia. The poet Walt Whitman described the United States as "not merely a nation but a teeming nation

Why It Matters

The Birth of Nationalism

What are the long-term consequences of deciding who "belongs" in a nation? The United States offers a case study. During the nineteenth century, white males of European ancestry used their powerful position in society to define the nation in terms of the legacies of the American revolution and a common western European heritage. By imagining the nation this way, this group also actively resisted the idea that people from different backgrounds— including formerly enslaved people, immigrants from Asia and southern Europe, and Native Americans— "belonged" in the nation or should gain access to its privileges. Indeed, white men went to great lengths to ensure the exclusion of those they believed did not belong, using violence, the law, politics, and social pressure. Their tactics shaped the history of the United States right down to the present, demonstrating the long-term, destructive potential of nationalism when it is used for exclusionary purposes.

of nations." Yet political and economic power rested almost exclusively with white male elites of European ancestry. The United States experienced tension and occasional conflict as members of various constituencies worked for dignity, prosperity, and a voice in society.

Native Peoples As they expanded to the west, Euro-American settlers and ranchers pushed indigenous peoples off their own lands and onto marginal tracts of land called reservations. Begrudging Native Americans even those meager lands, the United States embarked in the latter half of the nineteenth century on a policy designed to reduce native autonomy even further through laws and reforms aimed at assimilating native groups to American culture and destroying Native American cultural traditions. The U.S. government and private citizens acted to undermine or destroy outright the bases of native cultural traditions. For example, government officials removed native children from their families and groups and enrolled them in white-controlled boarding schools. These schools, such as the Carlisle Indian School and the Toledo Indian School, illustrated the extent to which white society sought to eliminate tribal influences and inculcate Christian, U.S. values. Native languages as well as dress and hair fashions were banned, further distancing the children from their cultures. Native Americans, however, resisted those forms of assimilation, and over the following decades native groups rebuilt and reaffirmed native identities.

Freed African-Americans The Civil War ended slavery, but it did not bring about equality for formerly enslaved African-Americans and their descendants. In an effort to establish a place for formerly enslaved people in American society, northern forces sent armies of occupation to the southern states and forced them to undergo a program of social and political **reconstruction** (1867–1877). They extended civil rights to formerly enslaved people and provided Black men with voting rights.

The Apache youths at the Carlisle Indian School offer stark faces to the camera, suggesting their discontent with reform efforts directed at assimilation through education.
Historical/Corbis Historical/Getty Images

What's Left Out?

The practice of separating indigenous children from their parents was not just a U.S. policy. In fact, most of the white settler colonies—including the United States, Canada, and Australia—used child separation as a tool of colonial rule in the late nineteenth and twentieth centuries. One of the primary goals of settler colonies was to dispossess indigenous populations of their lands and then to repopulate them with settlers of European descent. In spite of trying to accomplish this goal by battling with, murdering, and forcibly removing indigenous people, indigenous populations persisted. By the late nineteenth century, this persistence led agents of the settler colonies to attempt to eradicate indigenous culture by the forcible and systematic assimilation of children. In Australia, aboriginal people were removed to isolated areas, where children were separated from their parents in segregated dormitories. In the United States, settlers had founded 154 boarding schools for Native American children by 1902, each located far from their home communities. In Canada, authorities studied the U.S. model and established a network of boarding schools for indigenous children. Once removed from their homes, children were taught to adopt the language and behavior of the settler culture in the hope that this would permanently eliminate their own cultures and customs. But indigenous people seldom gave up their children voluntarily. In fact, so many resisted that most were taken by force or the threat of force. In the United States, for example, authorities often withheld food rations on reservations until communities gave up their children. When thinking about this global practice of child separation, it is worth considering that the 1948 United Nations Convention on Genocide defined one of the methods of genocide as "forcibly transferring children of one group to another group."

Source: Margaret D. Jacobs. *White Mother to a Dark Race: Settler Colonialism, Maternalism, and the Removal of Indigenous Children in the American West and Australia, 1880–1940.* Lincoln: University of Nebraska Press, 2009.

People in southern states elected biracial governments for the first time in U.S. history, and formerly enslaved people participated actively in the political affairs of the republic.

After reconstruction, however, the armies of occupation went home, and a violent backlash soon dismantled the reforms of reconstruction. By the turn of the century, U.S. Blacks faced violence and intimidation when they tried to vote. Southern states fashioned a rigidly segregated society that deprived the African-American population of educational, economic, and political opportunities. Although freedom was better than slavery, it was far different from the hopeful visions of the enslaved people who had won their emancipation.

Women Even before the Civil War, a small but growing women's movement had emerged in the United States. At the **Seneca Falls Convention** in 1848, feminists issued a declaration arguing "that all men and women are created equal" and demanding equal political and economic rights. Some groups of women fought for equal rights throughout the nineteenth century, and new opportunities for education and employment slowly began to offer alternatives to marriage and domesticity. Women's colleges, reform activism, and professional industrial jobs allowed some women to pursue careers instead of marriage. Yet meaningful economic and political opportunities for women awaited the twentieth century, and even these mainly benefited white women rather than women of color.

A lithograph from *Harper's Weekly* after the Civil War. An artisan, a middle-class African-American, and a Black Union soldier are in the process of voting, perhaps for the first time in their lives.
Historical/Corbis Historical/Getty Images

SOURCES FROM THE PAST

The Meaning of Freedom

Once an enslaved man in Tennessee on the plantation of Colonel P. H. Anderson, Jourdan Anderson gained his freedom in 1864, before the conclusion of the Civil War. He and his family then relocated to Dayton, Ohio. The following letter is a response to a letter from Colonel Anderson, who asked Jourdan to return to the Tennessee plantation. Jourdan's thoughtful reply, tinged with sarcastic humor, underscores his sense of dignity and self-worth.

Dayton, Ohio, August 7, 1865

To my Old Master, Col. P. H. Anderson, Big Spring, Tennessee

Sir: I got your letter and was glad to find that you had not forgotten Jourdan, and that you wanted me to come back and live with you again, promising to do better for me than anybody else can. I have often felt uneasy about you. I thought the Yankees would have hung you long before this for harboring Rebs they found at your house. I suppose they never heard about your going to Col. Martin's to kill the Union soldier that was left by his company in their stable. Although you shot at me twice before I left you, I did not want to hear of your being hurt and I am glad you are still living. . . . I would have gone back to see you all when I was working in the Nashville Hospital, but one of the neighbors told me Henry intended to shoot me if he ever got the chance.

> What indications does Jourdan Anderson give here about the kind of treatment he received from Colonel Anderson while he was enslaved?

I want to know particularly what the good chance is you propose to give me. I am doing tolerably well here; I get $25 a month, with victuals and clothing; have a comfortable home for Mandy (the folks here call her Mrs. Anderson) and the children, Milly, Jane, and Grundy, go to school and are learning well; the teacher says Grundy has a head for a preacher. They go to Sunday-School, and Mandy and me attend church regularly. We are kindly treated. . . . Now, if you will write and say what wages you will give me, I will be better able to decide whether it would be to my advantage to move back again.

As to my freedom, which you say I can have, there is nothing to be gained on that score, as I got my free-papers in 1864 from the Provost-Marshal-General of the Department at Nashville. Mandy says she would be afraid to go back without some proof that you are sincerely disposed to treat us justly and kindly— and we have concluded to test your sincerity by asking you to send us our wages for the time we served you. This will make us forget and forgive old scores, and rely on your justice and friendship in the future. I served you faithfully for thirty-two years, and Mandy twenty years, at $25 a month for me, and $2 a week for Mandy. Our earnings would amount to $11,680. . . . Please send the money by Adams Express, in care of V. Winters, esq., Dayton, Ohio.

> Do you think Jourdan Anderson was serious about this request or that he made it to make a point about how much the labor of enslaved people was worth?

If you fail to pay us for faithful labors in the past we can have little faith in your promises in the future. We trust the good Maker has opened your eyes to the wrongs which you and your fathers have done to me and my fathers, in making us toil for you for generations without recompense. . . . Surely there will be a day of reckoning for those who defraud the laborer of his hire.

In answering this letter please state if there would be any safety for my Milly and Jane, who are now grown up and both good looking girls. . . . I would rather stay here and starve and die if it come to that than have my girls brought to shame by the violence and wickedness of their young masters. You will also please state if there has been any schools opened for the colored children in your neighborhood, the desire of my life now is to give my children an education, and have them form virtuous habits.

From your old servant, Jourdan Anderson.

P. S.—Say howdy to George Carter, and thank him for taking the pistol from you when you were shooting at me.

For Further Reflection

■ What does Colonel Anderson's request for Jourdan Anderson to return tell us about the colonel's understanding of what slavery had been like? What does Jourdan Anderson's response tell us about what it meant to him to be free?

■ In what clever ways does Jourdan Anderson test the seriousness of his former shalveholder's offer of employment, and what does his approach say about the meaning of Black freedom?

Source: "Letter from a Freedman to His Old Master." *New York Daily Tribune,* 22 August 1865, p. 7.

Migrants Between 1840 and 1914 some twenty-five million European migrants landed on American shores, and by the late nineteenth century most of them hailed from southern and eastern European countries. Migrants introduced new foods, music, dances, holidays, sports, and languages to U.S. society and contributed to the cultural diversity of the western hemisphere. Yet white, native-born citizens of the United States often did not welcome the newer arrivals. Indeed, concerns about growing numbers of migrants with different cultural and social traditions eventually led to the exclusion of new arrivals from Asian lands: the U.S. government ordered a complete halt to migration from China in 1882 and from Japan in 1908.

Canadian Cultural Contrasts

Ethnic Diversity British and French settlers each viewed themselves as Canada's founding people. That cleavage, which profoundly influenced Canadian political development, masked much greater cultural and ethnic diversity in Canada. French and British settlers displaced the indigenous peoples, who remain a significant minority of Canada's population today. Slavery likewise left a mark on Canada. Slavery was legal in the British empire until 1833, and many early settlers brought enslaved people with them to Canada. After emancipation, Black people in Canada were free but not equal, segregated and isolated from the political and cultural mainstream. Chinese migrants also came to Canada: lured by gold rushes such as the Fraser River rush of 1858 and by opportunities to work on the Canadian Pacific Railway in the 1880s, most Chinese migrants lived in segregated Chinatowns in the cities of British Columbia, and like Black people they had little voice in public affairs. Between 1896 and 1914 three million migrants from Britain, the United States, and eastern Europe arrived in Canada, bringing even greater ethnic diversity with them.

Despite the diversity of Canada's population, communities descended from British and French settlers dominated Canadian society, and conflict between the two communities was the most prominent source of ethnic tension throughout the nineteenth and twentieth centuries. After 1867, as British Canadians led the effort to settle the Northwest Territories and incorporate them into the Dominion, frictions between the two groups intensified. Westward expansion brought British Canadian settlers and cultivators into conflict with French Canadian fur traders, lumberjacks, and *métis* of mixed French and Indian ancestry.

The *Métis* and Louis Riel Indeed, a major outbreak of civil strife took place in the 1870s and 1880s. Indigenous peoples and *métis* had moved west throughout the nineteenth century to preserve their land and trading rights, but the drive of British Canadians to the west threatened them. **Louis Riel** (1844–1885), who was himself a *métis*, emerged as the leader of the *métis* and indigenous peoples of western Canada. Of particular importance was his leadership in the resistance to the Canadian Pacific Railroad—and the white settlement it promised to bring—during the 1880s. In 1885 he organized a military force of *métis* and native peoples in the Saskatchewan river country and led an insurrection known as the **Northwest Rebellion**. Canadian forces quickly subdued the makeshift army, and government authorities executed Riel for treason. Although the Northwest Rebellion never had a chance of success, the execution of Riel nonetheless threatened to undermine the beginnings of Canadian national unity and foreshadowed a long term of cultural conflict between Canadians of British, French, and indigenous ancestry.

Ethnicity, Identity, and Gender in Latin America

The heritage of Spanish and Portuguese colonialism and the legacy of slavery inclined Latin American societies toward the establishment of hierarchical distinctions based on ethnicity and color. At the top of society stood the creoles, individuals of European ancestry born in the Americas; indigenous peoples, formerly enslaved people, and their Black descendants occupied the lowest rungs of the social ladder. In between were

An 1868 photograph of an Argentinian gaucho dressed in typical gear.

Historic Collection/Alamy Stock Photo

traditions. The migration of European workers to Argentina brought a lively diversity to the capital of Buenos Aires, which was perhaps the most cosmopolitan city of nineteenth-century Latin America. With its broad avenues, smart boutiques, and handsome buildings graced with wrought iron, Buenos Aires enjoyed a reputation as "the Paris of the Americas."

Gauchos One prominent symbol of Latin American identity was Argentina's **gauchos** (cowboys). Most, but not all, gauchos were of mixed race, but race was not the determining factor in becoming a gaucho. Instead, anyone who adopted gaucho ways became a gaucho, and gaucho society acquired an ethnic egalitarianism rarely found elsewhere in Latin America. Gauchos were most prominent in the Argentine pampas, but their cultural practices linked them to the cowboys, or vaqueros, found throughout the Americas. As pastoralists herding cattle and horses on the pampas, gauchos stood apart from both the indigenous peoples and the growing urban and agricultural elites who gradually displaced them with large landholdings and cattle ranches that spread to the pampas.

Male Domination Even more than in the United States and Canada, male domination was a central characteristic of Latin American society in the nineteenth century. Women could not vote or hold office, nor could they work or manage estates without permission from their male guardians. In rural areas, women were liable to rough treatment by gauchos and other men steeped in the values of *machismo*—a social ethic that honored male strength, courage, aggressiveness, assertiveness, and cunning. Women did carve spaces for themselves outside or alongside the male world of *machismo,* and this was especially true in the home and in the marketplace, where Latin American women exerted great influence. In addition, although Latin American states did not generate a strong women's movement, they did begin to expand educational opportunities for girls and young women after the mid-nineteenth century. In large cities most girls received some formal schooling, and women usually filled teaching positions in the public schools that proliferated throughout Latin America in the late nineteenth century.

various groups of mixed ancestry. Although most Latin American states ended the legal recognition of these groups, the distinctions themselves persisted and limited their opportunities.

Migration and Cultural Diversity Large-scale migration brought cultural diversity to Latin America in the nineteenth century. Indentured laborers who went from parts of Asia to Peru, Brazil, Cuba, and other Caribbean destinations carried with them many of their native cultural practices. When their numbers were relatively large, as in the case of Indian migrants to Trinidad and Tobago, they formed distinctive communities in which they observed their inherited cultural and social

gauchos (GAHW-chohs)
vaqueros (bah-KEH-rohs)

CONCLUSION

After gaining independence from European colonial powers, the states of the western hemisphere worked to build stable and prosperous societies. The independent American states faced difficult challenges as they sought to construct viable societies based partly on the Enlightenment principles of freedom, equality, and constitutional government. People in the United States and Canada built large federal societies in North America, whereas people in Latin America built a series of smaller states. Throughout the hemisphere descendants of European settlers violently conquered indigenous American peoples and built societies dominated by Euro-Americans. They established agricultural economies, exploited natural resources, and in some places launched processes of industrialization. Millions of people from Europe and Asia migrated to the Americas, contributing to American cultural diversity. All American states experienced tensions arising from social, economic, cultural, and ethnic differences, which led occasionally to violent civil conflict and often to smoldering resentments and grievances. Although the making of independent American societies was not a smooth process, it reflected the increasing interdependence of all the world's peoples.

STUDY TERMS

Abraham Lincoln (486)
Antonio López Santa Anna (489)
battle of Little Bighorn (485)
Benito Juárez (489)
British North America Act of 1867 (487)
Canadian Pacific Railroad (493)
Civil War (486)
Dominion of Canada (487)
Emancipation Proclamation (486)
Emiliano Zapata (491)
Francisco (Pancho) Villa (491)
gauchos (499)
Guadalupe Hidalgo (486)
Indian Removal Act of 1830 (485)
John A. Macdonald (487)
Juan Manuel de Rosas (489)
La Reforma (489)
Louis Riel (498)
machismo (499)
manifest destiny (485)
Mexican-American War (486)
National Policy (493)
Northwest Rebellion (498)
Porfirio Díaz (491)
railroad time (493)
reconstruction (495)
Seneca Falls Convention (496)
Trail of Tears (485)
War of 1812 (487)
Wounded Knee (485)

FOR FURTHER READING

David Barry Gaspar and Darlene Clark Hine, eds. *Beyond Bondage: Free Women of Color in the Americas*. Chicago, 2004. A collection of essays on free Black women and their unique abilities to negotiate social and legal institutions in the era of slavery.

Pekka Hämäläinen. *The Comanche Empire*. New Haven, 2008. An ambitiously revisionist history that challenges the accepted understanding of colonial America and westward expansion.

Tom Holm. *The Great Confusion in Indian Affairs: Native Americans and Whites in the Progressive Era*. Austin, 2005. A study of Native American resistance to the American government's attempts at subjugation.

Patricia Nelson Limerick. *The Legacy of Conquest: The Unbroken Past of the American West*. New York, 1987. A provocative work exploring the influences of race, class, and gender in the conquest of the American west.

Adam McKeown. *Melancholy Order: Asian Migration and the Globalization of Borders*. New York, 2008. Documents the global scale of Asian migration in the nineteenth and twentieth centuries and argues that it triggered exclusionary border policies in the United States and Europe.

J. R. Miller. *Skyscrapers Hide the Heavens: A History of Indian-White Relations in Canada*. 3rd ed. Toronto, 2000. An important study of Canadian policies toward indigenous peoples.

Desmond Morton. *A Short History of Canada*. 6th ed. Toronto, 2006. A well-balanced, popular history of Canada.

Paul Ortiz. *An African American and Latinx History of the United States*. Boston, 2018. A radical revisionist exploration of U.S. history from the perspective of marginalized people in a global context.

Robert L. Scheina. *Latin American Wars. Vol. 1: The Age of the Caudillos, 1791–1899*. Washington, D.C., 2003. By examining the wars of independence, this work uncovers the reasons behind the failures of Latin American state building.

Allison Sneider. *Suffragists in an Imperial Age: US Expansion and the Woman Question, 1870–1929*. Oxford, 2008. Explores the women's suffrage movement in the United States and U.S. imperialism as intertwined and inseparable phenomena.

ZOOMING IN ON ENCOUNTERS
Emperor Menelik II of Ethiopia and His Warning to European Empire Builders

In 1889 Emperor Menelik II (1844–1913) came to the throne of the independent state of Ethiopia, in the horn of Africa. Long before taking the throne, Menelik had focused on obtaining the most up-to-date European firearms as a means of strengthening his power. In the wake of the Berlin West Africa Conference (1884–1885)—in which European powers divided up the continent of Africa between them—Menelik observed with increasing concern the violent conquest of huge portions of African territory. In 1891 Menelik decided to make his position about attempts to conquer Ethiopia clear by sending a letter to the European heads of state, in which he said that "if powers at a distance come forward to partition Africa between them, I do not intend to be an indifferent spectator."

Menelik then set about stockpiling more than eighty thousand European rifles and other weapons, including a cannon. So when an Italian army—with the blessing of the British and French governments—invaded Ethiopia in 1896, the Ethiopians were ready. On 1 March, they routed the Italians in the Battle of Adwa, killing almost 40 percent

Emperor Menelik II of Ethiopia (reigned 1889–1913) on the throne in coronation garb.
MARKA/Alamy Stock Photo

of the force (about five thousand men). The battle was decisive: the Italians retreated, and the European nations formally recognized Ethiopian sovereignty and independence.

But Menelik's success against European invaders was unique in the late nineteenth and early twentieth centuries. Resistance to conquest was nearly universal among African leaders, but no other state or group had been able to purchase and stockpile such a large quantity of the latest weaponry, nor had they been able to command a large, unified army to use it. As a result, Europeans maintained a technological advantage in most of the rest of Africa and used it to conquer more than 90 percent of the continent by 1910.

CHAPTER OVERVIEW

From the days of ancient Mesopotamia and Egypt to the present, strong societies have often sought to dominate their neighbors by subjecting them to imperial rule. But in the second half of the nineteenth century, a handful of western European states wrote a new chapter in the history of imperialism. Industrialization equipped them with the most effective tools and the most lethal weapons available anywhere in the world. Strong nationalist sentiments enabled them to mobilize their populations for purposes of overseas expansion. Three centuries of experience with maritime trade in Asia, Africa, the Americas, and Oceania provided them with extensive knowledge of the world and its peoples. With those advantages, western European peoples conquered foreign armies, dominated foreign economies, used their economic power, and imposed their hegemony throughout the world. Toward the end of the century, the United States and Japan joined European states as imperial powers.

The establishment of global empires in this period had far-reaching effects. In many ways, imperialism forcibly tightened links between the world's societies. Imperial powers demanded trade between dominant states and their overseas colonies, for example, and they organized mass migrations of laborers to work in agricultural and industrial ventures. Yet imperialism also fostered divisions between the world's peoples. Powerful tools, deadly weapons, and global hegemony led European peoples to consider themselves superior to their subjects throughout the world. In fact, modern racism is one of the legacies of imperialism. Another effect of imperialism was the development of anticolonial resistance in subject territories, including nationalism. Although the formal empires of this period were relatively short-lived and nearly all colonies had won their independence by 1970, the influence of global imperialism continues to shape the contemporary world.

CHRONOLOGY	
1805–1848	Reign of Muhammad Ali in Egypt
1808–1839	Reign of Sultan Mahmud II
1824	Founding of Singapore by Thomas Stamford Raffles
1839–1842	Opium War
1839–1876	Tanzimat era
1850–1864	Taiping rebellion
1857	Sepoy rebellion
1859–1869	Construction of the Suez Canal
1860–1864	Land wars in New Zealand
1860–1895	Self-Strengthening Movement
1884–1885	Berlin West Africa Conference
1894–1895	Sino-Japanese War
1897–1901	Term of office of U.S. president William McKinley
1898–1899	Spanish-Cuban-American War
1899–1902	South African War (Boer War)
1901–1909	Term of office of U.S. president Theodore Roosevelt
1904–1905	Russo-Japanese War
1904–1914	Construction of the Panama Canal
1905–1906	Maji-Maji rebellion
1908–1918	Young Turk era

FOUNDATIONS OF EMPIRE

In nineteenth-century Europe, proponents of empire advanced a variety of political, economic, and cultural arguments to justify the conquest or economic control of foreign territories. The imperialist ventures they promoted enjoyed such dramatic success largely because of the military, transportation, and communications technologies developed by European industry in the first half of the nineteenth century.

Motives of Imperialism

Modern Imperialism The building of empires is an old story in world history. By the nineteenth century, however, even contemporary observers recognized that empires of their day were different from those of earlier times. About mid-century they began to speak of *imperialism,* and by the 1880s the recently coined term had made its way into popular speech and writing throughout western Europe. In contemporary usage, *imperialism* referred to domination over subject territories, usually overseas. Sometimes that domination came through **formal imperialism**, which involved military conquest and the establishment of political control. Frequently, however, it arose through what is known as **informal imperialism**: that is, the domination of trade, investment, and business activities that enabled imperial powers to profit from subject societies and influence their affairs without going to the trouble of exercising direct political control.

Modern Colonialism Like the building of empires, the establishment of colonies in foreign territories is a practice dating from ancient times. Here, however, *colonialism* refers not just to the settlement of colonists in new lands but also to the political, social, economic, and cultural structures that enabled imperial powers to dominate subject lands. In some places, such as North America, Chile, Argentina, Australia, New Zealand, and South Africa, European powers established settler colonies populated by large numbers of migrants from the home societies. Yet contemporary scholars also speak of European colonies in India, southeast Asia, and sub-Saharan Africa, even though European migrants did not settle there in large numbers. In such places, European agents and officials established political control and controlled domestic and foreign policy, integrated local economies into the network of global capitalism, and promoted European educational and cultural preferences. Contemporary scholars also speak of areas, particularly in the Ottoman empire and China, where Europeans did not establish formal colonies but nevertheless dominated finances, economy, and foreign policies to such a degree that they represented the form of imperial domination known as informal imperialism.

Economic Motives of Imperialism During the second half of the nineteenth century, many Europeans came to believe that imperial expansion and colonial domination were crucial for the survival of their societies. A wide range of motives encouraged European peoples to launch imperialist campaigns of domination, conquest, and control. Some advocates argued that imperialism was in the economic interests of European societies as well as individuals. They pointed out that overseas colonies could serve as reliable sources of raw materials: rubber, tin, and copper were vital industrial products, for example, and by the late nineteenth century petroleum had also become a crucial industrial resource.

Geopolitical Motives of Imperialism In the last half of the nineteenth century, geopolitical concerns became one of the most influential motivations for imperialism. Advocates argued that even if colonies were not always economically beneficial, they were crucial for political and military reasons. Territories that occupied strategic sites on the world's sea lanes or harbors ideal for supplying commercial and naval ships attracted particular attention. Proponents of imperialism sought to acquire these sites for their own states and especially to deny them to other states. The British occupation of Egypt in 1882 is a good example of this, because the British government was extremely anxious to protect the Suez Canal—the main route to India from Britain—from falling into the hands of a rival.

Imperialism had its uses also for domestic politics. In an age when socialists and communists directly confronted industrialists, European politicians and national leaders sought to defuse social tension and inspire patriotism by focusing public attention on imperialist ventures.

Why It Matters ▷▷▷▷▷▷▷

The Birth of Nationalism

How did imperialism affect ordinary people in the colonizing countries? One way is that some governments used imperial campaigns to manipulate political opinion at home. The Abyssinian campaign of 1862 is one example of this phenomenon: during an election year, the British Conservative Party used an incident in which several British citizens had been taken hostage by the Ethiopian king as a way to whip up nationalist outrage against both the Ethiopians and the British Liberal Party that was in power. In part because of this nationalist fervor, the Liberals were defeated, and the Conservatives were voted into power, thus changing the political leadership of the country. This is only one instance in which governments manipulated public opinion by using events, such as wars or campaigns of expansion, that occurred in the colonies.

Cultural Motives of Imperialism

Cultural motivations also helped justify imperial expansion in this period. European missionaries, for example, believed it was their duty to seek out converts to Christianity around the world, and imperial expansion allowed them the protection of European governments as they did so. European missionaries did not always see eye to eye with European entrepreneurs or colonial officials and were sometimes deeply critical of aspects of colonial rule. Nevertheless, they often facilitated communications between imperialists and subject peoples, and they sometimes provided European officials with information they needed to maintain control of overseas colonies. Missionary settlements also served as convenient meeting places for Europeans overseas and as distribution centers for European manufactured goods. While missionaries sought to introduce Christianity to subject peoples, their goals were compatible with those of other Europeans who sought to bring them "civilization" in the form of political order and social and cultural enlightenment. French imperialists routinely invoked the *mission civilisatrice* ("civilizing mission") as justification for their expansion into Africa and Asia, and other European powers routinely justified foreign intervention as their duty to civilize "backward" peoples.

Tools of Empire

Even the strongest motives would not have enabled imperialists to impose their rule throughout the world without the powerful technological advantages of industrialization. During the nineteenth century, industrialists devised effective technologies of war, transportation, communication, and medicine that enabled European imperialists to exert enormous influence in the world.

Military Technologies

By the middle of the nineteenth century, European armies were using breech-loading firearms with rifled bores that were far more accurate and reliable than any other firearm. By the 1870s Europeans were experimenting with rifled machine guns, and in the 1880s they adopted the Maxim gun, a light and powerful weapon that fired eleven bullets per second.

When European states sought to impose their will against others that did not yet have the latest rifles or machine guns, as they often did in this period, they were able to inflict devastating defeats. In 1898, for example, a British army with twenty machine guns and six gunboats engaged a Sudanese force at **Omdurman**, near Khartoum on the Nile River. During five hours of fighting, the British force lost 368 men, whereas machine guns and explosive charges fired from gunboats killed some 11,000 Sudanese. The battle of Omdurman became the first step in the establishment of British colonial rule in Sudan.

Transportation Technologies

The most important innovations in transportation as they related to imperial expansion involved steamships and railroads. During the 1830s British naval engineers adapted steam power to military uses and built large, ironclad ships equipped with powerful guns. These steamships traveled much faster than sailing vessels, and as an additional advantage they could ignore the winds and travel in any direction. Because of that, they could travel much farther upriver than sailboats, which enabled imperialists to project power deep into the interior regions of foreign lands.

The construction of new canals enhanced the effectiveness of steamships. Both the **Suez Canal** (constructed 1859–1869) and the **Panama Canal** (constructed 1904–1914) facilitated the building and maintenance of empires by enabling naval vessels to travel more rapidly than ever before between the world's seas and oceans. They also lowered the costs of trade between imperial powers and subject lands.

Once imperialists had gained control of overseas lands, they often constructed railroads to help them maintain their hegemony and organize local economies to their own advantage. Rail transportation enabled colonial officials and armies to travel quickly through the colonies. It also facilitated the exploitation of raw materials and the distribution of European manufactured goods in the colonies.

Communications Technologies

Communications also benefited from industrialization and in turn aided European imperial expansion. In the 1830s it took as long as two years for a British correspondent to receive a reply to a letter sent to India by sailing ship. By the 1850s, after the introduction of steamships, correspondence could make the round-trip between London and Bombay in four months. With the opening of the Suez Canal in 1869, steamships traveled from Britain to India in less than two weeks.

The invention of the telegraph made it possible to exchange messages even faster. By 1870 submarine cables carried messages between Britain and India in about five hours. By 1902 cables linked all parts of the British empire throughout the world, and other European states maintained cables to support communications with their own colonies. Their monopoly on telegraphic communications allowed imperial officials to rapidly mobilize forces to deal with troubles, and the telegraph allowed merchants to respond quickly to developments of economic and commercial significance. Rapid communication was an integral structural element of empire.

Imperial Medical Technologies

When Europeans traveled to the tropical and subtropical regions where they

---

mission civilisatrice (mee-see-on sih-vihl-ihs-a-trihs)

Omdurman (om-door-MAHN)

Khartoum (khar-TOOM)

A British Maxim gun at Chilas Fort on India's Northwest Frontier in the late nineteenth century.

Hulton Archive/Getty Images

intrusion into central Asia, the establishment of colonies in southeast Asia, and interference in the Ottoman and Qing empires in southwest and east Asia. Fearful that rivals might gain control over remaining regions, European states embarked on a campaign of frenzied expansion in the 1880s that brought almost all of Africa and Pacific Ocean territories into their empires. Throughout this period, Europeans were engaged simultaneously in projects of settler colonialism, formal imperialism without large numbers of settlers, and informal imperialism in which sovereignty was compromised by widespread economic interference. Whether European powers engaged in one kind or another of imperial project depended largely on rivalries with other European powers, the strategic or economic importance of a given area, and the level and type of resistance offered by indigenous peoples.

sought to impose their rule, they frequently became ill and died from malaria, a mosquito-borne disease. When they discovered an effective treatment for the disease in the form of quinine, it became a powerful weapon in the European quest to conquer and rule distant lands during the nineteenth century.

The remedy for malaria came to Europe from Peru, where indigenous peoples used the bark from the cinchona tree to treat various fevers, including malaria. In 1820, two French chemists, Pierre Pelletier and Joseph Caventou, extracted the alkaloid of quinine from cinchona bark, and by the 1840s European colonizers kept quinine pills by their bed stands. The use of quinine proved to be a major force in the expansion of European empires and ultimately permitted small European populations to survive in tropical regions.

EUROPEAN IMPERIALISM

Aided by powerful technologies, European states launched an unprecedented round of empire building in the second half of the nineteenth century. Imperial expansion began with the British conquest of India. Competition between imperial powers led to European

The British Empire in India

The British empire in south Asia and southeast Asia grew out of the mercantile activities of the English East India Company, which enjoyed a monopoly on English trade with India. In 1600, the East India Company obtained permission from the Mughal emperors of India to build fortified posts on the coastlines. In the seventeenth century, company merchants traded mostly for Indian pepper and cotton, Chinese silk and porcelain, and spices from southeast Asia. During the eighteenth century, tea and coffee became the most prominent trade items, and European consumers acquired a permanent taste for both beverages.

Company Rule   After the death of the emperor Aurangzeb in 1707, the Mughal state entered a period of decline. The East India Company took advantage of Mughal weakness to strengthen and expand its trading posts. In the 1750s, company merchants began campaigns of outright conquest in India, largely to protect their commercial interests. From their forts at Calcutta, Madras, and Bombay, the merchants extended their authority inland and won official rights to rule from the Mughal emperors and local authorities. They enforced their rule with armies composed mostly of Indian soldiers known as sepoys.

The British imposition of rule in south Asia was often insulting to both Hindu and Muslim religious traditions

Qing (ching)
Mughal (MOO-guhl)

and frequently cut off the political ambitions of influential leaders without any kind of political compensation. Discontent with the British reached even to the sepoys of the East India Company, and in 1857 large portions of the army rebelled. The **Sepoy rebellion**, as it became known, was quickly augmented by civilian peasants and disgruntled elites in north-central India who were deeply dissatisfied with recent British policies regarding taxation and law. To regain control, the British waged a bloody campaign of retribution in which many thousands of Indians—including civilians not directly involved in the rebellion—lost their lives through summary hangings and the destruction of villages. Once order was restored in 1858, the British government abolished the East India Company and assumed direct rule over the subcontinent.

British Imperial Rule Under the new administration, Queen Victoria (reigned 1837–1901) assigned responsibility for Indian policy to the newly established office of secretary of state for India. A viceroy represented British royal authority and administered the colony through an elite Indian civil service staffed almost exclusively by the English. Indians served in low-level bureaucratic positions, but British officials formulated all domestic and foreign policy in India.

Under both company rule and direct colonial administration, British rule transformed India. To profit from India's enormous size and wealth, British officials cleared forests and encouraged the cultivation of crops, such as tea, coffee, and opium, that were especially valuable trade items. They restructured landholdings and ensured that land taxes financed the costs of British rule. They built extensive railroad and telegraph networks that tightened links between India and the larger global economy. They also constructed new canals, harbors, and irrigation systems to support commerce and agriculture.

Especially after 1857, British colonial authorities made little effort to promote Christianity. They did, however, establish English-style schools for the children of Indian elites, and they suppressed Indian customs that conflicted with European law or values. Most prominent of those customs were **sati** (the practice of widows burning themselves on their husbands' funeral pyres), infanticide, and slavery.

Troops loyal to the British hang two participants of the Sepoy rebellion on a makeshift gallows. During the rebellion, British forces frequently resorted to summary execution without trial for those they suspected of involvement.
Felice Beato/Universal History Archive/Universal Images Group/Getty Images

Imperialism in Southeast Asia

The Dutch East Indies As the East India Company and British colonial agents tightened their grip on India, competition among European states kindled further empire-building efforts. In southeast Asia, Dutch officials tightened their control and extended their authority throughout the Dutch East Indies, the archipelago that makes up the modern state of Indonesia. Along with cash crops of sugar, tea, coffee, and tobacco, exports of rubber and tin made the Dutch East Indies a valuable and productive colony.

British Colonies in Southeast Asia In the interests of increasing trade between India, southeast Asia, and China, British imperialists moved in the nineteenth century to establish a presence in southeast Asia. By the 1880s they had established colonial authority in Burma, which became a source of teak, ivory, rubies, and jade. In 1824 Thomas Stamford Raffles founded the port of Singapore, which soon became the busiest center of trade in the Strait of Melaka. Administered by the colonial regime

sati (suh-TEE)

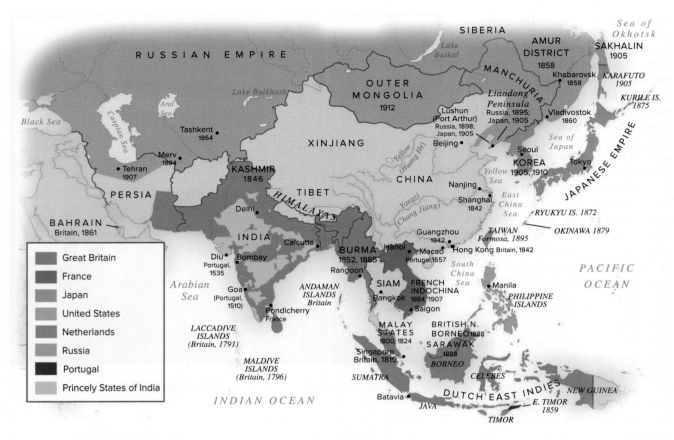

MAP 28.1 Imperialism in Asia, ca. 1914

Date is year of conquest. Note the claims made by various industrial powers.

Which territories remained unclaimed, and why? Which power claimed the most imperial territory in Asia?

in India, Singapore served as the base for the British conquest of Malaya (modern Malaysia) in the 1870s and 1880s. Besides offering ports that enabled the British navy to control sea lanes linking the Indian Ocean with the South China Sea, Malaya provided abundant supplies of tin and rubber.

French Indochina French imperialists built the large southeast Asian colony of French Indochina, consisting of the modern states of Vietnam, Cambodia, and Laos, between 1859 and 1893. Like their British counterparts in India, French colonial officials introduced European-style schools and sought to establish close connections with indigenous elites. Unlike their rivals, French officials also encouraged conversion to Christianity, and as a result the Roman Catholic church became prominent throughout French Indochina, especially Vietnam. By century's end, all of southeast Asia had come under European imperial rule except for the kingdom of Siam (modern Thailand), which preserved its independence

largely because colonial officials regarded it as a convenient buffer state between British-dominated Burma and French Indochina.

Informal Imperialism in the Ottoman and Qing Empires

As in India, the Indonesian islands, and Vietnam, European powers in the nineteenth century frequently seized territories outright and ruled them as colonies. More frequently, however, European (and later U.S.) forces used their economic and military power to force concessions out of militarily weak societies. They won rights for businesses to seek opportunities on favorable terms, gained influence in political affairs, and enabled industrial capitalists to realize huge profits without going to the trouble and expense of establishing formal colonies. In the last half of the nineteenth century, two formerly powerful societies—the Ottoman and the Qing empires—increasingly came under such informal imperialism as each struggled with military weakness and internal problems in contrast to the industrialized and competitive nation-states of Europe. Although reform movements emerged in both places, the results were inadequate, and by the early twentieth century both empires were still firmly in the grip of foreign domination.

Ottoman Military Difficulties By the late seventeenth century, it was already clear that Ottoman forces lagged behind European armies in strategy, tactics, weaponry, and training. Loss of military power translated into declining effectiveness of the central government, which was losing power in the provinces to its own officials. In addition, although the Ottoman government managed to maintain its authority in Anatolia as well as in Iraq, it suffered serious territorial losses in the Caucasus, central Asia, and the Balkan provinces of Greece (independent 1830) and Serbia (independent 1867).

Most significant, however, was the loss of Egypt. In 1798 the ambitious French general Napoleon invaded Egypt in hopes of using it as a springboard for an attack on the British empire in India. His campaign was a miserable failure, but the invasion sparked turmoil in Egypt, as local elites battled to seize power after Napoleon's departure. The ultimate victor was the energetic general Muhammad Ali, who built a powerful army modeled on European forces and ruled Egypt from 1805 to 1848. He also launched a program of industrialization, concentrating on cotton textiles and armaments. Although he remained nominally subordinate to the Ottoman sultan, by 1820 he had established himself as the effective ruler of Egypt, which was the most powerful land in the Muslim world. He even invaded Syria and Anatolia, threatening to

Caucasus (KAW-kuh-suhs)

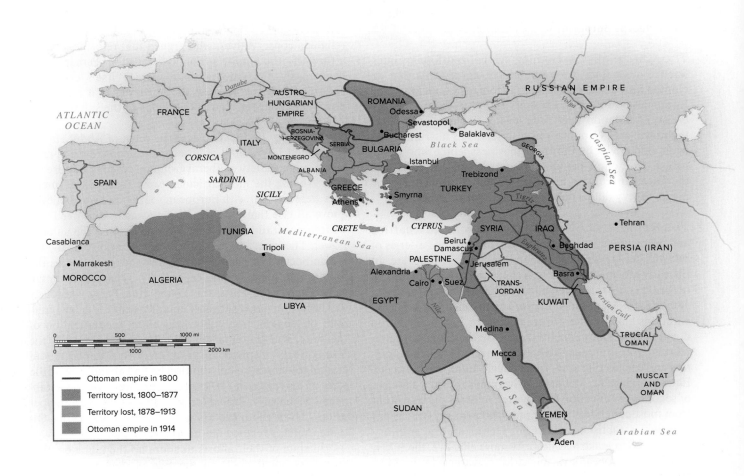

MAP 28.2   Territorial losses of the Ottoman empire, 1800–1923
Compare the borders of the Ottoman empire in 1800 with what was left of the empire in 1914.

What might have been the strategic value of the remaining Ottoman territories?

capture Istanbul and topple the Ottoman state. Indeed, the Ottoman dynasty survived only because British forces intervened out of fear that Ottoman collapse would result in a sudden and dangerous expansion of Russian influence.

Economic Difficulties

Meanwhile, European textiles and manufactured goods began to flow into the Ottoman empire in the eighteenth and nineteenth centuries. Because these items were inexpensive and high-quality products, they were in high demand by Ottoman consumers. At the same time, they placed considerable pressure on Ottoman artisans and crafts workers. Gradually, the Ottoman empire moved toward financial dependency on Europe. After the middle of the nineteenth century, economic development in the Ottoman empire depended heavily on foreign loans, as European capital financed the construction of railroads, utilities, and mining enterprises. Interest payments grew to the point that they consumed more than half of the empire's revenues. In 1882 the Ottoman state was unable to pay interest on its loans and had no choice but to accept European administration of its debts.

The Capitulations

Nothing symbolized foreign interference more than the **capitulations**, agreements that exempted European visitors from Ottoman law and provided European powers with extraterritoriality—the right to exercise jurisdiction over their own citizens according to their own laws. Capitulations also served as instruments of economic power by European businesspeople who established tax-exempt banks and commercial enterprises in the Ottoman empire, and they permitted foreign governments to levy duties on goods sold in Ottoman ports.

The Reforms of Mahmud II

In response to recurring and deepening crises, Ottoman leaders launched a series of reforms designed to strengthen and preserve the state. In the early nineteenth century, a significant period of reform occurred under the leadership of Sultan **Mahmud II** (reigned 1808-1839). Mahmud's program remodeled Ottoman institutions along western European lines, especially in the creation of a more effective army. Before long, Ottoman recruits wore European-style uniforms and studied at military and engineering schools that taught European curricula. Equally important, Mahmud's government created a system of secondary education for boys to facilitate the transition from mosque schools (which provided primary education) to newly established scientific, technical, and military academies. To make his authority more effective, the sultan established European-style ministries, constructed new roads, built telegraph lines, and inaugurated a postal service. By the time of Mahmud's death in 1839, the Ottoman empire had

shrunk in size, but it was also more manageable and stronger than it had been since the early seventeenth century.

The Tanzimat Era

Continuing defeats on the battlefield and the rise of separatist movements among subject peoples, however, prompted the ruling classes to undertake even more radical reforms during the **Tanzimat** ("reorganization") era (1839-1876). In designing their program, Tanzimat reformers drew considerable inspiration from Enlightenment thought and the constitutional foundations of western European states. One of their primary aims was to make Ottoman law more acceptable to Europeans, so that they could have the capitulations lifted and recover Ottoman sovereignty. Among the most important Tanzimat reforms were those that guaranteed public trials, rights of privacy, and equality before the law for all Ottoman subjects, whether Muslim or not. By 1869 educational reforms also provided free and compulsory primary education for all children. Yet even though reform and reorganization strengthened Ottoman society, the Tanzimat also provoked spirited opposition. Harsh criticism came from religious conservatives, who argued that reformers posed a threat to the empire's Islamic foundation. Perhaps most dangerously, the Ottoman bureaucracy itself criticized Tanzimat reforms because they believed that too much power was concentrated in the hands of the sultan.

The Young Turks

The despotic reign of Abdül Hamid II (reigned 1876-1909) only seemed to confirm such criticisms, and a variety of liberal groups grew up to oppose his rule. Among the most articulate were those whose members were familiar with European society and who believed above all else that Ottoman society was in dire need of a written constitution that defined and limited the sultan's power. The most active dissident organization was the Ottoman Society for Union and Progress, better known as the **Young Turk Party**. Founded in 1889 by exiled Ottoman subjects living in Paris, the Young Turk Party vigorously called for universal suffrage, equality before the law, freedom of religion, free public education, secularization of the state, and the emancipation of women. In 1908 the Young Turks inspired an army coup that forced Abdül Hamid to reinstate a constitution he had abandoned at the start of his reign. In 1909 they dethroned him and established Mehmed V. Rashid (reigned 1909-1918) as a puppet sultan. Throughout the Young Turk era (1908-1918), Ottoman sultans reigned but no longer ruled.

In spite of their efforts to shore up the ailing empire, reformers could not turn the tide of decline: Ottoman armies continued to lose wars, and subject peoples continued to seek autonomy or independence. By the early twentieth century, the Ottoman empire survived principally because European governments could not agree on how to dismantle the empire without upsetting the European balance of power.

Mahmud II (mah-MOOD)
Tanzimat (TAHNZ-ee-MAT)

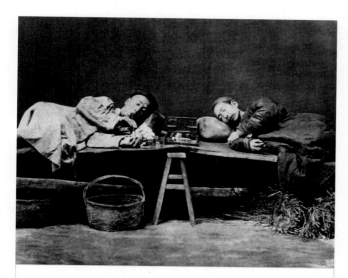

Chinese opium smokers around 1870. The Chinese government's attempt to stop the importation of opium resulted in a major defeat in the Opium War of 1839–1842. Here, opium smokers recline and sleep on the hard beds characteristic of opium dens.
Chronicle/Alamy Stock Photo

The Chinese Empire and The Opium Trade The Chinese empire experienced even more difficulties than the Ottoman empire in the nineteenth century. Qing problems became serious in the early nineteenth century when officials of the British East India Company began to trade in opium—rather than silver—in exchange for the Chinese silks, porcelains, and teas so coveted by Europeans. Trade in opium was illegal in China, but it expanded rapidly for decades because of the efforts of European and Chinese smugglers, and because some Chinese authorities benefited from the trade. By the late 1830s, however, government officials had become aware that opium had caused both a trade problem and a drug problem in China. In 1839 the government took active steps to halt the trade, which included the destruction of some twenty thousand chests of opium.

The Opium War Despite their awareness that the trade was illegal, outraged British commercial agents pressed their government into a military retaliation designed to reopen the opium trade. The ensuing conflict, known as the **Opium War** (1839–1842), made plain the military power differential between Europe and China. The Chinese navy and infantry were no match for their British counterparts, who relied on steam power and modern firearms, and in 1842 the Chinese government sued for peace. China experienced similar military setbacks throughout the second half of the nineteenth century in conflicts with Britain and France (1856–1858), France (1884–1885), and Japan (1894–1895).

Unequal Treaties In the wake of those confrontations came a series of pacts collectively known in China as **unequal treaties**, which curtailed China's sovereignty. The Treaty of Nanjing (1842), which ended the British war against the Chinese, ceded Hong Kong Island to Britain, opened five Chinese ports to foreign commerce and residence, compelled the Qing government to extend most-favored-nation status to Britain, and granted extraterritoriality to British subjects. In later years France, Germany, Denmark, the Netherlands, Spain, Belgium, Austria-Hungary, the United States, and Japan concluded similar unequal treaties with China. By 1900 ninety Chinese ports were under the effective control of foreign powers, foreign merchants controlled much of the Chinese economy, Christian missionaries sought converts throughout China, and foreign gunboats patrolled Chinese waters.

To make matters more difficult, China was convulsed by several large-scale rebellions in the nineteenth century, all of which reflected the increasing poverty and discontent of the Chinese peasantry. After 1850, rebellions erupted throughout China: the Nian rebellion (1851–1868) in the northeast, the Muslim rebellion (1855–1873) in the southwest, and the Tungan rebellion (1862–1878) in the northwest. Most dangerous of all was the **Taiping rebellion** (1850–1864), which raged throughout most of China and brought the Qing dynasty to the brink of collapse.

The Taiping Rebellion The village schoolteacher **Hong Xiuquan** provided both inspiration and leadership for the Taiping rebellion. He called for the destruction of the Qing dynasty and for the radical transformation of Chinese society, including the abolition of private property, the creation of communal wealth to be shared according to needs, the prohibition of foot binding and concubinage, free public education, simplification of the written language, literacy for the masses, and equality of the sexes. After sweeping through southeastern China, Hong and his followers in the Society of God Worshipers took Nanjing in 1853 and made it the capital of their Taiping ("Great Peace") kingdom. In 1855 a million Taipings were poised to attack Beijing, and in 1860 they threatened Shanghai. Although the rebellion was eventually crushed in 1864 with the aid of European advisors and weapons, in all it claimed between twenty and thirty million lives and devastated part of the Chinese countryside.

The Self-Strengthening Movement The Taiping rebellion altered the course of Chinese history. Contending

Nian (neen)
Tungan (tuhn-gahn)
Taiping (TEYE-pihng)
Hong Xiuquan (hoong shee-OH-chew-an)

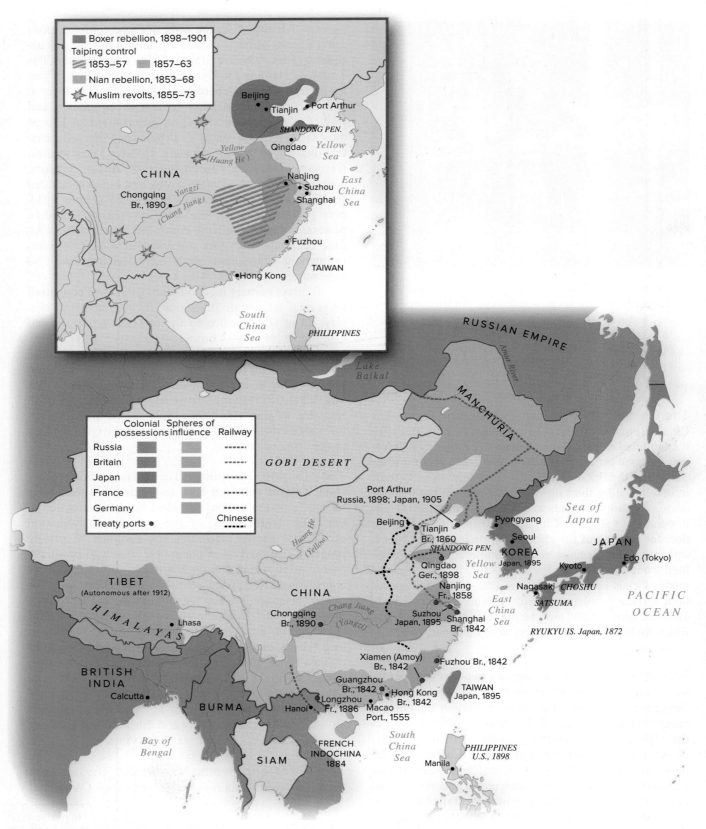

MAP 28.3   East Asia in the nineteenth century

Notice the division of China, which technically remained a sovereign nation, into spheres of influence by various European nations and Japan.

What impact would such spheres of influence have had on the Chinese government in Beijing?

with aggressive foreign powers and lands ravaged by domestic rebellion, Qing rulers recognized that reforms were necessary for the empire to survive. Most imaginative of these programs was the **Self-Strengthening Movement** (1860–1895). While holding to Confucian values and seeking to reestablish a stable agrarian society, movement leaders built modern shipyards, constructed railroads, established weapons industries, opened steel foundries with blast furnaces, and founded academies to develop scientific expertise.

Yet the Self-Strengthening Movement did not introduce enough industry to bring real military and economic strength to China. It also did not prevent continuing foreign intrusion into Chinese affairs. During the latter part of the nineteenth century, foreign powers began to dismantle the Chinese system of tributary states. In 1885 France incorporated Vietnam into its colonial empire, and in 1886 Great Britain detached Burma from Chinese control. In 1895 Japan forced China to recognize the independence of Korea and cede the island of Taiwan and the Liaodong peninsula in southern Manchuria. By 1898 foreign powers had carved China itself into spheres of economic influence, and only distrust among them prevented the total dismemberment of the Middle Kingdom.

The Hundred Days Reforms These setbacks sparked the ambitious but abortive **Hundred Days reforms** of 1898, whose purpose was to turn China into a powerful modern industrial society. Impressed by the ideas of reform-minded scholars, the young and open-minded Emperor **Guangxu** launched a sweeping program to transform China into a constitutional monarchy, guarantee civil liberties, root out corruption, remodel the educational system, modernize military forces, and stimulate economic development. Yet these reform efforts produced a violent reaction from members of the imperial household, from their allies in the gentry, and especially from the young emperor's aunt, the ruthless and powerful empress dowager **Cixi**. After a period of 103 days, Cixi nullified the reform decrees, imprisoned the emperor in the Forbidden City, and executed six leading reformers.

The Boxer Rebellion Cixi then threw her support behind an antiforeign uprising known as the **Boxer rebellion**, a violent movement spearheaded by militia units calling themselves the Society of Righteous and Harmonious Fists. The foreign press referred to the rebels as Boxers. In 1899 the Boxers organized to rid China of "foreign devils" and their influences. With the empress dowager's encouragement, the Boxers went on a rampage in northern China, killing foreigners and Chinese who had ties to foreigners. Confident that foreign weapons could not harm them, some one hundred forty thousand Boxers besieged foreign embassies in Beijing in the summer of 1900. They were crushed, however, by a heavily armed force of British,

French, Russian, U.S., German, and Japanese troops. After the rebellion, the Chinese government was forced to allow foreign powers to station troops at their embassies in Beijing and along the route to the sea. When Cixi died in 1908, anti-Qing revolutionary movements that sought alternative methods to deal with foreign and domestic crises were active throughout China. Indeed, revolution broke out in the autumn of 1911, and by early 1912 the child Puyi—the last emperor of the Qing dynasty—had abdicated his throne.

The Scramble for Africa

Even as European powers sponsored informal imperialism in the Ottoman and Qing empires in the last half of the nineteenth century, they also embarked on a striking expansion of formal imperialism in Africa. This was all the more remarkable, since as late as 1875 European peoples maintained a limited presence in Africa: their only sizable possessions were the Portuguese colonies of Angola and Mozambique, the French settler colony in northern Algeria, and a cluster of settler colonies populated by British and Dutch migrants in south Africa.

Between 1875 and 1900, however, the relationship between Africa and Europe dramatically changed. Within a quarter century European imperial powers partitioned and colonized almost the entire African continent. Prospects of exploiting African resources and geopolitical rivalries between European powers help explain this frenzied quest for empire, often referred to as the **scramble for Africa**.

The Belgian Congo In the 1870s **King Leopold II** of Belgium (reigned 1865–1909) employed the American journalist Henry Morton Stanley to help develop commercial ventures and establish a colony called the Congo Free State (modern-day Democratic Republic of the Congo) in the basin of the Congo River. To forestall competition from Belgium's much larger and more powerful European neighbors, Leopold announced that the Congo region would be a free-trade zone accessible to merchants and businesspeople from all European lands. In fact, however, he carved out a personal colony with the sole purpose of extracting lucrative rubber using forced labor. Working conditions in the Congo Free State were so brutal, taxes so high, and abuses so many that four to eight million Africans died under Leopold's personal rule. Once those abuses became public, humanitarian pressure induced the Belgian government to take control away from Leopold in 1908 and administer the colony directly.

While Leopold colonized central Africa, Britain established an imperial presence in Egypt. In an effort to build up their army, strengthen the economy, and distance themselves from Ottoman authority, Egypt's leaders had

Liaodong (lyou-dawng)
Guangxu (wang-soo)

This 1912 photograph shows a stark portrait of the Belgian king's inhumane treatment of Africans in the Congo. When Africans in the Congo did not collect their allotted quotas of rubber for the state, they or their relatives were liable to have their hands or feet amputated as punishment.

Cultural Heritage Images/Universal Images Group/Newscom

borrowed heavily from European lenders in the mid-nineteenth century. By the 1870s crushing debt had forced Egyptian officials to impose high taxes, which provoked popular unrest and a military rebellion. Concerned over the status of their financial interests and the security of the Suez Canal, British forces occupied Egypt in 1882.

The Berlin Conference The British occupation of Egypt intensified tensions between those European powers who were seeking African colonies. To avoid war, delegates from fourteen European states and the United States—not a single African was present—met at the Berlin West Africa Conference (1884–1885) to devise ground rules for the division of African territories by outsiders. According to those rules, any European state could establish African colonies after notifying the others of its intentions and occupying previously unclaimed territory.

Khoikhoi (KOI-koi)

Xhosa (KOH-suh)

Ndebele (uhn-duh-BEE-lee)

During the 1890s European imperialists sent armies to impose colonial rule on the African territories they claimed. Although resistance to colonial rule was often fierce, European cannons and machine guns rarely failed to defeat African forces. By the turn of the century, European colonies embraced all of Africa except for Ethiopia, where native forces fought off Italian efforts at colonization in 1896, and Liberia, a small republic in west Africa that was effectively a dependency of the United States.

Direct and Indirect Rule In the wake of rapid conquest, Europeans struggled to identify the most cost-effective and efficient system of rule in Africa. By the early twentieth century, after some experimentation, most European governments sought to establish their own rule, which took the form of either **direct rule**, typical of French colonies, or **indirect rule**, characteristic of British colonies. Under direct rule, colonies were headed by European personnel who assumed responsibility for tax collection, labor and military recruitment, and the maintenance of law and order. Administrative boundaries intentionally cut across existing African political and ethnic boundaries to divide and weaken potentially powerful indigenous groups. In contrast, indirect rule sought to exercise control over subject populations through indigenous institutions such as "tribal" authorities and "customary laws." Both methods of government were flawed: under direct rule, imperial powers struggled with a constant shortage of European personnel, which undermined the effectiveness of rule, and indirect rule imposed erroneous and rigid European ideas about what constituted tribal categories and boundaries onto African societies.

South Africa Although already inhabited by Europeans long before the scramble for Africa, the southern tip of the African continent did not escape conflict at the close of the nineteenth century. In this case, however, the main antagonists were both of European descent: one side was composed of the descendants of Dutch settlers who had founded Cape Town in 1652 (called "Boers" or "Afrikaners") and the other of British settlers who had taken control of the Cape in 1815. Relations between the two groups had never been good. When the British established themselves at the Cape, they subjected Afrikaners to British language and law—including the abolition of slavery when it became law in 1833. The abolition of slavery was particularly contentious, as Afrikaners believed that God had given them the right to exploit both the people and the resources of the Cape—the results of which left the indigenous **Khoikhoi** and **Xhosa** peoples decimated and virtually landless. Chafing under British rule, Afrikaners left their farms in Cape Colony and gradually migrated east in what they called the Great Trek. By the mid-nineteenth century, after fierce conflict with the Ndebele and Zulu

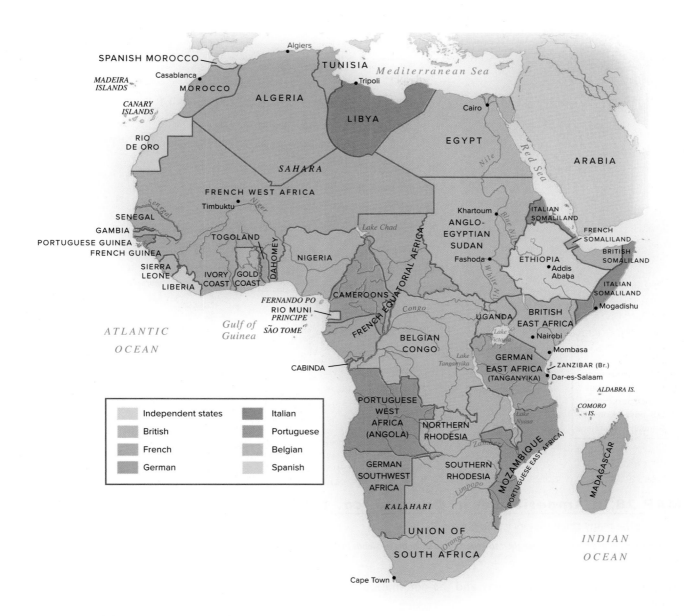

MAP 28.4   Imperialism in Africa, ca. 1914

By 1914, only Ethiopia and Liberia remained free of European control.

How was it possible for Europeans to gain such domination?

peoples indigenous to the interior of the region, the Afrikaners created several independent republics: the Republic of Natal, annexed by the British in 1843; the Orange Free State in 1854; and in 1860 the South African Republic (Transvaal territories).

Britain's lenient attitude toward Afrikaner statehood took a drastic turn with the discovery of diamonds (1867) and gold (1886) in Afrikaner territories. The influx of thousands of British miners and prospectors led to tensions between British authorities and Afrikaners,

culminating in the **South African War** (1899–1902), sometimes called the Boer War. Although the brutal conflict pitted whites against whites, it also took a large toll on Black Africans, who served both sides as soldiers and laborers. The Afrikaners conceded defeat in 1902, and by 1910, the British government had reconstituted the four former colonies as provinces in the Union of South Africa, a largely autonomous British dominion. British attempts at improving relations between English speakers and Afrikaners centered on shoring up the

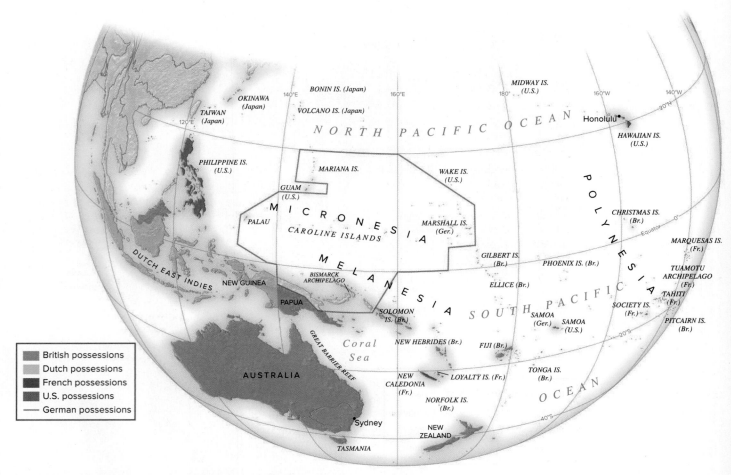

MAP 28.5   Imperialism in Oceania, ca. 1914

Observe the many small, distant islands of the Pacific.

Why would imperial powers have thought it so important to claim these islands in the late nineteenth and early twentieth centuries?

---

privileges of white colonial society and the domination of Black Africans.

European Imperialism in the Pacific

European imperial powers did not overlook opportunities to establish their presence in the Pacific Ocean basin even as they divided Africa between themselves. Imperialism in the Pacific took two main forms. In Australia and New Zealand, European powers established settler colonies and dominant political institutions. In most of the Pacific islands, however, they sought commercial opportunities and reliable bases for their operations but did not wish to go to the trouble or expense of outright colonization. Only in the late nineteenth century did they begin to impose direct colonial rule on the islands.

Settler Colonies in the Pacific Settlers began to arrive in Australia in 1788, nearly two decades after Captain James Cook reported that the region would be suitable for settlement. In that year, a British fleet with about one thousand settlers, most of them convicted criminals, arrived at Sydney harbor and established the colony of New South Wales. By the 1830s voluntary migrants outnumbered convicts, and the discovery of gold in 1851 brought a surge in migration to Australia. European settlers established communities also in New Zealand, where the islands' fertile soils and abundant stands of timber drew large numbers of migrants.

European migration devastated the indigenous societies of Australia and New Zealand, partially as a result of the introduction of European diseases such as smallpox and measles. The aboriginal population of Australia fell from about 650,000 in 1800 to 90,000 in 1900, whereas the European population rose from a few thousand to 3.75 million during the same period. Similarly, the population of indigenous **Maori** in New Zealand fell from

---

Maori (MAY-oh-ree)

about 200,000 in 1800 to 45,000 a century later, whereas European numbers climbed to 750,000.

Increasing migration also fueled conflict between European settlers and native populations. Large settler societies pushed indigenous peoples from their lands, often following violent confrontations. Because the nomadic foraging peoples of Australia did not occupy lands permanently, British settlers considered the continent *terra nullius*—"land belonging to no one"—that they could seize and put to their own uses. Despite strong resistance, by 1900 the British had succeeded in brutally displacing most indigenous Australians from their traditional lands and dispersing them throughout the continent.

A similarly disruptive process transpired in New Zealand, where Maori leaders organized effective and long-lasting opposition to British attempts to usurp their land and sovereignty. Conflicts over land confiscations and disputed land sales, for example, helped spark the New Zealand Wars, a series of confrontations between the Maori and the British that flared from the mid- to late nineteenth century. Despite that resistance, by the end of the century the British had managed to force many Maori into poor rural communities separated from European settlements.

Pacific Islands On the smaller Pacific islands, the picture was quite different. Although indigenous peoples were ravaged by European diseases, the imperial powers had little interest in establishing direct colonial rule over the islands. Rather, they were content to use the islands as naval ports, as coaling stations, and sometimes as producers of primary products. The situation changed, however, in the late nineteenth century, as European nationalist rivalries encouraged the imperial powers to stake their claims in the Pacific as they had done in Africa. Thus, although France had established a protectorate in Tahiti, the Society Islands, and the Marquesas as early as 1841, it only imposed direct colonial rule in 1880. Britain made Fiji a crown colony in 1874, and Germany annexed several of the Marshall Islands in 1876 and 1878. At the Berlin Conference, European diplomats agreed on a partition of Oceania as well as Africa, and Britain, France, Germany, and the United States proceeded to claim almost all the Pacific islands. By 1900 only the kingdom of Tonga remained independent, and even Tonga accepted British protection against the possibility of encroachments by other imperial powers.

THE EMERGENCE OF NEW IMPERIAL POWERS

Nineteenth-century imperialism was mostly a European affair until the end of the century. At that point, two new imperial powers joined Europeans in their efforts to divide the world into colonies: the United States and Japan.

Both states experienced rapid industrialization in the late nineteenth century, and both built powerful armed forces. As European imperial powers forcibly claimed territories throughout the world, leaders of the United States and Japan decided that they, too, needed to establish an imperial presence overseas.

U.S. Imperialism in Latin America and the Pacific

The very existence of the United States was due to European imperialism. After the new republic had won its independence, U.S. leaders brought almost all the temperate regions of North America under their authority. Indeed, all westward movement in the United States involved the forcible and violent removal of indigenous populations from their hereditary lands. In that sense, the settlement of the United States was no different from the settler colonialism

Queen Lili'uokalani, last monarch of Hawai'i, before her deposition in 1893. Wearing a European dress (she had received a Western education by missionaries and had traveled widely in Europe and America), the queen sits on a throne covered with a traditional royal cape made of bird feathers.
Everett Collection Inc/Alamy Stock Photo

SOURCES FROM THE PAST

Queen Lili'uokalani's Protest against the Annexation of Hawai'i

Queen Lili'uokalani (1838–1917) was the last monarch of the Kalakaua dynasty, which had ruled the Hawaiian Islands since 1810. Before taking the throne in 1891, Lili'uokalani had traveled extensively in the United States and Europe and had served in the royal court. In 1887, American businessmen forced King Kalakaua, her older brother, to sign a constitution (called the "Bayonet Constitution") that limited the powers of the monarchy. Lili'uokalani adamantly opposed this constitution, and when she acceded to the throne, she tried to implement a new constitution that would return her power. But in 1893, a group of European and American businessmen—with the help of U.S. Marines—staged a coup and deposed Lili'uokalani. Even after she was deposed, the queen continued to protest to the U.S. government against the loss of her power and against the rise of American power in Hawai'i. Her efforts were in vain, however, as the government of President William McKinley annexed Hawai'i in July 1898. Following is her letter of protest to the U.S. House of Representatives from December of that year.

I, Liliuokalani of Hawaii, named heir apparent on the 10th day of April, 1877, and proclaimed Queen of the Hawaiian Islands on the 29th day of January, 1891, do hereby earnestly and respectfully protest against the assertion of ownership by the United States of America of the so-called Hawaiian Crown Lands amounting to about one million acres and which are my property, and I especially protest against such assertion of ownership as a taking of property without due process of law and without just or other compensation.

Therefore, supplementing my protest of June 17, 1897, I call upon the President and the National Legislature and the People of the United States to do justice in this matter and to restore to me this property, the enjoyment of which is being withheld from me by your Government under what must be a misapprehension of my right and title.

Done at Washington, District of Columbia, United States of America, this nineteenth day of December, in the year one thousand eight hundred and ninety-eight. ———————————————

> What is the significance of the fact that Lili'uokalani went to Washington, D.C., to make this protest?

For Further Reflection

■ What, according to Lili'uokalani, is the nature of the injustices she has had to endure? Why does she say that the government must not understand her right and title?

Source: https://www.archives.gov/historical-docs/todays-doc/?dod-date=707. Records of the U.S. House of Representatives, HR 55A-H28.3, Record Group 233, National Archives.

---

of Australia or New Zealand, even though Americans obscured these similarities by claiming they had a "manifest destiny" to settle North America from coast to coast.

The fledgling United States also tried to wield power outside North America. In 1823 President James Monroe (in office 1817–1825) issued a proclamation that warned European states against imperialist designs in the western hemisphere. The **Monroe Doctrine**, as it came to be known, later served as a justification for U.S. intervention in hemispheric affairs.

As the United States consolidated its continental holdings, U.S. leaders became interested in acquiring

territories beyond the temperate regions of North America. The United States purchased Alaska from Russia in 1867 and in 1875 claimed a protectorate over the islands of Hawai'i, where U.S. entrepreneurs had established highly productive sugarcane plantations. The Hawaiian kingdom survived until 1893, when a group of American and European planters and businesspeople overthrew the last monarch, Queen **Lili'uokalani** (reigned 1891–1893), and invited the United States to annex the islands. In 1898 the pro-expansion president William McKinley (in office 1897–1901) agreed to acquire the islands.

The Spanish-Cuban-American War The United States emerged as an important imperial and colonial

---

Lili'uokalani (lee-lee-oo-oh-kah-lah-nee)

power after the brief **Spanish-Cuban-American War** (1898–1899). War broke out as anticolonial tensions mounted in Cuba and Puerto Rico—the last remnants of Spain's American empire—where U.S. business interests had made large investments. In 1898 the U.S. battleship *Maine* exploded and sank in Havana harbor. U.S. leaders claimed sabotage and declared war on Spain. The United States quickly defeated Spain and took control and possession of Cuba and Puerto Rico. U.S. leaders then turned their attention to Spain's Pacific colonies: Guam and the Philippines. After the U.S. Navy destroyed the Spanish fleet at Manila in a single day, the United States took possession of both colonies to prevent them from falling under German or Japanese control.

The consolidation of U.S. authority in the Philippines was an especially difficult affair. The Spanish-Cuban-American War coincided with a Filipino revolt against Spanish rule, and U.S. forces promised to support independence of the Philippines in exchange for an alliance against Spain. After the victory over Spain, however, President McKinley decided to bring the Philippines under American control instead. In response, Filipino rebels—led by **Emilio Aguinaldo**—turned their arms against the new intruders. The result was a bitter insurrection that raged until 1902 and claimed the lives of forty-two hundred American soldiers, fifteen thousand rebel troops, and some two hundred thousand Filipino civilians.

The United States also intervened in the affairs of Caribbean and Central American lands, even those that were not U.S. possessions, to prevent rebellion and protect American business interests. In the early twentieth century, U.S. military forces occupied Cuba, the Dominican Republic, Nicaragua, Honduras, and Haiti.

The Panama Canal To facilitate communication and transportation between the Atlantic and Pacific oceans, the United States sought to build a canal across the Isthmus of Panama in northern Colombia. However, Colombia was unwilling to cede land for the project. Under President Theodore Roosevelt (in office 1901–1909), an enthusiastic champion of imperial expansion, the United States supported a rebellion against Colombia in 1903 and helped rebels establish the breakaway state of Panama. In exchange for that support, the United States won the right to build a canal across Panama and to control the adjacent territory, known as the Panama Canal Zone. Roosevelt then added a corollary to the Monroe Doctrine in 1904, which stated that the United States has the right to intervene in the domestic affairs of nations within the hemisphere if they demonstrate an inability to maintain the security deemed necessary to protect U.S. investments. The **Roosevelt Corollary**, along with the Panama Canal when it opened in 1914, strengthened U.S. military and economic claims in the region.

Imperial Japan

Strengthened by the rapid industrialization during the Meiji era, Japan also joined the ranks of imperial powers in the late nineteenth century. Indeed, while founding representative political institutions to demonstrate their trustworthiness to American and European diplomats, Japanese leaders also made a bid to stand alongside the world's great powers by launching a campaign of imperial expansion.

Early Japanese Expansion The Japanese drive to empire began in the east Asian islands. During the 1870s Japanese leaders consolidated their hold on Hokkaido and the Kurile Islands to the north, and they encouraged Japanese migrants to populate the islands to forestall Russian expansion there. By 1879 they had also established their hegemony over Okinawa and the Ryukyu Islands to the south.

Emilio Aguinaldo (ee-MEE-lyaw AH-gee-NAHL-daw)

Japanese painting of a Japanese naval victory over a Chinese vessel. China's defeat in the Sino-Japanese War showed how the Qing dynasty had been weakened militarily, especially by the Opium War, and demonstrated how successful modernization had been for Japan since the Meiji restoration.
The Artchives/Alamy Stock Photo

The Sino-Japanese War In 1876 Japan purchased modern warships from Britain, and the newly strengthened Japanese navy immediately began to pursue military intervention in Korea. In 1894 conflict erupted between Japan and China over the status of Korea. When an antiforeign rebellion broke out in Korea in 1893, Qing rulers sent an army to restore order and reassert Chinese authority. However, Japanese businesses had built substantial interests in Korea, and Meiji leaders were unwilling to recognize Chinese control over such an economically important land. Thus in August 1894 they declared war on China. The Japanese navy quickly gained control of the Yellow Sea and demolished the Chinese fleet in a battle lasting a mere five hours. Within a few months the conflict was over. When the combatants made peace in April 1895, Qing authorities recognized the independence of Korea, thus making it essentially a dependency of Japan. They also ceded Taiwan, the Pescadores Islands, and the Liaodong peninsula (in northeastern China), which strengthened Japanese control over east Asian waters. Alongside territorial acquisitions, Japan gained unequal treaty rights in China like those enjoyed by European and American powers.

The Russo-Japanese War The unexpected Japanese victory startled European imperial powers, especially Russia. Tensions between Japan and Russia soon mounted, because both imperial powers had territorial ambitions in the Liaodong peninsula, Korea, and Manchuria. War broke out in 1904, and Japanese forces overran Russian outposts before reinforcements could arrive from Europe. The Japanese navy destroyed the Russian Baltic fleet, which had sailed halfway around the world to support the war effort. By 1905 the war was over, and Japan won international recognition of its colonial authority over Korea

and the Liaodong peninsula. Furthermore, Russia ceded the southern half of Sakhalin island to Japan, along with a railroad and economic interests in southern Manchuria. Victory in the **Russo-Japanese War** transformed Japan into a major imperial power.

LEGACIES OF IMPERIALISM

Imperialism and colonialism profoundly influenced the development of world history. In some ways they tightened links between the world's peoples: trade and migration increased dramatically as imperial powers exploited the resources of subject territories and recruited laborers to work in colonies throughout the world. Yet imperialism and colonialism also brought peoples into conflict and heightened senses of difference between peoples. European, Euro-American, and Japanese imperialists all came to think of themselves as superior to the peoples they conquered. Meanwhile, foreign intrusion stimulated the development of resistance in colonized territories, which over time served as a foundation for anticolonial movements.

Empire and Economy

One of the principal motives of imperialism was the desire to gain access to natural resources and agricultural products. As imperial powers consolidated their hold on foreign territories, colonial administrators reorganized subject societies, so that they would become efficient suppliers of timber, rubber, petroleum, gold, silver, diamonds, cotton, tea, coffee, cacao, and other products. As a result, global trade in those commodities surged during the nineteenth and early twentieth centuries. However, profits

What's Left Out?

Colonial policies seemingly unrelated to gender nevertheless frequently altered gender relations between colonized men and women. For example, the imposition of new systems of taxation often went hand in hand with European assumptions that men should be heads of households and thus the responsible parties for paying taxes to the state. In places where both women and men had held property and produced crops, such as colonial Tanganyika (modern Tanzania), these assumptions led to tax collection policies that put economic responsibility in the hands of men. This resulted in the marginalization of colonized women in public life and a rise in the political and economic power of colonized men, thus changing the gender dynamics between the sexes. The imposition of colonial law also led to changes in gender relations. In northern Ghana, for example, even though marriage practices in the region had given women an extraordinary amount of autonomy in both choosing and changing partners, British notions about the authority of husbands increasingly led to legal decisions that enforced the idea that wives were the property of their husbands. Over time, the colonial justice system allowed men to claim increasing legal control over their wives. It is important to remember that the imposition of economic and legal policies could impact seemingly unrelated—and quite intimate—issues such as gender relations.

Source: Jean Allman, Susan Geiger, and Nakanyike Musisi. *Women in African Colonial Histories.* Bloomington: Indiana University Press, 2002.

from this trade went mostly to the colonial powers, which exported raw materials for processing in the industrialized societies of Europe, North America, and Japan.

Introduction of New Crops In some cases, colonial rule led to the introduction of new crops that transformed both the landscape and the social order of subject lands. In the early nineteenth century, for example, British colonial officials introduced tea bushes from China to Ceylon and India. The effect on Ceylon was profound. British planters felled trees on much of the island, converted rain forests into tea plantations, and recruited Ceylonese women by the thousands to carry out the labor-intensive work of harvesting mature tea leaves.

Consumption of tea in India and Ceylon was almost negligible, but increased supplies met the growing demand for tea in Europe, where the beverage became accessible to individuals of all social classes. The value of south Asian tea exports rose from about 309,000 pounds sterling in 1866 to 6.1 million pounds sterling in 1900. Malaya and Sumatra underwent a similar social transformation after British colonial agents planted rubber trees there in the 1870s and established plantations to meet the growing global demand for rubber products.

Labor Migrations

Efforts to exploit the natural resources and agricultural products of subject territories led imperial and colonial powers to encourage mass migrations of workers during the nineteenth and early twentieth centuries. Two patterns of labor migration were especially prominent during this period. European migrants went mostly to temperate places, where they worked as free cultivators or industrial laborers. In contrast, migrants from Asia, Africa, and the Pacific islands moved largely to tropical and subtropical lands, where they worked as indentured laborers on plantations or manual laborers for mining enterprises or large-scale construction projects.

European Migration Between 1800 and 1914 some fifty million European migrants left their homes and sought opportunities overseas. Most of those migrants left the relatively poor agricultural societies of southern and eastern Europe, especially Italy, Russia, and Poland, although sizable numbers came also from Britain, Ireland, Germany, and Scandinavia. A majority of the migrants—about thirty-two million—went to the United States. Settler colonies in Canada, Argentina, Australia, New Zealand, and south Africa also drew large numbers of European migrants.

Indentured Labor Migration In contrast to their free European counterparts, migrants from Asia, Africa, and the Pacific islands generally traveled as indentured laborers.

As the institution of slavery went into decline, planters sought laborers from poor and densely populated lands who could replace enslaved people. Between 1820 and 1914 about 2.5 million indentured laborers left their homes to work in distant parts of the world. Labor recruiters generally offered workers free passage to their destinations and provided them with food, shelter, clothing, and modest compensation for their services in exchange for a commitment to work for five to seven years.

The majority of the indentured laborers came from India, but sizable numbers also came from China, Japan, Java, Africa, and the Pacific islands. Indentured laborers went mostly to tropical and subtropical lands in the Americas, the Caribbean, Africa, and Oceania. Large numbers of Indian laborers went to work on rubber plantations in Malaya and sugar plantations in south Africa, the Pacific island of Fiji, the Guianas, and the Caribbean islands of Trinidad, Tobago, and Jamaica. After the Opium War ended in 1842, large numbers of Chinese laborers went to sugar plantations in Cuba and Hawai'i, guano mines in Peru, tin mines in Malaya, gold mines in south Africa and Australia, and railroad construction sites in the United States, Canada, and Peru. After the Meiji restoration in Japan, a large contingent of Japanese laborers migrated to Hawai'i to work on sugar plantations, and a smaller group went to work in guano mines in Peru. Indentured laborers from Africa went mostly to sugar plantations in Réunion, the Guianas, and Caribbean islands. Those from Pacific islands went mostly to plantations on other Pacific islands and in Australia.

Empire and Migration All of the large-scale migrations of the nineteenth century reflected the global influence of imperial powers. European migrations were possible only because European and Euro-American peoples had established settler societies in temperate regions around the world. Movements of indentured laborers were possible because colonial officials were able to recruit workers and dispatch them to distant lands where their compatriots had already established plantations or opened mines. In combination, the nineteenth-century migrations profoundly influenced societies around the world by establishing large communities of people with distinctive ethnic identities in places far from their original homes.

Empire and Society

Colonial Conflict The policies adopted by imperial powers and colonial officials forced peoples of different societies to deal with one another on a regular and systematic basis. Their interactions often led to violent conflicts between colonizers and subject peoples. Indeed, the Sepoy rebellion was only one among many insurrections organized by discontented Indian subjects between the mid-nineteenth and the mid-twentieth centuries. Colonized

Connecting the Sources

Thinking about colonized peoples' responses to colonization

The problem   For many years, the history of imperialism and colonialism was written from the point of view of the various colonizing powers. Colonial officials produced copious amounts of official and unofficial documents about colonial policies, their own experiences, and their opinions of colonized peoples. Not surprisingly, the histories written about colonialism using such sources tended to be biased in favor of the colonizers and frequently marginalized the experiences of colonized peoples themselves. In the last four decades, however, a plethora of histories have appeared that explore the colonial past from the point of view of colonized peoples, relying on previously underutilized sources such as court records, letters, memoirs, oral interviews, and fiction. Such sources have altered the way historians understand the massive imperial expansion that occurred in Asia and Africa in the nineteenth and first half of the twentieth centuries.

Let us consider two sources generated by people responding to British policies—one from China, the other from southern Africa—in order to think about what sources generated by the people who experienced colonialism can and cannot tell us.

The British ironclad steamship HMS *Nemesis* destroying Chinese ships during the Opium War in 1841.
Dea Picture Library/De Agostini/Getty Images

The documents   Read the following documents, and consider carefully the questions that follow.

Document 1:

The following resolution was produced in 1842—just after the defeat of the Chinese empire by the British in the Opium War—by Chinese citizens at a large public meeting in the city of Canton (Guangzhou).

> Behold that vile English nation! Its ruler is at one time a woman, then a man, and then perhaps a woman again; its people are at one time like vultures, and then they are like wild beasts, with dispositions more fierce and furious than the tiger or wolf, and natures more greedy than anacondas or swine. These people having long steadily devoured all the western barbarians, and like demons of the night, they now suddenly exalt themselves here.
>
> During the reigns of the emperors Kien-lung [Qianlong] and Kia-king [Jiaqing] these English barbarians humbly besought an entrance and permission to deliver tribute and presents; they afterwards presumptuously asked to have Chu-san [the city of Zhoushan]; but our sovereigns, clearly perceiving their traitorous designs, gave them a determined refusal. From that time, linking themselves with traitorous Chinese traders, they have carried on a large trade and poisoned our brave people with opium.
>
> Verily, the English barbarians murder all of us that they can. They are dogs, whose desires can never be satisfied. Therefore we need not inquire whether the peace they have now made be real or pretended. Let us all rise, arm, unite, and go against them.
>
> We do here bind ourselves to vengeance, and express these our sincere intentions in order to exhibit our high principles and patriotism. The gods from on high now look down upon us; let us not lose our just and firm resolution.

> Which actions of the British caused the authors to find them so untrustworthy?

Document 2:

The following letter was written in 1858 by Moshweshewe I, founder of Basutoland and chief of the Basuto people in South Africa. It was directed to Sir George Grey, then governor of the Cape Colony and high commissioner of South Africa, regarding Moshweshewe's treatment at the hands of white South African Afrikaners (called Boers by Moshweshewe).

. . . *About twenty-five years ago my knowledge of the White men and their laws was very limited. I knew merely that mighty nations existed, and among them was the English. These, the blacks who were acquainted with them, praised for their justice. Unfortunately it was not with the English Government that my first intercourse with the whites commenced. People who had come from the Colony first presented themselves to us, they called themselves Boers. I thought all white men were honest. Some of these Boers asked permission to live upon our borders. I was led to believe they would live with me as my own people lived, that is, looking to me as to a father and a friend.*

About sixteen years since, one of the [British] Governors of the [Cape] Colony, Sir George Napier, marked down my limits on a treaty he made with me. I was to be ruler within those limits. A short time after, another Governor came, it was Sir P. Maitland. The Boers then began to talk of their right to places I had then lent to them. Sir P. Maitland told me those people were subjects of the Queen, and should be kept under proper control; he did not tell me that he recognized any right they had to land within my country, but as it was difficult to take them away, it was proposed that all desiring to be under the British rule should live in that part near the meeting of the Orange and Caledon rivers. _____

Then came Sir Harry Smith, and he told me not to deprive any chief of their lands or their rights, he would see justice done to all, but in order to do so, he would make the Queen's Laws extend over every white man. He said the Whites and Blacks were to live together in peace. I could not understand what he would do. I thought it would be something very just, and that he was to keep the Boers in my land under proper control, and that I should hear no more of their claiming the places they lived on as their exclusive property. But instead of this, I now heard that the Boers consider all those farms as their own, and were buying and selling them one to the other, and driving out by one means or another my own people.

In vain I remonstrated. Sir Harry Smith had sent Warden to govern in the Sovereignty. He listened to the Boers, and he proposed that all the land in which those Boers' farms were should be taken from me. . . . One day he sent me a map and said, sign that, and I will tell those people . . . to leave off fighting: if you do not sign the map, I cannot help you in any way. I thought the Major was doing very improperly and unjustly. I was told to appeal to the Queen to put an end to this injustice. I did not wish to grieve Her Majesty by causing a war with her people. I was told if I did not sign the map, it would be the beginning of a great war. I signed, but soon after I sent my cry to the Queen. I begged Her to investigate my case and remove "the line," as it was called, by which my land was ruined. I thought justice would soon be done, and Warden put to rights. [Hostilities then broke out between the Boers and Moshweshewe's people, and Moshweshewe was thus requesting arbitration by Grey, the high commissioner]

Moshweshewe I, 1786–1870.
A Short History of Lesotho by Stephen Gill

What was the main issue between Moshweshewe and the Boers (Afrikaners)?

Questions

1. What can these documents definitively tell you about their respective writers' situations? What *facts* can be gleaned from these brief sources?

2. In Document 1, how do the Chinese who produced the resolution feel about the recent British victory? What have the British done to deserve such condemnation, in the group's view? How does the group propose to remedy the problem of the British in China?

3. In Document 2, why does Moshweshewe carefully recount his interactions with the various British officials who oversee the area in which Basutoland is situated? What kind of tone does Moshweshewe take in this letter, and why? Do you think Moshweshewe believes he has been treated fairly by the Boers and the British? What do you think happened when he signed the map?

4. What can these two documents tell us about the experience of colonialism in general? Do you imagine that the responses to domination suggested by these documents were common reactions to colonial expansion, or do you think responses would differ depending on the interests of the colonized group?

5. Sources such as these make up the building blocks on which historians base their interpretations of the past. In most cases, however, historians discover that they must use a variety of primary and secondary sources in order to make accurate interpretations.

Source: **Document 1:** Eva March Tappan, ed. *China, Japan, and the Islands of the Pacific, Vol. I of The World's Story: A History of the World in Story, Song, and Art.* Boston: Houghton Mifflin, 1914. p. 197. **Document 2:** G. M. Theal, ed. *Records of Southeastern Africa.* Capetown: Government of Capetown, 1898–1903.

places in southeast Asia and Africa also strongly resisted foreign rule, the tyrannical behavior of colonial officials, the introduction of European schools and curricula, high taxation, and requirements that subject peoples provide compulsory labor for colonists' enterprises.

Many rebellions drew strength from traditional religious beliefs, and priests or prophets often led resistance to colonial rule. In Tanganyika, for example, a local prophet organized the huge **Maji-Maji rebellion** (1905–1906) to expel German colonial authorities from east Africa. Rebels sprinkled themselves with *maji-maji* ("magic water"), which they believed would protect them from German weapons. Although the rebellion failed and resulted in the deaths of as many as seventy-five thousand insurgents, it testified to the fact that rebellion was a constant threat to colonial rule. Even when subject peoples dared not revolt, they resisted colonial rule by boycotting European goods, organizing political parties and pressure groups, and pursuing anticolonial policies through churches and religious groups.

Scientific Racism Social and cultural differences were the foundation of an academic pursuit known as **scientific racism**, which became prominent especially after the 1840s. Theorists such as the French nobleman Count Joseph Arthur de Gobineau (1816–1882) took race as the most important index of human potential. In fact, there is no basis for separating humans into separate races, because differences such as skin color are purely physical and do not signal differences in biological makeup. Nevertheless, nineteenth-century theorists assumed that the human species consisted of several distinct racial groups. Throughout the later nineteenth and early twentieth centuries, racial theorists sought to identify racial groups on the basis of skin color, bone structure, nose shape, cranial capacity, and other physical characteristics. Although they did not always agree on the details about racial differences, one thing they did agree on was the superiority of Europeans to all others—a belief that seemed to be justified by the dominance of European imperial powers in the larger world.

After the 1860s scientific racists drew heavily from the writings of Charles Darwin (1809–1882), an English biologist whose book *On the Origin of Species* (1859) argued that all living species had evolved over thousands of years in a ferocious contest for survival. Species that adapted well to their environment survived, reproduced, and flourished, according to Darwin, whereas others declined and went into extinction. The slogan "survival of the fittest" soon became a byword for Darwin's theory of evolution. Theorists known as social Darwinists seized on those ideas, which Darwin had applied exclusively to biological matters, and adapted them to explain the development of human societies. For example, the English philosopher Herbert Spencer (1820–1903) relied on

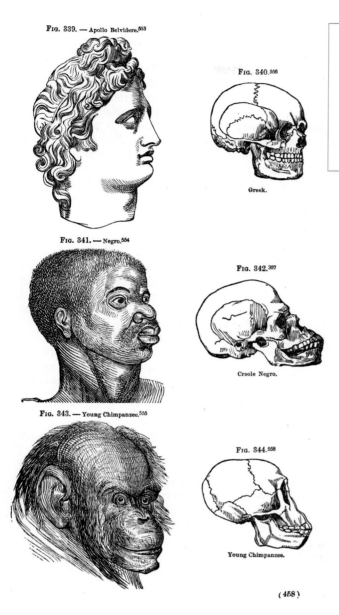

FIG. 339. — Apollo Belvidere.[553]

FIG. 340.[556]

Greek.

FIG. 341. — Negro.[554]

FIG. 342.[357]

Creole Negro.

FIG. 343. — Young Chimpanzee.[555]

FIG. 344.[558]

Young Chimpanzee.

(458)

Scientific racists often argued that Europeans had reached a higher stage of evolution than other peoples. An illustration from a popular book by Josiah Clark Nott and G. R. Glidden, *Indigenous Races of the Earth,* deliberately distorted facial and skull features to suggest a close relationship between African peoples and chimpanzees.
Science Source

theories of evolution to explain differences between the strong and the weak: successful individuals and races had competed better in the natural world and consequently evolved to higher states than did other, less fit peoples. On the basis of that reasoning, Spencer and others justified the domination of European imperialists over subject peoples as the inevitable result of natural scientific principles.

Racist views were by no means a monopoly of European imperialists: U.S. and Japanese empire builders also developed a sense of superiority over the peoples they conquered and ruled. U.S. forces in the Philippines disparaged the rebels with racial slurs, and they did not hesitate to torture enemies in a conflict that was supposed to "civilize and Christianize" the Filipinos. In the 1890s Japanese newspapers portrayed Chinese and Korean people as dirty, backward, stupid, and cowardly. After their victory in the Russo-Japanese War, political and military leaders came to believe that Japan had an obligation to oversee the affairs of their backward neighbors and help civilize their "little Asian brothers."

CONCLUSION

The construction of global empires in the nineteenth century noticeably increased the tempo of world integration. Armed with powerful transportation, communication, and military technologies, European peoples imposed their rule on much of Asia and almost all of Africa. Toward the end of the nineteenth century the United States and Japan joined European states as global imperialists. All the imperial powers profoundly influenced the development of the societies they ruled. They shaped the economies and societies of their colonies by pushing them

to supply natural resources and agricultural commodities in exchange for manufactured products. They created multicultural societies around the world by facilitating the movement of workers to lands where there was high demand for labor on plantations or in mines. They also developed racist ideologies that sought to justify conquest and brutal violence. In response, colonized people developed increasingly strong anticolonial and nationalist movements whose goal was to remove the imperial powers altogether. From the early twentieth century forward, much of global history has revolved around issues stemming from the world order established by imperialism and colonialism.

STUDY TERMS

Boxer rebellion (513)
capitulations (510)
Cixi (513)
direct rule (514)
Emilio Aguinaldo (519)
formal imperialism (504)
Guangxu (513)
Hong Xiuquan (511)
Hundred Days reforms (513)
indirect rule (514)
informal imperialism (504)
Khoikhoi (514)
King Leopold II (513)
Lili'uokalani (518)
Mahmud II (510)
Maji-Maji rebellion (524)
Maori (516)
mission civilisatrice (505)
Monroe Doctrine (518)
Omdurman (505)

On the Origin of Species (524)
Opium War (511)
Panama Canal (506)
Roosevelt Corollary (519)
Russo-Japanese War (520)
sati (507)
scientific racism (524)
scramble for Africa (513)
Self-Strengthening
    Movement (513)
Sepoy rebellion (507)
South African War (515)
Spanish-Cuban-American
    War (519)
Suez Canal (506)
Taiping rebellion (511)
Tanzimat (510)
unequal treaties (511)
Xhosa (514)
Young Turk Party (510)

FOR FURTHER READING

Clare Anderson. *Subaltern Lives: Biographies of Colonialism in the Indian Ocean World, 1790–1920*. Cambridge, 2012. Explores the experience of colonialism through the perspective of convicts, sailors, enslaved people, and indentured laborers.

Tony Ballantyne and Antoinette Burton. *Bodies in Contact: Rethinking Colonial Encounters in World History*. Durham, N.C., 2005. A collection of essays that explore the body as a critical site of cultural encounter in the context of colonialism.

Sugata Bose. *A Hundred Horizons: The Indian Ocean in the Age of Global Empires*. Cambridge, Mass., 2006. A bold, interregional history that argues that the peoples of the Indian Ocean littoral shared a common historical destiny.

Jane Burbank and Frederick Cooper. *Empires in World History: Power and the Politics of Difference*. Princeton, 2010. A major study that considers modern empires in historical context.

Ken S. Coates. *A Global History of Indigenous Peoples: Struggle and Survival*. Houndmills, U.K., 2004. Stressing the active role of indigenous peoples, this work examines the dynamics of colonial encounters.

John Darwin. *Unfinished Empire: The Global Expansion of Britain*. London and New York, 2013. A marvelous, sweeping, and sober account of one of the longest-lived and most influential empires in world history.

Daniel R. Headrick. *Power over Peoples: Technology, Environments, and Western Imperialism, 1400 to the Present*. Princeton, 2009. Explores the central role of technological innovation in the rise and fall of imperialism.

Eric T. L. Love. *Race over Empire: Racism and U.S. Imperialism, 1865–1900*. Chapel Hill, N.C., 2004. In this critical reinterpretation, the author challenges the prevailing notion that racism abetted imperialism, notwithstanding the fact that many imperialists were racists.

Heather Streets-Salter and Trevor Getz. *Empires and Colonies in the Modern World*. Oxford, 2015. Explores the structures and ideologies of imperialism and colonialism since 1400 from a global perspective.

H. L. Wesseling. *The European Colonial Empires: 1815–1919*. New York, 2004. Puts the process of colonization into a comparative and long-term perspective.

Chapter 29

The Great War:
The World in Upheaval

ZOOMING IN ON ENCOUNTERS

A Young Woman's Experience of the War

On 3 August 1914, twenty-one-year-old English college student Vera Brittain was playing tennis at her local club. She had just learned that France and Germany had declared war on one another, but the news seemed distant from her middle-class world on that bright summer day. In her diary that evening, she wrote, "I do not know how we managed to play tennis so calmly and take quite an interest in the result. I suppose it is because we all know so little of the real meaning of war that we are all so indifferent."

Like millions of other people around the world, the relative calm of the immediate pre-war world would soon seem like a surreal memory to Brittain. Looking back years later, she wrote, "How fortunate we were who still had hope I did not then realize; I could not know how soon the time would come when we should have no more hope, and yet be unable to die." In late 1915 her fiancé, Roland, died in the fighting on the western front. In 1917 the war also took her only brother, Edward, as well as her two closest male friends. After these losses, she said, "There seemed to be nothing left in the world, for I felt that

This contemporary painting by C. R. W. Nevinson, called *The Paths of Glory*, testifies to the appalling scale of death and destruction during the battles of World War I.
Photo12/Universal Images Group/Getty Images

Roland had taken with him all my future and Edward all my past."

Brittain herself waded through the years of the war in a state of deep disillusion and grief. Hoping to alleviate some of the suffering of the soldiers, in the summer of 1915 she withdrew from college and joined the Voluntary Aid Detachment (VAD) to become a nurse. She served initially at the First London General Hospital and then in France, where she saw firsthand the horrific wounds modern warfare inflicted on human bodies. She wished the people who spoke of the war as a glorious cause could see just one case of a mustard gas attack, that they could witness "the poor things all burnt and blistered all over with great suppurating blisters, with blind eyes . . . all sticky and stuck together, and always fighting for breath . . . saying their throats are closing and they know they are going to choke." At times her disillusion bordered on despair. After assisting at a particularly distressing amputation, she emerged "with my hands covered with blood and my mind full of a passionate fury at the wickedness of war, and I wished I had never been born."

Vera Brittain's experiences mirrored those of countless families who lost fathers, sons, brothers, and friends to the fighting between 1914 and 1918. These many millions paid the price of interstate conflict in Europe that boiled over from the assassination of the Austrian archduke Franz Ferdinand and his wife, Sophie, by a Serbian nationalist on 28 June 1914. As the various European powers took sides in the aftermath of the assassination, the stakes far outgrew Austro-Serbian conflicts. Nationalist aspirations, international rivalries, and an inflexible alliance system transformed that conflict into a general European war and ultimately into a global struggle involving thirty-two nations. Twenty-eight of those nations, collectively known as the **Allies** and the Associated Powers, fought the coalition known as the **Central Powers**, which consisted of Germany, Austria-Hungary, the Ottoman empire, and Bulgaria. The shell-shocked generation that survived the carnage called this clash of arms the Great War. A subsequent generation of survivors renamed the conflict World War I, because it was only the first of two wars that engulfed the world in the first half of the twentieth century.

CHAPTER OVERVIEW

Although the Great War only lasted four years, from August 1914 to November 1918, it deserves special attention because the processes of nationalism, industrialization, and imperialism all coalesced in one massive explosion of global violence, ushering in history's most violent century. In geographic extent the conflict surpassed all previous wars, compelling men, women, and children on five continents to participate directly or indirectly in a struggle that many did not understand. The Great War also had the distinction of being the first total war in human history, as governments mobilized every available human and material resource for the conduct of war. Moreover, the industrial nature of the conflict meant that it was the bloodiest in the annals of organized violence. The military casualties passed a threshold beyond previous experience: approximately fifteen million soldiers died, and an additional twenty million combatants suffered injuries.

The war of 1914–1918 did more than destroy individual lives. It seriously damaged national economies, it led to the redrawing of European boundaries, and it caused the demise of four dynasties and their empires—the Ottoman empire, the Russian empire, the Austro-Hungarian empire, and the German empire. The war also helped unleash the **Bolshevik revolution** of 1917, which set the stage for an ideological conflict between capitalism and communism that endured to the end of the twentieth century. Finally, the Great War was responsible for an international realignment of power. It undermined the preeminence and prestige of European society, signaling an end to Europe's global primacy.

CHRONOLOGY	
1914	Assassination of Archduke Francis Ferdinand
1915	Japan makes twenty-one demands on China
1915	Gallipoli campaign
1916	Battles at Verdun and the Somme
1917	German resumption of unrestricted submarine warfare
1917	United States declaration of war on Germany
1917	Bolshevik revolution
1918	Treaty of Brest-Litovsk
1918	Armistice suspends hostilities
1919	Paris Peace Conference
1920	First meeting of the League of Nations

THE DRIFT TOWARD WAR

Although the catalyst for war was the assassination of Archduke **Francis Ferdinand**, the assassin's bullets would have had limited effect if there had not been deeper reasons for war. Indeed, the underlying causes for the war of 1914–1918 were many, including intense nationalism, abrasive colonial rivalries, and a general struggle over the balance of power in Europe and in the world at large. Between 1871 and 1914, European governments adopted foreign policies that increased the likelihood of a general war between them. So as to not find themselves alone in a hostile world, national leaders sought alignments with other powers. The establishment and maintenance in Europe of two hostile alliances—the Allies and the Central Powers—helped spread the war from the Balkans to most of the rest of the world.

Nationalist Aspirations

The nationalist fervor that spread throughout most of Europe in the nineteenth century had led many Europeans to rally behind the idea of **self-determination**, or the idea that peoples with the same ethnic origins, language, and political ideals had the right to form sovereign states. In fact, that idea helped inspire the nationalist movements that led to the creation of the new nations of Belgium (1830), Italy (1861), and Germany (1871). Yet, at the end of the nineteenth century, the issue of nationalism remained unresolved in other areas of Europe, most notably in eastern Europe and the Balkans. There the nationalist aspirations of subject minorities threatened to tear apart the multinational empires of the Ottoman and Habsburg dynasties and with them the regional balance of power.

The Ottoman empire had controlled the Balkan peninsula since the fifteenth century, but after 1829 the Turkic empire lost huge portions of its territories. Greece was the first to gain independence (in 1830), and within a few decades Serbia, Romania, and Bulgaria followed suit. Austria-Hungary also confronted nationalism within its realms, especially the aspirations of Slavic peoples—Poles, Czechs, Slovaks, Serbs, Croats, and Slovenes. Most militant were the Serbs, who pressed for unification with the now-independent kingdom of Serbia. Russia and Germany added fuel to this volatile situation by supporting opposing sides. Russia supported Serbia and the notion of Slavic cultural unity, and Germany backed Austria-Hungary. Thus the stage was set for international conflict.

National Rivalries

Aggressive nationalism was also manifest in economic competition and colonial conflicts, fueling dangerous rivalries among the major European powers. All the industrialized nations of Europe competed for foreign markets and engaged in tariff wars, but the most unsettling economic rivalry involved Great Britain and Germany. By the twentieth century, Germany's rapid industrialization threatened Britain's long-standing economic predominance. Indeed, by 1914 Britain's share of global industrial output had declined to a level roughly equal to Germany's 13 percent. British reluctance to accept the relative decline of British industry vis-à-vis German industry strained relations between the two economic powers.

The Naval Race An expensive naval race worsened tensions between the two nations. When Germany's political and military leaders announced their program to build a fleet with many large battleships, they seemed to undermine Britain's longtime mastery of the seas. The British government moved to meet the German threat through the construction of battleships known as **dreadnoughts**. Rather than discouraging the Germans, the British determination to retain naval superiority stimulated the Germans to build their own flotilla of dreadnoughts. As the two nations raced to outdo each other, international hostilities boiled under the surface.

Colonial Disputes National rivalries also encouraged colonial competition. During the late nineteenth and early twentieth centuries, European nations searched aggressively for new colonies or dependencies to bolster economic performance. In their haste to conquer and colonize, the imperial powers sometimes stumbled over one another, repeatedly clashing in one or another corner of the globe: Britain and Russia competed for influence in Persia (modern-day Iran) and Afghanistan; Britain and France both sought a controlling influence in Siam (modern-day Thailand) and the Nile valley; Britain and Germany competed for territory in east and southwest Africa; Germany and France almost came to blows over attempts to influence affairs in Morocco and west Africa.

Between 1905 and 1914, a series of international crises and two local wars raised tensions and almost precipitated a general European war. The first crisis resulted from a French-German confrontation over Morocco in 1905. When the German government announced its support of Moroccan independence, which French encroachment endangered, the French responded by threatening war. An international conference in the following year prevented a clash of arms, but similar crises threatened the peace in subsequent years. Contributing to the growing tensions in European affairs were the Balkan wars. Between 1912 and 1913, the states of the Balkan peninsula—including Bulgaria, Greece, Montenegro, Serbia, and Romania—fought two wars for possession of the remaining European territories held by the Ottoman empire. The Balkan wars strained European diplomatic relations and helped shape the tense circumstances that led to the outbreak of the Great War.

Public Opinion Public pressure also contributed to national rivalries. New means of communication—especially

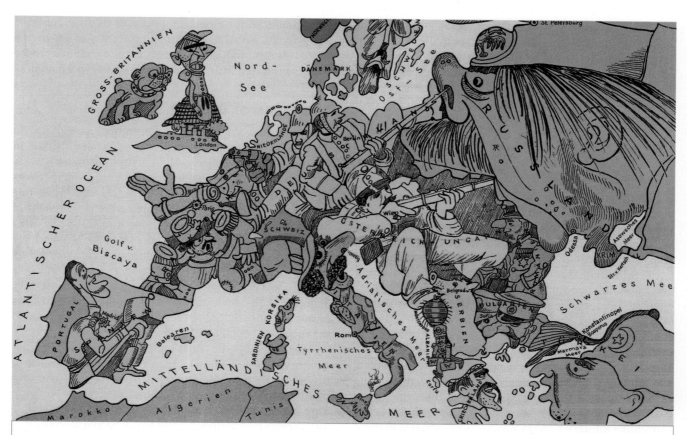

Dissident German cartoonist Walter Trier's satirical map of Europe in 1914. Trier's work stands in stark contrast to the press of the time, which fueled the chauvinist desires of competing national publics. What message was Trier trying to convey with this map?

akg-images/Alamy Stock Photo

inexpensive, mass-produced newspapers—nourished the public's desire to see their country "come in first," whether in the competition for colonies or in the race to the South Pole. However, public pressure calling for national greatness placed policymakers and diplomats in an awkward situation. Compelled to achieve headline-grabbing foreign policy successes, these leaders ran the risk of paying for short-lived triumphs with long-lasting hostility from other countries.

Understandings and Alliances

Escalating national rivalries and nationalist aspirations of subject minorities led to a system of entangling alliances. Fundamental to all of these alliances was that they outlined the circumstances under which countries would go to war to support one another. Although they were meant to preserve the peace, rival alliance systems created a framework whereby even a small international crisis could set off a chain reaction leading to global war. In 1914 the Great War erupted in large part because Europe's major powers had aligned into two hostile camps—the Triple Alliance and the Triple Entente.

The Central Powers The Triple Alliance, also known as the Central Powers, grew out of the close relationship that developed between the leaders of Germany and Austria-Hungary during the last three decades of the nineteenth century. In 1879 the governments of the two empires entered into the Dual Alliance, a defensive pact that ensured reciprocal protection from a Russian attack and neutrality in case of an attack from any other power. Fear of a hostile France motivated Germans to enter into this pact, whereas Austrians viewed it as giving them a free hand in pursuing their Balkan politics without fear of Russian intervention. Italy, fearful of France, joined the Dual Alliance in 1882, thereby transforming it into the Triple Alliance.

The Allies Meanwhile, the leaders of other nations viewed this new constellation of power with suspicion. This response was especially true of French leaders, who still remembered France's humiliating defeat during the Franco-Prussian War of 1870–1871. The czarist regime of Russia was equally disturbed by the new alignment of

Triple Entente (ahn-TAHNT)

powers, especially by Germany's support of Austria, and British leaders were traditionally suspicious of any arrangement that seemed to threaten the balance of power on the Continent. The result was an alliance called the Triple Entente, a combination of nations that had once been rivals (commonly referred to as the Allies). The construction of such alliances made it difficult for diplomats to contain what otherwise might have been relatively small international crises.

War Plans The preservation of peace was also difficult because the military staffs of each nation had devised inflexible military plans and timetables to be carried out in the event of war. German war plans, in particular, played a crucial role in the events leading to the Great War. Germany's fear of encirclement by France and Russia encouraged its military planners to devise a strategy that would avoid a war on two fronts. It was based on a strategy developed in 1905 by General Count Alfred von Schlieffen (1833–1913). The **Schlieffen plan** called for a swift attack on France, followed by defensive action against Russia. German planners predicated their strategy on the knowledge that the Russians could not mobilize their soldiers and military supplies as quickly as the French, thus giving German forces a few precious weeks during which they could concentrate their full power on France. However, Germany's military strategy was a serious obstacle to those seeking to preserve the peace. In the event of Russian mobilization, Germany's leaders would feel compelled to stick to their war plans by attacking France first, thereby setting in motion a military conflict of major proportions.

GLOBAL WAR

In the capitals of Europe, some people danced in the streets when their governments announced formal declarations of war. When the first contingents of soldiers left for the front, jubilant crowds threw flowers at the feet of departing men, who expected to return victorious after a short time. However, reality crushed any expectations of a short and triumphant war. On most fronts the conflict quickly bogged down and became a war of attrition (gradually wearing down the enemy) in which the firepower of modern weapons slaughtered soldiers by the millions. For the first time in history, belligerent nations engaged in total war. Even in democratic societies, governments assumed dictatorial control to marshal the human and material resources required for continuous war. One result was increased participation of women in the labor force. Total war had repercussions that went beyond the borders of Europe.

Imperial ties drew millions of Asians, Africans, and residents of the British dominions into the war to serve as soldiers and laborers. Struggles in and over colonies fur-

ther underlined the global dimension of this war. Last, the war gained a global flavor through the entry of Japan, the United States, and the Ottoman empire, nations whose leaders professed little direct interest in European affairs.

The Guns of August

Declarations of War The shots fired from Gavrilo Princip's revolver on that fateful day of 28 June 1914 set in motion a flurry of diplomatic activity that quickly escalated into war. Austrian leaders in Vienna were determined to teach the unruly Serbs a lesson, and on 23 July the Austrians issued an ultimatum to the government of Serbia. When the Serbian government rejected one of its terms, Austria-Hungary declared war on Serbia. The war had begun. The subsequent sequence of events was largely determined by two factors: complex mobilization plans and the grinding logic of the alliance system. Military planners were convinced that the timing of mobilization orders and adherence to precise timetables were crucial to the successful conduct of war.

On 29 July the Russian government under Czar Nicholas II (1868–1918) began mobilizing its troops to defend its Serbian ally and itself from Austria. The czar then ordered mobilization against Germany. Nicholas took that decisive step reluctantly and only after his military experts had convinced him that a partial mobilization might invite defeat, should the Germans enter the war on the side of Austria. His action precipitated a German ultimatum to Russia on 31 July, demanding that the Russian army cease its mobilization immediately. Another ultimatum addressed to France demanded to know what France's intentions were in case Germany and Russia went to war. The Russians replied with a blunt "impossible," and the French never answered. Thus on 1 August the German government declared war on Russia, and France started to mobilize.

On 3 August the Germans declared war on France. On the same day, German troops invaded Belgium in accordance with the Schlieffen plan. Key to this plan was an attack on the weak left flank of the French army by an imposing German force through neutral Belgium. On 4 August the British government sent an ultimatum to Germany demanding that Belgian neutrality be respected. When Germany's wartime leaders refused, the British immediately declared war. A local conflict had become a general European war.

Mutual Butchery

Everyone expected the war to be brief. In the first weeks of August 1914, twenty million young men donned uniforms, took up rifles, and left for the front. Many of them looked forward to heroic charges, rapid promotions, and a quick homecoming. Some dreamed of glory and honor, and they believed that God was on their side. Their visions could hardly have been more wrong.

SOURCES FROM THE PAST

Dulce et Decorum Est

The Great War produced a wealth of poetry. The poetic response to war covered a range of moods, from early romanticism and patriotism to cynicism, resignation, and the angry depiction of horror. One of the best-known war poets was Wilfred Owen (1893–1918), whose poems are among the most poignant of the war. Owen, who enlisted for service on the Western Front in 1915 at the age of twenty-two, was injured in March 1917 and sent home. Declared fit for duty in August 1918, he returned to the front. German machine-gun fire killed him on 7 November, four days before the armistice that ended the war, when he tried to cross the Sambre Canal. This poem was published in 1920, two years after his death.

Bent double, like old beggars under sacks,
Knock-kneed, coughing like hags, we cursed through sludge,
Till on the haunting flares we turned our backs
And towards our distant rest began to trudge.
Men marched asleep. Many had lost their boots
But limped on, blood-shod. All went lame; all blind;
Drunk with fatigue; deaf even to the hoots
Of gas-shells dropping softly behind.

> What is Owen trying to convey about the physical demands of service during the war?

Gas! GAS! Quick, boys!—An ecstasy of fumbling,
Fitting the clumsy helmets just in time;
But someone still was yelling out and stumbling
And floundering like a man in fire or lime.—
Dim, through the misty panes and thick green light
As under a green sea, I saw him drowning.

In all my dreams, before my helpless sight,
He plunges at me, guttering, choking, drowning.
If in some smothering dreams you too could pace
Behind the wagon that we flung him in,
And watch the white eyes writhing in his face,

> How does Owen describe the effects of a gas attack? Is his literary depiction more or less effective than detached descriptions of war's effects?

His hanging face, like a devil's sick of sin;
If you could hear, at every jolt, the blood
Come gargling from the froth-corrupted lungs,
Obscene as cancer, bitter as the cud
Of vile, incurable sores on innocent tongues,—
My friend, you would not tell with such high zest
To children ardent for some desperate glory,
The old Lie: Dulce et decorum est
Pro patria mori.*

Author's note: "Sweet and fitting is it to die for one's country" comes from a line by the Roman poet Horace (65–8 B.C.E.).

For Further Reflection

■ What is Owen's overall message in this poem? Do you think he intended to take a political stand on war or that he was simply describing his experience?

Source: Wilfred Owen. "Dulce et Decorum" (1918).

The Western Front The initial German march toward Paris in August 1914 was stopped by the French army (with British support) along the river Marne, after which each side tried to outflank the other in a race to the Atlantic coast. For the next three years, the battle lines remained virtually stationary, as both sides dug vast networks of defensive trenches and slugged it out in a war of attrition that lasted until the spring of 1918. Each belligerent tried to break through the other's defensive lines and to inflict continuous damage and casualties, only to

Why It Matters

▷ ▷ ▷ ▷ ▷ ▷ ▷

The Destructive Potential of Industrial Technologies

Was industrialization a net benefit or a net loss for humanity and for the planet more generally? A study of global history since the beginning of the industrial revolution demonstrates how difficult—and how important—it is to answer this crucial question at this moment of scientifically observable climate change.

By the late nineteenth century a variety of European and American intellectuals believed that industrialization—which resulted in mass-produced goods, new and more rapid forms of communication, and all manner of mechanized devices—had led to a marked improvement in the human condition, and that industrialization would continue to contribute to the overall progress of humanity into the distant future. And in many ways their expectations were realized: during the twentieth century, industrial machinery made it possible to feed billions of people, build vast networks of roads, and create hundreds of millions of cars and airplanes. Mass-produced medicines made it possible to eliminate smallpox and a variety of other health scourges from much of the world, and mass-produced consumer goods allowed people to purchase, at relatively low cost, a huge variety of items designed to make them more comfortable. At an aggregate level, humans in the twentieth century lived longer, were less poor, were more connected to one another, and had access to more everyday comforts than their predecessors in previous centuries.

But the twentieth century also revealed the enormous costs of industrialization—costs that echo right up to the present. That is because although industrialization allowed the manufacture of goods and materials that made life more convenient, it also allowed for the manufacture of items designed for destruction on a previously unimaginable scale. In this chapter we have already seen how the nations involved in World War I marshaled their industrial power to manufacture deadly weapons, ammunition, chemical gases, tanks, and submarines. Few humans alive even in 1900 could have imagined the devastation—in both life and property—made possible when industrial powers put their energies toward destruction during World War I. And humans did not stop there. During World War II, opposing sides used

industrial technology to kill ever more efficiently and quickly. In Germany, Adolf Hitler took industrialized killing to a chilling new level when he authorized the use of advanced industrial techniques to kill millions of people (chapter 32). After the war, the creation of the atom bomb, used with such devastating effect in Hiroshima and Nagasaki, made it clear that scientists had designed industrial weaponry capable of destroying entire populations in one blow. From that point until the dissolution of the Soviet Union in 1991, the threat of mass destruction via industrial technologies was a reality that the world's people had to live with.

Industrial technologies have also proven to be extremely destructive in terms of their environmental impact. Since the nineteenth century industrial economies have relied on fossil fuels to function. In addition, industrial manufacturing requires the widespread exploitation of raw materials such as cotton and timber. During the nineteenth and twentieth centuries, industrializing states operated as though fossil fuels and raw materials would be endlessly available. Over time, however, it became clear not only that fossil fuels will eventually run out but also that large-scale industrialization resulted in air and water pollution, as well as in deforestation, erosion, and the loss of biodiversity. By the end of the twentieth century, the majority of the world's scientists had concluded that the pollution generated by more than a century of industrialization had caused changes in climate on a planetary scale. The ultimate impact of these changes remains unclear, although many scientists fear that it may be too late to undo the damage that has been set in motion from industrialization, and that the fate of humanity and of the planet is in grave danger.

Given the current crisis of climate change, then, how do we evaluate the history of industrialization? Should we focus on its innovations, benefits, and conveniences, or should we focus on the ways in which industrialization has led us to the point of endangering the planet? Often we learn from history that there are no easy answers, especially because we do not yet know what the future holds. We do know, however, that understanding the history of industrialization *matters*, both for our present and for our future.

have its own forces suffer heavy losses in return. Trenches on the **western front** ran from the English Channel to Switzerland. Farther south, Italy left the Triple Alliance and then entered the war on the side of the Allies in 1915. Allied hopes that the Italians would pierce Austrian de-

fenses quickly faded. After a disastrous defeat at Caporetto in 1917, Italian forces maintained a defensive line only with the help of the French and the British.

Stalemate and New Weapons The stalemate on the western and southern fronts reflected technological developments that favored defensive tactics. Barbed wire proved highly effective in frustrating the advance of soldiers across

---

Caporetto (kap-uh-RET-oh)

no-man's-land, the deadly territory between opposing trenches. In addition, the rapid and continuous fire of machine guns turned infantry charges across no-man's-land into suicide missions. Both sides developed weapons to break the deadly stalemate and reintroduce movement into the war. Gas often proved lethal, and it caused its victims excruciating pain. Mustard gas, for example, rotted the body from both within and without. After blistering the skin and damaging the eyes, the gas attacked the bronchial tubes, stripping off the mucous membrane. Death could occur in four to five weeks. Yet, although both sides suffered heavy casualties, totaling about eight hundred thousand soldiers, gas attacks failed to deliver the promised strategic breakthroughs. Other novel weapons developed during the war included tanks and airplanes. Submarines had made earlier appearances in warfare but were most effectively used by the German navy against Allied commercial shipping in the Great War.

War casualties on the western front. This photograph depicts a mutilated body among barbed wire in no-man's-land. akg-images/Newscom

No-Man's-Land The most cour-ageous infantry charges, even when preceded by pulverizing artillery barrages and clouds of poisonous gas, were no match for determined defenders. Shielded by the dirt of their trenches and by barbed wire and gas masks, they unleashed a torrent of lethal metal with their machine guns and repeating rifles. In every sector of the front, those who fought rarely found glory. Instead, they encountered death. No-man's-land was strewn with shell craters, cadavers, and body parts. The grim realities of trench warfare—the wet, cold, waist-deep mud; lice; and corpse-fed rats—contrasted sharply with the encouraging and optimistic phrases of politicians and generals justifying the unrelenting slaughter.

Bloodletting Many battles took place, but some were so horrific, so devastating, and so futile that their names are synonymous with human slaughter. The casualty figures attested to this bloodletting. In 1916 the Germans tried to break the deadlock with a huge assault on the fortress of Verdun. The French rallying cry was "They shall not pass," and they did not—but at a tremendous cost: whereas the defeated Germans suffered a loss of 280,000, the victorious French counted 315,000 dead. To relieve the pressure on Verdun, British forces counterattacked at the Somme, and by November they had gained a few thousand yards at the cost of 420,000 casualties. The Germans suffered similar losses, although in the end neither side gained any strategic advantage.

The Eastern Front In eastern Europe and the Balkans, the battle lines were more fluid. After a staunch defense, a combination of Austrian and German forces overran Serbia, Albania, and Romania. Farther north, Russia took the offensive early by invading Prussia in 1914. The Central Powers recovered quickly, however, and in the summer of 1915 combined German and Austrian forces drove the Russian armies out of East Prussia and then out of Poland, establishing a defensive line extending from the Baltic to the Ukraine. Russian counterattacks in 1916 and 1917 collapsed in a sea of casualties. The huge scale of Russian defeats in turn undermined the popularity of the czar and his government and played a significant role in fostering revolutionary ferment within Russian society.

New Rules of Engagement The Great War established rules of engagement that made civilians targets of warfare, both from air attacks and from naval blockades. Indeed, military leaders on both sides used blockades to deny food to whole populations, hoping that starving masses would force their governments to capitulate. The British blockade of Germany during the war contributed to the deaths of an estimated half million Germans.

Total War: The Home Front

As the Great War ground on, it became a conflict of attrition in which the organization of material and human resources was of paramount importance. War became total, fought between entire societies, and total victory was the only acceptable outcome that might justify the terrible sacrifices made by all sides. The nature of total war created a military front and a home front. The term **home front** expressed the important reality that the outcome of the war hinged on how effectively each nation mobilized its economy and activated its noncombatant citizens to support the war effort.

The Home Front As the war continued beyond 1914 and as war weariness and a decline in economic capability set in, the response of all belligerents was to limit individual freedoms and give control of society increasingly to military leaders. Initially ministers and generals were

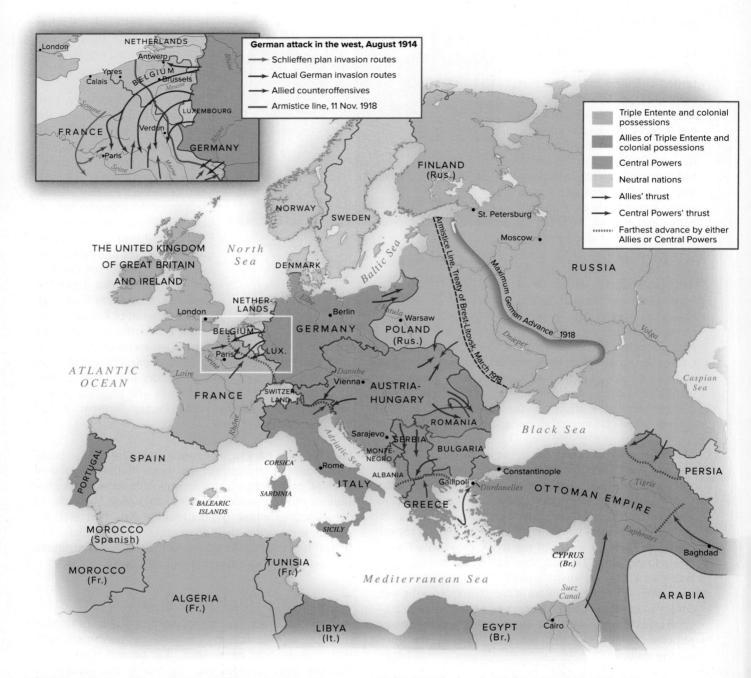

MAP 29.1   The Great War in Europe and Southwest Asia, 1914–1918

Note the locations of both the eastern and the western fronts in Europe during the war.

Why didn't the same kind of trench warfare immobilize opposing armies on the eastern front the way it did on the western front?

luctant to resort to compulsive measures, even conscription of recruits, but they quickly changed their minds. Each government eventually militarized civilian war production by subordinating private enterprises to governmental control and imposing severe discipline on the labor process.

Economic measures were foremost in the minds of government leaders because the war created unprecedented demands for raw materials and manufactured goods. Planning boards reorganized entire industries, set production quotas and priorities, and determined what would be produced and consumed. Government authorities also established wage and price controls, extended work hours, and in some instances restricted the movement of workers. Because bloody battlefields caused an insatiable appetite for soldiers, nations responded by extending the age range for compulsory military service. In Germany, for example, men between the ages of sixteen and sixty were eligible to serve at the front. By constantly tapping into the available male population, the war created an increasing demand for workers at home. Unemployment—a persistent feature of all pre-war economies—vanished virtually overnight.

Women at War As men went to war, women replaced them at work. Conscription took men out of the labor force, and wartime leaders exhorted women to fill the gaps in the workforce. A combination of patriotism and high wages drew women into many formerly "male" jobs in a wide variety of industries and public sectors. Perhaps the most crucial work performed by women during the war was the making of shells. Several million women, and some children, put in long, hard hours in munitions factories. That work exposed them to severe dangers, not to mention death, from explosions and poisoning from long-term exposure to TNT.

Although some middle- and upper-class women reported that the war was a liberating experience in regard to personal and economic freedom, most working-class women found little that was liberating in war work. Most of the belligerent governments promised equal pay for equal work, but in most instances that promise remained unfulfilled. Moreover, female employment was a transitory phenomenon. Once the war was over, many women workers—especially those in traditionally male occupations—found themselves forced to concede their jobs to men. Nevertheless, the extension of voting rights to women shortly after the war—in Britain (1918, for women thirty years and older), Germany (1919), and Austria (1919)—was an acknowledgment of the important roles women assumed during the Great War.

Propaganda To maintain the spirit of the home front and to counter threats to national unity, governments resorted to the restriction of civil liberties, censorship of bad news, and vilification of the enemy through propaganda campaigns. While government officials busily censored war news, people who had the temerity to criticize their nation's war effort were prosecuted as traitors. Meanwhile, the propaganda offices of the belligerent nations tried to convince the public that military defeat would mean the destruction of everything worth living for, and to that end they did their utmost to discredit and dehumanize the enemy.

German propaganda depicted Russians as semi-Asiatic "barbarians," and French authorities chronicled

This French propaganda poster, "The Heroes of Belgium, 1914," was intended to rouse French patriotism by depicting German soldiers as inhuman monsters.
Library of Congress Prints & Photographs Division [LC-DIG-ppmsca-57998]

One of the most crucial works performed by women during the war was the making of shells. This photograph shows a female assembly-line worker in a munitions factory in England in 1917.
Hulton Deutsch/Corbis Historical/Getty Images

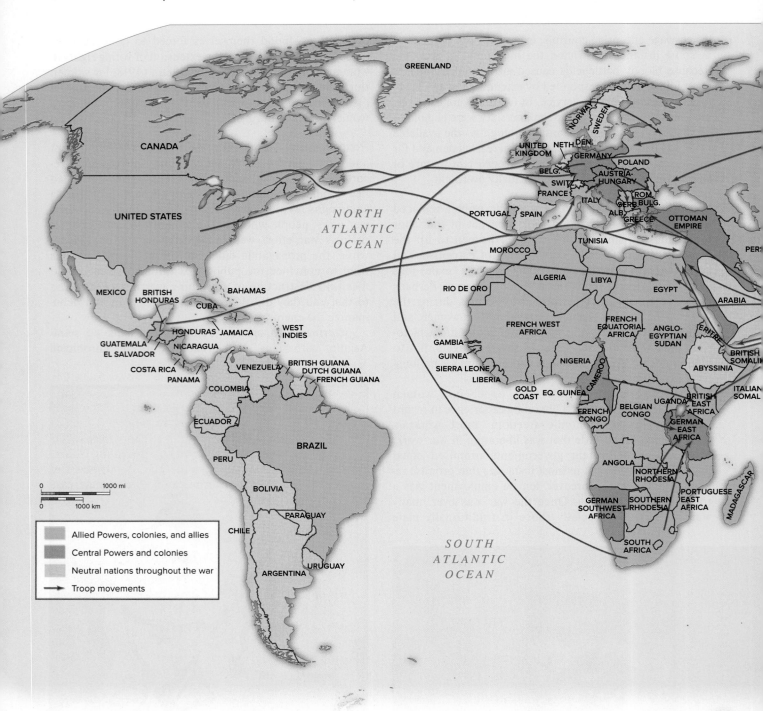

MAP 29.2   The global scope of the Great War

the atrocities committed by the German "Hun" in Belgium. In 1917 the *Times* of London published a story claiming that Germans converted human corpses into fertilizer and food. In Germany, one widely distributed poster invoked images of Black Allied soldiers raping German women to suggest what would follow if the nation's war effort failed. Most atrocity stories were patently false, and they eventually engendered public skepticism and cynicism. Ironically, public disbelief of wartime propaganda led to reluctance to believe in the abominations perpetrated in later wars.

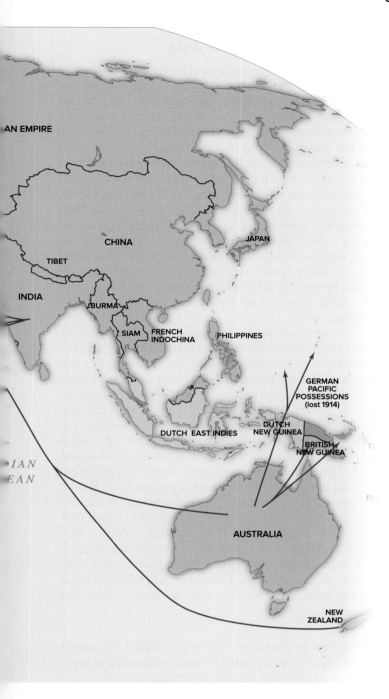

the French employed laborers from Algeria, west Africa, and French Indochina, and the British recruited more than a million Indian soldiers as well as African troops for combat. The British also relied on troops furnished by the dominion lands, including Australia, New Zealand, Canada, Newfoundland, and South Africa. Third, the Great War assumed global significance because of the entrance into the war of Japan, the Ottoman empire, and the United States.

On 15 August 1914 the Japanese government sent an ultimatum to Germany demanding the handover of the German-leased territory of Jiaozhou (northeastern China) to Japanese authorities without compensation. The same note also demanded that the German navy unconditionally withdraw its warships from Japanese and Chinese waters. When the Germans refused to comply, the Japanese—who had already been allied with Great Britain since 1902—entered the war on the side of the Allies on 23 August 1914. Japanese forces then proceeded to seize German territories in China and—aided by forces from New Zealand and Australia—in the Pacific. Next Japan shrewdly exploited Allied support and European preoccupation to advance its own imperial interests in China. On 18 January 1915 the Japanese presented the Chinese government with twenty-one secret demands. The terms of that ultimatum, if accepted, would have reduced China to a protectorate of Japan. Chinese diplomats leaked the note to the British authorities, who spoke up for China, thus preventing total capitulation. The **Twenty-one Demands** reflected Japan's determination to dominate east Asia and served as the basis for future Japanese pressure on China.

Africa and Africans in the War

The geographic extent of the conflict also broadened beyond Europe when the Allies targeted German colonies in Africa. When the war of 1914–1918 erupted in Europe, all of sub-Saharan Africa (except Ethiopia and Liberia) consisted of European colonies, with the Germans controlling four: Togoland, the Cameroons, German Southwest Africa, and German East Africa.

Thus one immediate consequence of war for Africans in 1914 was that the Allies invaded German colonies. The British anticipated that victory in the German colonies would mean the acquisition of German territory in Africa after the war. France's objective was to recover territory in Cameroon that it had ceded to Germany in 1911. The Germans, in contrast, simply tried to hold on to what they had.

Although their position in Africa was far less powerful than either the British or the French, by resorting to

Conflict in East Asia and the Pacific

The Great War quickly turned from a European war into a global conflict. There were three reasons for the war's expansion. First, European governments carried their animosities into their colonies, embroiling them in their war. Second, because of massive casualties among European recruits, the British and the French augmented their ranks by recruiting men from their colonies. Millions of Africans and Asians were drawn into the war. Behind their trenches

Jiaozhou (jyou-joh)

An Indian gun crew in the Somme area, 1916. During the Great War, colonial powers relied on millions of Asian and African men to fight or labor for their respective sides.
National Archives (165-BO-1602)

guerrilla tactics, some fifteen thousand German troops tied sixty thousand Allied forces down for the duration of the war.

Unlike the capture of German colonies in the Pacific, which Allied forces accomplished during the first three months of the war with relative ease, the conquest of German colonies in Africa was difficult. Fighting took place on land and sea; on lakes and rivers; in deserts, jungles, and swamps; and in the air. Indeed, the German flag did not disappear from Africa until after the armistice took effect on 11 November 1918.

More than one million African soldiers participated directly in military campaigns, in which they witnessed firsthand the spectacle of white people fighting one another. They fought on African soil, in the lands of southwest Asia, and on the western front in Europe. Even more men, as well as women and children, served as carriers to support armies in areas where supplies could not be hauled by conventional methods such as road, rail, or pack animal. The colonial powers raised recruits for fighting and carrier services in three ways: on a purely voluntary basis, in levies supplied by African chiefs that consisted of volunteer and impressed (coerced) personnel, and through formal conscription. Ultimately more than one hundred fifty thousand African soldiers and carriers lost their lives, and many more suffered injuries or became disabled.

Battles in Southwest Asia

The most extensive military operations outside Europe took place in the southwest Asian territories of the Ottoman empire, which aligned itself with the Central Powers on 28 October 1914. Seeing an opportunity to gain back some of its lost territories if Germany were to win the war, the Ottoman government sought to work with their German allies to undermine their enemies' war-making ability where they were weakest—in the colonies. In particular, the Ottomans—with overt German support—worked to turn the millions of Muslim subjects in British, French, and Russian territories against their rulers by declaring a *jihad* on the Allied Powers. Although these efforts were ultimately unsuccessful, they did necessitate that the Allies spend precious resources monitoring attempts by the Central Powers to foment rebellion in colonies from central Asia to Africa, and from east to southeast Asia.

Notwithstanding the aggravation and worry caused by the Ottoman call to *jihad,* the British believed that the Ottomans were a weak ally in the Central Powers. For this reason, **Winston Churchill** (1874–1965) proposed a plan to break the bloody stalemate on the western front by striking against Ottoman territory. Early in 1915 the British navy conducted an expedition to seize the approach to the Dardanelles Strait in an attempt to open a warm-water supply line to Russia through the Ottoman-controlled strait. The campaign was a disaster. Turkic defenders, ensconced in the cliffs above, quickly pinned down the Allied troops on the beaches. Trapped between the sea and the hills, Allied soldiers dug in and engaged in their own version of trench warfare. The resulting stalemate produced a total of two hundred fifty thousand casualties on each side. Despite the losses, Allied leaders took nine months to admit that their campaign had failed and that the Ottoman forces had not been as weak as they had imagined.

Armenian Massacres The war provided the pretext for the Ottoman government to begin a campaign of extermination against two million Armenians living under its rule. Friction between Christian Armenians and Muslim Ottoman authorities went back to the nineteenth century, when distinct nationalist feelings stirred many of the peoples who lived under Ottoman rule. After 1913 the Ottoman state adopted a new policy of Turkic nationalism intended to shore up the crumbling imperial edifice. The new nationalism stressed Turkic culture and traditions and regarded Christian minorities as obstacles to Turkism. During the Great War, the Ottoman government branded Armenians as traitorous internal enemies. The government then unleashed a murderous campaign against the Armenians, which included mass evacuations that were

What's Left Out? ■ ■ ■ ■ ■ ■

For decades after the Great War, historians focused on it as a European war. But such a focus obscured the profound ways World War I affected even neutral territories such as the Dutch East Indies, Siam, China, and the United States (the last three neutral until 1917) thousands of miles away. This was so because the German government established the principle of instigating revolutions in Allied colonies as an explicit war aim. Germany was especially interested in starting a revolution in India, Britain's most important colony. Thus the German Foreign Office created the Committee for Indian Independence, staffed it with active Indian revolutionaries, and provided them with money, weapons, and logistical support. During the war, Germans and Indian revolutionaries worked together to start a revolution in India by establishing a secret training base for Indians in Siam (Thailand) and smuggling weapons and propaganda to India from the United States via China and the Dutch East Indies. All of these efforts required revolutionaries to move around the world and to coordinate their efforts with German consuls in neutral territories. These contacts, in turn, brought the politics of the war right into neutral territories, because officials in those places feared they would be dragged into the war if the Central Powers were caught plotting against the Allies on their soil. As a result, each had to devote significant energy toward stopping German coordination with colonial revolutionaries. This example helps us see that the enmities between the Allied and the Central Powers were not simply fought out on European battlefronts and in European colonies but even in neutral territories halfway across the world.

Source: Heather Streets-Salter. *World War One in Southeast Asia.* Cambridge: Cambridge University Press, 2017.

accompanied by starvation, dehydration, and exposure. Equally deadly were government-organized massacres that claimed victims through mass drowning, incineration, or assaults with blunt instruments. Best estimates suggest that close to a million Armenians perished between 1915 and 1917 in what has become known as the **Armenian genocide**. Although it is generally agreed that the Armenian genocide did occur, the Turkic government denies the label of state-sponsored genocide, arguing instead that the deaths occurred as a result of communal warfare, disease, and famine.

The Arab Revolt against Ottoman Rule After successfully fending off Allied forces on the beaches of Gallipoli in 1915 and in Mesopotamia in 1916, Ottoman armies retreated slowly on all fronts. The British, in particular, were instrumental in coordinating multiple attacks against the Ottomans, using armies that drew heavily on recruits from Egypt, India, Australia, and New Zealand. As the armies smashed the Ottoman state—one entering Mesopotamia and the other advancing from the Suez Canal toward Palestine—they received significant support from an Arab revolt against the Turks. In 1916, aided by the British, the nomadic Bedouin of Arabia under the leadership of Hussein bin Ali, sharif of Mecca and king of the Hejaz (1856–1931), and others rose up against Turkic rule. The motivation for the Arab revolt centered on securing independence from the Ottoman empire and subsequently creating a unified Arab nation spanning lands from Syria to Yemen. The British government did not keep its promise of Arab independence after the war.

THE END OF THE WAR

The war produced strains within all the belligerent nations, but most of them managed, often ruthlessly, to cope with food riots, strikes, and mutinies. In the Russian empire, the war amplified existing stresses to such an extent that the Romanov dynasty was forced to abdicate in favor of a provisional government in the spring of 1917. Eight months later, the provisional government yielded power to Bolshevik revolutionaries, who took Russia out of the war early in 1918. This blow to the Allies was more than offset by the entry of the United States into the conflict in 1917, which turned the tide of war in 1918. The resources of the United States finally compelled the exhausted Central Powers to sue for peace in November 1918.

In 1919 the victorious Allies gathered in Paris to hammer out a peace settlement. The settlements that resulted were compromises that pleased few of the parties involved. The most significant consequence of the war was Europe's diminished role in the world. The war of 1914–1918 undermined Europe's power and simultaneously promoted nationalist aspirations among colonized peoples, who clamored for self-determination and national independence. For the time being, however, the major imperialist powers kept their grip on their overseas holdings.

Romanov (ROH-mah-nahv)
Bolshevik (BOHL-shih-vehk)

Revolution in Russia

The Great War had seriously undermined the Russian state. In the spring of 1917, disintegrating armies, mutinies, and food shortages provoked a series of street demonstrations and strikes in Petrograd (St. Petersburg). The inability of police forces to suppress the uprisings, and the subsequent mutiny of troops garrisoned in the capital, persuaded Czar Nicholas II (reigned 1894–1917) to abdicate the throne.

The Struggle for Power After its success in Petrograd, this **February revolution** spread throughout the country, and political power in Russia shifted to two new agencies: the provisional government and the Petrograd soviet of Workers' and Soldiers' Deputies. Soviets, which were revolutionary councils organized by socialists, surfaced all over Russia in 1917, wielding considerable power through their control of factories and segments of the military. The period between February and October witnessed a political struggle between the provisional government and the powerful Petrograd soviet. At first the new government enjoyed considerable public support as it eliminated the repressive institutions of the czarist state, but it failed to satisfy popular demands for an end to war and for land reform. It claimed that, being provisional, it could not make fundamental changes such as confiscating land and distributing it among peasants. The government also promised to continue the war and to bring it to a victorious conclusion. The Petrograd soviet, in contrast, called for an immediate peace.

Lenin Into this tense political situation stepped **Vladimir Ilyich Lenin** (1870–1924), a revolutionary Marxist and the leader of the small but radical Bolshevik socialist party. Although Lenin had been living in enforced exile in Switzerland, early in 1917 the German High Command helped him return to Russia in the hope that he would foment revolution and bring about Russia's withdrawal from the war. He did. Already in April 1917 Lenin began calling for the transfer of legal authority to the soviets and advocated uncompromising opposition to the war.

Under Lenin's leadership, the Bolsheviks eventually gained control of the Petrograd soviet. Crucial to this development was the provisional government's insistence on continuing the war, its inability to feed the population, and its refusal to undertake land reform. Workers and peasants became increasingly convinced that their problems could be solved only by the soviets. In September, Lenin persuaded the Central Committee of the Bolshevik Party to organize an armed insurrection and seize power in the name of the All-Russian National Congress of Soviets, which was then convening in Petrograd. Dur-

Vladimir Lenin (1870–1924) makes a speech in Red Square on the first anniversary (1918) of the Bolshevik revolution.
Hulton Deutsch/Corbis Historical/Getty Images

ing the night of 24 October and the following day, armed workers, soldiers, and sailors stormed the Winter Palace, the home of the provisional government. By the afternoon of 25 October, the virtually bloodless insurrection had run its course, and power passed from the provisional government into the hands of Lenin and the Bolshevik Party.

Treaty of Brest-Litovsk The Bolshevik rulers then ended Russia's involvement in the Great War by signing the **Treaty of Brest-Litovsk** with Germany on 3 March 1918. The treaty gave the Germans possession or control of one-third of Russia's territory (the Baltic States, the Caucasus, Finland, Poland, and the Ukraine) and one-quarter of its population. Although the terms of the treaty were harsh and humiliating, taking Russia out of the war gave the new government an opportunity to deal with internal problems. Russia's departure from the war also meant that Germany could concentrate all its resources on the western front.

U.S. Intervention and Collapse of the Central Powers

The year 1917 was crucial for another reason: it marked the entry of the United States into the war on the side of the Allies. In 1914 the American public firmly opposed intervention in a European war. That sentiment soon changed. After the outbreak of the war, the United States pursued a neutrality that favored the Allies, and as the war progressed, the United States became increasingly committed economically to an Allied victory.

Vladimir Ilyich Lenin (VLAD-uh-meer IL-yich LEHN-in)

German prisoners of war in 1917. Over six million prisoners of war were captured by both sides during the conflict, creating strains on wartime economies. Imprisoned enlisted men were put to work to supplement labor shortages by both the Allies and the Central Powers.
GL Archive/Alamy Stock Photo

America Declares War The official factor in the United States' decision to enter the war, however, was Germany's resumption of **unrestricted submarine warfare** in February 1917—a practice that had aroused American outrage in the early years of the war. Germany's leaders took this decisive step because they were desperate to break the British blockade that threatened to starve the Central Powers and hoped to use their submarines to do so. German military experts calculated that submarine attacks against the ships of Great Britain and all the ships headed to Great Britain would bring about the defeat of Great Britain in six months. By that time, however, both the American public and its leadership were invested in an Allied victory, and thus Germany's decision brought the United States into the war in April 1917.

Collapsing Fronts The corrosive effects of years of bloodletting showed. For the first two years of the conflict, most people supported their governments' war efforts, but the continuing ravages of war took their toll everywhere. The Central Powers suffered from food

shortages as a result of the British blockade, and increasing numbers of people took to the streets to demonstrate against declining food rations. Food riots were complemented by strikes as pre-war social conflicts reemerged. Governments reacted harshly to these challenges by suppressing demonstrators and jailing dissidents. Equally dangerous was the breakdown of military discipline on both sides. In France, for example, a mutiny in the spring of 1917 involved 50,000 soldiers, resulting in 23,385 courts-martial and 432 death sentences.

Against that grim background, Germany took the risk of throwing its remaining might at the western front in the spring of 1918. The gamble failed, and as the offensive petered out, the Allies—strengthened by fresh U.S. troops—broke through the front and started pushing the Germans back. By that time Germany had effectively exhausted its human and material means to wage war. Meanwhile, Bulgaria capitulated to the invading Allies on 30 September, the Ottomans concluded an armistice on 30 October, and Austria-Hungary surrendered on 4 November. Finally, the Germans accepted an armistice, which took effect on 11 November 1918. At last the guns went silent.

After the War

The immediate effects of the Great War were all too obvious. Aside from the physical destruction, which was most visible in northern France and Belgium, the war had killed, disabled, orphaned, or rendered homeless millions of people. Conservative estimates suggest that the war killed fifteen million people and wounded twenty million others. Many of the combatant survivors were unable to adjust back into civilian life after the horrors of what they had seen in battle. Survivors frequently displayed symptoms that contemporaries labeled "shell shock" (known today as post-traumatic stress disorder), which ranged from horrific nightmares, to uncontrollable shaking, to an inability to interact with others. Moreover, in the immediate postwar years, millions of people—noncombatants as well as combatants—succumbed to the effects of starvation, malnutrition, and epidemic diseases.

The Influenza Pandemic of 1918

The end of the Great War coincided with the arrival of one of the worst pandemics ever recorded in human history. No one knows its origins or why it vanished in mid-1919, but by the time this virulent influenza disappeared, it had left more than twenty million dead. This exceptionally lethal virus hit young adults—a group usually not severely affected by influenza—with particular ferocity.

The Great War did not cause the flu pandemic of 1918–1919, but wartime traffic on land and sea contributed to the spread of the infection. From the remotest villages in Arctic climates and crowded cities in India and the United States to the battlefields of Europe, men and women were struck down by high fever. Within a few days they were dead. In Calcutta, India, the postal service and the legal system ground to a halt. The Pacific islands suffered worst of all as the flu wiped out up to 25 percent of the entire population. Indeed, the influenza plague did not discriminate between the rich and poor, men and women, or the sick and healthy.

Before the costs of the war were assessed fully, world attention shifted to Paris. There, in 1919 the victorious powers convened to arrange a postwar settlement and set terms for the defeated nations. At the outset, people on both sides of the war had high hopes for the settlement, but in the end it left a bitter legacy. Ultimately, **Georges Clemenceau** (1841–1929), **David Lloyd George** (1863–1945), and **Woodrow Wilson**—the representative leaders of France, Great Britain, and the United States—dominated the deliberations. The Allies did not permit representatives of the Central Powers to participate, and the Soviet Union was not invited to the conference. Throughout this time the British blockade of Germany remained in effect, adding a sense of urgency to the proceedings.

Georges Clemenceau (jawrj klem-uhn-SOH)
Treaty of Sèvres (SEV-ruh)

Wilson's Fourteen Points

One year before the opening of the **Paris Peace Conference**, in January 1918, U.S. president Woodrow Wilson had forwarded a proposal for a just and enduring postwar peace settlement. Wilson's postwar vision subsequently prompted the defeated Central Powers to announce their acceptance of his so-called **Fourteen Points** as the basis for the armistice. They also expected the Allies to use them as the foundation for later peace treaties. Key among Wilson's Fourteen Points were the following recommendations: open covenants (agreements) of peace, openly arrived at; absolute freedom of navigation upon the seas in peace and war; the removal of all economic barriers and the establishment of an equality of trade conditions among all nations; adequate guarantees for a reduction in national armaments; adjustments of colonial disputes to give equal weight to the interests of the controlling government and the colonial population; and a call for "a general association of nations."

The idealism expressed in the Fourteen Points gave Wilson a position of moral leadership among the Allies. The same allies also opposed various points of Wilson's peace formula, because those points compromised the secret wartime agreements by which they had agreed to distribute among themselves the territories and possessions of the defeated nations. The defeated powers, in turn, later felt betrayed when they faced the harsh peace treaties that so clearly violated the spirit of the Fourteen Points.

The Peace Treaties

The final form of the treaties represented a series of compromises among the victors. The hardest terms originated with the French, who desired the destruction or the permanent weakening of German power. Thus, in addition to requiring Germany to accept sole responsibility and guilt for causing the war, the victors demanded a reduction in the military potential of the former Central Powers. In addition, the Allies prohibited Germany and Austria from entering into any sort of political union. The French and the British agreed that the defeated Central Powers must pay for the cost of the war and required the payment of reparations either in money or in kind.

The Paris Peace Conference resulted in additional treaties with Bulgaria, Austria, Hungary, and the Ottoman empire. Whereas Bulgaria lost only small portions of territory as a result, the Austro-Hungarian empire was destroyed: in separate treaties both Austria and Hungary suffered severe territorial losses. Arrangements between the defeated Ottoman empire and the Allies proved to be a more complicated and protracted affair that involved two treaties. In 1920 the **Treaty of Sèvres** effectively dissolved the empire, calling for the surrender of Ottoman Balkan and Arab provinces and the occupation of eastern and southern Anatolia by foreign powers. However, Turkic nationalists—led by the war hero Mustafa Kemal—set out to defy those terms. Kemal organized a national army that drove out Allied occupation forces, abolished the sultanate, and replaced it with the Republic of Turkey, with Ankara as its capital. In a great diplomatic victory for Turkic nationalists, the Allied powers officially recognized the Republic of Turkey in a final peace agreement, the **Treaty of Lausanne** (1923).

The League of Nations Although the war was over, the peace settlement that resulted from it was weak. To be sure, some efforts to avoid future conflicts were made. At the urging of U.S. president Woodrow Wilson, the Covenant of the **League of Nations** was made an integral part of the peace treaties, and every signatory to a peace treaty had to accept this new world organization. However, the league suffered from fundamental weaknesses that made it unable to enforce its decisions. Over the next two decades, it became clear that the league could not stop the aggression that would lead to World War II, and the institution closed its doors in 1940. Nevertheless, the league did establish the pattern for a permanent international organization and served as a model for its successor, the United Nations.

Self-determination Another weakness of the peace was the uneven way in which key ideas of the peacemaking process—especially the idea of national self-determination—were put into practice around the world. In Europe, the peacemakers in Paris did, in fact, try to apply the principle of self-determination and nationality to a variety of peoples, such as Slavs, Czechs, and Slovaks, although the results were far from perfect. Yet in other instances peacemakers pushed the principle aside for strategic and security reasons, such as in Austria and Germany, whose peoples were denied the right to form one nation.

The Mandate System In other parts of the world, however, peacemakers did not even try to apply the principle of self-determination. This unwillingness to apply the principle of self-determination became most obvious when the victors confronted the issue of what to do with Germany's former colonies and the Arab territories of the Ottoman empire. Because the United States rejected the establishment of new colonies, the European powers came up with the idea of trusteeship. Article 22 of the Covenant of the League of Nations referred to the colonies and territories of the former Central Powers as areas "inhabited by peoples not yet able to stand by themselves under the strenuous conditions of the modern world." As a result, "the tutelage of such peoples should be entrusted to the advanced nations who . . . can best undertake this responsibility." The administration of the mandates fell to the victorious powers of the Great War.

The Germans rightly interpreted the **mandate system** as a division of colonial booty by the victors, who had conveniently forgotten to apply the tutelage provision to their own colonies. German cynicism was more than matched by Arab outrage. The establishment of mandates in the former territories of the Ottoman empire violated promises by French and British leaders during the war. They had promised Arab nationalists independence from the Ottoman empire and had promised Jewish nationalists in Europe a homeland in Palestine. Where the Arabs hoped to form independent states, the French (in Lebanon and Syria) and the British (in Iraq and Palestine) established mandates. The Allies viewed the mandate system as a reasonable compromise between the reality of imperialism and the ideal of self-determination. To the peoples who were directly affected, the mandate system was simply continued imperial rule draped in a cloak of respectability.

Challenges to European Preeminence

When the war ended, it seemed to most Europeans that their global hegemony was more secure than ever. But the Great War did irreparable damage to European power and prestige and set the stage for a process of decolonization that gathered momentum during and after the Second World War. The decline in European power was closely related to diminished economic stature, a result of the commitment to total war. Nothing was more indicative of Europe's reduced economic might than the reversal of the economic relationship between Europe and the United States. Whereas the United States was a debtor nation before 1914, owing billions of dollars to European investors, by 1919 it was a major creditor.

The war also weakened the European hold over colonial territories. Colonial subjects in Africa, Asia, and the Pacific tended to view the Great War as a civil war among the European nations, a bloody spectacle in which the haughty bearers of an alleged superior society vilified and slaughtered one another. Because Europe seemed weak, divided, and vulnerable, the white colonizers appeared far less powerful than before. The colonial subjects who returned home from the war in Europe and southwest Asia reinforced those general impressions with their own firsthand observations. In particular, they were less inclined to be obedient imperial subjects.

The war also helped spread revolutionary ideas to the colonies. The U.S. war aims spelled out in the Fourteen Points raised the hopes of peoples under imperial rule and promoted nationalist aspirations. The peacemakers repeatedly invoked the concept of self-determination, and Wilson publicly proposed that in all colonial questions "the interests of the native populations be given equal weight with the desires of European governments." Nationalists struggling to organize anti-imperialist resistance also sought inspiration from the Soviet Union, whose leaders denounced all forms of imperialism and pledged their support to independence movements. Taken together, those messages were subversive to imperial control and had a great appeal for colonial peoples. Although nationalist movements endured many setbacks, the days of European global dominance were numbered.

Mustafa Kemal (MOOS-tah-fah kuh-MAHL)

MAP 29.3   Territorial changes in Europe after the Great War

Observe the territories ceded by the Central Powers and the Soviet Union.

Which power lost the most territory, and why?

CONCLUSION

The assassination of the Austrian archduke Francis Ferdinand had a galvanizing effect on a Europe torn by national rivalries, colonial disputes, and demands for self-determination. In the summer of 1914, inflexible war plans and a tangled alliance system transformed a local war between Austria-Hungary and Serbia into a European-wide clash of arms. With the entry of the Ottoman empire, Japan, and the United States, the war of 1914–1918 became a truly global conflict. Although many belligerents organized their societies for total war and drew on the resources of their overseas empires, the war in Europe remained at a bloody stalemate until the United States entered the conflict in 1917. The tide turned, and the combatants signed an armistice in November 1918. The Great War, a brutal encounter between societies and peoples, inflicted ghastly human casualties, severely damaged national economies, and discredited established political and cultural traditions. The war also altered the political landscape of many places as it destroyed four dynasties and their empires, fostered the creation of several new European nations, and created new protectorates called mandates. In Russia the war served as a backdrop for the world's first successful socialist revolution. In the end the Great War sapped the strength of European colonial powers while it promoted nationalist aspirations among colonized peoples.

STUDY TERMS

Allies (529)
Armenian genocide (541)
Bolshevik revolution (529)
Central Powers (529)
David Lloyd George (544)
dreadnoughts (530)
February revolution (542)
Fourteen Points (544)
Francis Ferdinand (530)
Georges Clemenceau (544)
home front (535)

League of Nations (545)
mandate system (545)
no-man's-land (535)
Paris Peace Conference (544)
Schlieffen plan (532)
self-determination (530)
Treaty of Brest-Litovsk (542)
Treaty of Lausanne (545)
Treaty of Sèvres (544)
Twenty-one Demands (539)

unrestricted submarine warfare (543)
Vladimir Ilyich Lenin (542)
western front (534)
Winston Churchill (540)
Woodrow Wilson (544)

FOR FURTHER READING

Mustafa Aksakal. *The Ottoman Road to War in 1914: The Ottoman Empire and the First World War*. Cambridge, 2008. Uses previously untapped sources to explore how and why the Ottomans entered the Great War on the side of the Central Powers.

Christopher Clark. *The Sleepwalkers: How Europe Went to War in 1914*. New York, 2013. The best researched, most readable one-volume account of a very contentious subject.

Peter Gatrell. *Russia's First World War: A Social and Economic History*. London, 2005. Traces the impact of World War I on Russian society before the revolution.

Robert Gerwarth and Erez Manela. *Empires at War, 1911–1923*. Oxford, 2014. An edited collection of top-notch essays that explore the Great War as a fundamentally imperial and global conflict.

Susan R. Grayzel. *Women and the First World War*. New York, 2002. An excellent introduction to the experiences and contributions of women during the war.

Margaret MacMillan. *Paris 1919: Six Months That Changed the World*. New York, 2002. The most engaging and lucid analysis written on the subject of the peace settlement.

John H. Morrow. *The Great War: An Imperial History*. New York, 2003. A global history of the Great War that places the conflict squarely in the context of imperialism.

Michael S. Neiberg. *Fighting the Great War*. Cambridge, Mass., 2005. A good blend of narrative and analysis highlighting the global reach of the conflict.

Susan Pedersen. *The Guardians: The League of Nations and the Crisis of Empire*. Oxford, 2015. A comprehensive study of the history of the League of Nations and its creation as well as management of the mandate system.

Hew Strachan. *The First World War*. New York, 2004. One of the leading historians of WWI offers a one-volume version of his projected three-volume work, treating the war in a global rather than European context.

Anxieties and Experiments in Postwar Europe and the United States

New Intellectual Frontiers
- Postwar Pessimism
- New Visions in Physics, Psychology, and Art

Global Depression
- The Great Depression
- Despair and Government Action
- Economic Experimentation

Challenges to the Liberal Order
- Communism in Russia
- The Fascist Alternative
- Italian Fascism
- German National Socialism

ZOOMING IN ON TRADITIONS
The Evolution of a Dictator

Born on a lovely spring day in 1889, in a quaint Austrian village, he was the apple of his mother's eye. He basked in Klara's warmth and indulgence as a youth, enjoying the fine life of a middle-class child. As he grew older, however, he sensed a tension between the competing expectations of his parents. Contented with being spoiled by Klara, he bristled at the demands of his father, Alois, who expected him to enter the Austrian civil service. He had no desire to become a bureaucrat. In fact, he envisioned a completely different life for himself as an artist.

Alois's unexpected death in 1903 freed him from a future as a bureaucrat. He left school in 1905 with a ninth-grade education and moved to Vienna with plans to study to become an artist. But the Vienna Academy of Fine Arts rejected him in 1907. His beloved Klara died the following year, and he meandered the city streets of Vienna, admiring the architecture of the city and attending the opera when his funds permitted.

Eventually, he hit bottom and began staying at a homeless shelter. There, he was exposed to a variety of political

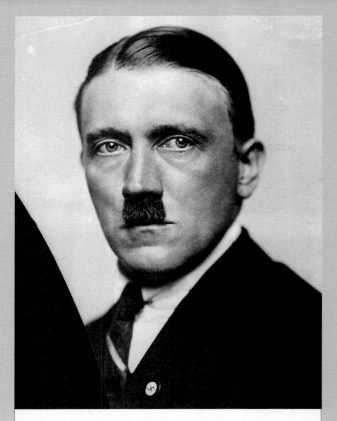

This is one of the few known photographs of a young Adolf Hitler, taken in 1923.
Bettmann/Getty Images

ideologies held by the shelter's other inhabitants. They discussed compelling issues of the day, and he was particularly attracted to the viewpoints of those who hailed the supremacy of the Aryan race and the inferiority of the Jews. He came to hate Jews and Marxists, who he thought had formed an evil union with the goal of destroying the world. He also despised liberalism and democracy.

In 1913 he left his Austrian homeland and found refuge in Munich, Germany. In Germany he volunteered for service in the army, which had just entered what later became known as World War I. He discovered in himself a talent for military service, and he remained in the army for the duration of the war, 1914–1918. Twice wounded and decorated for bravery, he nonetheless found himself in despair at war's end. He learned of Germany's defeat in the war while being treated in a hospital for exposure to mustard gas. Enraged, he believed with all his being that the Jews were responsible for this humiliation, and he also knew that he had to enter the political arena in his chosen fatherland and save the nation. **Adolf Hitler** had finally found his mission in life, a mission that would have a devastating and deadly effect for millions of people.

CHAPTER OVERVIEW

Badly shaken by the effects of war, Europeans experienced a shock to their system of values, beliefs, and traditions. Profound intellectual, scientific, and cultural transformations in the postwar decades also contributed to a sense of loss and anxiety. Then, as peoples in Europe and around the world struggled to come to terms with the aftermath of war, an unprecedented economic contraction gripped the international community.

Against the background of the Great Depression, dictators in Russia, Italy, and Germany tried to translate blueprints for utopias into reality. Those political innovations unsettled many Europeans and much of the world, contributing significantly to the anxiety of the age.

CHRONOLOGY	
1905	Einstein publishes special theory of relativity
1907	Picasso paints *Les demoiselles d'Avignon*
1918–1920	Civil war in Russia
1919	Mussolini launches fascist movement in Italy
1921–1928	Lenin's New Economic Policy
1927	Heisenberg establishes "uncertainty principle"
1928–1932	First Soviet Five-Year Plan
1929	U.S. stock market crash
1929	Beginning of Great Depression
1929	Hemingway and Remarque publish antiwar novels
1933–1945	Hitler is ruler in Germany
1935–1938	Stalin's "Great Purge" in the Soviet Union

NEW INTELLECTUAL FRONTIERS

The Great War discredited established social and political institutions and long-held beliefs about the superiority of European society. Although some European intellectuals and leaders had been anxious about the future of their society since the end of the nineteenth century, in the aftermath of the Great War the tendency for writers, poets, theologians, and other intellectuals to lament the decline and imminent death of their society increased markedly. Yet not everyone was so pessimistic: indeed, while some wrote obituaries, others embarked on bold new cultural paths that established the main tendencies of contemporary thought and taste. Both trends, however, turned many established beliefs, traditions, and certainties on their heads in the years after the Great War.

The discoveries of physicists undermined the Newtonian universe, in which a set of inexorable natural laws governed events, with a new and disturbing cosmos. Equally discomfiting were the insights of psychoanalysis, which suggested that human behavior was fundamentally irrational. Disquieting trends in the arts paralleled developments in science and psychology. Especially in painting, an aversion to realism and a pronounced preference for abstraction heralded the arrival of new aesthetic standards.

Why It Matters

The Destructive Potential of Industrial Technologies

Did World War I permanently alter intellectual and popular culture in Europe and the United States? Prior to the war, many artists and intellectuals believed that the technologies associated with industrialization would ultimately lead to greater human comfort, prosperity, and happiness. But the role of mass-produced war matériel in the huge scale of slaughter during the war caused many to believe that industrial technologies had created a monster that would ultimately bring about more death and destruction than happiness. Their works began to reflect ambivalence, revulsion, and pessimism about modern technologies, and the realities of the war made it impossible for them to return to the optimism of the nineteenth century. This shift, in turn, became an important feature of intellectual and popular culture, not only in interwar Europe and the United States but also in many parts of the world right up to the present.

Postwar Pessimism

"You are all a lost generation," noted Gertrude Stein (1874–1946) to her fellow American writer Ernest Hemingway (1899–1961). Stein had given a label to the group of American intellectuals and literati who congregated in Paris in the postwar years. This "lost generation" expressed in poetry and fiction the malaise and disillusion that characterized U.S. and European thought after the Great War. The brutal realities of industrialized warfare left no room for heroes or glory, and during the 1920s artists and intellectuals spat out their revulsion in a host of war novels, such as Hemingway's *A Farewell to Arms* (1929) and Erich Maria Remarque's *All Quiet on the Western Front* (1929)—works overflowing with images of meaningless death and suffering. Postwar writers lamented the decline of Western society. A retired German schoolteacher named Oswald Spengler (1880–1936) made headlines when he published *The Decline of the West* (1918–1922). In this work, which was seen as an obituary of civilization, Spengler proposed that all societies pass through a life cycle of growth and decay comparable to the biological cycle of living organisms. His analysis of the history of western Europe led him to conclude that European society had entered the final stage of its existence. All that remained was irreversible decline, marked by imperialism and warfare.

Theologians joined the chorus of despair. In 1919 Karl Barth (1886–1968), a notable Christian theologian, published a religious bombshell titled *Epistle to the Romans*. In his work Barth sharply attacked the liberal Christian theology that embraced the idea of progress, or the tendency of European thinkers to believe in limitless improvement as the realization of God's purpose. The Augustinian, Lutheran, and Calvinist message of original sin—the idea that humans are doomed to lives of sin as a result of Adam and Eve's disobedience—fell on receptive ears as many Christians refused to accept the idea that contemporary human society was in any way a realization of God's purpose. The Russian orthodox thinker Nikolai Berdiaev (1874–1948) summed up those sentiments: "Man's historical experience has been one of steady failure, and there are no grounds for supposing it will be ever anything else."

The Great War destroyed long-cherished beliefs, such as belief in the universality of human progress. Many idols

One of the best-known faces of the twentieth century, Albert Einstein (1879–1955) was the symbol of the revolution in physics.
Bettmann/Getty Images

Nikolai Berdiaev (nih-koh-LYE ber-dee-ev)

of nineteenth-century progress came under attack, especially science and technology. The scientists' dream of leading humanity to a beneficial conquest of nature seemed to have gone awry, because scientists had spent the war making poisonous gas and high explosives. Democracy was another fallen idol. The idea that people should have a voice in selecting the leaders of their government had enjoyed widespread support in European societies. By the early twentieth century, such sentiments had led to universal male suffrage in most societies, and after the Great War many societies also extended the franchise to women. However, many intellectuals abhorred what they viewed as weak political systems that championed the tyranny of the average person. In Germany, for example, a whole school of conservatives lamented the "rule of inferiors."

New Visions in Physics, Psychology, and Art

The postwar decade witnessed a revolution in physics that transformed the character of science. **Albert Einstein** (1879–1955) struck the first blow with his theory of special relativity (1905), showing that there is no single spatial and chronological framework in the universe. According to the theory, it no longer makes sense to speak of space and time as absolutes, because the measurement of those two categories always varies with the motion of the observer. That is, space and time are relative to the person measuring them. To the layperson such notions suggested that a commonsense universe had vanished, to be replaced by a radically new one in which reality or truth was merely relative.

The Uncertainty Principle More disquieting even than Einstein's discoveries was the theory formulated by Werner Heisenberg (1901–1976), who in 1927 established the **uncertainty principle**. According to Heisenberg, it is impossible to specify simultaneously the position and velocity of a subatomic particle. The more accurately one determines the position of an electron, the less precisely one can determine its velocity, and vice versa. In essence, he argued that scientists cannot observe the behavior of electrons objectively, because the act of observation interferes with them.

It quickly became evident that the uncertainty principle had important implications beyond physics. Indeed, Heisenberg's theory called into question established notions of truth. Likewise, objectivity was no longer a valid concept, because the observer was always part of the process under observation. Accordingly, any observer—an anthropologist studying another society, for instance—had to be alert to the fact that his or her very presence became an integral part of the study.

Sigmund Freud (1856–1939) formulated psychoanalysis, a theory and clinical practice to explore the mind and, by extension, its creations, such as literature, religion, art, and history.
Imagno/Getty Images

Freud's Psychoanalytic Theory As equally unsettling as the advances in physics were developments in psychology that challenged established concepts of morality and values. Beginning in 1896, the Austrian medical doctor **Sigmund Freud** (1856–1939) embarked on research that focused on psychological rather than physiological explanations of mental disorders. Through his clinical observations of patients, Freud identified a conflict between conscious and unconscious mental processes that lay at the root of neurotic (mentally unbalanced) behavior. That conflict, moreover, suggested to him the existence of a repressive mechanism that keeps painful memories away from the conscious mind. Freud believed that dreams held the key to the deepest recesses of the human psyche. Using the free associations of patients to guide him in the interpretation of dreams, he identified sexual drives and fantasies as

Werner Heisenberg (VER-nuhr HAHY-zuyn-burg)
Sigmund Freud (SIG-muhnd froid)

Edgar Degas's *The Dance Foyer at the Opera* (1872). Degas was known as an impressionist, part of a French movement that experimented with light and shadow, influencing the modern art of the early twentieth century.
Laurent Lecat/Electa/Getty Images

generally agreed on a program "to abolish the sovereignty of appearance." Paintings no longer depicted recognizable objects from the everyday world, and beauty was expressed in pure color or shape. Some painters sought to express feelings and emotions through violent distortion of forms and the use of explosive colors; others, influenced by Freudian psychology, tried to tap the subconscious mind to communicate an inner vision or a dream.

Artistic Influences The artistic heritages of Asian, Pacific, and African societies shaped various strains of contemporary painting. Nineteenth-century Japanese prints, for example, influenced French impressionists such as Edgar Degas (1834–1917). The deliberate violation of perspective by Japanese painters and their stress on the flat, two-dimensional surface of the picture; their habit of placing figures off center; and their use of primary colors encouraged European artists to take similar liberties with realism. In Germany a group of young artists known as the "Bridge" made a point of regularly visiting the local ethnographic museum to be inspired by the boldness and power of indigenous art. The early works of Pablo Picasso (1881–1973), the leading proponent of cubism, displayed the influence of African art forms.

By the third decade of the twentieth century, it was nearly impossible to generalize about contemporary painting. All artists were acknowledged to have a right to their own reality, and generally accepted standards that distinguished between "good" and "bad" art disappeared.

the most important source of repression. For example, Freud claimed to have discovered a so-called Oedipus complex, in which male children develop an erotic attachment to their mother and hostility toward their father.

In the end, Freudian ideas shaped the psychiatric profession and established a powerful presence in literature and the arts. During the 1920s, novelists, poets, and painters acknowledged Freud's influence as they focused on the inner world of their characters. The creators of imaginative literature used Freud's bold emphasis on sexuality as a tool for the interpretation and understanding of human behavior.

Experimentation in Art The roots of contemporary painting go back to nineteenth-century French avant-garde artists who disdained realism and instead were concerned with freedom of expression. The aversion to visual realism was heightened by the spread of photography. When everyone could create naturalistic landscapes or portraits with a camera, it made little sense for artists to do the same with paint and brush. Thus painters began to think that the purpose of a painting was not to mirror reality but to create it.

At the beginning of the twentieth century, this new aesthetic led to the emergence of a bewildering variety of pictorial schools, all of which promised an entirely new art. Regardless of whether they called themselves expressionists, cubists, abstractionists, dadaists, or surrealists, artists

Edgar Degas (ED-gahr day-GAH)

GLOBAL DEPRESSION

After the horrors and debilitating upheavals of the Great War, much of the world yearned for a return to normality and prosperity. By the early 1920s the efforts of governments and businesses to rebuild damaged economies seemed to be bearing fruit. Prosperity, however, was short-lived. In 1929 the world plunged into an economic depression that was so long-lasting, so severe, and so global that it has become known as the **Great Depression**. The old capitalist system of trade and finance collapsed, and until a new system took its place after 1945, a return to worldwide prosperity could not occur.

The Great Depression

By the middle of the 1920s, most countries seemed on the way to economic recovery, and industrial productivity had returned to prewar levels. But that prosperity was fragile, perhaps even false, and many serious problems and dislocations remained in the international economy.

Economic Problems The economic recovery and well-being of Europe, for example, was tied to a tangled and interdependent financial system. In essence, the governments of Austria and Germany relied on U.S. loans and investment capital to finance reparation payments to France and England. The French and British governments, in turn, depended on those reparation payments to pay off loans taken out in the United States during the Great War. Strain on any one part of the system, then, inevitably strained them all.

There were other problems as well. Improvements in industrial processes reduced worldwide demand for certain raw materials, which had devastating consequences for export-dependent areas. Technological advances in the production of automobile tires, for instance, permitted the use of reclaimed rubber. The resulting glut of natural rubber badly damaged the economies of the Dutch East Indies, Ceylon, and Malaysia, which relied on rubber exports. Similarly, the increased use of oil undermined the coal industry, and the growing adoption of artificial nitrogen virtually ruined the nitrate industry of Chile.

One of the nagging weaknesses of the global economy in the 1920s was the depressed state of agriculture. During the Great War, when Europe's agricultural output declined significantly, farmers in the United States, Canada, Argentina, and Australia expanded their own production. At the end of the war, European farmers resumed their agricultural activity, thereby contributing to worldwide surpluses. As production increased, prices collapsed throughout the world. By 1929 the price of a bushel of wheat was at its lowest level in four hundred years, and farmers everywhere became impoverished. The reduced income of farm families contributed to high inventories of manufactured goods, which in turn caused businesses to cut back production and dismiss workers.

The Crash of 1929 The United States enjoyed a boom after the Great War, which prompted many people in the

Soup kitchens and breadlines became commonplace in the United States during the earliest, darkest years of the Great Depression. They fed millions of starving and unemployed people.
Bettmann/Getty Images

United States to invest their earnings and savings in speculative and risky financial ventures, particularly in stocks. In October 1929, warnings from experts that stock prices were overvalued prompted investors to pull out of the market. On **Black Thursday** (24 October), a wave of panic selling on the New York Stock Exchange caused stock prices to plummet. Investors who had overextended themselves through speculative stock purchases watched in agony. Thousands of people, from poor widows to industrial tycoons, lost their life savings, and by the end of the day eleven financiers had committed suicide. The crisis deepened when lenders called in loans, thereby forcing more investors to sell their securities at any price.

Economic Contraction Spreads In the wake of this financial chaos came a drastic decrease in business activity, wages, and employment. When businesses realized that shrinking consumer demand meant they could not sell their inventories, they responded with layoffs. With so many people unemployed, demand plummeted further, causing more business failures and soaring unemployment. In 1930 the slump deepened, and by 1932 industrial production had fallen to half of its 1929 level. National income had dropped by approximately half, and 44 percent of U.S. banks were out of business. Because much of the world's prosperity depended on the export of U.S. capital and the strength of U.S. import markets, the contraction of the U.S. economy created a ripple effect that circled the globe.

Most societies experienced economic difficulties throughout the 1930s. Virtually every industrialized society saw its economy shrivel, but nations that relied on exports of manufactured goods to pay for imported fuel and food—Germany and Japan, in particular—suffered the most. The depression also spread to primary producing economies in Latin America, Africa, and Asia. Hardest hit were countries that depended on the export of a few primary products such as coffee, sugar, minerals, ores, and rubber.

U.S. investors, shaken by the collapse of stock prices, tried to raise money by calling in loans and liquidating investments, and Wall Street banks refused to extend short-term loans as they became due. Banking houses in Austria and Germany became vulnerable to collapse, because they had been major recipients of U.S. loans. Devastated by the loss of U.S. capital, the German economy experienced a precipitous economic slide, which by 1932 resulted in 35 percent unemployment and a 50 percent decrease in industrial production. As the German economy—which had remained a leading economic power in Europe throughout the postwar years—ground to a virtual halt, the rest of Europe sputtered and stalled with it. Likewise, because of its great dependence on the U.S. market, the Japanese economy felt the depression's effects almost immediately. Unemployment in export-oriented sectors of the economy skyrocketed as companies cut back on production.

Economic Nationalism The Great Depression destroyed the international financial and commercial network of the capitalist economies. As international cooperation broke down, governments turned to their own resources and practiced **economic nationalism**. By imposing tariff barriers, import quotas, and import prohibitions, politicians hoped to achieve self-sufficiency. Yet economic nationalism invariably backfired. Each new measure designed to restrict imports provoked retaliation by other nations whose interests were affected. After the U.S. Congress passed the **Smoot-Hawley Tariff Act** in 1930, which raised duties on most manufactured products to prohibitive levels, the governments of dozens of other nations retaliated by raising tariffs on imports of U.S. products. The result was a sharp drop in international trade. Between 1929 and 1932, world production declined by 38 percent and trade dropped by more than 66 percent.

Despair and Government Action

By 1933 unemployment in industrial societies had reached thirty million, more than five times higher than in 1929. Both men and women lost their jobs, and over the course of the depression most governments enacted policies restricting female employment, especially for married women. Indeed, the notion that a woman's place was in

Human faces of the Great Depression. This 1936 photograph of a mother with her two children in Oklahoma, taken by photographer Dorothea Lange, documented the extreme poverty of the Great Depression.
Pictorial Press Ltd/Alamy Stock Photo

the home was already widespread and gained even further currency during the depression. Some, such as the French physician Charles Richet (1850–1935), even insisted that removing women from the workforce would solve the problem of male unemployment.

The Great Depression caused enormous personal suffering. The stark statistics documenting the failure of economies do not convey the anguish and despair of those who lost their jobs, savings, and homes. For millions of people the struggle for food, clothing, and shelter grew desperate. Shantytowns appeared overnight in urban areas, and breadlines stretched for blocks. Marriage, childbearing, and divorce rates declined, and suicide rates rose. Those simply trying to survive came to despise the wealthy, who, despite their own reduced incomes, remained shielded from the worst impact of the economic downturn. Adolescents completing their schooling faced an almost nonexistent job market.

Economic Experimentation

Classical economic thought held that capitalism was a self-correcting system that operated best when left to its own devices. Thus, in the initial stages of the depression, most governments did nothing, hoping that the crisis would resolve itself. Faced with such human misery, however, some governments assumed more active roles, pursuing deflationary measures by balancing national budgets and curtailing public spending. Rather than lifting national economies out of the doldrums, however, those remedies only worsened the depression's impact. Far from self-correcting, capitalism seemed to be dying. Many people called for a fundamental revision of economic thought.

Keynes **John Maynard Keynes** (1883–1946), the most influential economist of the twentieth century, offered a novel solution. In his seminal work *The General Theory of Employment, Interest, and Money* (1936), he argued that the fundamental cause of the depression was not excessive supply but inadequate demand. Accordingly, he urged governments to stimulate the economy by increasing the money supply, thereby lowering interest rates and encouraging investment. He also advised governments to undertake public works projects to provide jobs and redistribute incomes through tax policy. Such intervention would result in reduced unemployment and increased consumer demand, which in turn would lead to economic revival. These measures, Keynes argued, were necessary even if they caused governments to run deficits and maintain unbalanced budgets.

The New Deal Although Keynes's theories did not become influential with policymakers until after World War II, the administration of U.S. president **Franklin Delano Roosevelt** (1882–1945) anticipated his ideas. Roosevelt took aggressive steps to reinflate the economy and ease the worst of the suffering caused by the depression. His program for dealing with the national calamity—called the **New Deal**—included legislation designed to prevent the collapse of the banking system, to provide jobs and farm subsidies, to guarantee minimum wages, and to provide social security in old age. Its fundamental premise, that the federal government was justified in protecting the social and economic welfare of the people, represented a major shift in U.S. government policy and started a trend toward social reform legislation that continued long after the depression years.

CHALLENGES TO THE LIBERAL ORDER

Even prior to the gloom and despair of the Great Depression, it seemed to many that the capitalism and liberalism that had come to characterize much of western Europe and the United States no longer worked. At the same time, some voices promised to guide the way to more effective alternatives. Marxists, for example, believed that capitalist society was on its deathbed, and they sought to demonstrate that a new and better system based on rule by the proletariat (the working class) was being born out of the ashes of the Russian empire. The new rulers of Russia, Vladimir Ilyich Lenin and then Joseph Stalin, transformed the former czarist empire into the world's first communist society, the Union of Soviet Socialist Republics (1922). Other people found solace in fascist movements, which seemed to offer revolutionary answers to the economic, social, and political problems of the day. Among these fascist movements, the Italian and German ones figured most prominently.

Communism in Russia

In 1917 Lenin and his fellow Bolsheviks had taken power in the name of the Russian working class, but socialist victory did not bring peace and stability to the lands of the former Russian empire. After seizing power, Lenin and his supporters had to defend the world's first "dictatorship of the proletariat" against numerous internal and external enemies.

Civil War Opposition to the Bolshevik Party—by now calling itself the Russian Communist Party—erupted into a civil war that lasted from 1918 to 1920. In response, Lenin's government began a policy of terror in which two hundred thousand suspected anticommunists (known as Whites) were arrested, tried, and executed. In July 1918 the Bolsheviks executed Czar Nicholas II, Empress Alexandra, and their five children because they feared that the

Charles Richet (shawrl ri-SHEY)

Romanov family could strengthen counterrevolutionary forces. The peasantry, meanwhile, largely supported the Bolsheviks, fearing that a victory by the Whites would result in the return of the brutally oppressive czarist system. Indeed, White terror was often as brutal as Red (communist) terror.

But the fight between the Whites and the Reds inside Russia was only part of the conflict. Russia's former allies—Britain, France, Japan, and the United States—were deeply opposed to the assumption of Bolshevik power. Thus, in 1918, just as the Great War was ending, the Allies assembled an international coalition and sent troops to support the Whites. But the coalition was poorly organized, the troops were tired from four years of war, and their numbers were small. After three years of brutal civil war, the Whites were decisively defeated by the Red Army in 1920. One of the lasting legacies of the civil war was that the methods of terror the Reds resorted to in order to defeat the Whites—including the creation of a powerful secret police—now became a permanent part of communist rule in Russia.

War Communism

The need for access to funds to fight the civil war led the new Soviet government to embark on a hasty and unplanned course of nationalization, known as **war communism**. After officially annulling private property, the Bolshevik government assumed control of banks, industry, and other privately held commercial properties. Landed estates and the holdings of monasteries and churches also became national property. Private trade was abolished, and the party seized crops from peasants to feed people in the cities. This last measure proved especially unpopular and caused peasants to drastically reduce their production. By 1920 industrial production had fallen to about one-tenth of its pre-war level and agricultural output to about half its pre-war level.

The Communist International

The communist revolution in Russia also had a global dimension almost from its beginning. From 1919 to 1943, Moscow organized the World Congress of the Communist International, also known as the Comintern, which was supposed to be composed of communist parties everywhere. When the Comintern was founded in 1919, its purpose was to defeat the international bourgeoisie through revolution and to replace it with an international Soviet republic. Little was said about the colonies, because it was assumed that revolution would begin with the industrialized proletariat of Europe. But at the second meeting of the Comintern in 1920, Lenin argued—in his *Theses on National and Colonial Questions*—that communists in the west should partner with communists in the colonies in order to damage the economic foundations of the capitalist powers. To bring about this end, communist parties in the colonies were to be formally incorporated into the Comintern alongside European communist parties and would thus be subject to Comintern supervision as well as direction. This rhetorical commitment to supporting communism in the colonies became a reality when colonial subjects began almost immediately to form communist parties of their own. The first to form was the Parti Komunis Indonesia (PKI) in 1920. By 1930, communist parties had formed in most colonies, including South Africa, India, Algeria, Korea, Malaya, Indochina, and the Philippines, to name only a few. Although Comintern control over colonial communist parties was far from complete, colonial parties did establish direct connections with Moscow. In addition, colonial communist parties often received funds and operatives from the Comintern and sent their own representatives to Moscow for training. This support by Moscow for international communist movements led most of the colonial powers—including especially Britain, France, and the United States—to believe that communism was a deeply destructive force long before the Cold War.

The New Economic Policy

In 1921, as the Reds consolidated their military victories after the civil war, the Soviet economy was in a shambles. Workers were on strike, cities were depopulated, and factories were destroyed. Faced with economic paralysis, in the spring of 1921 Lenin decided on a radical reversal of war communism. In its place he implemented the **New Economic Policy (NEP)**, which temporarily restored the market economy and some private enterprise in Russia. Large industries and banks remained under state control, but the government returned small-scale industries to private ownership. The government also allowed peasants to sell their surpluses at free-market prices. Other features of the NEP included a vigorous program of electrification and the establishment of technical schools to train technicians and engineers. Lenin did not live to see the success of the NEP. After suffering three paralytic strokes, he died in 1924.

Josef Stalin

After a bitter political struggle for power, **Josef Stalin** (1879–1953), general secretary of the Communist Party, emerged as the new leader of the Soviet Union in 1928. A Georgian by birth, an Orthodox seminarian by training, and a Russian nationalist by conviction, Stalin indicated his unified resolve to gain power in his surname, which meant "man of steel." His first economic program, which replaced Lenin's NEP, was both ambitious and ruthless. Indeed, Stalin's **First Five-Year Plan**, implemented in 1929, aimed at nothing less than transforming the Soviet Union from a predominantly agricultural country to a leading industrial power. The First Five-Year Plan set targets for increased productivity in all spheres of the economy but emphasized heavy industry—especially steel and machinery—at the expense of consumer goods. As the rest of the world teetered on the edge

SOURCES FROM THE PAST

M. N. Roy: The Awakening of the East

Narendra Nath Battacharya, who later adopted the name M. N. Roy, was born near Calcutta, India, in 1887. He began his political life as a radical Indian nationalist but became a Marxist while living in the United States during World War I. After helping found the Mexican Communist Party in 1917, he was invited to Moscow to attend the Second World Congress of the Communist International in 1920. In Moscow, Roy became an influential leader in the Communist International. His ideas about the importance of the colonial world in the future communist revolution helped shape Comintern policy toward the colonial world.

The world revolution, in order to accomplish its great mission must cross the borders of the so-called Western Countries where capitalism has reached its climax. Until very recently this truth was almost entirely unknown among the revolutionaries of Europe and America, who hardly gave a moment's thought to the social and economic conditions of the Asiatic generally. It was generally maintained that, owing to their industrial backwardness, the hundreds of millions of the masses in the East would not count for anything in the great struggle between the exploiter, and the exploited. Consequently the "World" of the world revolution was limited to Europe and America. ⸻

> Why did revolutionaries in Europe and the United States disregard the revolutionary potential of people from the "East," according to Roy?

But revolution is the result of objective conditions; it breaks out in the least suspected place if the dynamic forces are there. The inevitable result of oppression is that sooner or later the oppressed rebel. This is happening to-day in the Eastern countries, where the myriads of toilers, have been groaning under the same exploitation against which their more fortunate and less downtrodden comrades of the Occident have been carrying on an heroic fight. The East is awakening: and who knows if the formidable tide, that will sweep away the capitalist structure of Western Europe, may not come from there. . . . ⸻

> Which group of revolutionaries does Roy believe is the most oppressed under world capitalism?

. . . During almost a century World Capitalism kept on invigorating itself by sucking the blood of the colonial toilers. But along with the bloody sword of organised exploitation, it carried in its womb the incipient forces that were destined to rise against it and build the new society upon its ruins. To-day these forces are manifesting themselves in the growing revolutionary fermentation among the Eastern peoples, who were considered till the other day negligible factors in the World Revolution. This awakening of the East must open a new vision before the revolutionary leaders of Europe. It ought to show them the way through which the retreat of the cunning enemy can be cut. A formidable upheaval of the colonial and "protected" peoples will take away from under the feet of Imperialist Capitalism, the rock of super-profit which has helped so far offset the effects of overproduction. . . . The disruption of Empire is the only thing that will complete the bankruptcy of European capitalism; and the revolutionary upheavals in the Asiatic countries are destined to bring about the crumbling of the proud imperial structure of capitalism.

For Further Reflection

■ Why does Roy believe that the awakening of the East is essential to the undermining of the capitalist world order? How have the European colonies helped preserve this world order, in his view?

Source: The Call, July 15, 1920, p. 5. Marxists Internet Archive (2007). https://www.marxists.org/archive/roy/1920/07/15.htm

of economic collapse, Stalin's plan offered a bold alternative to market capitalism. Stalin repeatedly stressed the urgency of this monumental endeavor, telling his people, "We are 50 to 100 years behind the advanced countries. Either we do it, or we shall go under."

Collectivization of Agriculture

Integral to the drive for industrialization was the **collectivization of agriculture**. The Soviet state expropriated privately owned land to create collective, or cooperative, farm units whose profits were supposed to be shared by all farmers. Stalin and his regime viewed collectivization as a means of increasing the efficiency of agricultural production and ensuring that industrial workers would be fed.

In some places, outraged peasants reacted to the government's program by slaughtering their livestock and burning their crops. Faced with enforced collectivization, millions of farmers left the land and migrated to cities in search of work. Those who stayed behind were often unable to meet production quotas and starved to death on the land they once owned. When Stalin called a halt to collectivization in 1931, half the farms in the Soviet Union had been collectivized. Estimates of the cost in number of peasant lives lost have fluctuated wildly, but even the most cautious place it at three million. Among them, the *kulaks*—relatively wealthy peasants who had risen to prosperity during the NEP—were nearly eliminated.

The Soviet leadership proclaimed the First Five-Year Plan a success after only four years. The Soviet Union industrialized under Stalin even though the emphasis on building heavy industry first and consumer industries later meant that citizens postponed the gratifications of industrialization. However, the scarcity or nonexistence of such consumer goods as refrigerators, radios, and automobiles was to some degree balanced by full employment, low-cost utilities, and cheap housing and food. Set against the economic collapse of the capitalist world, the ability of a centrally planned economy to create more jobs than workers could fill made it appear an attractive alternative.

The Great Purge

Nevertheless, the disaster of collectivization and the ruthlessness with which it was carried out had raised doubts about Stalin's administration. As

Josef Stalin (1879–1953) at a Soviet congress in 1936. By 1928 Stalin had prevailed over his opponents to become the dictator of the Soviet Union, a position he held until his death in 1953.
Bettmann/Getty Images

the Communist Party prepared for its seventeenth congress in 1934, the "Congress of Victors," Stalin learned of a plan to bring more pluralism back into leadership. The Congress of Victors quickly became the "Congress of Victims" as Stalin purged two-thirds of the delegates from the Communist Party (in what became known as the **Great Purge**). Between 1935 and 1938 Stalin removed from posts of authority all persons suspected of opposition, including more than half the army's high-ranking officers. According to declassified Soviet archives, during 1937 and 1938 Soviet security forces detained 1,548,366 persons, of whom 681,692 were shot.

The outside world watched the events unfolding within the Soviet Union with a mixture of contempt, fear, and admiration. The establishment of the world's first dictatorship of the proletariat challenged the values and institutions of liberal society all over the world and seemed to demonstrate the viability of communism as a social and political system.

The Fascist Alternative

While socialism was transforming the former Russian empire, another political force swept across Europe after the Great War. **Fascism**, a far-right, ultranationalist political movement and ideology that sought to create a new type of society, developed as a reaction against liberal democracy and the spread of socialism and communism. In 1919 Benito Mussolini founded the first fascist party. Movements comparable to Italian fascism subsequently developed in many European societies, most notably in Germany in the guise of **national socialism** (Nazism). Although fascism enjoyed widespread popularity in many European countries, it rarely threatened the political order and overthrew parliamentary systems only in Italy and Germany. Although potential fascist movements sprang up during the 1930s in Japan, China, and South Africa; in Latin American societies such as Brazil and Argentina; and in several Arab territories, fascism nevertheless remained basically a European phenomenon in the era between the two world wars.

During the 1920s and 1930s, fascist movements in Europe attracted millions of followers and proved especially attractive to middle classes and rural populations.

Those groups became radicalized by economic and social crises and were especially fearful of the perceived threat from the political left, especially communism. Fascism also proved attractive to nationalists of all classes. Asserting that society faced a profound crisis, fascists sought to create a new national community, which they defined either as a nation-state or as a unique ethnic or racial group. Although each fascist movement had its own unique characteristics, most shared certain features, such as veneration of the state, devotion to a strong leader, and an emphasis on ultranationalism, ethnocentrism, and militarism.

Fascist ideology consistently invoked the central role of the state, which stood at the center of the nation's life and history. Strong and charismatic leaders, such as Benito Mussolini in Italy and Adolf Hitler in Germany, embodied the state and claimed indisputable authority. Consequently, fascists were hostile to liberal democracy, which they viewed as weak. Fascism was also extremely hostile to socialism and communism. Fascist movements emphasized an aggressive form of nationalism (**chauvinism**) and a fear of foreign people (**xenophobia**). The typical fascist state also embraced militarism, a belief in the rigors and virtues of military life as an individual and national ideal. In practice, militarism meant that fascist regimes maintained large and expensive military establishments, tried to organize much of public life along military lines, and generally showed a fondness for uniforms, parades, and monumental architecture.

Benito Mussolini and Adolf Hitler watch a Nazi parade staged for the Italian dictator's visit to Germany in the fall of 1937. Hitler ordered a major display of military power for Mussolini, and by the end of the visit Mussolini was convinced that an alliance with Germany would lead to Italy becoming more powerful in Europe.
Bettmann/Getty Images

Italian Fascism

The first fascist movement developed in Italy after the Great War. Italians in 1918 were deeply disilluisioned with their uninspired political leadership and ineffective government, extensive economic turmoil and social discontent, and a growing fear of what seemed like a threatening rise of socialist movements. In addition, Italians were extremely disappointed with Italy's territorial spoils from the peace settlement after the Great War, as many believed Italy should have received significant chunks of Austrian territory.

Benito Mussolini The guiding force behind Italian fascism was **Benito Mussolini**, a former socialist who turned, after the Great War, to a political program that emphasized virulent nationalism, demanded repression of socialists, and called for a strong political leader. In 1919 he established the Fasci Italiani di Combattimento (Italian Combat Veteran League). Mussolini's movement gained widespread support after 1920, and by 1921 his league managed to have thirty-five fascists elected to the Italian parliament. Much of the newly found public support resulted from the effective use of violence against socialists by fascist armed squads known as Blackshirts. In 1922 Mussolini and his followers decided the time was ripe for a fascist seizure of

power, and on 28 October they staged a march on Rome. While Mussolini stayed safely in Milan, thousands of his black-shirted troops converged on Rome. Rather than calling on the military to oppose the fascist threat, King Victor Emmanuel III hastily asked Mussolini on 29 October to become prime minister and form a new government. Mussolini inaugurated a fascist regime in 1922.

The Fascist State Between 1925 and 1931, Italy's fascists consolidated their power through a series of laws that transformed the nation into a one-party dictatorship. In 1926 Mussolini seized total power as dictator and subsequently ruled Italy as Il Duce ("the leader"). The regime moved quickly to eliminate all other political parties, curb the freedom of the press, and outlaw free speech and association. A Special Tribunal for the Defense of the State, supervised by military officers, silenced political dissent. Thousands of Italians were marked as antifascist subversives and found themselves imprisoned or exiled on remote islands. Others faced capital punishment. Allying himself and his movement with business and landlord

---

chauvinism (SHOH-vuh-niz-uhm)
xenophobia (zen-uh-FOH-bee-uh)

interests, Il Duce also crushed labor unions and prohibited strikes. In 1932, on the tenth anniversary of the fascist seizure of power, Mussolini felt confident enough to announce that "the twentieth century will be a century of fascism, the century of Italian power."

Although racism and anti-Semitism (prejudice against Jews) were never prominent components of Italian fascism, in 1938 the government suddenly issued a series of anti-Semitic laws. That development was likely occasioned by Mussolini's newly found friendship with fellow dictator Adolf Hitler. In 1936 Mussolini told his followers that from now on, world history would revolve around a Rome-Berlin axis. In May 1939 the leaders of fascist Italy and Nazi Germany formalized their political, military, and ideological alliance by signing a ten-year Pact of Steel.

German National Socialism

Hitler and the Nazi Party After Adolf Hitler's postwar political awakening, he came into contact with an obscure political party sympathetic to his ideas. In 1921 he became chairman of the party now known as the National Socialist German Workers' Party. National socialism (the Nazi movement) made its first major appearance in 1923 when party members and Hitler attempted to overthrow the democratic Weimar Republic, which had replaced the German empire in 1919. The revolt was a failure, however, and Hitler was jailed. When Hitler emerged from prison in 1924, he resolved to gain power legally through the ballot box and, once successful, to discard democracy altogether.

The Struggle for Power National socialism made rapid gains after 1929 because it had broad appeal. Hitler attracted disillusioned people, many of whom blamed the young German democracy for Germany's misfortunes: a humiliating peace treaty—the Treaty of Versailles—that identified Germany as responsible for the Great War and assigned reparation payments to the Allies; the hyperinflation of the early 1920s that wiped out the savings of the middle class; and the suffering brought on by the Great Depression. Adolf Hitler promised an end to all those misfortunes by creating a new order that would lead to greatness for Germany. While anti-Semitism remained a fundamental part of Hitler's own beliefs, until he came to power in 1933 the **Nazi Party** downplayed this aspect of its ideology in its propaganda as it attempted to gain a wide base of support among the German population. Anti-Semitism and racist doctrines were consistently important to the party's base, however, which mainly consisted of members of the lower-middle classes: ruined shopkeepers, impoverished farmers, discharged white-collar workers, and disenchanted students.

As Germany slipped into the Great Depression, the government's inability to find solutions to unemployment and impoverishment radicalized the electorate and caused them to lose faith in the democratic system. Both communists, on the far left, and fascists, on the far right, increasingly vied for the allegiance of Germans who sought alternatives to what was perceived as the failures of democracy. Between 1930 and 1932 the Nazi Party became the largest party in parliament, and the reactionary and feeble president, Paul von Hindenburg (1847–1934), decided to offer Hitler the chancellorship. Hitler lost little time in transforming the dying republic into a single-party dictatorship. He promised a German **Reich**, or empire, that would endure for a thousand years.

Consolidation of Power Under the guise of a state of national emergency, the Nazis used all available means to impose their rule. They began by eliminating all working-class and liberal opposition. The Nazis suppressed the German communist and socialist parties and abrogated virtually all constitutional and civil rights. Subsequently, Hitler made the National Socialist Party the only legal party. Between 1933 and 1935 the regime replaced Germany's federal structure with a highly centralized state. The National Socialist state then guided the destruction of trade unions and the elimination of collective bargaining, including the prohibition of strikes and lockouts. The Nazis also purged the judiciary and the civil service, took control of all police forces, and removed enemies of the regime—both real and imagined—through imprisonment or murder.

The Racial State Once securely in power, the Nazi regime translated its racist ideology, especially the notions of racial superiority and racial purity, into practice. The leaders of the Third Reich pursued the creation of a race-based

A Nazi "racial expert" uses a caliper to measure the racial purity of a German, in this case as expressed in his facial features.
Henry Guttmann Collection/Hulton Archive/Getty Images

"Mother and Child" was the slogan on this poster, idealizing and encouraging motherhood. The background conveys the Nazi predilection for the wholesome country life, a dream that clashed with the urban reality of German society.
akg-images/Newscom

12 August—the birth date of Hitler's mother—women who bore many children received the Honor Cross of the German Mother in three classes: bronze for those with more than four children, silver for those with more than six, and gold for those with more than eight. By August 1939 three million women carried this prestigious award, which many Germans cynically called the "rabbit decoration." In the long term, however, these pronatalist measures failed, and the birthrate remained below replacement level.

The quantity of offspring was not the only concern of the new rulers, who were obsessed with "quality." Starting in 1933, the regime initiated a compulsory sterilization program for men and women the regime had identified as having "hereditarily determined" sicknesses, including schizophrenia, manic depression, hereditary blindness, hereditary deafness, and serious physical deformities. Between 1934 and 1939 more than thirty thousand men and women underwent compulsory sterilization. The mania for "racial health" culminated in a state-sponsored euthanasia ("mercy killing") program that was responsible for the murder of approximately two hundred thousand women, men, and children. Between 1939 and 1945 the Nazis systematically killed those people judged useless to society, especially the physically and mentally disabled.

Anti-Semitism was a key element in Nazi designs to achieve a new racial order. Immediately after coming to power in 1933, the Nazis initiated systematic measures to suppress Germany's Jewish population. A flood of discriminatory laws and directives designed to humiliate, impoverish, and segregate Jews from the rest of society followed. In 1935 the notorious **Nuremberg Laws** deprived German Jews of their citizenship and prohibited marriage and sexual intercourse between Jews and other Germans. The Nazi Party, in cooperation with government agencies, banks, and businesses, took steps to eliminate Jews from economic life and expropriate their wealth. Party authorities also supervised the liquidation of Jewish-owned businesses or argued for their purchase—at much less than their true value—by companies owned or operated by non-Jews.

The official goal of the Nazi regime, at least initially, was Jewish emigration. Throughout the 1930s thousands of Jews left Germany, depriving the nation of many of its leading intellectuals, scientists, and artists. The exodus gained urgency after what came to be known as "the night of broken glass" (**Kristallnacht**). During the night of 9–10 November 1938, the Nazis arranged for the destruction of thousands of Jewish stores, the burning of most synagogues, and the murder of more than one hundred Jews throughout Germany and Austria. This *pogrom* (a Yiddish term for devastation) was a signal that the position of Jews in Hitler's Reich was about to deteriorate dramatically. Indeed, approximately two hundred fifty thousand Jews had left Germany by 1938. Those staying behind, especially the poor and the elderly, would face a troubling and potentially deadly future.

national community by introducing measures designed to improve both the quantity and the "quality" of the German "race." Implicit in this racial remodeling was the conviction that there was no room for the "racially inferior" or for "biological outsiders." The racial program of the Nazis, implemented as early as 1933, was based on a diffuse mixture of racial anthropological, pseudo-scientific, and anti-Semitic theories that harkened back to the nineteenth century.

Alarmed by declining birthrates, the Nazis launched a campaign to increase births of "racially valuable" children. Through tax credits, special child allowances, and marriage loans, the authorities tried to encourage marriage and, they hoped, procreation among young people. At the same time, the regime outlawed abortions, restricted birth control devices, and made it difficult to obtain information about family planning. The Nazis also became enamored of pronatalist (to increase births) propaganda and set in motion a veritable cult of motherhood. Annually on

What's Left Out?

Although Nazi Germany is most closely associated with the application of **eugenics** policies (the advocacy of controlled selective breeding of human populations to improve the population's genetic composition), in the 1920s and 1930s the United States also enacted a series of eugenics laws. Like Nazi Germany, eugenics in the United States—as promoted by the American Eugenics Society (founded in 1922)—focused mostly on eliminating negative traits from the population. Also like Nazi Germany, proponents of eugenics in the United States located most of these negative traits in minority populations. In the United States, poor and non-white populations were targeted as "undesirables," as were the mentally ill. In an effort to ensure that the people in these groups did not reproduce, the eugenics movement in the United States focused on forced sterilization. Indiana was the first state to enact a forced sterilization law in 1907, but by 1935 thirty-one other states had followed suit. In total, more than sixty thousand American citizens were sterilized against their will as a result of such laws. In one landmark 1927 case that made it to the Supreme Court, Chief Justice Oliver Wendell Holmes justified the practice by writing, "It is better for all the world, if instead of waiting to execute degenerate offspring for crime, or to let them starve for their imbecility, society can prevent those who are manifestly unfit from continuing their kind. . . . " Hitler himself boasted of studying American eugenics laws when developing his own programs of forced sterilization and euthanasia in the 1930s. When thinking about the crimes against humanity committed by Nazi Germany, it is worth remembering that these were justified by racist thinking masquerading under the guise of "scientific" ideas such as eugenics, and that such racist thinking was also widely believed—and put into practice—in the United States during the interwar period.

Source: Adam Cohen. *Imbeciles: The Supreme Court, American Eugenics, and the Sterilization of Carrie Buck.* New York: Penguin Press, 2016.

CONCLUSION

In the decades after the Great War, European intellectuals questioned and challenged established traditions. While scientists and social thinkers conceived new theories that reshaped the ways humans encountered knowledge and perceptions, artists forged a contemporary aesthetic. In an age of global interdependence, the U.S. stock market crash of 1929 ushered in a period of prolonged economic contraction and social misery that engulfed much of the world. As most of the industrialized world reeled under the impact of the Great Depression, the leadership of the Soviet Union embarked on a state-sponsored program of rapid industrialization that despite causing widespread suffering transformed the Soviet Union into a major industrial and military power and offered an alternative to liberal democracy.

European fascist regimes also offered alternatives to liberal democracy. Italians under the leadership of Mussolini rebuilt their state through fascist policies and imperial expansion. In Germany the effects of the Great Depression paved the way for the establishment of the Nazi state, which was based on the principle of racial inequality. Although many different peoples suffered under the new regime, Jews were the principal victims of the Nazi racial state. Ultimately, Adolf Hitler's vision of a powerful and racially pure German state—crafted in an age of anxiety and uncertainty—helped lead to another world war less than two decades after the end of World War I.

STUDY TERMS

Adolf Hitler (549)
Albert Einstein (551)
Benito Mussolini (559)
Black Thursday (554)
chauvinism (559)
collectivization of agriculture (558)
economic nationalism (554)
eugenics (562)
fascism (558)
First Five-Year Plan (556)
Franklin Delano Roosevelt (555)
Great Depression (552)
Great Purge (558)

John Maynard Keynes (555)
Josef Stalin (556)
Kristallnacht (561)
national socialism (558)
Nazi Party (560)
New Deal (555)
New Economic Policy (NEP) (556)
Nuremberg Laws (561)
Reich (560)
Sigmund Freud (551)
Smoot-Hawley Tariff Act (554)
uncertainty principle (551)
war communism (556)
xenophobia (559)

FOR FURTHER READING

H. H. Arnason and Elizabeth C. Mansfield. *History of Modern Art.* 7th ed. 2012. A comprehensive source for students studying the art of the late nineteenth to the twenty-first centuries.

R. J. B. Bosworth. *Mussolini's Italy: Life under the Fascist Dictatorship, 1915-1945.* New edition. New York, 2011. One of the world's leading authorities on modern Italian history successfully explores the complexities of Il Duce and his times.

Peter J. Bowler and Iwan Rhys Morus. *Making Modern Science: A Historical Survey*. Chicago, 2005. Examines the relationship between science and modern thought more thoroughly than a typical survey.

Richard Evans. *The Third Reich in Power, 1933–1939*. New York, 2005. The second work in a three-volume series, starting with the Nazis' assumption of power and ending at the beginning of World War II in Europe.

Ian Kershaw. *Hitler: A Biography*. Reprint edition. New York, 2010. The definitive biography of Adolf Hitler, penned by one of the foremost historians of the Nazi era.

George Makari. *Revolution in Mind: The Creation of Psychoanalysis*. New York, 2008. A comprehensive history of the development of psychoanalysis and how it gained influence during the first half of the twentieth century.

John Moser. *Global Great Depression and the Coming of World War II*. London, 2015. Explores the ways various states responded to the crisis of the Great Depression and how these responses helped lead to World War II.

Norman Naimark. *Stalin's Genocides*. Princeton, N.J., 2010. A lucid analysis of Stalin's terror and brutal mass killings.

Robert Paxton. *The Anatomy of Fascism*. New York, 2004. Groundbreaking work focusing on what fascists did rather than on what they said.

Robert Service. *Stalin: A Biography*. Cambridge, Mass., 2005. The most complete portrait available of Lenin, from the author of an acclaimed biography of the Soviet ruler.

Chapter 31

Revolutionaries and Nationalists in the Colonial and Neocolonial World

ZOOMING IN ON ENCOUNTERS

Shanfei Becomes a New and Revolutionary Young Woman in China

Shanfei lived in a time of great political turmoil. The daughter of a wealthy landowning man of the Chinese gentry, she grew up with luxuries and opportunities unknown to most girls. Her father reluctantly allowed her to attend school, and her mother clothed her in beautiful silk dresses. Shanfei's formative years, however, were marked by the unsettling cultural and political changes that engulfed the globe in the wake of the Great War. The rise of nationalism and communism in China after the revolution of 1911 and the Russian revolution in 1917 transformed Shanfei into an active revolutionary dedicated to freeing her country as a member of the Chinese Communist Party.

With the exception of Shanfei's father, the members of her family in Hunan province took in the new spirit of the first decades of the twentieth century. Her brothers, for example, returned from school with ideas that challenged the subordinate position of women in China. Shanfei's mother listened quietly to her sons as they discussed new views, and then she used every means at her disposal to persuade her husband to educate their daughter. He eventually

In this cigarette advertisement from 1935, Chinese women are shown wearing modern styles and smoking cigarettes. They would have been recognized around the world as "modern girls," who increasingly challenged traditional gender expectations in their choices of clothing, behavior, and occupation.
swim ink 2 llc/Corbis Historical/Getty Images

agreed but still insisted that Shanfei receive an old-fashioned education and submit to foot binding and childhood betrothal.

When Shanfei was eleven years old, her father suddenly died. Her mother then ripped the bandages off Shanfei's feet and sent her to a modern school far from home. In the lively atmosphere of her school, Shanfei became an activist. At sixteen she incited a student strike against the school administration and later became famous as a leader in the student movement. In 1926 Shanfei abandoned her studies to join the Communist Youth, and she gave up the fiancé who had been arranged for her for a free marriage to the man she loved: a peasant leader in the communist movement.

CHAPTER OVERVIEW

The twists of fate that altered the destiny of Shanfei had parallels throughout the colonial and neocolonial world after 1914. Two major events, the Great War and the Great Depression, defined much of the turmoil of those years. As peoples around the world struggled to come to terms with the aftermath of war, an unprecedented economic contraction gripped the international community. The Great Depression complicated peoples' struggles for national sovereignty and financial solvency, especially in Asia, where Japan's militarist leaders sought to build national strength through imperial expansion. Latin American states worked to resist the economic domination of the United States, and people in sub-Saharan Africa suffered devastating economic consequences when European powers were no longer able to buy and use the raw materials produced in their colonies.

European empires still appeared to dominate global relations in the 1920s and 1930s, but the Great War had opened fissures within the European and U.S. spheres of influence. Nationalist and communist movements were already active in most colonial and neocolonial territories, and now they gathered strength. Movements to throw off foreign domination were especially strong in India and China, where various visions of national identity competed, but they also took on new momentum in sub-Saharan Africa and Latin America. And although we know that resistance to colonialism was not new, the trauma of the Great War and the Depression that followed helped convince more people than ever before to try to secure the self-determination they desired.

CHRONOLOGY	
1909–1955	Life of Carmen Miranda
1912	Taft establishes dollar diplomacy as U.S. foreign policy
1919	May Fourth Movement in China
1920	Non-Cooperation Movement in India
1921	Rivera returns to Mexico to paint
1928	Socialist Party of Peru is founded
1929	Beginning of Great Depression
1930	Civil Disobedience Movement in India
1930s–1940s	Vargas's *estado novo* in Brazil
1931	Japanese invasion of Manchuria
1933	Roosevelt begins practice of the Good Neighbor Policy
1934	Long March by Chinese Communists
1934	Sandino is murdered in Nicaragua
1935	Government of India Act
1938	Cárdenas nationalizes oil industry in Mexico

PATHS TO AUTONOMY IN SOUTH AND EAST ASIA

In the decades following the Great War, nationalism and revolutionary anticolonialism developed into powerful political forces in Asia, especially in India, China, and Japan. Achieving the twin ideals of independence from foreign powers and national unity became a goal of intellectuals, new political leaders, and ordinary people alike. In India the quest for national identity focused on gaining independence from British rule, a pursuit that was complicated by sectarian (religious) differences between Hindus and Muslims. The Chinese path to national identity was fraught with foreign and civil war as two principal groups—the Nationalist and Communist Parties—contended for power and sought a unified Chinese state.

Japanese militarists made China's quest for national unity more difficult, because Japan struggled to overcome its domestic problems and enhance its national identity through conquests that focused on China.

India's Quest for Home Rule

By the beginning of the twentieth century, Indian nationalism already threatened the British empire's hold on India. The construction of a vast railway network across India to facilitate the export of raw materials contributed to the idea of national unity by bringing the people of the subcontinent within easy reach of one another. Moreover, the British had trained an elite class of English-speaking, educated Indian administrators to help them rule. A European system of education familiarized the local middle-class intelligentsia with the political and social values of European society. However, those values—democracy, individual freedom, and equality—were the antithesis of empire, and Indians educated within this system realized their fundamental contradiction with the injustices of imperial rule.

Indian National Congress Of all the associations dedicated to the struggle against British rule, the most influential was the **Indian National Congress**, founded in 1885. This organization, which enlisted the support of many prominent Hindus and Muslims, at first sought collaboration with the British to bring self-rule to India, but after the Great War the congress pursued that goal in opposition to the British.

During the Great War, more than one million Indians—Hindus and Muslims—served in the armies of the British at the western front and in Mesopotamia. During the war, the Indian National Congress supported the British and suspended its campaigns for self-rule. Many Indians hoped their active support in the war effort would result in British willingness to allow greater Indian autonomy. But once the war was over the British dashed these hopes. In April 1919, British-led troops opened fire on a group of unarmed Indian demonstrators in the city of Amritsar, killing 379 and wounding 1,200 more. This massacre prompted Indian political leaders to call not just for home rule but for total independence.

Mohandas K. Gandhi Into this turmoil stepped **Mohandas Karamchand Gandhi** (1869–1948), a remarkable and charismatic leader. Gandhi grew up in a prosperous and pious Hindu household, married at thirteen, and left his hometown in 1888 to study law in London. In 1893 he went to South Africa, part of the British empire, to

Mohandas Karamchand Gandhi
(moh-huhn-DAHS kuhr-uhm-CHUND GAHN-dee)
satyagraha (suh-TYA-gruh-hah)

accept a position with an Indian firm, and there he quickly became involved in organizing the local Indian community against a system of racial segregation that made Indians second-class citizens. During the twenty-five years he spent in South Africa, Gandhi embraced a moral philosophy of ahimsa (tolerance and nonviolence) and developed the technique of passive resistance that he called *satyagraha* ("truth and firmness"). His belief in the virtue of simple living led him to renounce material possessions, dress in the garb of a simple Indian peasant, and become a vegetarian.

Gandhi returned to India in 1915, where he became active in Indian politics. He succeeded in transforming the Indian National Congress from an elitist institution into a

Leader of the Indian civil disobedience revolt Mohandas Gandhi marched to the shore at Dandi, a coastal village located on the Arabian Sea, to collect salt without paying taxes. This Salt March, also known as the Salt Satyagraha, sparked large-scale acts of civil protest against the British Raj (rule) and changed both global and British attitudes about Indian independence. On his left is Sarojini Naidu (1879–1949), a feminist activist who in 1925 was elected the first female president of the Indian National Congress.
Bettmann/Getty Images

mass organization. His unique mixture of spiritual intensity and political activism appealed to a broad section of the Indian population, and in the eyes of many he quickly achieved the stature of a political and spiritual leader, their Mahatma, or "great soul."

Under Gandhi's leadership the congress launched two mass movements: the Non-Cooperation Movement of 1920–1922 and the Civil Disobedience Movement of 1930. Convinced that economic self-sufficiency was a prerequisite for self-government, Gandhi called on the Indian people to boycott British goods and return to wearing rough, homespun cotton clothing. Gandhi furthermore admonished Indians to boycott institutions operated by the British in India, such as schools, offices, and courts. Despite Gandhi's cautions against the use of force, violence often accompanied the protest movement, both by Indians who were protesting and by the British who sought to stop them.

The India Act The Indian National Congress, led by Gandhi in the 1920s and 1930s, was only one of the movements seeking independence from Britain. Various revolutionary groups and the Indian Communist Party (founded in 1925) also agitated in favor of independence, sometimes using violence. In an attempt to maintain some control over India, then, the British offered a political compromise. After years of commissions, reports, and tense conversations with Indian political leaders (including Gandhi), in 1935 the British Parliament enacted the **Government of India Act**. The act established in India the institutions of a self-governing state, including autonomous legislative bodies in the provinces of British India and a bicameral (two-chambered) national legislature. On the urging of Gandhi, the majority of Indians approved the measure, which went into effect in 1937.

The Government of India Act proved unworkable, however, because India's six hundred nominally sovereign princes refused to cooperate and because Muslims feared that Hindus would dominate the national legislature. These latter fears were exacerbated by the Great Depression, because Muslims constituted the majority of indebted tenant farmers in India, and they found themselves increasingly unable to pay rents and debts during the economic crisis. And because most of their landlords were Hindus, Muslims increasingly perceived their experiences during the depression as stemming from economic exploitation by Hindus. They were encouraged in these perceptions by **Muhammad Ali Jinnah** (1876–1948), an eloquent and brilliant lawyer who headed the Muslim League. Jinnah warned that a unified India represented nothing less than a threat to the Muslim faith and its Indian community. Jinnah proposed that British India be divided into two independent states: India, for India's Hindus, and Pakistan, for India's Muslims. Thus, in spite of hundreds of years of Hindus and Muslims living peace-

fully together, these increasing sectarian tensions in the interwar period came to dominate the independence process on the Indian subcontinent.

China's Campaigns to End Foreign Domination

During the first half of the twentieth century China was in a state of almost continual revolutionary upheaval. The conflict's origins dated from the nineteenth century, when the Chinese empire came under relentless pressure from imperialist powers that rushed in to fill the vacuum created by China's internal political disintegration. As revolutionary and nationalist uprisings gained widespread support, a revolution in 1911 forced the **Xuantong** emperor (also known as Puyi), to abdicate at the age of five. The Qing empire fell with relative ease. Dr. **Sun Yatsen** (1866–1925), a leading opponent of the old regime, proclaimed a Chinese republic in Nanjing in 1912 and briefly assumed the office of president.

The Republic The revolution of 1911 did not establish a stable government. Sun Yatsen controlled only a portion of China around Nanjing, whereas many others in different parts of the country had their own claim to leadership. As a result, the republic soon plunged into a state of political anarchy and economic disintegration marked by the rule of disaffected generals from the old imperial Chinese army and their troops who established themselves as provincial or regional rulers. Yet the rule of the generals was just one symbol of the disintegration of the political order. The fragmented relationship between Chinese authority and foreign powers was another. Since the nineteenth century, a collection of treaties, known in China as the unequal treaties, had guided Chinese relations with foreign countries. Those treaties had established a network of foreign control over the Chinese economy and permitted foreigners to intervene in Chinese society to protect their own interests. Although foreigners did not control every aspect of the state, they greatly impaired its sovereignty.

Chinese Nationalism After the Great War, nationalist sentiment developed rapidly in China. Youths and intellectuals, who in the previous decade had looked to Europe and the United States for models and ideals for the reform of China, eagerly anticipated the results of the 1919 Peace Conference in Paris. They expected the U.S. government to support the termination of the treaty system and the restoration of full Chinese sovereignty. Instead, the peacemakers approved increasing Japanese interference in China. That decision gave rise to the

Muhammad Ali Jinnah (moo-HAHM-ahd ah-lee JIN-uh)
Xuantong (shoo-ahn-tohng)

Adversaries in the struggle for power in China: at left, Jiang Jieshi (Chiang Kai-shek) (1887–1975); at right, Mao Zedong (1893–1976).
Bettmann/Getty Images

May Fourth Movement. Spearheaded by students and intellectuals in China's urban areas, the movement galvanized the country against foreign, especially Japanese, interference. In speeches, newspapers, and novels, the movement's leaders pledged themselves to rid China of imperialism and reestablish national unity.

Disillusioned by the cynical self-interest of the United States and the European powers, some Chinese became interested in Marxism and the social and economic experiments under way in the Soviet Union. The anti-imperialist rhetoric of the Soviet leadership inspired the founding of the **Chinese Communist Party (CCP)** in Shanghai in 1921. Among its early members was **Mao Zedong** (1893–1976), a former teacher and librarian who viewed a Marxist-inspired social revolution as the cure for China's problems.

Sun Yatsen Even before the founding of the Chinese Communist Party, Sun Yatsen—who had helped bring down the Qing government—sought to organize Chinese people into a party based on nationalism and modernization. In 1912 he founded the *Guomindang* (Nationalist People's Party), which was based on Sun's ideology, which called for elimination of special privileges for foreigners, national reunification, economic development, and a democratic republican government based on universal suffrage. Although Sun was not a communist, he recognized the utility of forming an alliance with the powerful Soviet Union and the Chinese Communist Party in order to achieve his goals. In 1923 the Soviet Union brokered a deal in which the *Guomindang* and the Chinese Communist Party agreed to a partnership (now known as the First United Front), in which both would use Soviet training and aid to work toward the common goal of uniting China and driving out foreign imperialists. This part-

nership was deeply alarming to the foreign powers active in China, because none of them wanted a strong Chinese state to limit their profits or privileges.

Civil War When Sun Yatsen died in 1925, leadership of the *Guomindang* fell to **Jiang Jieshi** (Chiang Kai-shek, 1887–1975), a young general who had been trained in Japan and the Soviet Union and who deeply distrusted the Chinese communists he was supposed to be working with. In 1926 Jiang maintained the partnership of the United Front in order to wage a political and military offensive, known as the Northern Expedition, to unify the nation and bring China under *Guomindang* rule. But once the offensive had proven successful, Jiang's forces brutally and unexpectedly turned against his former communist allies. On 12 April 1927 Jiang unleashed armed men on communists in the city of Shanghai, murdering thousands and arresting many more over the two weeks that followed. In the following year, nationalist forces occupied Beijing, set up a central government in Nanjing, and declared the *Guomindang* the official government of a unified and sovereign Chinese state. Meanwhile, the badly mauled communists retreated to a remote area of southeastern China, where they tried to reconstitute and reorganize their forces.

The nationalist government had to deal with many concerns, but Chinese leaders evaded one major global crisis—the Great Depression. Foreign trade in such items as tea and silk, which did decline, made up only a small part of China's economy, which was otherwise dominated by its large domestic markets. Although the new government in China generally avoided having to contend with global economic devastation, it did have to confront three major problems during the 1930s. First, the nationalists actually controlled only part of China, leaving the remainder of the country in the hands of various generals. Second, in the early 1930s communist activity in China again became a major threat. Third, the *Guomindang* faced increasing

---

Guomindang (GWOH-mihn-dahng)
Jiang Jieshi (jyahng jeh-she)

MAP 31.1 The struggle for control in China, 1927–1936

Compare the continental territories controlled by Japan and the *Guomindang* in 1934.

How would the size of Japan's territories in Manchuria and Korea influence Chinese abilities to challenge Japanese expansion?

Japanese aggression. In dealing with those problems, Jiang Jieshi gave priority to eliminating the CCP. No longer able to ward off the relentless attacks of nationalist forces, the communists took flight in October 1934 to avoid annihilation, and some eighty-five thousand troops and auxiliary personnel of the Red Army began the legendary **Long March**, an epic journey of 10,000 kilometers (6,215 miles).

After traveling across difficult terrain and fighting for survival against hunger, disease, and *Guomindang* forces, those marchers who had not died of hardship arrived in a remote area of Shaanxi province in northwestern China in October 1935 and established headquarters at Yan'an. During the Long March, Mao Zedong emerged as the leader and the principal theoretician of the Chinese communist movement. He came up with a Chinese form of Marxist-Leninism, or Maoism, an ideology grounded in the conviction that peasants rather than urban proletarians were the foundation for a successful revolution.

Imperial and Imperialist Japan

After the Great War, Japan achieved great power status and appeared to accept the international status quo that the major powers fashioned in the aftermath of war. After joining the League of Nations as one of the "big five" powers, the Japanese government entered into a series of international agreements that sought to improve relations among countries with conflicting interests in Asia and the Pacific. As a signatory to several Washington Conference treaties in 1922, Japan agreed to limit naval development, pledged to evacuate Shandong province in China, and guaranteed China's territorial integrity. In 1928 the Japanese government signed the Kellogg-Briand Pact, which renounced war as an instrument of national policy.

During the Great War, Japanese businesses profited from selling munitions and other goods to the Allies throughout the war, and they gained a bigger foothold in Asia as the war led Europe's trading nations to neglect Asian markets. But rapid inflation and labor unrest set in by 1918, followed by a series of recessions that culminated in a giant economic slump caused by the Great Depression. Like the economies of other industrial nations tied into the global economy, Japan's economy experienced plummeting industrial production, huge job layoffs, declining trade, and financial chaos. Economic contraction set the stage for social unrest and radical politics.

Public demands for sweeping reforms, including a broadening of the franchise, protection for labor unions, and welfare legislation, figured prominently in Japanese domestic politics throughout the 1920s. Yet conservatives blocked any major reforms beyond the suffrage law of 1925, which established universal male suffrage. By the early 1930s an increasingly frustrated public blamed its government for the nation's continuing economic problems. Right-wing political groups called for an end to party rule, and xenophobic nationalists dedicated themselves to the preservation of a unique Japanese culture and the eradication of Western influences. A campaign of assassinations, targeting political and business leaders, culminated in the murder of Prime Minister **Inukai Tsuyoshi** (1855–1932).

Politicians who supported Japan's role in the international industrial-capitalist system faced increasing opposition from those who were inclined toward a militarist vision of a self-sufficient Japan that would dominate east Asia. Meanwhile, China's unification threatened Japan's economic interests in Manchuria. Manchuria had historically been Chinese territory, but by the twentieth century

Inukai Tsuyoshi (ee-NO-kigh ts-yo-she)

it had become a sphere of influence where Japan maintained the Manchurian Railroad (built in 1906), retained transit rights, and stationed troops.

The Mukden Incident On the night of 18 September 1931, Japanese troops used explosives to blow up a few feet of rail on the Japanese-built South Manchuria Railway north of Mukden. They accused the Chinese of attacking their railroad. This **Mukden incident** became the pretext for war. Although the civilian government in Japan tried to halt this military incursion, by 1932 Japanese troops controlled all of Manchuria. The Japanese established a puppet state called Manchukuo, but in reality Japan had absorbed Manchuria into its empire. In response to the Manchurian invasion, the *Guomindang* (Nationalist Party) leader Jiang Jieshi appealed to the League of Nations to halt Japanese aggression. After a lengthy investigation, the league called for the withdrawal of Japanese forces and the restoration of Chinese sovereignty. The Japanese responded by leaving the league, and nothing was done to stop the aggression. This reaction set the pattern for future responses to the actions of expansionist nations such as Japan. Embarking on conquests in east Asia, Japanese militarists found a sure means of promoting a new militant Japanese national identity. They also helped provoke a new global war.

SUB-SAHARAN AFRICA UNDER COLONIAL DOMINATION

The Great War and the Great Depression similarly complicated quests for national independence and unity in sub-Saharan Africa. The colonial ties that bound African colonies to European powers had ensured that Africans became participants in the Great War, willing or not. As in India, Africans expected that their participation in the Great War on behalf of the various colonial powers would lead to greater control over their governments and economies.

Rather than retreating, colonialism consolidated its hold on the African continent, including sub-Saharan Africa. In the decades following the Paris Peace Conference, the European powers focused on the economic exploitation of their colonies. The imposition of a rapacious form of capitalism caused African economies to become enmeshed in the global economy. The persistence of colonialism led to the development of African anticolonial movements and the establishment of nationalist parties. During the decades following the Great War, African intellectuals searched for new national identities and looked forward to independence from colonial rule.

The Colonial Economy

The decades following the Great War witnessed a thorough transformation of economic life in sub-Saharan

Africa. Colonial powers pursued two key economic objectives: they wanted to make sure that colonized people paid for the institutions—bureaucracies, the judiciary, the police, and military forces—that kept them in subjugation; and they developed export-oriented economies characterized by the exchange of unprocessed raw materials or minimally processed cash crops for manufactured goods from abroad. In pursuit of those goals, colonial authorities imposed economic structures that altered, subordinated, or destroyed preexisting economies in sub-Saharan Africa and then tightly integrated them into the European-dominated global economy. The Great Depression of the 1930s exposed the vulnerability of dependent colonial economies. As international markets for primary products shrank under the impact of the depression, European companies that controlled the export of African products suffered accordingly. Trade volume often fell by half, and commodity prices dropped even more sharply.

Infrastructure The economic integration of sub-Saharan Africa required investment in infrastructure in the form of port facilities, roads, railways, and telegraph wires. Transportation and communication networks not only facilitated conquest and rule but also linked the agricultural or mineral wealth of a colony to the outside world. Although Europeans later claimed that they had "given" sub-Saharan Africa its first modern infrastructure, Europeans and their businesses were its main beneficiaries. Indeed, although Africans paid for the infrastructure with their labor and taxes, Europeans did not consider the needs of local African economies.

Farming and Mining Colonial taxation was an important tool designed to drive Africans into the labor market. To earn the money to pay the taxes colonial powers levied on land, houses, livestock, and people themselves, African farmers had to become cash crop farmers or seek wage labor on plantations and in mines. Cash crop farming embraced the largest proportion of sub-Saharan Africans. In most colonies, farmers who had their own land specialized in one or two crops, generally destined for export to the country governing them. Farmers in

Two workers in a diamond mine in northern Rhodesia. Although this photograph was taken in the 1950s, it depicts the difficult conditions involved in the mining industries of sub-Saharan Africa in the interwar period.
INTERFOTO/Alamy Stock Photo

sub-Saharan Africa grew a variety of cash crops for the international marketplace, among them peanuts from Senegal and northern Nigeria, cotton from Uganda, cocoa from the Gold Coast, rubber from the Congo, and palm oil from the Ivory Coast and the Niger delta. In areas with extensive white settlement, such as in Kenya, Rhodesia, and South Africa, settlers expropriated African lands and grew cash crops—using African labor—themselves. In British-controlled Kenya, for example, four thousand white farmers seized the Kikuyu highlands, which comprised seven million acres of the colony's richest land. In South Africa, the government reserved 88 percent of all land for whites, who made up just 20 percent of the total population.

Colonial mining enterprises relying on African labor loomed large in parts of central and southern Africa. These enterprises usually involved the extraction of mineral wealth such as copper, gold, and diamonds, and they required vast numbers of laborers from rural areas who were paid minimal wages. These recruitment practices set in motion a vast pattern of labor migration that persisted throughout the twentieth century. The absence of male labor and the payment of minimal wages had the effect of impoverishing the rural areas.

Labor Practices Where taxation failed to create a malleable native labor force, colonial officials resorted to outright forced labor. Indeed, projects such as the construction of railways and roads commonly depended on forced labor regimes. When the French undertook construction of the Congo-Ocean railway from Brazzaville to the port at Point-Noir, for example, they rounded up some ten thousand workers annually. Labor practices were so brutal that within a few years between fifteen and twenty thousand African laborers had perished from starvation, disease, and maltreatment. A white settler in Kenya candidly expressed the view held by many colonial administrators: "We have stolen his land. Now we must steal his limbs. Compulsory labor is the corollary to our occupation of the country."

African Nationalism

In the decades following the Great War, many Africans were disappointed that their contributions to the war went unrewarded. In place of anticipated social reforms or some degree of greater political participation came an extension and consolidation of the colonial system. This reality, coupled with an awareness of the demands of anticolonial movements in other parts of the world, led Africans in sub-Saharan colonies to develop their own anticolonial movements. An emerging class of urban intellectuals, frequently educated in Europe, became especially involved in the formation of ideologies that sought freedom from colonialism and promoted new national identities.

What's Left Out?

As we have seen in this chapter, the interwar period was characterized by numerous anticolonial movements. It is impossible to capture all of these anticolonial movements in one chapter, but it is even more difficult to capture the ways in which the people involved in these movements were not only aware of each other but often knew each other personally. One of the primary reasons for this was that many anticolonial activists in this period spent time living in European cities such as Paris, Berlin, and London, often while attending university. People from all over the colonized world lived in these cities, as did people from places such as Latin America and China. As a result, people from diverse areas came into contact with one another through their participation in student groups, social activities, and political movements. When they interacted, they learned about colonial and neocolonial conditions in other places, helping them see imperialism as a global problem rather than as a problem specific to a particular imperial power. One organization designed for just this purpose was the League Against Imperialism, which held its first major conference in Brussels, Belgium, in 1927. In February of that year, 174 delegates from the colonial and neocolonial world (including India's Jawaharlal Nehru, Indonesia's Mohammad Hatta, Senegal's Lamine Senghor, and Algeria's Messali Hadj) gathered together with leftist Europeans to make resolutions calling for an end to imperialism. Through connections like these, anticolonial activists were inspired by each other, gained information about events happening elsewhere, and learned new techniques to fight against colonialism. When they returned home, they took this knowledge with them and used it in their own anticolonial struggles. It was thus no accident that so many anticolonial movements flourished at roughly the same time in the interwar period.

Source: Michael Goebel. *Anti-Imperial Metropolis: Interwar Paris and the Seeds of Third World Nationalism.* Cambridge, Mass.: Cambridge University Press, 2015.

Sub-Saharan Africa's New Elite Colonialism prompted the emergence of a new African social class, sometimes called the "new elite." This elite derived its status and place in society from employment and education. The upper echelons of this elite class included high-ranking civil servants, physicians, lawyers, and writers, most of whom had studied abroad either in western Europe or in the United States. For example, **Jomo Kenyatta** (1895–1978) spent almost fifteen years in Europe, during which time he attended various schools and universities, including the London School of Economics. Later, Kenyatta led Kenya to independence from the British. Other members of the new elite included teachers, clerks, and interpreters who had obtained a European-derived primary or secondary education. These were the Africans who spoke European languages and outwardly adopted European cultural norms such as wearing European-style clothes or adopting European names. It was within the ranks of this new elite that anticolonial mass movements emerged.

Alternatives to the Nation Because colonialism had introduced Africans to European ideas and ideologies, African nationalists frequently embraced the European concept of the nation as a means of forging unity—as well as colonial resistance—among disparate African groups. But some anticolonial sub-Saharan Africans were not convinced that independent nations—especially as constituted within borders drawn by European colonizers—were what anticolonial movements should be striving for. Instead, some looked to the precolonial past for inspiration. There they found identities based on ethnicity, religion, and languages, and they believed that any future state must reconstitute institutions crucial to those identities. Race had provided colonial powers with one rationale for conquest and exploitation; hence it was not surprising that some anticolonial activists used the concept of an African race as an important concept in an important strain of African anticolonialism, which originated in the western hemisphere among the descendants of enslaved people. Pan-Africanists thought of Africans and African-descended peoples from around the world as members of a single race and promoted the unification of all people of African descent into a single African state. Many pan-Africanists came from North America and the Caribbean, though the idea also attracted followers in Africa. Some of the most well-known representatives of this **pan-Africanism** were the Black U.S. activist and intellectual **W.E.B. DuBois** (1868–1963) and the Jamaican nationalist leader **Marcus Garvey** (1887–1940), who preached Black pride and called on Blacks living in the African diaspora to go "Back to Africa." However, the need to oppose colonial powers from within existing colonial borders made it difficult to enact proposed alternatives that moved across them.

Portrait of the Jamaican pan-Africanist Marcus Garvey (1887–1940), taken in 1924.
Library of Congress, Prints and Photographs Division [LC-USZ61-1854]

LATIN AMERICAN STRUGGLES WITH NEOCOLONIALISM

Having gained their independence in the nineteenth century, most sovereign nations in Latin America thereafter struggled to achieve political and economic stability in the midst of interference from foreign powers. The era of the Great War and the Great Depression proved crucial to solidifying and exposing the neocolonial structures that dominated affairs in Latin America. Generally seen as an indirect and more subtle form of imperial control, neocolonialism usually took shape as foreign economic domination but did not exclude more typically imperial actions such as military intervention and political interference. In Central and South America, as well as in Mexico and the Caribbean, this imperial influence came not from former colonial rulers in Spain and Portugal but, rather, from wealthy, industrial-capitalist powerhouses such as Great Britain and, especially, the United States. Neocolonialism impinged on the independent political

SOURCES FROM THE PAST

Africa for Africans

Marcus Garvey (1887–1940) is best remembered as a pivotal figure in the pan-African movement. He inspired many African leaders. A powerful orator, Garvey preached the greatness of the African heritage and called on European colonial powers to leave Africa. Convinced that Blacks in the diaspora could never secure their rights as minorities, Garvey rejected the idea of integration and instead championed a "Back to Africa" movement. According to Garvey, a Jamaican who also lived for a time in the United States, only in Africa would it be possible to establish an autonomous Black state that featured its own, unique culture. In the following excerpt, Garvey addressed the Second International Convention of Negroes in New York City in 1921.

George Washington was not God Almighty. He was a man like any Negro in this building, and if he and his associates were able to make a free America, we too can make a free Africa. Hampden, Gladstone, Pitt and Disraeli were not the representatives of God in the person of Jesus Christ. They were but men, but in their time they worked for the expansion of the British Empire, and today they boast of a British Empire upon which "the sun never sets." As Pitt and Gladstone were able to work for the expansion of the British Empire, so you and I can work for the expansion of a great African Empire. Voltaire and Mirabeau were not Jesus Christs, they were but men like ourselves. They worked and overturned the French Monarchy. They worked for the Democracy which France now enjoys, and if they were able to do that, we are able to work for a democracy in Africa. Lenin and Trotsky were not Jesus Christs, but they were able to overthrow the despotism of Russia, and today they have given to the world a Social Republic, the first of its kind. If Lenin and Trotsky were able to do that for Russia, you and I can do that for Africa. Therefore, let no man, let no power on earth, turn you from this sacred cause of liberty. I prefer to die at this moment rather than not to work for the freedom of Africa. If liberty is good for certain sets of humanity it is good for all. Black men, Colored men, Negroes have as much right to be free as any other race that God Almighty ever created, and we desire freedom that is unfettered, freedom that is unlimited, freedom that will give us a chance and opportunity to rise to the fullest of our ambition and that we cannot get in countries where other men rule and dominate.

> Why is it important to Garvey to point out that the various leaders listed here were not gods?

We have reached the time when every minute, every second must count for something done, something achieved in the cause of Africa. . . . It falls to our lot to tear off the shackles that bind Mother Africa. Can you do it? You did it in the Revolutionary War. You did it in the Civil War; You did it at the Battles of the Marne and Verdun; You did it in Mesopotamia. You can do it marching up the battle heights of Africa. Let the world know that 400,000,000 Negroes are prepared to die or live as free men. Despise us as much as you care. Ignore us as much as you care. We are coming 400,000,000 strong. We are coming with our woes behind us, with the memory of suffering behind us—woes and suffering of three hundred years—they shall be our inspiration. My bulwark of strength in the conflict of freedom in Africa, will be the three hundred years of persecution and hardship left behind in this Western Hemisphere.

> What is the three hundred years of suffering to which Garvey refers here?

For Further Reflection

■ In his speech, how does Marcus Garvey convey the significance of Africa for both Africans and those involved in the Black diaspora?

Source: Marcus Garvey. *The Philosphy and Opinions of Macus Garvey*, Amy Jacques Garvey. New Preface by Tony Martin. Dover, Mass.: The Majority Press Inc., 1986, pp. 95–96.

and economic development of Latin American states, but it did not prevent nationalist leaders from devising strategies to combat it.

The Impact of the Great War and the Great Depression

Reorientation of Political and Nationalist Ideals

The Great War and the Russian revolution, along with the ongoing Mexican revolution, spread radical ideas and the promise of new political possibilities throughout Latin America. The disparate ideals emerging from this time of political ferment found receptive audiences in Latin America before but especially during the global economic crisis of the Great Depression. Marxism, Vladimir Lenin's theories on capitalism and imperialism, and a growing concern for the impoverished indigenous population as well as exploited peasants and workers in Latin American societies informed the outlooks of many intellectuals and artists who sought a path to greater social and political equality. Although those revolutionary doctrines did not achieve full-scale adoption by Latin American states during the interwar era, their increasing popularity and perceived viability as political options suggested the alternatives open to nations in the future.

University Protests The Great War had propelled the United States into a position of world economic leadership. The peoples of Latin America came to experience this increased U.S. economic power most intensely, and it was no coincidence that the capitalism embraced by the United States came under attack. Some of the most radical responses to U.S. economic domination came from Latin American universities, where students in the 1920s began to demand reforms in their own countries. Universities thereafter became training grounds for future political leaders, including the Cuban **Fidel Castro** (1926-2016), and the ideas explored within an academic setting—from Marxism to anti-imperialism—exerted great influence on those budding politicians.

Diego Rivera and Radical Artistic Visions The ideological transformations apparent in Latin America became stunningly and publicly visible in the murals painted by famed Mexican artist **Diego Rivera** (1886-1957). After studying art in Mexico in his youth, Rivera went to study in Europe in 1907 and did not return to Mexico until 1921. Influenced by the art of both Renaissance artists and cubists, Rivera also experienced the turmoil and shifting political sensibilities taking place in Europe during the Great War and its aftermath. He blended his artistic and political visions in vast murals that he intended for viewing and appreciation by the masses. He believed that art should be on display for working people. Along with other Mexican muralists, Rivera shaped the politicized art of Mexico for decades.

Diego Rivera celebrated indigenous Mexican art and pre-Columbian folk traditions, and he incorporated radical political ideas into his approach to mural painting. In the late 1920s and 1930s the government commissioned him to create large frescoes for public buildings, and Rivera transcribed the history of Mexico, replete with its social ills, on the walls of such structures as the National Palace and the Ministry of Education in Mexico City. In 1933 Rivera received a request to paint murals for the RCA building in Rockefeller Center in New York City. He included in one panel a portrait of Vladimir Lenin, which caused John D. Rockefeller himself to order the mural to be plastered over and replaced. In response, Rivera undertook a series of twenty-one paintings on U.S. history titled *Portrait of America.* He labeled one of the most pointed and critical paintings *Imperialism,* which visualized and advertised the economic interference and political repressiveness engendered by U.S. neocolonialism in Latin America.

The Evolution of Economic Imperialism

U.S. Economic Domination Latin American states were no strangers to foreign economic domination in the nineteenth and early twentieth centuries. Their export-oriented economies had long been tied to global finances and subject to controls imposed by foreign investors, largely those from Great Britain, the United States, France, and Germany. The major evolution in economic neo-colonialism during this period concerned the growing predominance of the United States in the economic affairs of Latin American nations. The Great War sealed this transition to U.S. supremacy, and U.S. investments in Latin America soared in the 1920s. Between 1924 and 1929, U.S. banks and businesses more than doubled their financial interests in Latin America as investments grew from $1.5 billion to $3.5 billion. Much of that money went toward the takeover of businesses extracting vital minerals, such as copper-mining firms in Chile and oil-drilling concerns in Venezuela.

Dollar Diplomacy That U.S. neocolonialism was meant to be largely economic became evident in the policies of President William Howard Taft (1857-1931). In his final address to Congress in 1912, Taft argued that the United States should substitute "dollars for bullets" in its foreign policy. He wanted businesses to develop foreign markets through peaceful commerce and believed that expensive military intervention should be avoided as much as possible. This new vision of U.S. expansion abroad, dubbed **dollar diplomacy** by critics, encapsulated the gist of what those in Latin America perceived as "Yankee imperialism."

The cover of American humor and satire magazine *Puck*, from 6 April 1901, featured Columbia wearing a warship bearing the words "World Power" as her Easter bonnet. Columbia is the female personification of the United States of America.

Library of Congress, Prints and Photographs Division [LC-DIG-ppmsca-25515]

Economic Depression and Experimentation The economic crisis of the Great Depression demonstrated the extent to which Latin America had become integrated into the world economy. Indeed, the Great Depression halted fifty years of economic growth in Latin America and illustrated the region's susceptibility to global economic crises. The increasing U.S. capital investments for budding industries and other financial concerns during the 1920s could not be maintained during this catastrophic economic downturn. Further, most Latin American states, because they exported agricultural products or raw materials, suffered from plummeting prices. The prices of sugar from the Caribbean, coffee from Brazil and Colombia, tin from Bolivia, nitrates from Chile, and

Getúlio Dornelles Vargas (zhi-TOO-lyoo door-NEH-lis VAHR-guhs)

many other products fell sharply after 1929, and throughout Latin America unemployment rates increased rapidly. The drastic decline in the price of the region's exports and the drying up of foreign capital prompted Latin American governments to raise tariffs on foreign products and impose various other restrictions on foreign trade.

Although the weaknesses of export-oriented economies and industrial development financed by foreigners became evident during the Great Depression, the international crisis also allowed Latin American nations to take alternative paths to economic development. Economic policy stressing internal economic development was most visible in Brazil, where dictator-president (1930–1945, 1950–1954) **Getúlio Dornelles Vargas** (1883–1954) turned his nation into an *estado novo* ("new state"). Ruling with the backing of the military but without the support of the landowning elite, during the 1930s and 1940s Vargas and his government embarked on a program of industrialization that created new enterprises. Key among them was the iron and steel industry. The Vargas regime also implemented protectionist policies that shielded domestic production from foreign competition, which pleased both industrialists and urban workers. Social welfare initiatives accompanied industrial development, protecting workers with health and safety regulations, minimum wages, limits on working hours, unemployment compensation, and retirement benefits. The Great Depression contributed in many ways to the evolution of both economic neocolonialism and economic experimentation within Latin American states.

Conflicts with a "Good Neighbor"

The Good Neighbor Policy The pressures of the Great Depression and the instability of global politics led to a reassessment of U.S. foreign policy in Latin America during the late 1920s and 1930s. U.S. leaders realized the costliness and ineffectiveness of their previous direct interventions in Latin America, especially when committing U.S. Marines as peacekeeping forces. To extricate U.S. military forces and rely more fully on dollar diplomacy, policymakers instituted innovations that nonetheless called into question any true change of heart among U.S. neocolonialists. They approved "sweetheart treaties" that guaranteed U.S. financial control in the Caribbean economies of Haiti and the Dominican Republic, for example, and the U.S. Marines provided training for indigenous police forces to keep the peace and maintain law and order. This revamped U.S. approach to relations with Latin America became known as the **Good Neighbor Policy**, and it was most closely associated with the administration of Franklin D. Roosevelt (1882–1945).

Mexico under Cardenas's Rule Under Roosevelt, the Good Neighbor Policy evolved into a more conciliatory U.S. approach to Latin American relations. The interventionist corollary to the Monroe Doctrine enunciated previously by President Theodore Roosevelt (1859–1919) was formally renounced in December 1933, when Secretary of State Cordell Hull attended the Seventh International Conference of American States in Montevideo, Uruguay. Hull signed the Convention on the Rights and Duties of States, which held that "no state has the right to intervene in the internal or external affairs of another." That proposition faced a severe challenge in March 1938 when Mexican president **Lázaro Cárdenas** (1895–1970) nationalized the oil industry, much of which was controlled by foreign investors from the United States and Great Britain.

Given the history of tempestuous relations between the United States and Mexico, including multiple U.S. military incursions into Mexico during the revolution, there was little chance for a peaceful resolution to this provocative move by Cárdenas. Cárdenas took this step after Mexican oil workers went on strike in protest of their difficult working conditions and low pay. The Mexican government intervened and drew up a new labor agreement between Mexican workers and the foreign oil companies, but the foreign oil companies refused to abide by it. Cárdenas took this as a direct challenge to Mexican sovereignty and thus resolved to nationalize the oil industry. Despite calls for a strong U.S. and British response, Roosevelt and his administration officials called for a cool, calm response and negotiations to end the conflict. This plan prevailed, and the foreign oil companies ultimately had to accept only $24 million in compensation rather than the $260 million they initially demanded. The nationalization of Mexican oil proved popular with Mexican people, not least because it had demonstrated Mexico's ability to stand up to the exploitative capitalist economies of the United States and western Europe.

Lázaro Cárdenas (LAH-sah-roh CAR-deh-nahs)

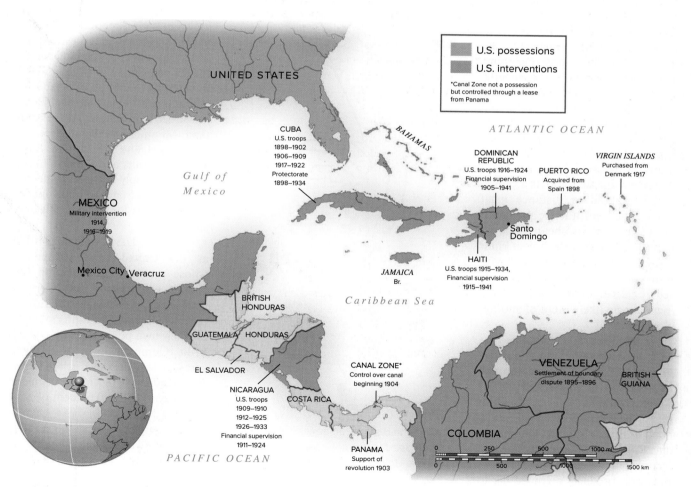

MAP 31.2   The United States in Latin America, 1895–1941

Note the number of Latin American states where U.S. troops intervened in local politics.

On what basis did U.S. policymakers justify those interventions?

Why It Matters ▶▶▶▶▶▶▷

The Destructive Potential of Industrial Technologies

Can nationalism affect the environment? Events in the mid-twentieth century demonstrated that it can. One of the features of many of the nationalist movements discussed in this chapter was an emphasis on economic development through industrialization. The reasons were clear: nationalists around the world objected strongly to economic exploitation by the industrial powers of Europe, Japan, and the United States. To fight back against such exploitation, nationalists wanted to produce their own industrial goods and exploit their own natural resources by becoming industrial powers themselves. But the model of industrialization established by the powers that had already industrialized had paid little attention to the environmental consequences of resource extraction or industrial pollution. Instead, they depleted resources without a plan to sustain them, they eroded the soils, and they polluted the air, water, and soil. As increasing numbers of states tried to gain control of their own sovereignty by industrializing like the Western powers and Japan, they also perpetuated these destructive environmental patterns. The result, as we know, has had planetary consequences right up to the present.

Neighborly Cultural Exchanges? Although the nationalization crisis in Mexico ended in a fashion that suggested the strength of the Good Neighbor Policy, a good deal of the impetus for that policy came from economic and political concerns associated with the Great Depression and the deterioration of international relations in the 1930s. The United States wanted to cultivate Latin American markets for its exports, and it wanted to distance itself from the militarist behavior of Asian and European imperial powers. The U.S. government knew it needed to improve relations with states in Latin America, if only to secure those nations' support in the increasingly likely event of another global war.

Hollywood added to this process by promoting more positive images of Latin America through its adoption of singer and dancer **Carmen Miranda** (1909–1955). Born in Portugal but raised from childhood in Brazil, Miranda found fame on a Rio de Janeiro radio station and recorded hundreds of hit songs. A Broadway producer recruited her to the United States, where she then became a popular sensation. Carmen Miranda appeared as an exotic Latin American woman, usually clothed in

Chiquita Banana, an advertising icon used to promote a good image of the United Fruit Company, was a replica in fruit of the singing and acting sensation Carmen Miranda.
Fort Worth Star-Telegram/Tribune News Service/Getty Images

sexy, colorful costumes that featured headdresses adorned with the fruits grown in Latin America—such as bananas. She softened representations of Latin Americans for audiences in the United States, providing a less threatening counterpoint to laboring migrants or women guerrilla fighters in Mexico's revolution. At the same time, Miranda's deliberately sexualized image and her use of Latin American fruits and symbols in her costumes simply encouraged people in the United States to trade one set of stereotypes for a more palatable alternative.

Indeed, U.S. companies such as the **United Fruit Company**—whose profits were based on the brutal exploitation of Central Americans on banana plantations—co-opted Carmen Miranda's image for their own purposes. The United Fruit Company owned 160,000 acres of land in the Caribbean by 1913, and by 1918 U.S. consumers were buying fully 90 percent of Nicaragua's bananas. In 1944 United Fruit Company advertising executives crafted "Chiquita Banana," a female banana look-alike of Carmen Miranda. This singing banana promoted the sales of United Fruit Company bananas, and for consumers in the United States, it gave the prototypical neocolonial company in Latin America an image that challenged the more ideologically raw representation in Diego Rivera's *Imperialism*.

While Hollywood and U.S. companies were softening images of Latin American people and products for their own reasons, the treatment of Mexican migrants to the United States revealed the persistence of negative attitudes toward Latin American people. During the Great War, hundreds of thousands of Mexican men, women, and children migrated to the United States to work. In spite of the fact that their work was desperately needed, many Mexican migrants were treated poorly by U.S. citizens. These attitudes hardened further during the Great Depression, when federal and local officials managed to deport thousands of Mexicans who had come to the United States at the urging of agricultural and industrial companies.

CONCLUSION

In the decades after the Great War, and in the midst of the Great Depression, intellectuals and political activists in Asia, sub-Saharan Africa, and Latin America challenged the ideological and economic underpinnings of empire and neocolonialism. Often embracing the ideas and theories that activists encountered in their travels and around the globe as a result of the war—including self-determination, socialism, communism, and anti-imperialism—radicals and nationalists crafted new visions of a future in which political and economic independence was possible.

Meanwhile, the Japanese government embarked on a policy of militarism in east Asia, and the United States increased its efforts to intervene in Latin American economies. European colonial rulers also continued to limit, often brutally, the freedom of peoples in Asia and Africa. Yet, like Shanfei, young intellectuals and older political leaders alike fought against these trends during the interwar period. Although their efforts to achieve economic and political autonomy did not come to fruition until after World War II, this period was critical to formulating their social, political, and economic responses to all forms of imperial control.

STUDY TERMS

Carmen Miranda (578)
Chinese Communist Party (CCP) (568)
Diego Rivera (575)
dollar diplomacy (575)
estado novo (576)
Fidel Castro (575)
Getúlio Dornelles Vargas (576)
Good Neighbor Policy (576)
Government of India Act (567)
Guomindang (568)
Indian National Congress (566)
Inukai Tsuyoshi (570)
Jiang Jieshi (568)

Jomo Kenyatta (573)
Lázaro Cárdenas (577)
Long March (569)
Mao Zedong (568)
Marcus Garvey (573)
May Fourth Movement (568)
Mohandas Karamchand Gandhi (566)
Muhammad Ali Jinnah (567)
Mukden incident (570)
pan-Africanism (573)
satyagraha (566)
Sun Yatsen (567)
United Fruit Company (578)
W.E.B. DuBois (573)
Xuantong (567)

FOR FURTHER READING

Victor Bulmer-Thomas. *The Economic History of Latin America since Independence* (Cambridge Latin American Studies). 3rd ed. New York, 2014. A well-known classic, which remains the best economic history of Latin America.

Ian Buruma. *Inventing Japan, 1853-1964.* New York, 2003. A century of complex history compressed into a short and elegant book by a respected journalist.

Toyin Falola. *Nationalism and African Intellectuals.* Rochester, 2002. Explores the ways African intellectuals shaped anticolonial nationalist movements in the colonial period and then state-building movements after independence.

William Gould. *Hindu Nationalism and the Language of Politics in Late Colonial India.* New York, 2004. A political history of India on the eve of independence.

Robert E. Hannigan. *The New World Power: American Foreign Policy, 1898-1917.* Philadelphia, 2002. A detailed account of U.S. foreign relations that links class, race, and gender influences to policymakers.

Michele Louro. *Comrades against Imperialism: Nehru, India, and Interwar Nationalism.* Cambridge, 2018. Argues that Jawaharlal Nehru, the first president of independent India, was deeply shaped by the internationalism of the interwar period—particularly by the League Against Imperialism.

Roland Oliver and Anthony Atmore. *Africa since 1800.* 5th ed. Cambridge, 2005. An updated version of a well-regarded survey.

S. C. M. Paine. *The Wars for Asia, 1911-1949.* Cambridge, 2012. Explores the competing visions of Chinese, Japanese, and Russians for the future of China in the period encapsulated by the two world wars.

Steve Striffler and Mark Moberg, eds. *Banana Wars: Power, Production, and History in the Americas.* Durham, N.C., 2003. An interdisciplinary analysis of the transformative impact of the banana industry on global trade and the consequences for Latin American societies and economies.

Odd Arne Westad. *Decisive Encounters: The Chinese Civil War, 1946-1950.* Stanford, 2003. An engaging work that introduces the salient political and military events that led to the eventual defeat of the *Guomindang*.

ZOOMING IN ON ENCOUNTERS
Victor Tolley Finds Tea and Sympathy in Nagasaki

On 6 August 1945, as he listened to the armed services radio on Saipan (a U.S.-controlled island in the north Pacific), U.S. marine Victor Tolley heard the news: the president of the United States announced that a "terrible new weapon" had been deployed against the city of Hiroshima, Japan. Tolley and the other marines rejoiced, realizing that the terrible new weapon—the atomic bomb—might end the war. A few days later Tolley heard that the city of Nagasaki had also been hit with an atomic bomb and that radio announcers suggested it might be decades before the cities would be inhabitable.

Imagine Tolley's astonishment when a few weeks later he and his fellow marines were assigned to the U.S. occupation forces in Nagasaki. Assured by a superior officer that Nagasaki was "very safe," Tolley lived there for three months, during which he became very familiar with the devastation wrought by the atomic bomb. Tolley also became acquainted with some of the Japanese survivors in Nagasaki, which proved to be an eye-opening experience. After seeing "young children with sores and burns all over," Tolley, having become separated from his

A Japanese child cries in the rubble of Hiroshima in the aftermath of the atomic bombing, expressing the profound sadness of war and its devastating weapons.
Bettmann/Getty Images

unit, befriended a young boy, who took Tolley home to meet his surviving family. Tolley recalled that while speaking to the boy's father about his missing son-in-law, "it dawned on me that they suffered the same as we did. They lost sons and daughters and relatives, and they hurt too."

Before his chance meeting with this Japanese family, Tolley had felt nothing except contempt for the Japanese. He pointed out, "We were trained to kill them. . . . They asked for it and now we're gonna give it to 'em. That's how I felt until I met this young boy and his family." But after coming face-to-face with his enemies, Tolley saw only their common humanity, their suffering, and their hurt.

CHAPTER OVERVIEW

The civility that reemerged at the end of the war was barely evident during the war itself. The war began and ended with Japan. In 1931 Japan invaded Manchuria, and the United States concluded by dropping atomic bombs on Hiroshima and Nagasaki. By 1941 World War II was a truly global war. Hostilities spread from east Asia and the Pacific to Europe, north Africa, and the Atlantic. Beyond its immense geographic scope, World War II exceeded even the Great War (1914–1918) in demonstrating the enormous sacrifices in lives and other resources required for achieving complete victory. At least sixty million people perished in the war, with civilian deaths outnumbering military casualties. World War II also redefined gender roles and relations between colonial peoples and colonizers. The cold war and the atomic age that began almost as soon as World War II ended also inaugurated a new global order. In particular, the United States and the Soviet Union gained geopolitical strength during the early years of the cold war as they competed for global influence.

CHRONOLOGY	
1937	Invasion of China by Japan, the "Rape of Nanjing"
1939	Nazi-Soviet pact, invasion of Poland by Germany
1940	Fall of France, Battle of Britain
1941	German invasion of the Soviet Union, attack on Pearl Harbor by Japan
1942	U.S. victory at Midway
1943	Soviet victory at Stalingrad
1944	D-Day, Allied invasion at Normandy
1945	Capture of Berlin by Soviet forces, atomic bombing of Hiroshima and Nagasaki, establishment of United Nations
1947	Truman Doctrine
1948	Marshall Plan
1949	Division of Berlin and Germany, establishment of the People's Republic of China
1950–1953	Korean War
1961	Construction of Berlin Wall
1962	Cuban missile crisis

ORIGINS OF WORLD WAR II

In 1941 two major alliances squared off against each other. Japan, Germany, and Italy, along with their conquered territories, formed the **Axis powers**. The **Allied powers** included France and its empire, Great Britain and its empire and Commonwealth allies (such as Canada, Australia, and New Zealand), the Soviet Union, China, and the United States and its allies in Latin America. Driven in part by a desire to revise the peace settlements that followed the Great War and affected by the economic distress of the worldwide depression, Japan, Italy, and Germany engaged in a campaign of territorial expansion that ultimately broke apart the structure of international cooperation that had kept the world from violence in the 1920s. These **revisionist powers**, so called because they overthrew the terms

of the post–Great War peace, confronted nations that were committed to the avoidance of another world war. To expand their global influence, the revisionist nations remilitarized and conquered territories they believed were central to their needs. The Allies did not resist the revisionist powers' early aggressive actions, but in the late 1930s and early 1940s they felt compelled to engage the Axis powers in a total war.

Japan's War in China

The global conflict opened with Japan's attacks on China in the 1930s: the conquest of Manchuria between 1931 and 1932 was the first step in Japan's goal of expansion. In 1933, after the League of Nations condemned its actions in Manchuria, Japan withdrew from the league and followed an ultranationalist and promilitary policy. Four years later, Japan launched a full-scale invasion of China. Japanese troops first took Beijing and then moved south toward Shanghai and Nanjing, the capital of China. Japanese naval and air forces bombed Shanghai, killing thousands of civilians, and secured it as a landing area for armies bound for Nanjing. By December 1937 Shanghai and Nanjing had fallen, and during the following six months Japanese forces won repeated victories.

The Rape of Nanjing China became the first nation to experience the horrors of World War II in the form of brutal warfare against civilians and repressive occupation. Chinese civilians were among the first to feel the effects of aerial bombing of urban centers; the people of Shanghai died by the tens of thousands when Japanese bombers attacked the city to soften Chinese resistance. What became known as the **Rape of Nanjing** demonstrated the horror of the war as the residents of Nanjing became victims of Japanese troops inflamed by a sense of racial superiority. Over the course of two months, Japanese soldiers raped seven thousand women, murdered hundreds of thousands of unarmed soldiers and civilians, and burned one-third of the homes in Nanjing. Four hundred thousand Chinese lost their lives as Japanese soldiers used them for bayonet practice and machine-gunned them into open pits.

Chinese Resistance Despite Japanese military successes, Chinese resistance persisted throughout the war. Japanese aggression aroused feelings of nationalism among the Chinese that continued to grow as the war wore on. By September 1937 nationalists and communists, who had spent the past decade fighting one another, put aside their differences to fight the Japanese together in a combined army of 1.7 million soldiers. Although Chinese forces were not able to defeat the Japanese, by 1941 the Japanese had to engage half of their land army, 750,000 soldiers, in order to maintain control in China.

Throughout the war, the coalition between nationalists and communists was fragile, and both groups competed for control of enemy territory and political control within China. Their clashes rendered Chinese resistance less effective. The nationalists kept the *Guomindang* government alive by moving far inland to Chongqing while the communists carried on guerrilla operations against the Japanese invaders. Although the guerrillas did not defeat the Japanese, they captured the loyalty of many Chinese peasants through their resistance to the Japanese and their moderate policies of land reform in territories they controlled.

The Japanese invasion of China met with intense international opposition, but other world powers—distracted by depression and military aggression in Europe—could offer little in the way of an effective response to Japanese actions. The government of Japan aligned itself with the

Japanese soldiers execute Chinese prisoners in 1937. In the Japanese invasion of China that year, four hundred thousand Chinese people were brutally murdered.
Hulton-Deutsch Collection/Corbis Historical/Getty Images

other revisionist nations, Germany and Italy, by signing a ten-year military pact, the Tripartite Pact, in September 1940. Japan also cleared the way for further empire building in Asia and the Pacific basin by concluding a neutrality pact with the Soviet Union in April 1941, thereby precluding hostilities in Manchuria. Japan did not face determined opposition to its expansion until it ran into conflict with the United States in December 1941.

Italian and German Aggression

Italy's expansionism helped destabilize the post–Great War peace. Italians suffered tremendously in World War I. Six hundred thousand Italian soldiers died, and the national economy was badly damaged. Many Italians expected far greater recompense and respect than they received at the conclusion of the Great War.

Italy Benito Mussolini (1883–1945) promised to bring glory to Italy through the acquisition of territories that it had been denied after the Great War. Italy's conquest of Ethiopia in 1935 and 1936, when added to the previously annexed Libya, created an overseas empire. Italy also intervened in the Spanish Civil War (1936–1939) on the side of General Francisco Franco (1892–1975), and it annexed

Albania in 1939. The invasion and conquest of Ethiopia, in particular, infuriated other nations, but, as with Japan's invasion of Manchuria, the League of Nations was not able to offer effective opposition.

Outsiders—from state leaders to ordinary people—were horrified by Italy's conquest of Ethiopia because of Italy's excessive use of force during the invasion. Mussolini sent an army of two hundred fifty thousand soldiers armed with tanks, poison gas, artillery, and aircraft to conquer the Ethiopians, who were entirely unprepared for the assault. The mechanized troops mowed them down. Italy lost two thousand soldiers, and Ethiopia lost two hundred seventy-five thousand.

Germany Japan and Italy were the first nations to challenge the post-World War I settlements through territorial conquest, but it was Germany that systematically undid the Treaty of Versailles and the fragile peace of the interwar years. Most Germans and their political leaders resented the harsh terms imposed on their nation in 1919. Adolf Hitler (1889–1945) came to power in 1933, riding a wave of public discontent with Germany's postwar position of powerlessness and the suffering caused by the Great Depression. Hitler referred to the signing of the 1918 armistice as the "November crime" and blamed it on those he viewed as Germany's internal enemies: Jews, communists, and liberals of all sorts. Hitler's scheme for ridding Germany of its enemies and reasserting its power was remilitarization—which was legally denied to Germany under the Versailles treaty. After withdrawing Germany from the League of Nations in 1933, his government carried out an ambitious plan to strengthen the German armed forces. Hitler reinstated universal military service in 1935, and in the following year his troops entered the previously demilitarized Rhineland that bordered France. Germany joined with Italy in the Spanish Civil War, during which Hitler's troops, especially the air force, honed their skills. In 1938 Hitler began the campaign of expansion that ultimately led to the outbreak of World War II in Europe.

Hitler began with the forced annexation of Austria (known as the *Anschluss*) in March 1938. He justified this annexation as an attempt to unite all Germans into a single homeland. Europe's major powers, France and Britain, did not respond by taking action against Germany, thus enhancing Hitler's reputation in the German military. Soon thereafter, using the same rationale of uniting Germans, the Nazis attempted to gain control of the Sudetenland, the western portion of Czechoslovakia, which was inhabited largely by ethnic Germans. Against the desires of the Czechoslovak government, the leaders of France and Britain accommodated Hitler and allowed Germany to annex the Sudetenland. Neither the French nor the British were willing to risk a military confrontation with Germany to defend Czechoslovakian territory.

At a conference in Munich in September 1938, European politicians anxious to avoid war consolidated the policy that came to be known as **appeasement**. At the **Munich Conference**, representatives of Italy, France, and Great Britain conceded to (or "appeased") Hitler's demands in return for a promise that Hitler would not expand German territorial aims beyond the Sudetenland. Their goal was to keep peace in Europe, even if it meant making major concessions. Britain's prime minister, Neville Chamberlain (1869–1940), arrived home from Munich to announce that the meeting had achieved "peace for our time." Unprepared for war and distressed by the depression, nations sympathetic to Britain and France also embraced peace as an admirable goal in the face of aggression by the revisionist nations.

Hitler, however, quickly broke the promises he made in the Munich agreement, and in March 1939 German troops occupied and annexed most of Czechoslovakia. But when Hitler appeared ready to invade Poland just a short time later, the European nations that had supported appeasement realized that the policy had failed. Britain and France therefore guaranteed the security of Poland, which meant that they would declare war against Germany if it decided to invade. Meanwhile, in August 1939 Hitler and the Soviet Union's Josef Stalin (1879–1953) concluded the German-Soviet Non-Aggression Pact. By the terms of the pact, the two nations agreed not to attack each other, and they promised neutrality in the event that either of them went to war with a third party. Additionally, a secret protocol divided eastern Europe into German and Soviet spheres of influence. Hitler was now ready to conquer Europe.

TOTAL WAR: THE WORLD UNDER FIRE

Two months after the United States became embroiled in World War II, President Franklin Roosevelt (1882–1945) delivered one of his famous radio broadcasts, known as fireside chats. In it he explained the nature of the war: "This war is a new kind of war," he said. "It is warfare in terms of every continent, every island, every sea, every air lane." There was little exaggeration in FDR's analysis. Before World War II was over, almost every nation and colonial territory in the world had participated in it, and virtually every weapon known to humanity had been used. Even more than the Great War, this was a conflict in which entire societies engaged in warfare and mobilized every available material and human resource.

Japan and China had already been at war for over eight years when, between 1939 and 1941, nations and territories inside and outside Europe were drawn into the

Anschluss (AHN-shloos)
Sudetenland (soo-DEYT-n-land)

conflict. They included the French and British colonies in Africa and India as well as the British Dominion allies of Canada, Australia, and New Zealand. Germany's stunning military successes in 1939 and 1940 focused attention on Europe, but after the Soviet Union and the United States entered the war in 1941, the conflict took on global proportions.

Blitzkrieg: **Germany Conquers Europe**

During World War II it became common for aggressor nations to avoid overt declarations of war. Instead, the new armed forces relied on surprise and swiftness for their conquests. Germany demonstrated the advantages of that strategy in Poland, when its air force and *Panzer* ("armored") columns moved into Poland unannounced on 1 September 1939. Within a month they subdued its western expanses while the Soviets took the eastern sections in accordance with the Nazi-Soviet pact. The Germans stunned the world with their *Blitzkrieg* ("lightning war") and sudden victory.

The Fall of France With Poland subdued, Germany prepared to break through European defenses. In April 1940 the Germans occupied Denmark and Norway,

Adolf Hitler proudly walks through conquered Paris in 1940, with the Eiffel Tower as a backdrop.
Harwood/Keystone/Hulton Archive/Getty Images

German dive-bombers like this one dominated the early air war in World War II and played a significant role in the German technique known as *Blitzkrieg*.
Bettmann/Getty Images

then launched a full-scale attack on western Europe. The German offensive against Belgium, France, and the Netherlands began in May, and again the Allies were overwhelmed by *Blitzkrieg* tactics. Belgium and the Netherlands fell in May, whereas the French signed an armistice in June. The fall of France convinced Italy's Benito Mussolini to enter the conflict on the side of the Germans in the hopes of reaping any potential benefits the partnership might offer.

Before the battle of France, Hitler had boasted to his staff, "Gentlemen, you are about to witness the most famous victory in history!" Given France's rapid fall, Hitler was not far wrong. In a moment of exquisite triumph, Hitler had the French sign their armistice in the very railroad car in which the Germans had signed the armistice in 1918. Trying to rescue some Allied troops before the fall of France, the British engineered a retreat at the coastal town of Dunkirk, but it could not hide the bleak failure of the Allied troops in their mission to defend Europe from Germany. Britain now stood alone against the German forces.

The Battle of Britain The Germans next turned their attention to defeating Britain. In July 1940 they launched the Battle of Britain, led by the German air force, the *Luftwaffe*. The goal was to defeat Britain almost solely through air attacks. "The Blitz," as the British called this air war, rained bombs on heavily populated metropolitan areas, especially London, and killed more than forty thousand British civilians. The Royal Air Force staved off defeat, however, and by the end of October 1940 Hitler had abandoned plans to invade Britain. But Hitler's successes continued elsewhere. By the summer of 1941 his conquests included the Balkans, and the battlefront extended to north Africa, where the British fought both the Italians and the Germans.

The German Invasion of the Soviet Union

Flush with victory in the spring of 1941, Hitler next turned his attention to the Soviet Union. Hitler had long coveted Soviet territory, where Jews, Slavs, and Bolsheviks could be expelled or exterminated to create more *Lebensraum* ("living space") for resettled Germans. Believing firmly in the bankruptcy of the Soviet system, Hitler said, "You only have to kick in the door, and the whole rotten structure will come crashing down."

Operation Barbarossa On 22 June 1941 Adolf Hitler ordered his armed forces to invade the Soviet Union. To do so, the German military assembled the largest and most powerful invasion force in history, attacking with 3.6 million soldiers, thirty-seven hundred tanks, and twenty-five hundred planes. Military contingents from Italy, Romania, Hungary, Slovakia, Croatia, and Finland—totaling some thirty divisions—augmented the German invasion force. The invasion, along a front of 3,000 kilometers (1,900 miles), took Stalin by surprise and caught the Red Army off guard. By December 1941 German troops had reached the gates of Moscow. Germany seemed assured of victory.

But the German *Blitzkrieg* tactics that had earlier proved so effective in Poland and western Europe failed in the vast expanses of Russia. Hitler and his military leaders underestimated Soviet personnel reserves and industrial capacity. Within a matter of weeks, the 150 German divisions faced 360 divisions of the Red Army. By the time the German forces reached the outskirts of Moscow, fierce Soviet resistance had produced eight hundred thousand German casualties.

The arrival of winter—the most severe in decades—helped Soviet military efforts. The Germans had been so sure of a quick victory that they did not bother to supply their troops with winter clothing and boots. One hundred thousand German soldiers suffered frostbite, and two thousand of them un-derwent amputation. The Red Army, in contrast, prepared for winter and found further comfort as the United States manufactured thirteen million pairs of felt-lined winter boots. By early December, Soviet counterattacks along the entire front had halted German advances.

In the spring of 1942 the Germans briefly regained the military initiative, and by June they were approaching the city of **Stalingrad**. At this point the Soviets dug in. "Not a step back," Stalin ordered. The Russians did hold Stalingrad, but only at the price of a bloody, street-by-street defense of the city until the Red Army could regroup for a counterattack.

Battles in Asia and the Pacific

The United States, though officially neutral, inched toward greater involvement in the war between 1939 and 1941. In 1939 it instituted a cash-and-carry policy of supplying the British, in which the British paid cash and carried the materials across the Atlantic on their ships. More significant was the lend-lease program initiated in 1941, in which the United States "lent" destroyers and other war goods to the British in return for the lease of naval bases. The program later extended such aid to the Soviets, the Chinese, and many others.

Pearl Harbor German victories in 1940 and Great Britain's precarious military position in Europe and in Asia encouraged the Japanese to project their influence into southeast Asia. In September 1940, with the blessings of the German-backed **Vichy** government in France, Japanese forces began to occupy French Indochina (now Vietnam, Laos, and Cambodia). The government of the United States responded to that situation by freezing Japanese assets in the United States and imposing a complete embargo on oil. To Japanese militarists faced with the alternatives of succumbing to U.S. demands—which included the withdrawal of Japanese forces from China and southeast Asia—or of engaging the United States in war, war seemed the lesser of two evils.

The Japanese hoped to quickly destroy American naval capacity in the Pacific with an attack at **Pearl Harbor**. On 7 December 1941 more than three hundred fifty Japanese bombers, fighters, and torpedo planes attacked the Hawaiian naval base in two waves, sinking or disabling eighteen ships and destroying more than two hundred aircraft. Except for the U.S. aircraft carriers, which were out of the harbor at the time, American naval power in the Pacific was devastated. The next day, on 8 December, the United States and Great Britain declared war on Japan.

Luftwaffe (LOOFT-vaff-uh)
Lebensraum (LAY-behnz-rahwm)
Vichy (vee-shee)

Flames consumed U.S. battleships in Pearl Harbor after the Japanese attack on
7 December 1941.
Bettmann/Getty Images

On 11 December 1941, though not compelled to do so by treaty, Hitler and Mussolini declared war on the United States. That move provided the United States with the only reason it needed to declare war on Germany and Italy. The United States, Great Britain, and the Soviet Union came together in a coalition that linked two vast and interconnected theaters of war, the European and Asian-Pacific theaters. Winston Churchill (1874–1965), prime minister of Britain, expressed a vast sense of relief when he said, "So we had won after all!"

Japanese Victories After Pearl Harbor the Japanese swept on to one victory after another. They coordinated their strike against Pearl Harbor with simultaneous attacks against the Philippines, Guam, Wake Island, Midway Island, Hong Kong, Thailand, and British Malaya. For the next year the Japanese military maintained the initiative in southeast Asia and the Pacific, capturing Borneo, Burma, the Dutch East Indies, and several Aleutian islands off Alaska. Australia and New Zealand were now in striking distance. The humiliating surrender of British-held Singapore in February 1942 dealt a blow to British prestige and shattered any myths of European military invincibility.

The slogan under which Japan pursued expansion in Asia was "Asia for Asians," implying that the Japanese would lead Asian peoples to independence from the despised European imperialists and the international order they dominated. In this struggle for Asian independence, Japan required the region's resources and therefore sought to build what it called a Greater East Asia Co-Prosperity Sphere. The appeal to Asian independence at first struck a responsive chord among some anticolonial activists such as Sukarno in the Dutch East Indies, but conquest and brutal occupation soon made it obvious to most Asians that the real agenda was "Asia for the Japanese." Proponents of the Greater East Asia Co-Prosperity Sphere advocated Japan's expansion in Asia and the Pacific while cloaking their territorial and economic designs with the idealism of Asian nationalism.

Defeat of the Axis Powers

The entry of the Soviet Union and the United States into the war in 1941 was decisive, because personnel reserves and industrial capacity were the keys to the Allied victories in the European and Asia-Pacific theaters. The U.S. automotive industry alone, for instance, produced more than four million armored, combat, and supply vehicles of

After the Pearl Harbor attack, Americans expressed great hostility toward the Japanese nationals and Japanese Americans living in the United States, primarily on the west coast. In 1942 President Franklin Roosevelt authorized the forcible removal of approximately one hundred twenty thousand Japanese and Japanese Americans to relocation or internment camps. This photograph shows interned Japanese people behind barbed wire at the Santa Anita camp in California.
Everett Collection Historical/Alamy Stock Photo

all kinds during the war. In the Atlantic, although German submarines sank a total of 2,452 Allied merchant ships and 175 Allied warships over the course of six years, after 1942 U.S. naval shipyards simply built more "Liberty Ships" than the Germans could sink.

Allied Victory in Europe By 1943 German forces faced bleak prospects. Moscow never fell, and the battle for Stalingrad, which ended in February 1943, marked the first large-scale victory for Soviet forces. The Red Army, drawing on enormous personnel and material reserves, then pushed the German invaders out of Russian territory. By April 1945 the Soviets had reached the suburbs of Berlin. At that point, the Soviets had inflicted more than six million casualties on the German enemy—twice the number of the original German invasion force. The Red Army had broken the back of the German war machine.

With the eastern front disintegrating under the Soviet onslaught, British and U.S. forces attacked the Ger-

mans from north Africa and then through Italy. In August 1944 the Allies forced Italy to withdraw from the Axis and to join them. In the meantime, the Germans also prepared for an Allied offensive in the west, where the British and U.S. forces opened a front in France. On **D-Day**, 6 June 1944, British and U.S. troops landed on the French coast of Normandy. With the two fronts collapsing around them and round-the-clock strategic bombing by the United States and Britain leveling German cities, German resistance faded. Indeed, the British firebombing raid on Dresden alone killed one hundred thirty-five thousand people in February 1945. A brutal street-by-street battle in Berlin between Germans and Russians, along with a sweep through western Germany by British and U.S. troops, forced Germany's unconditional surrender on 8 May 1945. A week earlier, on 30 April, Hitler had committed suicide. He did not live to see the Soviet red flag flying over the Berlin *Reichstag*, Germany's parliament building.

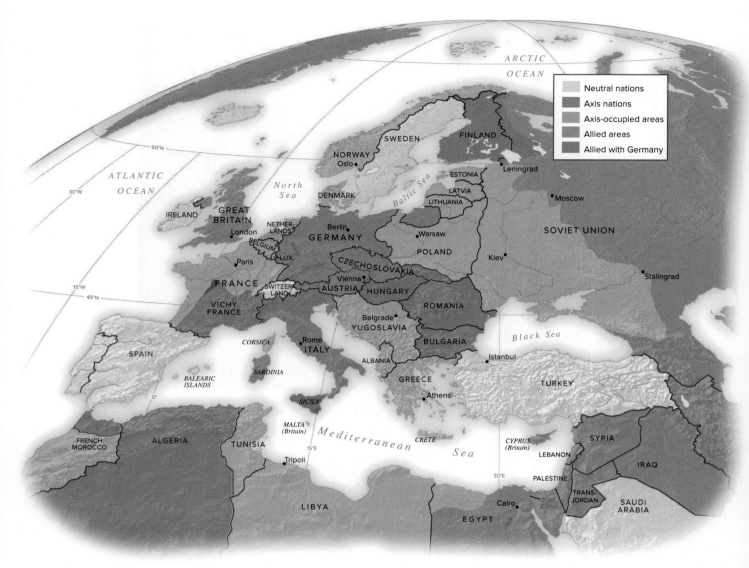

MAP 32.1   High tide of Axis expansion in Europe and north Africa, 1942–1943

Observe the number of nations occupied by or allied with the Axis powers.

Given Axis dominance in Europe, what factors finally allowed the Allies to turn the tide of war in their favor?

Turning the Tide in the Pacific The turning point in the Pacific war came in a naval engagement near the Midway Islands on 4 June 1942. The victory was accomplished by a code-breaking operation known as *Magic,* which enabled a cryptographer monitoring Japanese radio frequencies to discover the plan to attack Midway. On the morning of 4 June, thirty-six carrier-launched dive-bombers attacked the Japanese fleet, sinking three Japanese carriers in one five-minute strike and a fourth one later in the day. After Midway, the Allies took the offensive in the Pacific. They adopted an island-hopping strategy, capturing islands from which they could make direct air assaults on

Japan. Deadly fighting characterized these battles in which the United States and its allies gradually retook islands in the Marianas and the Philippines and then, early in 1945, moved toward areas more threatening to Japan: the islands of Iwo Jima and Okinawa.

The fighting on Iwo Jima and Okinawa was savage. On Okinawa the Japanese introduced the *kamikaze*—pilots who "volunteered" to fly planes with just enough fuel to reach an Allied ship and dive-bomb into it. In the two-month battle, the Japanese flew nineteen hundred kamikaze missions, sinking dozens of ships and killing more than five thousand U.S. soldiers. The *kamikaze,* and the defense mounted by Japanese forces and the one hundred ten thousand Okinawan civilians who died refusing to

kamikaze (KAH-mih-kah-zee)

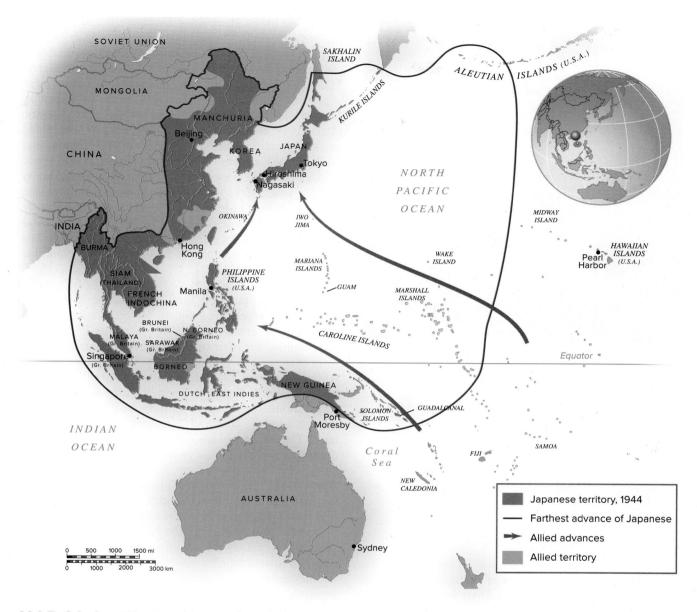

MAP 32.2   World War II in Asia and the Pacific

Compare the geographic conditions of the Asian-Pacific theater with those of the European theater.

What kinds of resources were necessary to win in the Asian-Pacific theater as opposed to the European theater?

surrender, convinced many people in the United States that the Japanese would never willingly surrender.

Japanese Surrender   The fall of Saipan in July 1944 and the subsequent conquest of Iwo Jima and Okinawa brought the Japanese homeland within easy reach of U.S. strategic bombers. The release of napalm firebombs during low-altitude missions at night met with devastating success. The firebombing of Tokyo in March 1945 destroyed 25 percent of the city's buildings, killed approximately one hundred thousand

people, and made more than a million people homeless. The final blows came on 6 and 9 August 1945, when the United States used a revolutionary new weapon, the atomic bomb, against the cities of Hiroshima and Nagasaki. The atomic bombs either instantaneously vaporized or slowly killed by radiation poisoning upward of two hundred thousand people.

The Soviet Union declared war on Japan on 8 August 1945, and this new threat, combined with the devastation caused by the bombs, persuaded Emperor Hirohito (1901–1989) to surrender unconditionally. The Japanese

A photograph titled *Planes over Tokyo Bay*, taken from the U.S.S. *Missouri*, visually captured a sense of U.S. power and victory on V-J Day (Victory over Japan Day), 1945.
Hulton Deutsch/Corbis Historical/Getty Images

surrendered on 15 August, and the war was officially over on 2 September 1945.

LIFE DURING WARTIME

The widespread bombing of civilian populations during World War II, from its beginning in China to its end in Hiroshima and Nagasaki, meant that there was no safe home front during the war. In this total war, civilian death tolls far exceeded military casualties. Yet alongside such terrible brutality remains the record of human endurance, personified in the contributions of resistance groups battling occupying forces, in the determination of mobilized civilians, and in the survivors of bombings or concentration camps.

Occupation, Collaboration, and Resistance

The administration imposed on conquered territories by Japanese and German forces varied in character. In territories such as Manchukuo, Japanese-controlled China, Burma, and the Philippines, Japanese authorities installed puppet governments. Other conquered territories either were considered too unstable or unreliable for self-rule or were deemed strategically too important to be left alone. Thus territories such as Indochina (Laos, Cambodia, and Vietnam), Malaya, the

Dutch East Indies, Hong Kong, Singapore, Borneo, and New Guinea came under direct military control.

In Europe, Hitler's racist ideology played a large role in determining how occupied territories were administered. Hitler intended that most areas of western and northern Europe—populated by people he believed to be "racially valuable"—would become part of a greater Germanic empire. Accordingly, Denmark retained its elected government and monarchy under German supervision. In Norway and Holland, the Germans left the civilian administration intact. Though northern France and the Atlantic coast came under military rule, the Vichy government remained the civilian authority in the unoccupied southeastern part of the country. In contrast, most conquered territories in eastern Europe and the Balkans came under direct military rule as a prelude to brutal occupation, economic exploitation, and German settlement.

Exploitation Japanese and German authorities administered their respective empires for economic gain and proceeded to exploit the resources of the lands under their control for their own benefit. The most notorious form of economic exploitation involved the use of slave labor. By August 1944 more than seven million foreign workers labored inside Germany's Third Reich. And in China alone, the Japanese military mobilized more than ten million civilians and prisoners of war for forced labor. These enslaved laborers worked under horrific conditions and received little in the way of sustenance.

Atrocities The treatment of prisoners of war (POWs) by German and Japanese authorities was brutal. The death rate among soldiers in Japanese captivity averaged almost 30 percent, and 2 million of the 3.3 million Soviet soldiers in German custody died from starvation, exposure, disease, or outright murder.

Beyond the mistreatment of POWs, both German and Japanese authorities engaged in painful and often deadly medical experiments on thousands of unwilling subjects. In China, special Japanese military units, including infamous Unit 731, conducted cruel experiments on civilians and POWs. Tens of thousands of Chinese became victims of germ warfare experiments after they were deliberately infected with bubonic plague, cholera, anthrax, and other diseases. German physicians carried out similar medical experiments in concentration camps. Experimentation ranged from performing bone-grafting surgeries without anesthesia to exposing victims to phosgene and mustard gas in order to test possible antidotes. German doctors also directed painful experiments to determine how different "races" withstood various contagious diseases.

Collaboration The majority of people resented occupation forces but tried, if possible, to go on with life. That response was especially true in many parts of Japanese-occupied lands in Asia, where local populations

The writing on the board displayed by German security forces in Minsk, Belarus, reads, "We are partisans who shot at German soldiers." The Germans murdered some seven hundred thousand civilians, mostly Belarusians and Poles, in so-called antipartisan reprisals. Women and children were included in the "reprisal" because they were considered an encumbrance. Sueddeutsche Zeitung Photo/Alamy Stock Photo

found little to resent in the change from one colonial administration to another. In both Asia and Europe, local notables sometimes joined the governments sponsored by the conquerors because collaboration offered them the means to gain power. Businesspeople and companies sometimes collaborated because they prospered financially from foreign rule. Still other people became collaborators and assisted occupation authorities by turning in friends and neighbors to get revenge for past grievances. In western Europe, anticommunism motivated Belgians, French, Danish, Dutch, and Norwegians to join units of Hitler's elite military formations, the Waffen SS, creating in the process a multinational army tens of thousands strong. In violation of its own racial policies, the SS also accepted volunteers from the Balkans, eastern Europe, and the Caucasus. In China several *Guomindang* generals went over to the Japanese, and local landowners and merchants in some regions of

China set up substantial trade networks between the occupiers and the occupied.

Resistance Occupation and exploitation also created an environment for resistance that took various forms. The most dramatic forms of resistance were campaigns of sabotage, armed assaults on occupation forces, and assassinations. Resistance fighters as diverse as Filipino guerrillas and Soviet partisans harassed and disrupted the military and economic activities of the occupiers by blowing up ammunition dumps, destroying communication and transportation facilities, and sabotaging industrial plants. Less conspicuously, other resisters gathered intelligence, hid and protected refugees, or passed on clandestine newspapers. Even more subtle were simple acts of defiance such as scribbling anti-German graffiti or walking out of bars and restaurants when Japanese soldiers entered. Despite the deadly retaliation meted out to

Why It Matters

The Destructive Potential of Industrial Technologies

World War I demonstrated that human societies around the world were prepared to use industrial technologies to kill maximum numbers of people. Although many people reacted with horror at this use of technology, it did not end there. Less than two decades later, during World War II, states unleashed even more destructive technologies on their enemies than they had in World War I. More chilling still, they now specifically targeted civilian populations in

addition to enemy combatants. Poison gas, aerial bombardment, and atomic bombs could now wipe out thousands—even millions—of people at one time. Consider whether or not it is possible, or even desirable, to guide the development of technology in ways that can prevent such destructive outcomes. Why and how does that matter as humans develop new technologies such as gene editing, space travel, and face recognition?

people who were caught openly resisting occupation, widespread resistance movements grew throughout the war. This was so in spite of the great hardships people involved in resistance movements endured, including changing identities, hiding out, and risking capture and death.

German and Japanese citizens faced different decisions about resistance than conquered peoples did. For them, any form of noncompliance constituted an act of treason. Moreover, many institutions that might have formed the core of resistance in Japan and Germany, such as political parties, labor unions, or churches, were weak or had been destroyed. As a result, there was little overt opposition to the state in Japan, and in Germany resistance remained sparse and ineffective. The most spectacular act of resistance against the Nazi regime came from a group of officers and civilians who tried, but failed, to assassinate Adolf Hitler on 20 July 1944.

The Holocaust

By the end of World War II, the Nazi regime and its accomplices had murdered millions of Jews, Slavs, Roma (Gypsies), and others targeted as undesirables. Jews were the primary target of Hitler's racially motivated genocidal policies. These policies resulted in what has come to be known as the **Holocaust**, or the near elimination of European Jews by Germany.

The murder of European Jews was preceded by a long history of vilification and persecution. By the time the Nazi regime assumed power in 1933, anti-Semitism had contributed significantly to widespread tolerance for anti-Jewish measures. Nazi determination to destroy the Jewish population in Europe and Europeans' passive acceptance of anti-Semitism had laid the groundwork for genocide.

During the 1930s the German government encouraged Jewish emigration. Although tens of thousands of

MAP 32.3   The Holocaust in Europe, 1933–1945

Observe the geographic locations of the concentration and extermination camps.

Why were there more concentration camps in Germany and more extermination camps in Poland?

SOURCES FROM THE PAST

"We Will Never Speak about It in Public"

On 4 October 1943, Heinrich Himmler, leader of the SS and chief of the German police, gave a three-hour speech to an assembly of SS generals in the city of Posen (Poznan), in what is now Poland. In the following excerpt, Himmler justified Nazi anti-Jewish policies that culminated in mass murder. The speech, recorded on tape and in handwritten notes, was entered into evidence at the Nuremberg war crimes trials in 1945.

I also want to speak to you here, in complete frankness, of a really grave chapter. Amongst ourselves, for once, it shall be said quite openly, but all the same we will never speak about it in public. . . .

I am referring here to the evacuation of the Jews, the extermination of the Jewish people. This is one of the things that is easily said: "The Jewish people are going to be exterminated," that's what every Party member says, "sure, it's in our program, elimination of the Jews, extermination—it'll be done." And then they all come along, the 80 million worthy Germans, and each one has his one decent Jew. Of course, the others are swine, but this one, he is a first-rate Jew. Of all those who talk like that, not one has seen it happen, not one has had to go through with it. Most of you men know what it is like to see 100 corpses side by side, or 500 or 1,000. To have stood fast through this and except for cases of human weakness to have stayed decent, that has made us hard. This is an un-written and never-to-be-written page of glory in our history. . . .

> What was Himmler's point here about "decent" Jews?

The wealth they possessed we took from them. I gave a strict order, which has been carried out by SS *Obergruppenfuehrer* Pohl, that this wealth will of course be turned over to the Reich in its entirety. We have taken none of it for ourselves. Individuals who have erred will be punished in accordance with the order given by me at the start, threatening that anyone who takes as much as a single Mark of this money is a dead man. A number of SS men, they are not very many, committed this offense, and they shall die. There will be no mercy. We had the moral right, we had the duty towards our people, to destroy this people that wanted to destroy us. But we do not have the right to enrich our-selves by so much as a fur, as a watch, by one Mark or a cigarette or anything else. We do not want, in the end, because we destroyed a bacillus, to be in-fected by this bacillus and to die. I will never stand by and watch while even a small rotten spot develops or takes hold. Wherever it may form we will together burn it away. All in all, however, we can say that we have carried out this most difficult of tasks in a spirit of love for our people. And we have suffered no harm to our inner being, our soul, our character. . . .

> Why was it so important to Him-mler that individual Germans not take the wealth of murdered Jews?

For Further Reflection

■ Himmler argued that SS officers and soldiers "stayed decent" while overseeing the extermination of the Jews; how, according to him, was this possible?

Source: Heinrich Himmler. " We Will Never Speak about It in Public" (*The Complete Text of the Poznan Speech*), 4 October 1943, Translation used with permission of the Holocaust History Project (www.holocaust-history.org).

Jews availed themselves of the opportunity to escape from Germany and Austria, many more were unable to do so. Most nations outside the Nazi orbit limited the migration of Jewish refugees. In any case, German armies brought an ever-larger number of Jews under Nazi control as they ex-panded into Europe. Nazi "racial experts" toyed with the idea of deporting Jews to Nisko, a proposed reservation in eastern Poland, or to the island of Madagascar, near Africa. Those ideas, however, proved to be impractical.

The Final Solution The German occupation of Po-land in 1939 and invasion of the Soviet Union in the

Connecting the Sources

Exploring perspective and neutrality in the historical interpretation of World War II

The problem   More than sixty million people died in World War II. Millions more suffered intensely but ultimately survived the ordeal. Because World War II occurred within living memory, millions of individuals around the world still feel intimately connected with it—if not through their own experiences, then through the stories of their family members of an older generation. As a result, it is still understandably difficult for historians and nonhistorians alike to consider the war from a neutral perspective. Moreover, although all the countries that actively participated in the war engaged in brutalities, both the German and the Japanese states sanctioned extreme brutalities against civilian populations—which included massive campaigns of genocide, forced prostitution, forced labor, and medical experiments. These appalling events have resulted in a marked reluctance to discuss the suffering of ordinary Germans not targeted by the Holocaust or of ordinary Japanese, because doing so has been associated with cheapening the experience of the millions who suffered and died as a result of German and Japanese national policies. The implication, though not usually stated explicitly, is that not all human suffering in World War II should be explored equally. Let us consider two sources as a way of considering how our own proximity to traumatic historical events might affect the ways we interpret the past.

Indonesians who were recruited by the Japanese to work as *romushas* (forced laborers).
Image bank WW2 – NIOD

The documents   Read the following documents, and consider carefully the questions that follow.

Document 1:

Dulrahman, a Javanese farmer born in 1920, was one of approximately two hundred fifty thousand laborers forced by the Japanese to work on various war-related projects in southeast Asia during World War II. These work battalions were called romushas. *Although* romushas *were told they would receive pay when they were recruited, instead they found themselves working without pay in extremely difficult conditions and with little food. As a result, over half did not survive the war.*

> In June 1942, a Japanese soldier by the name of Kawakubu came to our village and asked
> my father if there were any people who could work, for wages, of course. My father then gave
> him my name. They first assigned me to help build a tunnel at Parangtritis, south of Yogya,
> on the coast. We didn't get paid at all, however, and they told my father they'd kill him if
> he'd come to fetch me. Sure, the Japanese told us repeatedly: "We've come to free you from
> colonial oppression." But meanwhile they forced us to work for them!
>
>   We left from Gunung Kidul for Parangtritis with about 500 people. My estimate is
> that about 300 survived. It's hard to be precise, for people were not buried but simply
> tossed into the sea. Some eight months later they shipped us out by the hundreds,
> including about 100 people belonging to the Gunung Kidul group. It turned out that they
> had taken us to Digul (in Irian Jaya, a former Dutch penal colony in what was then
> New Guinea) to cut trees for building a road and a prison. Compared to this place,
> Parangtritis had been pleasant. There at least we got a piece of cassava the size of my
> fist, and we could fetch water from a small mountain lake. In Digul, however, we were
> left to our own devices and so we had to forage for ourselves. For food, you had to look
> in the jungle. We ate leaves, and any snake you'd find was good for roasting.
>
>   Finally, they told us we could go home. Everybody was elated. . . . But about
> halfway, in the middle of the ocean, we began to ask ourselves: "Where on earth are

> Why did Dulrahman's father agree to let his son work for the Japanese in 1942?

they taking us this time?" There was no land to be seen anywhere. The voyage took a month. We finally arrived and got off the ship and that's when we panicked: Where on earth were we? This wasn't Indonesia, but then what country was it? After one week, I found out that we were in Burma.

In Burma, life for a romusha was terrible. But compared to Digul it was better. . . . If we did anything wrong, [the Japanese would] beat us up vigorously with their rubber truncheons. That was no joke. If you got beaten with that truncheon it would remove your skin when bouncing back, and that caused a lot of pain.

We spent exactly one year in Burma. . . . One day, our foreman let it slip that we'd be going home in two weeks. . . . When I arrived [back home], everybody cried. They thought I'd been dead long since. I certainly looked quite different. . . . During the first month, my family treated me a bit like a retiree, as it were. I was not allowed to work and they fed me very well. . . .

I still dream a lot about those days, especially about the work we did: dragging stones, that sort of thing. And about that voyage across the sea. Those high waves. That results in a nightmare once in a while, and then I find myself screaming out loud. . . . My gosh, to think that after 50 years I'm still dreaming about that!

Document 2:

Devastation in the aftermath of the bombing of Hiroshima.
Bettmann/Getty Images

Kosaku Okabe was a young Japanese soldier who had seen combat many times over the course of the war. The day after the Hiroshima bombing, on 7 August, he and some fellow soldiers took the train to Hiroshima, knowing only that a bomb had been dropped on the city. The passengers were told to get out on the outskirts of the city, as the train was going no farther. Once Kosaku got out, he realized it was because the train tracks had been completely destroyed. What follows is what Kosaku saw as he moved closer to the epicenter.

In front of me, smoke still overhung the city, and there was increasing confusion as the people leaving the city met those trying to enter it. I began to come across people with tattered clothing and injuries of a kind I had never seen before. By now the area around me was a burned-out wasteland, with no houses standing. It was when I crossed what I think was the Ota River, though, that I really seemed to step into hell. . . . Dead bodies lay where they had fallen. The great cherry trees that had lined the embankment were stripped of their branches, which were now hanging down in shreds from their trunks. Looking downstream to the river mouth, I saw strange black shapes almost obliterating the sparkling sandbars . . . . As I drew nearer I realized that in reality they were dead bodies, possibly deposited there by the river. . . . Farther on, in the water, floated countless bodies of men, women, and children. The misery was indescribable.

> What difference does it make to read about civilian deaths versus those of military combatants? Is it more difficult or the same for both groups? Why?

Questions

1. What can these documents definitively tell you about their respective situations? What facts can be gleaned from these brief sources?

2. In Document 1, what was it like for Dulrahman to serve as a *romusha*? According to this source, how did the experience affect him after the war? Does Dulrahman's story elicit your sympathy, even though he was working in a Japanese-led work battalion? If yes, are you able to determine what factors of the story make you sympathetic? If no, are you able to determine the reasons why not?

3. In Document 2, does Kosaku's story elicit your sympathy, even though he was a Japanese soldier who had actively supported the Japanese war effort? If yes, what parts of his story make you feel sympathetic? If no, are you able to determine the reasons?

4. Taking both documents together, do you believe that either Dulrahman or Kosaku deserves more sympathy than the other? Do you find that your answer to this question is affected by the nationality of either person? Do you think it

would be difficult for individuals who had experienced the war to be impartial about the suffering of individuals in enemy nations? Why or why not?

5. Sources such as these make up the building blocks on which historians base their interpretations of the past. When interpreting the relatively recent past, it is especially important that historians remain aware of the ways in which their own personal and national backgrounds affect both the sources they use and their interpretations of them.

Source Citations: **Document 1:** http://www.opendemocracy.net/arts-photography/war_2764.jsp, from Open Democracy, Jan Banning exhibition, 2005: Traces of War: Dutch and Indonesian Survivors. **Document 2:** Gaynor Sekinori and Naomi Shohno. *Hibakusha: Survivors of Hiroshima and Nagasaki.* Tokyo: Kosei, 1989, pp. 33–34.

summer of 1941 gave Hitler an opportunity to solve what he considered the problem of Jews in Germany and in Europe. When German armies invaded the Soviet Union in June 1941, the Nazis dispatched three thousand troops in mobile detachments known as SS *Einsatzgruppen* ("action squads") to kill entire populations of Jews, Roma (Gypsies), and many non-Jewish Slavs in the newly occupied territories. By the spring of 1943 the special units had killed over one million Jews, as well as tens of thousands of Soviet citizens and Roma.

Sometime during 1941 the Nazi leadership committed to what they called the "final solution" of the Jewish question, a plan to murder every Jew living in Europe. At the Wannsee Conference on 20 January 1942 fifteen leading Nazi bureaucrats agreed to evacuate all Jews from Europe to camps in eastern Poland, where they would be worked to death or exterminated. Soon German forces—aided by collaborating authorities in foreign countries—rounded up Jews and deported them by rail to specially constructed concentration camps in occupied Poland. The Jewish victims packed into these suffocating railway cars never knew their destinations, but rumors of mass deportations and mass deaths nonetheless spread among Jews remaining at large and among the Allied government leaders, many of whom were apathetic to the fate of Jews.

In camps such as Kulmhof (Chelmno), Belzec, Majdanek, Sobibor, Treblinka, and Auschwitz, the final solution took on an organized and technologically sophisticated character. Nazi camp personnel subjected victims from all corners of Europe to industrial work, starvation, medical experiments, and outright extermination by gassing. The German commandant of **Auschwitz**—the largest camp, where at least one million Jews perished—explained proudly how his camp became the most efficient at killing Jews: by using the fast-acting crystallized prussic acid Zyklon B as the gassing agent, by enlarging the size of the gas chambers, and by lulling victims into thinking they were going through a delousing process. At Auschwitz and elsewhere, the Germans also constructed large crematories to incinerate the bodies of gassed Jews and hide the evidence of their crimes.

Jewish Resistance Jews fiercely resisted throughout the war. Thousands of Jews joined anti-Nazi partisan groups, and others led rebellions in concentration camps or participated in ghetto uprisings from Minsk to Krakow. The best-known uprising took place in the Warsaw ghetto in the spring of 1943. Even though the resisters were not well armed, it still took German security forces using tanks and flamethrowers three weeks to crush the uprising. In total, approximately 5.7 million Jews perished in the Holocaust.

Women and the War

Observing the extent to which British women mobilized for war, the U.S. ambassador to London noted, "This war, more than any other war in history, is a woman's war." While hundreds of thousands of women in Great Britain, the United States, and the Soviet Union joined the armed forces or entered war industries, women around the world were affected by the war in a variety of ways. Some nations, including Great Britain and the United States, barred women from engaging in combat or carrying weapons, but Soviet and Chinese women took up arms, as did women in resistance groups. In fact, women often excelled at resistance work, because they were less suspect in the eyes of occupying security forces and less subject to searches. Nazi forces did not discriminate, though, when rounding up Jews for transport and extermination: Jewish women and girls died alongside Jewish men and boys.

Women's Roles Women who joined military services or took jobs on factory assembly lines gained an independence and confidence previously denied them, but so did women who were forced to act as heads of household in the absence of husbands killed or away at war, captured as prisoners of war, or languishing in labor camps. Women's roles changed during the war, often in dramatic ways, but those new roles turned out to be temporary. After the war,

---

Einsatzgruppen (INE-zahts-GROO-pen)

women warriors and workers were expected to resume their traditional roles as wives and mothers. In the meantime, women made the most of their opportunities. In Britain, women served as noncombatant pilots, drove ambulances and transport vehicles, and labored in the fields to produce foodstuffs. More than five hundred thousand women joined British military services, and approximately three hundred fifty thousand women did the same in the United States. In the Soviet Union, about eight hundred thousand women enlisted in the armed forces during the war. Although many served as medics and nurses, thousands also served in active combat as pilots, snipers, and machine gunners.

Natalya Kravtsova (left) and Irina Sebrova (right) were pilots in the Soviet air force's 588th Night Bomber Regiment and are pictured here in front of a PO 2 aircraft. Sebrova flew 825 bombing missions during World War II and in 1945 was awarded the title "Hero of the Soviet Union" for her service.
ITAR-TASS News Agency/Alamy Stock Photo

Comfort Women Women's experiences in war were not always empowering. The Japanese army forcibly recruited, conscripted, and coerced as many as two hundred thousand women aged fourteen to twenty to serve in military brothels, called "comfort houses" or "consolation centers." The army presented the women to the troops as a gift from the emperor. The majority of women came from China and the Japanese colony of Korea, although others were from Japanese colonies and occupied territories in Taiwan, Manchuria, the Philippines, and elsewhere in southeast Asia.

Once forced into this imperial prostitution service, the "comfort women" catered to between twenty and thirty men each day. Stationed in war zones, the women often confronted the same risks as soldiers, and many became casualties of war. Others were killed by Japanese soldiers, especially if they tried to escape or contracted venereal diseases. At the end of the war, soldiers massacred large numbers of comfort women to cover up the operation. The impetus behind the establishment of comfort houses for Japanese soldiers came from the horrors of Nanjing, where the mass rape of Chinese women had taken place. In trying to avoid such atrocities, the Japanese army created another horror of war. Comfort women who survived the war experienced deep shame and hid their past or faced being shunned by their families. They found little comfort or peace after the war.

THE COLD WAR

The end of World War II produced moving images of peace, such as Soviet and U.S. soldiers clasping hands in camaraderie at the Elbe River, celebrating their victory over the Germans. But by the time Germany surrendered in the spring of 1945, the wartime alliance between the Soviet Union, the United States, and Great Britain was disintegrating. Within two years the alliance forged by mutual danger gave way to a cold war between the United States and the Soviet Union and their allies that lasted almost five decades and affected every part of the world; however, in the end, a direct clash of arms between the two principal powers was always avoided, hence the term *cold war*.

The cold war was responsible for the formation of military and political alliances, the creation of client states, and an arms race of unprecedented scope. It engendered diplomatic crises, spawned military conflicts, and at times brought the world to the brink of nuclear annihilation. Among the first manifestations of the cold war was the division of the European continent into competing political, military, and economic blocs—one dependent on the United States and the other subservient to the USSR—separated by what Winston Churchill in 1946 famously called an "iron curtain."

What's Left Out?

Historians used to assume that antagonism between capitalist and communist systems was natural and, therefore, the intense rivalry that emerged between the United States and the Soviet Union during the cold war needed no historical explanation. But cold war antagonisms had a history that predated the end of World War II by almost three decades. The leading capitalist powers—including Great Britain and the United States—had actively tried to put an end to the Russian revolution in 1918 when they sent troops to help overthrow the Bolsheviks as World War I was ending. In 1919 they grew even more alarmed about the Soviet state when it established the Communist International (Comintern), whose express purpose was to provide funds and strategies for colonized and marginalized people to overthrow capitalism through violent revolution. In fact, it is no exaggeration to say that metropolitan and colonial authorities—especially from Great Britain and France—were convinced that international communism posed a fundamental danger to the stability of the Euro-American global system in the interwar period. During the 1920s and 1930s, both Britain and France expended enormous energy and capital trying to root out and persecute communists around the world (especially in their colonies). British authorities, in particular, were influential in shaping the anticommunist attitudes of U.S. authorities at this time, encouraging them to fear the influence of communism both in their own overseas empire and among U.S. workers. So, even though the capitalist powers were able to put aside their animosity toward the Soviet Union in order to fight the Axis powers, it is hardly surprising that this decades-long rivalry flared up again at the end of the war. The difference now was that the United States, rather than Great Britain or France, was leading the campaign. What is important to remember is that the United States took over the campaign but did not invent it and that the struggle between communism and anticommunism was critical to international politics long before the United States became the primary adversary of the Soviet Union.

Source: Anne Foster, "Secret Police Cooperation and the Roots of Anti-Communism in Interwar Southeast Asia," *Journal of American-East Asian Relations* 4:4 (1995).

The Origins of the Cold War

The United Nations Despite their many differences, the Allies were among the nations that agreed to the creation of the **United Nations (UN)** in October 1945, a supranational organization dedicated to keeping world peace and security. Unlike its predecessor, the League of Nations (1920), which failed in its basic mission to prevent another world war, the United Nations created a powerful Security Council responsible for maintaining international peace. Recognizing that peace could be maintained only if the great powers were in agreement, the UN founders made certain that the Security Council consists of five permanent members and six rotating elected members. The United States, the Soviet Union, Great Britain, France, and China—the members of the full Allied alliance in World War II—are the five permanent powers, and their unanimous vote is required on all substantive matters. The decisions of the Security Council are binding on all members.

Despite this initial cooperation, the wartime unity of the former Allies began to crack. At the end of the war the Allies were already expressing differences over the future of Poland and eastern Europe. On the surface, all sides agreed at the wartime conference at Yalta (4–11 February, 1945) to "the earliest possible establishment through free elections of governments responsive to the will of the people." But the Soviet Union had just suffered a devastating invasion by the German army through this territory, and Josef Stalin was determined that postwar governments in the region would not threaten Soviet security again. From the American and British perspectives, Stalin's intentions threatened the expansion of communism in Europe. Their fears were realized in 1946 and 1947, when the Soviets helped bring communist governments to power in Romania, Bulgaria, Hungary, and Poland. Communists had previously gained control in Albania and Yugoslavia in 1944 and 1945.

Truman Doctrine The enunciation of the **Truman Doctrine** on 12 March 1947—partly in response to crises in Greece and Turkey—starkly drew the battle lines of the cold war. As President Harry Truman (1884–1972) explained to the U.S. Congress, "At the present moment in world history nearly every nation must choose between alternative ways of life. I believe that it must be the policy of the United States to support free peoples who are resisting attempted subjugation by armed minorities or by outside pressures." The United States then committed itself to an interventionist foreign policy, dedicated to the "containment" of communism, which meant preventing any further expansion of Soviet influence.

Marshall Plan Just after the announcement of the Truman Doctrine, the U.S. government developed a plan to help shore up the destroyed infrastructures of western Europe and, in the process, to make communism less appealing to Europeans. The European Recovery Program,

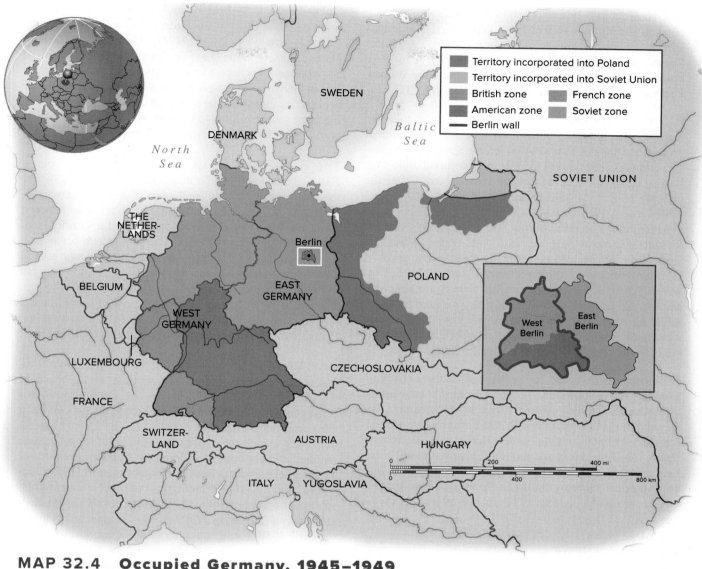

MAP 32.4   Occupied Germany, 1945–1949

Locate the city of Berlin in Soviet-controlled territory.

How was it possible for the British, the Americans, and the French to maintain their zones of control in Berlin, given the geographic distance from West Germany?

commonly called the **Marshall Plan** after U.S. secretary of state George C. Marshall (1880–1959), proposed to rebuild European economies through cooperation and capitalism. Beginning in 1948, the Marshall Plan provided more than $13 billion to reconstruct western Europe. Although initially included in the nations invited to participate in the Marshall Plan, the Soviet Union became infuriated over what it correctly saw as a U.S. attempt to combat communism in the parts of Europe devastated by the war. In response, the Soviet government came up with its own aid program for the satellite nations around it, establishing an economic Council for Mutual Economic Assistance (**COMECON**) in 1949. COMECON offered increased trade within the Soviet Union and eastern Europe as an alternative to the Marshall Plan, which Soviet officials denounced.

Military Alliances   In 1949 the United States established the North Atlantic Treaty Organization (**NATO**) as a regional military alliance against Soviet aggression. The original members included Belgium, Canada, Denmark, France, Great Britain, Iceland, Italy, Luxembourg, the Netherlands, Norway, Portugal, and the United States. The intent of the alliance was to maintain peace in postwar Europe through collective security, which implied that a Soviet attack on any NATO member was an attack against all of them. NATO assumed a more military focus with the Soviet Union's detonation of its first atomic bomb in 1949 and with the outbreak of the Korean War in 1950. When NATO admitted West Germany and allowed it to rearm in 1955, the Soviets formed the Warsaw Pact as a countermeasure. A military alliance of seven communist European nations, the Warsaw Pact matched the collective defense policies of NATO.

A Divided Germany

The fault lines of early cold war Europe were most visible in Germany. An international crisis arose there in 1948–1949 when the Soviet Union pressured the western powers to give up their jurisdiction over Berlin, which sat deep within the Soviet sector. After the collapse of Hitler's Third Reich, the forces of the United States, the Soviet Union, Britain, and France occupied Germany and its capital, Berlin, both of which they divided for administrative purposes into four zones. When the western powers decided to merge their occupation zones in Germany—including their sectors in Berlin—the Soviets were alarmed that their former allies were trying to re-create a strong German state. The Soviets retaliated by blockading all road, rail, and water links between Berlin and western Germany in the hope of at least forcing their opponents to surrender their control over the city of Berlin.

Blockade and Airlift

In the first serious test of the cold war, the Americans and the British responded with an airlift designed to keep West Berlin's inhabitants alive. For eleven months American and British aircrews flew around-the-clock missions to supply West Berlin with the necessities of life. Tensions remained high during the airlift, but the cold war did not turn hot. Unable to force the British and Americans to leave Berlin, the Soviet leadership called off the blockade in May 1949. In the aftermath of the

Barbed wire and a concrete wall in front of the Brandenburg Gate in Berlin symbolized the cold war division of Europe.
Keystone-France/Gamma-Keystone/Getty Images

blockade, the U.S., British, and French zones of occupation coalesced to form the Federal Republic of Germany (West Germany) in May 1949. In October the German Democratic Republic (East Germany) emerged out of the Soviet zone of occupation. A similar process repeated itself in Berlin. The Soviet sector formed East Berlin and became the capital of the new East Germany. The remaining three sectors united to form West Berlin, and the West German capital moved to the small town of Bonn.

The Berlin Wall

By 1961 nearly 3.5 million people in East Germany had fled en masse to West Germany, where the quality of life was higher. To stop people from leaving, in August 1961 the communists reinforced the border between East and West Germany and constructed a fortified wall that divided the city of Berlin. The wall, which began as a layer of barbed wire, quickly turned into a barrier several layers deep, with watchtowers, searchlights, antipersonnel mines, and border guards who had orders to shoot to kill. The **Berlin Wall** accomplished its purpose of stemming the flow of refugees, although at the cost of shaming a regime that seemed to be unpopular even among its own people.

Cold War Culture and Censorship

Somewhat ironically, despite their intense competition, during the cold war societies in the Soviet Union and the United States came to resemble one another in some ways, especially in their internal censorship policies. In the United States, cold war concerns about the spread of communism reached deeply into the domestic sphere. Politicians, agents of the Federal Bureau of Investigation (FBI), educators, and social commentators warned of communist spies trying to undermine the institutions of U.S. life. Senator **Joseph McCarthy** (1909–1957) became infamous in the early 1950s for his quest to expose communists in the U.S. government. Thousands of citizens who supported any radical or liberal cause—especially those who were or once had been members of the Communist Party—lost their jobs and reputations. Hollywood, in particular, came under great scrutiny for its suspected ties to left-wing politics, which had the effect of limiting overt criticism of the United States and its foreign policies.

In the Soviet Union and Eastern Europe, cold war ideologies also profoundly influenced domestic culture and politics. After the war, Stalin imposed Soviet economic planning on governments in Eastern Europe and expected the peoples of the Soviet Union and Eastern Europe to conform to anticapitalist ideological requirements. Rebellious artists and novelists found themselves silenced or denounced. This policy of repression relaxed somewhat after Stalin's death in 1953, but there remained limits on Soviet liberalization. Soviet troops cracked down on Hungarian rebels in 1956, and Soviet novelist Boris Pasternak (1890–1960), author of *Doctor Zhivago,* was not allowed to receive his Nobel Prize in Literature in 1958.

The Globalization of the Cold War

The People's Republic of China The establishment of a communist China in 1949 simultaneously ended a long period of imperialist intrusion in China and further transformed the cold war. When World War II broke out, the opposing nationalist and communist groups in China came together to fight against the Japanese invasion (see chapter 31). Once World War II was over, however, civil war ensued. In 1948 and 1949, the communists inflicted heavy military defeats on the nationalists. With the communist People's Liberation Army controlling most of mainland China, the nationalist government under Jiang Jieshi (Chiang Kai-shek) sought refuge on the island of Taiwan, taking along most of the nation's gold reserves. Although Jiang Jieshi continued to proclaim that the government in Taiwan was the legitimate government of all China, Mao Zedong, chairman of the Chinese Communist Party, proclaimed the establishment of the People's Republic of China on 1 October 1949. That declaration brought to an end the long period of imperialist intrusion in China and spawned a close relationship between the world's largest and most powerful socialist states.

Fraternal Cooperation China and the Soviet Union drew closer during the early years of the cold war. This relationship was hardly surprising, because the leaders of both communist states felt threatened by the United States, which sought to establish anticommunist bastions throughout Asia. Most disconcerting to Soviet and Chinese leaders was the American-sponsored rehabilitation of their former enemy, Japan, and the forming of client states in South Korea and Taiwan. The Chinese-Soviet partnership matured during the early 1950s and took on a distinct form when China recognized the Soviet Union's undisputed authority in world communism in exchange for Russian military equipment and economic aid.

Confrontations in Korea In conjunction with the communist victory in China, the outbreak of hostilities on the Korean peninsula in the summer of 1950 shifted the focus of the cold war from Europe to east Asia. At the end of World War II, the leaders of the Soviet Union and the United States had partitioned Korea along the thirty-eighth line of latitude into a northern Soviet zone and a southern U.S. zone. Because the superpowers were unable to agree on a framework for the reunification of the country, in 1948 they consented to the establishment of two separate Korean states: in the south, the Republic of Korea, with Seoul as its capital, and in the north, the People's Democratic Republic of Korea, with Pyongyang as its capital. After arming their respective clients, each of which claimed sovereignty over the entire country, U.S. and Soviet troops withdrew.

On the early morning of 25 June 1950 the unstable political situation in Korea came to a head. Determined to unify Korea by force, the Pyongyang regime in North Korea ordered more than one hundred thousand troops across the thirty-eighth parallel in a surprise attack, quickly pushing back South Korean defenders and capturing Seoul on 27 June. Convinced that the USSR had given its blessing for the invasion, the United States persuaded the United Nations to adopt a resolution to drive the North Koreans out. Armed with a UN mandate, the U.S. military went into action and within months had pushed the North Koreans back to the thirty-eighth parallel. However, sensing an opportunity to unify Korea under a pro-U.S. government, they pushed on into North Korea and within a few weeks occupied Pyongyang. But subsequent U.S. advances toward the Yalu River on the Chinese border brought the Chinese into the war. A combined force of Chinese and North Koreans pushed U.S. forces and their allies back into the south, and the war settled into a stalemate near the original border at the thirty-eighth parallel. After two more years of fighting, which raised the number of deaths to three million—mostly Korean civilians—both sides finally agreed to a cease-fire in July 1953.

Beyond the human casualties and physical damage it wrought, the Korean conflict also encouraged the globalization of the U.S. strategy of containment. Viewing the North Korean offensive as part of a larger communist conspiracy to conquer the world, the U.S. government extended military protection and economic aid to noncommunist governments in the rest of Asia. It also entered into security agreements that culminated in the creation of the Southeast Asian Treaty Organization (SEATO), an Asian counterpart of NATO. By 1954 U.S. President Dwight D. Eisenhower (1890–1969) asserted the famous **domino theory**. This strategic theory rationalized worldwide U.S. intervention on the assumption that if one country became communist, neighboring ones would collapse to communism the way a row of dominoes falls sequentially. Subsequent U.S. administrations extended the policy of containment to areas beyond the nation's vital interests and applied it to local or imagined communist threats in Central and South America, Africa, and Asia.

Cracks in the Soviet-Chinese Alliance In spite of the fact that the Soviet Union had given valuable economic and technical assistance to China after the war, and that it had become China's principal trading partner by the mid-1950s, the friendly relationship between the two states did not last. By 1960, the Chinese government had grown increasingly angry at the Soviet Union's refusal to share the technology for nuclear weapons. In 1962, the Chinese were furious when the Soviet Union did not support them in their war with India. By the end of 1964, the rift between the Soviet Union and the

A nuclear test in the Marshall Islands in 1954. Between World War II and the end of the twentieth century, nations with the capacity to produce nuclear weapons conducted more than two thousand tests. Although most tests were conducted in remote regions, they inflicted severe damage on animal populations and the environment.
Galerie Bilderwelt/Getty Images

People's Republic of China had become embarrassingly public, with both sides engaging in name-calling. In addition, both nations openly competed for influence in Africa and Asia, especially in the nations that had recently gained independence. The fact that China conducted successful nuclear tests in 1964, without the help of the Soviet Union, enhanced its prestige. An unanticipated outcome of the Chinese-Soviet split was that many countries gained an opportunity to pursue a more independent course by playing capitalists against communists and by playing Soviet communists against Chinese communists. It also opened the door for an eventual truce between China and the United States, because both countries now saw the Soviet Union as their principal enemy.

The Nuclear Arms Race   A central feature of the cold war world was a costly arms race and the terrifying proliferation of nuclear weapons. The Soviet Union had broken the U.S. monopoly on atomic weaponry by testing its own atomic bomb in 1949, but because the United States was determined to retain military superiority and because the Soviet Union was equally determined to reach parity with the United States, both sides amassed enormous arsenals of nuclear weapons and developed a multitude of systems for deploying those weapons. In the 1960s and beyond, the superpowers acquired so many nuclear weapons that they reached the capacity for mutually assured destruction, or MAD.

Cuba: Nuclear Flashpoint Ironically, the cold war confrontation that came closest to unleashing nuclear war took place not at the expected flashpoints in Europe or Asia but on the island of Cuba. In 1959 a revolutionary movement headed by Fidel Castro Ruz (1926–2016) overthrew the autocratic Fulgencio Batista y Zaldivar (1901–1973), whose regime had gone to great lengths to maintain the country's subservient relationship with the United States, especially with the U.S. sugar companies that controlled Cuba's economy. Fidel Castro's new regime gladly accepted a Soviet offer of massive economic aid—including an agreement to purchase half of Cuba's sugar production—and arms shipments. In return for Soviet aid, Castro declared his support for the USSR's foreign policy. In December 1961 he confirmed the U.S. government's worst suspicions when he publicly announced, "I have been a Marxist-Leninist all along, and will remain one until I die."

Bay of Pigs Invasion Cuba's alignment with the Soviet Union spurred newly elected president John F. Kennedy (1917–1963) to authorize a clandestine invasion of Cuba to overthrow Castro and his supporters. In April 1961 a force of fifteen hundred anti-Castro Cubans trained, armed, and transported by the Central Intelligence Agency (CIA) landed on Cuba at a place called the **Bay of Pigs**. The arrival of the invasion force failed to incite a hoped-for internal uprising, and when the promised American air support failed to appear, the invasion quickly fizzled. Within three days, Castro's military had either captured or killed the entire invasion force. The Bay of Pigs fiasco strengthened Castro's position in Cuba and encouraged him to accept the deployment of Soviet nuclear missiles in Cuba as a deterrent to any future invasion.

Cuban Missile Crisis On 26 October 1962 the United States learned that Soviet technicians were assembling launch sites for medium-range nuclear missiles on Cuba that could reach targets in the United States within minutes. President John F. Kennedy responded by issuing an ultimatum, calling on the Soviet leadership to withdraw all missiles from Cuba and stop the arrival of additional nuclear armaments. To back up his demand, Kennedy im-

posed an air and naval quarantine on the island nation. The superpowers seemed poised for nuclear confrontation, and for two weeks the world's peoples held their collective breath. After two weeks, the Soviet government yielded to the U.S. demands. In return, Soviet premier Nikita Khrushchev (1894–1971) extracted an open pledge from Kennedy to refrain from attempting to overthrow Castro's regime and a secret deal to remove U.S. missiles from Turkey. The world trembled during this **Cuban missile crisis**, awaiting the apocalypse that potentially lurked behind any superpower encounter.

Dissent, Intervention, and Rapprochement

De-Stalinization Within three years of Josef Stalin's death in 1953, several communist leaders startled the world when they openly attacked Stalin and questioned his methods of rule. The most vigorous denunciations came from Stalin's successor, Soviet premier Nikita Khrushchev, who embarked on a policy of **de-Stalinization**, or the end of the rule of terror and the partial liberalization of Soviet society. Government officials removed portraits of Stalin from public places, renamed institutions and localities bearing his name, and commissioned historians to rewrite textbooks to deflate Stalin's reputation. The de-Stalinization period, which lasted from 1956 to 1964, also resulted in the release of millions of political prisoners. With respect to foreign policy, Khrushchev emphasized the possibility of "peaceful coexistence" between different social systems and the achievement of communism by peaceful means. This change in Soviet doctrine reflected the recognition that a nuclear war was more likely to lead to mutual annihilation than to victory.

Soviet Intervention The new political climate in the Soviet Union tempted eastern European states to gain a measure of autonomy from the Soviet Union. They did not fare well in those endeavors. East Germans staged an unsuccessful uprising in 1953, but the most serious challenge to Soviet control came in 1956 from nationalist-minded communists in Hungary. When the communist regime in Hungary embraced the process of de-Stalinization, large numbers of Hungarian citizens demanded democracy and the breaking of ties to Moscow and the Warsaw Pact. Soviet leaders viewed those moves as a serious threat to their national security. In the late autumn of 1956, Soviet tanks entered Budapest and crushed the Hungarian uprising.

In 1968 Soviets again intervened in eastern Europe, this time in Czechoslovakia. The Communist Party leader there, Alexander Dubček (1921–1992), supported a liberal movement known as the Prague Spring and promised his fellow citizens "socialism with a human face." The Czechs' move toward liberal communism aroused fear in the Soviet Union, because such ideas could lead to the unraveling of Soviet control in eastern Europe. Intervention by Soviet and Warsaw Pact forces brought an end to the Prague Spring. Khrushchev's successor, Leonid Ilyich Brezhnev (1906–1982), justified the invasion of Czechoslovakia by the Doctrine of Limited Sovereignty. This policy, more commonly called the **Brezhnev doctrine**, reserved the right to invade any socialist country that was deemed to be threatened by internal or external elements "hostile to socialism."

Détente Realizing the extreme danger posed by mutually assured destruction, in the late 1960s the leaders of the Soviet Union and the United States agreed on a policy of **détente**, or a reduction in hostility, in which they tried to slow the costly arms race and decrease their competition in developing countries. Although détente did not resolve the deep-seated antagonism between the superpowers, it did signal a relaxation of cold war tensions and prompted a new spirit of cooperation. The spirit of détente was most visible in negotiations designed to reduce the threat posed by strategic nuclear weapons. The two cold war antagonists cooperated despite the tensions caused by the U.S. incursion into Vietnam, Soviet involvement in Angola and other African states, and continued Soviet repression of dissidents in eastern Europe. Likewise symbolic of the relaxation of tensions between democratic and communist nations were the state visits in 1972 to China and the Soviet Union made by U.S. president Richard Nixon (1913–1994). Nixon had entered politics in 1946 on the basis of his staunch belief in anticommunism, and his trips to the two global centers of communism suggested a possible beginning to the end of cold war divisions.

CONCLUSION

World War II was a total global war that forced violent encounters between peoples and radically altered the political shape of the world. Beginning in Japan and China in 1931, this global conflagration eventually engulfed Europe and its empires, the Pacific Ocean, and the rest of Asia. Men, women, and children throughout the world were subjected to the horrors of war as victims of civilian bombing campaigns, as soldiers and war workers, and as slave laborers and comfort women. When the Allies defeated the Axis powers in 1945, destroying the German and Japanese empires, the world had to rebuild just as another conflict began. The end of the war saw the breakup of the alliance that had defeated Germany and Japan, and within a short time the United States and the Soviet Union, and their respective allies, squared off against each other in a cold war, a rivalry waged on political, economic, and propaganda fronts, as well as via proxy wars with client states. When former colonial territories began to win their independence in the postwar period, they emerged as new nations into this bipolar world: a reality that limited their choices and shaped their futures.

STUDY TERMS

Allied powers (581)	Brezhnev doctrine (603)
appeasement (583)	COMECON (599)
Auschwitz (596)	Cuban missile crisis (603)
Axis powers (581)	D-Day (587)
Bay of Pigs (602)	de-Stalinization (603)
Berlin Wall (600)	détente (603)
Blitzkrieg (584)	domino theory (601)

Holocaust (592)	Rape of Nanjing (582)
Joseph McCarthy (600)	revisionist powers (581)
kamikaze (588)	Stalingrad (585)
Marshall Plan (598)	Truman Doctrine (598)
Munich Conference (583)	United Nations (UN) (597)
NATO (599)	Vichy (585)
Pearl Harbor (585)	

FOR FURTHER READING

Svetlana Alexievich. *The Unwomanly Face of War: An Oral History of Women in World War II*. New York, 2017. A meticulously researched history of Soviet women's contributions to the war effort.

Christopher Bayly and Tim Harper. *Forgotten Armies: The Fall of British Asia, 1941-1945*. Cambridge, 2005. A broad study of the impact of World War II on Britain's Asian empire.

John Lewis Gaddis. *The Cold War: A New History*. New York, 2005. A fresh and concise history of the cold war by the dean of cold war historians.

Brian Masaru Hayashi. *Democratizing the Enemy: The Japanese American Internment*. Princeton, N.J., 2004. An important account of the experience of Japanese Americans in World War II.

Waldo Heinrichs and Marc Gallicchio. *Implacable Foes: War in the Pacific, 1944-1945*. Oxford, 2017. Explores both the battles and the bitter debates over strategy in the last eighteen months of the Pacific war.

Keith Lowe. *Savage Continent: Europe in the Aftermath of World War II*. New York, 2012. An absorbing and chilling picture of a continent brutalized by war.

Rana Mitter. *Forgotten Ally: China's World War II, 1937-1945*. Boston, 2013. An important account of how a brutal conflict shaped modern China.

Richard Overy. *The Bombers and the Bombed: Allied Air War over Europe 1940–1945.* New York, 2014. An impressive work in which the author explores the military, technological, and ethical issues of strategic bombing and challenges the notion that the Allies fought a "moral" war.

Timothy Snyder. *Bloodlands: Europe between Hitler and Stalin.* New York, 2010. A nuanced and pathbreaking study of Europe's killing fields, where the murderous regimes of Hitler and Stalin claimed the lives of fourteen million noncombatants.

Odd Arne Westad. *Global Cold War: Third World Interventions and the Making of Our Times.* New York, 2007. A reexamination of the global conflict between the United States and the Soviet Union, in which the author argues that cold war interventionism helped shape present-day international affairs.

ZOOMING IN ON ENCOUNTERS

Mohandas Gandhi's Last Words

"**H**é Ram" were the last words that escaped Gandhi's lips after three bullets ripped through his frail body. Roughly translated, he uttered, "O! God," and then died. It had begun as a day much like any other in the life of **Mohandas K. Gandhi** (1869–1948), or "Bapuji" (dear father), as he was fondly called. On the morning of 30 January 1948, a few months after India gained its independence from Great Britain, he labored on a draft of a new constitution for the **Indian National Congress**, stressing as usual his major concerns that villages be empowered, that discrimination based on the caste system be abolished, and that religious intolerance and violence between Hindus and Muslims cease. Still distraught over the partitioning of his land into a Hindu India and Muslim Pakistan, he had weakened himself after independence through fasts and hunger strikes in protest against the killings of Hindus and Muslims and the

mistreatment of Pakistan. He weighed a mere 107 pounds that day.

Alternating between working, talking with visitors, and napping, Gandhi finally took a meal at 4:30 P.M. A little over half an hour later, he made his way to the evening prayer meeting he was to lead. As he approached the dais, he stopped to press his palms together, offering the traditional Hindu greeting to the crowd waiting at the

An American air strike against anti-American Viet Cong positions during the Vietnam War results in the destruction of a Vietnamese village.
Pictures From History/CPA Media Pte Ltd/Alamy Stock Photo

meeting. At that moment, Nathuram Godse—a Hindu extremist—stepped out of the crowd, pulled a pistol from his pants pocket, and fired the three shots that ended the life of the man many saw as the soul and conscience of India. The force of the shots crumpled Gandhi's thin body. As he slumped to the ground, large, crimson bloodstains spread starkly over his white, homespun shawl. After he whispered "Hé Ram," his breathing stilled. Godse's actions made it clear that not all Hindus agreed with Gandhi's lifelong rejection of violence and his insistence that Hindus and Muslims should tolerate one another's religious beliefs. Indeed, before he was executed by hanging in 1949, Godse declared Gandhi a "curse for India, a force for evil."

CHAPTER OVERVIEW

Gandhi's murder suggested the troubles and traumas faced by nations and peoples adjusting to independence from colonial rule, a process that occurred in almost every colonized territory in the three decades after World War II. Although most colonies won their independence in this period, few colonial powers transferred power willingly. During this period of decolonization, those fighting for independence not only had to actually win but also had to determine who would be included in and excluded from the new states, whether or not established colonial borders would be adequate, how ethnic and religious minorities would be treated, and what kind of governments would be established in place of colonial rule.

Although colonized subjects resisted colonial rule from its very beginnings, by 1945 anticolonial movements in a number of places had grown very strong. Over the next fifty years these movements swept away colonial rule around the world and gave birth to ninety new nations. Decolonization was aided by several factors. First, it became increasingly apparent that there was a significant growth of democratic and anti-imperialist sentiments within imperial countries themselves, and political leaders could no longer count on a war-weary public to make serious sacrifices to maintain overseas colonies. Second, the short-lived Japanese empire contributed to colonial revolutions throughout Asia, where European military prestige had been severely and permanently damaged after the Japanese defeated the British in Burma and Malaya, the French in Indochina, the Dutch in Indonesia, and the United States in the Philippines. Finally, with the emergence of the two postwar superpowers, the United States and the Soviet Union, both of which opposed European colonialism, the stage was set for a drastic overturning of colonial rule.

However, decolonization frequently did not lead to the kind of freedom and stability most formerly colonized people had fought for. In some places this was because the withdrawal of colonial rule brought religious, ethnic, or cultural divisions into high relief as once-colonized people struggled over who would take power. In other places, newly independent people realized that colonial rule had left them impoverished and without adequate infrastructure to compete in an increasingly globalized world. In still others, independence threw new states right into the midst of cold war competition between the United States and the Soviet Union. This competition frequently entailed intervention and influence by one of the cold war powers, which limited the ability of new states to determine their own futures. Thus, although freedom did not remain elusive for colonized people, peace and prosperity often did.

CHRONOLOGY	
1940s–1970	El Milagro Mexicano
1947	Partition of India
1948	Creation of Israel
1948–1989	Apartheid in South Africa
1954	French defeat at Dien Bien Phu
1954–1962	Algerian war of liberation
1955	Bandung Conference
1956	Suez crisis
1957	Ghana gains independence
1958–1961	Great Leap Forward in China
1963	Founding of Organization of African Unity
1973	Arab-Israeli War
1976	Reunification of Vietnam
1979	Revolution in Iran
1980–1988	Iran-Iraq War
1997	Transfer of British Hong Kong to People's Republic of China

INDEPENDENCE IN ASIA

In the wake of World War II, the power of Asian anticolonial movements was irrepressible. In the decades that followed, new states emerged in south, southwest, and southeast Asia. Although colonized people faced different kinds of struggles in each territory, ranging from civil disobedience to guerrilla warfare, the end result across the whole region was independence from colonial rule.

India's Partitioned Independence

In the 1930s Indians had fought for, and won, numerous reforms from the British colonial government. The most significant of these reforms was the India Act of 1935, which laid out a structure for Indian home rule (control over internal affairs). But the India Act faced challenges in the form of increasing calls for independent yet separate Hindu and Muslim states, and the eruption of World War II suspended home rule altogether.

The Coming of Self-Rule After the war, however, British resistance to independence evaporated. Faced with the necessity of waging a costly war to maintain British rule against strong Indian resistance, the war-weary and economically weakened British government decided to work toward independence.

The issue of Muslim separatism grew in importance as Indian independence became more certain. In particular, Muslims expressed concerns about their minority status in a free India dominated by Hindus. **Muhammad Ali Jinnah** (1876–1948), leader of the Muslim League, argued that these concerns could only be met through the establishment of a separate Muslim state, even as Congress Party leaders such as **Jawaharlal Nehru** (1889–1964) and Gandhi urged all Indians to act as one nation, undivided by communalism (emphasizing religious over national identity). In August 1946, in the midst of negotiations with the British to reach terms regarding independence, the Muslim League called for a Day of Direct Action. Some six thousand people died in the rioting that ensued—called the Great Calcutta Killing—further fueling communal feeling and adding weight to Jinnah's claim: "The only solution to India's problem is Pakistan."

Partition and Violence Gandhi and Nehru only reluctantly came to accept the notion of a divided and independent India. Gandhi condemned what has come to be known as the **partition of India**, glumly prophesying that "rivers of blood" would flow in the wake of partition. Indeed, both Hindus and Muslims were involved in propaganda campaigns intended to stir up animosities between the two religious traditions, and rumors about the dire consequences of remaining in the "wrong" state inspired fear and uncertainty among ordinary people. To make matters worse, the British government did not make it clear exactly where the boundaries of the new states would be, leaving that task to the new Indian government two days after independence. Hindus and Muslims who lived in the areas that would likely be affected were terrified that they would suddenly be in hostile territory once independence was declared, and thus millions began to move to what they hoped would be "safe" territory during the summer of 1947. Muslims and Hindus who had once been neighbors and friends now began to see one another as the enemy, and in the highly charged atmosphere, individuals began to resort to violence. By mid-1948 an estimated ten million refugees had made the torturous journey to one state or the other, and between half a million and one million people died in the violence that accompanied those massive human migrations. The hostility between migrating Hindus and Muslims spilled over into the enmity between the two states, complicating efforts to build their independent nations.

In spite of the tragic violence of partition, Indian independence became a reality with momentous consequences for the process of decolonization. India was the most important British colony, and its breakaway encouraged anti-imperial movements throughout Asia and Africa. Indian independence also provided inspiration for other states grappling with decolonization in the midst of the cold war because of Jawaharlal Nehru's promotion of a nonalignment strategy. In his role as the first president of independent India, Nehru became an impassioned defender of nonalignment for newly independent nations caught in the cold war superpower tug-of-war for the loyalties of new nations.

Nonalignment Leaders of new African and Asian countries—including Nehru—first discussed nonalignment at the Bandung Conference. In April 1955 leaders from twenty-three Asian and six African nations met in Bandung, Indonesia, to find an alternative to aligning with either the United States or the Soviet Union. Bandung was the precursor of the broader **Nonaligned Movement**, which held occasional meetings so that its members could discuss matters of common interest, particularly their relations with the United States and the Soviet Union. The movement's primary goal was to maintain formal neutrality. However, the Nonaligned Movement suffered from a chronic lack of unity among its members and ultimately failed to present a genuinely united front. Although theoretically nonaligned with either cold war superpower, many member states did, in fact, maintain close ties to one or the other.

Nationalist Struggles in Vietnam

In contrast to India, the Vietnamese struggle for independence became deeply enmeshed in the politics of the

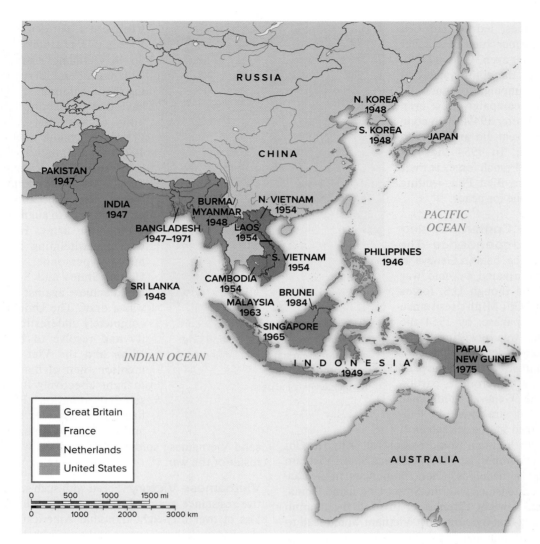

MAP 33.1 Decolonization in Asia; date is year of independence

Note the dates of independence for the colonies of Great Britain, the Netherlands, the United States, and France.

Why did independence occur in such a short time span for most of these colonies?

cold war. As a result, Vietnam's independence occurred only after decades of bloody wars to defeat first the French and then the Americans.

Fighting the French Vietnamese anticolonial activists had been fighting against French rule in Indochina since the late nineteenth century. By the 1930s the Indochinese Communist Party was among the groups fighting to drive out the French. **Ho Chi Minh** (1890–1969), the man who would become the first president of North Vietnam, had helped found the Indochinese Communist Party but spent the 1930s in exile as a wanted man in his home country. When the Japanese invaded Indochina in 1940, Ho was infuriated that after so many years of fighting French colonizers, the Vietnamese now faced another. In that year

he returned to Indochina and worked with U.S. operatives from the Office of Strategic Services to undermine their common enemy. By 1945, when it was clear that Japan was going to lose the war and before the French could return to reclaim Indochina, Ho and his party proclaimed Vietnam an independent republic. However, the French, humiliated by their country's easy defeat and occupation by the Germans, sought to reclaim their world-power status through their imperial possessions. By October 1945 the French had retaken Saigon and much of southern Vietnam, and by 1946 war had broken out between the French and the Vietnamese communist forces of the north, known as the Viet Minh. By 1947 the French appeared to have secured their power, especially in the cities, but that security proved to be temporary. Vietnamese resistance forces, led by Ho Chi Minh and former history teacher General Vo Nguyen Giap (1912–2013), took to the countryside and mounted a campaign of guerrilla warfare. This campaign grew even more effective after 1949, when communist China sent aid and arms to the Viet Minh. In 1954 the Viet Minh defeated French forces at their fortress at Dien Bien Phu, leading the French to sue for peace.

The Geneva Conference and Partial Independence The peace conference, held in Geneva in 1954, was dominated by cold war concerns. Even though U.S. forces had aided Ho Chi Minh's resistance against the Japanese, by 1954 the United States was unwilling to accept that French defeat would leave Ho's Communist Party in control of Vietnam. As a compromise, participants in the **Geneva Conference** agreed that Vietnam should be temporarily divided at the seventeenth

Ho Chi Minh, leader of North Vietnam from 1945 to 1969 and one of southeast Asia's most influential communist leaders.
Bettmann/Getty Images

parallel; North Vietnam would be controlled by Ho Chi Minh and the communist forces, whereas South Vietnam would remain in the hands of noncommunists. In the context of growing tensions with the Soviet Union and China, U.S. president Dwight Eisenhower invoked the domino theory, arguing that a communist Vietnam would lead to the spread of communism throughout southeast Asia. Because of this, the United States supported a South Vietnamese anticommunist leader, and together both ignored calls for new elections, which likely would have brought Ho to power over a unified Vietnam. But Ngo Dinh Diem (1901–1963), the first president of the Republic of (South) Vietnam, was dictatorial, corrupt, and deeply unpopular with the people, and growing discontent sparked the spread of guerrilla war in the south.

In 1960, Vietnamese nationalists in the south formed the National Liberation Front (NLF) to fight for freedom from South Vietnamese rule (the military arm of the NLF became known as the Viet Cong). Although Vietnamese from the south made up the majority in this organization, it received direction, aid, weapons, and ultimately troops from the north. In turn, the government in the north received economic and military assistance from the Soviet Union and China, and a cold war stalemate ensued.

Vietnam's "American War" The Viet Cong's attacks against the South Vietnamese government met with considerable success. Believing that a communist victory would have dire consequnces for the stability of southeast Asia, in 1965 President **Lyndon Johnson** (1908–1973) exponentially increased U.S. involvement in Vietnam. He ordered a bombing campaign against North Vietnam and sent U.S. ground troops to augment the South Vietnamese army. However, even with overwhelming firepower and military personnel, the best the United States and South Vietnam could achieve against the Viet Cong was a draw. The United States had completely underestimated the ability and resolve of both the Viet Minh and the Viet Cong—not to mention their civilian supporters—to fight effectively for Vietnamese self-determination. But the sacrifices were terrible: between 1965 and 1975, nearly nine hundred thousand Vietnamese soldiers and civilians were killed as a result of the war.

Vietnamese Victory Faced with such strong and effective resistance against U.S. intervention, incensed by the loss of over fifty-eight thousand American soldiers, and shocked by daily depictions of the war's brutality on American television, public opinion in the United States began to turn against the war. In 1968 the war had become so divisive that President Lyndon Johnson pledged not to run for reelection, and Richard Nixon successfully campaigned on a pledge to end the war. During Nixon's administration, U.S. troops gradually withdrew from the conflict, and in January 1973 the "American War," as the Vietnamese termed it, ended with the Paris Peace Accords. With the Americans out of the way, forces from North Vietnam, in partnership with the Viet Cong, began to move south. In April 1975 North Vietnamese tanks rolled into Saigon. War itself did not end, however, as forces from North Vietnam and the NLF continued their struggle to conquer South Vietnam. They achieved their goals with the military defeat of South Vietnam in 1975 and with national reunification in 1976.

Arab National States and the Problem of Palestine

With the exception of Palestine, the Arab states of southwest Asia had little difficulty freeing themselves from the

---

Vo Nguyen Giap (voh winn zahp)

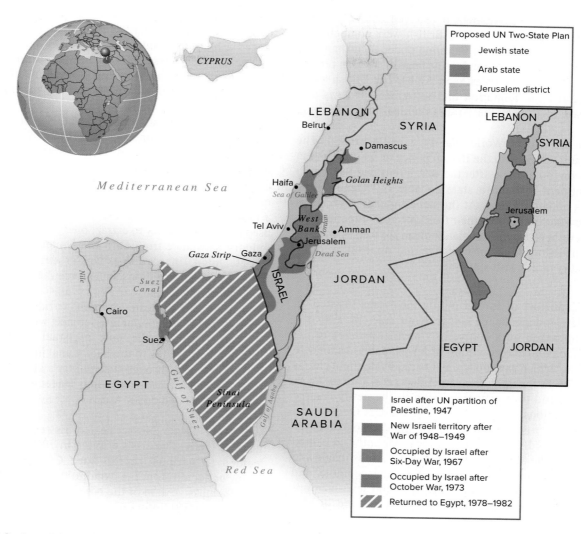

MAP 33.2   The Arab-Israeli conflict, 1947–1982

Compare the boundaries proposed by the UN partition of Palestine with the substantially larger territories claimed by Israel after 1948–1949.

What were the strategic advantages of the extra territories claimed by Israel in 1948–1949?

colonial powers of France and Britain by the end of World War II. Before World War II, anticolonial activists in Arab states had already won concessions for self-rule under the mandate system established after the Great War. For example, Egyptians had won almost complete autonomy from British rule, although this autonomy continued to be limited by British military control of the strategic Suez Canal and the oil-rich Persian Gulf.

Arab Independence

By 1946 Syria, Iraq, Lebanon, and Jordan had gained complete independence. However, as in Egypt, significant vestiges of imperial rule impeded Arab sovereignty. The battle to rid southwest Asia of those remnants of imperialism was deeply complicated by the cold war, as both the United States and the Soviet Union sought

influence in the region because of its vast reserves of oil, the lifeblood of the cold war's military-industrial complexes. Throughout, one ambiguous legacy of imperialism, Palestine, absorbed much of the region's energies and emotions.

Palestine

Great Britain served as the mandate power in Palestine after the Great War and made conflicting promises to both the Palestinian Arabs and to Jews migrating to Palestine to establish a secure homeland where they could avoid persecution. With the Balfour Declaration of 1917, the British government committed itself to the support of a homeland for Jews in Palestine, a commitment engendered in part by the vibrant Zionist movement that had been growing in Europe since the 1890s. The Zionist dream of establishing a national state in Palestine, the site of the original Jewish homeland, received a boost from the Balfour Declaration. Thus the British were compelled to allow Jewish migration to Palestine under their mandate, but they also had to respond to the fears of those in possession of the land—the Palestinian Arabs. The British therefore limited the migration and settlement of Jews and promised to protect the Arabs' political and economic rights.

At the end of World War II, a battle brewed. The Holocaust, along with the British policy of limiting Jewish migration to Palestine after the war, intensified the Jewish commitment to build a state capable of defending the world's remaining Jews. At the same time, as Arab states around Palestine gained their freedom from imperial rule, they developed a pan-Arab nationalism sparked by support for their fellow Arabs in Palestine and opposition to the possibility of a Jewish state there.

The Creation of Israel While the Arabs insisted on complete independence under Arab rule, in 1945 the Jews embarked on a course of violent resistance to the British to compel recognition of Jewish demands for self-rule. The British gave up trying to adjudicate these claims in 1947, stating that they intended to withdraw from Palestine and turn over the region to the newly created United Nations. In November 1947 the UN General Assembly announced a proposal for the division of Palestine into two distinct states, an idea that both the United States and the Soviet Union supported. Arabs inside and outside Palestine found that solution unacceptable, and in late 1947 civil war broke out. Arab and Jewish troops battled each other as the British withdrew, and in May 1948 the Jews in Palestine proclaimed the creation of the independent state of Israel before the UN proposal could be enacted.

Israel's proclamation of statehood provoked a series of military conflicts between Israeli and various Arab forces spanning decades, most notably in 1948–1949, 1956, 1967, 1973, and 1982. As a result of those wars, Israel substantially increased the size of its territory beyond the area granted to it by the original UN partition proposal and forced hundreds of thousands of Palestinians to become refugees outside the state of Israel. Violence continues well into the twenty-first century, and the future of the occupied territories remains undetermined.

Egypt and Arab Nationalism Egyptian military leaders, under the direction of **Gamal Abdel Nasser** (1918–1970), committed themselves to opposing Israel and taking command of the Arab world. When Israel declared independence in 1948, Egypt—along with Jordan, Iraq, Syria, and Lebanon—declared war against the new state. However, instead of defeating Israel, the Arab coalition lost both the war and territory. In response,

Egyptians staged a number of riots against the monarch, King Farouk. In July 1952 Nasser and other officers staged a bloodless coup that ended the monarchy, and two years later Nasser named himself prime minister. He then labored to develop Egypt economically and militarily and make it the fountainhead of pan-Arab nationalism.

In his efforts to strengthen Egypt, Nasser adopted an internationalist position based, like India's Nehru, on the idea of nonalignment (in fact, Nasser attended the Bandung Conference on nonalignment in 1955). Nasser condemned states that joined with either the United States or the Soviet Union in military alliances as participants in a new form of imperialism. In practice, however, Nasser used his political savvy to extract pledges of economic and military assistance from both the United States and the Soviet Union. In so doing, Nasser demonstrated how newly independent nations could force the superpowers to compete for influence.

Nasser also dedicated himself to ridding Egypt and the Arab world of imperial interference, which he believed included destroying the state of Israel and abolishing British military rights to the Suez Canal in 1954. Through such actions and through his country's antipathy toward Israel, he laid claim to pan-Arab leadership throughout southwest Asia and north Africa.

The Suez Crisis Nasser sealed his reputation during the **Suez crisis**. The crisis erupted in 1956, when Nasser decided to nationalize the Suez Canal and use the money collected from the canal to finance the construction of a massive dam of the Nile River at Aswan. When he did not bow to international pressure to provide multinational control of the vital Suez Canal, British, French, and Israeli forces conspired to wrest control of the canal away from him. Their military campaign was successful, but they failed on the diplomatic level and tore at the fabric of the cold war world system. They had not consulted with the United States, which strongly condemned the attack and forced them to withdraw. The Soviet Union also objected forcefully, thereby gaining a reputation for being a staunch supporter of Arab nationalism. Nasser gained tremendous prestige, and Egypt solidified its position as a leader against imperialism in the region.

Despite Nasser's successes, he did not achieve his goal of defeating Israel, which instead continued to grow stronger and gain more territory. Although Nasser succeeded in playing the cold war powers off one another, the superpowers continued to intervene in the region because of its strategic value as an oil-producing region. These interventions, along with the continuation of the Arab-Israeli conflict, contributed to long-term instability in southwest Asia long after the end of empire.

DECOLONIZATION IN AFRICA

Independence struggles in Africa took many forms—some peaceful and some violent—depending on the type of colony, the colonial power, and the nature of opposing anticolonial movements. In some colonies, such as Angola, the colonial powers refused to relinquish their power without long and bloody wars. In others, such as Ghana, decolonization was seen as an inevitability. In colonies where imperial rule had the support of European settlers, as in Algeria or Kenya, decolonization often became violent. Complicating the decolonization process were ethnic, religious, and linguistic divisions in African societies, which undermined attempts to forge national or pan-African identities. Whatever the path and in spite of many challenges, between 1957 and 1980 Africans from every region had won their independence.

Forcing the French Out of North Africa

In 1956 Morocco and Tunisia peacefully won their independence from France. Four years later thirteen French colonies in west and equatorial Africa also won their independence, leading some to dub 1960 as "the year of Africa." However, in Algeria, the French resisted decolonization, sparking a brutal war that lasted eight years.

France and Algeria The French government treated Algeria differently than its other African colonies for two reasons. First, Algeria was a settler colony, which more than two million French and other Europeans had made their permanent home by the mid-1940s. Second, unlike its other colonies in Africa, the French constitution of 1848 had incorporated Algeria as a region of France rather than as a separate colony. Thus, when Algerian nationalists began to advocate for independence from France just after World War II, the French government saw their actions as a threat to the integrity of France itself.

Two female members of the National Liberation Army in combat gear during the war for Algerian independence. Thousands of women were active participants in the fight for independence from the French.
Keystone-France/Gamma-Keystone/Getty Images

War in Algeria The event that touched off the Algerian revolt came in May 1945. French colonial police in the town of Sétif fired shots into an otherwise peaceful demonstration in support of Algerian and Arab nationalism.

Why It Matters ▶▶▶▶▶▶

The Destructive Potential of Industrial Technologies

What does it take to win a war? Several conflicts during the period of decolonization demonstrate that sophisticated weaponry and a superior military force do not guarantee victory. The examples of Algeria and Vietnam are cases in point, as neither were defeated by French or American military might in spite of long and costly conflicts. The reasons included military aid (indirect and direct) from the Soviet Union (and China, in the case of Vietnam) but also a willingness by Algerians and Vietnamese to resort to guerrilla warfare, suicide bombings, or sabotage to maximize the effectiveness of individual efforts in fighting against massive force. This matters because history can provide valuable lessons for states considering military intervention against smaller or less powerful states—including, in more recent times, Afghanistan.

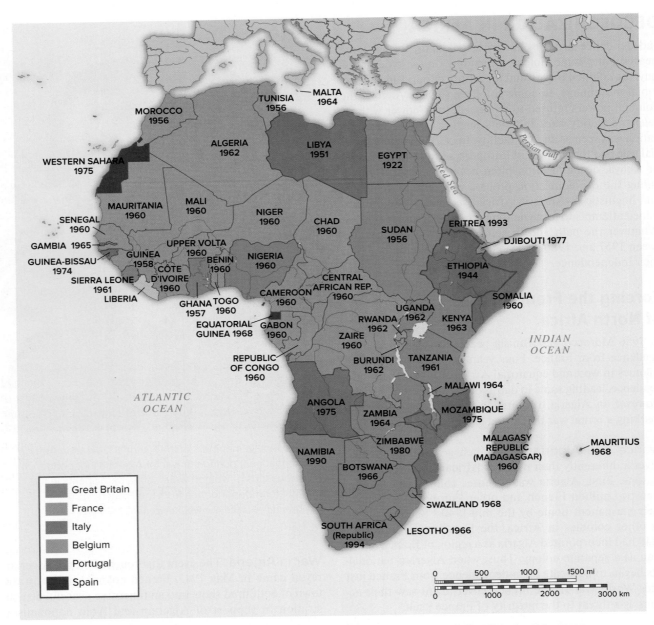

MAP 33.3   Decolonization in Africa; date is year of independence

Compare this map with Map 28.4.

How do the borders of the newly independent African states compare with those drawn by European powers in the late nineteenth century?

More than eight thousand Algerian Muslims died in rioting that took place in the wake of the shootings, along with approximately one hundred French. Discontent simmered following the disaster, but it was only in 1954 that the Algerian war of liberation began in earnest under the command of the Front de Libération Nationale (FLN, or National Liberation Front). At first, the FLN operated mostly in outlying, mountainous areas and resorted to guerrilla warfare. Then in 1955 the FLN moved into more urbanized areas. At that point France sent thousands of troops to Algeria to put down the revolution, and by 1958 it had committed half a million soldiers to the war. The war was brutal and ugly: Algerians serving with the French had to kill fellow Algerians or be killed by them; Algerian civilians became trapped in the crossfire of war, often accused of and killed for aiding FLN guerrillas; thousands of French soldiers died. By the war's end in 1962, when the Algerians gained independence from France, hundreds of thousands of Algerians had died.

Black African Nationalism and Independence

Anticolonial movements were widespread in sub-Saharan Africa by the end of World War II. Some of these movements drew from the pan-African movements that emerged in the early twentieth century. For example, African intellectuals, especially in French-controlled west Africa, established a movement to promote *Négritude* ("Blackness"). Reviving Africa's great traditions, poets and writers expressed a widely shared pride in the rich and diverse cultures and histories of Africa.

Growth of African Nationalism This celebration of African culture was accompanied by grassroots protests against European imperialism in nearly every colony. A new urban African elite created organizations that held demonstrations and protests and put pressure on colonial governments. Workers also organized strikes against oppressive labor practices and low wages, especially in areas such as the Gold Coast and northern Rhodesia. Some independent Christian churches also provided avenues for anticolonial agitation, as prophets such as Simon Kimbangu in the Belgian Congo promised his churchgoers that God would deliver them from imperial control. And in the years after World War II, African poets associated with the *Négritude* movement continued to encourage Africans to turn away from European culture and colonial rule.

African Independence European colonizers frequently tried to stall independence in sub-Saharan Africa. Often assuming that Black Africans were incapable of self-government, imperial powers planned for a slow transition to independence. The presence of white settlers in certain African colonies also complicated the process of decolonization. The politics of the cold war allowed imperial powers to justify oppressive actions in the name of rooting out a subversive communist presence. Despite delays, however, sub-Saharan states slowly but surely won their independence as each newly independent nation inspired and often aided other territories to win their freedom.

Freedom and Conflict in Sub-Saharan Africa

Ghana Ghana, an important center for growing and exporting cacao in west Africa, was the first sub-Saharan country to achieve independence from colonial rule. Ghana's success in achieving its freedom from British rule in 1957 served as a hallmark in Africa's end of empire.

Under the leadership of **Kwame Nkrumah** (1909–1972), political parties and strategies for mass action took shape. Although the British subjected Nkrumah and other nationalists to jail terms and repressive control, they eventually conceded to reforms and negotiated the transfer of power in their Gold Coast colony.

After it became independent in 1957, Ghana emboldened and inspired other African anticolonial movements. More than thirty other African countries followed Ghana's example and won their own independence within the next decade. Nkrumah, as a leader of the first sub-Saharan African nation to gain independence from colonial rule, became a persuasive spokesperson for pan-African unity. These efforts were aided by the optimism for the future in Ghana, whose immediate postcolonial economic prospects were bright. Indeed, in 1957 Ghana's gross domestic product was roughly equal to that of South Korea and was only slightly behind Portugal. Nkrumah's leadership of this prosperous new state symbolized the changing times in Africa.

Anticolonial Rebellion in Kenya The process of attaining independence was sometimes extremely violent. The battle for independence that took place in the British colony of Kenya in east Africa was one of these cases. The situation in Kenya turned violent in a clash between powerful white settlers and their elite, land-holding African allies on the one hand and landless Africans who had been impoverished by colonial rule on the other. Most of those involved were Kikuyu, one of Kenya's largest ethnic groups, because the British had disproportionately dispossessed the Kikuyu from their lands in the fertile Kenyan highlands. Beginning in 1947, Kikuyu seeking to drive out the British embarked on an intermittently violent campaign against both Europeans and the Africans who had allied themselves with them. The settlers who controlled the colonial government in Nairobi refused to see the uprisings as a legitimate expression of discontent with colonial rule and branded the Kikuyu rebels as **Mau Mau** subversives who should be eliminated.

Kikuyu who became involved in the Mau Mau movement were deeply dissatisfied with British rule in Kenya. Their resentment originated, in particular, from their treatment in the 1930s and 1940s, when white settlers pushed them off the most fertile highland farm areas, relegating them to overcrowded "tribal reserves." Resistance began in the early 1940s with labor strikes and violent direct action campaigns designed to force or frighten the white settlers off the land. In the 1950s, attacks on white settlers—and on Africans the Kikuyu believed were collaborating with them—escalated, and in 1952 the British established a state of emergency to crush the movement through a violent counterinsurgency program that involved rounding up and imprisoning over a hundred thousand Kikuyu in detention camps. Conditions inside the camps were dismal, and many thousands died from abuse, disease, and execution. Unable or unwilling to distinguish violent activism

Kwame Nkrumah (KWAH-mee en-KROO-mah)

from nonviolent agitation, the British moved to suppress all anticolonial groups and jailed Kenyan nationalist leaders, including Jomo Kenyatta (1895–1978) in 1953. Amid growing resistance to colonial rule, the British mounted major military offenses against rebel forces, supporting their army troops with artillery, bombers, and jet fighters. By 1956 the British had effectively crushed all military resistance in a conflict that claimed the lives of twelve thousand Africans and one hundred Europeans.

Despite military defeat, Kikuyu fighters broke British resolve in Kenya and gained increasing international recognition. The British resisted the radical white supremacism and political domineering of the settlers in Kenya and instead responded to calls for Kenyan independence. In 1959 the British lifted the state of emergency, and nationalist leaders such as Kenyatta reemerged to lead the independence movement. By December 1963 Kenya had negotiated its independence.

Internal Colonialism in South Africa As elsewhere in Africa, the presence of large numbers of white settlers in South Africa long frustrated, complicated, and delayed the arrival of freedom for Black South Africans. Even though Black South Africans made up almost 70 percent of the population by 1946, white settlers had violently driven them off the best lands and deprived them of political rights. Anticolonial agitation thus was significantly different in South Africa than in the rest of sub-Saharan Africa: it was a struggle against internal colonialism, against an oppressive white regime that denied basic human and civil rights to tens of millions of South Africans.

Apartheid The ability of whites to resist majority rule was aided by the South African economy, the strongest on the continent. That strength had two sources: extraction of minerals and industrial development, which received a huge boost during World War II. The growth of the industrial sector opened many jobs to Black South Africans, allowing some to build wealth, to organize into labor unions, and to demand serious political reform. These changes deeply alarmed white South Africans, who had built their rule on the political and economic oppression of Black South Africans. In 1948 the Afrikaner National Party, which was dedicated to quashing any move toward Black equality, came to power. Under the National Party the government instituted a harsh new set of laws designed to extend their control over the increasingly organized Black population; these new laws constituted the system known as **apartheid**, or "separateness."

The system of apartheid institutionalized the racial segregation established in the years before 1948. The government designated approximately 87 percent of South Africa's territory for white residents. Remaining areas were left as homelands for Black and mixed-race (called "colored" by the government) citizens. Nonwhites were classified and separated according to a variety of ethnic, racial, and tribal identifications in order to prevent the rise of unified liberation movements. The apartheid system was a system designed to keep Blacks in a position of political, social, and economic subordination.

Black South Africans resisted apartheid, just as they had resisted oppressive laws prior to 1948. The African National Congress (ANC), formed in 1912, gained new young leaders such as **Nelson Mandela** (1918–2013), who inspired direct action campaigns to protest apartheid. In 1955 the ANC (itself inspired by the Indian National Congress) published its Freedom Charter, which proclaimed the ideal of multiracial democratic rule for South Africa. Because its goals directly challenged white rule, the ANC and all Black activists in South Africa faced severe repression. The government declared all its opponents communists and escalated its actions against Black activists. Protests increased in 1960, the so-called year of Africa when multiple African nations won their independence from European colonial powers, and on 21 March 1960 white police gunned down unarmed Black South African demonstrators in Sharpeville, near Johannesburg. Sixty-nine people, among them young adults and ten children, were killed and almost two hundred more were wounded. Sharpeville, however, only increased radical activism by Black South Africans.

At the same time, the egregious use of violence and repression by the white regime in South Africa also increased international opposition to white South African rule. Newly independent nations in Asia and Africa called for UN sanctions against South Africa, and anticolonial and antiracist activists sought to publicize the government's repeated human rights violations. In 1963 government forces captured the leaders of the ANC's military unit, including Nelson Mandela, and sentenced them to life in prison. Thereafter, Mandela and others became symbols of oppressive white rule. Protests against the system persisted in the 1970s and 1980s, spurred especially by student activism and awareness of successful independence struggles in neighboring states. The combined effects of widespread resistance and agitation with a powerful international antiapartheid boycott eventually led to a growing recognition that if it was to survive, South Africa had to change.

The End of Apartheid When **F. W. de Klerk** (1936–) became president of South Africa in 1989, he and the National Party began to dismantle the apartheid system. De Klerk released Mandela from jail in 1990, legalized the ANC, and worked with Mandela and the ANC to negotiate the end of white minority rule. The National Party, the ANC, and other African political groups created a new constitution and in April 1994 held elections that were open to people of all races. The ANC won overwhelmingly, and Mandela became the first Black president of South Africa. Echoing the words of Martin Luther King Jr., President Mandela could finally proclaim his nation "free at last."

This sign in English and Afrikaans instructs visitors that the beach is for white persons only (from the Cape province in South Africa in 1974, during the period of apartheid).

Jonathan C. Katzenellenbogen/ Getty Images

AFTER INDEPENDENCE: LONG-TERM STRUGGLES IN THE POSTCOLONIAL ERA

Political and economic stability proved elusive after independence, particularly in those nations struggling to build systems free from the domination of more powerful nations. The legacies of imperialism, either direct or indirect, hindered the creation of democratic institutions in many parts of the world—from recently decolonized nations, such as those of Africa, to nations that had won their independence a century earlier, such as those in Latin America. Continued interference by the former colonial powers or the cold war superpowers impeded stability and prosperity all over the world. Indeed, few developing or newly independent nations escaped the legacies of imperialism or the new realities of cold war rivalries as they sought to find their place in the postcolonial world.

Communism and Democracy in Asia

Except for Japan and India, the developing nations in south, southeast, and east Asia adopted some form of authoritarian or militarist political system, and several followed a communist or socialist path of political development. Under Mao Zedong (1893–1976), China served as a guide and inspiration for those countries

A 1966 poster shows Mao Zedong (1893–1976) inspiring young people to launch the Great Proletarian Cultural Revolution (1966–1976).

Hulton Archive/Getty Images

seeking a means of political development distinct from the ways of the former colonial powers.

Mao's China Mao reunified China for the first time since the collapse of the Qing dynasty, transforming European communist ideology into a distinctly Chinese communism. After 1949 he embarked on programs designed to accelerate development in China. The economic and social transformation of Chinese society centered on rapid industrialization and the collectivization of agricul-

ture (making landownership collective, not individual). Emulating earlier Soviet experiments, the Chinese introduced their first Five-Year Plan in 1955. Designed to speed up economic development, the Five-Year Plan emphasized improvements in infrastructure and the expansion of heavy industry at the expense of consumer goods. The government also confiscated the landholdings of rich peasants and landlords and redistributed the land, so that virtually every peasant had at least a small plot of land. Between 1954 and 1960, however, the government over-

SOURCES FROM THE PAST

China's Marriage Law, 1949

When the Chinese Communist Party came into power under Mao Zedong in 1949, the new government quickly instituted the "Marriage Law," which made Chinese men and women legal equals in marriage. This was truly revolutionary, because women traditionally held very low status in China's highly patriarchal social structure. Although actual equality was more elusive than legal equality, the Marriage Law marked a significant step toward granting women more rights in Chinese society.

Chapter I. General Principles

Article 1. The arbitrary and compulsory feudal marriage system, which is based on the superiority of man over woman and which ignores the children's interests, shall be abolished. The new democratic marriage system, which is based on free choice of partners, on monogamy, on equal rights for both sexes, and on protection of the lawful interests of women and children, shall be put into effect.

> Why might this article have seemed revolutionary in 1949?

Article 2. Bigamy, concubinage, child betrothal, interference with the remarriage of widows, and the exaction of money or gifts in connection with marriage shall be prohibited. . . .

Chapter III. Rights and Duties of Husband and Wife

Article 7. Husband and wife are companions living together and shall enjoy equal status in the home.

Article 8. Husband and wife are in duty bound to love, respect, assist, and look after each other, to live in harmony, to engage in production, to care for the children, and to strive jointly for the welfare of the family and for the building up of a new society.

Article 9. Both husband and wife shall have the right to free choice of occupation and free participation in work or in social activities.

> Why might it have seemed important to the authors of this law to include this article?

Article 10. Both husband and wife shall have equal right in the possession and management of family property.

Article 11. Both husband and wife shall have the right to use his or her own family name.

Article 12. Both husband and wife shall have the right to inherit each other's property.

For Further Reflection

■ In what ways were these marriage laws similar to or different from the demands for gender equality made by feminists in the United States and western Europe during the 1960s and 1970s?

Source: Dennis Sherman. *World Civilizations: Sources, Images, and Interpretations*, 3rd ed., Volume 2. New York: McGraw-Hill, 2002.

saw the gradual collectivization of individual landhold-ings into agricultural communes in which landownership existed only at the level of the commune. In the same period the government took over the grain market and prohibited farmers from marketing their own crops. Col-lectives also became responsible for the provision of health care and primary education, which permitted the extension of social services to larger segments of the pop-ulation. In the wake of economic reforms came social re-forms, many of which challenged and often eliminated Chinese family traditions. Supporting equal rights for women, Chinese authorities introduced marriage laws that eliminated practices such as child or forced mar-riages, gave women equal access to divorce, and legalized abortion. Foot binding, a symbol of women's subjugation, was outlawed.

Mao's drive for development and revolutionary change was epitomized by the **Great Leap Forward** (1958–1961) and the **Great Proletarian Cultural Revolution** (1966–1976). These were far-reaching movements in-tended to bring rapid progress to China. In practice, how-ever, they undermined the very political and economic development that Mao sought.

Mao envisioned his Great Leap Forward as a way to quickly overtake the industrial production of more devel-oped nations. To achieve this, Mao extended the program of agricultural collectivization. Private ownership was abolished, and both farming and industry became commu-nal. But the Great Leap Forward—or "Giant Step Back-ward," as some have dubbed it—failed. Most disastrous was its impact on agricultural production in China: the peas-ants did not meet production quotas set by the govern-ment, and a series of bad harvests contributed to one of the deadliest famines in history. Between 1959 and 1962 as many as twenty million Chinese may have died of star-vation and malnutrition in this crisis.

The Cultural Revolution In 1966 Mao tried again to mobilize the Chinese and reignite the revolutionary spirit with the inauguration of the Great Proletarian Cultural Revolution. Designed to root out the revisionism (antirev-olutionary sentiment) Mao perceived in Chinese life, es-pecially among Communist Party leaders and others in positions of authority, the Cultural Revolution subjected millions of people to humiliation, persecution, and death. The elite—intellectuals, teachers, professionals, managers, and anyone associated with foreign or bourgeois values—constituted the major targets of the Red Guards, teenagers Mao had empowered to cleanse Chinese society of oppo-nents to his rule. Victims were beaten and killed, jailed, or sent to corrective labor camps or to toil in the countryside. The Cultural Revolution, which cost China years of stable development and gutted its educational system, did not end until after Mao's death in 1976. It fell to one of Mao's political heirs, Deng Xiaoping, to begin to heal the nation.

Deng's Revolution Although he was a colleague of Mao, **Deng Xiaoping** (1904–1997) suffered the same fate as millions of other Chinese during the Cultural Revolu-tion: he had to identify himself as a petit-bourgeois intel-lectual and labor in a tractor-repair factory. When a radical faction failed to maintain the Cultural Revolution after Mao's death, China began its recovery from the turmoil. Deng came to power in 1981, and the 1980s are often re-ferred to as the years of "Deng's Revolution." Deng mod-erated Mao's commitment to Chinese isolation and engineered China's entry into the international financial and trading system, a move that was facilitated by the nor-malization of relations between China and the United States in the 1970s.

Tiananmen Square To facilitate China's economic de-velopment, Deng opened the nation to the influences that had been suspect under Mao as foreign, capitalist values. His actions included sending tens of thousands of Chi-nese students to foreign universities to rebuild the profes-sional, intellectual, and managerial elite needed for modern development. But Deng's openness to foreign val-ues only extended so far. When some of the students who had studied abroad staged prodemocracy demonstrations in Beijing's **Tiananmen Square** in 1989, Deng approved a bloody crackdown. The issue facing China as it entered the global economy was how (or whether) to reap eco-nomic benefits without compromising its identity and its authoritarian political system. This issue gained added urgency as Hong Kong, under British administration since the 1840s and in the throes of its own democracy movement, reverted to Chinese control in 1997. Chinese leaders in the twenty-first century have managed to main-tain both centralized political control over China and im-pressive economic growth and development, although political control has depended on swift repression of dis-senting voices.

Indian Democracy Whereas other nations turned to dictators, military rule, or authoritarian systems, India was able to maintain its political stability and its demo-cratic system after gaining independence in 1947. Even when faced with ethnic and religious conflict, wars, pov-erty, and overpopulation, India remained committed to free elections and a critical press. Its first postindependence prime minister, Jawaharlal Nehru, guided this commit-ment to democratic rule for seventeen years, until his death in 1964.

In 1966 **Indira Gandhi** (1917–1984), Nehru's daughter (and no relation to Mohandas K. Gandhi), became leader of the Congress Party. She served as prime minister of In-dia from 1966 to 1977 and from 1980 to 1984, and under her leadership India embarked on the "green revolution"

Deng Xiaoping (duhng show-ping)

that increased agricultural yields for India's eight hundred million people. However, the new agricultural policies mostly helped wealthier farmers and only increased the poverty of India's poorest farmers.

To tackle India's persistent problems with poverty, overpopulation, and sectarian conflicts, Indira Gandhi resorted to decidedly undemocratic measures. To quell growing opposition to her government, she declared a national emergency that suspended democratic processes from 1975 until 1977. She used her powers under the emergency to move forward with one of India's most needed social reforms, birth control. However, rather than persuading Indians to control the size of their families, the government engaged in repressive birth control policies, including forced sterilization. A record eight million sterilization operations were performed in 1976 and 1977, prompting huge riots.

When Indira Gandhi allowed elections to be held in 1977, Indians voted against her because of her violation of democratic principles and her harsh birth control policies. But she was voted back into power in 1980, this time in the midst of fierce religious, ethnic, and secessionist movements. One such movement was an uprising by Sikhs who wanted greater autonomy in the Punjab region. The Sikhs, representing perhaps 2 percent of India's population, practiced a monotheistic religion, maintained a distinctive physical appearance, and had a history of serving in the Indian army. When partition occurred, the traditional Sikh homeland had been split between India and Pakistan, leaving Sikhs to desire its reunification under Sikh rule. When Sikh separatists occupied the sacred Golden Temple in Amritsar and began stockpiling weapons, Indira Gandhi ordered the Indian army to attack, killing hundreds of separatists. In retaliation, two of her Sikh bodyguards—hired for their martial skills—assassinated her a few months later in 1984.

Indira Gandhi's son Rajiv Gandhi (1944–1991) took over the leadership of India in 1985 and offered reconciliation to the Sikhs. However, he was assassinated by a terrorist in 1991 while attempting to win back the office he lost in 1989. Despite assassinations, violations of democratic rule, and continued problems with poverty and sectarian division, India has maintained its democratic institutions into the twenty-first century.

Pan-Arab and Islamic Resurgence in Southwest Asia and North Africa

The geographic convergence of the Arab and Muslim worlds in southwest Asia and north Africa encouraged the development of Arab nationalism in states of those regions that gained independence after World War II. Indeed, members of Arab nations were attracted by the idea of pan-Arab unity as a way of fending off European, U.S.,

and Soviet influence in the region. In north Africa, Egypt's Gamal Abdel Nasser provided the leadership for this pan-Arab nationalism, and Arab opposition to the state of Israel held the dream together.

The hopes attached to pan-Arab unity did not materialize. Although Arab lands shared a common language and religion, divisions were frequent and alliances shifted over time. The cold war split the Arab world; some states allied themselves with the United States, whereas others allied with the Soviet Union. Some countries also shifted between the two. Governments in these nations included military dictatorships, monarchies, and revolutionary Islamist regimes.

Islamism In the 1970s, **Islamism**—or the revival of Islamic values in the political and social sphere—emerged as an alternative to pan-Arab unity. Some Islamic thinkers called for the rigorous enforcement of the sharia (Islamic law), emphasized pan-Islamic unity, and urged the elimination of non-Muslim economic, political, or cultural influences. Many Muslims had become skeptical about European and American models of economic development and political and cultural norms, which they blamed for economic and political failure as well as for secularization and its attendant breakdown of traditional social and religious values. Disillusionment and anger with European and American societies, and especially with the United States, became widespread. The solution to the problems faced by Muslim societies lay, according to Islamists, in the revival of Islamic identity, values, and power. A small minority of Islamists argued that these goals could only be realized through violence.

The Iranian Revolution The **Iranian Revolution** that took place in 1979 demonstrated the power of Islam as a means of staving off secular foreign influences. Islamist influences emerged in Iran during the lengthy regime of Shah Mohammed Reza Pahlavi (1919–1980), whom the United States helped bring to power in 1953 in a CIA-engineered coup. The shah used the money from Iran's vast supply of oil to industrialize the country, and the United States provided the military equipment that enabled Iran to become a bastion of anticommunism in the region. But devout Muslim leaders despised the shah's secular regime, Iranian small businesses detested the influence of U.S. corporations on the economy, and leftist politicians rejected the shah's repressive policies. When the shah left Iran to get medical treatment in 1979, Ayatollah Ruhollah Khomeini (1900–1989) coordinated an Islamist revolution that deposed the shah.

The revolution took on a strongly anti-U.S. cast. During the revolution, Iranians captured sixty-nine hostages at the U.S. embassy in Tehran, fifty-five of whom remained captives until 1981. In the meantime, Iranian leaders shut U.S. military bases and confiscated U.S.-owned economic

Iranian women and men protesting in favor of the revolution to remove the shah from power, Tehran 1979. Thousands of women took an active part in the Iranian revolution. Several people hold posters depicting Ayatollah Khomeini.
Michael Norcia/Sygma/Getty Images

ventures. This Islamic power play against a developed nation such as the United States inspired other Muslims to stand up for themselves as well. Yet the resurgent Islamism of Iran did not lead to a new era of solidarity. Iranian Islam was the minority sect of Shia Islam, and one of Iran's neighbors, Iraq, attempted to take advantage of the revolution to invade Iran.

By the late 1970s Iraq had built a formidable military machine, largely owing to oil revenues and the efforts of **Saddam Hussein** (1937–2006), who became president of Iraq in 1979. Hussein launched his attack on Iran in 1980, believing that victory would be swift. Although they were initially successful, during the **Iran-Iraq War** Iraqi troops faced a determined counterattack by Iranian forces, and the conflict became a war of attrition that killed as many as one million soldiers before the war ended in 1988.

The Iran-Iraq and Gulf Wars Signs of recovery and a relaxation of Islamist strictness appeared in Iran in the late 1990s, but the destruction from war also remained visible. Islamism has reemerged in twenty-first-century Iran and has aroused some international concern, particularly for the United States. A conservative supreme leader, the Ayatollah Khamenei (1939–), and a conservative president, **Mahmoud Ahmadinejad** (1956–), represented this trend. Ahmadinejad took office in 2005 and touted Iran's nuclear program and his antipathy to the state of Israel, which had the effect of increasing his status in the Islamic world while intensifying tensions with the United States.

Iraqis continued on a militant course. Two years after the end of the Iran-Iraq War, Hussein's troops invaded

Kuwait (1990) and incited the Gulf War (1991). The result was a decisive military defeat for Iraq, at the hands of an international coalition led by the United States, and further hardships for the Iraqi people.

Colonial Legacies in Sub-Saharan Africa

The optimism that accompanied decolonization in sub-Saharan Africa faded as the prospects for political stability gave way in some areas to civil wars and territorial disputes. This condition largely reflected the impact of colonialism. As European powers departed their decolonized lands, they left behind territories whose borders were artificial conveniences that did not correspond to indigenous economic or ethnic divisions. Historically distinct communities found themselves jammed into a single "national" state. In other instances, populations found themselves in newly independent states whose borders were unacceptable to neighboring states. As a result, decolonization was sometimes accompanied or followed by civil wars and border disputes that resisted resolution.

The **Organization of African Unity (OAU)**, created in 1963 by thirty-two member states, recognized some of those problems and attempted to prevent conflicts that could lead to intervention by former colonial powers. The artificial boundaries of African states, although acknowledged as problematic, were nonetheless held inviolable by the OAU to prevent disputes. The OAU also promoted

---

Mahmoud Ahmadinejad (mah-MOOD ah-mah-DIH-nee-zhahd)

pan-African unity, at least in the faction headed by Kwame Nkrumah, as a vehicle for African states to resist interference and domination by foreign powers. In its early years the OAU successfully mediated border disputes between Morocco and Algeria (1964–1965) and between Somalia and its neighbors (1965–1967). But the drive for African political unity by leaders such as Kwame Nkrumah of Ghana was not always appreciated. It was so unpopular in Ghana that it contributed to Nkrumah's overthrow in a military coup in 1966. In addition, the OAU could not prevent extensive interference by the cold war superpowers in places such as the Democratic Republic of the Congo, Angola, and Mozambique. Nevertheless, in spite of continuing instability and poverty, African leaders in the early postcolonial period sought to integrate their new nations into the global economy by making the most of their rich mineral deposits, raw materials, and agricultural products.

Politics and Economics in Latin America

The uneasy aftermath of independence visible throughout Asia and Africa also affected states on the other side of the world—states that had gained their freedom from colonial rule more than a century before postwar decolonization. Nations in Central and South America along with

Mexico grappled with the conservative legacies of Spanish and Portuguese colonialism, particularly the political and economic power of the landowning elite of European descent. Latin America, moreover, had to deal with neocolonialism, because the United States not only intervened militarily when its interests were threatened but also influenced economies through investment and full or part ownership of enterprises such as the oil industry. In the nineteenth century, Latin American states may have looked to the United States as a model of liberal democracy, but by the twentieth century U.S. interference provoked negative reactions. That condition was true after World War I, and it remained true during and after World War II.

Mexico Only President Lázaro Cárdenas (in office 1934–1940) had substantially invoked and applied the reforms guaranteed to Mexicans by the Constitution of 1917. He brought land reform and redistribution to a peak in Mexico, returning forty-five million acres to peasants, and he wrested away control of the oil industry from foreign investors. Cárdenas's nationalization of Mexico's oil industry allowed for the creation of the Petróleos Mexicanos (PEMEX), a national oil company in control of Mexico's petroleum products. The revenues generated by PEMEX contributed to what has been called "El Milagro Mexicano," or the Mexican economic miracle, a period of

What's Left Out? ■■ ■■■■■ ■■■■ ■■■ ■■■

Although textbooks often discuss how the process of decolonization became entangled with the cold war, few offer extended treatment of the Portuguese colony of Angola. Yet Angola endured more than thirty years of war when a local communist anticolonial movement became enmeshed in a complex web of international aid and interference during the cold war. Anticolonial activists in Angola began a widespread rebellion against Portuguese rule in 1961, just as Britain and France were in the process of decolonizing nearby territories in sub-Saharan Africa. War broke out when it became clear that Portugal would not even consider a path to Angolan independence. But Angolans were not united in their vision of independence and broke into three factions, one of which was communist in orientation. The factions turned to outside allies for help, with the result that the communist faction drew aid from communist Cuba and Yugoslavia, whereas the noncommunist factions drew aid from the United States and South Africa. Outside aid ensured that the war would be long and bloody. But after fourteen years of fighting, new leadership in Portgual led the government to abruptly agree to Angolan independence. Before independence could even be declared, however, the three Angolan factions erupted in civil war as each sought sole control of the new country. Seeing an opportunity to determine the ideological allegiance of independent Angola, the United States and the South African government sent weapons, advisors, and (South African) troops to support the noncommunist factions. In response, Cuba sent its own weapons and troops to support the communist faction. With Cuban help, by 1976 the communist faction had won control of now-independent Angola, but even then the South African government continued to provide weapons to noncommunists. This, in turn, led both Cuba and the Soviet Union to continue providing material and financial aid to the victorious communist factions until the cold war ended in 1991. By then, the Angolan civil war had resulted in massive destruction to the land and infrastructure, and a half million were dead. Thanks to the politics of the cold war, the struggle for Angolan independence and power in the postcolonial era ended in the virtual destruction of the country.

Source: Jonathan Reynolds. *Sovereignty and Struggle: Africa and Africans in the Era of the Cold War, 1945–1994.* New York and Oxford: Oxford University Press, 2015.

In this 1950 photo taken in Buenos Aires, Eva Perón (1919–1952) waves to adoring *descamisados*, or "shirtless ones," to whose poverty she ceaselessly ministered. Although many thought of Eva Perón as a "saint," others viewed her own extravagant lifestyle as a sign of her opportunism. Keystone/Hulton Archive/Getty Images

prosperity that lasted until the 1970s. Conservative governments thereafter, controlled by the one-party rule of the Institutional Revolutionary Party (PRI), often experimented with various economic strategies that decreased or increased Mexico's reliance on foreign markets and capital. The PRI came under attack in the 1990s as Mexican peasants in the Chiapas district protested their political oppression. Cuauhtémoc Cárdenas, the son of Lázaro Cárdenas, took on the leadership of an opposition party, the Democratic Revolutionary Party (PRD), and this shift to democratic political competition and multiparty elections has continued into the twenty-first century.

Argentina Mexico served as one model for political development in Latin America, and Argentina seemed to be another candidate for leadership in South America. It had a reasonably expansive economy based on cattle raising and agriculture, a booming urban life, the beginnings of an industrial base, and a growing middle class in a population composed mostly of migrants from Europe. Given its geographic position far to the south, Argentina remained relatively independent of U.S. control and became a leader in the Latin American struggle against U.S. and European economic and political intervention in the region. A gradual shift to free elections and a sharing of political power beyond that exercised by the landowning elite also emerged.

However, during World War II, nationalistic military leaders gained power in Argentina and established a government controlled by the army. In 1946 **Juan Perón** (1895–1974), a former colonel in the army, was elected president. Although he was a nationalistic militarist, his regime garnered immense popularity among large segments of the Argentine population, partly because he

appealed to ordinary Argentines. He promoted a nationalistic populism, calling for industrialization, support of the working class, and protection of the economy from foreign control.

Peron's wife, Eva (1919–1952), helped foster that popularity, as Argentines warmly embraced their "Evita" (little Eva). She rose from the ranks of the desperately poor. An illegitimate child who migrated to Buenos Aires at the age of fifteen, she found work as a radio soap-opera actress. She met Perón in 1944, and they were married shortly thereafter. Reigning in the Casa Rosada (the Pink House) as Argentina's first lady from 1946 to 1952, Eva Perón transformed herself into a talented and fashionable political leader. While pushing for her husband's political reforms, she also tirelessly ministered to the needs of the poor. Endless lines of people came to see her in her offices at the labor ministry—asking for dentures, wedding clothes, medical care, and the like. Eva Perón accommodated those demands and more: she bathed lice-ridden children in her own home, kissed lepers, and created the Eva Perón Foundation to institutionalize and extend such charitable endeavors. When she died of uterine cancer at the age of thirty-three, the nation mourned the tragic passing of a woman who came to be elevated to the status of "Santa Evita."

Some saw Eva Perón not as a saint but as a grasping social climber and a fascist sympathizer and saw her husband as a political opportunist, but after Juan Perón's ouster from office in 1955, support for the Perónist party remained strong. However, with the exception of a brief return to power by Perón in the mid-1970s, brutal military dictators held sway in Argentina for the next three decades. Military rule took a sinister turn in the late 1970s and early 1980s when dictators approved the creation of death squads that fought a "dirty war" against suspected subversives. Between six thousand and twenty-three thousand people disappeared between 1976 and 1983.

Liberation for Nations and Women Revolutionary ideologies and political activism provided opportunities for Latin American women to agitate for both national and women's liberation. Nicaraguan women, for example, established the Association of Women Concerned about National Crisis in 1977 and fought as part of the Sandinista Front for National Liberation (FSLN). The FSLN was named in honor of the martyred Augusto Cesar Sandino (1893–1934), murdered for his opposition to U.S. intrusion in Nicaragua by the forces of Nicaraguan leader and U.S. ally Anastacio Somoza Garcia (1896–1956). Somoza's sons followed their father's brutal leadership practices, and Nicaraguan women dedicated themselves to ridding their nation of Somoza rule. In 1979 they renamed the organization the Luisa Amanda Espinoza Association of Nicaraguan Women (AMNLAE) to acknowledge the first woman who died in the battle against the Somoza regime. The group's slogan—"No revolution without women's emancipation: no emancipation without revolution"—suggested the dual goals of Nicaraguan women. By the mid-1980s AMNLAE had over eighty thousand members. Despite facing problems typical of women's movements trying to navigate between national and personal needs, AMNLAE has been credited with forwarding women's participation in the public and political spheres, an impressive accomplishment in a region where woman suffrage had often been delayed.

The Search for Economic Equity The late twentieth century witnessed a revival of democratic politics in Latin America, but economic problems continued to limit the possibility of widespread change or the achievement of economic and social equity. In many Latin American nations, the landowning elites who gained power during the colonial era were able to maintain their dominant position, which resulted in societies that remained divided between the few rich and the masses of the poor. It was difficult to structure such societies without either keeping the elite in power or promoting revolution on behalf of the poor, and the task of fashioning workable state and economic systems was made even more troublesome, given the frequency of foreign interference by the United States. Indeed, in addition to long-standing economic interference, during the cold war the U.S. government sanctioned either overt or covert military interference in multiple Latin American states, including Cuba, Guatemala, Brazil, the Dominican Republic, Chile, Nicaragua, and Grenada. In spite of such obstacles to stability, some Latin American states prospered in the mid-twentieth century. During and after World War II, nations in the region experienced sustained economic growth through expanded export trade and diversification of foreign markets. Exports included manufactured goods and traditional export commodities such as minerals and foodstuffs such as sugar, fruits, and coffee.

Latin American economies have continued to show resilience in the late twentieth and early twenty-first centuries, and Latin American nations have maintained links to global markets and money. Their economies appeared strong enough to limit the effects of their export-oriented systems and their use of foreign investment monies. Especially since the end of the cold war and the resulting decline in military interference by the United States, further economic growth should aid in the search for social and economic stability in Latin America.

CONCLUSION

In the years immediately before and after World War II, a few nations claimed imperial territories that spanned much of the world. But the decades following 1945 witnessed the stunningly rapid demise of the European, Japanese, and U.S. empires as colonized people everywhere fought for—and won—their independence. The process of decolonization was not easy and was frequently made more complicated by the presence of settlers, cold war politics, and internal divisions. Nevertheless, by 1980 decolonization was nearly complete, and the world's peoples sought to reshape their identities and build relations with the rest of the world. This process was frequently hampered, however, by legacies of imperialism, such as lack of infrastructure, economic underdevelopment, poverty, and religious or ethnic conflict. Additionally, since decolonization occurred at precisely the same time as the cold war, newly independent nations found their freedoms and stability compromised by the insistence of the two superpowers that they choose sides. Nevertheless, the global balance of power had been irrevocably altered by this attainment of worldwide independence and pointed to the emergence of a new kind of world order leading into the twenty-first century.

STUDY TERMS

apartheid (616)
Deng Xiaoping (619)
F. W. de Klerk (616)
Gamal Abdel Nasser (612)
Geneva Conference (610)
Great Leap Forward (619)
Great Proletarian Cultural
    Revolution (619)
Ho Chi Minh (609)
Indian National Congress
    (606)
Indira Gandhi (619)
Iranian Revolution (620)
Iran-Iraq War (621)
Islamism (620)
Jawaharlal Nehru (608)

Juan Perón (623)
Kwame Nkrumah (615)
Lyndon Johnson (610)
Mahmoud Ahmadinejad (621)
Mau Mau (615)
Mohandas K. Gandhi (606)
Muhammad Ali Jinnah (608)
Nelson Mandela (616)
Nonaligned Movement (608)
Organization of African Unity
    (OAU) (621)
partition of India (608)
Saddam Hussein (621)
Suez crisis (612)
Tiananmen Square (619)

FOR FURTHER READING

Abdel Monem Said Aly, Shai Feldman, and Khalil Shikaki. *Arabs and Israelis: Conflict and Peacemaking in the Middle East.* New York, 2013. An insightful book by three eyewitnesses who represent multiple perspectives on a controversial topic.

Nancy L. Clark and William H. Worger. *South Africa: The Rise and Fall of Apartheid.* New York, 2004. A survey of the history of the apartheid regime from 1948 to its collapse in the 1990s.

Prasenjit Duara, ed. *Decolonization (Rewriting Histories).* New York, 2004. The perspective of the colonized is privileged through a selection of writings by leaders of the colonizing countries.

Carlene J. Edie. *Politics in Africa: A New Beginning?* New York, 2002. Examines the domestic and external pressures that have transformed postcolonial African states and societies.

Caroline Elkins. *Imperial Reckoning: The Untold Story of Britain's Gulag in Kenya.* New York, 2005. Exposes the extreme violence and brutality of the British response to the Mau Mau rebellion in Kenya.

Rebecca Karl. *Mao Zedong and China in the Twentieth-Century World.* New Haven, 2010. Explores Mao and the Chinese revolution in a global context of imperialism, decolonization, and the cold war.

Yasmin Khan. *The Great Partition: The Making of India and Pakistan.* New Haven, 2007. A thoughtful analysis of the context in which partition occurred, as well as its execution and legacy into the present.

Todd Shepherd. *Voices of Decolonization: A Brief History with Documents.* Boston, 2014. An excellent summary of decolonization with a variety of supporting documents authored by colonizers and anticolonial activists.

Martin Shipway. *Decolonization and its Impact: A Comparative Approach to the End of the Colonial Empires.* Hoboken, 2008. Explores the process of decolonization across all of the empires, with a special emphasis on understudied areas.

Thomas E. Skidmore and Peter H. Smith. *Modern Latin America.* 8th ed. New York, 2013. A thorough and comprehensive overview of the region.

ZOOMING IN ON ENCOUNTERS

Kristina Matschat and a Falling Wall

On 9 November 1989 Kristina Matschat felt excitement and tension in the night air of Berlin. She had joined thousands of other East Germans at Checkpoint Charlie, one of the most famous crossing points in the Berlin Wall. Anticipating that the wall might come down that night, she also shivered in fear at the proximity of the *Volkspolizei* ("people's police")—the same force who since 1961 gunned down East Germans attempting to escape to freedom in

Neon McDonald's sign in Arabic, Amman, Jordan. Critics of globalization often point to the spread of McDonald's restaurants as both a sign of globalization and a sign of the Americanization of global culture. Proponents of globalization point out that people in different cultures experience McDonald's differently and that they make the restaurant chain their own by adding culturally specific foods and drinks to the menu. As of 2020, McDonald's had restaurants in one hundred countries around the world, with over thirty-eight thousand individual locations.
A. Astes/Alamy Stock Photo

West Berlin. She wore running shoes in case she needed to sprint away if shooting broke out.

Matschat remembered that "everybody was full of fear—but also full of hope." She could see that on the other side of the wall massive crowds of West Berliners had gathered to join their demonstration. Thrilled by this open protest against an iconic symbol of the cold war, she was nonetheless unprepared for how quickly victory came. Just before midnight East German soldiers suddenly began not only opening gates in the wall but also gently helping East Germans cross to the west, many for the first time in their lives.

Matschat remained at the wall until 3:00 or 4:00 A.M., celebrating with the hundreds of thousands of other Berliners who now mingled, drinking champagne and dancing on top of the wall. While celebrating the fall of the barbed wire and mortar structure, she became aware of the significance of what had just happened: "Suddenly we were seeing the West for the first time, the forbidden Berlin we had only seen on TV or heard about from friends. When we came home at dawn, I felt free for the first time in my life. I had never been happier." The fall of the Berlin Wall brought down one of the world's most notorious borders and symbolized the start of a new era in the contemporary world.

CHAPTER OVERVIEW

The fall of the Berlin Wall signaled the end of the cold war, a phenomenon that had shaped the world in multiple ways for more than forty years. The post-cold war era that followed was characterized by an increased level of economic interaction between countries and a tighter economic integration of the world. The forces driving the world economy in this direction, often referred to as *globalization*, included advances in communication technology, an enormous expansion of international trade, and the emergence of new global enterprises that favored market-oriented economics.

Cultural integration also resulted from the never-ending stream of ideas, information, and values spreading from one society to another. Consumer goods, popular culture, television, computers, and the Internet spread outward from advanced capitalist and industrialized nations but also increasingly moved the other way as well.

But the post-cold war era was also characterized by a host of urgent issues, including climate change, women's rights, terrorism, mass migration, and global disease. Each of these issues crosses national boundaries and requires global, interconnected responses. Almost a quarter of the way into the twenty-first century, none have yet been solved. Although no one can predict the future, the ability of the world's peoples to deal with these issues will determine how historians in the future will describe the successes and failures of the post-cold war era.

CHRONOLOGY	
1947	Establishment of GATT
1948	UN adopts Universal Declaration of Human Rights
1950	World population at 2.5 billion
1960	Introduction of birth control pill, creation of OPEC
1967	Establishment of ASEAN, birth of European Community
1981	Identification of AIDS
1989	Fall of Berlin Wall
1991	Collapse of Soviet Union
1992	Beginning of socialist market economy in China
2000	World population at 6 billion
2001	Terrorist attacks against the United States and war against Afghanistan
2003–2011	U.S. war in Iraq
2011	U.S. killing of Osama bin Laden
2012	Aung San Suu Kyi elected to Burmese parliament
2014	President Obama withdraws American troops from Afghanistan
2020	World population at 7.8 billion

THE END OF THE COLD WAR AND THE EMERGENCE OF A UNIPOLAR WORLD

Between 1989 and 1991 the Soviet system in Europe collapsed. In this period, through a series of mostly nonviolent revolutions, the peoples of eastern and central Europe regained their independence, instituted democratic forms of government, and adopted market-based economies.

The downfall of communist regimes in Europe was the direct consequence of interrelated economic and political developments. The United States, particularly under President Ronald Reagan (in office 1981–1989), kept relentless pressure on the Soviet Union to match the enormous military spending of the United States. At the same time, internal economic difficulties in the communist regimes of central Europe and the Soviet Union became so apparent as to require reforms. The policies espoused by a new Soviet leader, Mikhail S. Gorbachev (1931–), who came to power in 1985, represented an effort to address these massive economic challenges, but they also unleashed a tidal wave of revolution that brought down communist governments. Although Gorbachev desperately tried to save the Soviet Union from disintegration by restructuring the economy and liberalizing society there was little he could do except watch as events unfolded beyond his control. By the time the Soviet Union collapsed in 1991, the cold war system of states and alliances had become irrelevant.

Revolutions in Eastern and Central Europe

The inability to connect communism with national identities left communist regimes vulnerable throughout eastern and central Europe. To most eastern and central Europeans, the Soviet-imposed governments lacked legitimacy from the beginning, and despite the efforts of local communist leaders, the regimes never became firmly established.

By the 1980s economic stagnation and an accelerated arms race with the United States that strained the Soviet economy had led to obvious discontent in eastern and central Europe. It remained for Gorbachev to unleash the forces that resulted in the disappearance of the Soviet empire in Europe. By 1989 Gorbachev had committed himself to a restructuring of the Soviet Union and to unilateral withdrawal from the cold war. In public

interviews he surprised his hosts with the announcement that the Brezhnev Doctrine (in which the Soviet Union reserved the right to intervene in any eastern European nation if it compromised Soviet domination) was no longer in force and that from then on each country would be responsible for its own destiny. The new Soviet orientation led in rapid succession to the collapse or overthrow of regimes in Poland, Bulgaria, Hungary, Czechoslovakia, Romania, and East Germany.

Poland, Bulgaria, and Hungary The end of communism came first in Poland, where Solidarity—a combined trade union and nationalist movement—put pressure on the crumbling rule of the Communist Party. The Polish government legalized the previously banned Solidarity movement and agreed to multiparty elections in 1989 and 1990. The voters favored Solidarity candidates, and Lech Walesa (1943–), the movement's leader, became president of Poland. In Bulgaria popular unrest forced Todor Zhivkov (1911–1998), eastern Europe's longest-surviving communist dictator, to resign in November 1989. Hungarians tore down the Soviet-style political system between 1988 and 1989. In 1990 they held free elections and launched their nation on the rocky path toward democracy and a market economy.

Velvet and Violent Revolutions The disintegration of communism continued elsewhere in eastern Europe. In Czechoslovakia a "velvet revolution"—which meant that little violence was associated with the transfer of power—had swept communists out of office and restored democracy by 1990. In 1993, disagreements over the time frame for shifting to a market economy led to a "velvet divorce," breaking Czechoslovakia into two new nations, the Czech Republic and Slovakia. In Romania, by contrast, the regime of dictator Nicolae Ceaușescu (1918–1989) refused to acknowledge the necessity of reform. In 1989 *Securitate,* a brutal secret police force, savagely repressed demonstrations, setting off a national uprising that ended within four days and left Ceaușescu and his wife dead.

Fall of the Berlin Wall East Germany had long been a staunchly communist Soviet satellite. Its aging leader, Erich Honecker (1912–1994), openly objected to Gorbachev's ideas. When he showed genuine bewilderment at the fact that East German citizens fled the country by the thousands through openings in the iron curtain in Hungary and Czechoslovakia, his party removed him from power. When the East German regime decided to open the Berlin Wall to intra-German traffic on 9 November 1989, the end of the German Democratic Republic was in sight. In 1990 the two Germanies, once divided by the cold war, formed again as a united nation.

Lech Walesa (LEHK wah-LEHN-sah)

Todor Zhivkov (TO-dohr JHIF-kof)

Nicolae Ceaușescu (nih-kuh-LIE chow-SHESS-koo)

Men and women climb atop the Berlin wall on 9 November 1989.
picture alliance/Getty Images

The Collapse of the Soviet Union

The desire to concentrate attention and resources on urgent matters at home motivated Gorbachev's decision to disengage his nation from the cold war. When he came to power in 1985, Gorbachev was keenly aware of the need for economic reform and the liberalization of Soviet society, although he never intended the collapse of the whole system. Yet it proved impossible to fix parts of the system without undermining the whole.

Gorbachev's Reforms Gorbachev's reform efforts first focused on the ailing economy. Antiquated industrial plants and inefficient government control of production resulted in shoddy and outmoded products. The diversion of crucial resources to the military in order to keep up with U.S. military spending made it impossible to produce enough consumer goods, regardless of their quality. The failure of state and collective farms to feed the population compelled the Soviet government to import grains from abroad. By 1990 the government had imposed rationing to cope with the scarcity of essential consumer goods and food. Ominous statistics documented the disintegration of the state-sponsored health care system: infant mortality increased while life expectancy decreased. Funding of the educational system dropped precipitously, and pollution threatened to engulf the entire country.

Perestroika* and *Glasnost Under the slogan of *uskorenie,* or "acceleration," Gorbachev tried to shock the economy out of its coma. Yet the old methods of boosting production and productivity through bureaucratic

exhortation and harassment proved ineffective. Gorbachev then introduced the concept of *perestroika,* or "restructuring," to describe his efforts to decentralize the economy. To make *perestroika* work, the Soviet leader linked it to *glasnost,* the opening of Soviet society to public criticism and admission of past mistakes.

Perestroika proved more difficult to implement than Gorbachev imagined, and *glasnost* unleashed a torrent of criticism that shook the Soviet state to its foundations. When Gorbachev pushed economic decentralization, the profit motive and the cost-accounting methods he instituted engendered the hostility of those whose privileged positions depended on being protected by the old system. Meanwhile, *glasnost* not only opened the door to public criticism of party leaders and Soviet institutions but also allowed long-repressed ethnic and nationalist sentiments to bubble to the surface, posing a threat to the multiethnic Soviet state. Only half of the 285 million Soviet citizens were Russian. The other half included numerous ethnic minorities, most of whom never fully reconciled themselves to Soviet dominance.

The pressures on the Soviet system were exacerbated by a costly Soviet military intervention in 1979 to save a Marxist regime in Afghanistan. For nine years well-equipped Soviet forces fought a brutal, unsuccessful campaign against Afghan *mujahideen,* or Islamic warriors, who gradually gained control of most of the countryside. The Central Intelligence Agency of the United States supplied

perestroika (pehr-eh-STROY-kuh)
glasnost (GLAHS-nost)
mujahideen (moo-jah-hih-deen)

the decisive weapons in the war: ground-to-air Stinger missiles, which could be used to shoot down heavily armored Soviet helicopters, and thousands of mules to haul supplies from Pakistan. In 1986 the Kremlin decided to pull its troops out of the costly, unpopular, and unwinnable war. A cease-fire negotiated by the United Nations in 1988 led to a full Soviet withdrawal in 1989.

Collapse By the summer of 1990, as industrial and agricultural production continued their downward slide against a backdrop of skyrocketing inflation, the Soviet economy disintegrated. Inspired by the end of the Soviet empire in eastern and central Europe, Baltic peoples—Estonians, Latvians, and Lithuanians—began to secede from the Soviet Union in 1991. In the following months the remaining twelve republics of the Soviet Union followed suit. The largest and most prominent of the Soviet republics, the Russian Soviet Federated Socialist Republic, and its recently elected president, Boris N. Yeltsin (1931–2007), led the drive for independence.

Although the pace of reform was neither quick nor thorough enough for some, others convinced themselves that reforms had gone too far. While Gorbachev was vacationing in the Crimea in August 1991, a group of conspirators—including discontented party functionaries, disillusioned KGB (secret police) officials, and dissatisfied military officers—decided to seize power. Although Boris Yeltsin crushed the coup with the help of Red Army units, it was clear in the aftermath of the event that Gorbechev's political career had ended. He watched from the sidelines as Yeltsin dismantled the Communist Party and pushed the country toward market-oriented economic reforms. On 25 December 1991 the Soviet flag fluttered for the last time atop the Kremlin, and by the last day of that year the Union of Soviet Socialist Republics had ceased to exist.

The Unipolar Moment

With the demise of the Soviet Union, the cold war suddenly ended. For forty years the bipolar rivalry between the United States and the Soviet Union had dominated global politics and resulted in countless deaths as a result of "hot" proxy wars. And although millions of people rejoiced that nuclear war no longer seemed likely, this

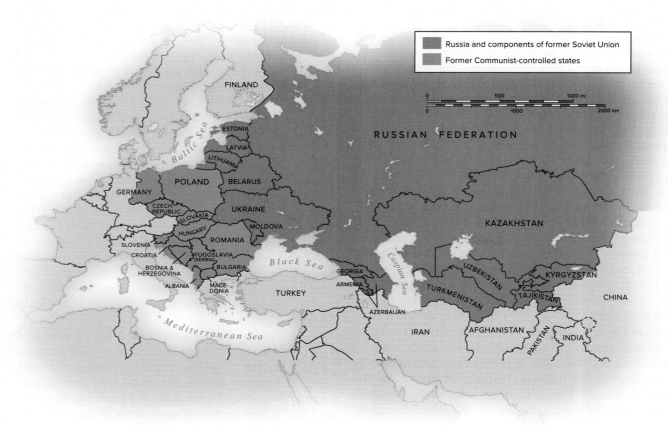

MAP 34.1 The collapse of the Soviet Union and European communist regimes, 1991
Note the number of states suddenly created by the breakup of the Soviet Union.
How would this affect the ability of each to survive, both economically and politically?

massive shift in the global balance of power left a vacuum. In the three decades following 1991, the United States sought to influence world politics as the sole remaining superpower, whereas Russia sought to return to stability and to regain its earlier prestige. These efforts caused relations between the United States and Russia to deteriorate dramatically in the opening decades of the twenty-first century. At the same time, the end of the cold war seemed to open space for other powers, especially China, to play major roles in global politics.

Instability versus Overconfidence In spite of initial optimism in and outside Russia in 1991, by the mid-1990s it was clear that the shift to a market economy could not immediately fix the country's many economic problems. Both industrial and agricultural production had dropped significantly, and one-third of the Russian population had sunk below the poverty line. Crime was pervasive. To make matters worse, Boris Yeltsin—who became the first popularly elected president in Russia in 1991—proved to be an erratic ruler.

In the midst of these difficulties, the U.S. government saw an opportunity to become the only world superpower. In 1992 Paul Wolfowitz, President George H. W. Bush's undersecretary for defense, wrote a post–cold war policy statement that advocated unilateral action and the use of the military force to prevent the reemergence of another superpower. This aggressive stance receded somewhat during President Bill Clinton's administration (1993–2001), but in 1999 the United States alarmed Russian leaders by inviting the former Soviet satellite states of Hungary, Poland, and the Czech Republic to join NATO. Given that NATO's original purpose at its founding in 1949 was to form a defensive alliance against the Soviet Union, the Russian government saw the incorporation of its traditional buffer states as a clear threat to national security.

The Bush Doctrine Under the administration of President George W. Bush (2001–2009), the U.S. government returned to an overtly aggressive foreign policy. The president's policies, which became known collectively as the **Bush Doctrine**, affirmed the legitimacy of the United States acting alone to pursue its own interests, even to the point of engaging in preemptive strikes. At this time the U.S. government regarded Russia as a second-rate power, and its leaders continued the policy of inviting former Soviet satellites into NATO. In 2004 NATO admitted Bulgaria, Estonia, Latvia, Lithuania, Romania, Slovakia, and Slovenia, further alarming and angering the Russian government.

Deteriorating Relations in the Early Twenty-First Century Meanwhile, Vladimir Putin, Boris Yeltsin's former prime minister, was elected to the Russian presidency in 2000. After stepping down in 2008, in 2012 he returned to the presidency, and in 2018 he was reelected for another six-year term. Putin focused on winning back the prestige Russia had lost after the collapse of the Soviet Union, demonstrating to the world that Russia would not tolerate unilateral action by the United States, and gaining control over domestic politics.

Relations between the United States and Russia deteriorated in 2014, when the pro-Russian president of Ukraine fled to Russia in response to popular protests against his rule. Putin's government then massed its forces along the Ukrainian border and annexed the Ukrainian region of Crimea, which had been part of the independent nation of Ukraine since 1991. In response, both the United States and the European Union imposed sanctions on Russian individuals and financial institutions. Confrontational relations between Russia and the United States continued in 2016, when the FBI announced an investigation of Russian hacking into the Democratic National Committee's computer system, and the Democratic Party accused Russia of meddling in the 2016 presidential election. The fraught relationship between Russia and the United States hit a new low when Vladimir Putin directed his armed forces to invade the rest of Ukraine on February 24, 2022. Although Putin expected a quick victory, Ukrainian resistance was strong and was aided by war materiel and aid from the U.S. and the European Union. Additionally, both the United States and European Union imposed harsh sanctions on Russia in an attempt to damage its economic ability to make war. In spite of these efforts, the invasion resulted in millions of Ukrainian refugees and thousands of civilian and military deaths.

THE GLOBAL ECONOMY

With the collapse of the Soviet Union, the potential for a truly globalized economy expanded to the former communist world. Economists pointed to a new economic order characterized by the growth of foreign investments, the unfettered movement of capital, the privatization of former state enterprises, and the emergence of a new type of corporation. Supporting the new global economy were technological developments in communications that virtually eliminated geographic distances. The forces driving the world economy toward increased economic integration have been responsible for a process termed *globalization*.

Economic Globalization

Globalization is a widely used term that can be defined in a number of ways. There is general agreement, however, that in an economic context *globalization* refers to the reduction and removal of barriers between national borders to facilitate the flow of goods, capital, services, and labor. Although global economic interaction and integration is not a new phenomenon, the more recent

Nestlé global corporate headquarters in Vevey, Switzerland. Nestlé is the largest food company in the world and has corporate offices all over the globe. In 2018 Nestlé generated sales of $93.4 billion. Gunter Fischer/Education Images/Universal Images Group/Getty Images

phenomenon of globalization since 1945 has been different and unprecedented in both scope and speed, and it has transformed the social and political as well as the economic contours of the world.

GATT and WTO At the end of World War II, the victors sought to establish an international trading system that would facilitate economic recovery after the destruction of the war. Believing that the protective tariffs characteristic of national policies during the Great Depression had only worsened the global economic crisis, they pushed instead for the elimination of restrictive trading practices that stood in the way of **free trade** (freedom from state-imposed constraints on trade across borders). The main vehicle for the promotion of unrestricted global trade was the **General Agreement on Tariffs and Trade (GATT)**, which was signed by the representatives of 23 noncommunist nations in 1947. In 1994 the member nations of GATT signed an agreement to establish the **World Trade Organization (WTO)**, which took over the activities of GATT in 1995. The WTO has developed into a forum for settling international trade disputes, with the power to enforce its decisions. The WTO has 164 member nations and 23 observer nations, which accounts for 99 percent of all world trade.

Global Corporations The emergence of global corporations played another key role in the development of the new economic order. Since the end of the twentieth century, the transformation of the corporate landscape has resulted in the birth of some fifty thousand global corporations. In contrast to multinational corporations, which

operate in several countries but have to abide by the laws and customs of a given society, the typical global corporation relies on a small headquarters staff while dispersing all other corporate functions around the globe in search of the lowest possible operating costs. Global corporations treat the world as a single market and act as if the nation-state no longer exists. Many multinational corporations, such as General Motors, Siemens AG, and Nestlé, have transformed themselves into global enterprises, both benefiting from and contributing to the ongoing process of globalization.

Global corporations have become the symbols of the new economy. They also have begun to transform the political and social landscape of many societies. Since the end of World War II, major corporations throughout the developed world have been required to contribute to the welfare of their respective home communities through a combination of collective bargaining agreements, tax laws, and environmental regulations. Highly mobile global corporations that are no longer bound to any particular location have managed, however, to escape those obligations. Competing with companies around the world, global corporations have moved jobs from high-wage facilities to foreign locations where wages are low and environmental laws are weak or nonexistent.

Economic Growth in Asia

Globalization and the acceleration of worldwide economic integration also benefited from economic developments in east and southeast Asia, where the economies of Japan, China, and the so-called **little tigers** (Hong Kong,

Singapore, South Korea, and Taiwan) underwent dramatic economic growth. This Asian "economic miracle" was largely a result of economic globalization.

Japan U.S. policies jump-started Japan's economic revival after its defeat in 1945, and by 1949 the Japanese economy had already attained its pre-war level of productivity. Just as western European countries had benefited from the Marshall Plan, so Japan benefited from direct U.S. financial aid ($2 billion) and investment. In addition, the United States placed no restrictions on the entry of Japanese products into the U.S. market. Finally, because a 1952 treaty stipulated that the United States would be the military protector of Japan and that Japan could never spend more than 1 percent of its gross national product on defense, the country's postwar leaders were able to channel the savings into economic development.

By the 1960s the Japanese had used the profits from their economic development policies to switch from producing manufactured goods such as textiles, iron, and steel to manufacture more capital-intensive goods such as radios, television sets, motorcycles, and automobiles. Then in the 1970s Japanese corporations took advantage of a highly trained and educated workforce and shifted their economic resources toward technology-intensive products such as random access memory chips, liquid crystal displays, and CD-ROM drives. By that time the label "Made in Japan," once associated with cheap manufactured goods, signified state-of-the-art products of the highest quality. Japan's economic achievements gave its banks, corporations, and government an increasingly prominent voice in global affairs. By the 1980s Japan seemed poised to overtake the United States as the world's largest economy. In the 1990s, however, it became clear that postwar growth rates were not sustainable, and the Japanese economy entered a deep recession, which continued into the second decade of the twenty-first century. Nevertheless, the postwar Japanese success story served as an inspiration for other Asian countries.

The Little Tigers The earliest and most successful imitators of the Japanese model for economic development were Hong Kong, Singapore, South Korea, and Taiwan. By the 1980s these newly industrializing countries had become major economic powers. By the 1990s the four little tigers were no longer simply imitators of Japan but had become serious competitors. As soon as new Japanese products had carved out market niches, corporations based in the four little tigers moved in and undercut the original item with cheaper versions. By the turn of the millennium, Indonesia, Thailand, and Malaysia had joined the original tigers in their quest for economic development and prosperity.

Perils of the New Economy For the supporters of the new global economy, the spectacular economic development of so many Asian societies was proof that globalization could deliver on the promise of unprecedented prosperity. By the late 1990s, however, it seemed clear that globalization could also lead to economic ruin.

At the center of this bust was a financial crisis that came to a head in 1997. In the preceding twenty years, the developing Asian economies had started to embrace the market, opening their borders to imports and courting foreign investments. After years of generous lending and growing national debts, the international investment community suddenly lost confidence in the booming economies and withdrew support. The crisis began in Thailand in mid-1997, when the government decided to discontinue its policy of pegging the Thai national currency (the baht) to the U.S. dollar. This led many investors to turn to other markets, which in turn caused the value of the baht to plummet. The Thai stock market quickly lost 75 percent of its value, and the country found itself in the grip of a depression. For no obvious reason, the financial panic—and with it economic contraction—then moved to Malaysia, Indonesia, the Philippines, and South Korea. In each instance, the rise and fall of the individual economy resulted from its integration in the new global economy, which rewarded and punished its new participants with equal ease.

BRICs Contrary to all expectations, the nations hit so hard by the financial crisis recovered quickly. Their recovery was matched by other emerging economies, often identified as BRICs because they include the fast-growing and developing economies of Brazil, Russia, India, and China. In the aftermath of the cold war, the governments composing the BRICs initiated political and economic reforms that allowed their countries to join the world economy. To make these nations more competitive, their leaders have simultaneously emphasized education, domestic entrepreneurship, foreign investment, and domestic consumption, with varying levels of success. China is already the leading global supplier of manufactured goods, whereas Brazil and Russia supply much of the world's raw materials.

The Rise of China After the death of Mao Zedong in 1976, China's leaders launched economic reforms that opened Chinese markets to the outside world, encouraged foreign investment, and imported foreign technology. These changes promoted rapid economic growth, and in 1992 the Chinese government labeled its new economic model a "socialist market economy." In such a model, the government retains control over political life while allowing a functioning market economy. In the economic realm, demand for goods and services determines production and pricing, and the role of the government is limited to providing a stable but competitive environment. Besides acting as a major exporter, China benefited from its large pool of cheap labor, and its enormous domestic markets have made the Chinese economy the destination of choice for foreign investment capital. In December 2001 China became a member of the World Trade Organization, and in 2010 it overtook Japan as the second largest economy in the world after the United States.

Trading Blocs

In the rapidly changing global economy, some groups of nations have sought to reduce risk, achieve advantages,

and gain economic strength for their partners by entering into economic alliances known as trading blocs.

European Union The most strongly integrated regional bloc is the **European Union**. In March 1957, representatives of France, West Germany, Italy, the Netherlands, Belgium, and Luxembourg took a significant step in this direction by signing the Treaty of Rome. This treaty established the European Economic Community—renamed the European Community in 1967. At the heart of this new community of nations lay the dismantling of tariffs

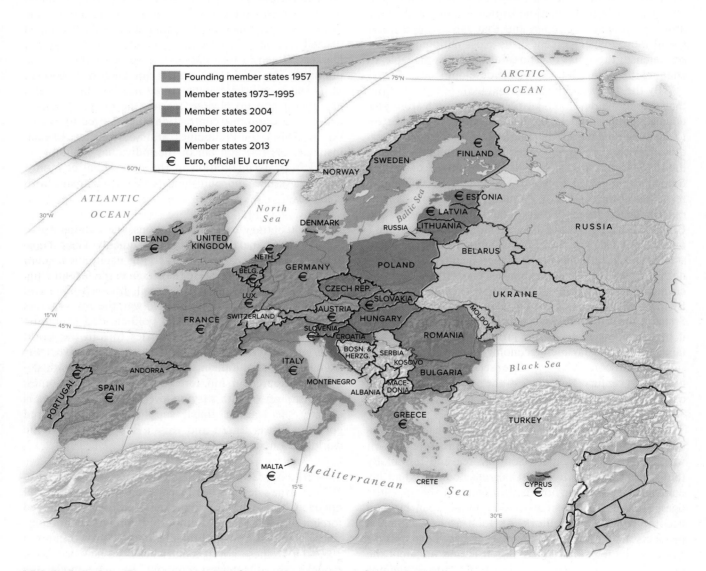

MAP 34.2   European Union membership, 2020

In 2007 the European Union celebrated the fiftieth anniversary of its founding as a supranational and intergovernmental organization. The euro (sign: €) is the official currency of the eurozone, which consists of eighteen of the twenty-eight member states of the European Union. Note that Great Britain is no longer a member state, having left the European Union on 31 January 2020.

What major challenges face the European Union in the twenty-first century?

and other barriers to free trade among member nations. Subsequent treaties created political institutions such as the Council of Ministers and the European Parliament. The development of a supranational organization dedicated to increasing European economic and political integration culminated in the Maastricht Treaty of 1993, which established the European Union. By 2013, twenty-eight European nations had submerged much of their national sovereignty in the European Union, and since 1999 eighteen members have adopted a common currency.

Despite the European Union's many achievements, it has had its share of problems in the twenty-first century. Among the most serious have been concerns within member countries about the loss of control over social, political, and economic policies. Indeed, these concerns led to the first withdrawal from the EU by a member state when the United Kingdom voted to leave the union in 2016. "Brexit," as it has become known, was initiated by Britons who argued that the economic benefits of EU membership were no longer worth the price of a submerged British sovereignty. In addition, deep concerns over the movement of people across the European Union—particularly migrants from parts of Africa and the Middle East—triggered nationalist, xenophobic responses that called for reasserting control over Britain's borders. The British withdrawal became final on 31 January 2020.

OPEC One of the earliest and most successful economic alliances was the **Organization of Petroleum Exporting Countries (OPEC),** a producer cartel established in 1960 by the oil-producing states of Iran, Iraq, Kuwait, Saudi Arabia, and Venezuela, later joined by Qatar, Libya, Indonesia, Abu Dhabi, Algeria, Nigeria, Ecuador, Congo, Equatorial Guinea, the United Arab Emirates, and Gabon. The purpose of OPEC is to control and negotiate the price of oil through cooperation with its mostly Arab or Muslim members. During the Arab-Israeli War of 1973, however, OPEC demonstrated that its economic control over oil prices could be used for political purposes. Because the United States supported Israel, the political enemy of many OPEC member nations, the cartel ordered an embargo on oil shipments to the United States and quadrupled the price of oil between 1973 and 1975. The huge increase in the cost of petroleum triggered a global economic downturn. OPEC's policies therefore demonstrated how the alliance could exert control over the more developed world and its financial system. OPEC's influence diminished in the 1980s and 1990s as a result of overproduction and dissension among its members over the Iran-Iraq War and the Gulf War. Additionally, in the twenty-first century, the increased use of hydraulic fracturing (often called "fracking") to extract oil from shale has allowed the United States to become the world's largest oil-producing country, with ten million

barrels a day. Because this allows the United States to be less dependent on OPEC, it has also muted the political potential of OPEC actions. Nevertheless, OPEC members continue to control around 72 percent of the world's crude oil reserves and thus remain a critical trading bloc.

ASEAN Another well-established economic partnership is the **Association of Southeast Asian Nations,** or **ASEAN.** Established in 1967 by the foreign ministers of Thailand, Malaysia, Singapore, Indonesia, and the Philippines, its principal objectives were to accelerate economic development and promote political stability in southeast Asia. Originally conceived as a bulwark against the spread of communism in the region, the economic focus of ASEAN became sharper after it signed cooperative agreements with Japan in 1977 and the European Community in 1980. In 1992 member states agreed to establish a free-trade zone and to cut tariffs on industrial goods over a fifteen-year period. By 2020, ASEAN member states had expanded to include Brunei, Cambodia, Laos, Vietnam, and Myanmar.

NAFTA Beginning in the 1980s, leaders of the North American nations of the United States, Canada, and Mexico also began to discuss the creation of a trading bloc to increase their economic competitiveness in the global marketplace. The result was the **North American Free Trade Agreement (NAFTA),** which went into effect on 1 January 1994 during the administration of U.S. president Bill Clinton. NAFTA worked toward the elimination of trade barriers among the three nations, allowing goods and services to move freely across borders, and set up mechanisms to resolve trade disputes. By 2018 NAFTA had quadrupled trade among the three nations, up from $290 billion in 1993 to $1.23 trillion. But NAFTA has been criticized, especially in the United States, for causing a loss in U.S. jobs and for keeping wages in the United States artificially low. In 2018 U.S. president Donald Trump sought the renegotiation of NAFTA for the specific purposes of reducing the U.S. trade deficit with its partners and safeguarding U.S. jobs. The new agreement, called the United States Mexico Canada Agreement (USMCA), was signed in the United States in December 2019 and had been ratified by all three countries by March 2020.

Globalization and Its Critics The global economy is still very much a work in progress, and it is not clear what the long-term effects will be on the economies and societies it touches. To its supporters, the global economy delivers markets that operate with efficiency, speedily directing goods and services wherever there is demand for them and always expecting the highest returns possible. Proponents of globalization also argue that the new economy is the only way to bring prosperity to the less developed world. Detractors of globalization claim that the hallmark of globalization—rapid economic development—is responsible for the destruction of the environment; the widening gap between rich and poor societies; and the worldwide homogenization of local, diverse, and indigenous cultures. It is certain that globalization has been accompanied by major social and economic changes. But it is too soon to tell if these changes will be overwhelmingly destructive for the world's lands and peoples.

CROSS-CULTURAL EXCHANGES AND GLOBAL COMMUNICATIONS

Like trade and business organizations, cultural practices have become globalized, thriving on a continuous flow of information, ideas, tastes, and values. At the turn of the twentieth century, local traditions—commonly derived from gender, social class, or religious affiliation—still determined the cultural identity of the vast majority of people. At the end of the twentieth century, thanks in part to advances in technology and communications, information and cultural practices were becoming truly global and more people than ever were aware of events and issues occurring far away.

Consumption and Cultural Interaction

New communications media have tied the world together and have promoted a global cultural integration whose hallmark is consumption. Although the desire to consume is hardly novel, the modern consumer culture means that consumers want more than they need and that the items they consume take on symbolic value. Consumption, in other words, has become a means of self-expression as well as a source of personal identity and social differentiation. The peculiar shape of this consumer culture resulted from two seemingly contradictory trends: a tendency toward homogenization of cultural products and heightened awareness of local tastes and values. Critics sometimes refer to the homogenizing aspect of global culture as the "Americanization" or **McDonaldization** of the world.

Those terms suggest that the consumer culture that developed in the United States during the mid-twentieth century has been exported throughout the world. Thus it is no accident that young people clad in blue jeans and T-shirts sing the same Usher or Eminem lyrics in San Francisco, Sarajevo, and Beijing. Still, nothing symbolizes the global marketing of U.S. mass culture more than the spread of its food and beverage products. While Pepsi and Coca-Cola fight battles over the few places on earth that their beverages have not yet dominated, fast-food restaurants such as Burger King, McDonald's, and Pizza Hut sell their standardized foods throughout the world. The closing of many bistros and cafés in France, for instance, is the result of more French people opting for fashionable fast food instead of taking the time for more traditional and lengthy lunches. So successful has the global spread of U.S. mass culture been that it seems to threaten local cultures everywhere.

However, because contemporary consumer culture stresses minute differences between products and encourages consumers to make purchase decisions based on brand names designed to evoke particular tastes, fashions, or lifestyles, it also fosters differentiation. Indeed, global marketing often emphasizes the local value of a product. Genuinely Australian products, such as Drizabone wet-weather gear and Foster's Lager, have become international commodities precisely because they are Australian in origin. Likewise, young, upwardly mobile consumers continue to prefer Rolex watches from Switzerland, Armani clothes from Italy, and Perrier mineral water from France.

Multilateral Globalization It would be a mistake to conceive of the globalization of culture as a one-way street emanating mainly from the United States. For example, reggae music became a worldwide phenomenon after the Jamaican musician Bob Marley partnered with British-based Island Records in 1972 to produce the album *Catch a Fire*. Although reggae was a complex, hybrid musical style particular to Jamaica, its protest lyrics and beat found eager audiences in countercultures in almost every continent from North and South America to Europe and Africa, and it profoundly influenced musical traditions in the late twentieth century. Sushi consumption in the United States provides another example of the multidirectional nature of globalization. In the 1990s sushi suddenly caught on outside major metropolitan areas as a healthy alternative to fatty, American-style food. In the last thirty years, sushi—which had been prepared in Japan since the eighth century—could be found in local Japanese restaurants across the United States, in airports, in the prepared foods section of grocery stores, and even in the refrigerated section of gas station convenience stores. Not only that, but Americans have altered and modified sushi recipes to reflect ingredients more familiar in the United States or to give the varieties American-sounding names. Thus it is important to remember that many societies are able to successfully blend and absorb a variety of foreign and indigenous practices.

The Networked World

Today virtually instantaneous electronic communications have dissolved time and space. Since the mid-1990s the rise of the Internet and smartphones has swept away the social, economic, and political isolation of the past.

Communications technologies underwent a fundamental transformation during the 1990s with the rapid spread of the Internet. The Internet had arisen from cold war imperatives: U.S. defense specialists wanted to establish a way to disseminate information after a nuclear attack and ultimately created a network (the Advanced Research Projects Agency Network, or ARPANET) in which computers at different locations could communicate with one another. In 1983 researchers began to use a communications protocol (called TCP/IP) by which different kinds of computers on different networks could communicate, and the Internet was officially born. However, it was not until 1991 that a platform for public use, called the World Wide Web, became available. When the institution that developed the World Wide Web (CERN) announced in 1993 that the platform was free for everyone to develop, its use exploded around the world. In 1998 Google went live, changing the way millions of people searched for information, and in 2004 Facebook launched its social media platform. By the second decade of the twenty-first century, the Internet had become fully integrated into the lives of most people living in more developed nations.

Although the Internet fundamentally changed the way in which people communicated around the world, at first it was available only to people or companies who owned computers or who could pay to use them in "Internet cafés." But access to the Internet gradually became more democratized through the use of smartphones, mobile phones that could access wireless networks and thus the Internet. The introduction of the first iPhone in 2007 revolutionized smartphone use: in little more than the span of a decade, a huge percentage of the human population had gained access to relatively inexpensive mobile phones that could function as telephones, computers, cameras, and video recorders, with ever-increasing coverage areas in nearly every part of the world. The Pew Research Center estimated that by 2019 five billion people, including 45 percent of those in less developed nations, had mobile phones and that half of these were smartphones.

The use of the Internet, and especially of smartphones, has not only accelerated communications and proved convenient for everyday life activities but also changed the way people organize social movements. For example, during the social protests that swept the Arab world during the "Arab Spring" of 2011, activists used social media to advertise the locations of protests and to communicate what was happening with the outside world. Additionally, individuals have used social media as a platform to publicize human rights abuses they have filmed on their smartphones, often leading to public outcry and even policy changes.

International Organizations

As the world's peoples are becoming increasingly connected and interdependent as a result of new technologies,

many have realized that they face issues that extend well beyond national borders. Since the end of World War II, this recognition has led to an increase in the number of organizations dedicated to solving global problems through international coordination and action. These institutions are important, because they have the potential to tackle issues that do not respect territorial boundaries and thus cannot be effectively addressed by individual national governments.

Intergovernmental Organizations One type of international body is the intergovernmental organization, meaning that membership is made up of sovereign states rather than individuals or private groups. These organizations include the North Atlantic Treaty Organization (NATO), the African Development Bank, and the European Union, to name a few. The main purposes behind intergovernmental organizations are to provide mechanisms for member states to work together to find solutions to maintain peace and security and to enhance economic and social stability across national borders.

The best known intergovernmental organization is the United Nations (UN), which was established at the end of World War II to replace the League of Nations (1920–1946). Unlike a national government, the UN does not legislate. Yet representatives of the vast majority of the world's countries (193 out of 195 total) have a voice and a vote in shaping the international community of nations. Under its charter, a principal purpose of the UN is "to maintain international peace and security." It has not been able to achieve this goal, however, partly because member states have often chosen to embark on wars or hostilities in spite of UN opposition. And unless all members of the UN Security Council (whose permanent members are made up of the five most powerful nations in the world) agree, the UN cannot send peacekeeping troops to help end a conflict.

But the UN has compiled an enviable record with respect to another role defined in its charter, "to achieve international cooperation in solving international problems of an economic, social, cultural, or humanitarian character." Quietly and often without attracting attention from the international news media, the specialized agencies of the UN have achieved numerous successes. For example, in 1980 the World Health Organization (a division of the UN) proclaimed the worldwide eradication of smallpox as a result of its thirteen-year global program. On other fronts, UN efforts resulted in more than a 50 percent decrease in both infant and child mortality rates in less developed countries between 1960 and 2002. The organization's efforts also promoted an increase in female literacy, especially in Africa, where for the first time in history the majority of women—53.6 percent in 2010—were deemed to be literate. The UN also worked to provide access to safe water for over one billion people living in rural areas.

Nongovernmental Organizations Another type of international body is the nongovernmental organization; such an organization operates independently of any government. NGOs typically are nonprofit organizations focusing on a social, economic, environmental, or humanitarian issue that transcends national borders. Many NGOs have focused on the protection of human rights or the notion that all persons are entitled to some basic rights. Universal recognition and acceptance of the concept of human rights came in the aftermath of World War II with the exposure of Nazi crimes. In 1948 the National Assembly of the UN adopted the **Universal Declaration of Human Rights**, which contributed to the codification of international human rights laws. The declaration singled out specific human rights violations such as summary executions, arbitrary arrest and torture, and slavery or involuntary servitude. Since then, concerned individuals and groups have formed human rights NGOs with the goal of ensuring that these laws are upheld. For example, Amnesty International (founded 1961) seeks to expose human rights violations all over the world through massive media and lobbying campaigns, as well as to provide legal defense where possible. Amnesty International has counted among its many victories campaigns on behalf of groups as well as individuals, from compelling Shell Oil to pay $55 million to the Nigerian government for oil spills to freeing a young woman in El Salvador who was imprisoned on suspicion of inducing an abortion.

In 2015 it was estimated that there are ten million NGOs operating around the world. It is thus not surprising that they focus on many issues besides human rights. Many focus on global health, including organizations such as Partners in Health (founded 1987), whose mission is to provide health care to the most marginalized populations in the world. Others focus on the environment and solutions to climate change. The Environmental Defense Fund (founded 1967), for example, seeks solutions to the most urgent environmental problems, whether in the air, in the oceans, or on land.

Given the intensity and acceleration of global interaction after World War II, the possibilities for solving global problems through international coordination is increasingly imaginable. Although both intergovernmental and nongovernmental international organizations are far from perfect, for the present they represent the closest thing humanity has to a global system of governance that can help the world's peoples meet the challenges of international problems.

URGENT GLOBAL ISSUES IN THE EARLY TWENTY-FIRST CENTURY

By the twenty-first century, it had become clear that the new millennium would bring with it a multitude of issues whose solution would require both a global perspective and global responses. Each of these issues—from climate change to women's empowerment to global pandemics—has the potential to affect all the world's people, and none have easy solutions.

Climate Change

The post–World War II period has been accompanied by vast population increases. As the result of advances in agriculture, industry, science, and medicine, global population increased from 2.5 billion in 1950 to 7.8 billion in 2020. As increasing numbers of people are born, pollution levels increase, more habitats and animal and plant species disappear, and more natural resources are consumed. In recent decades one environmental issue related to human population growth has taken center stage: climate change. In the context of environmental debates and policymaking, *climate change* usually refers to a human-induced climate change known as **global warming**.

Global warming is the phenomenon of increasing average air temperature near the surface of the earth over the past two centuries. On the basis of detailed observations, scientists have concluded that the influence of human activities since the beginning of industrialization have altered the earth's climate. More specifically, they believe that most of the observed temperature increases since the middle of the twentieth century are caused by increasing concentrations of greenhouse gases. Like the glass panes in a greenhouse, hydrocarbon emissions from automobiles, and methane emitted from animal dung on commercial farms, trap heat within the atmosphere, leading to a rise in global temperatures. An average rise of global temperature by more than 2°C (3.6°F) would cause significant economic and ecological damage, particularly because this would cause a rise in sea levels as a result of melting in the polar ice caps.

A vigorous debate is in progress over the extent and seriousness of rising surface temperatures, their consequences for the environment, and the necessity to limit further warming. In the ancient Japanese capital of Kyoto, at a conference dedicated to climate change, the delegates from 187 nations agreed in 1997 to cut greenhouse emissions blamed for global warming. The Kyoto protocol went into force in 2005 and imposed targets for carbon emission reductions on more developed countries until 2012. The protocol did not require less developed countries—some of them major polluters, such as India and China—to reduce their emissions. The world's second-largest polluter after China, the United States, did not sign the protocol, because it required nothing of less developed countries. Since Kyoto, global carbon-dioxide emissions have risen by a third.

International efforts in dealing with climate change have been hampered by the fact that less developed

Most scientists argue that emissions such as these, carbon-dioxide emissions from smokestacks in Siberia, along with other hydrocarbon emissions and methane, contribute to global climate change.
Peter Turnley/Corbis/VCG/Getty Images

nations have been reluctant to commit themselves to cutting emissions. In part this is because their leaders believe that the only way to remain economically competitive in the globalized world is to continue industrializing. Additionally, some leaders resent being told they must cut back on emissions to solve environmental problems caused by more developed nations over the span of more than a century. As a result, less developed nations have insisted that more developed nations bear the costs of reducing emissions. Efforts to find solutions have also been hampered by one of the most powerful nations and one of the world's greatest polluters: the United States. Politicians in the United States have worried about the economic effects of reducing emissions, and some have expressed skepticism about the existence of climate

change at all. In spite of these obstacles, in December 2015 the United Nations Framework on Climate Change produced the Paris Agreement, which set global goals of capping greenhouse emissions. The Paris Agreement commits signatories to reducing emissions and to publicly tracking their progress in doing so. Unlike the Kyoto protocol, the Paris Agreement was signed by nearly every less developed country (including China and India) as well as the United States. Under the administration of President Donald Trump, who cited concern for American jobs and businesses, the United States withdrew from the Paris Agreement on 1 June 2017. However, Under Joe Biden's administration, the United States once again joined the Paris Agreement on 19 February 2021.

Why It Matters

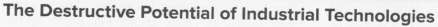

The Destructive Potential of Industrial Technologies

Should humans try to anticipate unintended consequences of their actions as well as intended consequences? In the nineteenth century, advocates of industrialization envisioned a world in which mechanization and new technologies would lead to improvements in the human condition over the long term. They did not, however, anticipate that the resource extraction and pollution associated with

industrialization might have disastrous consequences for the whole planet only two centuries later. This matters because the unintended consequence of global climate change can provide a model for how we might think about some of the potential unintended consequences of technological advances in our own time, including space travel, artificial intelligence, and gene editing.

Economic Inequities and Labor Servitude

The unequal distribution of resources and income and the resulting poverty have materialized as key concerns of the contemporary world. Several hundred million people, especially in the less developed areas of eastern Europe, Africa, Latin America, and Asia, struggle daily for sufficient food, clean water, adequate shelter, and other basic necessities. Malnutrition among the poor has led to starvation and death. As one of the most persistent effects of poverty, malnutrition is accompanied by vitamin and mineral deficiencies, which in turn cause mental disorders, organ damage, and vision failure among poor children and adults. Because of inadequate shelter, lack of safe running water, and the absence of sewage facilities, the poor have been exposed disproportionally to bacteria and viruses carried by other people, insects, and rodents. Poverty has correlated strongly with higher than average infant mortality rates and lower than average life expectancies.

The Causes of Poverty The division between rich and poor has been a defining characteristic of all complex societies. Although relative poverty levels within a given society remain a major concern, it is the continuing division between rich and poor societies that has attracted the attention of the international community. The uneven distribution of resources has figured as a major cause of poverty and has divided nations into the haves and have-nots. Excessively high population densities and environmental degradation have caused the depletion of available resources, leading to shortages of food, water, and shelter and ultimately to poverty. A major cause of this unequal distribution of resources is five hundred years of colonialism, defined by the appropriation of labor and natural resources. Pervasive poverty characterizes many former colonies and dependencies. All of these less developed societies have tried to raise income levels and eliminate poverty through diversified economic development, but only a few, such as South Korea, Singapore, and Malaysia, have accomplished their aims. In the meantime, economic globalization has generated unprecedented wealth for more developed nations, creating an even deeper divide between rich and poor countries. A report issued by the antipoverty charity Oxfam noted that in 2018, 82 percent of the world's total wealth went to the richest 1 percent of the population.

Labor Servitude Poor economic conditions have been closely associated with forms of servitude similar to slavery. Although legal slavery ceased to exist when Saudi Arabia and Angola abolished slavery officially in the 1960s, forced and bonded labor practices continue to affect millions of poor people in the less developed world. Of particular concern is child-labor servitude. According to the International Labor Organization, a specialized agency of the United Nations, more than two hundred fifty million children between ages five and fourteen work around the world, many in conditions that are harmful to their physical health and emotional well-being. Child-labor servitude is most pronounced in south and southeast Asia, affecting an estimated fifty million children in India alone. Most child labor occurs in agriculture, domestic service, family businesses, and the sex trade, making it difficult to enforce existing prohibitions and laws against those practices. Many children are born into a life of bonded labor because their parents are impoverished and have been forced to pledge their labor to others.

Trafficking A growing and related global problem that touches societies on every continent is the trafficking of persons. In this insidious form of modern slavery, one to two million human beings annually are bought and sold across and within national boundaries. Trafficking has appeared in many forms. In Russia and the Ukraine, for example, traffickers lure victims with the promise of well-paying jobs abroad. Once the victims arrive in the countries of their destination, they become captives of ruthless traffickers who force them into bonded labor, domestic servitude, or the commercial sex industry through threats and physical brutality—including rape, torture, starvation, incarceration, and death. Most of the victims of trafficking are girls and women, which is a reflection of the low social and economic status of women in many countries. In south Asia, for instance, it is common for poverty-stricken parents or other relatives to sell young women to traffickers for the sex trade or forced labor. The trafficking industry is one of the fastest growing and most lucrative criminal enterprises in the world, generating billions of dollars annually in profits.

The Continuing Inequality of Women

The status of women in many places around the world began changing after World War II. Women gained more economic, political, social, and sexual rights in highly industrialized states than in less developed nations, but nowhere have they achieved full social, political, and economic equality with men. Agitation for gender equality is often linked to women's access to employment, which is highest in industrialized nations. Women constitute 40 to 50 percent of the workforce in industrial societies, compared with only 20 percent in less developed countries. However, in all countries, most women who do work for pay are engaged in low-paying jobs such as teaching, service, and clerical work. In addition, 40 percent of all farmers in the world are women. Rural African women, for example, produce more than 70 percent of Africa's food. Whether they are industrial, service, or agricultural workers, women earn less than men earn for the same work and are generally kept out of the highest-paid professional careers.

In addition, a report issued by the UN and the World Bank in 2017 argued that more women than men live in extreme poverty in the world. At the same time, data collected by both the UN and many NGOs have demonstrated that programs to improve overall public health, improve access to education, and promote sustainable development in societies around the world meet with greater success when steps are taken to improve the status of women.

The Struggle for Equality in Industrialized Nations

The discrimination that women faced in the workplace was a major stimulus for the **feminist movement** in industrialized nations. After World War II, when more and more women went to work, women started to protest job discrimination, pay differentials between women and men, and their lack of legal equality. In the 1960s those complaints expanded into a feminist movement that criticized all aspects of gender inequality. In the United States, the civil rights movement that demanded equality for African Americans influenced the women's movement and provided a training ground for many women activists.

In addition to demanding equality in the workplace, women in industrialized countries demanded full control over their bodies and their reproductive systems. The introduction of the birth control pill in the 1960s gave millions of women the power to protect themselves from unwanted pregnancies. Shortly thereafter, beginning with the United Kingdom in 1967 and then extending to Canada (1967), the United States (1973), and many European countries, women won the fight to legalize abortion. But even though these developments provided women in industrialized nations with a measure of sexual freedom, women continue to lag behind men in terms of access to political power and equal wages for equal work. In addition, women often face sexual harassment in the workplace.

Gender Equality in China

Legally, the position of women most closely matches that of men in communist or formerly communist countries such as Cuba and China. "Women hold up half the sky," Mao Zedong had declared, and that eloquent acknowledgment of women's role translated into a legal commitment to fairness. The communist dedication to women's rights led to improvement in the legal status of Chinese women once the communists gained power in China. In 1950, communist leaders passed a Marriage Law, which mandated the protection of the interests of both men and women within marriage, legalized divorce, and abolished patriarchal practices such as child betrothal. It also upheld equal rights for men and women in the areas of work, property ownership, and inheritance.

Critics argue that despite such laws Chinese women have never gained true equality with men. Few women have gained high status in the Communist Party's leadership, and Chinese working women do not receive wages equal to those of men. They do most of the work at home as well.

Young girls study the Qu'ran at a madrassa (school) in Pakistan, 2005.
Robert Nickelsberg/Getty Images

Long-standing cultural values continue to degrade the status of women, especially in rural areas. For example, parents have traditionally much preferred boy children over girls. One unintended consequence of China's population policies, which until 2016 limited couples to one child, was the mysterious disappearance of a large number of baby girls. Demographers estimate that annually more than one-half million female births went unrecorded in government statistics. Some population experts speculate that a continued strong preference for male children caused parents to send baby girls away for adoption, to be raised secretly, or in some cases to single them out for infanticide.

Domesticity and Abuse Although girls and women in industrial and communist nations are guaranteed basic if not fully equal legal rights and are educated in roughly the same numbers as boys and men, women in other areas of the world have long been denied access to education. Indeed, of the world's remaining 774 million illiterate adults, two-thirds of these are women.

In India, for example, the literacy gap between men and women is stark, at 81.5 percent for men compared to 64.6 percent for women. Moreover, the participation of Indian women in the labor force is very low, at about 25 percent for rural women and 15 percent for urban women. At the same time, birthrates in India remain high in spite of greater access to birth control, at 2.33 births per woman as compared to 1.8 in the United States. These conditions have ensured a life of dependence for many Indian women. One indicator of the low social status of Indian women is the continued occurrence of dowry deaths. It is customary among many Indian communities to pay a dowry (gifts of money or goods) to the husband and his family upon a woman's marriage, although this requirement is difficult for many Indian families to meet. If the husband and his family become dissatisfied with the woman, her new family sets her on fire, so that her death can be explained as a cooking accident. Although this practice is illegal, it is still widespread enough to make women's precarious position in society clear. In 2016 the government of India reported 7,621 dowry deaths, although unofficial estimates put the number closer to twenty-five thousand.

Women Leaders By 2015, women had gained the right to vote in almost every country in the world. In general, they do not exert political power commensurate with their numbers, although some women have attained high political offices or impressive leadership positions. Some-

Indira Gandhi (in-DEE-rah GAHN-dee)
Benazir Bhuto (BEN-ah-zeer BOO-toh)
Chandrika Bandaranaike Kumaratunga (CHAHN-dree-kah BAHN-dah-rah-nigh-kee koo-mah-rah-TOONG-ah)
Aung San Suu Kyi (ong sahn soo chee)

what ironically, the same south Asia that revealed so many continued barriers to women's rights on a day-to-day basis also elevated some women from powerful political families to power. Indira Gandhi (1917–1984) and Benazir Bhuto (1953–2007), both of whose fathers had been prime ministers, served as prime minister for India and Pakistan, respectively. Yet both women were controversial figures, and both were assassinated while in office. In 1994 Chandrika Bandaranaike Kumaratunga (1945–) became the first female president of Sri Lanka. Both her parents had previously served as prime ministers; her mother, Sirimavo Bandaranaike (1916–2000), became the first elected woman prime minister in 1960.

In Myanmar (formerly Burma), Aung San Suu Kyi (1945–) emerged as a leader, also deriving her political authority from her father, Aung San, who was assassinated in 1947. Assuming the leadership of the democracy movement after her return from exile in 1988, Suu Kyi called for a nonviolent revolution against what she called Myanmar's "fascist government." The government placed her under house arrest in 1989, where she remained for most of the next twenty-one years until she was released in 2010. During that time her party won an election (1990), but Suu Kyi was not allowed to come to power. After her release, Suu Kyi was elected to the Burmese parliament in 2012, and in 2015 she led her party to a landslide victory in Myanmar's first openly contested elections. Although not allowed to serve as president because she has foreign-born children, she served as de facto leader of the country beginning in 2016. Beginning in 2017 Suu Kyi has come under international criticism for her failure to stop attacks by Myanmar's army on Burma's indigenous Muslim minority, the Rohingya. Suu Kyi was imprisoned again in 2021 in a military coup at the age of seventy-six.

In spite of the fact that some women have served as leaders of their countries, by the end of the second decade of the twenty-first century, women still are vastly underrepresented as political leaders in nearly every nation. Worldwide, there have been only nineteen female heads of state since 2000, and in 2020 only one in five members of lower or single houses of parliament were women. Women remain a small minority of corporate managers and senior officials everywhere in the world, and only 50 percent of working-age women are in the labor force compared to 77 percent of men. We have seen that women are more likely to live in poverty than men, which has clear implications for their access to adequate health care, housing, and nutrition. Additionally, a UN report indicates that about one-third of women in the world have experienced sexual or physical violence by an intimate partner or have experienced sexual violence by a nonpartner at some point in their lives. Thus, if it is true that programs for improving public health and sustainable development succeed best when women are empowered through access to education and work, much remains to be done.

SOURCES FROM THE PAST

Malebogo Molefhe on Being a Woman of Courage

Malebogo Molefhe (1980–) began playing professional basketball in her home country of Botswana at the age of eighteen. When she was twenty-nine, her boyfriend attacked her, shot her eight times, and then killed himself. Malebogo survived the attack, but is confined to a wheelchair due to spinal injuries. Since her recovery, Malebogo has been an outspoken advocate for survivors of gender-based violence, and has created programs designed to educate and aid young women at risk. In 2017 she was recognized by the United States Department of State as an International Woman of Courage. Below are excerpts of the speech she gave on accepting the award.

Often times, when walking in the street, people ask, "What happened to you? Why are you in a wheelchair?" Once I tell them that I've been shot–they say, "What did you do to him?" The journey to my recovering, as well as to the point of who I am, has not been an easy one. Being a woman and being in a wheelchair is not the easiest of things. Not all women are lucky. Some have lost their lives, and most have lost their sanity.

> What does Molefhe mean by 'lucky,' given that she was shot and is confined to a wheelchair?

My goals in Botswana is to see the life of young girl changed. Is to see a brave girl who is courageous enough to walk out when they're in situations of violence. I want to see a young girl who is educated. And who is proud of themselves enough to say, "I did this." And they don't need any validation from anyone.

I take pride in knowing that I didn't lose my strength. And I continued to use my story to inspire other women, and to learn from me. To partake in changing, and helping change the lives of others. My name is Malebogo Molefhe from Botswana. I am a woman of courage.

For Further Reflection

■ How does Molefhe wish to see young girls' lives changed? Why does education play a role in those changes?

Source: https://eca.state.gov/video/international-women-courage-malebogo-molefhe. International Women of Courage, Malebogo Molefhe.

Global Terrorism

Terrorism has become a persistent feature of the globalized world since 1945. Heightened media awareness, especially the ubiquity of worldwide television coverage, has exposed the grievances and demands of terrorists to millions of viewers, but it has also transformed the practice of terrorism. Acts of terror therefore punctuated the era following World War II, as individuals and groups the world over attempted to destabilize or overthrow political systems within or outside the borders of their countries. Terrorism figured prominently in anticolonial conflicts in Algeria and Vietnam; in struggles over a homeland between national groups such as Israelis and Palestinians; in clashes between religious denominations such as Protestants and Catholics in Northern Ireland; and between revolutionary forces and established regimes in states such as Indonesia, Iran, and Nicaragua.

Defining Terrorism Experts agree that a key feature of terrorism is the deliberate and systematic use of violence against civilians, with the aim of inspiring terror to advance political, religious, or ideological causes. Terrorists use violent means—from hijackings and hostage-taking to assassinations and mass murder—to magnify their influence and power. In contrast to the populations and institutions they fight, terrorist organizations are usually limited in size and resources. During the last decades of the twentieth century and the first decade of the twenty-first century, terrorism increasingly assumed a global character, because terrorist networks brought violence thousands of miles away to strike at the heart of their perceived enemies. To do this, they relied on the same sophisticated financial networks, modern modes of transportation, and communications technologies used by billions of other people in a globalized world. This relatively novel kind of terrorism was typified by the 11 September attacks in the United States.

The north face of the south tower immediately after being struck by United Airlines flight 175 on 11 September, 2001.

Laperruque/Alamy Stock Photo

11 September On the morning of 11 September 2001, New York City and Washington, D.C., became the targets of a coordinated terrorist attack that was unprecedented in scope, sophistication, and destructiveness. Hijackers seized four passenger jetliners and used them as guided missiles. Two of the planes crashed into the World Trade Center towers in New York City, causing the collapse of the two towers, the ancillary destruction of adjacent skyscrapers, and more than twenty-five hundred deaths. Before the morning was over, another plane crashed into the Pentagon, killing 125 people, and the fourth jet crashed into a field outside Pittsburgh, Pennsylvania. Intended for another Washington, D.C., landmark, the fourth jet was thwarted in its mission when passengers stormed the hijackers and forced the plane to crash. As millions around the world watched events unfold on television, the U.S. government launched an intensive investigation and identified the Islamic militant Osama bin Laden (1957–2011) as the mastermind behind the attacks. Officials also accused bin Laden of directing previous attacks on U.S. interests in Africa and

southwest Asia. Before the dust of the collapsed World Trade towers had settled, U.S. president George W. Bush (1946–) declared war on Osama bin Laden and global terrorism itself.

Osama bin Laden headed *al-Qaeda* ("the base"), the core of a global terrorist network. Although he had once received U.S. aid as a *mujahideen* (Islamic warrior) fighting the Soviets in Afghanistan, by the end of the Persian Gulf War (1990–1991) he had come to see the United States as an unqualified enemy. The stationing of U.S. troops on what he regarded as the holy soil of Saudi Arabia, the bombing of Iraq, and support for Israeli oppression of Palestinians, bin Laden claimed, were tantamount to a declaration of war against God. He went to Afghanistan in 1996 at the invitation of the radical and violent **Taliban** Party, after being expelled from both Saudi Arabia and Sudan. From his base in Afghanistan in 1998, bin Laden publicly called on every Muslim to kill Americans and their allies "wherever he finds them and whenever he can."

War in Afghanistan and Iraq The Taliban itself emerged out of the disorder and devastation of the Afghan-Soviet War (1979–1988). In their pursuit of what they claimed would be the purest Muslim state on earth, Taliban intolerance figured prominently, and the party's austere interpretation of Islam quickly alienated people both inside and outside Afghanistan. Dominated by Pashtuns—the majority ethnic group of Afghanistan—the Taliban, under its leading *mullah* (male religious leader), Mohammed Omar, fought a series of holy wars against other ethnic and Muslim groups. At the same time, the Taliban provided sanctuary and training grounds for Islamist fighters such as Osama bin Laden.

The Taliban enforced a strict interpretation of Islam that barred women from education and the workplace. All forms of European and American dress became taboo: women had to be completely veiled in *burkas,* and men had to stop wearing neckties and grow full, untrimmed beards. The Taliban also called for a ban on television, movie theaters, photographs, and most styles of music. A religious police, the Ministry of the Promotion of Virtue and Prevention of Vice, enforced these rules with an extremely harsh code of justice. The United Nations did not recognize the Taliban as Afghanistan's legitimate government. Instead, it recognized the Northern Alliance, which was composed of the country's smaller religious and ethnic groups. The Northern Alliance became a crucial ally of the United States in its mission to find and punish those responsible for the 11 September attacks.

When the U.S. government announced its war against global terrorism, it also pointedly targeted governments and states that supported and provided sanctuary for terrorists. The refusal of the Taliban government to surrender Osama bin Laden prompted the United States and its allies to begin military operations against

Taliban military positions and terrorist training camps on 7 October 2001. The U.S. military and its international allies generally limited their operations to intelligence missions and massive air strikes, fighting the war on the ground through Afghan proxies, most notably the forces of the Northern Alliance. By November, U.S.-led bombardments permitted Northern Alliance troops to capture Kabul and other key Afghan cities.

Another international action against terrorism separate from the war in Afghanistan came in March 2003, when President Bush coordinated what he termed **Operation Iraqi Freedom**. A multinational coalition force some three hundred thousand strong, largely made up of U.S. and British troops but also including those from approximately two dozen other nations, carried out an invasion of Iraq designed to wage further war on terrorism by ousting the regime of Saddam Hussein. The coalition argued they had firm evidence that Hussein possessed a huge stockpile of chemical and biological weapons that could be employed by global terrorists to wreak destruction on a scale even greater than that of 11 September 2001. Coalition forces managed to establish their military supremacy in Iraq, but they did not uncover any such cache of weapons. President Bush declared an end to major battle operations on 1 May 2003, and coalition forces since that time have struggled in their efforts to occupy and stabilize Iraq. Hussein was finally caught in December 2003 and executed in 2006, but deadly resistance in Iraq persisted.

The costs of the Iraq War were enormous. Tens of thousands of Iraqi military personnel and civilians died, as had more than forty-seven hundred coalition soldiers by mid-2010. The United States spent approximately $4 billion per month to maintain troops in Iraq. Seen as an expression of the "Bush Doctrine of Deterrence," this preemptive strike against Iraq—which had not overtly committed a terrorist act or been proven to harbor terrorists—set a troubling precedent in U.S. foreign policy. Moreover, the increased presence of foreign military personnel in Iraq appeared to intensify the sort of Islamist fervor already fanned by Osama bin Laden. U.S. president Barack Obama (president 2008–2016) shifted the war on terror away from Iraq and back to Afghanistan and bin Laden. Obama announced in May 2011 that elite forces had fulfilled a major mission in the war on terror by carrying out the U.S.-sanctioned killing of Osama bin Laden in Pakistan. Further, the United States declared the war in Iraq over in December 2011, at least as far as U.S. troops were concerned, although Iraqis continued to face intense civil conflict.

Meanwhile, in Afghanistan President Obama announced first the draw-down (2011) and then the withdrawal of U.S. troops in 2014, leaving only about ten thousand advisors. In December 2019, President Donald Trump withdrew about half of these and promised to withdraw the rest in 2020. When Joe Biden was inaugurated as president in January 2021, his administration announced that the remaining U.S. troops in Afghanistan would be withdrawn by 11 September 2021. Once they were withdrawn, however, the Taliban almost immediately resumed control over the country. Critics argued that Biden's administration mishandled the withdrawal by failing to ensure the safety of Afghans who aided the United States and were now left behind to be ruled by the Taliban. Moreover, the war, which resulted in around two hundred forty-one thousand deaths and cost $2.3 trillion, ultimately did not keep the Taliban from resuming control of Afghanistan.

Migration

Migration, the movement of people from one place to another, is as old as humanity and has shaped the formation and identity of societies throughout the world. With the advent of industrialization during the eighteenth century, population experts distinguished between two types of migration: internal migration and external or international migration. Internal migration is the flow of people from rural to urban areas within one society, whereas external migration is the movement of people across long distances and international borders. Lack of resources such as land or adequate food supplies, population pressure, religious or political persecution, and discriminatory practices aimed at ethnic minorities push people to move. Conversely, opportunities for better employment, the availability of arable land, and better services such as health care and education pull people to move.

Internal Migration The largest human migrations in recent history are rural-urban flows. During the second half of the twentieth century, these internal migrations led to rapid urbanization in much of the world. Today the most highly urbanized societies are those of western and northern Europe, Australia, New Zealand, and temperate South America and North America. In these societies the proportion of people living in urban areas exceeds 75 percent; in some countries, such as Belgium, it exceeds 97 percent. In many countries in Africa and Asia, the process of urbanization is at a relatively early stage. Even though most people still reside in rural areas, the rate of urbanization is very high.

Urbanization In Latin America, Africa, and south Asia, large numbers of people have migrated to metropolitan areas in search of relief from rural poverty. Once in the cities, though, they often find themselves equally destitute. Life is bleak in the slums outside Mumbai and in the *barriadas, barrios,* and *villas miserias* of Lima, Mexico City, and Buenos Aires. More than ten million people cram the environs of cities such as Calcutta, Cairo, and Mexico City, straining those cities' resources. The few services originally available to those who moved to slum

Migrants from Libya on an overcrowded boat trying to reach Europe in 2017. These passengers were rescued by a Spanish NGO, but many thousands died trying to cross the Mediterranean from North Africa to Europe. Samuel Nacar/SOPA Images/LightRocket/Getty Images

areas—potable water, electricity, and medical care—have diminished with the continuous influx of new people. Among the unemployed or underemployed, disease runs rampant, and many suffer from malnutrition.

External Migration During World War II the Nazi regime initiated the largest mass expulsions of the twentieth century, deporting eight million people to forced-labor sites and extermination camps. Following the war, the Soviet regime expelled ten million ethnic Germans from eastern and central Europe and transported them back to Germany. The largest migrations in the second half of the twentieth century consisted of refugees fleeing war. For example, the 1947 partition of the Indian subcontinent into two independent states resulted in the exchange of six million Hindus from Pakistan and seven million Muslims from India. According to recent United Nations figures, by 2013 more than forty-five million people worldwide had been forcibly displaced as a result of conflict and persecution. More than fifteen million of the uprooted were refugees who fled their home countries, and another thirty million were people who remain displaced by conflict within their homelands. These numbers were amplified in the second decade of the twenty-first century by a new wave of migrant refugees seeking safety and stability in the wake of civil war in Syria and instability in Afghanistan and Iraq. In 2015 alone, more than one million people sought refuge in Europe, and several hundred thousand followed in the ensuing four years. Many were desperate and allowed themselves to be illegally transported by human traffickers, and more than fifteen thousand died in the process. Although a variety of European countries initially agreed to take in migrants (especially Germany but also France, Sweden, Italy, and Austria), their presence has triggered a xenophobic backlash in many countries. Indeed, controversy over taking in migrants is believed to have contributed to the calls for British withdrawal from the European Union in 2016, and fear of migrants has led to an upsurge in right-wing parties across Europe whose rhetoric is openly racist.

Across the Atlantic, in 2012 many tens of thousands of refugees left their home countries in El Salvador, Guatemala, and Honduras for the United States. Although migration from Central America and Mexico was not a new phenomenon (over ten million Mexican migrants have settled in the United States since 1960), the rate of migration increased in that year from Central America because of extremely dangerous internal conditions. As in Europe, though, this surge in migration stimulated controversy in the United States, as many Americans began to call for closing the border between Mexico and the United States to prevent migration from the south. In fact, President Donald Trump ran his presidential campaign in 2016 on a promise to build a wall between Mexico and the United States to keep migrants out.

In general, migrants leave their home countries because they seek a better life in countries with a higher standard of living and stable legal and political systems. They want better jobs and more readily available health care, educational opportunities, and a safe place to raise their children. Thus most contemporary mass migrations involve movement from less developed countries to more developed ones. Given the disparities and inequities between more developed and less developed countries, it seems likely that migration will continue to be a major issue in the short and long terms.

Global Diseases

For thousands of years, disease has played a significant role in the development of human communities. Its impact has been as dramatic as it has been destructive. For example, during the Columbian exchange the introduction of diseases to populations that lacked any form of immunity killed perhaps as many as 90 percent of Native Americans in the span of one hundred fifty years. More recently, an influenza pandemic that swept the globe in 1918 and 1919 killed between twenty and forty million people, far more than died as the result of the Great War that had just ended. Since then, medical experts, public health officials, and scientists have scored major victories in their fight against diseases, eradicating smallpox and diphtheria, for example. Buoyed by those successes, the United Nations in 1978 called for the elimination of all infectious diseases by the year 2000. Instead, however, ancient diseases once thought under control, such as malaria, tuberculosis, and even measles, are on the rise again. Moreover, the recent past has demonstrated the deadly potential of new diseases.

HIV/AIDS One of the most serious new diseases to emerge was acquired immunodeficiency syndrome (AIDS). This fatal disorder of the immune system is caused by the human immunodeficiency virus (HIV), which slowly attacks and destroys the immune system, leaving the infected individual vulnerable to diseases that eventually cause death. The HIV infection is spread through sexual contact with an infected person, contact with contaminated blood, and transmission from mother to child during pregnancy and breast feeding.

Medical experts identified AIDS for the first time in 1981 among homosexual men and intravenous drug users in New York and San Francisco. Subsequently, evidence for an epidemic appeared among heterosexual men, women, and children in sub-Saharan Africa, and rather quickly AIDS developed into a worldwide epidemic affecting virtually every nation. At the end of 2019 the number of people living with HIV/AIDS was 37.9 million, and more than 32 million AIDS deaths had occurred since the beginning of the epidemic.

When scientists first identified AIDS, there was no treatment for the disease. By 1995, though, researchers had succeeded in developing a new class of drugs known as protease inhibitors to produce what is now known as **highly active antiretroviral therapy**, or **HAART**. In most cases, HAART can prolong life indefinitely. Antiretroviral therapy not only prevents AIDS-related illness and death but also has the potential to significantly reduce the risk of HIV transmission and the spread of tuberculosis. The high cost of these sophisticated drugs initially prevented poor people from sharing in their benefits, but this is changing. By 2018, 62 percent of the world's people living with HIV were receiving antiretroviral therapy. However, the epidemic continues to disproportionately affect sub-Saharan Africa, home to 1.1 million new HIV infections in 2017. Equally worrisome, new infections have been on the rise in eastern Europe, central Asia, southwest Asia, and north Africa.

Present and Future Concerns In spite of significant successes in the battle against HIV infection, global disease remains an urgent concern in the twenty-first century. Globalization has allowed ever more rapid

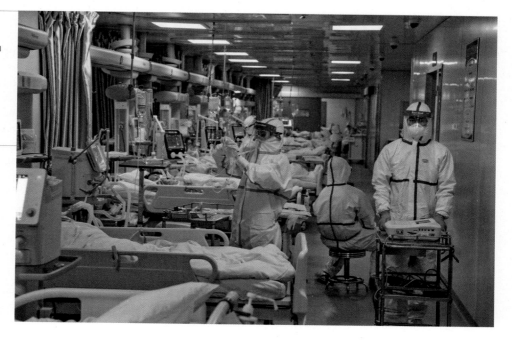

In February 2020, medical staff in Wuhan, China work in an isolated intensive care unit for the treatment of patients with COVID-19.
Feature China/Barcroft Media/Getty Images

circulations of people, meaning that new or mutated viruses—especially those spread through the air—can travel around the world in a few hours. This was the case with the outbreak of the severe acute respiratory syndrome (SARS) virus in 2003 and the Middle East respiratory syndrome (MERS) virus in 2012. Viruses such as these have the potential to infect many thousands of people on every continent and require intensive international cooperation if a global pandemic is to be halted.

The incredible speed with which viruses can travel in an era of globalization was clearly demonstrated at the end of 2019, when authorities in China reported that a mysterious form of pneumonia had infected a cluster of people in the city of Wuhan. By 7 January 2020 the illness was identified as a novel coronavirus, which later became known as COVID-19. Case numbers rose quickly in China, and in an attempt to halt the spread of the epidemic, the government took drastic steps to place the city of Wuhan (with eleven million people) under strict quarantine. A week later the United States and other nations halted travel to and from China. But these efforts were too late. The speed at which people travel ensured that individuals infected with the extremely contagious virus had already traveled to North America, southeast Asia, Europe, and other countries in Asia. By 11 March, the World Health Organization had declared COVID-19 a pandemic, meaning that it was an uncontrolled disease that affected the whole world.

COVID-19 revealed the weaknesses of international cooperation in halting pandemics. The World Health Organization, which was designed to coordinate international response to situations like this, was accused of moving too slowly to communicate the level of threat posed by the virus. Even more important, many countries, including the United States, failed to heed warnings about the virus until it had already spread widely and thus failed to prepare by ensuring adequate levels of medical supplies or tests. Some countries sought to shift the blame for the virus to China, thus calling attention away from their own mismanagement. The pandemic also brought social inequalities into sharp relief, as it became clear that the poor and the marginalized died in far greater numbers than the rich and healthy. The worldwide lack of preparedness for dealing with a pandemic such as COVID-19 meant that the only way to decrease the infection and death rates was to lock down societies by closing stores, halting gatherings and travel, and requiring people to stay at home. Indeed, by 31 March nearly one-third of humanity was living under some kind of lockdown. Although lockdowns were largely successful at reducing new infections, their negative impact on both local and global economies was enormous.

Although more than 272,000 people had been infected by the virus and 5.3 million had died by December 2021, the pandemic has also given us reason to be hopeful. In spite of political squabbles at the highest levels, tens of thousands of scientists, researchers, and health care workers raced at record speed to develop effective treatments and vaccines to eliminate the threat of COVID-19. Indeed, the first vaccines were introduced in December 2020, and a year later nearly 58 percent of the world's population

What's Left Out? ■ ■ ■ ■ ■

Historians are comfortable writing about events that happened long ago, even though they understand they can never fully comprehend the vast complexities of the past. But they are often far less comfortable writing about events that occurred in their own living memory—and grow increasingly uncomfortable as they move closer to the present. There are good reasons for this discomfort. The task of writing history is much easier when historians have perspective, which in this case means knowing what happened *after* the period under discussion. Perspective can also mean having distance from the events under discussion, so that writers of history are not personally invested in the outcomes of their stories. When writing about the very recent past, it is difficult for historians to maintain either kind of perspective. This is because they might have been active participants in some of the events they write about, or because they personally knew active participants, or simply because they remember hearing about and reacting to events as they were happening. It is also because the events of the immediate past happened so recently that not enough time has elapsed to say with any certainty what their long-term effects will be. In both scenarios, it is extremely difficult for historians to remain personally uninvolved in the way the story of the past is told. Of course, the personality and point of view of historians are always present in the histories they write. But it is worth thinking about how much more this is true when the subject matter is the very recent past.

Source: David Lowenthal. *The Past Is a Foreign Country Revisited*, 2nd ed. Cambridge: Cambridge University Press, 2015, chapter 8.

had received at least one dose. But there have also been stark discrepancies in how vaccines have been distributed worldwide, with richer nations having far greater access to the vaccines than poorer nations. This not only mirrors the problem of global inequalities more generally but also makes it far more likely that new variants of the disease will develop among populations with low vaccination rates. At the same time, scientists, researchers, and health care workers continue to work across national borders to find ways to beat the virus. Let us hope that we might learn from their example, in the likely event that a global pandemic will strike again in the future.

CONCLUSION

In 1989 ordinary Germans such as Kristina Matschat toppled the Berlin wall—an event that signaled the impending collapse of the Soviet Union and the end of the cold war. The end of the cold war changed the global balance of power in favor of the United States, although its unilateral actions in the following decades led to deteriorating relations with a variety of states, especially Russia. The decades after the end of the cold war were also characterized by increasing globalization, which accelerated economic, political, and cultural connections between the world's peoples. Although these connections and encounters in many cases aided economic growth and allowed for rich cultural exchanges, they also brought a host of urgent issues into high relief, including climate change, continuing inequalities, terrorism, migration, and global disease. Each of these issues continues to affect the whole world (although sometimes in different ways), and each appears unlikely to be solved in the short term. One thing is clear, however: if any solutions are to be found, they will require that nations work in cooperation with one another. Given the extremely violent and destructive twentieth century, in which nations killed tens of millions of people to achieve their goals, such cooperation would truly signal a new era in the history of the world.

STUDY TERMS

al-Qaeda (644)
Association of Southeast Asian Nations (ASEAN) (635)
Bush Doctrine (631)
European Union (634)
feminist movement (641)
free trade (632)
General Agreement on Tariffs and Trade (GATT) (632)
globalization (631)
global warming (638)
highly active antiretroviral therapy (HAART) (647)
little tigers (632)
McDonaldization (636)
North American Free Trade Agreement (NAFTA) (635)
Operation Iraqi Freedom (645)
Organization of Petroleum Exporting Countries (OPEC) (635)
Taliban (644)
terrorism (643)
Universal Declaration of Human Rights (638)
World Trade Organization (WTO) (632)

FOR FURTHER READING

Jagdish Bhagwati. *In Defense of Globalization.* New York, 2007. A convincing rebuttal to popular fallacies about global economic integration.

Gregory C. Chow. *China's Economic Transformation.* Oxford, 2007. The most accepted reference for understanding the world's most dynamic economy.

Jussi Hanhimäki and Bernhard Blumenau. *An International History of Terrorism: Western and Non-Western Experiences.* London, 2013. Analyzes the history and uses of terrorism for the last one hundred fifty years years from a variety of perspectives.

Mark Harrison. *Contagion: How Commerce Has Spread Disease.* New Haven, 2013. A scholarly examination of the connections between trade and infectious diseases, as well as the measures taken to limit the spread of disease.

Jason Hickel. *The Divide: Global Inequality from Conquest to Free Markets.* New York, 2018. An anthropologist explores the complex historical reasons behind the vast global inequalities between more developed and less developed countries.

Edward Luce. *In Spite of the Gods: The Rise of Modern India.* New York, 2008. A keen assessment of an up-and-coming economic and geopolitical giant.

David Marples. *The Collapse of the Soviet Union, 1985–1991.* London, 2015. A revisionist look at the collapse of the Soviet Union that emphasizes the role of Soviet national republics and Boris Yeltsin instead of the arms race with the United States.

J. R. McNeill. *Something New under the Sun: An Environmental History of the Twentieth-Century World.* New York, 2000. A brilliant but dark tale of the past century's interaction between humans and the environment.

Anne Sisson Runyan and V. Spike Peterson. *Global Gender Issues in the New Millennium.* London, 2019. Looks at the ways ideologies of gender have been used to perpetuate inequalities between men and women on a global stage and feminist resistance and action to counteract these uses.

Joseph Stiglitz, *Globalization and Its Discontents Revisited: Anti-Globalization in the Era of Trump.* New York, 2017. An updated and revised edition of the classic 2007 book that argued for the destructive impact of the International Monetary Fund (IMF), World Bank, and trade agreements on less developed nations.

Glossary & Pronunciation Key

AH *a* sound, as in *car, father*
IH short *i* sound, as in *fit, his, mirror*
OO long *o* sound, as in *ooze, tool, crew*
UH short *u* sound, as in *up, cut, color*
A short *a* sound, as in *asp, fat, parrot*
EE long *e* sound, as in *even, meet, money*
OH long *o* sound, as in *open, go, tone*
EH short *e* sound, as in *ten, elf, berry*
AY long *a* sound, as in *ape, date, play*
EYE long *i* sound, as in *ice, high, bite*
AW diphthong *a* sound, as in *awful, paw, law*
OW diphthong *o* sound, as in *cow, how, bow*

Note on emphasis: Syllables in capital letters receive the accent. If there is no syllable in capitals, then all syllables get equal accent.

Abbasid dynasty (ah-BAH-sihd) Cosmopolitan Arabic dynasty (750–1258) that replaced the Umayads; it was founded by Abu al-Abbas and reached its peak under Harun al-Rashid.

Absolutism Political philosophy that stressed the divine-right theory of kingship: the French king Louis XIV was the classic example.

Abu Bakr (ah-BOO BAHK-uhr) First caliph after the death of Muhammad.

Achaemenid empire (ah-KEE-muh-nid) First great Persian empire (558–330 B.C.E.), which began under Cyrus and reached its peak under Darius.

Adolf Hitler (1889–1945) German politician and leader of the Nazi Party who came to power in 1933; he initiated the European theater of World War II by invading Poland in 1939 and oversaw the establishment of death camps that resulted in more than ten million deaths.

Aegean Sea Sea located between the mainlands of modern Greece and Turkey.

Afonso d'Albuquerque (1453–1515) Commander of the Portuguese forces in the Indian Ocean in the early sixteenth century; he was responsible for seizing Hormuz, Goa, and Malacca, which allowed the Portuguese to control Indian Ocean trade.

Age grades Bantu institution in which individuals of roughly the same age carried out communal tasks appropriate for that age.

Ahimsa (uh-HIM-suh) Jain term for the principle of nonviolence to other living things or their souls.

Ahura Mazda (uh-HOORE-uh MAHZ-duh) Main god of Zoroastrianism, who represented truth and goodness and was perceived to be in an eternal struggle with the malign spirit Angra Mainyu.

Akbar Mughal emperor from 1556 to 1605; he was known for his tolerance for religion and thought to be one of the greatest Mughal emperors.

Al-Andalus (al-ANN-duh-luhs) Islamic Spain.

Albert Einstein (1879–1955) German-born physicist who developed the theory of relativity and whose ideas had a profound influence on the development of science in the twentieth century.

Alexander II (1818–1881) Emperor of Russia from 1855 until his assassination; he was best known for his emancipation of the serfs in 1861.

Alexander of Macedon King of the ancient Greek kingdom of Macedon from 336 to 323 B.C.E.; he was responsible for creating one of the largest ancient empires, stretching from Greece to Egypt and northern India.

Alexandria Important city of the ancient world, founded by Alexander on the Mediterranean coast of Egypt during the fourth century B.C.E.

Ali'i nui Hawaiian class of high chiefs.

Allah Standard Arabic word for God, the supreme divinity of the Muslim faith.

Amon-Re (AH-muhn RAY) Egyptian god; a combination of the sun god Re and the air god Amon.

Analects Collection of the sayings and teachings of the fifth-century B.C.E. Chinese philosopher Confucius, collected by his students.

Angkor (AHN-kohr) Southeast Asian Khmer kingdom (889–1432) that was centered on the temple cities of Angkor Thom and Angkor Wat.

Anti-Semitism Term coined in the late nineteenth century; prejudice against Jews and the political, social, and economic actions taken against them.

Antonio López de Santa Anna (1794–1896) Mexican army officer and politician best known for his efforts to prevent Spain from recapturing Mexico; he served as president of Mexico several times.

Apartheid (ah-PAHR-teyed) South African system of "separateness" implemented in 1948; it maintained the Black majority in a position of political, social, and economic subordination.

Appeasement British and French policy in the 1930s that tried to maintain peace in Europe in the face of German aggression by making concessions.

Aristotle (384–322 B.C.E.) Athenian Greek philosopher who was a pupil of Plato.

Armenian Genocide Campaign of extermination undertaken by the Ottomans against two million Armenians living in Ottoman territory during World War I.

Artha Hindu concept of the pursuit of economic well-being and honest prosperity.

Arthashastra (AR-thah-sha-strah) Ancient Indian political treatise from the time of Chandragupta Maurya; its authorship was traditionally ascribed to Kautalya, and it stressed that war was inevitable.

Asceticism (uh-SET-uh-sizm) Severe self-discipline and avoidance of all forms of indulgence, typically for religious reasons.

Ashoka Third monarch of the Mauryan dynasty—also known as Ashoka the Great—who ruled most of the Indian subcontinent from 269 to 232 B.C.E.

Assyrians (uh-SEAR-ee-uhns) Southwest Asian people who built an empire that reached its height during the eighth and seventh centuries B.C.E.; their empire was known for its powerful army and well-structured state.

Astrolabe Navigational instrument for determining latitude.

Aten Monotheistic god of Egyptian pharaoh Akhenaten (reigned 1353–1335 B.C.E.).

Athens Important city-state of ancient Greece located in the Attica region.

Attila Warrior king of the Huns who ruled the confederation from 434 to 453.

Audiencias Spanish courts in Latin America.

Augustus Grand-nephew and protégé of Julius Caesar; he served as de facto ruler of the Roman state from 27 B.C.E. until his death in 14 C.E.

Aurangzeb Sixth Mughal emperor, who reigned from 1658 to 1707; under his reign the empire stretched to its largest extent, covering most of the Indian subcontinent.

Auschwitz Camp established by the Nazi regime in occupied Poland; it functioned as both a concentration camp and an extermination camp, where approximately one million Jews were killed.

Austronesian-speaking peoples Peoples who as early as 2000 B.C.E. began to explore and settle the islands of the Pacific Ocean basin.

Avesta Book that contains the holy writings of Zoroastrianism.

Axum African kingdom, centered in Ethiopia, that became an early and lasting center of Coptic Christianity.

Aztec empire Central American empire constructed by the Mexica and expanded greatly during the fifteenth century during the reigns of Itzcoatl and Motecuzoma I.

Babur Central Asian conqueror who founded the Mughal dynasty in northern India; he reigned 1519–1530.

Bakufu Feudal style of government that ruled Japan under the direction of shoguns from 1603 until the Meiji restoration in 1868.

Ban Zhao (45–115) Renowned female historian and scholar of the Han dynasty and author of the *Book of Han*.

Bantu (BAN-too) African peoples who originally lived in the area of present-day Nigeria; around 2000 B.C.E. they began a centuries-long migration to most of sub-Saharan Africa; they were very influential, especially linguistically.

Battle of Gaugamela (1 October 331 B.C.E.) Final meeting between Alexander of Macedon and King Darius III of Persia, in which Alexander was victorious.

Battle of Marathon Battle fought in 490 B.C.E. between Greek and Persian forces, from which the Greeks emerged victorious.

Bedouin (BEHD-oh-ihn) Nomadic Arabic tribespeople.

Benito Juárez Mexican lawyer of Zapotec origin who served as president of Mexico for five terms, the first beginning in 1858 and the last ending in 1872.

Benito Mussolini Italian politician and leader of the National Fascist Party, who ruled the country from 1922 until his removal from the post in 1943.

Bhagavad Gita (BUH-guh-vahd GEE-tuh) "Song of the Lord," an Indian short poetic work drawn from the lengthy *Mahabharata*; it expressed basic Hindu concepts such as karma and dharma and was finished around 400 C.E.

Bhakti movement (BAHK-tee) Indian movement that attempted to transcend the differences between Hinduism and Islam.

Blitzkrieg German style of rapid attack through the use of armor and air power; it was used in Poland, Norway, Denmark, Belgium, the Netherlands, and France in 1939–1940.

Bloodletting rituals Rituals involving the shedding of human blood as a form of sacrifice to the gods; practiced by the Maya and Aztec, among many other societies.

Bodhisattva (BOH-dih-SAT-vuh) Buddhist concept of an individual who has reached enlightenment but stays in this world to help people.

Book of Songs Oldest existing collection of Chinese poetry, dating from the eleventh to the seventh century B.C.E.

Boxer rebellion Uprising by a secret Chinese society called the Society of the Righteous and Harmonious Fists; it lasted from 1900 to 1901.

Brahman Central concept of classical Vedic religion; it is the name of the "universal soul" at the heart of the cosmos.

Brahmins (BRAH-minz) Hindu caste of priests.

Brezhnev Doctrine Policy developed by Leonid Brezhnev (1906–1982) that claimed for the Soviet Union the right to invade any socialist country faced with internal or external enemies; the doctrine was best expressed in the Soviet invasion of Czechoslovakia.

Buddha (BOO-duh) The "enlightened one"; the term applied to Siddhartha Gautama after his discoveries that would form the foundation of Buddhism.

Buddhism (BOO-dizm) Religion, based on Four Noble Truths, associated with Siddhartha Gautama (563–483 B.C.E.), or the Buddha; its adherents desire to eliminate all distracting passion and reach nirvana.

Bunraku (boon-RAH-koo) Japanese puppet theater.

Bush Doctrine Set of policies during the administration of American president George W. Bush (2001–2009) that advocated preemptive strikes by the United States against potential enemies instead of containment or deterrence.

Byzantine empire (BIHZ-ann-teen) Long-lasting empire centered at Constantinople; it grew out of the end of the Roman empire, carried the legacy of Roman greatness, and was the only ancient society to survive into the early modern age; it reached its early peak during the reign of Justinian (483–565).

Cahokia (kuh-HOH-kee-uh) Large structure in modern Illinois that was constructed by the mound-building peoples; it was the third-largest structure in the Americas before the arrival of the Europeans.

Caliph (KAL-ihf) "Deputy"; Islamic leader after the death of Muhammad.

Cambyses (kam-BIE-sees) Son of Cyrus and second ruler of the Achaemenid Persian empire, who reigned 530–522 B.C.E.

Camillo di Cavour (1810–1861) Prime minister to King Vittorio Emmanuel II of Piedmont and Sardinia and a key figure in bringing about the unification of Italy.

Capetian (cah-PEE-shuhn) Early French dynasty that started with Hugh Capet.

Capitalism Economic system, with origins in early modern Europe, in which private parties make their goods and services available in a free market.

Capitulations Highly unfavorable trading agreements that the Ottoman Turks signed with the Europeans in the nineteenth century, symbolizing the decline of the Ottomans.

Captain James Cook (1728–1779) British explorer, navigator, and cartographer who served in the British Royal Navy; he was famous for his expeditions to the Pacific Ocean in the eighteenth century.

Carolingian empire Germanic dynasty named after its most famous member, Charlemagne.

Carthage Northern African kingdom, a main rival of early Roman expansion, that was defeated by Rome in the Punic Wars.

Caste System of social distinction, which emerged in South Asia late in the second millennium B.C.E., that divides the population into a series of classes, or varnas.

Çatal Hüyük Important neolithic settlement in Anatolia (7250–6150 B.C.E.).

Catherine the Great (1729–1796) Catherine II, the longest-serving female ruler of Russia (from 1762 to 1796); she came to power by overthrowing her husband, Peter III, in a coup.

Catholic Reformation Sixteenth-century Catholic attempt to cure internal ills and confront Protestantism; it was inspired by the reforms of the Council of Trent and the actions of the Jesuits.

Caudillos (KAW-dee-ohs) Latin American term for nineteenth-century local military leaders.

Central Powers World War I alliance of Germany, Austria-Hungary, and the Ottoman empire.

Chan (CHAHN) Influential branch of Buddhism in China, with an emphasis on intuition and sudden flashes of insight instead of textual study.

Chanchan (chahn-chahn) Capital of the pre-Inca South American Chimu society that supported a large population of fifty thousand.

Chandragupta Maurya (chuhn-dra-GOOP-tah MORE-yuh) Founding ruler of the South Asian Mauryan dynasty, who reigned from 321 to 297 B.C.E.

Chang'an (chahng-ahn) Capital city for various early Chinese dynasties, including the Qin, Han, and Tang.

Charlemagne King of the Franks, who ruled most of western Europe in the late eighth and early ninth centuries C.E.

Chavín culture Mysterious but very popular South American religion (1000–300 B.C.E.).

Chichén Itzá (chee-CHEN eet-SAH) Major Maya city located in the northern Yucatan Peninsula of modern Mexico.

Chimu Pre-Inca South American society that fell to the Inca in the fifteenth century.

Chinampa Agricultural garden used by the Mexica (Aztec) in which fertile muck from lake bottoms was dredged and built up into small plots.

Chinggis Khan (1206–1227) Founder of the Mongol empire and conqueror of most of Eurasia.

Chivalry European medieval code of conduct for knights based on loyalty and honor.

Chola kingdom Southern Indian Hindu kingdom (850–1267); a tightly centralized state that dominated sea trade.

Christopher Columbus (1451–1506) Italian explorer and colonizer who made four trans-Atlantic voyages from Europe to the Americas beginning in 1492.

Chucuito Pre-Inca South American society that rose in the twelfth century and fell to the Inca in the fifteenth century.

Civil Code Civil law code promulgated by Napoleon Bonaparte in 1804.

Civil service examinations Grueling tests given at district, provincial, and metropolitan levels that determined entry into the Chinese civil service during the Ming and Qing dynasties.

Cixi (1835–1908) Former imperial concubine who established herself as effective ruler of the Qing dynasty in the fifty years prior to the end of Qing rule in 1908; she was hated by millions for her lavish spending, corruption, and resistance to reform.

Collectivization of agriculture Process beginning in the late 1920s by which Stalin forced the Russian peasants off their own land and onto huge collective farms run by the state; millions died in the process.

Colossal human heads Large, carved heads made of basalt, which were produced by the Olmec during the late-second and early-first millennia B.C.E.

COMECON Council for Mutual Economic Assistance, which offered increased trade within the Soviet Union and eastern Europe; it was the Soviet alternative to the United States' Marshall Plan.

Confucianism (kuhn-FYOO-shuhn-izm) Philosophy, based on the teachings of the Chinese philosopher Kong Fuzi (551–479 B.C.E.), or Confucius, that emphasizes order, the role of the gentleman, obligation to society, and reciprocity.

Congress of Vienna Gathering of European diplomats in Vienna, Austria, from October 1814 to June 1815; the representatives of the "great powers" that defeated Napoleon—Britain, Austria, Prussia, and Russia—dominated the proceedings, which aimed to restore the prerevolutionary political and social order.

Conquistadores (kohn-KEE-stah-dohrayz) Spanish adventurers, such as Cortés and Pizarro, who conquered Central and South America in the sixteenth century.

Constantine Roman emperor who reigned from 306 to 337 and moved the capital of the empire from Rome to Constantinople.

Corpus iuris civilis (KOR-puhs yoor-uhs sih-VEE-lihs) *Body of the Civil Law,* the Byzantine emperor Justinian's attempt to codify all Roman law.

Council of Nicaea (nahy-SEE-uh) Assembly of leading theologians that convened in the city of Nicaea in 325 to determine the orthodox position of the church on a range of contentious theological matters.

Council of Trent (1545–1563) Assembly of high Roman Catholic church officials that met over a period of years to institute reforms in order to increase morality and improve the preparation of priests.

Criollos (kree-OH-lohs) Creoles; people born in the Americas of Spanish or Portuguese ancestry.

Ctesiphon (TES-uh-phon) Capital city of the Sasanian empire from the mid-third to mid-seventh century C.E.

Cuneiform Written language of the Sumerians; probably the first written script in the world.

Cyrus Founder and first ruler of the Persian Achaemenid empire, who reigned from 548 to 530 B.C.E.

Daimyo (DEYEM-yoh) Powerful territorial lords in early modern Japan.

Daodejing (DOW-DAY-JIHNG) Book that is the fundamental work of Daoism.

Daoism (DOW-izm) Chinese philosophy with origins in the Zhou dynasty and associated with legendary philosopher Laozi; it called for a policy of noncompetition.

Dar al-Islam "House of Islam," a term for the Islamic world.

Darius Third ruler of the Achaemenid Persian empire, who reigned from 521 to 486 B.C.E.

Dasas Ancient Aryan Indian term for enemies or subject peoples.

Decolonization Process by which former colonies achieved their independence, as with the newly emerging African nations in the 1950s and 1960s.

Deng Xiaoping (duhng show-ping) (1904–1997) Chinese politician who led the People's Republic of China from 1978 to his retirement in 1992.

Détente Reduction in cold war tension between the United States and the Soviet Union from 1969 to 1975.

Devshirme Ottoman requirement that the Christians in the Balkans provide young boys to be enslaved to the sultan.

Dharma (DAHR-muh) Hindu concept of obedience to religious and moral laws and order; also the basic doctrine of Buddhism.

Dhimmi (dihm-mee) Islamic concept of a protected people that was symbolic of Islamic toleration during the Mughal and Ottoman empires.

Diocletian (dah-yuh-KLEE-shuhn) Roman emperor who reigned from 284 to 305.

Dreadnoughts British battleships whose heavy armaments made all other battleships obsolete overnight.

Dunhuang Oasis in modern western China that had become a site of Buddhist missionary activity by the fourth century C.E.

Dutch learning European knowledge that reached Tokugawa Japan.

East India Company British joint-stock company that grew to be a state within a state in India; it possessed its own armed forces.

Economic nationalism Economic policies, pursued by many governments affected by the Great Depression, in which nations try to become economically self-sufficient by imposing high tariffs on foreign goods; it exacerbated the damaging effects of the Great Depression around the world.

Emiliano Zapata (eh-mee-LYAH-no zuh-PAH-tuh) (1879–1919) Mexican revolutionary and leader of the peasant revolution during the Mexican revolution whose followers were called Zapatistas.

Emilio Aguinaldo (eh-MEE-lyoh AH-gee-NAHL-doh) (1869–1964) Filipino revolutionary who declared independence from Spain and then fought against the United States during its war of occupation.

Encomienda (ehn-KOH-mee-ehn-dah) System that gave Spanish settlers *(encomenderos)* the right to compel the indigenous peoples of the Americas to work in the mines or fields.

Engenho Brazilian sugar mill; also, the entire complex world relating to the production of sugar.

English Civil War (1642–1649) Series of armed conflicts between the English crown and the English Parliament over political and religious differences.

Enlightenment Eighteenth-century philosophical movement that began in France, with an emphasis on the preeminence of reason rather than faith or tradition; it spread concepts from the scientific revolution.

Epicureans (ehp-ih-kyoo-REE-uhns) Hellenistic philosophers who taught that pleasure—as in quiet satisfaction—was the greatest good.

Equal-field system Chinese system during the Tang dynasty in which the goal was to ensure an equitable distribution of land.

Estates General French legislative assembly, prior to 1789, that consisted of three classes (estates) of men: the clergy, aristocracy, and commoners.

Etruscans (ih-TRUHS-kuhns) Northern Italian society that initially dominated the Romans; the Etruscans helped convey Greek concepts to the expanding Romans.

Eugenics Late-nineteenth- and early-twentieth-century movement that sought to improve the gene pool of the human race by encouraging those deemed fit to have more children and by discouraging those deemed unfit from reproducing; the movement was deeply tied to racism and was eventually adopted by the German Nazi regime to justify the extermination of "undesirable" populations.

Eunuchs (YOO-nihks) Castrated males, originally in charge of harems, who grew to play major roles in government; eunuchs were common in China and other societies.

Fascism Political ideology and mass movement prominent in many parts of Europe between 1919 and 1945; it sought to regenerate the social, political, and cultural life of societies, especially in contrast to liberal democracy and socialism; fascism began with Mussolini in Italy and reached its peak with Hitler in Germany.

Ferdinand Magellan (1480–1521) Portuguese explorer who organized the expedition that completed the first circumnavigation of the earth.

Filippo Brunelleschi (1377–1446) Italian architect, designer, and sculptor, considered one of the founding fathers of Renaissance architecture; he is most famous for designing the dome of the Florence cathedral.

Five Pillars of Islam Foundation of Islam: (1) profession of faith, (2) prayer, (3) fasting during Ramadan, (4) almsgiving, and (5) pilgrimage, or hajj.

Foot binding Historical Chinese custom of breaking and tightly binding young girls' feet to change their shape and size.

Four Noble Truths Foundation of Buddhist thought: (1) life is pain, (2) pain is caused by desire, (3) elimination of desire will bring an end to pain, and (4) living a life based on the Noble Eightfold Path will eliminate desire.

Francisco Pizarro (1478–1541) Spanish *conquistadore* whose military expeditions led to the fall of the Inca empire.

Franklin Delano Roosevelt (1882–1945) American politician who served as the thirty-second president of the United States from 1933 until his death.

Franks Germanic peoples who founded a successful dynasty in France, which went on to rule a substantial European empire in the eighth and ninth centuries.

Friedrich Engels (1820–1895) German socialist philosopher who, with Karl Marx, founded modern communism and

co-authored *The Communist Manifesto* (1848).

Funan Southeast Asian state that ruled the lower reaches of the Mekong River (including parts of modern Cambodia and Vietnam) between the first and sixth centuries C.E.

Galileo Galilei (1564–1642) Italian astronomer, engineer, and physicist, from the town of Pisa, whose observations had a huge impact on the development of modern science.

Gamal Abdel Nasser (1918–1970) Second president of Egypt; he led the overthrow of the monarchy in 1952 and served from 1954 until his death.

Gathas (GATH-uhs) Zoroastrian hymns believed to be compositions by Zarathustra.

Gauchos (GOW-chohz) Argentine cowboys, who were highly romanticized figures.

Ghana (GAH-nuh) Kingdom in west Africa during the fifth through the thirteenth centuries whose rulers eventually converted to Islam; its power and wealth were based on dominating trans-Saharan trade.

Ghazi (GAH-zee) Islamic religious warrior.

Ghaznavids Turkish tribe under Mahmud of Ghazni, who moved into northern India in the eleventh century and began a period of greater Islamic influence in India.

Gilgamesh Legendary king of the Mesopotamian city-state of Uruk (ca. 3000 B.C.E.); he was the subject of the "Epic of Gilgamesh," the world's oldest complete epic literary masterpiece.

Giovanni Pico della Mirandola (1463–1494) Italian humanist who sought to harmonize the various religions and philosophies of the world.

Golden Horde Mongol tribe that controlled Russia from the thirteenth to the fifteenth century.

Great Zimbabwe Large sub-Saharan African kingdom in the fifteenth century.

Greek fire Devastating incendiary weapon used mainly at sea by Byzantine forces in the seventh and eighth centuries C.E.

Griots Professional singers, historians, and storytellers in sub-Saharan Africa.

Gupta dynasty (GOOP-tah) Dynasty (320–550) that briefly reunited India after the collapse of the earlier Mauryan dynasty.

Guru Kabir (1440–1518) Blind weaver who became the most important teacher in the bhakti movement, which sought to harmonize Hinduism and Islam.

Hacienda (HAH-see-ehn-dah) Large Latin American estate.

Hadith Collection of the sayings of the Prophet Muhammad and the accounts of his deeds.

Hagia Sophia (HAH-yah SOH-fee-uh) Massive Christian church constructed by the Byzantine emperor Justinian and later converted into a mosque.

Hajj (HAHJ) Pilgrimage to Mecca.

Hammurabi's code (hahm-uh-RAH-beez) Sophisticated law code associated with the Babylonian king Hammurabi (reigned 1792–1750 B.C.E.).

Han Feizi (hahn fay-zi) Third-century B.C.E. scholar credited as one of the founders of the ideology of Legalism.

Han Wudi One of the most important emperors of the Early Han dynasty, who reigned from 141 to 87 B.C.E.

Hangzhou Capital of the Southern Song dynasty in the late thirteenth century.

Hanseatic League Commercial confederation of guilds and market towns that dominated trade in coastal northern Europe from the thirteenth to the seventeenth century.

Harsha Ruler of northern India from 606 to 648.

Harun al-Rashid Powerful ruler of the Abbasid Caliphate who reigned from 789 to 809.

Hebrews Semitic-speaking, nomadic tribe influential for their monotheistic belief in Yahweh.

Heian Japan (HAY-ahn) Japanese period (794–1185), a brilliant cultural era notable for the world's first novel, Murasaki Shikibu's *The Tale of Genji*.

Hieratic Simplified writing script used for day-to-day administration in Egypt.

Hieroglyphics (heye-ruh-GLIPH-iks) Ancient Egyptian written language.

Hijra Muhammad's migration from Mecca to Medina in 622, which is the beginning point of the Islamic calendar and is considered to mark the beginning of the Islamic faith.

Hinayana (HEE-nah-yah-nuh) Branch of Buddhism known as the "lesser vehicle" and Theravada Buddhism, popular in South and southeast Asia; its beliefs include a strict, individual path to enlightenment.

Hinduism Main religion of India, a combination of Dravidian and Aryan concepts; Hinduism's goal is to reach spiritual purity and union with the great world spirit; its important concepts include *dharma*, karma, and samsara.

Hittites Indo-European-speaking peoples who constructed a powerful empire in Anatolia and Mesopotamia in the mid-second millennium B.C.E.

Ho Chi Minh (1890–1969) North Vietnamese revolutionary and politician who first fought the French and then the Americans, then became the first prime minister of North Vietnam in 1945.

Holocaust German attempt in World War II to exterminate the Jews of Europe.

Home front During World War I and World War II, the civilian "front" that was symbolic of the greater demands of total war.

Hominid (HAWM-ih-nihd) Creature belonging to the family Hominidae, which includes human and humanlike species.

Homo sapiens (HOH-MOH SAY-pee-uhns) "Consciously thinking human," which first appeared around two hundred and fifty thousand years ago and used sophisticated tools.

Hongwu (1328–1398) Personal name: Zhu Yuanzhang; he was the founding emperor of the Ming dynasty in China (reigned 1368–1398).

Huitzilopochtli (wee-tsee-loh-pockt-lee) Sun god and patron deity of the Aztec.

Hundred Days Reform Chinese reforms of 1898 led by Kang Youwei and Liang Qichao in their desire to turn China into a modern industrial power.

Hundred Years' War (1337–1453) Series of intermittent wars between France and England over the control of modern France.

Huns Militarized confederation of central Asian nomads whose westward migration helped precipitate the collapse of the western Roman empire.

Hyksos (HICK-sohs) Invaders who seized the Nile delta and helped bring an end to the Egyptian Middle Kingdom.

Ibn Rushd (IB-uhn RUSHED) Known as Averroes in the West, an important Islamic philosopher whose intellectual contributions were also appreciated by many European scholars; he lived from 1126 to 1198.

Ilkhanate (EEL-kahn-ate) Mongol state that ruled Persia after abolition of the Abbasid empire in the thirteenth century.

Inca empire Powerful South American empire that reached its peak in the fifteenth century during the reigns of Pachacuti Inca and Topa Inca.

Indentured servants Labor source for plantations; wealthy planters paid the laboring poor to sell a portion of their working lives, usually seven years, in exchange for passage.

Indira Gandhi (1917–1984) Indian politician and daughter of Jawaharlal Nehru, who became the first Indian female prime minister in 1966.

Indo-Aryans Indo-European-speaking pastoral nomads who migrated from central Asia to South Asia in the second millennium B.C.E.

Indra Early Indian god associated with the Aryans; he was the king of the gods and was associated with warfare and thunderbolts.

Iron metallurgy Adoption and use of iron for weapons and tools.

Iroquois (EAR-uh-kwoi) Eastern Native American confederation made up of Mohawk, Oneida, Onondaga, Cayuga, and Seneca.

Isaac Newton (1643–1727) English mathematician, physicist, and astronomer who played a key role in the scientific revolution.

Isfahan Capital city of the Safavid empire (modern Iran), which was founded by Shah Abbas in the early seventeenth century.

Islam Monotheistic religion announced by the prophet Muhammad (570–632); influenced by Judaism and Christianity, Muhammad was considered the final prophet because the earlier religions had not seen the entire picture; the Quran is the holy book of Islam.

Israelites Branch of the Hebrews who settled in Palestine (modern-day Israel) after 1200 B.C.E.

Jainism (JEYEN-izm) Indian religion, associated with the teacher Vardhamana Mahavira (ca. 540–468 B.C.E.), in which every physical object possesses a soul; Jains believe in complete nonviolence to all living beings.

Janissaries Highly respected, elite infantry units of the Ottoman empire, who formed the first modern standing army in Europe.

Jati Indian word for a Hindu subcaste.

Jawaharlal Nehru (1889–1964) Indian activist and politician who fought for decades for Indian independence and became the first prime minister of India.

Jenne Also known as Jenne-jeno; settlement in the middle Niger River region in Africa that flourished from the fourth to the eight century C.E.; it was known for iron production.

Jesus of Nazareth Charismatic Jewish teacher who lived from 4 B.C.E. to the early 30s, recognized as the founder of the religion of Christianity.

Jiang Jieshi (jyahng jeh-she) (1887–1975) Also known as Chiang Kai-Shek; Chinese nationalist revolutionary, military leader, and politician who led the Republic of China from 1928 to 1975, first in mainland China and then in Taiwan after the Communist Party won the civil war between them in 1949.

Jihad Arabic term for "struggle"; it has various meanings to Muslims, each referring to the imperative to spread Islam throughout the world.

Jizya (JIHZ-yuh) Tax in Islamic empires that was imposed on non-Muslims.

Joint-stock company Early forerunner of the modern corporation; individuals who invested in a trading or exploring venture could make huge profits while limiting their risk.

Jomo Kenyatta (1891–1978) Kenyan independence leader and politician who governed Kenya from its independence in 1963 until his death.

Josef Stalin (1878–1953) Soviet revolutionary who led the Soviet Union from the mid-1920s to his death, whose policies resulted in the deaths of twenty million people.

Julius Caesar Major late-Republican Roman ruler who served as consul and later as dictator of the Roman state; he was assassinated in 44 B.C.E.

Ka'ba (KAH-buh) Main shrine in Mecca, the goal of Muslims embarking on the hajj.

Kabuki (kah-BOO-kee) Japanese theater in which actors were free to improvise and embellish the words.

Kama Hindu concept of the enjoyment of physical and sexual pleasure.

Kamikaze (KAH-mih-kah-zee) Japanese term, meaning "divine wind," related to the storms that destroyed Mongol invasion fleets; the term is symbolic of Japanese isolation and was later taken up by suicide pilots in World War II.

Kangxi (kahng-shee) (1654–1722) Fourth emperor of China's Qing dynasty, whose sixty-one-year rule was the longest in Chinese history.

Kapu Hawaiian concept of something being taboo.

Karl Marx (1818–1883) German philosopher and socialist revolutionary who founded, with Friedrich Engels, the modern communist movement and co-authored *The Communist Manifesto* (1848).

Karma (KAHR-mah) Hindu concept that the sum of good and bad in a person's life will determine his or her status in the next life.

Khoikhoi South African people referred to pejoratively as the Hottentots by Europeans.

Khubilai Khan (KOO-bih-lie kahn) (1215–1294) Grandson of Chinggis Khan and founder of the Yuan dynasty in China in 1271.

King Nzinga Mbemba (IN-zinga MEHM-bah) (1456–1543) Also known as Afonso I; ruler of Kongo in the first half of the sixteenth century who became the first vassal king to Portugal.

Kinship groups Families, clans, or other groups based on kinship relationships.

Kong Fuzi (551–479) Original name of Confucius, Chinese philosopher and teacher of ethics.

Kongo Central African state that began trading with the Portuguese around 1500; although their kings, such as King Affonso I (reigned 1506–1543), converted to Christianity, they nevertheless suffered from the slave trade.

Koumbi-Saleh Important trading city along the trans-Saharan trade route from the eleventh to the thirteenth century.

Krishna One of the incarnations of the Hindu god Vishnu, who appears in the *Bhagavad Gita* as the teacher of Arjuna.

Kshatriyas (KSHAHT-ree-uhs) Hindu caste of warriors and aristocrats.

Kush Nubian African kingdom that conquered and controlled Egypt from 750 to 664 B.C.E.

Kushan empire Major Eurasian empire that controlled much of central Asia and modern Pakistan and South Asia during the first three centuries of the Common Era.

Kwame Nkruhmah (KWAH-mee en-KROO-mah) (1909–1972) Ghanaian politician and revolutionary who led the Gold Coast to independence in 1957 and served as the new country of Ghana's first prime minister.

La Reforma Political reform movement of Mexican president Benito Juárez (1806–1872) that called for limiting the power of the military and the Catholic church in Mexican society.

Laozi Semilegendary sixth-century B.C.E. Chinese philosopher traditionally recognized as the founder of the ideology of Daoism.

Lapita Earliest-known Austronesian migrants to sail out into the Pacific Ocean and establish settlements on Pacific islands.

Latifundia (LAT-ih-FOON-dee-uh) Huge, state-run farms worked by enslaved people in ancient Rome.

League of Nations Forerunner of the United Nations, the dream of American president Woodrow Wilson, although its potential was severely limited by the refusal of the United States to join.

Legalism Chinese philosophy from the Zhou dynasty that called for harsh suppression of the common people.

Leonardo da Vinci (1452–1519) Noted Italian painter, sculptor, architect, and engineer of the Renaissance period.

Lili'uokalani (1838–1917) The first and only queen of Hawaii and the last Hawaiian sovereign to rule the islands.

Little ice age Period, beginning about 1300, when global temperatures declined for about five hundred years.

Louis Riel (1844–1885) Leader of *méis* and indigenous people who organized the unsuccessful Northwest Rebellion against Canadian settlement in 1885; he was executed by Canadian authorities.

Louis XIV (LOO-ee) (1638–1715) Also known as the Sun King; his seventy-two-year reign was the longest of any monarch in European history.

Louis XVI French king from 1774 until his deposition in 1792; he was executed in 1793 during the French revolution.

Luddites Early-nineteenth-century artisans who were opposed to new machinery and industrialization.

Machismo (mah-CHEEZ-moh) Latin American social ethic that honored male strength, courage, aggressiveness, assertiveness, and cunning.

Madrasas (MAH-drahs-uhs) Islamic institutions of higher education that originated in the tenth century.

Magi Members of a priestly caste in ancient Persia.

Mahabharata (mah-hah-BAH-rah-tah) Massive ancient Indian epic that was developed orally for centuries; it tells of an epic civil war between two family branches.

Mahayana Buddhism (mah-huh-YAH-nah) "Greater vehicle," a more metaphysical and more popular northern branch of Buddhism.

Maize Plant whose domestication was crucial to the emergence of complex states in early Mesoamerica.

Majapahit (MAH-ja-PAHT) Southeast Asian kingdom (1293–1520) centered on the island of Java.

Mali (MAH-lee) West African kingdom founded in the thirteenth century by Sundiata; it reached its peak during the reign of Mansa Musa.

Malintzin (1500–1529) Nahua woman who acted as interpreter and advisor for Hernan Cortes.

Mandate system System that developed in the wake of World War I when the former colonies ended up mandates under European control, a thinly veiled attempt at continuing imperialism.

Manichaeism (man-ih-KEE-izm) Religion founded by the prophet Mani in the third century C.E.; a syncretic version of Zoroastrian, Christian, and Buddhist elements.

Manors Large estates of the nobles during the European middle ages; home for the majority of the peasants.

Mansa Musa (MAHNsuh MOO-suh) (Reigned 1312–1337) Ruler of the wealthy and powerful Mali empire in west Africa.

Maori (MOW-ree) Indigenous people of New Zealand.

Marae Polynesian temple structure.

Marco Polo (1254–1324) Italian merchant whose account of his travels to China and other lands became legendary.

Marshall Plan U.S. plan, officially called the European Recovery Program, that offered financial and other economic aid to all European states that had suffered from

World War II, including Soviet bloc states.

Martin Luther (1483–1546) German monk and Catholic priest who became a critical figure in what became known as the Protestant Reformation after challenging the corruption of the church in his *Ninety-five Theses,* published in 1517.

Matteo Ricci (maht-TAY-oh REE-chee) (1552–1610) Italian Jesuit who was one of the founders of the Jesuit China missions.

Mauryan dynasty Indian dynasty (321–185 B.C.E.) founded by Chandragupta Maurya and reaching its peak under Ashoka.

Maya (MYE-uh) Brilliant Central American society (300–1100) known for math, astronomy, and a sophisticated written language.

Mecca City in modern Saudi Arabia that was the birthplace of Mohammed and remains the holiest Muslim pilgrimage site.

Medes (meeds) Indo-European branch that settled in northern Persia and eventually fell to another branch, the Persians, in the sixth century B.C.E.

Medina City, 345 kilometers (214 miles) north of Mecca, to which the Prophet Muhammad and his followers migrated in 622; *Medina* means "the city," as in "the city of the prophet."

Meiji restoration (MAY-jee) Restoration of imperial rule under Emperor Meiji in 1868 by a coalition led by Fukuzawa Yukichi and Ito Hirobumi; the restoration enacted western reforms to strengthen Japan.

Melaka (may-LAH-kah) Southeast Asian kingdom that was predominantly Islamic.

Mencius (MEN-shi-us) Late fourth/early third century B.C.E. Chinese philosopher recognized as one of the most important followers of Confucius.

Menes (mee-neez) Egyptian conqueror who, according to tradition, unified Upper and Lower Egypt ca. 3100 B.C.E. (sometimes identified with Narmer).

Mesoamerica (mez-oh-uh-MER-i-kuh) Central America.

Mesopotamia Term meaning "between the rivers," in this case the Tigris and Euphrates; Sumer and Akkad are two of the earliest societies.

Mestizo (mehs-TEE-zoh) Latin American term for children of Spanish and native parentage.

Métis (may-TEE) Canadian term for individuals of mixed European and indigenous ancestry.

Mexica (MEHK-si-kah) Nahuatl-speaking people from the Valley of Mexico who were the rulers of the Aztec empire.

Millet Autonomous, self-governing community in the Ottoman empire.

Ming dynasty Chinese dynasty (1368–1644) founded by Hongwu and known for its cultural brilliance.

Minoan society (mih-NOH-uhn) Society, located on the island of Crete (ca. 2000–1100 B.C.E.), that influenced the early Mycenaeans.

Missionaries People who travel on religious missions to help spread their faith.

Mithradates I (mihth-rah-DAY-teez) Powerful ruler of the Parthian empire, who reigned from 171 to 132 B.C.E.

Mithraic religion Mystery religion based on worship of the sun god Mithra; it became popular among the Romans because of its promise of salvation.

Mochica (moh-CHEE-kuh) Pre-Incan South American society (300–700) known for its brilliant ceramics.

Modu (210–174 B.C.E.) Highly successful leader of the Xiongnu peoples of the central Asian steppes.

Mohandas Karamchand Gandhi (1869–1948) Indian nationalist, politician, and lawyer who led the campaign against British rule by employing methods of nonviolent confrontation.

Moksha Hindu concept of the salvation of the soul.

Monotheism (MAW-noh-thee-izm) Belief in only one god, a rare concept in the ancient world.

Monsoon systems Seasonal winds that blow across the Indian subcontinent and Indian Ocean basin; they facilitated maritime trade during the early Silk Roads eras.

Motecuzoma II (mo-tek-oo-ZO-mah) (1466–1520) Aztec emperor at the time of Hernan Cortes's invasion.

Mughal empire (MOO-guhl) Islamic dynasty that ruled India from the sixteenth through the eighteenth century; construction of the Taj Mahal is representative of its splendor; with the exception of the enlightened reign of Akbar, the increasing conflict between Hindus and Muslims was another of its legacies.

Muhammad (muh-HAH-mehd) Prophet of Islam (570–632).

Muhammad Ali (Reigned 1805–1848) Egyptian general who built a powerful army on the European model and became the effective ruler of Egypt in spite of its official status as an Ottoman territory.

Muhammad Ali Jinnah (moo-HAHM-ahd ah-lee JIN-uh) (1876–1948) Politician and independence fighter who led the All-India Muslim League from 1913 until the founding of Pakistan in 1947 and then served as the first leader of independent Pakistan until his death.

Munich Conference 1938 meeting of Germany, Great Britain, Italy, and France in which attendees agreed to German expansion in Czechoslovakia; it

is considered part of the policy of appeasement that led Adolf Hitler to believe he had a free hand in Europe.

Muslim Follower of Islam.

Mutsuhito (MOO-tsoo-HEE-taw) (1852–1912) First Meiji emperor of Japan, who reigned from 1867 until his death; during his reign Japan transformed from a feudal to an industrial economy.

Mycenaean society (meye-seh-NEE-uhn) Early Greek society on the Peloponnese (1600–1100 B.C.E.) that was influenced by the Minoans; the Mycenaeans' conflict with Troy is immortalized in Homer's *Odyssey.*

Nara period Japanese period (710–794), centered on the city of Nara, that was the highest point of Chinese influence.

National Policy Nineteenth-century Canadian policy designed to attract migrants, protect industries through tariffs, and build national transportation systems.

NATO North Atlantic Treaty Organization; it was established by the United States in 1949 as a regional military alliance against Soviet expansionism.

Ndongo (n-DAWN-goh) Angolan kingdom that reached its peak during the reign of Queen Nzinga (reigned 1623–1663).

Nebuchadnezzar (neb-uh-kud-NEZ-er) King of the Babylonian empire who reigned between 600 and 550 B.C.E.

Nelson Mandela (1918–2013) South African revolutionary and politician who consistently fought against the apartheid state until its demise in 1994; he became the first Black president of South Africa and served from 1994 to 1999.

Neo-Confucianism (nee-oh-kuhn-FYOO-shuhn-izm) Philosophy that attempted to merge certain basic elements of Confucian and Buddhist thought; the most important of the early neo-Confucianists was the Chinese thinker Zhu Xi (1130–1200).

Neolithic era New Stone Age (10,000–4000 B.C.E.), which was marked by the discovery and mastery of agriculture.

Nestorians (neh-STOHR-ee-uhns) Early branch of Christianity, named after the fifth-century Greek theologian Nestorius, that emphasized the human nature of Jesus Christ.

New Economic Policy (NEP) Plan, implemented by Lenin, that called for minor free-market reforms.

Nicolaus Copernicus (1473–1543) Polish astronomer who theorized that the sun, rather than the earth, lay at the center of the universe.

Nile River World's longest river; it flows 6,695 kilometers (4,160 miles) from Lake Victoria through Egypt to the Mediterranean Sea.

Nirvana (nuhr-VAH-nuh) Buddhist concept of a state of spiritual perfection and enlightenment in which distracting passions are eliminated.

Noble Eightfold Path Final truth of the Buddhist Four Noble Truths, which call for leading a life of balance and constant contemplation.

Nonaligned Movement Movement in which leaders of former colonial states sought to assert their independence from either Soviet or U.S. domination; the initial meeting was held in 1955 in Bandung, Indonesia.

Nubia (NOO-bee-uh) Area south of Egypt; the kingdom of Kush in Nubia invaded and dominated Egypt from 750 to 664 B.C.E.

Oceania Pacific Ocean basin and its lands.

Odovacer Germanic general who deposed Romulus Augustus in 476, thus bringing about the end of the western Roman empire.

Olaudah Equiano (oh-LAU-duh eh-kwee-AHN-oh) (1745–1797) Writer and abolitionist from the kingdom of Benin who was sold into slavery but purchased his freedom in 1766.

Olmecs Early Mesoamerican society (1200–100 B.C.E.) that centered on sites at San Lorenzo, La Venta, and Tres Zapotes and influenced later Maya.

Olympe de Gouges (1748–1793) French feminist who authored *Declaration of the Rights of Woman and the Female Citizen,* which advocated for equal rights for women, at the start of the French revolution in 1789; she was later executed by the Jacobins.

Olympic Games Pan-Hellenic festival in which competitors from all over ancient Greece competed in athletic competitions; it was founded according to tradition in 776 B.C.E.

Oracle bones Chinese Shang dynasty (1766–1122 B.C.E.) means of foretelling the future.

Organization of African Unity (OAU) Organization started in 1963 by thirty-two newly independent African states and designed to prevent conflict that would lead to intervention by former colonial powers.

Osiris Ancient Egyptian god that represented the forces of nature.

Osman Bey (os-MAHN bay) (1258–1326) Also known as Osman Gazi; founder of the Ottoman dynasty and the Ottoman state.

Ottoman empire Powerful Turkic empire that lasted from the conquest of Constantinople (Istanbul) in 1453 until 1918 and reached its peak during the reign of Süleyman the Magnificent (reigned 1520–1566).

Paleolithic era Old Stone Age, a long period of human development before the development of agriculture.

Parsis (pahr-SEES) Indian Zoroastrians.

Parthians Persian dynasty (247 B.C.E.–224 C.E.) that reached its peak under Mithradates I.

Partition of India Period immediately following Indian and Pakistani independence in 1947 in which millions of Muslims sought to move to Pakistan from India and millions of Hindus sought to move from Pakistan to India; it was marked by brutal sectarian violence and the deaths of five hundred thousand to one million people.

Pataliputra (pah-tal-ih-puh-tra) Purpose-built capital city of the South Asian Mauryan and Gupta empires.

Patriarch (PAY-tree-ahrk) Leader of the Greek Orthodox church, which in 1054 officially split with the pope and the Roman Catholic church.

Patriarchy Social and political system in which power is held by men through cultural norms and customs that privilege men and withhold opportunities from women.

Patricians Roman aristocrats and wealthy classes.

Pax romana (pahks roh-MAH-nah) "Roman peace," a term that relates to the period of political stability, cultural brilliance, and economic prosperity beginning with unification under Augustus and lasting through the first two centuries C.E.

Peloponnesian War Bitter and destructive civil war fought between Sparta and its allies, and Athens and its allies, between 431 and 404 B.C.E.

Peninsulares (pehn-IHN-soo-LAH-rayz) Latin American officials from Spain or Portugal.

Pericles Athenian statesman who ruled his city from 461 until 429 B.C.E.

Period of the Warring States Last centuries of the Zhou dynasty (403–221 B.C.E.), when wars divided the region until the establishment of the Qin dynasty ended the disunity.

Persian Royal Road Long-distance road, partly paved with stone, built by the Persian Achaemenid empire; it stretched for 2,575 kilometers (1,600 miles) from the Mediterranean coast to the Persian heartland in modern Iran.

Peter the Great (Reigned 1682–1725) Russian czar of the Romanov family who sought to remake Russia on the model of the western European states.

Pharaoh (FARE-oh) Egyptian king considered to be a god on earth.

Plato Athenian Greek philosopher, a pupil of Socrates, who lived from 430 to 347 B.C.E.

Plebians (plih-BEE-uhns) Roman common people.

Polis (POH-lihs) Greek city-state.

Pope Gregory I Important pope whose papacy lasted from 590 to 604; he was well known for his prolific writings.

Popol Vuh (paw-pawl vuh) Mayan creation epic.

Porfirio Diaz (pohr-FEER-eeo DEE-ahs) (1830–1915) Mexican general and politician who served seven terms as president, for a total of thirty-one years.

Potosi (paw-taw-SEE) City in the central highlands of modern-day Bolivia that became the world's largest silver-producing area after silver was discovered in 1545.

Protestant Reformation Sixteenth-century European movement during which Luther, Calvin, Zwingli, and others broke away from the Catholic church.

Protoindustrialization Also called the "putting-out system"; entrepreneurs delivered raw materials to families in the countryside, who then spun and wove the materials into garments; the entrepreneurs then picked up the garments, paid the families, and sold the garments on the market.

Ptolemaic dynasty (TAWL-oh-may-ihk) Egyptian kingdom founded by Alexander the Great's general Ptolemy and the thought of the philosopher Ptolemy of Alexandria (second century C.E.), who used mathematical formulas in an attempt to prove Aristotle's geocentric theory of the universe.

Punic Wars Series of three wars fought between the Roman Republic and Carthage between 264 and 146 B.C.E.

Punt Land that traded with the ancient kingdoms of Egypt; its exact whereabouts are unknown but may be in or near modern Eritrea.

Qadis Islamic judges.

Qanat (kah-NAHT) Persian underground canal.

Qianlong (chyahn-lawng) (1711–1799) Sixth emperor of China's Qing dynasty and grandson of Kangxi.

Qin (chihn) Chinese dynasty (221–207 B.C.E.) founded by Qin Shihuangdi and marked by the first unification of China and the early construction of defensive walls.

Qing dynasty (chihng) Chinese dynasty (1644–1911) that reached its peak during the reigns of Kangxi and Qianlong.

Qin Shihuangdi (chihn she-huang-dee) First emperor of the short-lived but highly influential Qin dynasty; he reigned from 221 to 210 B.C.E.

Qizilbash (gih-ZIHL-bahsh) "Red heads"; Turkic tribes that were important allies of Shah Ismail in the formation of the Safavid empire.

Quetzalcoatl (keht-zahl-koh-AHTL) Aztec god, the "Feathered Serpent," who was borrowed originally from the Toltecs; Quetzalcoatl was believed to have been defeated by another god and exiled, and he promised to return.

Quinto (KEEN-toh) One-fifth of Mexican and Peruvian silver production, which was reserved for the Spanish monarchy.

Quipu (KEE-poo) Inca mnemonic aid comprising different-colored strings and knots; it was used to record events in the absence of a written text.

Quran (koo-RAHN) Islamic holy book believed to contain the divine revelations of Allah as presented to Muhammad.

Raja Sanskrit term for "king."

Ramayana (rah-mah-yah-nah) Ancient Indian masterpiece about the hero Rama; it symbolized the victory of *dharma* (order) over *adharma* (chaos).

Rape of Nanjing Japanese conquest and destruction of the Chinese city of Nanjing in the 1930s.

Reconquista (ray-kohn-KEE-stah) Crusade, ending in 1492, to drive Islamic forces out of Spain.

Reconstruction System, implemented in the American south (1867–1877), that was designed to bring the Confederate states back into the union and to extend civil rights to formerly enslaved people.

Relics Physical remains of saints or other religious figures assembled by churches for veneration.

Rhapta Port that emerged as a principal commercial center in east Africa.

Roman empire Empire that succeeded the Roman republic during the reign of Augustus, which dates from 27 B.C.E. to 395 C.E.

Romanov (ROH-mah-nahv) Russian dynasty (1610–1917) founded by Mikhail Romanov and ending with Nicholas II.

Sakk Letters of credit that were common in the medieval Islamic banking world.

Samsara (sahm-SAH-ruh) Hindu term for the concept of transmigration, the soul passing into a new incarnation.

Samurai (SAM-uhr-eye) Japanese warrior.

Sanskrit Original and "sacred" language of the Indo-Aryans.

Sargon of Akkad Ruler of the Mesopotamian city of Akkad who conquered most of the other city-states of the region to establish the first empire in world history.

Sasanians (suh-SAH-neeuns) Powerful Persian dynasty (224–651) that would reach its peak under Shapur I and later fall to Arabic expansion.

Sati (SUH-tee) Also known as *suttee;* the Indian practice of a widow throwing herself on the funeral pyre of her husband.

Satrapies (SAY-trap-ies) Persian administrative districts, usually ruled by members of the royal family who governed as satraps.

Schism Mutual excommunication of the Roman pope and Byzantine patriarch in 1054 over ritual, doctrinal, and political differences between the two Christian churches.

Scholasticism Medieval attempt of thinkers such as St. Thomas Aquinas to merge the beliefs of Christianity with the logical rigor of Greek philosophy.

Scientific racism Nineteenth-century attempt to justify racism by scientific means; an example is Gobineau's *Essay on the Inequality of the Human Races.*

Seleucid empire Persian empire (323–83 B.C.E.) founded by Seleucus after the death of Alexander of Macedon.

Self-determination Belief, popular in World War I and after, that every people should have the right to determine their own political destiny; the belief was often cited but ignored by the Great Powers.

Self-Strengthening Movement Chinese attempt (1860–1895) to blend Chinese cultural traditions with European industrial technology.

Seljuqs (sehl-JYOOKS) Turkic tribe that gained control over the Abbasid empire and fought with the Byzantine empire.

Semitic (suh-MIHT-ihk) Relating to the Semites, ancient nomadic herders who spoke Semitic languages; examples were the Akkadians, Hebrews, Aramaics, and Phoenicians, who often interacted with the more settled societies of Mesopotamia and Egypt.

Serfs Peasants who, although not enslaved persons, were tied to the land and owed obligation to the lords on whose land they worked.

Sergei Witte (SAYR-gay VIHT-tee) Late-nineteenth-century Russian minister of finance who pushed for industrialization.

Sericulture Cultivation of silkworms for the production of silk.

Shamans Religious specialists who possessed supernatural powers and communicated with the gods and the spirits of nature.

Shang dynasty Dynasty of ancient China that ruled, according to tradition, from 1766 to 1122 B.C.E.

Shang Yang (390–338 B.C.E.) Minister to the duke of Qin state in western China and important developer of the political philosophy of Legalism.

Sharia (shah-REE-ah) Islamic holy law, drawn up by theologians from the Quran and accounts of Muhammad's life.

Shia (SHEE-ah) Islamic minority in opposition to the Sunni majority; their belief is that leadership should reside in the line descended from Ali.

Shinto (SHIHN-toh) Indigenous Japanese religion that emphasizes purity, clan loyalty, and the divinity of the emperor.

Shiva (SHEE-vuh) Hindu god associated with both fertility and destruction.

Shogun (SHOH-gun) Japanese military leader who ruled in place of the emperor.

Shudras (SHOO-druhs) Hindu caste of landless peasants and serfs.

Siddhartha Gautama (sih-DHAR-tuh GOW-tau-mah) Indian kshatriya who achieved enlightenment and became known as the Buddha, the founder of Buddhism.

Sikhs (sihks) Adherents of an Indian syncretic faith that contains elements of Hinduism and Islam.

Silk Roads Extensive network of trade routes that linked much of Eurasia with north Africa during the classical period.

Silla dynasty Important early Korean dynasty that flourished during the seventh and eighth centuries.

Sima Qian Major ancient Chinese historian who lived during the second and early first centuries B.C.E. and wrote the first complete history of China to that point, the *Shiji.*

Socialism Political and economic theory of social organization based on collective ownership of the means of production; its origins were in the early nineteenth century, and it differs from communism by a desire for slow or moderate change compared with the communist call for revolution.

Socrates (SAHK-rah-teez) Athenian Greek philosopher who lived from 470 to 399 B.C.E.

Solon Aristocrat in Athens in the sixth century B.C.E. who forged a compromise between wealthy aristocrats and discontented common and landless classes who threatened rebellion.

Song dynasty (SOHNG) Chinese dynasty (960–1279) marked by an increasingly urbanized and cosmopolitan society.

Song Taizu (sawng tahy-zoo) First emperor of the Chinese Song dynasty, who reigned from 960 to 976.

Spanish Inquisition Institution organized in 1478 by Fernando and Isabel of Spain to detect heresy and the secret practice of Judaism or Islam.

Sparta Important city-state of ancient Greece located in the Peloponnesus region.

Srivijaya (sree-VIH-juh-yuh) Southeast Asian kingdom (670–1025), based on the island of Sumatra, that used a powerful navy to dominate trade.

St. Augustine (354–430) Bishop of the north African diocese of Hippo; one of the leading intellectuals of the late Roman empire.

St. Basil (329–379) Byzantine Christian reformer who prepared regulations for monasteries emphasizing poverty, charity, and chastity.

St. Thomas Aquinas (uh-KWIY-nuhs) (1225–1274) Italian Dominican friar and Catholic priest whose religious writings became enormously influential in the school of Scholasticism.

Stoicism Hellenistic philosophy that strongly appealed to the Romans; it focused on recognizing a set of universal moral standards by which to live.

Stupas (STOO-pahs) Buddhist shrines.

Sufis (SOO-fees) Islamic mystics who placed more emphasis on emotion and devotion than on strict adherence to rules.

Sui dynasty (sway) Chinese dynasty (589–618) that constructed the Grand Canal, reunified China, and allowed for the splendor of the Tang dynasty that followed.

Sui Yangdi (sway yahng-dee) Second emperor of the Chinese Sui dynasty, responsible for the construction of the Chinese Grand Canal system; he reigned from 604 to 618.

Süleyman the Magnificent (SOO-lee-mahn) Ottoman Turkic ruler (reigned 1520–1566); the most powerful and wealthy ruler of the sixteenth century.

Sumerians (soo-MEHR-ee-uhns) Earliest Mesopotamian society.

Sundiata (soon-JAH-tuh) (Reigned 1230–1255) Founder of the Mali empire and the inspiration for the Sundiata, an African literary and mythological work.

Sunni (SOON-nee) "Traditionalists," the most popular branch of Islam; Sunnis believe in the legitimacy of the early caliphs, compared with the Shiite belief that only a descendant of Ali can lead.

Swahili (swah-HEE-lee) East African city-state society that dominated the coast from Mogadishu to Kilwa and was active in trade; also a Bantu language of east Africa or a member of a group who speaks this language.

Taino (TEYE-noh) Caribbean tribe who were the first indigenous peoples from the Americas to come into contact with Christopher Columbus.

Taiping rebellion (TEYE-pihng) Rebellion (1850–1864) in Qing China led by Hong Xiuquan, during which twenty to thirty million were killed; the rebellion was symbolic of the decline of China during the nineteenth century.

Tang dynasty Powerful and wealthy Chinese dynasty that ruled a vast east Asian empire from 618 to 907.

Tang Taizong (TAHNG TEYE-zohng) Chinese emperor (reigned 627–649) of the Tang dynasty (618–907).

Tanzimat "Reorganization" era (1839–1876); an attempt to reorganize the Ottoman empire on Enlightenment and constitutional forms.

Temüjin (TEM-oo-chin) Mongol conqueror (ca. 1167–1227) who later took the name Chinggis Khan, "universal ruler."

Tenochtitlan (the-NOCH-tee-tlahn) Capital of the Aztec empire, later Mexico City.

Teotihuacan (tay-uh-tee-wah-KAHN) Central American society (200 B.C.E.–750 C.E.); its Pyramid of the Sun was the largest structure in Mesoamerica.

Three estates Three classes of European society, composed of the clergy (the first estate), the aristocrats (the second estate), and the common people (the third estate).

Tikal (tee-KAHL) Maya political center from the fourth through the ninth century.

Timbuktu (tim-buhk-TOO) City in the Mali empire known for its large population, wealth, and places of learning.

Timur (ca. 1336–1405) "Timur the Lame," who conquered an empire ranging from the Black Sea to Samarkand.

Toltecs Central American society (950–1150) centered in the city of Tula.

Trail of Tears Forced relocation of the Cherokee from the eastern woodlands to Oklahoma (1837–1838); it was symbolic of U.S. expansion and destruction of indigenous societies.

Tribunes Officials elected by plebians (commoners) in the Roman republic to represent their interests in the Roman government.

Truman Doctrine U.S. policy, instituted in 1947 by President Harry Truman, in which the United States would follow an interventionist foreign policy to contain communism.

Twelver Shiism (SHEE-izm) Branch of Islam that stressed there were twelve perfect religious leaders after Muhammad and that the twelfth went into hiding and would return someday; Shah Ismail spread this variety through the Safavid empire.

Uighurs (WEE-goors) Turkic tribe.

Ulama Islamic officials; scholars who shaped public policy in accordance with the Quran and the sharia.

Umayyad dynasty (oo-MEYE-ahd) Arabic dynasty (661–750), with its capital at Damascus, that was marked by a tremendous period of expansion to Spain in the west and South Asia in the east.

Umma (UM-mah) Islamic term for the "community of the faithful."

United Nations (UN) Successor to the League of Nations, an association of sovereign nations that attempts to find solutions to global problems.

Upanishads (oo-PAHN-ee-shahds) Indian reflections and dialogues (800–400 B.C.E.) that reflected basic Hindu concepts.

Utopian socialists Members of a movement that emerged around 1830 to establish ideal communities that would provide the foundation for an equitable society.

Vaishyas (VEYES-yuhs) Hindu caste of cultivators, artisans, and merchants.

Varna (VAHR-nuh) Hindu word for "caste."

Versailles (vehr-SEYE) Palace of French king Louis XIV.

Vijayanagar (vee-juh-yah-NAH-gahr) Southern Indian kingdom (1336–1565) that later fell to the Mughals.

Vishnu (VIHSH-noo) Hindu god, preserver of the world, who was often incarnated as Krishna.

Volta do mar (VOHL-tah doh MAHR) "Return through the sea"; a fifteenth-century Portuguese sea route that took advantage of the prevailing winds and currents.

Voltaire (vohl-TAIR) (1712–1778) French Enlightenment writer and philosopher famous for his wit and criticism of the Catholic church; his real name was François-Marie Arouet.

Wanli (wahn-LEE) Chinese Ming emperor (reigned 1572–1620) whose refusal to meet with officials hurried the decline of the Ming dynasty.

War chariot Ancient, horse-drawn, two-wheeled vehicle used in war.

War communism Bolshevik policy of nationalizing industry and seizing private land during the civil war.

William the Conqueror (Reigned 1066–1087) William I, the first Norman king of England after the Norman invasion in 1066.

Woodrow Wilson (1856–1924) President of the United States during World War I and author of the Fourteen Points, one of which envisioned the establishment of the League of Nations.

Wuwei (woo-WAY) Daoist concept of disengagement from the affairs of the world.

Wu Zhao (626–706) Concubine of Emperor Tang Taizong who seized imperial power for herself in 690 after Taizong became debilitated.

Xia dynasty (shyah) Early Chinese dynasty (2200–1766 B.C.E.).

Xianyang (shyahn-yahng) Capital city of the Qin empire.

Xiao (SHAY-OH) Confucian concept of respect for one's parents and ancestors.

Xiongnu (SHE-OONG-noo) Confederation of militarized pastoral nomads that were the dominant power on the steppe of central Asia during the reign of the Chinese Han dynasty.

Xuanzang (SHWEN-ZAHNG) Seventh-century Chinese monk who made a famous trip to India to collect Buddhist texts.

Xunzi (SHOON-dzuh) Third-century B.C.E. Chinese philosopher and administrator recognized as one of the most important followers of Confucius.

Yahweh (YAH-way) God of the monotheistic religion of Judaism that influenced later Christianity and Islam.

Yang Jian (yahng jyahn) First emperor of the short-lived but effective Sui dynasty, which united China after centuries of division; he reigned from 589 to 604

Yangzi River (YAHNG-zuh) River in central China.

Yellow Turban Rebellion Major peasant revolt that broke out in the last decades of the Later Han dynasty and was partly responsible for that dynasty's collapse.

Yongle (YAWNG-leh) Chinese Ming emperor (reigned 1403–1424) who pushed for foreign exploration and promoted cultural achievements such as the *Yongle Encyclopedia*.

Young Turk Party Nineteenth-century Turkic reformers who pushed for changes within the Ottoman empire, such as universal suffrage and freedom of religion.

Yuan dynasty (yoo-AHN) Chinese dynasty (1279–1368) founded by the Mongol ruler Khubilai Khan.

Yurts (yuhrts) Tents used by nomadic Turkic and Mongol tribes.

Zaibatsu (zeye-BAHT-soo) Japanese term for "wealthy cliques," which are similar to American trusts and cartels but are usually organized around one family.

Zambos (ZAHM-bohs) Latin American term for individuals born of indigenous and African parents.

Zarathustra (zar-uh-THOO-struh) Persian prophet (ca. sixth century B.C.E.) who founded Zoroastrianism.

Zhang Qian (jung-chen) Han dynasty explorer and ambassador who was dispatched by Emperor Wudi.

Zheng He (1371–1433) Admiral in China's Ming dynasty who carried out seven extensive oceanic voyages in the early fifteenth century.

Zhou dynasty (joh) Chinese dynasty (1122–256 B.C.E.) that was the foundation of Chinese thought formed during this period: Confucianism, Daoism, Zhou Classics.

Zhu Xi (ZHOO SHEE) Neo-Confucian Chinese philosopher (1130–1200).

Ziggurats (ZIG-uh-rahts) Mesopotamian temples.

Zionism National movement for the return of Jewish people to the historic land of Israel, founded in the 1890s by Theodor Herzl.

Zoroastrianism (zohr-oh-ASS-tree-ahn-izm) Persian religion based on the teaching of the sixth-century B.C.E. prophet Zarathustra; its emphasis on the duality of good and evil and on the role of individuals in determining their own fate would influence later religions.

Index

In this index, letters following a page locater are as follows: the letter *d* denotes a document, *f* denotes a figure, *m* denotes a map, and *t* denotes a table.